TIME AND PHILOSOPHY

TIME AND PHILOSOPHY
A History of Continental Thought

John McCumber

ACUMEN

First published in 2011 by Acumen

Acumen Publishing Limited
4 Saddler Street
Durham
DH1 3NP
www.acumenpublishing.co.uk

ISBN: 978-1-84465-275-4 (hardcover)
ISBN: 978-1-84465-276-1 (paperback)

British Library Cataloguing-in-Publication Data
A catalogue record for this book is available
from the British Library.

Typeset in Minion Pro.
Printed and bound in the UK by MPG Books Group.

CONTENTS

Acknowledgements   vii

Abbreviations and note on texts   ix

Introduction   1

I. Germany, 1790–1890

1. The collapse of Kant   15
2. Hegel discovers the past   31
3. Marx, capitalism and the future   57
4. Kierkegaard's dreadful future   77
5. Nietzsche and the boundless future   97

II. Germany and America, 1900–1968

6. The return of traditional philosophy: Edmund Husserl   127
7. The finite future: Martin Heidegger   159
8. Activity and mortality: Hannah Arendt   201
9. The twilight of Enlightenment: Theodor W. Adorno
   and Max Horkheimer   225

III. France, 1945–2004

10. The future and freedom: Jean-Paul Sartre   253
11. The future and the disclosure of being: Simone de Beauvoir   287
12. The future as rupture: Michel Foucault   313
13. The future and hope: Jacques Derrida   331

IV. Onwards, 2011–

14. Badiou, Rancière, and the time of equality   351
15. Life and gender in Agamben and Butler   373

   Further reading   394
   Bibliography   399
   Index   404

ACKNOWLEDGEMENTS

Charlton Payne compiled the suggestions for further reading. I am indebted to my department chairs, Hans Wagener and James Schultz, and to my Dean, Timothy Stowell, for arranging my teaching as to both time and topic so that it could contribute to this volume. Brenda Wirkus and Dianna Taylor afforded me the privilege of a term at John Carroll University, during which this project had its genesis. Tristan Palmer performed near-miraculous feats as my editor, rounding up four excellent readers from whose reports I learned much.

Jeffrey Rice and my colleagues in the UCLA German Department have provided ongoing inspiration and encouragement, as has Françoise Lionnet. My greatest debt is to my students at John Carroll University, Northwestern University and UCLA. They have taught me far more than I have taught them, and I aspire to be their worthy disciple.

ABBREVIATIONS AND NOTE ON TEXTS

AA   Kant, Akademie Ausgabe
BE   Badiou, *Being and Event*
BT   Heidegger, *Being and Time*
BW   Sartre, *Basic Writings*
CD   Kierkegaard, *The Concept of Anxiety*
CJ   Kant, *Critique of Judgment*
CM   Husserl, *Cartesian Meditations*
DE   Horkheimer & Adorno, *Dialectic of Enlightenment*
EA   Beauvoir, *The Ethics of Ambiguity*
EPM   Marx, *Economic and Philosophical Manuscripts of 1844 and the Communist Manifesto*
ES   Rancière, *The Emancipated Spectator*
FR   Foucault, *The Foucault Reader*
GM   Nietzsche, *On the Genealogy of Morality*
GT   Butler, *Gender Trouble*
HC   Arendt, *The Human Condition*
HS   Agamben, *Homo Sacer*
KPV   Kant, *Critique of Practical Reason*
KRV   Kant, *Critique of Pure Reason*
OWA   Heidegger, "The Origin of the Work of Art"
PA   Rancière, *The Politics of Aesthetics*
PF   Derrida, *The Politics of Friendship*
PhS   Hegel, *Phenomenology of Spirit*
QT   Heidegger, "The Question Concerning Technology"
RH   Hegel, *Reason in History*
SAT   Agamben, *The Signature of All Things*
SE   Agamben, *State of Exception*

A NOTE ON TEXTS

Works by Kant are cited by volume and page number in the Berlin Academy edition, the Akademie Ausgabe (*Immanuel Kants gesammelte Schriften*, 28 vols [Berlin, 1902–]), except for the *Critique of Pure Reason*, which is cited by page numbers to the "A" and "B" editions in the Akademie Ausgabe edition (vols IV and III, respectively).

References to Heidegger's *Being and Time* are to the marginal pagination, which follows that of the German edition of 1927.

References to Aristotle and Plato use Bekker and Stephanus numbering, respectively, which is given marginally in most translations. Abbreviations follow those used in the *Oxford Classical Dictionary*.

Except for primary texts, all translations are my own.

INTRODUCTION

True madness lies primarily in immutability.
Horkheimer & Adorno (*DE* 194)

THE PARADOX OF CONTINENTAL PHILOSOPHY

Continental philosophy is the most important intellectual tradition of the past two centuries. Billions – not millions – of people the world over have not only studied it in detail, but have tried to live by it. It has transformed our understanding of God, of society, of art and literature, of minority groups and of human life in general. It has provided much of the vocabulary in which educated people from Buenos Aires to Hanoi, from Moscow to Cairo, from Mexico City to Mauritius, from Shanghai to Brussels, think about their lives and communities. The only intellectual project that can rival it in importance is the "rise of science", but science is far too huge and diverse to be a single tradition. The representatives of continental philosophy, by contrast, form a relatively cohesive group whose later members read and learnt from the earlier ones, and often knew them personally.

The claims I made in the previous paragraph are immense, but the name of just one of continental philosophy's practitioners, Karl Marx, is enough to establish them. Adding the other continental philosophers to be discussed in this book gives us one of the greatest collections of intellectual superheroes ever to storm the heavens of the mind: Adorno, Agamben, Arendt, Badiou, Beauvoir, Butler, Derrida, Foucault, Hegel, Heidegger, Horkheimer, Husserl, Kierkegaard, Nietzsche, Rancière and Sartre. And there are many more.

In spite of its importance, however, continental philosophy remains little understood today, particularly in the anglophone world. What connects these thinkers? Why do we think of Hannah Arendt together with Marx and Jacques Derrida but not with John Stuart Mill or Bertrand Russell? This is no small mystery, but one of the central paradoxes of contemporary intellectual life. How can something so important be so little understood?

There are a number of explanations. First, continental philosophy *looks* weird. It is far too radical to look any other way, for it violates one of the deepest postulates of contemporary science and philosophy: that intellectual enquiry can have no goal other than the provision of true assertions (beliefs, propositions or sentences). Continental philosophy, while at its best accepting that goal, insists on having other ones as well. This means (as we shall see) that it does not move merely by constructing arguments or verifying hypotheses, as science and philosophy traditionally have done. This strangeness, in turn, allows exponents of more traditional philosophical approaches to claim that continental philosophy is not as rigorous as their own, more familiar forms of enquiry. Many dismiss it on these grounds, while others claim, with equal fervour, that continental philosophy's lack of rigour signals profundity, and so is a reason to uphold it. In fact, the whole debate is moot. As we shall see, continental philosophy is an extremely rigorous approach to philosophy.

In addition to looking weird, continental philosophy is risky – as is all philosophy that critically raises fundamental questions, or, in short, all real philosophy. The risks are often political. Almost every philosopher in the list above had problems with political authorities. Several, being European Jews, had to flee the Nazis; one, Heidegger, *was* a Nazi. Hegel and Kierkegaard had to tread carefully around the established churches in their respective countries. Nietzsche attracted the condemnation of a leading authority in his field, Ulrich von Wilamowitz-Moellendorff. Derrida actually spent a few hours in a Communist jail, in Prague. Badiou, Beauvoir, Butler, Foucault, Marx, Rancière and Sartre lived (and live) lives of political activism. While these political engagements help explain the unparalleled influence continental philosophy has gained worldwide, they also give it enough of a critical bite to be just a little dangerous.

The third, and perhaps most shocking, reason for the widespread ignorance of continental philosophy, however, is that continental philosophers themselves have not explained it very well. Until surprisingly recently, anglophone continental philosophers have not written introductory works explaining just what continental philosophy is, and why it is so important the world over. In the wake of Robert Solomon's pioneering study, *Continental Philosophy since 1750* (1988) this situation is now being remedied by people such as Simon Critchley (2001), Andrew Cutrofello (2005), Karen Feldman and Will O'Neill (1998), Simon Glendinning (2006), William Schroeder (2004) and David West (1996). It is my hope that this book, with its strict attention to the texts and its critical account of the ways they connect into a coherent tradition, will deserve a place in classrooms and studies alongside those efforts.

Finally, the lack of understanding of continental philosophy as a unified tradition also stems from our usual ways of configuring the history of philosophy. We tend to see it, not as a set of multigenerational traditions, but as an unrelated sequence of Great Minds: unique thinkers who stand alone before the mysteries of existence. But philosophers are not like that, for the simple reason that no humans are. According to theologians, God can create *ex nihilo*, from nothing. It was a deeply delusional moment when humans decided they could do so as well. Human creativity is really never more than a *reshaping* of one's conceptual heritage.

To see this, we need only remember that all philosophers write and think in one of several languages; a *wholly* original thinker would have to invent her own, *ex nihilo*. Philosophers do not do this. The most any philosopher ever manages is to define a few new words, and even those are usually taken from the store she has inherited. When Plato decided, for example, that true reality resided in an unchangeable domain of beings that could be known with the intellect but not via the five senses, he used a word from standard Attic Greek to name those beings: *eidos*, "that which is seen", the shape or form of something. And when Aristotle relocated Plato's *eidē* to the sensible world, as the unchanging essences of the changing things we live among, he used another standard Attic word for them: *ousia*, "that which is one's own", or one's property. Subsequent metaphysics has largely consisted in playing with, or reshaping, these two fundamental notions.

No philosopher, then, stands alone before reality. She reshapes the work of other thinkers, as deposited in the conceptual heritage conveyed to her through her language. Sometimes, if she is linguistically gifted, she also reshapes the thought of people who worked in other languages, as when Hegel rethinks Aristotle or Sartre rethinks Husserl. The set of thinkers that a given thinker reshapes can be called her "tradition", and continental philosophy is a distinct philosophical tradition in this sense. Continental philosophers reshape continental philosophers who have gone before, and are in turn reshaped by continental philosophers who come after.

There ought to be a reason for this. There ought to be some common project that leads Beauvoir, for example, to choose to reshape Hegel, Heidegger and Nietzsche, and Heidegger to reshape Nietzsche, but neither of them to reshape, say, Jeremy Bentham. What is distinctive enough about these thinkers to make them all so important to one another? What distinguishes continental philosophers from other philosophers?

TRADITIONAL PHILOSOPHY

It is not yet clear that anything does. It may be, in other words, that continental philosophy is simply too diverse in itself to contrast meaningfully with any other approach. This view is well stated by Critchley:

> Continental philosophy is a highly eclectic and disparate series of intellectual currents that could hardly be said to amount to a unified tradition.

> ... There is simply no category that would begin to cover the diversity
> of work produced by thinkers as methodologically and thematically
> opposed as Hegel and Kierkegaard, Freud and Martin Buber, Heidegger
> and Theodor Adorno, as Jacques Lacan and Deleuze.   (2001: 32–3)

Critchley is certainly right to stress the enormous diversity of continental philosophy, with respect to both themes and methods. Nonetheless, I maintain that
the philosophers I am going to discuss in this volume form a unified tradition
that, while not encompassing the entire diversity of continental philosophy,
serves as a sort of backbone for it. These two claims – the relative unity of the
tradition and its fundamental importance to continental philosophy as a whole
– can only be established by the book itself. For the moment, we can best understand the basic nature of this tradition by contrasting it with a more familiar
version of philosophy, which I shall call "traditional philosophy". Traditional
philosophy has many different shapes and tactics, but Heidegger understood its
basic nature: it is philosophy that locates true reality in an atemporal domain
(*BT* 18). In traditional philosophy, we first establish (or postulate) a domain that
is not subject to time, be it God, the Platonic Forms, Aristotelian essences, the
transcendental structures of the human mind or even, most recently of all, the
magnificent (but empty) apparatus of contemporary logic. Then we attempt to
use whatever knowledge we can gain of that atemporal domain to explain the
lives we live – as much as we can.

Parmenides started this off. His Way of Truth, which never changed, was
developed out of a love of unity, for something truly unified cannot change.[1] If
it did, it would bifurcate into two things: itself-as-it-was-before-the-change and
itself-as-it-is-after-the-change. Such internal opposition is incompatible with
true being, so what we find on the Way of Truth, the "One" of Parmenides, never
changes. And we ourselves? We are not unified or atemporal for Parmenides, but
dikranoi, two-minded, wandering along his "Way of Seeming". Everything on
this path is in a process of change, and so exhibits internal opposition. Beyond
this path is the Way of Non-Being, which is without unity and cannot even be
spoken of.

And how do these three ways relate to one another? How, in particular, are
they unified? The question is an important one for a philosopher who prizes
unity as much as Parmenides did, but it receives no discussion at all in his works
as we have them today.

Plato critically reshaped Parmenides by articulating our relation to the Way
of Truth as a *moral* one (something evident from Parmenides' writings, for who
does not value such things as truth, being and unity?). For Plato, the atemporal
realm became a whole congeries of moral values. It was not merely one perfect

---

1. Parmenides' poem is presented in Kirk & Raven (1960: 263–85).

4

unity, but a whole set of them, the Forms. We mortals are supposed to escape from Seeming: not a "way" now, but a whole domain of coming to be and passing away, of what Plato called *ta gignomena*, the things-which-become. Our moral task is to rise intellectually from *ta gignomena* to the contemplation of unchanging truth.

But the question that stumped Parmenides now arises again: how do these two worlds, the one of unchanging Forms and the one of things that become, relate to one another? Plato sees this question as primarily a moral one: the Forms somehow make our world what it is, but their more important role is to be what we are to seek. For our bodies situate us among *ta gignomena*. We cannot even know the Forms in detail until we are dead. Their moral function is to call us elsewhere, and their ontological function is to *be* elsewhere. Instead of explanations, we get exhortations. The problem becomes most acute when we ask about non-moral beings: chairs and horses and mud (cf. Pl. *Prm.* 130c–e). Is their relation to the world of Forms also primarily moral? Do they too somehow seek the Forms?

Plato never arrived at an answer, and this was not good enough for his pupil Aristotle. Aristotle's reshaping of Plato began by claiming that Plato should have given us an explanation of how *ta gignomena* relate to Forms, but instead he provided only a word – and a metaphor at that: *methexis*, sharing or (as it is usually translated) "participation" (*Metaph.* I.9 991a21). So Aristotle denied that there are two different worlds, one atemporal and the other full of things that change and become. But he still maintained, with Plato, that the true natures of things are unchanging. He thus came up with "essences", the unchanging basic components of our changing world. The task of these essences, instead of preparing our escape from the temporal world, was to dominate it from within (see McCumber 1999: chs 1, 2).

And now we ask the same question again, but in Aristotle's reshaped vocabulary: what is the relation of an atemporal essence to the thing of which it is the essence? It is no surprise that when Aristotle tried to specify this, he failed completely. Unlike Plato, he tried mightily. Instead of a single word, he gave us a whole soup of words: the central books (Z, H and Θ) of his *Metaphysics*, where, as the industrious Elizabeth Anscombe and Peter Geach put it, "There is hardly a statement about form in the *Metaphysics* that is not contradicted, at least verbally, by some other statement" (1961: 75).

We are not yet beyond the Greeks, and we already have three philosophical ways for handling the relation between the unchanging domain of "real" beings and the changing, unpredictable world in which we all live: ignore, flee and dominate. All of them, in the eyes of later philosophers, are failures. Do their failures cast doubt on the overall project of traditional philosophy itself? Should it be carried forwards at all? One of the greatest philosophers of the twentieth century, W. V. Quine, thinks so:

> Our ordinary language shows a tiresome bias in its treatment of time. Relations of date are exalted grammatically as relations of position, weight, and color are not. This bias is of itself an inelegance, or breach of theoretical simplicity … Hence in fashioning canonical notations it is usual to drop tense distinctions. We may conveniently hold to the grammatical present as a form, but treat it as temporally neutral. Where the artifice comes in is in taking the present tense as timeless always, and dropping other tenses. This artifice frees us to omit temporal information, or, when we please, handle it like spatial information.
>
> (1960: 170)

This is the same old tradition in different dress. Now the atemporal entities are not Aristotelian essences, or Platonic Forms, or the mighty and mystical One of Parmenides. They are merely sentences stated in logically canonical notation, notation from which temporal indices have "conveniently" been dropped. The long and arduous Platonic struggle to the atemporal realm is now, in Quine's word, merely a professional "artifice", that is, a useful fabrication. And yet a moral dimension is still present, directed against philosophers who do not overcome the "bias" Quine detects in ordinary language:

> But if one pursues philosophy in a scientific spirit as a quest for truth, then tolerance of wrong-headed philosophy is as unreasonable as tolerance of astrology would be on the part of the astrophysicist, and as unethical as tolerance of Unitarianism would be on the part of hell-fire fundamentalists.
>
> (1987: 209)

Quine's "convenient" flight to the atemporal realm quickly turns into an attempt to dominate philosophy itself. This is all very traditional, and sadly misbegotten; Quine, one of the greatest modern philosophers, pronounces himself to share the intellectual exclusivity, and so the intellectual dishonesty, of hell-fire fundamentalists.

In between the Greeks and Quine stand many other philosophers. Almost all of them, however, are playing basically the same game: they are attempting to find an eternal order that explains the changing world we live in. Descartes, in the modern era, had sought, and believed he had found, a "certain and unshakeable" foundation for knowledge (1985: 16). Leibniz's Kingdom of Grace and Spinoza's substance are further examples. Even the greatest of modern sceptics, David Hume, found his unchanging order – not in some objective domain, for his sceptical arguments barred us from knowledge of any such domain, but within the human mind itself. As he puts it in his *Treatise of Human Nature*:

> I must distinguish in the imagination betwixt the principles which are permanent, irresistible, and universal … And the principles, which are

changeable, weak, and irregular .... The former are the foundation of all our thoughts and actions, so that upon their removal human nature must immediately perish and go to ruin. (1888: 225)

The man with whom our story of continental philosophy will begin, Immanuel Kant, took up the challenge of Hume's scepticism and met it with Hume's own weapon: he extended Hume's account of the "principles which are permanent, irresistible, and universal" from the imagination to the entire structure of the human mind. Kant's philosophy is thus, as we shall see, not as radically "critical" as many people think it is. It is really a last-ditch attempt to salvage a domain of timeless truth as the basis for philosophical thought by locating such truth within the human mind. But eventually Kant arrived at the same old question of how the atemporal order, conceived as a necessary creation of the human mind, is related to the temporal order within which we must live and act. He wrote the *Critique of Judgment* to answer this question. We shall see that, like his predecessors, he failed utterly. With that failure, the atemporal order could not be found either within the human mind or outside it, and the only way forward was to deny it altogether.

This is what the continental philosophers, in general, have done. For them, everything has come to be from something else and will pass away into something else. We cannot understand anything whatsoever without understanding where it has come from and where it is headed: its future and its past. This means that continental philosophers accept two principles deeply foreign to traditional philosophy: (a) that everything philosophy can talk about at all is in time, and (b) that philosophers must be faithful to this at all times.

This emphasis on temporality begins to explain the worldwide influence I have attributed to continental philosophy, for it means that continental philosophy, unlike traditional philosophy, cannot retreat to realms of eternal or atemporal truth, or to the various ivory towers that purport to represent that realm in the present day. Continental philosophy is always out there in the human struggles, whatever those struggles may be.

This influence comes at a price, however. As I remarked above – and as so many philosophers have found out – philosophy has always been a dangerous undertaking. But continental philosophy is particularly so, for it denies itself the traditional recourse of philosophers when political pressures threaten: escape to an abstract realm of necessary truth, different from, and superior to, the messy, conflicted, often violent realm in which we really live. When cold political winds start to blow, continental philosophers cannot escape them by talking about such high-minded things as Platonic Forms, Aristotelian essences, *a priori* truths or the "laws" of logic. They must remain with the joys, pains and dangers of *ta gignomena*.

Indeed, continental philosophy so understood is not only weird and risky, but also downright terrifying, for if everything is mortal, then we are mortal. Not only that, but everything we cherish and value – our families, tribes, nations, religions and the very gods they live and die for – is mortal as well.

THE CONTINENTAL ALTERNATIVE: A PRELIMINARY HISTORICAL SKETCH

If continental philosophy holds that everything must be understood in terms of its development, then this must hold most of all for continental philosophy itself. A brutally brief presentation would begin with Heraclitus, who was somewhat younger than Parmenides and the main ancient ancestor of continental philosophy. Just what he thought about anything is hard to say, for his writings share with those of his descendents the feature of looking extremely weird; the ancients called him *ho skoteinos*, "the obscure one". He was long believed to hold a doctrine of cosmic flux, that is, the view that all things change. Certainly he did not clearly articulate the atemporal truth claims characteristic of traditional philosophy.

With Plato, however, traditional philosophy became the norm. It was not until the collapse of Kant's philosophy in the *Critique of Judgment* that Hegel, who famously bragged that "there is no proposition of Heraclitus that I have not adopted in my Logic" (1974: I, 279) abandoned all appeal to an atemporal order and opened philosophy up to the past. His *Phenomenology of Spirit* is most easily understood as his argument for doing this, and his Introduction to the *Lectures on the Philosophy of History*, published separately as *Reason in History*, shows him actually doing it. Hegel does not abandon reason altogether, but he temporalizes it, so that for the first time we have in philosophy the distinction between an *eternal* order and a *rational* order.

But Hegel was drastically, although naturally, misread as a traditional philosopher. People thought that his system, which he began to construct after finishing the *Phenomenology*, undertook to establish a traditionally philosophical atemporal order, which they called "The Absolute". All subsequent philosophers in the story of continental philosophy, from Marx to Derrida, will read Hegel this way. By doing so, they will dissociate themselves from the founder of their own tradition, misunderstanding both that tradition and themselves.

Impelled by just this misunderstanding of Hegel, Marx undertook, in his *Economic and Philosophical Manuscripts of 1844* (also called the "Paris Manuscripts"), to see the categories of Hegel's system as grounded in historical processes. In this, he was unknowingly repeating what Hegel had done. He also attempted to make philosophy an active force in history, which meant that he needed to take some account of the future, which Hegel had avoided. But Marx did not see the future as intrinsically problematic; the problem as he saw it was merely to make the correct predictions about it, which he famously did not.

It is Kierkegaard who, in *The Concept of Dread*, establishes the future as intrinsically problematic: as something unfathomable, indeed full of dread, with which we must nonetheless reckon. Philosophy is incapable of such reckoning, for him, because the future can be appropriated only through the Christian Paradox: Jesus Christ.

Nietzsche's atheism is thus an antidote to Kierkegaard's Christianity, for those who need it; but more basic is his notion of "genealogy". As he pursues it in *On the Genealogy of Morality*, genealogy is a way of taking philosophical account of the past without ignoring the future as Hegel did. In Nietzsche's view, our future is infinite; it could contain anything whatever, even (in virtue of his doctrine of "eternal recurrence") the past; not only that, this radical openness is present at every stage of history. This means that the move from one historical event to the next is radically open, and so random. There is thus for Nietzsche no continuity in history; history contains no ongoing processes that are worth being carried forwards. Nietzsche's atheism is the strongest expression of this underlying treatment of the future.

Husserl attempts to put continental philosophy back on traditional footing by finding, as Kant did, atemporal truths in human cognitive activity, now construed as "consciousness" rather than as "the mind". Taking this approach as a foil, Heidegger seeks to show how philosophy can open itself up to the future in a methodical way, in "The Question Concerning Technology", by finding the right questions to ask. To be sure, the future thus opened is not the infinite future with which Nietzsche and Kierkegaard were concerned: it is a particular future, the specific future of this or that person or group. With this, continental philosophy makes a decisive move beyond the approaches of Kierkegaard and Nietzsche, but Heidegger did not understand his own thought well enough to make good use of it. When he applied his philosophy to his own time and place, he fell into the worst of philosophical and moral disasters: membership in the Nazi party.

Arendt takes from Heidegger and Nietzsche the view that if everything is in time, then all origins are temporal. The ultimate philosophical origin, as far as we are concerned, is thus Greek thought, the earliest philosophy that we have. In *The Human Condition*, Arendt therefore undertakes a critical meditation on Greek thought and how it has determined our current ways of living.

Horkheimer and Adorno, turning to Marx to consolidate their opposition to Heidegger, seek, like Hegel, to turn to the past without trying to see where things are going: without providing any kind of concrete predictions. But in a time of fascism, what they see awaiting us is not the infinite future but an empty one, the triumph of what they call "administrative reason". From the point of view of such reason, dialectics is paradoxical; *The Dialectic of Enlightenment* thus hovers between despair and paradox.

Working from the texts of the early Heidegger (and Husserl), Sartre and Beauvoir make his thought more concrete by developing his account of the human future into an account of radical freedom. Beauvoir is often viewed as merely Sartre's companion and defender or, more accurately, is recognized as the inspiration for much contemporary feminism. She is also, however, an original continental philosopher in her own right. Her *The Ethics of Ambiguity* reshapes Sartre in important ways, most crucially in undoing the Husserlian side of Sartre's project: his attempt to give a traditionally philosophical account of human being as founded on an essential characteristic of the human mind, its activity of "nihilation" or taking-distance-on-things. Because nihilation is a general and empty activity, it presupposes a perfectly empty, and so infinite, future. But because what it takes distance on is always something specific, it makes that future specific as well. Nihilation thus *finitizes* the future, and finitization is an interplay between the finite and infinite futures developed in previous continental philosophy.

Such interplay also characterizes the work of Foucault and Derrida. Working mainly from the thought of the later Heidegger, supplemented in Foucault's case by a large dose of Nietzsche, they locate us within historical developments, instead of seeing the individual in a solitary confrontation with time itself the way Sartre and Beauvoir do. For both, there is thus something the future will not contain: namely, what we are now. Hence, for Foucault history is not only characterized by, but actually *is*, a series of ruptures, and this guarantees that we will not remain as we are. For Derrida, in *The Politics of Friendship*, the unfathomable emptiness of what can happen allows, at least, for a kind of hope: the hope for "democratic friends".

CAVEAT LECTOR

Written texts, as Plato wrote in the *Phaedrus*, are like drugs: they can do us good or ill. Any book thus needs, like cigarette packs, some "product warnings"; and since the place for these is at the beginning, I shall issue a few here.

First, and most obviously, there are a number of people left out of this story. Any history must be selective, and some of those omitted, such as Franz Brentano, Eugen Fink, Roman Ingarden and Max Scheler, are simply minor figures. Others, although of the first importance, can be understood relatively easily once one has some acquaintance with the subjects of this book. Into this group I would put Gilles Deleuze, Hans-Georg Gadamer, Jacques Lacan, Emmanuel Levinas, Maurice Merleau-Ponty and Slavoj Žižek. Still others are using the insights and achievements of continental philosophy for special purposes within philosophy. Race theorists, from W. E. B. Dubois himself to Robert Gooding-Williams, Lewis Gordon and Lucius Outlaw, are crucially engaged in such efforts, as are feminist thinkers such as Linda Martín Alcoff, Michèle Le Doeuff, Monique Wittig and Iris Marion Young.

Another significant omission, that of Jürgen Habermas, follows from the unifying theme of the book. Not all the philosophers I shall be discussing reject atemporal truths. Husserl and Kant, in particular, represent attempts to vindicate traditional philosophy by relocating atemporal truths to the human mind itself, as *a priori* principles of its functioning (Kant) or as "eidetic" components of consciousness (Husserl). The reason for including them here is that their efforts provoked immediate reactions, pre-eminently on the parts of Hegel and Heidegger, which put continental philosophy back on its temporalized path. Hegel's reaction to Kant, and Heidegger's to Husserl, were so important that subsequent developments cannot be understood without them. This gives Husserl and Kant crucial roles in the development of continental philosophy, but as what I call "foils" to the main story.

When Habermas claims that *all* speech presupposes that the speaker is claiming to speak honestly, sincerely and in accordance with societal norms governing the situation in which she speaks (even if the claims are implicit and the presuppositions violated on occasion; Habermas 1979; 1984–87: I, 8–101), he too attempts a rehabilitation of traditional philosophy. As Raymond Geuss has put it:

> In the work of Habermas and his associates ... the Kantian themes of finding a fixed universal framework for theorizing, giving firm foundations for knowledge claims of various sorts, and investigating the conditions of the possibility of various human activities, structure much of the discussion. (1998: 727–8)

Habermas's proper position in the current story, then, would be, like those of Husserl and Kant, that of a foil. But unlike Husserl and Kant, Habermas provoked no significant temporalizing reaction;[2] his philosophy never found a Hegel or a Heidegger. Whether this means that Habermas's restoration of traditional philosophy was successful or not is a complex and important question; but, like his philosophy in general, it is not a topic for this book.

Continental philosophy is, I suggest, the philosophical resonance of time itself. This explains not only its influence but the boisterous diversity to which Critchley calls attention. For time is the slipperiest of topics, and one of its aspects – the future – is by definition unknowable, an inscrutable source of unimagined surprise. New ways of understanding it are thus inevitable. Moreover, if a single method, or even family of methods, for understanding the future could be settled on, continental philosophy would have discovered a truth or truths that held for all time, and would itself become traditional. The proliferation of different ways of conceiving not only the future, but also the past

---

2. For an early attempt at one, cf. McCumber (1989: 325–79).

and present, is thus part and parcel of continental philosophy's temporalized approach. This proliferation is ongoing, and in Part IV I shall briefly discuss how four contemporary thinkers – Giorgio Agamben, Alain Badiou, Judith Butler and Jacques Rancière – are, in very different ways, carrying it forwards.

My final set of product warnings concerns the fact that in writing this book I have aimed at clarity, and have been guided in my search for it by a number of maxims. The first was that I should not merely write *about* a given book or passage, but include enough quotations for the student to actually see on the page what I claimed was there. This is obviously most helpful in the cases of such people as Hegel and Heidegger, but all these philosophers are creative enough thinkers to be, at least on occasion, idiosyncratic writers.

Second, I have largely eschewed secondary literature and its controversies. Further reading is provided for each chapter at the end of the book, and the works suggested are representative of various viewpoints on the respective philosophers. But including discussions of those viewpoints would risk extending the book indefinitely, and to little purpose for it is rare that issues of scholarly interpretation have much bite at the basic textual level. Either what I claim each thinker says really *is* there on the page for the reader to see, once it is pointed out, or it is not. Beyond that, thankfully, we need rarely go.

I have mentioned the principles by which I have chosen the thinkers to include; my final three maxims involve the choice of which of their works to discuss. First, the works discussed should be truly representative of their authors' thought in general; second, I should be able to render them intelligible in relatively few pages; and third, they must be readily available to an anglophone audience. In most cases, other works could have been chosen, and would have worked equally well. But I think that none would work better. (The two philosophers to whom this will not apply are Michel Foucault and Jean-Paul Sartre; my choices among their texts will be keyed to standard anthologies of their works.)

This book, then, does not aim to tell the whole story of continental philosophy. What it does do is explain some of its most basic and representative texts in ways that allow us to appreciate the larger enterprise of which they are part, and to see the underlying rigour of that enterprise. And that, perhaps, is enough – for now.

PART I

GERMANY, 1790–1890

CHAPTER 1

THE COLLAPSE OF KANT

PRIMARY TEXT Immanuel Kant, *Critique of Judgment* (*CJ*; [1790] 1987)[1]

Immanuel Kant was hard at work – all the time. From his daily reveille at 4.55am until his bedtime at around 9.30pm, his entire day – with the exception of his afternoon walk through Königsberg, the far eastern German town in which he lived – was devoted to work. From 5.00am until 7.00am, he did his correspondence and investing. From 7.00 until noon, he lectured: five hours straight. After his walk, at around 4.00pm, he took up his labours again until fatigue forced him into bed. Even the guest lists for Kant's elaborate daily luncheon parties, which lasted for hours, were carefully designed to help Kant's work, by informing him of what was going on in scientific and political circles.[2]

Why was Kant working so very hard? He had not always done so. As a young, and even a youngish, man, he had been known in the taverns of Königsberg as *der galante Magister*, the gallant master; his grace and wit transformed many a convivial evening. Why had he changed?

The reason for the gloom was the Scotsman David Hume. Hume, Kant tells us in the *Prolegomena to Any Future Metaphysics*, had awakened him from his "dogmatic slumbers" (AA IV, 260). In the *Prolegomena*, Kant talks about Hume's sceptical treatment of the notion of causality, which resulted in the view that you could not come to know a cause by reasoning backwards from its effects. This meant, in particular, that you could not reason back from the universe (or any aspect of the universe) to God as its cause, which was shocking enough to a "dogmatist" such as Kant claims to have been. But Kant's intense reaction to Hume was hardly confined to the concept of causality. Hume's philosophy was, for Kant, as he tells us in the *Critique of Practical Reason*, nothing less than a global "assault on the rights of pure reason" (*KPV*, AA V, 550).

---

1. The *Critique of Judgment* (*CJ*) is in volume V of Kant's Akademie Ausgabe (AA).
2. For Kant's daily routine see Kuehn (2001: 222, 273).

If Hume's philosophy could be construed as an attack on reason in general, then Hume had made an end to, among other things, the area of Kant's main philosophical passion. This was ethics:

> The whole armament of reason, as worked through in what one could call philosophy, is in fact directed only upon these three problems [of God, the soul, and immortality]. These again have as their further aim [clarifying] *what is to be done* if the will is free and there is a future world. Since this concerns our behavior in relation to the highest purpose, the ultimate intention of a wisely provident nature in setting up our Reason was clearly directed to moral considerations alone.
>
> (*KRV* B 828–9)

Kant wanted passionately to make humanity better. He believed that philosophy, and philosophy alone, could do this properly, for true moral guidance must come from reason. Religion cannot provide it, if only because a true religion must be adopted freely, and a free act is a moral act. True religion thus presupposes morality (cf. Kant, *Religion Within the Limits of Mere Reason*, AA VI, 8). If there is to be any such thing as moral guidance, it can only come from reason.

If Hume's "assault" on reason were allowed to stand, nothing would be left to guide us in life but experience, our own and that of the people around us, that is, of the culture to which we belong. This, in fact, is precisely the conclusion that Hume had reached: "custom", he writes, "… is the great guide of human life" (1894: 44). The problem with this, of course, is that our experiences, and the customs they inculcate, may mislead us. Slavery, for example, was largely unobjectionable to Europeans for millennia. Someone who had the misfortune to grow up in Nazi Germany would have absorbed "ethical" customs that were, in fact, absolutely evil.[3] In order to have a morally trustworthy guide to life, then, we need knowledge that is independent of custom, which means not founded on experience. Only such knowledge can be valid no matter what our experience and upbringing tell us. Moral guidance is only possible, then, if we have access to a domain of truths that hold for all human beings over time: that is, which never change. It is such access that Hume's empiricism had denied to us. Hume's philosophy had to be answered because it endangered human morality itself.

It also endangered what, in the Introduction, I called "traditional philosophy". Ever since Plato came up with his theory of Forms – the view that moral values resided, pure and unchanging, in a realm beyond that of *ta gignomena*, things that come to be and pass away – philosophers had presumed that we have access to some sort of unchanging truth. So Kant's advocacy, against Hume, of

---

3. Hume's own "experiences" led him, on occasion, into horrifying views: "You may obtain anything of the NEGROES by offering them strong drink; and may easily prevail with them to sell, not only their children, but their wives and mistresses" (1985: 214).

atemporal knowledge hardly rendered him a philosophical innovator. He aimed to salvage traditional ethics, ethics that reposes on timeless moral truths, by showing that we do have knowledge of an atemporal realm. But Hume's arguments are good ones: good enough, in Kant's view, that the domain of atemporal truth could no longer be considered to be outside the mind. He therefore relocated it to the mind itself. The principles of morality, valid for all time, are given to us, not by reason's knowledge of some eternal and unchanging domain, but merely by reason itself. The core of Kant's philosophy is thus a study of the atemporal structure of the human mind: of the unchanging bounds, rules and limits of the mind's powers (*KRV* A xii, xvi). He called this study "critique".

Kant was thus working, night and day, to salvage philosophy's ancient claim to unchanging truth. As Theodor W. Adorno put it in the twentieth century, Kant "wishes to salvage the timeless, absolutely valid experience of independent truth. … The *Critique of Pure Reason* is in general a supreme attempt to salvage ontology on a subjectivist basis" (2001: 31).

Kant's effort at salvaging traditional philosophy, and with it morality, came to a head in a little noticed argument at the very end of the third and last of his great *Critiques*, the *Critique of Judgment*. It is not too much to say that continental philosophy itself is born from the failure of that argument. Before discussing it, however, I should provide some basic Kant.

SOME BASIC KANT

The gist of Kant's "critical" account of the mind is easily given, if we dispense with the hundreds of pages of excruciatingly difficult argumentation designed to establish it. Mind is both theoretical, directed to truth, and practical, directed to goodness. Theoretical mind, as Kant sometimes calls it, achieves cognition (*Erkenntnis*, often translated "knowledge") by a complex process:

1. First, the mind receives a completely unstructured "manifold" of sensory data from the senses: this is the function of the faculty of Sensibility.[4]
2. The mind then arranges that manifold in space and time. This is the job of the faculty of Intuition.
3. Finally, the mind constitutes the resulting sensory arrangements as experience of "objects". Our intuitions, laid out in space and time, yield experience of objects only when the Understanding structures them according to twelve "categories", such as unity, plurality, cause and effect. These categories inhere in the human mind as fundamental principles of its cognitive activity. According to Kant, they apply to any object, because it is only by

---

4. When I am using words as the names of Kantian faculties, I shall capitalize them.

applying them that the mind obtains objects at all. Any object is thus to some degree a unity and a plurality; it is a cause of some things and an effect of other things; and so on.

Space and time, it should be noted, have unequal statuses in Kant's philosophy. My intuitions of my own internal experiences, such as pains and pleasures and ideas that occur to me, are not located in space, but they do come and go in time. Hence, time is the form of all intuitions; space is merely the form of "outer" intuitions (*KRV* B 50–51).

Space, for Kant, is the principle by which the mind orders sensory data that are mutually compatible. That there is a tree in my yard does not make my house impossible, so as my Intuition structures the data it receives from Sensibility, it can place the tree next to the house. The state of the house as it exists now, however, is incompatible with the state of the house when it was first built, and both are incompatible with the way the plot existed before the house was built. These things, therefore, have to be structured by a temporal succession, in which one state of affairs replaces another state that is incompatible with it, and is replaced in turn by yet later states of affairs. Time is thus the "ordering of incompatibles" (*KRV* B 48). To exist in time therefore means to be part of a temporal sequence in which earlier and later phases differ from each other. This applies to all our intuitions.

And it also applies to all objects of our knowledge, because the categories give us knowledge only when they are applied to intuitions that are worked up from Sensibility: that is, to things that we experience as in time. Unless we limit their application to such material, our minds will spin the categories through the conceptual ether, inventing all sorts of pseudo-objects in which the categories are applied to entities that are themselves, at best, mere "figments of the brain". Thus, I can think of the archangel Gabriel as a unit, a cause, an effect and so on, but I can have no knowledge of him, because I can have no sensory experience of an archangel. The pseudo-science that purports to tell us about these pseudo-objects is "metaphysics". What Hume showed once and for all, in Kant's view, was that metaphysics is illegitimate. Kant agrees with Hume, then: we can have no knowledge of anything that is outside time.

All our ideas of atemporal objects are formed by Reason. If experience is one realm in which the mind functions, for Kant (the "cognitive" realm), the atemporal pseudo-objects created by Reason constitute the second realm. They can be said to exist in three senses. First, they exist in our minds, as what Kant calls "figments of the brain" (*Hirngespenster*), along with ghosts, witches and archangels. Second, unlike ghosts, witches and archangels, some of these pseudo-objects exist as *rationally constructed* figments of the brain, or what Kant calls "ideas of Reason" (*Vernunftideen*). Kant never considered metaphysics to be mere superstition, in the sense that it irrationally invented entities. Metaphysics – properly carried out – invents entities *rationally*, and that is a big difference.

The third sense in which these pseudo-objects can be said to exist is the trickiest. Kant's approach implies that our senses do not present us directly with things themselves; everything we know is to some extent a product of our own minds. Things such as the chairs we sit in and the streets we walk down, since they are arranged in space and time, are in part products of our faculty of Intuition. Since they are units, pluralities, causes, effects and so forth, they are also in part products of our Understanding. Our experiences of things in general are, then, at least partially structured by our minds. Kant's way of putting this is to say that our senses can only present us with "appearances" (*Erscheinungen*) of things as they exist outside our minds, and not with the things-in-themselves, that is, things as they are independently of the structuring activity of our minds.

With this, Kant gave final form to a model of knowledge so influential that Heidegger will still be quarrelling with it 146 years later. In rough terms, this model holds that knowledge is an indirect relation between the knowing mind and the objects it knows. In between the two, as products of their interaction, are appearances. It is appearances that we cognize directly; the nature and the very existence of objects "behind" them must be inferred by us. Because of the crucial role played by appearances in this model, I shall call it the "appearance" model.

On this model, there turns out to be a whole universe of things *of* which Sensibility gives us appearances, but which are not themselves appearances and so cannot be known by us. Kant calls these "things-in-themselves". Since we can never know those things in any way, it is possible that they are exactly like the appearances we have of them; it may be that when no human mind is around, stop lights turn red and cars are parked at the kerb just as they are when we are there. It is also possible that there is only one thing, a single Giant Fact, which our minds arranges as a succession of appearances in space and time. It is also possible that there are ghosts, witches and aliens. We just do not know.

This ignorance, grounded in the very nature of our minds, also holds for the rationally constructed pseudo-objects produced by Reason. Since we can know nothing at all about what exists outside our minds, we can hardly rule out that any one of them also exists as a thing outside our minds. Such a possible being is not merely a thing-in-itself but (because it was rationally constructed) is a rationally intelligible thing-in-itself: a "noumenon" (from the Greek for "thing thought"). Any such noumenon might, for all we know, actually exist in just the way we construct it. The only way we could know that a purported noumenon did not exist would be if its concept were self-contradictory, like that of a square circle, and that is impossible because a noumenon has, by definition, been rationally constructed. Such possibly existing noumena, not being appearances, need not be thought of as being in time. Kant thus arrives at the view that the great and eternal objects of metaphysics – such as God, the soul and, in

× Kant's 'categorical imperative'

particular, freedom of the will – exist uncontroversially as rationally constructed ideas in our minds, and it is at least *possible* that they exist outside it as well.[5]

Kant goes on to argue that such ideas of Reason as God, the soul and, especially, freedom are *necessary* to the functioning of the human mind: we must suppose God, the soul and freedom to be not mere *Hirngespenster*, but objectively existent as well. Not doing so is misusing the human mind, rather like grasping a knife by the blade instead of the handle. In order for these ideas to function properly in our minds, and so to make our minds themselves function properly, we must *think of* the objects designated by these ideas as actually existing, even though we can never *know* that they do. This, then, is the third sense in which the pseudo-objects of metaphysics can be said, although not known, to exist, in that they are capable of existing (i.e. do not contradict themselves, as a square circle does) and the nature of our mind requires us to view them as existing outside it.

Now Kant's whole ethical argument comes home. We must think, and then act, as if God existed, our souls were immortal and we were free beings, even though we can never know the truth of such matters. Acting as if we were free beings means respecting freedom itself, that is, the freedom of all human beings: their ability to set their own goals, or to be "ends in themselves". The demand that we treat all human beings as ends in themselves is the sum and substance of moral- *×* ity: the "categorical imperative". Morality is thus founded, not on divine commandments or on our knowledge of some purely logical, atemporal realm – and certainly not on our culture and experience – but on the activity of Reason itself.

Kant's two worlds Thus, there are two worlds. One is cognized through the senses in terms of space, time and the categories. The other is a rational postulate of reason, outside time and experience, an atemporal world that may not exist and of which no denizen can ever be known by us. Our cognition is *true* in so far as we relate correctly to the former world; our wills are *good* in so far as we relate correctly to the latter one. And never shall the twain meet: Kant's distinction between appearances and things-in-themselves brings with it a radical divorce between knowledge and will, between goodness and truth. It is the divorce between noumena and phenomena, between the world of things in time and an unchanging, atemporal world.

Kant's solution for morality Kant has salvaged morality, and the atemporal sphere in general, by moving it into our minds. He has done this because, after Hume, that is the only place left for it to be. If Kant's solution does not work, then the only way to salvage morality will be to abandon traditional philosophy altogether: to adopt an approach in which nothing is exempt from time, and try to found morality on that without reducing it to mere custom. Such an approach, rejecting the last

---

5. Technically, freedom of the will cannot exist "outside" the mind, for it is a property of the mind. It (possibly) exists outside the constructive activity of reason, as a "real" property of the mind.

vestige of an atemporal domain of eternal truth, would be a radical innovation within philosophy, the most radical innovation since Parmenides came up with that domain in the first place.

There is much riding on Kant's solution. Does it work?

EARLY REACTIONS TO KANT

Kant's philosophy provoked an impassioned reaction among Germans of his time. On the one hand, it expressed the liberation of the human mind from nature: not only were we not bound by moral strictures coming from social institutions and customs, but in fact nothing about nature could determine our actions or thought. Birth, for example, did not cause some people to be morally different from others: nobles and commoners all had the same mental faculties. Reason, the tribunal before which all social arrangements were to be brought for adjudication, could in fact be "limited" only by itself, that is, in virtue of its own nature. And that act of self-limitation had been carried out philosophically in the *Critique of Pure Reason*.

Beguiled by this, an entire young generation of German intellectuals threw itself into the study of Kant. But they quickly ran into serious problems with his philosophy: resounding failures to carry out what it had promised. Those failures had less to do with the quality of its argumentation, which is still a matter of endless debate, than with issues of organization and thoroughness.

Kant's most distinctive claim for his own thought is not that it is true, but that it is systematic. Here is a typical example:

> Pure speculative reason has a true structure (*Gliederbau*). In such a structure everything is an organ, i.e. everything is here for the sake of each member, and each individual member is there for the sake of all. Hence even the slightest defect, whether it be a mistake or an omission, must inevitably betray itself when we use that plan or system.
>
> (*KRV* B xxxvii–xxxviii)

This is an extreme claim, but without it Kant would not be Kant. He would, by his own account, be John Locke. Locke had undertaken, like Kant, to trace our concepts back to their sources. In so doing, however, he had proceeded unsystematically: he had not investigated those sources themselves. Thus, Locke traced all concepts back to experience. But experience is confused and messy; by starting from it and it alone, Locke had inevitably proceeded "inconsistently". He had, in sum, produced an "aggregate", where Kant seeks "system" (*KRV* A x; B 119, 127; *Prolegomena*, AA IV, 322–3). Kant claimed to be systematic, then. But when they got into his system, younger Germans found problems: not so much mistakes and fallacies as omissions. In some cases, Kant was actually refusing to give answers on grounds that seemed specious and overly convenient. Other questions were not only not being answered, but were not even being asked. Certain things that needed to be done were not even being attempted. This gave rise to an enormous and highly confused literature, as younger thinkers stumbled over holes in Kant's thought that were not supposed to be there. I shall give a brief and partial summary.

Problems with Kant

What, to begin with, is the relation between an "appearance" and the "thing-in-itself" of which it is an appearance? Kant claimed that things-in-themselves, things that exist independently of our minds, cannot be known because the objects of our knowledge are produced, in part, by our own mental activity. But then he did claim to know something about such things-in-themselves, namely that they existed. How could he know that?

He had three main arguments.

(a) It would be absurd for there to be appearances without anything for them to be appearance of (*KRV* B xxvii).

(b) The phrase "thing-in-itself" is merely a "boundary concept", without positive significance: it merely designates what we can never know, and thus keeps us aware of the limits of our cognition (*KRV* B 310–12).

(c) The concept of the thing-in-itself enables us to resolve a particularly important set of contradictions, the "antinomies" (*KRV* B 432–595).

I shall come back to the third of these arguments shortly. Of the other two, it is evident that (a) is not serious. As to (b), maybe there are other ways of doing that job. Does recognizing that there are limits to our knowledge really require us to postulate an unknowable something outside our minds? As to (c), the resolving of the antinomies, the question will be whether the concept of the thing-in-itself does that job at all.

Another nest of problems concerns the issue of why we have the faculties that we do: Sensibility, Reason, Intuition and the rest. Why does our Sensibility operate in terms of space and time? Why do we have a Reason that generates ideas? If critique is the study of the faculties, it seems that it simply presupposes them, as mathematics presupposes the existence of number, and biology that of living things. But should it not try to *explain* them?

One of Kant's answers to this is clear and, in the minds of many younger Germans, damning:

> But how this peculiar property of our Sensibility itself is possible, or that of our Understanding and of the apperception which is necessarily its

basis and that of all thinking, cannot be further analyzed or answered, because it is of them that we are in need for all our answers and for all our thinking about objects.

(Prolegomena, AA IV, 318–19; cf. KPV, AA V, 81)

In other words, any explanation of the faculties would require us to use our faculties and hence is circular. But this conflates an explanation of fact with one of validity, a distinction that Kant is normally very careful to make.[6] It would make sense to say that the validity of the categories, for example, cannot be established by using the categories. But an explanation of where the categories come from is unaffected by this. We cannot think without the Understanding, but we cannot think without our brains either: is Kant saying that brain research is impossible?

The other answer – not stated as succinctly by Kant, but implicit in his entire project – is that only if we have such an array of faculties can we be truly moral. But that presupposes that we *can* be truly moral, in Kant's sense, and that we want to be. Both of these views would come under attack. The latter, in particular, was skewered by one member of the next generation of Germans, the poet Friedrich Schiller. Kant himself often claims, Schiller noted, that by making morality an affair of Reason alone he has removed it from the emotions (or, as Kant calls them, the "inclinations" or *Neigungen*). This, to Schiller, made morality a coldly rational and, in the end, inhuman affair, which he captured in a famous piece of doggerel:

> I help my friends
> But I do it because I want to
> And it rankles me often
> That I am not virtuous.[7]

A further problem: the causality of Reason

The biggest and knottiest problem with Kant's critical philosophy, and the one he tried hardest to solve, concerns the causality of Reason. It first appears in the *Critique of Pure Reason*'s Third Antinomy (*KRV* B 472–80), which argues that (a) everything in the world has a cause that precedes it in time, and (b) some things – namely, free acts – have no causes preceding them in time. How can both be true? Kant's solution is to maintain, as we have seen, that the category of causality obtains only within experience. Free acts, however, are supposed to come about through freedom, which is a thing-in-itself. Thus, empirically

---

6. It may be that Kant's concept of critique, which aims to validate our cognition by tracing it back to its sources, contributes to his error here.

7. Schiller (1939: 138), my translation.

we are determined, as the Understanding tells us: that much we *know*. But we must nonetheless *think of* ourselves as "noumenally" free.

But how can a noumenon be the cause of anything? If causality is a category that properly applies only within appearances, it should be unthinkable that something outside our experience could cause anything. Yet if he is to salvage morality, Kant needs to say that our free decisions on our actions make a difference in the empirical world, so freedom itself can be said, in some sense, to cause, or at least causally condition, events in that world. The problem is sharpened because Kant seems to be operating with a view of causality as "efficient" causality. This view of causality, in turn, is an updating of Aristotle's doctrine of the "moving cause", according to which a form (or property) moves from one packet of matter to another, as when a fire heats water. The idea that a property was "passed along" from one thing to another was later edited out of the notion of efficient causality (by Hume, in fact); but what was not edited out was that efficient causes (a) are objects (and not, for example, events) and (b) precede their effects in time.[8]

At this point, the relation between causes and their causal action becomes problematic. As Kant puts it in the "Third Antinomy" of the *Critique of Pure Reason*, if A causes B (or something about B), there must be a moment when A begins to act as a cause (*KRV* B 474). Prior to that moment we have A, but it is A-not-yet-causing-B. A being changes, then, when it begins to act as a cause. This is tendentious in many cases: does it change the fire if water is placed above it? But Kant is thinking of the will, which is *defined* as a kind of causal power. For the will to begin willing something is thus a change in the will; indeed, it is very hard to see in what sense the will even exists if it is not actually willing something.

To sum this up, any cause has a cause, which precedes it in time, and has effects, which it precedes in time. All causes are therefore temporal in the sense I gave that term above: they came to be out of something else, and will pass away into something else. But Ideas of Reason are not empirical and so are not in time; they never change in any way. How, then, can they "cause" our actions? To say that the Idea of freedom, in particular, has a causal role in producing our actions would amount to placing the will into time, and so to denying its status as a thing-in-itself. Moreover, if Reason is in time, then the Understanding tells us that it is itself causally determined, so even our "free" actions would not be free!

Kant has a couple of answers here. First, and most simply, we cannot understand how Ideas of Reason can be causes: we cannot understand how we can be free. We can only know that it is not impossible that, somehow, we are

---

8. Sometimes the change is simultaneous, as with a stove heating a room, but the beginning of the causality of the cause then precedes the effect, so Kant's general point is unaffected (*KRV* B 247–8).

(*KPV*, AA V, 85). This, of course, is not a solution. Second, he can say it is not the Ideas of Reason that cause our actions anyway; we cause them, through our free will. Ideas of Reason such as the categorical imperative are merely *Bestimmungsgründe*: grounds that determine our will or what philosophers today might call "auxiliary conditions". But the problem comes back: how is it possible for something that is not in time (the categorical imperative) to condition something that is (the will)?

The problem thus remains. To put it in specifically ethical terms, our will for Kant has empirical determining grounds, the general name for which is "inclination". These are purely mechanical. When I am hungry, my empty stomach sends chemical message to my brain, and I eat. This sort of thing, being mechanical, is explainable through efficient causality: by causes that act within a temporal sequence, causing later components of the sequence and being caused themselves by earlier components. According to the Understanding, *only* such "efficient causes" exist: all determining grounds of our will and choices are mechanical inclinations. But for the will to be determined freely means for it to be determined independently of efficient causality, that is, independently of all inclination. Why should we think it is even possible for that to happen?

Kant gives an answer that echoes Aristotle. Aristotle had claimed that there is one form of causality that does not change the cause but only the effect, and that is final causality. The exemplary case of this is love (*Metaph.* XII.7 1072b1–13). Love is a case of final causality for Aristotle because nearness to the object of my love makes me more me: it is part of my inherent tendency to become myself. My beloved is thus a "final cause" of my actions. And, as a case of such final causality, or "teleology", my love for something does not necessarily change that thing. My love for quantum theory does not change quantum theory, and the universe's love for the Prime Mover, Aristotle's version of God, does not change the Prime Mover. The Prime Mover, who never changes in any way, is thus the final cause of the cosmos, but not its efficient cause.

Kant does not go so far as to say that the will "loves" the moral law, but in the *Critique of Practical Reason* he does introduce an analogous feeling, namely that of respect (*Achtung*) for the moral law (*KPV*, AA V, 132–40). When I think of the moral law, I am aware that it is far nobler than I am, and so I respect it. This feeling, Kant says, is brought about through Reason alone. It is our only *a priori* feeling, and it is also our "sole and simultaneously undoubted moral motivation" (*ibid.*). This may seem more than a bit weird and *ad hoc*, but there is a larger problem. The causality of Reason, so explained, extends only to the will itself: it tells us how the will can "determine itself" independently of desire. Such explanation, even if successful, would not explain action (cf. *KPV*, AA V, 23). I may *decide* to do the right thing, but any number of factors both inside and outside me – such as compelling countervailing inclinations, or sheer physical weakness, or unfavourable circumstances – may prevent me from even *attempting* to do it.

25

Action, decision and will in Kant's ethics

Kant has thus given an account of the causality of Reason that, if we accept his account of respect for the moral law, can show us how the Ideas of Reason, although they are not in time, can have causal effects on our will. But his account is wholly interior to us; it has to do with what goes on in our heart and will, not with empirical reality itself.

The account is so internalized, in fact, that it seems to offer an ethics that has nothing to do with making the world a better place, but only with the way I make my moral decisions. Schiller, then, was right: Kant abstracts away from all motivating factors except respect for the moral law. Love of others, sympathy, compassion, generosity and so on are all outside the domain of morality so defined. They are mere "inclinations". Kant's ethics therefore seems to have nothing to do with the lives we lead, and it has to be that way. For the lives we lead are in the empirical domain, which is governed by efficient causality rather than by freedom.

Kant has thus created an ethical theory that extends morality only to decisions, not to actions. There are times when he seems to suggest that this is enough – as when, at the beginning of the *Groundwork of the Metaphysics of Morals*, he claims that "It is impossible to think of anything at all in the world, or indeed even beyond it, that could be considered good without limitation, except a *good will*" (*Groundwork*, AA IV, 393). But this brings Kant's ethics into contradiction with itself, for the three formulations of the categorical imperative later in the book (*Groundwork*, AA IV, 421–36) do not enjoin us to "determine our will" in various ways; they enjoin us to *act* in certain ways. Why? Because the aim of morality is to make a difference in the world. Ethics is not just about changing our hearts and inner spiritual lives, but about getting us to behave in certain ways. Kant thus needs to get from "determination of the will" to action. But how can he do so?

The main impediment, once again, is the Understanding, which tells us that everything in the world comes about entirely through natural efficient causes, and that desire alone can therefore determine our acts. Even given the very odd "desire" that determines our will – respect for the moral law – we have no right to think that our determinations of will are going to change anything in the world.

Or, as Kant puts it in the Introduction to the *Critique of Judgment*, Reason and Understanding both "legislate" to the empirical world; they tell us that it has to have certain properties. For Reason, the "has to" is moral; but the Understanding says that whatever happens will happen independently of reason and of our "free" determinations of the will. And this, in Kant's scheme, is an unassailable truth grounded in the structure of the Understanding. The two "legislations" thus conflict.

In the *Critique of Judgment*, which he claims to have written precisely in order to solve this problem (*CJ* 174–9), Kant does exactly what we might expect him to do: he expands his account of the final causality of Reason from the interior of the human mind to empirical reality itself. He argues that the Ideas of Reason, and in particular freedom, are not merely final causes in that they evoke respect for the moral law within the human heart, but that they can and must be thought of as the final causes of nature itself.

Thus, Kant's answer to the third question about the thing-in-itself – that it can reconcile the contradiction between causality and freedom by allocating the former to the empirical world and the latter to the world of things-in-themselves – runs into severe difficulties. Once the two worlds (or frameworks) have been separated, they have to be brought back together. And that is the job of the *Critique of Judgment*.

THE FINAL COLLAPSE

[handwritten annotation: On external & internal teleology]

In §§82–4 of his *Critique of Judgment*, Kant completes his argument concerning the unification of the empirical and noumenal realms. His basic strategy is to show that the noumenal realm must be thought of as the final cause of the empirical realm. If it need not, or even cannot, be thought of in this way, then we are free to reject Kant's entire account of the moral will; it becomes just an edifying story. At that point, the fact that the Understanding tells us that there is no moral will, that we are completely determined in every respect, will require us to reject Kant's entire ethics.

Kant's argument is tortured and, frankly, full of holes; whether it can be salvaged is, to say the least, questionable.[9] I shall state here just enough of it to enable us to see why later thinkers rejected it, and Kant's entire moral theory with it.

Kant first distinguishes "external teleology", where something exists or happens for the sake of something else, from "internal teleology", in which a thing is its own purpose (*CJ* 426). One example of an internal *telos* would be the overall "purpose" of a horse. If a horse has such a purpose at all (which is for Kant another of the things we cannot know but only think about in certain ways), that purpose is to be a horse, that is, to be what it is. Rain falling on the

---

9. It is perhaps not surprising that this argument, so embarrassing yet so crucial to Kant's entire philosophy, should be widely ignored by Kant scholars. One of the few who discusses it in detail, Charles Nussbaum, notes that Kant's argument requires charity from the reader that "not everyone will be prepared to grant" (1996: 277–8). Another, Paul Guyer, recognizes that the argument represents the culmination of "the whole philosophy developed in Kant's three Critiques"; but his account of it uses some form of the word "assumes" four times, and "suggests" twice. Guyer's conclusion is that Kant's discussion is not really an argument at all, but a set of "important hints", and that Kant has taught us by means of those hints that we must "think systematically" about nature and our duties. But, I suggest, it is precisely systematic thinking itself that has failed here (Guyer 2006: 349–51, and esp. 358).

earth and causing plants to grow, by contrast, would be a case of "external teleology", in which one thing is useful for another thing.

Kant then asks whether the whole of nature can be considered to be a single teleologically organized being. If so, everything cannot be externally teleological: the final purpose of the entirety of nature must, it seems, be part of nature itself, and so internally teleological. If we look at things like that, there are two ways to go. One is to say (*CJ* 426) that *we* are the final purpose of nature: herbivores eat plants, and predators eat herbivores, for the sake of humans. For humans are "the only beings on earth who can form a concept of purposes and use their reason to turn an aggregate of purposively structured things into a system of purposes" (*CJ* 427). But there is evidence against this. Nature makes use of us, too: by killing predators we reduce their numbers, and so contribute to the overall order of nature. Moreover, our bodies fertilize the world after our death, as does any organic matter. In fact, nature treats us like any other beings: rocks fall and crush us, microbes attack us, and so on. It seems, then, that that overall natural order, and not we humans, would be the internal *telos* of nature as a whole. Hence, the following dilemma:

> An ultimate purpose of nature is certainly required for such a system to be possible, and we cannot posit it anywhere but in man. But man too is one of the many animal species, and nature has in no way exempted him from its destructive forces any more than from its productive forces, but has subjected everything to natural mechanism without a purpose.
>
> (*CJ* 427)

As §83 goes on to tell us in more detail, nothing else can be thought of as the ultimate purpose of nature, then; it has to be us, somehow. But it cannot *simply* be us, either. Perhaps, then, it is some quality or aspect of us that is the final purpose of nature, some aspect of ourselves that can survive our mistreatment at the hands of nature even when we ourselves do not. In virtue of what property of ours, then, can we be thought of as the ultimate purpose of nature?

There are only two possibilities: happiness and moral goodness (which Kant here, for complex reasons, calls "culture"). But our happiness cannot be coherently posited as the ultimate cause of nature, for three reasons. First, happiness just means the satisfaction of all desires for Kant, and that is an inherently changing and undefinable concept: it depends on what desires you happen to have at a given moment. So if *that* were the ultimate purpose of nature, nature "even it if were subjected completely to man's choice, still could not possibly adopt a definite and fixed universal law that would keep it in harmony with that wavering concept" (*CJ* 430).

But "nature" for Kant is defined in terms of law, as law-governed appearances, so nature, serving our happiness, would not even be natural. In addition, not only does nature in general take no regard for our happiness, as Kant has already argued, but our own human nature causes us much misery, in wars, oppression and so on: "man himself does all he can to work for the destruction of his own species" (*CJ* 430). Therefore, "in the chain of natural purposes man is never more than a link" (*CJ* 431). The final purpose of nature thus cannot be found in human happiness. What in us is left to be that final purpose, over and above that?

Our capacity to set our own purposes: to act freely. To view this as the final cause of nature means postulating that we can use nature as a means for freely setting our own purposes. The way we do this is through "culture". So, within nature, the expression of the final purpose of nature is human culture.

We must, then, view nature as providing us with the means to set our final purposes. But this includes the nature within us; so we must view human nature as amenable to the kind of society in which individuals are allowed to set their own purposes, that is, a free society or law-governed civil society (*CJ* 432). Therefore, when we "determine our will" freely to change the universe so that other people can freely determine their wills – when we choose to work for the establishment of a civil society – we are entitled to expect that we can actually accomplish something by that. Our determination of our wills will result in successful action.

But the ability of all people to freely set their own purposes, as §84 argues, is not something empirical; it can never be experienced. It is at most a noumenon, for it is nothing other than freedom. This is the final, ultimate purpose of nature, then. The final cause of nature is not an internal *telos*, but an external one: the noumenal realm is the final cause of the natural realm – or must be *thought of* as such!

AFTER THE COLLAPSE

Kant's final argument, to say the least, is unpersuasive. Why, for example, must we think of the entirety of nature as a single teleological system? Why does the final cause of that system have to be something about us? Why does that something have to be either happiness or freedom? Why is happiness defined as the satisfaction of all desires? Why, in sum, are human beings not merely parts of nature?

Kant's failure leaves the noumenal realm both in legislative conflict with the empirical realm and without any intelligible relation to it; the conflict, in other words, remains inscrutable. Since the relation between the realms is unintelligible, neither realm can explain anything about the other. We are thus free to resolve the conflict by dispensing with either realm. While rejecting the empirical realm does not make much sense, doing so with the noumenal realm allows us to formulate a consistent picture that solves three of the four difficulties with Kant that I listed above.

29

If we look back at those four problems, we see that there is a common thread in all but one of them: Kant's recurrent tendency to treat certain things as being outside time. The thing-in-itself, being non-empirical, is outside time, and there is a big problem about whether we should even say it is there. The principles of the faculties, and so the faculties themselves, are also treated as atemporal: hence Kant's refusal to talk about where they may have come from. And the problem of the causality of Reason is the problem of how something that is not itself temporal can have effects in the empirical, that is temporal, world. Of the four problems I have listed, the only one that is not generated by taking something to be atemporal is the problem of how the categories relate to one another.

Since all the other problems arose from claiming that there is something that is outside time, they can all be dismissed by denying that there is any such thing, at least as far as we are concerned. Our "pure concepts", as well as our moral ideas, and indeed our faculties themselves, would thus have origins in time: they would have come to be from something else, and would presumably pass away into something else. To be sure, such dismissal opens a difficult and painful path for philosophy. Freedom can no longer be assigned to a noumenal realm, and must be redefined in a way compatible with natural causality, or our view of natural causality itself must be modified. More generally, and indeed even more seriously, if everything we can concern ourselves with is in time, then everything we can concern ourselves with is mortal. Our basic moral standards, and indeed everything that we love and admire, has come to be from something else, and will, one day, turn into something else. That goes, in particular, for the kind of philosophy that Kant so loved, and which he tried so hard to salvage.

* our 'pure concepts'/moral
ideas & faculties have
to have their origins
in time — therefore
also mortal

CHAPTER 2

HEGEL DISCOVERS THE PAST

PRIMARY TEXTS G. W. F. Hegel, *Phenomenology of Spirit* (*PhS*; [1807] 1979) and *Reason in History* (*RH*; 1953)[1]

Kant died, worn out, in 1802. It is fortunate that he never lived to see what happened just four years later. The French Revolution, which in its beginnings had contained what Kant could recognize as a rational impulse towards freedom and goodness (Kant, *The Conflict of the Faculties*, AA VII, 85–7), had grown steadily more chaotic and violent until it was finally taken over by a young Corsican, Napoleon Bonaparte. Bonaparte, however, was riding a tiger. By 1806 the revolutionary impulse had coalesced into a mighty army, spreading the name of freedom – but the reality of conquest – to the east, which meant to Germany.

Germany was disunited and, in general, politically repressive; hereditary nobles squabbled with each other and controlled far too much of their subjects' lives. But to be taken over and forcibly "enlightened" by foreigners was not what the Germans wanted, and they fought back. The decisive battle came at Jena, in east central Germany, on 14 October 1806. It was a complete rout for the Germans, who suffered enormous casualties. Within six weeks, Napoleon would complete his conquest of Prussia.

The day before the battle, as the troops massed, Napoleon led part of his army through the city of Jena, sitting proudly on his great white horse. The fearful Germans stood silent in the streets to watch him as he rode by. The only sounds were the clopping of hooves and the rumbling of caissons.

Watching Napoleon from the crowd, wearing a threadbare old coat, was a thorough specimen of human failure. Just one year younger than Napoleon, George Wilhelm Friedrich Hegel had conquered nothing.[2] After spending his university years in something close to an alcoholic stupor, he had gone on to

---

1. References to *Phenomenology of Spirit* (*PhS*) are to paragraph numbers in Hegel (1979); references to *Reason in History* (*RH*) are to page numbers in Hegel (1953).
2. For information on Hegel's life see Pinkard (2000). The account of the battle of Jena is on pp. 228–9.

pass his twenties as a domestic tutor, educating the children of a well-to-do family several miles outside Berne, Switzerland; these were years of intense solitude and unrelieved boredom.

Hegel's many efforts to escape what Marx would call the "idiocy of rural life" all failed, but eventually his old college roommate, the poet Friedrich Hölderlin, got him a job as a domestic tutor in Frankfurt. Soon after Hegel's arrival, however, the two friends had a falling out, and Hegel was left alone again. In desperation, he appealed to his other college roommate, Friedrich Wilhelm Joseph Schelling, who by that time had become a famous philosopher at the university of Jena, and Schelling got him work as a *Dozent* in the university. A *Dozent*-ship in a German university at that time was basically a licence to starve, for *Dozenten* were unsalaried. They taught courses that the university officially recognized, but were paid directly by the students according to what the students considered the course had been worth. Hence Hegel's threadbare coat; hence his rented room in a shabby boarding house.

And things were not looking up. Although he had scheduled the examinations necessary to obtain a true professorial appointment, and had almost finished the book he needed to publish in order to qualify for it, the arrival of the French could only mean that the German educational system would undergo huge changes. Whether there would be a place for him under the new regime was doubtful. In the event, the university simply closed down for a while; Hegel went off to become a small-town newspaper editor in Bavaria.

Hegel's problems extended to his personal life as well: he had impregnated his landlady, Johanna Burckhardt. This man, nearing forty and without resources or prospects, was shortly to become a father, but not a true husband for there was no question of love here and Frau Burckhardt already had two illegitimate children (Pinkard 2000: 237).

There is a legend that Hegel, as he stood there in the street and watched Napoleon ride past, had under his arm the manuscript of a book he had written, the one that was supposed to win him a professorship. He probably did not, but if he did it was a messy manuscript. Written under conditions of the most extreme stress and duress, it is one of the most obscure and difficult books ever published, one of the most widely read, and one of the most controversial: *The Phenomenology of Spirit*. The *Phenomenology* would not make Hegel's career, for no one could understand it. It would be another ten years before he obtained an academic position, at the University of Heidelberg, and another two before he arrived in Berlin, where he spent the rest of his life lecturing to growing acclaim. Hegel died in 1832.

Because the *Phenomenology of Spirit*, or as I shall call it, the *Phenomenology*, is so confused and intricate – and so long – a true commentary on it would run to many hundreds of pages. My aim here is merely to illuminate its basic nature by discussing its two most important sections, the first and the last. This will suffice to clarify the basic claim of the book, which is that philosophy must abandon all hope of access to an atemporal domain. The *Phenomenology* is thus the first appearance in philosophy of what Kant had laboured so hard to stave off: the first appearance of continental philosophy.

WHAT IS THE *PHENOMENOLOGY OF SPIRIT*?

The least controversial thing about the *Phenomenology* is that it is supremely difficult. It is a series of portrayals or re-enactments of the adventures of something called *Geist*, or Spirit, which takes on different forms in different parts of the book. These constitute the series of its appearances: the "phenomena" of the title. The series is progressive: things get somehow better as it goes along. The progress is necessary in at least two senses: each stage could not be located elsewhere than it is in the overall development, and Spirit cannot simply stop and stay put at any stage but must move on to the next. This is because at each stage problems, often but not always "contradictions", arise that call forth a new stage in which those problems, and no others, are resolved. Because the sequence is necessary (in these senses at least), it has a "why and wherefore", or, to use the Greek term for this, a *logos*.

The book thus gives the why and wherefore of the appearances of Spirit, and in that sense is a "phenomenology" of it. As the progress unfolds, all sorts of familiar and unfamiliar things seem to appear and disappear, from ancient forms of slavery to the Roman *lares* and *penates* to medieval guilds and various philosophical positions.

The basic movement is from "Consciousness" (part A) to "Self-consciousness" (part B) and finally to Reason, Spirit and Absolute Spirit (part C). This movement is explicitly "dialectical", and if that means anything for Hegel, it has to do with defining things in terms of their opposites. This provides a clue for understanding the three basic parts of the book:

(A) The opposite of consciousness is the unconscious, not in any Freudian sense (which would, of course, be anachronistic) but simply as what is not itself conscious. We can consider this section to deal with the awareness of objects that are not themselves aware. Since the object and the awareness of it reciprocally define one another, the chapter titles here refer to both: "Opining" (*Meinen*) and its object, the "This"; "Perception" and the "Thing"; and "Understanding" and "Force".

(B) The opposite of self-consciousness is, we may say, other-consciousness, or the awareness of an object that is itself taken to be aware. Here, consciousness defines itself in terms of other consciousnesses as other (i.e. in so far as they are not similar to the first consciousness). The chapter headings thus refer to social relations that are more or less antagonistic: "Master" and "Bondsman"; the Stoic withdrawal from society; the sceptical denial of others' reality; and finally the unrequited yearning for God of the "Unhappy Consciousness".

Now let us consider the relation of parts (A) and (B), because they, too, if dialectical, are opposed. In (A), we just have consciousness and unconscious-ness, present in an interplay of abstract categories; there is no differentiation within consciousness, so to speak. In (B), consciousness is considered to be split up into a plurality of different, antagonistic individuals. What (A) and (B) would seem to have in common is an equation of distinction with antagonism: in (A) both are absent, while in (B) both appear.

We can thus expect (C) to explore the possibilities of distinction without antagonism. Spirit here is increasingly able to accept the other as other, without attempting to deny the otherness by either submerging it in a general category (such as "consciousness") or adopting an antagonistic attitude towards it. So we find (C) to be concerned with truly cooperative endeavours such as science, the family, society, religion and philosophy. The point of the whole book is correspondingly to provide a philosophical justification for philosophy as the understanding of, and as itself an exercise in, human cooperation. In contrast to the solitary doubter of Descartes' *Meditations*, Hegel's philosophical "I" is a "we" (*PhS* ¶177). But the different "I"s that make up this "we" are not united by the fact that their minds are all isomorphic, that is, exhibit the same basic struc-tures as they do in Kant; rather, their "we" is an achievement: a "commonality of consciousnesses which has been brought about" (*PhS* ¶69).

The overall purpose of the *Phenomenology* is usually taken to be, more trad-itionally, the overcoming of something called the "subject–object split". The idea that there is something intolerable about the gulf between the knowing mind and the objects it knows was certainly crucial to Hegel's friend and ben-efactor Schelling, and Schelling's standard response to the subject–object split was to invoke something that somehow combined both, which he called the Absolute. If we accept this as the concern of the *Phenomenology*, then Hegel can be viewed as carrying on Schelling's project by engaging in what John Findlay called "absolute-theory", an account of a sort of depersonalized pantheistic Godhead similar to Schelling's Absolute.[3]

Since the Absolute contains everything, this approach is basically pantheistic. Knowing the Godhead means knowing everything else as well. Absolute-theory would therefore be the knowledge, at one and the same time, both of self and of non-self. Hegel thus seeks to achieve, as Findlay puts it, "a pure knowledge of self, even of this individual self, which is also the knowledge of all the moments of content which self distinguishes from itself, and in comprehending brings

---

3. For this "metaphysical" take on Hegel, see Findlay (1958). For a historicized Absolute see Taylor (1975). For criticism of "large-entity" interpretations in general, see Kolb (1986).

back into self" (Findlay 1958: 590). As Findlay's confusing formulation here shows, it is very difficult to make this project intelligible, let alone plausible. In fact, Hegel's project is not a continuation of Schelling's, for Schelling's philosophy was yet another attempt to maintain traditional philosophy. In his *Treatise on Human Freedom*, published in 1809, he wrote, in words that could be a conscious reaction to the *Phenomenology*, published two years earlier:

> We entertain the greatest respect for the profound significance of historical investigations. … Nevertheless we believe that Truth lies nearer to us and that we should first seek the solution for the problems that have become vital in our time among ourselves and on our own soil, before we wander to such distant sources. The time of merely historical faith is past, as soon as the possibility of immediate knowledge is given. (Schelling 1936: 97–8)

The idea that "immediate knowledge", knowledge that simply presents itself as certain, could ward off history is certainly antithetical to the *Phenomenology*. As both Hegel and Schelling understood, the *Phenomenology* is a *farewell* to Schelling.[4] In a revealing note written a year before his death, in connection with a project to rewrite the *Phenomenology*, Hegel explains why he broke that project off, characterizing the *Phenomenology* as a "peculiar early work, not to be reworked – related to the time of its composition – in the Preface: the abstract [i.e. Schellingian] absolute ruled in those days".[5]

The Phenomenology's beginning: "Sense-Certainty"

If the *Phenomenology* is not a theory of the union of subject and object, what can it be? The book's opening chapter on "Sense-Certainty" provides some clues. There, consciousness confronts the first and rawest form of an opposition that will continue to plague it throughout the *Phenomenology*. It is not the opposition between subject and object, however, but one between space and time, on the one hand, and what fills them on the other. This turns out to be a specific form of a more general opposition, which I shall – for the moment – call that between universal and individual.

Space and time are infinite in extent, and infinitely divisible; no boundary can be found to them in either respect, and they are what may be called universal containers. To them corresponds the "pure self" of consciousness, likewise an

---

4. Concerning the *Phenomenology*'s effect on their friendship, see Pinkard (2000: 256–8).
5. "*Eigentümliche frühere Arbeit, nicht umzuarbetien – auf die damalige Zeit der Abfassung bezüglich – in Vorrede: das abstrakte Absolute herrschte damals*" (quoted by the editor, Johannes Hoffmeister, in Hegel [1952: 578]).

all-containing universality (*PhS* ¶91). Opposed to all three is their "concrete content" (*Inhalt*). This also appears, at first, as an infinitely extended (or divisible) richness. But on closer examination it turns out to be deeply impoverished: a mere "example" (*Beispiel*) of content that, local and transitory, "plays past" the pure self (*spielt … beiher*; *PhS* ¶92).

Among the "countless differences that crop up here" is that between the example, or "this", as the object, and the ego that, right here and now, confronts (or "senses") that object. As Hegel himself puts it, the "this" as self and the "this" as object "fall out of" pure being, the undifferentiated infinitude of space–time, to which they are both opposed (*PhS* ¶92). Space, time and the pure ego, or the I, are thus universal containers. What they contain is radically individual subjects and objects: passing, but concrete, "heres" and "nows".

Once these basic distinctions are clear, the actual movement of the section is relatively easy to follow. Consciousness is attempting, as it attempts throughout the *Phenomenology*, to attain ultimate truth. Such truth, the goal of consciousness's efforts, is here taken to be just what presents itself to sensation – the very "immediate knowledge" that Schelling, two years later, would claim frees us from history:

> The knowledge or knowing which is at the start or is immediately our object cannot be anything else but immediate knowledge itself, a knowledge of the immediate or of what simply *is*. Our approach to the object must also be immediate or receptive; we must alter nothing in the object as it presents itself. (*PhS* ¶90)

The concrete sensory object is taken to be ultimate, just as sensation presents it to us. This brings up the question of *what* that object is. Consciousness first attempts to answer this question by naming the object in temporal terms. The *Phenomenology*'s first definition of ultimate truth is thus, "now is night" (*PhS* ¶95).

Here, consciousness comes up against the contrast between the universal and the individual. This occurs when it accepts the demand – itself, like everything else here, immediate and peremptory – to *write the truth down*: "a truth cannot lose by being written down, any more than by being preserved by us" (*PhS* ¶95). When "now is night" is written down, its inadequacy as absolute truth is seen twelve hours later, when "night" has vanished and "day" has taken its place (*PhS* ¶¶95–6). The concrete object can hardly be ultimate truth, because it no longer exists at all. The same thing happens when consciousness tries to formulate ultimate truth in spatial terms: if it says that "here is a tree", all it has to do is turn around to see that "here" is (for example) a house (*PhS* ¶98).

At that point, consciousness changes direction and takes the subject, rather than the object, to be the primary truth. This move overcomes the problem of the vanishing objects, because the objects no longer count as ultimate: ultimate truth is what I say it is, *because* I say it is that. If I say it is a house, then it is a house; if I say it is a tree, then it is a tree. No matter what happens to the objects, no matter how fast they disappear, I and my utterances are still around.

But grounding ultimate truth in my ego will not work either, for I am not the only ego in the world. What happens when I say that here is a tree and some other I says that here is a house? Neither ego is special, and ultimate truth must really lie in a universal "ego as such", an I that is "A simple seeing which, though mediated by the negation of this house, etc. is all the same simple and indifferent to whatever happens in it. The 'I' is merely universal like 'Now', 'Here', or 'This' in general" (*PhS* ¶102).

But this is not ultimate truth either, for this universal ego is merely abstract, while ultimate truth was originally taken to be concrete. Consciousness therefore reverses itself again and takes the *relation* between I and object to be the truth. *Both* terms of that relation can change freely, then, as long as the relation remains the same: "Its truth preserves itself as a relation that remains self-identical, and which makes no distinction of what is essential and unessential, between the 'I' and the object, a relation therefore into which no distinction can penetrate" (*PhS* ¶104). But this still does not solve the underlying problem; indeed, it only makes it more evident. For we now see that the specific contents of the here and the now, be they objective or subjective, do not have any *staying power*:

> The now is pointed to, this "Now"; it has already ceased to be in the act of pointing to it. The Now that is [now] is another now than the one pointed to, and we see that the Now is just this: to be no more just when it is. The Now, as it is pointed out to us, is Now that *has been*, and this is its truth; it has not the truth of being. Yet this much is true, that it has been. (*PhS* ¶106)

Consciousness, then, can neither talk about nor know what is, but only what has been. Knowledge is not only *conditioned* by the past, but is directed *upon* it. The future is unknown, while the present does not stay long enough to be even pointed at; all that we have is the ongoing past. This ongoing past is now to count as ultimate truth. But because it extends over several moments, it is a universal; and the *Phenomenology* moves beyond the premise of sense-certainty, which was that ultimate truth was to be formulated as a concrete individual.

The Phenomenology's onward movement

Several important lessons can be learned about Hegel from these few ---
First, subject and object are distinguished from each other in that now now the other is identified either as universal or as individual: the subjec

distinction is not primary but presupposes the distinction between universal and individual. Moreover, in order for the subject–object distinction to function as it does within "Sense-Certainty", yet another opposition must come into play: that between basic and derivative. For throughout the section, one side of the more basic split – universal or individual – is always taken as primary and the other as secondary. Thus, at the beginning of the section, universal "pure consciousness" confronts an individual "this", and is either derived from it or vice versa; at the end, the object has become universal and the self is an individual pointing to it (*PhS* ¶110). The subject–object distinction is thus founded on not one but two more basic distinctions: that between universal and individual, and that between basic and derivative.[6]

Second, the distinction between the universal (space–time, ego) and individual (example) begins to cause problems when consciousness accepts the demand to *write the truth down*. This first attempt to write down the truth fails because of the discrepancy between universal and individual. It is this that disqualifies the vanishing concrete objects (night, day, tree and house) from being ultimate truths. Ultimate truth, then, must be permanent.

This brings us to a third point. The distinction between the universal and the individual operates here as a distinction between what does not change (the empty universal container) and that which simply is continuous change and nothing more (the *Bei-spiele* or "examples", the concrete, disappearing objects that are unsuccessfully talked about and pointed to). This distinction is even more basic than the distinction between universal and individual as such, because it persists throughout the *Phenomenology*. Each of the book's sections has the same general form. Something is taken to be unchanging and it is then opposed to a changing reality on which it is seen to depend; the discrepancy between changing and unchanging requires a redefinition of truth itself.

Thus, the beginning of each stage of the *Phenomenology*, as Hegel tells us in the "Introduction", is a "certainty": something that claims to be what Descartes, as I noted in the Introduction, called a "certain and unshakeable" foundation (*PhS* ¶¶81–6). That this putatively unchanging truth turns out to depend on something that does change undoes its claim to be "ultimate" truth, because ultimate truth – in the eyes of "consciousness", anyway – cannot change.

Here is a list, selected from some of the most famous stages of the *Phenomenology*, of such putatively unchanging "certainties":

- the empty ego of Desire, the "motionless tautology of 'I am I'", which requires satisfaction in objects that continually present themselves anew (*PhS* ¶167);

---

6. It follows that Hegel here, in the opening moves of his first major published work, is already beyond standard views of such "modern" philosophers as Descartes and Locke, for whom the opposition of subject and object is famously basic.

- the unchanging ego of the Lord, "the consciousness that exists for itself", which depends on the dynamic activity of the Bondsman (*PhS* ¶186);
- the annihilating activity of sceptical consciousness, "the unchanging and genuine certainty of itself", which depends on the "confused medley" of specific doctrines it must refute (*PhS* ¶205);
- the "simple Unchangeable" with which the changeable Unhappy Consciousness seeks – but cannot find – unity (*PhS* ¶¶208, 657);
- the "divine law" that comes into opposition to the prevailing (and so changeable) law of the state in "The Ethical Order" (*PhS* ¶449);
- the "Aether of pure consciousness" into which self-alienated Spirit projects its own activity in the real world (*PhS* ¶487);
- "Pure Insight", which, as Enlightenment, opposes the "twaddle of the moment" of belief (*PhS* ¶539);
- the moral soul, which can be moral only when it does not perform any actions – but finds it must act in order to be good (*PhS* ¶637);
- the "tranquil and positive" religious artificer, which becomes tranquil and positive only by transcending natural phenomena in favour of its own individual creations (*PhS* ¶690);
- the absolute self of revealed religion, which has "let content go free" (*PhS* ¶751); and so on.

What the *Phenomenology* is most basically about, then, is the very opposition that has bedevilled philosophy from Parmenides to Kant: that between the philosophical realm of unchanging truth and the changing world in which we live. Its ultimate claim, then, is somehow to resolve that opposition. To see what that "resolution" amounts to, we must turn to the book's end.

THE *PHENOMENOLOGY'S* FINAL OUTCOME

At each stage of the *Phenomenology*, then, consciousness begins by thinking that its voyage of discovery is over: that it has found some unchanging truth. But each time, this turns out not to be the case. This continues right up to the end, where – on most accounts – Hegel puts an end to the adventures of Spirit by, at last, climbing up out of history. Or he thinks he does: few have been willing to follow him in this, or to venture on into his system itself. Certainly, later exponents of continental philosophy will not. Whatever their disagreements, and however fierce, Marx, Kierkegaard, Nietzsche, Heidegger, Arendt, Horkheimer and Adorno, Sartre, Beauvoir, Derrida and Foucault all agree that Hegel tried to escape time and history in the final chapter of the *Phenomenology*, and failed. But escaping from time and history is not the only way to end Spirit's quest. Also possible is that consciousness simply gives up, once and for all, any hope of transcending them. Indeed, given how utterly all of its many previous attempts at such transcendence have failed, this is the more likely outcome.

"Absolute Knowing", the final chapter of the *Phenomenology*, was, like the rest of the book, written under extreme duress. It is even more confused and confusing than earlier sections. It begins by identifying its task as the "overcoming of its consciousness as such" (*PhS* ¶788). This, in turn, requires getting rid of the opposition that has defined consciousness throughout the book: that between temporal and atemporal being. Here, as a result of the (many) intervening developments, consciousness already sees itself as dynamic, and therefore as in time. Surmounting the opposition between subject and object thus means, in the first instance, showing that the object also is dynamic:

> [This surmounting] is to be taken more specifically to mean not only that the object presented itself to the Self as vanishing, but rather that it is the externalization of consciousness. ... This is the movement of consciousness, and in that movement consciousness is the totality of its moments. (*PhS* ¶788)

The specific way in which the object shows itself to be a "vanishing", and so as having the same dynamism as consciousness, lies in the object showing itself as the *interplay* of three levels: "[The object] is, as a whole, the *syllogism* or the movement of the universal through the particular to individuality, as [well as] the reverse, the movement from individuality through itself as sublated, the particular, to the universal" (*PhS* ¶789). Such, in outline, is what Hegel calls the "self-mediation" of the object. Its "vanishing" is thus the mediation, or interplay, of the three levels of individual, particular and universal. These three levels correspond, we are told here, to the three basic levels of consciousness as it has developed so far in the book: immediate (or sensuous) consciousness, perception and understanding. Consciousness and the object thus have the same tri-level dynamic structure. This, however, makes them isomorphic rather than identical, and so some disparity remains to be overcome. How does Hegel overcome it?

The remaining disparity lies in the fact that at the beginning of the chapter, the object is passive, while consciousness is active. Thus, Hegel says there that the "vanishing" of the object – the mediation of its three levels – is carried out in it, not merely or even primarily by the object, but "more specifically ... rather" by self-consciousness (*PhS* ¶788). If this final disparity is to be overcome, then, the object cannot remain passive. The interplay of its three levels must be something that it brings about itself, rather than something bestowed on it by consciousness. And indeed, as we just saw, Hegel says that the object "presented *itself* to the Self as vanishing" (*PhS* ¶788, emphasis added). We thus have two views of the self-mediation of the object: that it is brought about by consciousness, and that it is brought about by the object itself. How to reconcile them? What is plainly needed is to show, somehow, that the vanishing or self-mediation of the object is carried out by *both* it and by "us", or consciousness, together.

Here, something *really* strange happens, for Hegel's argument that the object carries out its own tri-level self-mediation turns out to be nothing but a short recapitulation of the *Phenomenology* up to that point (*PhS* ¶790–97). Instead of talking about the object, he talks about the *Phenomenology*: about the development of consciousness into self-consciousness and then into Spirit. The rest of the chapter, in fact, concerns the nature of the *Phenomenology* itself and its relation to science and to history: to time.

We can ask whether Hegel's recapitulation of the course of the *Phenomenology* is accurate or not, or whether the developments it recapitulates were themselves dialectically sound as originally presented. But such issues are less important at the moment than the fact that he should apply such a strategy at all. Why would he even think that a recapitulation of the *Phenomenology*'s development of consciousness would show us the self-mediation of the object? The answer has to be that the "object" in question here is the *Phenomenology* itself. The *Phenomenology*'s development, its own self-mediation, can then count as the self-mediation of the object, carried out by consciousness, for the *Phenomenology* is, most basically, the story of consciousness's own development or self-mediation.

If the *Phenomenology* and the self-mediation of the object were not identical, then the possibility would remain open that Hegel has in fact faithfully recapitulated his book, but that the book itself somehow did not really present the object's self-mediation. That Hegel does not even mention this possibility suggests that he sees no "gap" between the pathway of consciousness in the *Phenomenology* and the self-mediation of the object: that they are one and the same thing. What Hegel means by "the object" at the beginning of the chapter "Absolute Knowing" is not, then, objects as such or in general. It is the *Phenomenology* itself: consciousness's whole project of attaining unchanging truth.

Indeed, the pathway of the *Phenomenology*, the progression of Spirit from sense-certainty through consciousness, self-consciousness, reason and so forth, did not even exist until Hegel wrote the book: "As Spirit that knows what it is, it does not exist before, and [exists] nowhere at all until after the completion of its work … " (*PhS* ¶800).

There is, then, no antecedent reality in which, for example, stoicism gave way in succession to scepticism, the unhappy consciousness, and the contemplation of nature. If that sequence constitutes the self-mediation of the object, then the object cannot have mediated itself until the book was written. So again, the writing of the *Phenomenology* and the self-mediation of the object must be identical. The book's pathway does not *present* the self-mediation of the object; it *is* that self-mediation. It is now clear why, back in "Sense-Certainty", the truth could not be hurt by being written down: the truth, we now see, simply *is* what is written down. Considered in that way, truth could only be hurt if it were written down in a loose (unconnected or uncollected) way, or phrased in the wrong words, and so on: only if Hegel did not do what remains of his job as author.

The *Phenomenology* now seems more mysterious than ever, for it is now entirely self-referential. This presents us with a final mystery: what can Hegel possibly have thought he had achieved in writing a book that, at its end, turned out to be only about itself?

Recall what I said was the basic structure of each section of the book. Consciousness begins by declaring something to be a "certainty", some unchanging truth that will not, and need not, be transcended. Such a declaration can be shared by the reader, which means that it is the *reader*'s certainty that is undone. And if, as Hegel claims at the end of the "Introduction", the *Phenomenology* presents "the entire system of consciousness" (*PhS* ¶89), that is, considers all the possible ways of making such a declaration of certainty, then at its end all such declarations have been undone. Hegel has shown that there is no way for any reader to sustain such a declaration of certainty, and the *Phenomenology* becomes what he said it was in the beginning: a "thoroughgoing [self-completing] skepticism" (*sich vollbringende Skeptizismus*; *PhS* ¶78).

Scepticism, of course, is open to a vicious paradox: to claim that one knows nothing is to claim, at least, that one knows that. In Hegel's case, to claim that we cannot, ever, attain unchanging truth would be to establish at least one unchanging truth: that one. But Hegel has not shown that; he has shown only that *consciousness*, and the reader who identifies with it at any stage, cannot claim to attain such a truth. It is the difference between "there is no domain of unchanging truth" and "you, the reader who has bought into one of the *Phenomenology*'s certainties, cannot claim to attain such truth". Hegel has thus shown, not that there is no such thing as unchanging truth, but that all the many quests for such truth that the *Phenomenology* has explored have ended in failure; and until philosophers come up with a radically new way of conceiving such truth, and the quest for it, they must accept that there is no domain of unchanging truth to which they can have access. The state of things here and now is not an image of unchanging reality, as Plato thought, nor its materialization, as Aristotle thought, but simply the result of what has come before. The past – history – has swallowed reason.

REASON IN HISTORY

What this means is that, since we cannot gain access to a domain of unchanging truth, the very nature of reason itself must, like everything else, change over time. What counts as rational today would not have counted in the past, and presumably will not count in the future. For Hegel after the *Phenomenology*, then, *reason is historicized*. This seems to plunge him into an abyss of historical relativism, in which ancient Greek tolerance of slavery, for example, would be wholly justified for them, although wholly abhorrent to us.

But Hegel avoids the abyss, because for him there is another side to this: *history is rationalized*. He sees history in a way broadly analogous to what happens to consciousness in the *Phenomenology*: as a process in which basic ideas are tried and fail. In world history, humanity learns from that failure and moves on, just as consciousness did in the *Phenomenology*. History, for Hegel, is thus, at bottom, *idea driven*. His *Lectures on the Philosophy of World History* seek to vindicate this claim. *Reason in History* was originally the introduction to those lectures. It has the virtue of being much more readily intelligible than the *Phenomenology*, if only because it has the defect of not having actually been written by Hegel. It was pieced together by his students after his death, from notes they took at his lectures and from his own.

Hegel states his claim that history is rationalized as follows: "The sole thought which philosophy brings with it, in regard to history is the simple thought of reason – the thought that reason rules the world and that world history has therefore been rational in its course" (*RH* 11). This is one way of doing history, which Hegel calls "philosophical" or "speculative". In the opening pages of the book, Hegel contrasts it with two other ways of doing history: "original" and "reflective". "Original history" is history as told by eyewitnesses. An example would be Thucydides, writing down what he saw happening around him in the Peloponnesian War. This was the first kind of history to be done, because the other kind of history Hegel discusses here, "reflective history", needs it.

"Reflective history" is history that is done *subsequently* to the period in which it happens, as when someone today writes a history of ancient Greece: she needs eyewitness accounts as a database. Reflective history tries to tell history "as it happened", but is not restricted to eyewitness accounts. It is also not confined to the events occurring in some single lifespan, so it can have a long sweep. This is the kind of history usually written by historians today, and it has different subtypes. The historian can seek to recount history without any reference to her own period ("universal history"). Or she can seek to find lessons in history that can be of value for us today ("pragmatic history"). A third subtype is the history of history itself ("critical history"), in which the historian is concerned not with direct accounts of what happened in the past but with the ways other historians have written them up.

Reflective history, however much it aspires to be accurate and tell history "as it happened", cannot do this, if only because it is selective: to tell the whole history of Greece in a single book, you must leave a lot out (*RH* 7). Such omissions, moreover, must be guided by some sort of principle; one cannot just leave things out randomly. And this means that the reflective historian must have an idea, in advance of her work, of what the history she is going to recount was in fact all about. If we think ancient Greece was all about the birth of democracy, we will tell a different story than if we think it was all about the economics of slavery. So reflective history departs from the facts on the ground: it conveys a particular interpretation of those facts.

Like reflective history, philosophical history departs from the facts because it too has an idea that it brings to history. This, we have seen, is the idea that history is rational, which, as the *Phenomenology* suggests, is the idea that history is a process in which the human species learns from its mistakes. If we take this view to convey the facts of history, we will see history as many people think Hegel sees it: as a stately progression of the human mind towards higher and higher levels of philosophical comprehension. But Hegel sees the facts of history very differently. History, he says, bears a "universal taint of corruption" (*RH* 26). Indeed, it is "a slaughter bench at which the happiness of peoples, the wisdom of states, and the virtue of individuals have been sacrificed" (*RH* 27).

The "slaughter bench" of history is tremendously wasteful. Most people are born, lead their lives, die (violently or not) and are forgotten. And the lessons of history remain almost entirely unlearned:

> What experience and history teach us is this: that nations and govern-ments have never learned anything from history, nor acted in accord-ance with the lessons to be derived from it. Each era has such particular circumstances, such individual situations, that decisions can only be made from within the era itself.   (*RH* 8)

That is the problem with "pragmatic" history; it claims to give us useful lessons, but those lessons have *no effect* on politicians. So who learns from history? What do they learn? And, most importantly, if the philosophical his-torian cannot be absolutely faithful to the facts of history, how does she know that reason "rules" it? Hegel refuses to answer this question here. He says we cannot know, at the beginning of our study of history, that reason rules it: that is a truth that will emerge only at the end of the investigation (*RH* 12). So what for him is a *result* of his way of doing history is from the point of view of his audience a *hypothesis* that has to be proved to be true, by recounting history *as* rational. But Hegel must at least explain, here at the outset, what he means by "reason" and "rules" and even by "history". And it turns out (no surprise here) that what is meant by "reason" has changed in history. Hegel discusses three previous stages of the idea of reason.

Transformations in reason

To the ancients (*RH* 13–14), reason was not something in a conscious head: it was just the laws governing nature. So when the Greek philosopher Anaxagoras said that reason (*nous*) rules the world, he meant "reason" differently from Hegel when he says that reason (*Vernunft*) rules history. Anaxagoras just meant that there are natural patterns to things: that the universe is not chaotic. But (as Plato points out; *Phd.* 98b–c) Anaxagoras stopped there (*RH* 14). He did not try to show in detail how this works, that is, why things happen in rational ways, or just what those rational ways are, or why they are "rational" in the first place.

Later thinkers fleshed this out, but to do so they needed to view reason in a second way: as conscious – not as the laws of nature but as the ideas of God himself, who designed the laws of nature when he created the world. So we get a second view of reason, one that (unlike mere natural regularities) applies specifically to history: history is rational in that it is ruled by divine providence.

But the belief in a divine providence, as used by historians in Hegel's day, does not solve the problem with Anaxagoras. Historians of Hegel's time, he reports, either just say generally that God rules history, leaving things in the same vagueness as Anaxagoras did ("not a sparrow falls"), or they look at individual events and call them "providential" (how fortunate that Winston Churchill became Prime Minister on the day the Germans invaded Belgium!). Neither of these, Hegel says, is worthy of God: "God wants no narrow-minded souls and empty heads for his children" (*RH* 16). We humans are supposed to use our minds to understand what God does. This means discussing as many empirical facts as we can while not losing sight of the overall story we are telling about history. For the progress of reason lies *in* the facts of history; it is one thread in history's huge, bloody tapestry. It is the job of the philosophical historian to follow that single, but all-important, thread.

The reasons why Hegel's contemporaries cannot make effective use of the idea of divine providence is that they do not understand that idea rationally, and they do not understand it because they suppose that providence is somehow different from them: that God is other than, outside, the world. But the God that we know cannot be a god who is separate from the universe: "in placing the Divine beyond the reach of our knowing and beyond human affairs altogether, we gain the convenient license of indulging in our own imaginings" (*RH* 17). We are thus not going to learn from Hegel about an eternal God who existed before the world was created; we are going to learn about God's activity in history. In other words, even God, in so far as we humans can know him, changes: he acts differently in different historical periods. This changing, immanent deity is Hegel's third version of reason.

We still do not have a specific answer, however, to the question of what reason is. In order to see that, we must look further: to the nature of history's goal. So the next task (*Reason in History*, part 3) is to spell out what that goal is, the means by which reason achieves it and what sort of thing the process of that achievement is.

The overall process of history is what Hegel calls "Spirit", which includes whatever exists that is not merely part of nature (*RH* 20). According to Hegel, nature is the realm in which events merely repeat themselves according to law, but go nowhere, that is, there is no critical improvement going on: "Change in

Hegel's third version of reason

Hegel + process of history as spirit

45

nature, no matter infinitely varied it is, shows only a cycle of constant repetition. In nature, nothing new happens under the sun" (*RH* 68).

Hegel also goes on to say that nature is the realm of things that are determined from outside; a stone falls because of the laws of nature, and because of the specific events that cause this particular stone to fall. Spirit, in contrast to these two points, would be the realm of things that do not mindlessly repeat what has gone before, but determine themselves and so can transform themselves. So Spirit is the realm of *freedom*, and history, for Hegel, is the pursuit of freedom; the final goal is the state of complete freedom.

Here we first get Hegel's notorious ranking of civilizations as Oriental, where one person is free; Greek, where some people are free; and the modern world, concentrated in northern Europe, where all are free.[7] This modern world came about through Christianity; but Christianity at first construed freedom as existing only in the interior of the soul – you could be free even if you were a slave, if your soul was pure. Gradually we see in history the realization that freedom is not merely a matter of the interior of each individual, but of structures out there in the world, such as social structures (*RH* 23–4). The final goal of the world, then, is all humans being free and knowing that they are free; if you are free but do not know it, you cannot act freely, and your freedom is not real (*RH* 24). The specific idea that the philosophical historian brings to history is thus that it is "the progress of the idea of freedom" (*RH* 24). To say that "reason rules history" is to say that such progress can be found in the facts of history.

History as the development of freedom

The next question, then, is: what is freedom? Beyond the empty suggestion that freedom is the capacity to "determine oneself", Hegel defers this question as well: "The term 'freedom', without further qualification, is indefinite and infinitely ambiguous. … Yet for the time being we must content ourselves with this general, as yet undefined term" (*RH* 25). Hegel does not tell us the nature of freedom here because he cannot; as the goal of history, the nature of freedom must emerge from the facts of history as recounted by the philosophical historian. This does tell us something about the nature of freedom, however. For it means that the nature of freedom is relative to the process that brings freedom about; there is no eternal "essence of freedom", and different historical developments might well have given us a different concept of freedom.

Hegel makes another point, and a surprising one, to show how his own idea of reason follows on from what he has discussed previously: *God himself,*

---

7. Hegel does not identify the modern world with Germany, as is often alleged. His word for the modern world is *germanisch*, which means northern European, not merely German.

understood philosophically – that is, without religious "imagery" – is the "idea" of freedom. This means that he is the final goal of the world, plus the process of its realization. "Reason in history" is thus the God who changes and acts in the world (*RH* 25). Such freedom is not just an idea; it needs to become *actual* in human consciousness and social structures. The "rule of reason in history" is the process in which the idea of freedom is given this sort of actuality.

The need for freedom to become actual in social structures, rather than merely in the interior of the soul, returns us to the basic schema or intellectual pattern we saw at work in the *Phenomenology*. According to this pattern, something – anything – starts as a mere "certainty", a basic idea, which is then carried out into experience, refuted and reformulated in a richer way. Here, the schema starts, not with a supposedly unchanging definition of how the mind properly relates to ultimate reality, but more broadly with "a principle, a law, [which] is something implicit which, as such is not completely real" (*RH* 27). An example of this might be a projected law saying something like "anyone who enters another person's home without their knowledge or approval is liable to a jail term of three to five years". This is not real; as stated, it is merely a "possibility". It exists, at first, only in our thoughts and words.

In order to make it real, which is the next phase of the overall process, we must pass our law and then actually start sentencing to jail people who violated it. We have to get our hands dirty. We have to *will* the law. When we do that, we inevitably learn a great deal. Maybe the law is not so easy to enforce; maybe the sentences it proposes are too strict; maybe it is too vague. Then we have to move back and reformulate the law, then try again to carry it out as reformulated, that is as improved and enriched by our experience in trying to realize the earlier version. So we get a first moment of *subjectivity* and *abstractness*, a second moment of *struggle*, and a third moment of *reformulation* before trying again.

Hegel's account of history as the development of freedom, moving progressively through the notorious rank order of civilizations I mentioned above, fits it directly into this scheme. Like the idea of reason, the idea of freedom starts historically in a very crude way, with just one person in the society able to know himself as free: the "Oriental" emperor. Then it progresses by trial and error to the point where *some* members of society know themselves as free, in ancient Greece, and finally to a state of affairs where all do, in the modern world.

The *means* by which freedom advances, the beings that actually carry out the struggle that educates us all as to the meaning of freedom, are human individuals, and Hegel's conception of the human individual is one of his most important. Like other German philosophers, Hegel has an "active" view of the mind, so an "individual" is primarily a set of actions: you are what you do. The actions of a historical figure, Hegel is careful to insist, do not come from high motives, but from the desire for one's own gain as defined at the moment: "passions, private aims, and the satisfaction of selfish desires are, *on the contrary*, tremendous springs of action" (*RH* 26, emphasis added).

47

the 'additional results of history

This, then, is why history is a "slaughter bench". Historical actors are not trying to bring about the full consciousness of human freedom; nothing could be farther from their thoughts. They are trying to achieve ends that are often stupid and evil, and their actions often give rise to things that are stupid and evil: wars, pogroms, oppression of all sorts. But sometimes – if only sometimes – their actions have further results:

> Human actions in history produce additional results, beyond their immediate purpose and attainments, beyond their immediate knowledge and desire. They gratify their own interests but something more is thereby accomplished, which is latent in the action though not present in their consciousness and not included in their design. (RH 35)

Hegel's example is someone who wants to get even with his neighbours by setting fire to their house, and burns down the whole town. Hegel clearly does not think that there is some Spirit turning the local bonfire into a city-wide conflagration and so, correspondingly, there is not some Spirit out there consciously directing history. But the actions of a few, so to speak, "catch fire": they become known and disseminated widely to people. There may have been a hundred Athenians trying to write philosophical dialogues in Plato's day, but his, and his alone, have survived *in toto*. The "Spirit" that rules history is not some sort of great ghost over and above it, but just the tendency of human beings, at certain times, to value certain sorts of thing.

History's use of individuals proceeds via an internal dynamic of its own. The case of Socrates illustrates this even better than that of Plato. Greece was a slave economy. But the idea that all humans are siblings, that all are inherently free, was out there, waiting to be expressed, as it were. In order for it to be expressed, though, something else had to be articulated first. This was the idea that our society, in which we grow up and live our lives, is possibly not only wrong about various things but deeply, fundamentally, *very* wrong. That such a thing was even possible was a discovery that Socrates made by accident. As Plato has him tell the story in the *Apology of Socrates*, somebody went to the oracle at Delphi and asked the oracle who was the wisest person in Athens. The oracle said Socrates was. This surprised him, because he had always felt very ignorant. So he went out and started buttonholing those with reputations for wisdom – politicians, poets, philosophers – and it turned out that, indeed, they too were very ignorant people. So Socrates gradually came round to the idea, almost in spite of himself, that maybe society itself, in which these were the influential parties, was also pretty ignorant.

At that point, the world divided for Socrates, not into slaves and free people as it did for other Athenians, but into people who knew they were ignorant and people who did not. Slaves and free people could be found on both sides of that division; and since it was the only division among humans that mattered, the

example of history, Socrates & things being 'wrong' fundamentally → story of oracle as example

distinction between slaves and free people did not. Socrates, although he did not know it, had thus come up with a powerful argument against slavery, one that would take millennia to achieve existence in social structures. What he had also come up with, also without knowing it, was the view that Athens was set up in ways that were fundamentally wrong. When he expressed that idea openly in his own life, the Athenians killed him. But they could not kill the idea.

The passion for self-understanding

What people value changes over history, of course. Ancient Romans found Plato's story of Socrates important for reasons that are not the same as ours. But there is one most basic value that can be found at work in history, and we have already seen what it is: self-understanding, of the sort we have when we know that all humans are free. This explains why we need philosophical history. The point of it is not to give guidance to historical actors, to politicians and generals; rather, it is supposed to help individuals understand themselves.

To understand more fully the nature of such self-understanding, we must return to a passage I quoted above: "private aims, and the satisfaction of selfish desires are, *on the contrary*, tremendous springs of action" (*RH* 26, emphasis added). What, here, provokes the phrase "on the contrary"? It is a recognition that not all passions and aims are selfish: "It is true that this drama [of history] involves also universal purposes, benevolence, or noble patriotism. But such virtues and aims are insignificant on the broad canvas of history" (*RH* 26).

For Kant, all motivations save respect for the moral law were merely "inclinations", physiological cases of mechanical causality. It is important to Hegel's view of human individuality that this not be the case: that some motivations, but only some, are "true and substantial". "If someone wants to decide whether my conviction and passion are true and substantial, s/he must consider the content of my conviction and the aim of my passion. Conversely if they are true and substantial, they cannot but attain actual existence" (*RH* 30). What does it mean for a passion to be "true and substantial"? Clearly, it means for it not to be a passing whim. This, then, is the sort of difference we have between a childhood crush and lasting love. And for a passion to be "true and substantial" on a historical scale, it must *really* last: must outlive the person who feels it and go on, changing and growing, to influence later generations. Thus, Plato felt a passionate admiration for his teacher Socrates, and organized his life around that admiration: he undertook his life's work, wrote his dialogues, as memorials to Socrates' memory. Those dialogues, in turn, have been influential on a much larger, historical scale. They have had a profound influence on the Western world for the past 2400 years, precisely because what they memorialize about Socrates is not some passing thing like how funny he was, or what he looked like, but his own "true and substantial passion": the love of wisdom. So we read

✱ Key in understanding dif between Hegel & Kant

Plato's dialogues today in part because through them we can see what it *really* means to love wisdom: to be a philosopher.

An individual, then, is not merely a creature with a flock of interests and inclinations. She has a moral core. This is not, as it was for Kant, a faculty of reason that is somehow outside time and the world yet functions within them. It is her own true and substantial passions. A human being therefore needs to be able to tell the difference between what is true and substantial and what is not: to know what is really basic and important to her. And to know this is just to know yourself, to bring your own basic nature into consciousness. That effort takes a long time, longer, in fact, than any single human life. When we try to figure out what our lives are all about, for example, we must use words and categories that we have inherited from the efforts of others, over millennia, to do that same thing. We are leaning on history, which "begins its general aim – to realize the Idea of Spirit – only as an innermost unconscious instinct. And the whole business of history … is to *bring it into consciousness*" (RH 30, emphasis added).

So our individual self-understandings had their roots long before we were ever born: "[E]ach individual is the child of a people at a definite stage of its development. One cannot skip over the spirit of his people any more than one can skip over the earth. The individual does not invent his own content; he is what he is by acting out the universal as his own content" (RH 37–8). Every plan we make, every emotion we express, is conditioned by words that were invented and refined over thousands of years by poets, philosophers and so on. They are in part products of a very long past, one much longer than our own. But our actions also escape us in the other direction: they have consequences beyond what we can foresee. And, as I suggested above, the more "true and substantial" they are, the more they have this characteristic.

The human individual thus has a double status in Hegel's philosophy of history. On the one hand, the individual is the "means" of history: someone whose passions, however stupid and selfish, advance humanity when they catch fire in their culture. On the other hand, the self-knowing individual is the goal of Hegel's own efforts at philosophical comprehension. It is the individual who, as Hegel puts it in the "Preface" to the *Phenomenology*, "Has the right that Science should at least show him the ladder to [the absolute] standpoint, and show him this standpoint within himself" (PhS ¶26). On both counts, a human individual is someone who has a number of passions. Some of these are true and substantial: the ones that have historical "staying power". Such passions have such power because they do not remain the exclusive property of the (mortal) individual who feels them, but are passed on to others. Ultimately then, this staying power is multigenerational: staying power not merely in an individual or a people, but in history itself.

One particularly important passion is the desire to understand oneself – to understand which among one's passions are true and substantial – and for this

Society's role in establishing true & subst

the individual is not used by history, but uses it; she makes use of the conceptual and linguistic heritage that has come down to her to express her passions. Only history, and of the "philosophical" type, can truly teach us which of our passions are true and substantial. To be sure, not everybody wants or needs this level of self-understanding. The great actors in history, as we shall see, do not trouble themselves with it. Most of the time, for most people, their culture provides sufficient guidance in life:

> What special course of action is good or not, right or wrong, is deter-
> mined, for the ordinary circumstances of private life, by the laws and
> customs of a state. It is not too difficult to know them … Each individual
> has his position; he knows, on the whole, what lawful and honorable
> course of conduct is. *(RH 37)*

Your society, then, tells you what is to be taken as true and substantial in your own life. In the modern world, having an occupation and participating in some sort of family life obviously counts as "true and substantial", whereas taking drugs and having random sex do not. The educational and legal systems of modern states incorporate these values, and thus provide guidance to individuals. Hegel says that the guidance modern societies provide is, generally, good guidance. But how can Hegel be so sure of this? For that we must turn to another highly influential part of his philosophy: his theory of the state.

HEGEL'S THEORY OF THE HISTORICAL STATE

"What counts in a state is the practice of acting according to a common will and adopting universal aims" *(RH 50)*. Because the state operates, for Hegel, in accordance with "universal" aims, it is *rational*. What is a rational state? Consider the irrational state. This, for Hegel, is a society in which one will is subjected to another will: a despotism, where the ruler rules in his own interest and does not have to justify himself to the ruled, whose desires and passions will have no validity whatsoever *(RH 50)*. This *irrational* situation is where the *rational* state comes from, for it is "already a connection of wills" *(RH 60)*. When this connection ceases to be despotic and becomes rational, the state does not operate by whim and fancy but rules through and as law.

The law, in turn, is valid because it is rational, not just because the citizens have agreed to to be governed by laws *(RH 56–7)*. The "rational" chain of thought that Hegel has in mind works like this: we individuals need to act together; therefore we need to have commanders and followers *(RH 57)*. The next questions are: (a) what sorts of commands need to be given, that is, what kinds of office are needed in the state; and (b) to whom should those offices be given? The way a society answers these questions produces a set of governmental

51

institutions and practices that provide the members of that society with concrete ways in which those individuals can understand themselves. In modern societies, it provides them with a set of concrete ways in which individuals can know themselves to be free, and so provides them, finally, with freedom itself. The "constitution" of a society – the offices established in it and the way those offices are distributed – is thus *itself* the freedom that society conveys to its members.

So we can say that freedom for Hegel, the goal to which history has been working, is a certain sort of constitution. If we want to know what specifically Hegel thinks freedom is, then we must ask: what type of constitution is the freest? But once again, Hegel refuses to answer the question; no one type of state is valid for every people or in every circumstance (*RH* 58). Indeed, the same people can require a different sort of constitution at different times. As he puts it, "a constitution is therefore not a matter of choice but depends on the stage of the people's spiritual development" (*RH* 60).

So an important aspect of constitutions – of concrete social definitions of freedom – is, for Hegel, as we might expect, the question of how constitutions come about and are changed. Hegel refuses to say in general terms how this happens, but his general view of history, one that is carried out in the *Lectures* whose Introduction we are considering here, shows how it will work. Somebody has an idea for a new form of governance, or for a new law; they may propose it to others or they may (like Socrates) just start acting in accordance with it. If that idea is the right idea, it will catch on with others and become accepted.

This *could* happen through a constitutional convention, as it did in the United States; or it *could* come about through a series of adjustments of very different kinds, as in the United Kingdom; or it *could* come about through a violent revolution, as in France. But whatever is finally accepted is accepted because the *people* in general have accepted it; what succeeds in this way is true, substantial and rational. So not just any sort of constitution is rational; although the laws of the state are valid because they are rational and not just because people accept them, on a deeper level what makes them rational is that people accept them.

The constitution, and the specific laws that follow from it, thus arise, for Hegel, out of the specific needs and desires of the people. And the fact that a constitution can change, even in fundamental ways, means that the *people* can change in fundamental ways. For if the constitution "depends on the stage of the people's spiritual development", then a people can develop. This is what Hegel means when he says that a people is a "*spiritual* individual": "This spirit of a people is a *definite* spirit and is ... determined according to the historical state of its development" (*RH* 66).

Because the basic constitution of a state is accepted by the people in a given stage of its development, it is rational, at least while the people remain in that stage. It can thus give them concrete ethical guidance in the form of its laws. When people follow that guidance, life in the state "is the union of the subjective [individual] with the rational [universal] will. It is that actuality in which the individual has and enjoys his freedom, but only as knowing, believing, and willing the universal" (*RH* 49).

What we do *not* have here, then, is a claim that the rational life in the state today will always be so. When Hegel says that the state unites the individual with the universal, he is clearly using "universal" in an unusual way. For him the political universal, being merely what the laws codify, changes over time.[8] To be "universally" true means to be rationally accepted by an entire people or community *at a particular stage of its development*; it does not mean to be true for all time. For if reason itself is historical, nothing is exempt from time.

Rational guidance is not provided to individuals merely by the state in the restricted sense of their government. Hegel says that the main vehicle by which the state provides and requires *specific* ways for the individual to "will the universal" is, in fact, religion, for in religion "the will of man renounces particular interest" (*RH* 63). Thus, religion is the foundation of the state, from which it grows: "[The state] has arisen from [religion] and now and always continues to arise from it" (*RH* 65). Which religion?

Given that in this discussion Hegel mentions only Christianity, and within that harshly criticizes Catholicism, we may assume that he has Protestantism in mind as the foundation of the state. But in his *Philosophy of Right*, he specifically denies that people should be forced to join any Church: the state should require everyone to belong to a religion he says, but cannot specify which (Hegel 1991: 295). What is going on here?

The answer is that, once again, everything depends on the level of development. Europe has developed to the level of "modernity". In modernity, as Kant and Descartes showed, the individual reason is the criterion of what is right and wrong; a "modern" person is reluctant to accept what is true from anyone else, but demands to decide for himself or herself. And not just in matters of truth and falsity, but across the board, the individual wants to be allowed to be himself or herself: "the subjective element in [individuals], their interests, cravings, and impulses, their views and judgments [have] an *intrinsic* right to be satisfied" (*RH* 44).

The modern state is rational, at our stage of development, because it allows us the right to be ourselves. It offers us a variety of lifestyles, professions, religions and so on, among which we can (a) find those that suit *us* best as individuals, and (b) put them to use for the good of the whole. Modern states are "modern" because they allow a diversity of lifestyles, indeed, the greatest possible diversity, and they do that because their citizens will settle for nothing else. In the *Philosophy of Right*, Hegel identifies this as the "prodigious strength" of the

---

8. This harks back to the sort of "universal" that, in the final chapter of the *Phenomenology*, was constituted through its interplay with the particular and the individual.

modern state (1991: 161). This means that, for Hegel, a state is modern if it not only tolerates minorities but allows them, as minorities, to bring their special perspectives and insights to bear on the issues of common or universal interest. Hegel is thus the first Western thinker to appreciate and articulate the value of *diversity* within a state or culture.

The individual's life is to be guided, then, by the "state" in a wide sense, including subcommunities such as religion, family, ethnic group, workplace and so on. This guidance will be good because these structures have passed through the test of history: whatever the state or society tells you to do is something that has become accepted, in one way or another, by many people and so is "rational" and good.

That is usually the case. As we have seen, things change, and what is universal and rational has to change with them: the state "is essentially the medium of historical change" (*RH* 61). In general, we may say that Hegel has what can be called a "catastrophe" theory of history: things go along relatively smoothly for long periods, but every now and again the basic premises of society are called into question and the move to something new becomes imperative. When things get that critical, we find individuals who cannot follow the guidance of the state, and must act against it. They act in the service of the *next* stage of history: the "higher universal" (*RH* 39). They are what Hegel calls "world-historical individuals".

Such people do not act with a clear consciousness of what they are doing. Caesar had to destroy the Roman Republic because otherwise his political enemies within that republic would have destroyed him (*RH* 39). The Roman Republic had in fact been outgrown, and as it turned out Caesar's acts showed the way to the Empire, but Caesar did not know this, any more than Socrates had known that his ideas would eventually lead to the abolition of slavery. Caesar's "true and substantial passion" at that stage of his life was just to save his skin. He, and those he convinced to stand with him, had enough insight, perhaps, to know that the Republic was no longer worth very much, and to think that if saving Caesar's skin required overthrowing the whole thing, perhaps that was possible, but none of them, not even Caesar himself, knew in any detail where things were going (we never do, as my account above of Hegel's view of historical development showed).

These world-historical individuals are the great people of history, but their lot is not a happy one:

> They attained no calm enjoyment. Their whole life was labor and trouble, their whole being was in their passion. Once their objective is attained, they fall off like empty hulls from the kernel. They die early like Alexander, they are murdered like Caesar, transported to Saint Helena like Napoleon. This awful fact, that historical men were not what is called happy – for only private life in its manifold historical

circumstances can be "happy" – may serve as a consolation for those people who need it, the envious ones who cannot tolerate greatness and eminence. (*RH* 41)

So which is better: to be Napoleon, France's greatest general, on his way to another brilliant victory, or an impoverished *Dozent* in the street? The answer is clear. Hegel the philosopher understood Napoleon better than Napoleon did, and had the joys of private life to boot, even if they were not very joyful at that moment in Hegel's life.

CONCLUSION

[handwritten: history's impotence when considering early Continental philosophy]

Continental philosophy, here at the moment of its birth, has as yet no history, but only an ancient and obscure prehistory in the form of Heraclitus. And yet history is all-important to such philosophy; indeed, we may say here, in continental philosophy's first version, reason is swallowed up by the past. Everything around us, except for the unchanging laws of nature, *has come to be*. What is valid about our beliefs and ways of doing things – what we really are and want to be – is what has emerged from the rationalized course of history. It can be understood and evaluated only through an account of how it came to be, through what Hegel calls "philosophical history".

Such history, the first appearance of continental philosophy, begins with the current state of affairs: in Hegel's case, here, with the concrete concept of freedom embodied in the state. It asks how this has come to be, and seeks in the myriad facts of history those few that can be construed as having led up to it. This learning process – what Hegel calls "reason" – is always present in history, behind the scenes. It underlies the bloody chaos of history because it is what makes history historical; where it is absent, we do not have history but only a meaningless sequence of events. So the philosophical or "speculative" historian, although telling the immense story of the entire human race, is not just talking about past times: she is talking about something that is present and ongoing even as she writes. In that way, philosophical history is a combination of original and reflective history.

The final stage of history – up to now – is thus, for Hegel, modern society, in which all people are free and know it. But what about the future? We do not know, and should not care. Here is what Hegel has to say about the future:

> The past is the preservation of the present as reality, but the future is the opposite of this, the becoming of the present as possibility, and thus as formless (*gestaltlos*). From out of this formlessness the universal first comes into form in the present; and hence in the future no form can be perceived. (Hegel 1974: I, 434)

[handwritten: formless future]

"The past is the preservation of the present as reality": Hegel is saying here that something becomes "real" (*wirklich*) only when it is retained and remembered – another way of putting Hegel's argument in the *Phenomenology*'s section on "Sense-Certainty". Not surprisingly, given his view that the present becomes "real" only when connected to the past, Hegel has next to nothing to say about the future. Commenting on – and in the final sentence apparently endorsing – Epicurus' views on death, he writes:

> The negative, the nothing is not to be brought into life and fixed there, only the positive is; there is no reason to worry about it. ... It is no concern of ours whether [the future] is or is not; we are to have no uneasiness on that account. This is the correct way to think about the future. (Hegel 1974: II, 307, trans. mod.)

This applies to Hegel's own philosophy, which is not meant to stand for all time. Already in the Preface to the *Phenomenology*, he had claimed to hear at the door "the feet of those who will carry you out" (*PhS* §71). His system itself, then, is radically revisable; it does not provide any unchanging truth. But it also provides no guidance with respect to the future, and does not even see it as a problem. It would soon become one, in the future.

CHAPTER 3

MARX, CAPITALISM AND THE FUTURE

PRIMARY TEXT Karl Marx, *Economic and Philosophical Manuscripts of 1844 and the Communist Manifesto* (*EPM*; 1988)

In March 1843, eleven years after Hegel's death, authorities in the western German region of Westphalia closed down a newspaper called the *Rheinische Zeitung*, or the "Rhineland Gazette". Among the people thrown out of work by this was the paper's twenty-five-year-old editor, Karl Marx. The newspaper itself was not very radical; its main audience was originally supposed to be businessmen, although after Marx became editor it veered leftwards. That the authorities could not tolerate even something as mildly progressive as the *Gazette* so disenchanted its editor that he decided to move abroad. After marrying the following summer, Marx moved with his wife to Paris. This began a six-year migration, mostly forced, through Europe: in 1844 Karl and Jenny were expelled from France and moved to Brussels; a return to Germany in 1848 (to edit a revived version of the *Gazette*) did not work out; and in 1849 the couple arrived in London, where they lived for the rest of their lives. Marx died in 1883.[1]

AFTER HEGEL: PHILOSOPHY IN CONFUSION

That Marx was working at a newspaper at all calls for some explanation. He came from a family of distinguished rabbis, but had a father who, like many German Jews in those days, had converted to Christianity mainly for career reasons. Karl himself obtained a doctorate in philosophy from Jena, the university where Hegel had failed to become a professor, and had hoped to succeed, where Hegel had failed for so long, in finding an academic position. That Marx also failed, and definitively, had much to do with the philosophical reaction in Germany to Hegel's temporalizing of philosophy.

---

1. The classic English biography of Marx is Berlin (1996); also cf. Wheen (2001).

Continental philosophy, with its view that everything is mortal, is, to say the least, uncomfortable. As Marx himself sums it up in his *Capital*, such thought, which he calls "dialectics":

> includes, in its comprehension and affirmative recognition of the exist-ing state of things ... also the recognition of the negation of that state, of its inevitable breaking up; because [such thought] regards every his-torically developed social form as in fluid movement, and hence takes into account its transient nature not less than its momentary existence; because it lets nothing impose upon it, and is in its essence critical and revolutionary. (Marx 1906: 26)

This was as true of Hegel's philosophy as of Marx's, and among the people who were apparently discomfited by it was a group of Hegel's students and friends. After his untimely death, they constituted themselves as a group called the *Freunde des Verewigten*, the "Friends of the immortalized one", and undertook to publish a complete edition of the master's works. The name they chose for their group is telling. The German word "*verewigt*", which is usually translated as "immortalized" or "perpetuated", literally means "eternalized". Hegel's discom-fited friends undertook to render his philosophy as just what it was not: a tradi-tional philosophical account of eternal truth. It was they who "eternalized" him.

It may have been inevitable that Hegel's version of continental philoso-phy, seeking to understand history without as yet having a history of its own, should have been viewed as an attempt to understand history from outside: by using a conceptual framework intended to stand for all time, resting (to quote a claim Kant once made for his own philosophy) "on fully secured foun-dations, established forever" (Kant 1967: 254). Certainly the "friends of the eternalized" viewed Hegel's system – including all the works he wrote after the *Phenomenology* – as a timeless set of logical structures. As they saw it, the *Phenomenology* itself, instead of showing why the quest for such timeless truths must be abandoned, somehow showed how it could be successful. Instead of submitting to time and history at its end, the *Phenomenology* somehow used those final pages to climb up out of history altogether.

Or so the "Friends" thought. But their effort was wholly misguided. It was as if Darwin's friends and supporters had devoted their efforts to showing that *On the Origin of Species*, whatever it appears to be, is really a defence of the biblical account of creation. Although their project "normalized" Hegel's philosophical project into something fairly familiar to traditional philosophers, it also rendered it distinctly implausible, in at least two ways. First, if Hegel was saying what the "Friends" thought he was saying, he had done an extraordinarily bad job of saying it. His meaning, if that is what it was, bore little relation to the words actu-ally on the pages of his writings. An enormous field of scholarship opened up, as people attempted to force on to Hegel's writings views they never expressed.

Hegel's system, if construed in this way, also loses plausibility because his logic, and the further system that develops out of it, are very detailed. It would be quite a job for all reality, always, to conform to its basic structures. In fact, the only power great enough to guarantee such conformity is divine power. When Hegel said, in a *bon mot* regularly distorted by both later attackers and defenders, that "the real is rational and the rational is real" (Hegel 1991: 20), this was taken to affirm some kind of rationalist theology in which all that exists exhibits the eternal truths of reason. In fact, Hegel never meant to say anything like that; his original formulation, in his lecture course of 1819–20, was much more dynamic: "the real *becomes* rational, and the rational *becomes* real" (1983: 201, emphasis added; cf. also the Editor's Note, 389–90).

Still more unfortunate, but entirely to be expected, was that the misguided project of the "Friends" affected their editorial practices. Their edition of Hegel's works, published between 1840 and 1847 and the only one available until 1970, is so full of distortions that it has now had to be entirely redone by the Hegel-Archiv in Germany, a project that is still far from finished. The true radicality of Hegel's philosophy was thus covered over for generations to come. He appeared to be a traditional philosopher, but a very bizarre one.

This approach to Hegel was opposed, early on, by others of his friends, by his students and, especially, by his students' students. They saw his philosophy as providing, not a philosophical theology, but the basis for a thoroughgoing critique of religion. The main group of these alternative readers of Hegel is called the "Young Hegelians", and its numbers included Ludwig Feuerbach, Moses Hess, David Strauss, Max Stirner – and Marx.[2] These radical young philosophers were extremely courageous; all of them, Marx included, had the chance to keep their philosophizing within politically safe topics and bounds and gain professorships in an increasingly repressive German university system. None of them did so, and all of them failed to find academic employment as a result.

But the Young Hegelians, Marx also included, made one major mistake: when it came to Hegel himself, they bought the line of the "Friends", who, to be sure, had produced the only version of Hegel's works available to them. The critical potential the Young Hegelians found in Hegel's philosophy was there, they thought, in spite of Hegel's own conscious intentions. The Young Hegelians thus thought they were breaking with Hegel when they rejected timeless truth in favour of the kind of dialectical thinking that Marx advocates in the above quotation. In fact, they were carrying forwards Hegel's project, but in a way that obscured its true nature.

---

2. For more information on this extremely interesting group of thinkers, see Stepelevich (1983).

THE COMMUNIST MANIFESTO

The Communist Manifesto is a relatively early work, written when Marx was about thirty. Marx and his collaborator Friedrich Engels never repudiated it, however, although in 1872 Engels would admit that "here and there some detail might be improved", a point he reiterated in 1888 (*EPM* 205). It remains the best short statement of Marxist communism, and illustrates how Marx both takes over the basic gestures of Hegelian thought and recognizes some of its problems. The first part of the *Manifesto* is dedicated to the bourgeoisie, the leading class of the time (i.e. the mid-nineteenth century): "The bourgeoisie during its rule of scarce one hundred years has created more massive and more colossal productive forces than have all preceding generations put together" (*EPM* 214). We see from the start that Marx has a strong historical consciousness: the bourgeoisie is not ancient, much less eternal, for it has only been around for a century. The only way to understand the bourgeoisie, then, is to see what sort of thing it has come from: in particular, feudal society, which in turn replaced still more ancient forms.

True, Marx begins this section by asserting that all history has so far been a history of class struggle; every society in history has been divided between oppressed people and their oppressors, and either society itself was reconstituted by a revolution or both groups were ruined (*EPM* 209). But the omnipresence of this struggle is not a truth destined to stand for all time. It has only been the case "so far" that all history exhibits class struggle. Indeed, the overall similarities exhibited by different historical periods are less important to Marx than the concrete facts unique to each, and, in particular, to our present age. Each age has its own particular form of class struggle, which has developed from the forms that struggle took in previous ages.

The rise of the bourgeoisie

Comparing the present situation with earlier ones shows that the rise of the bourgeoisie has resulted in five important new things. First, what used to be a number of different classes and social formations – the "motley feudal ties" of one group to others – have been dissolved as the bourgeoisie has acquired more and more power:

> The executive of the modern state is but a committee for managing the common affairs of the whole bourgeoisie. … The bourgeoisie has stripped of its halo every occupation hitherto honored and looked up to with reverent awe. It has converted the physician, the lawyer, the priest, the poet, the man of science into its paid wage laborers.
>
> (*EPM* 211–12)

Small-business people are also being forced into bankruptcy and have to sell their labour, becoming workers (*EPM* 217). The result of all this is that what used to be a complex constellation of interacting power groups has been simplified by the power of the bourgeoisie into just the bourgeoisie, on the one hand, and everybody else on the other. Since what "everybody else" has in common is that they have lost their capital and become wage labourers, Marx calls them the "proletariat" (from the Latin *proletarius*, a free person without property – a wage labourer).

Second, and partly because of this simplification, the reality of oppression is clearer than it ever has been: exploitation formerly veiled by political and religious illusions has become "naked exploitation" (*EPM* 212).

Third, time itself has changed, for it now affects everything. The bourgeois must continually "revolutionize the instruments of production", and thereby the whole economy. There is nothing permanent anymore, and "everything solid melts into air". The bourgeoisie is both universally destructive and wildly innovative (*EPM* 212).

Fourth, and partly because of this, space has also changed. Because of the constant innovations of the bourgeoisie, we now have a world market and a world economy (globalization). Original communities – for example the countryside, the "idiocy of rural life" – have been placed under the control of the towns and cities: "We find new wants, requiring for their satisfaction the products of distant lands and climes. … In place of the old local and national self-seclusion and self-sufficiency we now have trade in every direction" (*EPM* 213).

Fifth, although the bourgeoisie initiated these developments, it is no longer able to control them (*EPM* 214). This is shown by the recurrent "general gluts", or depressions, into which the economy falls. These are bad for everybody, including the bourgeoisie itself. The reason for them, Marx thinks, is that the productive forces are *too* productive. Too many things are made, and so the value of all of them collapses: something the bourgeoisie can hardly desire (*EPM* 215). The bourgeois solution to this has been twofold: to destroy the overproduction, and also to expand its market, so that what the bourgeoisie cannot sell at home they can sell abroad (*EPM* 215). This strategy has now culminated in the global market, so it cannot be used again.

The proletariat

Opposing the bourgeoisie is the other class: the proletariat. Since it was created by the bourgeoisie, it is even younger than it. Where the bourgeoisie is painted by Marx as a stable group, the nature of the proletariat is more diffuse. Proletarians have come from the more unfortunate members of a variety of different groups: in Marx's listing, quoted above, physician, lawyer, priest and poet. They have little in common with one another; hence Marx's characterizations of the proletariat are mainly metaphorical or negative. Proletarians are:

- *Appendages of the machine*: they work on an assembly line, doing work that is monotonous, has no "individual character" and so is "charmless" (*EPM* 216). Women can do such work; old people and children can as well. And they must: for family ties are reduced to a "money relation" (*EPM* 212).
- Like *soldiers*: proletarians are under the command of a "perfect hierarchy" of officers and sergeants (who themselves, presumably are also proletarians; *EPM* 216).
- Virtual *slaves* of the bourgeois class and state, and also of the machine: the bourgeoisie and the economic machinery they have created exercise over the workers a "despotism" (*EPM* 216).
- *Completely different from the bourgeoisie*: law, morality and religion, the normative systems that shape our lives, do not speak to them. Their family life, too, has nothing in common with bourgeois family life, because when you are working to exhaustion every single day you do not have a family life at all. All you contribute to the family is what you earn (which is why Marx said earlier that "money relations" have replaced family ties; *EPM* 220).
- Finally, the proletarians are *starving*: the employer, in order to compete, must pay his workers the absolute minimum necessary to keep them alive, and must go even below that, so that the workers necessarily become paupers (*EPM* 221).

In spite of their diversity and penury, the proletarians are growing ever more united. Since the bourgeoisie are the main actors in the modern world, it is they who in large part are bringing this about: employers treat their employees as all alike, and they gradually come to be that way (*EPM* 218). Even workers of different nationalities, let alone those of different professions, are by now more like each other than like their employers (*EPM* 220), although the proletarians in each nation must "of course" liberate themselves separately (*EPM* 221). The proletarians are also growing more unified because they have been fighting the bourgeoisie from the start, although in diffuse and local ways (Marx gives a brief history of this at *EPM* 217–18). Their various local struggles, although they usually lose them, educate them about one another (*EPM* 217–18.). This, too, is in part brought about by the bourgeoisie. The means the capitalists use to expand their markets – railways, telegraphs and so on – are also ways the proletarians communicate with one another. But the bourgeoisie is not working alone here; as we shall see, there is another group at work in this educational process.

The unified proletariat, finally, is the *majority*. This, for Marx, is another new fact in history. All previous historical movements, such as the revolution by which the bourgeoisie themselves overcame feudalism, were movements of minorities. Because the proletariat are by far the majority, their struggle will transform all of society (*EPM* 220–21).

The communists

The third group acting in this situation, Marx says, is the communists. The communists are merely the theoretically informed branch of the proletariat, and their "theory" is simply the general features of the existing class struggle (*EPM* 223). Because of their awareness of this, the communists have an international perspective, and are bringing proletarians of various countries together. As they do this, they keep the interests of the "movement as a whole" in view for the various local conflicts that are arising all the time (*EPM* 222). The communists are thus primarily an educational force, teaching those engaged in local struggles the lessons of other such local struggles.

The immediate aim of the communists, and of all "proletarian parties", is the conquest of political power by the proletariat. This will be followed by the abolition, not of property generally, but of bourgeois private property: property that comes from the labour of others (*EPM* 223). The aim is to convert private property into the property of all by giving the workers enough of it to enable them to live decently, rather than merely subsist (*EPM* 224).

Marx against his critics

In the rest of the *Manifesto*, Marx responds to various criticisms that have been made of the proletarians' struggle for power. Will the proletariat, if it takes power, destroy all private property, so that individuals, we might say, sleep in common dormitories, eat in public cafeterias and get their clothes from some central clothing office? No. The abolition of capitalist property is not the same thing as confiscation of all property. Self-acquired private property, the property an individual has earned, will not be destroyed by the revolution; it is being destroyed *already*, by the bourgeoisie (*EPM* 223). When small-business owners are put out of business and have to join the proletariat, their property is in a sense confiscated by the bourgeoisie. Only about a tenth of the population, in fact, now owns anything (*EPM* 225).

Will the revolution hurt freedom? Only bourgeois freedom, the freedom to buy and sell without restraint: free trade. Will the revolution hurt the "individual"? Only the bourgeois individual, the man of ill-gotten property. Will the revolution, by eliminating the profit motive, instil universal laziness? The bourgeoisie are *already* lazy: they do not work. Will culture disappear? Only bourgeois culture, to be replaced by cultural forms everyone can enjoy. Will the family be destroyed? We have seen that, for Marx, the bourgeoisie is *already* destroying the family life of the proletarians; here, he adds that only the propertied bourgeois kind of family will be destroyed, the kind in which the wife is a mere "instrument of production" (of children). Will home education be destroyed? Only to be replaced by education for all. Will the revolution bring about the community of women? The bourgeoisie *already* has it; they tirelessly seduce one another's wives. Will country and nationality cease to exist? They are (as we saw) *already* gone, for the workers, and their complete disappearance will not be such a bad thing.

In these passages, we see Marx using two different argument forms over and over again. One is that the bourgeoisie, in making these charges against the revolution, has looked only to threats to its particular way of life. It has assumed that its ways of looking at things and doing things are eternal laws of nature, when in fact they are only "social forms springing from [the] present mode of production and form of property" (*EPM* 226). But history proves that this is false. The rise of Christianity in ancient Rome, the birth and death of feudalism, and other such historical transformations, prove that what seem to be eternal truths common across all epochs of history are merely social forms deriving from the single basic fact of all history up to now: the class struggle (*EPM* 229–30). The other argument form is that all the developments that the bourgeoisie fear are *already* taking place. Private property, family life and hard work are *already* being destroyed, by the bourgeoisie itself.

The revolution will be gradual, and different in different places. Some likely parts of it are listed (*EPM* 230–31):

- abolition of property in land;
- a heavy progressive income tax;
- abolition of all right of inheritance;
- confiscation of all property of "immigrants and rebels";
- establishment of a national bank;
- state control of all means of transportation and communication;
- increasing the number of factories owned by the state; agriculture to proceed on the basis of a common plan;
- equal liability of all to labour;
- combination of agriculture with industry, ending the distinction between town and countryside;
- free education for all children, and abolition of child labour.

The goal of all this, in one of Marx's most famous phrases, is: "an association in which the free development of each is the condition for the free development of all" (*EPM* 231).

MARX AND THE FUTURE

As I noted at the end of the previous chapter, Hegel did not discuss the future. Speculations such as Marx has just given about coming states of affairs are simply absent from his writings. This is because, for Hegel, as we first saw in discussing the *Phenomenology*'s opening section on "Sense-Certainty", all knowledge is hindsight. Not only can we not know the future, but we cannot know what is happening right now unless we know what has been, because the "now" is a fleeting moment that cannot be captured in words.

In most of the *Manifesto*, Marx has remained true to this insight. While the dominance of the bourgeoisie is not a mere passing moment – it has already lasted a hundred years – it cannot be understood except in terms of how it has come to be. Hence, Marx has compared the bourgeoisie to earlier ruling classes to show that its degree of dominance in society is unprecedented. With respect to the proletariat, he has argued that its own history so far has shown greater numbers, growing unity and increasing impoverishment. An index of the strength of this perspective in the *Manifesto* is Marx's recurrent use, when discussing the proletariat, of the word "already": the evils that communism is accused of bringing in the future are, he argues, "already" being brought about by the bourgeoisie.

As opposed to this orientation to history, Marx's discussions of the future are for the most part statements of intention or mere conjectures. The conquest of political power by the proletariat, for example, is presented as the "immediate aim" of the communists, while the list of future revolutionary measures I have just summarized is announced as "pretty generally applicable" (*EPM* 230). But these conjectures, weak as they are, show that Marx wants more than Hegel did. In his *Philosophy of Right*, Hegel explicitly refused to "issue instructions on how the world ought to be", and for just the reason we would expect: philosophy "always comes too late to perform this function" (Hegel 1991: 23). Philosophical construals of history, mere hindsight and always revisable, cannot provide guidance for the future. The function of the communists, however, is, for Marx, precisely to issue such instruction: to show the struggling proletarians how their local efforts are to fit into the larger struggle for political power. In order to do this, the communists must know where that struggle is going. They must be able, in other words, to predict the future.

But you cannot predict the future unless you know, for sure, where things are going, and that means knowing, for sure, where they are now, which, for Marx, means knowing how they got there. His views on history and society cannot, then, be mere construals; they must be objectively true. A philosophy of history like Hegel's, which knowingly distorts the facts of history in the service of other criteria (by, for example, eliding as we saw its "slaughter bench" character) will not suffice for Marx. Hence, he replaces Hegel's interpretive approach with an approach that claims objective truth:

> The theoretical conclusions of the communists are in no way based on ideas that have been invented, or discovered, by this or that would-be universal reformer. ... They merely express, in general terms, actual relations springing from an existing class struggle, from a historical movement going on under our very eyes. (*EPM* 223)

The story of class struggle, then, is *the* story of all history up to now, and it is the final story; new ones will not be told. It is not merely a good way to unify a large number of data, so as to give us an illuminating picture of where we have come from and so of where we are; it claims to be the *truth* about history. Only so can it be a basis for large-scale action.

As much of the history of the second half of the twentieth century teaches us, the problems with this view are enormous. One of Marx's favourite words points to them. "Proletarian" is his name for the wage labourers, those without property of their own who must hire themselves out to others; it comes, I noted, from Latin. But the Latin "*proletarius*" itself comes, of all things, from "*proles*", which means "that which surges forth" or "is cultivated". A *proletarius*, strictly speaking, was a man whose only state service lay in providing children. But the raising of children is not something Marx ever mentions in the *Manifesto*. Although he does refer to family life, he never suggests that the key function of the family is the raising of children. His references are only to show how degraded family life has become, for both proletarians and bourgeoisie.

Child-raising is, in particular (and contrary to what the Latin *proletarius* suggests), a function performed largely by women. The oppression of women throughout history is another of history's key elements, an important story to be told. No one even tried to tell it until the twentieth century. Marx missed it entirely, because he thought that the facts showed that history contained only one story, that of class struggle.

"ESTRANGED LABOUR"

This essay is one of the most philosophically informed writings of the early Marx. He begins it with a one paragraph summary of the classical political economists such as Adam Smith.[3] Even if you accept the writings of the political economists, as Marx claims to have done (*EPM* 69), you find that modern society is in much more trouble than they allow themselves to see. What you also find is that they have nowhere discussed a question Marx thinks is central. They all assume private property's existence, and then show how it works. But where does it come from? Where, moreover, does competition come from? Where does greed itself come from? What, in short, is the origin of private property? Marx is thus asking the same kind of question of the political economists that Hegel had asked of Kant. Both Kant and the political economists discuss certain present realities – the faculties of the mind in the one case, private property in the other – without

---

3. Smith is treated in more detail in the manuscript "Wages of Labor", which is also to be found in *EPM*.

asking where they came from. The result is a tendency to view them as permanent. And that is mystification, not knowledge.

The political economists cannot answer questions like Marx's for two reasons. First, they do not connect the dots. They discuss competition and monopoly separately, for example, without examining how one leads to the other (*EPM* 70). They fail to see this process *as* a process, and fail to see how its two ends are united. This failure is grounded in a deeper, more familiar error. What connects the various features of the modern economy with one another is a movement, a process. Political economy ignores this and is therefore ahistorical in its approach: "It expresses in general, abstract formulae the material process through which private property actually passes, and these formulae it then takes for *laws*. … [Political economy] does not grasp the connections within the movement" (*EPM* 69–70).

Political economy has adopted the view that all we have before us in the spheres of economic and social reality is a set of events that, one by one, instantiate universal laws. It does not see that even economic laws exist only in and through specific processes.

One set of these processes is historical: the processes that have produced the modern economy itself. The universal "laws" that political economy claims to have discovered are really nothing more than abstract statements of current economic realities, which have not always existed and will not continue forever. Political economists thus think that they have formulated the laws of all economic activity. In fact, they *have* successfully formulated laws, but only the laws of the current economy: the "laws of estranged labor" (*EPM* 81).

Marx is not supposing that before capitalism there was no private property, that the Romans did not own their togas or that no Greek was greedy. He is asking how these things came to be central to the economy: its mainsprings. And the answer, in a word, is "estranged labour". The key fact to uncovering this is a paradox: the more the worker produces, the poorer he gets (*EPM* 71). This, too, is largely ignored by political economists, who admit that workers are poor (that could hardly be denied), but do not see that they are growing poorer. The increasing poverty of the workers and their increasing capacity constitute for Marx a single process; neither side should be singled out and treated in abstraction from the other. Seen together, the increases in poverty and capacity constitutes a paradox that highlights a more general matter: that things are progressively being valued more highly than people. This, in concrete terms, is bringing all kinds of misery. How does it come about?

Labour produces commodities, things that can be bought and sold. In fact, that is what labour is: activity that results in commodities. Among the commodities it produces are (a) the *products* of labour as traditionally understood, the goods we buy and sell; and (b) *labour itself*, and the labourer whose activity it is (*EPM* 71). For in the modern economy, labour is wage labour: it is itself a commodity, something that can be bought and sold.

The products of such modern labour, for their part, appear to be other than – estranged from – the labour that produced them. If I am a handicraftsman, as all pre-industrial workers were, everything I make bears the stamp of my individuality. The arrowheads made by ancient humans, the sacred vessels used by the medieval popes and the huts of eighteenth-century Scottish weavers were all like that. But today things are different, because handicrafts today are only a small part of production. If I work on an automotive assembly line (to update Marx a bit), I do not feel that my personality has gone into the cars that come off the line. They would be exactly the same if other people made them. The workers have disappeared, "lost reality" (*EPM* 71). They have lost the objects that they produce, to the extent that those objects can be taken from them and sold by someone else, who pockets the proceeds. Why is this?

Labour requires matter, in two ways (*EPM* 72). First, it requires the matter on which the worker works, and which she transforms into an object: her raw materials. Second, it requires the matter that sustains the worker herself: her food and clothing, and so on. So the paradoxical fact with which Marx began can be expressed as: the more the worker gets of the first kind of matter, the more material she works on, the less she gets of the other kind of matter, the means of life. The more things the worker makes, the less she has.

Since labour is just activity that results in commodities or products, this situation must be the result either of the product of labour or of the activity of labouring itself. But the product is just matter plus the activity of the worker: "the product is after all but the summary of the activity or production" (*EPM* 74). Matter is merely passive, so if there is something wrong with the worker's relationship to the object she makes, it cannot be due to the matter. Therefore, the problem can only lie in the way she works on it. The problem must lie in something inherent to the labour process itself.

Human nature as species being

The basic presupposition Marx is working under here is stated at *EPM* 75: humans are "species beings". Because they constitute a part of nature, they *have* a nature. This is what estranged labour is estranged *from*. Under capitalism, labour does not belong to the "essential being", the nature, of the labourer; it is "external" to her (*EPM* 74). Estranged labour is thus labour that works against human nature. In a preliminary discussion of this, Marx makes four points:

(a) Labour is, as Marx will argue later, our essence – our nature. What we do by nature we like to do; as Marx puts it here, we "affirm" ourselves in doing it. But today, labour "mortifies the body and ruins the mind": it is not affirmative but mindless and backbreaking.

(b) Since such labour is not natural to the worker, it must be coerced (e.g. by fear of starvation).

(c) This kind of labour is not the satisfaction of a need (i.e. the need to affirm yourself by doing what nature meant you to do) but merely the means to such satisfaction (i.e. estranged labour is not fulfilling in itself but is merely a way to get money to buy food, clothing, etc.).

(d) The final level of estrangement is that the worker does not seem to have done this to herself; someone else appears to be responsible. For if you do not belong to yourself in working, you must belong to someone else: to the person who coerces you:

> Just as in religion the spontaneous activity of the human imagination, of the human brain and the human heart, operates independently of the individual – that is, operates on him as an alien, divine or diabolical activity – in the same way the worker's activity is not his spontaneous activity. It belongs to another; it is the loss of his self.   (*EPM* 74)

This means that the worker feels free, not as a human being, but only in animal functions: drinking, eating, procreating, and so on. But there is more to human nature than that, and it is this "more" that is missing from labour under capitalist conditions. So a deeper analysis requires sorting out what makes us different from animals: what is our particular nature.

First, however, Marx discusses some things we have in common with animals. He calls our human nature our *Gattungswesen*, which is usually translated "species being", but could also be rendered as "essence of the species". This means, for him, that our species is both our nature and our goal or "object". Just as a horse can be said to exist in order to be a horse (in what Kant called "internal teleology"), so humans exist, or should exist, in order to be human. We *are* humanity, each one of us (*EPM* 75). What does this entail? In general terms, it means that as with other animals, our "purpose" is our species: the fulfilment of human nature. This means, in turn, that the "purpose" of a human being is not his or her individual well-being. And it means that the deepest happiness that we humans can feel, the happiness that goes along with the fulfilment of our nature, comes from helping humanity.

This idea appears strange to those who live in a society dominated, as many societies now are, by the idea that what everyone pursues is, first and foremost, their own individual self-interest. But it is not a new idea with Marx. Nor is it merely the utopian fantasy of revolutionary theorists in general. It was aptly expressed by George Bernard Shaw, a socialist but no revolutionary, who wrote that the "true joy of life" is

> The being used for a purpose which is recognized by yourself as a mighty one, the being thoroughly worn out before you are thrown on

the scrap heap; the being a force of Nature instead of a feverish, selfish little clod of ailments and grievances complaining that the world will not devote itself to making you happy.   (Quoted in Kuehn 2001: 153)

On this basis, Marx argues that the relation of the human individual to human nature, and so the basic nature itself of each individual, is a kind of labour that engages us as whole beings: we transform nature with both our bodies and our minds. Physically, we transform "inorganic" nature, that is, nature that is not part of our bodies, because it furnishes the matter we live from and work: "matter" in the two senses mentioned above. We do it when we eat, drink or even breathe. Theoretically, we also transform matter; all the ideas we have, and all the beauty we create, are transformations of nature. Science, for example, "transforms" nature just in taking it as an object of study. When I run a rat through a maze, I am taking it not in its existence as an individual being but as an example of a certain kind of learning machine; when I look at a star through a telescope, I am also taking it in a certain way, as for example a red giant or blue dwarf. In both cases, and many others, I "work" on the object: I transform its significance for me, if not its actual nature out there in space and time.

Species being, labour and alienation

The transforming of nature – labour – is thus the most general thing we do, and in fact it is *all* that we do. Animals also labour, but we do it differently. Marx mentions six differences between our natural way of working (*praxis*) and the animal's way:

(a) We work on everything. The beaver chops down trees, and the mole digs tunnels, but we do both (and form scientific theories about the stars). Our labour is thus universal.

(b) We also work when there is no direct need. The animal works to feed itself and its offspring. We can work for strangers, as Michelangelo did when he carved the *Pietà*.

(c) Therefore we do not always immediately use or consume what we make. We can leave it around, as an object.

(d) Because of this, we can know that we are something over and above what we are involved in at the moment. We can become aware of our lives as wholes; we can make objects of them, too. We can become "conscious". It follows – and this is a key Marxist point – that we are only conscious beings because of the unique way we labour. The specific forms that labour takes in different historical and social circumstances are correlated with different forms of consciousness. Estranged labour, in particular, produces alienated consciousness, or what Marx calls "ideology".[4]

(e) When labour is viewed this global way, everything we know or make is the product of labour; we create through labour a whole second world, our human world.

(f) The labour that creates this whole world is communal. My individual labour can be understood without regard for other human beings only to the extent that it is animalistic: to satisfy my needs of the moment. As soon as it goes beyond that, it is not just for and about me alone. I am always part of a labour force, because my being as a labourer intersects with the being of other people who are also labourers.

Estranged labour is the opposite of all this. Because it is unnatural to us we have to decide to do it, whereas species labour is going on all the time. Estranged labour does not engage us globally; some people work solely with their bodies, others solely with their minds.[5] Estranged labour creates only certain kinds of thing: commodities. It is a means to an end: personal survival. Instead of pulling me into community with others, estranged labour isolates me from others. In particular, the product of labour, instead of being stamped with my nature that others can enjoy, stands over and against me as something foreign. It does not belong to me, and so appears as belonging to someone else.

Who is that someone else? Clearly not, for Marx, the gods (or God), and not nature, which is incapable of owning anything. It can only be another human being, one who has taken what I made and so confronts me as "alien, hostile, powerful, [and] independent of [me]" (*EPM* 80). The alienation of the labouring *activity* produces the same result: "If his own activity is to him an unfree activity, then he is treating it as an activity, performed in the service, under the domination, the coercion, and the yoke of another man" (*EPM* 80). Private property, the property of the dominant other or of the bourgeois, is, then, property that is the result of estranged labour.

Marx is emphatic that what does not happen in the contemporary economy is this: some awful capitalist snatches the product away from the worker who made it, thus creating private property. Rather, private property is itself created by estranged labour, which came first: "though private property appears to be the source, the cause, of alienated labor, it is really its consequence" (*EPM* 81). Only once estranged labour becomes generalized and you have a class of capitalists do they start snatching things away from the workers. At that point, private property assumes a causal role. But at bottom, it is not what is basic; estranged labour is.

---

4. For a discussion of the complex and difficult views of Marx on ideology, see Rosen (1996).
5. On the division of labour, cf. *EPM* 128–34.

The other thing that estranged labour leads to, in addition to private property, is wage labour, since you can buy my labour from me only if I am already alienated from it. The "private property" of the worker is his wages. When the capitalist, himself created by estranged labour, buys the labour of others, he turns them into proletarians, as we saw previously. Estranged labour thus indirectly brings about the proletariat itself. From this, it follows that the only way to emancipate society as a whole is through the political emancipation of the workers. For the bourgeoisie, too, are alienated from human nature by estranged labour – more so, in fact, than the workers, because they do not work at all: "Everything which appears in the worker as an *activity* of alienation, of estrangement, appears in the non-worker as a *state* of alienation, of estrangement" (*EPM* 83, emphasis added). The emancipation of the workers will, therefore, end estranged labour, which will in turn end private property and will emancipate all humanity. Two questions remain: what is the historical origin of estranged labour? And what is the relation of private property to good property, "human property"?

The manuscript breaks off here, but Marx's answer to the first question is well known.⁶ As we might expect, it is historical in nature, showing "how this estrangement is rooted in the nature of human development" (*EPM* 82). Basically, it goes like this: in earlier times, labour was an individual activity in the sense that the tools that were available could be used by only one person at a time. Each worker, in those days, owned his own tools, or did by the time he had finished his apprenticeship. A modern factory, however, must be operated by thousands of people working together; it is a giant communal tool. But the form of ownership has not changed. These giant tools are still owned by individuals. The key, then, is to restore harmony by making ownership of the means of production communal as well.

"PRIVATE PROPERTY AND COMMUNISM"

Marx attempts to answer the other question in his essay "Private Property and Communism". This essay was, according to legend, censored by the Soviet Union and not printed in the standard editions of Marx's works available there. It certainly shows the trouble Marx gets into when he tries to predict the future.

He begins by noting that the transcendence of self-estrangement, or estranged labour, "follows the same course" as self-estrangement itself (*EPM* 99). He obviously does not mean that it develops in exactly the same way as self-estrangement did, because then it would not be a "transcending" of it at all. What he means is that getting rid of estranged labour must respect its nature, and must be a step-by-step sequence of moves that go to its heart. Thus, simply

---

6. One place where it is given is "The German Ideology", in Marx (1994a: 107–11).

getting rid of capital altogether, as Pierre-Joseph Proudhon wants to do, will not get at the problem. Nor will abolishing some versions of estranged labour but retaining others, as Charles Fourier and Saint-Simon want to do. Only communism is the "positive expression of transcended private property". It becomes this by performing the simplest of moves – a one-step operation: it transfers all private property to the state, and makes the state the owner of everything derived from estranged labour. Property thus becomes "universal private property" via a huge act of confiscation (*EPM* 100).

This version of communism, however – Marx sometimes calls it "crude communism" – is not really new; universal private property is merely the final phase, the consummation, of private property in general, and Marx has some extremely harsh things to say about it:

- It requires the destruction of all property that cannot be public, including homes and personal possessions beyond the bare minimum.
- It also refuses to recognize and reward talent, because only the universal and "abstract" characteristics involved in estranged labour count for it; the ability to drive a screw is rewarded equally with the ability to write a play. It thus turns everyone into a worker.
- At the extreme it advocates "free love", or the "community of women", which denies to women the protections given them by bourgeois marriage (although that makes private property of them) and forces them into a sort of universal prostitution.

What is the underlying mistake of crude communism? It is the belief that the fundamental problem with capitalism is not estranged labour, but the capitalist himself. By confiscating the means of production without changing the nature of labour, it does away with the capitalist. The labour, however, remains estranged, and so private property is still being created, only it is now "universal private property". Crude communism can thus also be called "state capitalism", because in it the state is the owner of everything, Some quotations (all from *EPM* 101) will show how degraded Marx thinks it is:

> In negating the personality of man in every sphere, this type of communism is really nothing but the logical expression of private property which is this negation. General *envy* constituting itself as a power is the disguise in which *avarice* reestablishes itself.

> The envy and urge [to reduce everything to a common level] even constitute the essence of competition [i.e. people compete to do it].

> How little this annulment of private property is really an appropriation is in fact proved by the abstract negation of the entire world of culture and civilization.

> The community is only a community of *labor*, and an equality of wages paid out by the communal capital – the community as the universal capitalist.

The confiscation of all property would thus be the largest act of greed in history, the "consummation of envy". Truly human labour, by contrast, should be on the model of procreation. The "relation of man to woman" includes the relation of both to nature, for they are perpetuating their species (*EPM* 102). They come together out of love, not merely for pleasure but in order to bring something new; procreation is non-estranged labour. (This, presumably, is why Marx finds the community of women so vile.)

The next form of communism is political: democratic or despotic (*EPM* 102). In this form, as in the previous one, communism is trying to overcome human self-alienation, but it still has not seen how to overcome private property; it has just transferred it to the state.

The final stage of communism will overcome these problems (*EPM* 102–3). At this stage the state no longer owns things, so they are (presumably) usable by all without the permission of higher authority. Such communism is nothing other than "humanism" (*EPM* 102). In it, humans become truly social beings: society is not something over and above them, giving orders, but simply the community to which they belong. In everything I do, I work with and for the sake of others, without this being dictated by higher authority. Such labour is as spontaneous as the love relation. All activity is communal, and so is all consumption: "Activity and consumption, both in their content and in their *mode of existence*, are *social*: social *activity* and *social* consumption" (*EPM* 104).

This will require rethinking all forms of human activity. Family life, the state, law, science and art must all be reconceived as modes of social production, as labour in Marx's extended sense: as free communal activity (*EPM* 104). Religion must be reconceived socially as "philanthropic atheism", which (Marx notes) is much better than having some authoritarian God giving you orders (*EPM* 103–4). Natural science will be redirected, not to discovering how nature is when we are not around, as it is today, but to seeing how humans are in nature and are natural beings (*EPM* 110). Even our senses will be different: "The transcendence of private property is therefore the complete *emancipation* of all human senses and attributes. The eye has become a *human* eye, just as its *object* has become a social, *human* object – an object emanating from man for man" (*EPM* 107). We will enjoy our senses together, and so for the first time (*EPM* 109).

Communal activity and consumption can be direct or indirect. I can work together with others, for example at an Amish barn-raising, the kind of free, undirected communal activity that Marx apparently has in mind. Even in "scientific" (intellectual) activity that I perform alone, I am working with and on an inherited body of material (a poet works on, transforms, her language, for example), and with a view to communicating my results. But none of this is "communism" as construed in this essay. Here, communism is the immediate future of humanity, but as such is only the culminating, most degraded state of capitalism.

If Marx's aim is to show that the seizing of all property by the state is not what we should be working for, he has done his job. But to the extent that he needs to show how the third phase of communism, the positive reappropriation of all capital by humanity and of humanity by itself, is to come about from the first and second stages, he has completely failed. His account of this is not even coherent; the essay degenerates into a series of murky observations from which I have been forced to quote very selectively.

CONCLUSION

In Hegel's version of continental philosophy, the past swallowed the present and the future: we could understand what is only in terms of what has been; and what is to come we cannot philosophically understand at all. In his early *Economic and Philosophic Manuscripts*, Marx, in large part, adopts this general view. He believes that we cannot understand the present unless we see how even its most basic "laws" have come to be from the past; failure to do this lands us in political economy, with all its problems.

Marx seeks, then, to treat history largely as Hegel did: to extract from the facts of history the story of how the contemporary situation – in Marx's case, the modern economy – came to be. The result of this is the recognition of the unprecedented fact that estranged labour is now the dominant form of production, and a theory of how this fact can explain many other facets of economy and society. Communism thus has a historical justification:

> Communism is the riddle of history solved, and it knows itself to be this solution. The entire movement of history is, therefore, both [communism's] actual act of genesis (the birth act of its empirical existence) and also for its thinking consciousness, the comprehended and known process of its coming to be. (*EPM* 103)

But there is more. Marx's desire to understand – indeed, to shape – the future leads him to make claims about the present and the past that go well beyond the radically revisable, and so provisional, kind of interpretation of the past that Hegel presented. Marx comes to believe that he has attained a final truth, and so lapses into traditional philosophy.

That final truth can be expressed in at least two ways: either as the view that the mode of production dominant in society determines all other aspects of culture, or as Marx's claim that class struggle is the universal ground of all history. They work out to the same thing because the modes of production are always contested; this contest, the class struggle, shapes everything else. Even if we reduce this to the lesser claim that Marx actually makes – that all history *up to now* has been the history of class struggle – Marx presents it in a away that entails that further revisions to the way history is written will not be necessary. Marx, unlike Hegel, hears no footsteps in the next room; no one, he thinks, is going to carry out his intellectual corpse!

But they did, if only a couple of decades ago, and in part at least because of two problems with Marx's attempt to predict the future. This he can do only by seeing the future as a continuation of what he sees developing around him out of the past: class struggle. Hence, the conversion of all property to state property is the final stage of the class struggle; one could even call it the "grand finale". The prediction this leads to, which we saw in "Private Property and Communism", fails in two ways. First, the conversion of all capitalist property into state property never occurred as the result of a proletarian revolution. It was either imposed from outside, as in eastern Europe, or occurred in pre-capitalist societies such as Russia and China, in both of which cases Marx's dire predictions did become all too true. Second, because the conversion is the last act of the class struggle, Marx cannot see beyond it at all. Hence, the moment he tries to see how the first stages of communism will lead to a later, more wholesome and humanistic stage, his effort dissolves in a welter of incoherence.

Marx's narrative of the genesis of the modern economy tied enough things together in a compelling enough way to gain the allegiance, and focus the efforts, of millions of people. It is amazing how many of the reforms he advocates in *The Communist Manifesto* have been adopted, at least in part. But Marx's attempt to shape the efforts of revolutionaries by showing the directions in which history would move was a disastrous attempt to coerce history intellectually. It was taken up practically, in the most horrible of ways, by people who had learned from Marx every possible lesson except the one they most needed: that history cannot be coerced. As we shall see in discussing Horkheimer and Adorno, Marxism survives today primarily as a diagnostic tool, providing insights into the origins of cultural and other phenomena. It has been stripped of its claims to solve *the* riddle of history and thus to provide a secure basis for large-scale social action.

What Marx saw, more clearly than any of the other Young Hegelians (and far more clearly than the "Friends of the Immortalized", who did not see it at all) was *why* we have to go beyond Hegel. The reason is that philosophy cannot embrace the past while dismissing the future, as Hegel did. The future may not be as securely predictable as Marx thought it was; but it cannot be ignored. It must be recognized and dealt with somehow. Figuring out how to do this will occupy continental philosophy for the next hundred and fifty years.

CHAPTER 4

KIERKEGAARD'S DREADFUL FUTURE

PRIMARY TEXT Søren Kierkegaard, *The Concept of Anxiety* (*CD*; [1844] 1980)

One evening around 1850, a man named Otto Zinck had nothing to do. Zinck was a well known actor in Copenhagen, but this evening he had no perform-ance scheduled, nor any party. As he was casting about for a way to spend the evening it occurred to Zinck that he might drop in on the brother-in-law of a friend of his, who had come to be his friend as well: Søren Kierkegaard. As Zinck approached Kierkegaard's luxurious apartment on the Nørregade, one of Copenhagen's most elegant streets, he must have wondered if he was doing the right thing. Even from the street he could see that the apartment, where Kierkegaard lived alone, was all lit up, as if for a party. Zinck went up anyway, and found Kierkegaard dressed in festive clothing – he was a very fashionable dresser – but completely alone. He was, Zinck decided, clearly waiting for his guests to arrive; and, not having been invited, Zinck promptly excused himself.

Kierkegaard would not hear of it: yes, Zinck must stay and chat a while; and no, he was not waiting for anyone. "I never have parties," explained Kierkegaard, "but once in awhile it occurs to me to pretend that I am having one, and so I walk to and fro through the rooms, mentally greeting my imagined guests." At that, Zinck wanted more than ever to leave, but he stayed for an hour, and was royally entertained by Kierkegaard's charm and wit.[1]

There were few people who wanted to socialize with Kierkegaard in those days. A few years before, he had publicly attacked a Copenhagen newspaper, the *Corsair*, in the pages of another newspaper. In revenge, the *Corsair* had set out to make a laughing stock of him, and had succeeded entirely. Everything about him, from his odd physical appearance – he was a semi-hunchback – to his dandyesque bachelor lifestyle, had been ridiculed without mercy, to such an extent that Danish plays of the time regularly featured a comic character named

---

1. This story is told by Kirmmse (1996: 96–7). For Kierkegaard's life in general, see Garff (2005).

"Søren". Even his relatives turned away when they saw him coming down the street.

Kierkegaard had been born in 1813, five years before Marx. His father, Michael Pedersen Kierkegaard, had at one time been the wealthiest man in Denmark, thanks to wise investments in real estate. He had then retired from business, devoting himself to raising his seven children; by the somewhat gloomy standards of bourgeois Denmark, they were a happy family. But in the space of just a few years, Michael Pedersen's wife and five of his children died, leaving him alone with his oldest and youngest sons, Peter Christian and Søren. After completing studies at the university, Søren was ready for marriage and a career as a pastor. He went so far as to get engaged to an attractive young woman of Copenhagen, Regina Olsen, but suddenly broke off both engagement and career in order to devote himself to his writing. The break with Regina was a trauma from which neither of them ever really recovered. The affair with the *Corsair*, ten years later, was equally traumatic; Kierkegaard found himself without family or friends, totally alone in the midst of his native city. There was one more trauma in his adult life, like the other two provoked by him. This was his "attack upon Christendom" of 1855, a violent diatribe against the established Church of Denmark, which ended only with his death later that year.

I have suggested that Hegel set philosophy on a new path by taking everything to be temporal, never appealing to the invariance of anything. But he does so only to a point. Hegel's philosophy, as we saw, defines "truth" in temporal terms, as what amounts to the possession of a certain kind of past, and it is not surprising that his whole philosophy should be, so to speak, past-centred. Certainly Hegel himself almost never mentions the future or makes predictions, as Marx tried to do. The only thing that Hegel's philosophy can teach us about the future, we saw, is that it is philosophically irrelevant.

Together with this goes a kind of quietism, for we cannot act except on behalf of some future or other, which we hope to make real by our action; we always act for a purpose. Hegel's disregard for the future is thus entirely consistent with his view of philosophy as a purely theoretical enterprise that always comes on the scene too late to change anything about the world. Such quietism, we saw, is hardly enough for Marx, who wants to make philosophy into a revolutionary force and so must not only deal with the future, but specify it so that he and others can work towards it. But it was quite enough for Hegel, whose rejection of attempts to predict the future, let alone affect it, was a principled one.

But Hegel's position runs into trouble even if we accept his view that philosophy cannot change anything. The future for him, we saw towards the end of Chapter 2, is the "source" of form. It is, to quote him again, "the becoming of the present as possibility, and thus as formless (*gestaltlos*). From out of this formlessness the universal first comes into form in the present; and hence in the future no form can be perceived" (1974: I, 434).

As formless, and so radically indeterminate, the future for Hegel is something that philosophy cannot comprehend or define.[2] The problem is that the whole point of Hegel's turn to history was to establish history as the source of reason itself; that turn, as I presented it, was a revision of the search for origins that characterizes Kantian critique, but hardly a revocation of it. Now we see that the future, too, is a source: the source of form. So, for Hegel, it too ought to be something with which we must deal, something to which we are not only open but towards which we are unavoidably moving. How does our constant slippage towards a radically indeterminate future affect our efforts at philosophical comprehension? Kierkegaard is the first exponent of continental philosophy to pose this problem.

THE CONCEPT OF DREAD

The Concept of Dread appeared in 1844, under the Danish title *Begrebet Angest*, which in German becomes *Der Begriff der Angst*. Both *Angst* and *Angest* are stronger than the English "anxiety", which is used by the translation I reference here. The strength of Kierkegaard's *Angest* can be gathered if we remember the forcefulness of some of his other famous titles, such as *Fear and Trembling* and *The Sickness Unto Death*. I shall translate it as "dread".

Kierkegaard's dread is the first important appearance in philosophy of the famous existential *Angst*, which has been much derided by people who think that philosophy should be "objective", and who mean by this that it should be without affect. But Kierkegaard, like later existentialists who follow in his path, is not merely venting his feelings; he is writing about something that he thinks is so scary that merely to think about it honestly terrorizes you. That something is the future, and the cool calm of "objective" knowledge actually *blocks* the way to our knowledge of it.

There are three points to make about the kind of future Kierkegaard is talking about. First, it is not merely some state of affairs that has not yet come to be. It is *your* future, the one to which you are unavoidably moving. Second, part of what makes your future so scary is that it is radically unknowable. It is frightening to imagine the evils that may befall you in the future, but more frightening still to realize that you have no idea at all whether they, or perhaps other things so horrible you cannot even imagine them, will actually come to pass. And third, the future that we experience in this way is important, more important than

---

2. Contrary to popular belief and much of his own practice, philosophy for Hegel should aim at clarity and determinacy: "[Philosophy's] foremost requirement is that every thought shall be grasped in its full precision, and nothing allowed to remain vague and indefinite" (Hegel 1975b: 115).

the present or the past, Hegel to the contrary notwithstanding. Why? Because it incites in us dread (*Angest*).

What is dread? Kierkegaard defines his "Concept of Dread" in part I, §5, which I shall discuss first. He begins (*CD* 41) in a Hegelian way (and we shall see this again, for Kierkegaard is in many ways every bit as brilliant a dialectician as Hegel). What, he asks, would anxiety come to be *from*? From a state that knows no anxiety, which, therefore, knows nothing of the sorrows and troubles and difficulties of the world. This blissful ignorance is the state of "innocence" (*CD* 41). Innocence (Kierkegaard is thinking about the Garden of Eden) is all peace and repose, and contains no strife.

But there is something else about innocence: it will not last. Even Adam and Eve, who were as innocent as human beings could possibly be, saw an end to their innocence. And an innocent person can, on some level anyway, be *aware* of this. Innocence is not entirely at ease, then. Something more is going on: "In this state there is peace and repose, but there is simultaneously something else that is not contention and strife, for there is indeed nothing against which to strive. What, then, is it? Nothing. But what effect does nothing have? It begets dread" (*CD* 41). Innocence knows that it will come to an end because it is unable to *think* about the future; it is too ignorant of the world to make the predictions and extrapolations necessary for that. So innocence can only "dream" the future, as a simple prolongation of the present. And you have to be very innocent indeed not to know that dreams are even more untrustworthy than predictions.

The reason that dreams are so untrustworthy is that dreaming is not a normed activity: I can dream whatever I like, and the space of the dreamable – unlike that of the predictable – is infinitely open. Only when I can distinguish the languor of a dream from the rigour of a prediction can I see that dreams, being without norms, are not trustworthy; and I can only make that distinction if I know what norms are. It is thus the introduction of norms into human life that teaches us that dreaming is untrustworthy and ends our innocence. The moment we are given an ethical norm, we are presented with the possibility that bad things can happen to us, for a norm by definition is what has bad consequences if we violate it. In Kierkegaard's paradigm case of innocence, that of Adam and Eve, it is not their sin that ends their innocence and replaces it with dread. Even before they eat the apple, their innocence is over. God's commandment to them has already killed it.

What God commands seems straightforward enough: "Only from the tree of knowledge of good and evil you must not eat" (*CD* 44). In reality, it is highly paradoxical and, indeed, almost self-contradictory. It suggests to Adam that something bad will happen to him if he eats the fruit. But Adam, in his innocence, will not know what good and bad are until he has eaten the fruit, for the tree is the "tree of knowledge of good and evil". Hence Adam cannot understand this prohibition, or indeed any prohibition, until he has broken it. What he *can* understand right from the start, however, is that he is free: free to eat the fruit or not. And this is what really awakens dread: the thought that unknowable things will happen to you, in the future, because of what *you* decide to do.

KIERKEGAARD'S CRITICISM OF HEGEL

Now that we have some understanding of Kierkegaard's basic account of dread, we can go back and look at his criticism of Hegel in the "Introduction" to *The Concept of Dread* (i.e. *Anxiety*). Criticism of Hegel is an ongoing concern of Kierkegaard's: The Church of Denmark, against which he would later inveigh, was dominated by Hegelians very similar to the "friends of the eternalized" I discussed in Chapter 3; and Kierkegaard's critique of Hegel here is both lengthy and subtle. The discussion does not seem even to touch on the issues concerning time and the future I have just discussed. Kierkegaard begins instead by saying that Hegel's biggest mistake was that he entitled the last section of his Logic "Reality" (*CD* 9). In fact, says Kierkegaard, reality has no place in Hegel's system because logic has no room for the contingent, which is an "integral part of reality" (*CD* 9). So Kierkegaard, like Marx and so many others, thinks that Hegel has, in his system, set forth an eternally valid logical structure. Moreover (and this is also part of viewing Hegel as an Old Hegelian) he thinks that Hegel thinks that reality itself is somehow "part" of this eternal structure.

Is this fair to Hegel? Hardly. The logical category of "reality" concludes what Hegel calls the "Logic of Essence", the second book of Hegel's *Logic*. In both versions Hegel published of his *Logic* (1975b, 1976), it is followed by book III, the "Logic of the Notion". Kierkegaard, then, makes a very basic mistake when he says that Hegel ends his *Logic* with the category of "reality".

In any case, there is for Kierkegaard a great divide between the necessary, atemporal realm of logic and the changing, contingent world in which we live. Kierkegaard does not think that Hegel simply ignores the fact that this discrepancy is there, but he also does not think that Hegel takes it seriously enough. Echoing Aristotle's complaint about Plato, which I cited in the "Introduction", he says that Hegel tries to overcome the discrepancy between timeless realm of true being and the messy, changing world of contingency with a mere word, a word used, moreover, almost solely in "propaedeutic investigations", that is, when Hegel addresses the reader in an introductory and informal way, prior to actually doing philosophy. The word in question is "reconciliation" (*CD* 10). In the *Phenomenology*, Hegel used this word to denote our shared attitude towards our individual sins (cf. *PhS* ¶¶670–71). It was synonymous with "forgiveness", and mutual forgiveness was an essential part of human community. Kierkegaard takes it to denote, for Hegel, the relation of thought to reality, for if reality is rational, then we have no choice but to be "reconciled" to it.

Kierkegaard's critique of Hegel is already complex. The gist of it so far is that Hegel sets up a fictitious domain of logical structure, which, he thinks, is eternal, necessary. Such a domain is entirely different from the world in which we actually live, so Hegel is trapped for Kierkegaard in the same problem we saw besetting Plato, Aristotle, Kant and indeed the rest of traditional philosophy: how can two such different realms be related at all? Hegel cannot deny the gap, so he tries to cover it over with words like "reconciliation"; but those words are simply meaningless. Another such word, for Kierkegaard, is "mediation" (*CD* 11). This is ambiguous, says Kierkegaard, because Hegel takes it to denote both an action and the result of the action. Hegel, once again, was well aware of this; in his *Encyclopedia Logic*, he defines "mediation" as "a having-gone forward from a first to a second and coming to be from distinct things" (Hegel 1975b: 125). Mediation is thus for Hegel a movement that comes to an end: the conversion of a process to a state, not an ambiguous conflation of the two. What has been mediated is precisely what is present as the result of the past, an undeniably central theme of Hegel's philosophy, from "Sense-Certainty" on.[3]

Finally, the Hegelians – says Kierkegaard – introduce movement, or mediation, into logic (*CD* 12). The factor responsible for this, they say, is "the negative". This, in Hegelian, parlance, is once again ambiguous: to be "negative" is not merely to move on from something and arrive at an end, but also to produce something new.[4]

Behind all three Hegelian catchwords – reconciliation, mediation and negativity – lie attempts to introduce movement and change into logic. Logic, however, cannot contain movement: "logic is, and whatever is logical only *is*" (*CD* 13). In a move whose consequences we shall see later, Kierkegaard has here accepted the standard philosophical distinction between a temporal and an atemporal realm. He is, indeed, claiming that Hegelian logic is *not atemporal enough*. This criticism is no vindication of traditional logic as against the Hegelian variety, however, because it comes with a twist: if we subtract movement from the logical realm, and make it truly atemporal, it also ceases to be logical. Indeed, it becomes utterly unfathomable: Kierkegaardian eternity, the source of our dread.

Hegel's problems are not confined to his logic. In Hegelian ethics, Kierkegaard tells us, the negative is evil itself (*CD* 13).[5] But Hegel, in fact, did not write an ethics, and this is what Kierkegaard *really* holds against him. Why?

---

3. In a figure that Ludwig Wittgenstein, a twentieth-century admirer of Kierkegaard, will also use to describe philosophical problems in general, Kierkegaard concludes that Hegel's philosophy represents a "sabbatical year" for language (*CD* 12); cf. "philosophical problems arise when language goes on holiday" (Wittgenstein 1958: 19).

4. Kierkegaard is presumably thinking about Hegel's famous discussion, in the "Introduction" to the *Phenomenology*, of "determinate negation" (*PhS* ¶79).

5. Actually, when Hegel talks this, way (as at Hegel [1991: 28, 92–3], the passages referred to by Kierkegaard's editor in his note *ad loc*), he is talking from his caricature of Kant, not in his own voice.

For Kierkegaard, evil – sin – can only be defined negatively: "its idea is that its concept is annulled" (*CD* 15). What does this mean? That the true nature of sin is not merely eating fruit, or violating this or that commandment. Sin is *turning away from God*. Towards what? Towards what cannot be known, since knowledge is traditionally defined as coming from God. That is why sin is defined as "annulling" its own concept; in fact, the reality of sin annuls *every* concept. What cannot be known? Kierkegaard's answer, once again, is quite traditional. Indeed, it is the same as Aristotle's (cf. *Metaph.* VII.15 1039b27–20): the individual. "Sin does not belong in any science, but it is the subject of the sermon, in which the single individual speaks as the single individual to the single individual" (*CD* 16). Hegel could not write an ethics, in Kierkegaard's view, because his view that logical structure informs all of reality keeps him from seeing what Kierkegaard calls "existence": the plight of the individual in all of his or her contingency: that is, freedom; the capacity to sin; unknowability. This connects to the basic theme of dread, because dread is awakened by my realization that I can sin: that I am free to be me – sinful, unique, unfathomable me.

In his *Concluding Unscientific Postscript*, Kierkegaard writes that Hegelian philosophy is the "perfect victory" of pure thought, but that it has "nothing, nothing, nothing to do with existence" (1941a: 295; also cf. 100n.). Only an ethics founded on the Christian doctrine of original sin, says Kierkegaard there, can take sin seriously. Philosophical ethics, which aims at an atemporal realm where individuals count only as "mediated", "reconciled", and so on, cannot take sin seriously because it cannot really deal with individuals at all. Hegel's omission of an ethics from his system was at least honest, then; but his honesty only indicated his deeper failure to see the radical disparity between the temporal and the atemporal realms.

In chapter 3, Kierkegaard repeats this basic criticism. He says there that Hegel makes use of *three* terms that he never defines but only presupposes: "mediation", "negation" and "transition". Hegel, once again, uses theses terms to bring movement into his logic, and thereby to fudge the distinction between time and eternity: Hegel cannot accept the old and simple truth that "Man ... is a synthesis of psyche and body, but he is also *a synthesis of the temporal and the eternal*" (*CD* 85).

What, in Kierkegaard's view, is Hegel's basic mistake? So far, it is that he has not taken into account the true distinction between time and eternity. He has tried to fudge eternity by putting movement into his logic; and he has tried to fudge the individual by seeing human individuals as knowable and necessary. He has, therefore, failed to understand the nature of the human individual, as a being that can become radically different and thus has a radically open future: a future so open that it cannot even be understood.

KIERKEGAARD'S VIEW OF TIME

Because Hegel does not understand the true nature of the human individual, he is not able to show how time and eternity are brought together, or "synthesized", in such an individual. How is this? What is "time" for Kierkegaard?

In his treatment of time, Kierkegaard once again takes a basically Hegelian approach, in that he seeks to locate the origin of something in a temporally prior state of affairs or situation. In this case, what he seeks to explain is time itself. We generally consider time to consist of a past, a present and a future. But that, Kierkegaard says, is a confusion (*CD* 85). What time most basically is, is an "infinite vanishing" (*CD* 86): the continuous passing away of everything. Kierkegaard is going to argue that time as we experience it, time with a past, present and future, comes to be from this infinite vanishing.

One moment of the infinite vanishing is like another; no moment is special in any way: "Every moment, like the sum of all moments, is a process, a going-by" (*CD* 85). Time is therefore not merely an *infinite* vanishing but a *homogenous* vanishing. If the passage of time is perfectly homogenous, there are no privileged moments in time. It follows that the present moment cannot exist, for to be present makes a moment very privileged indeed. The future, after all, is what is not yet present, and the past is what once was present; since past and future are defined in terms of the present, if we have no present, we have no past or future either. Thus, Kierkegaard writes, when time is considered as homogenous infinite vanishing there is no "foothold" for the present: "The life which is in time, and is merely that of time, has no present" (*CD* 85, 86). I shall call this kind of time – a homogenous infinite vanishing without past, present or future – time A.[6]

The next step in the "genesis of time" that Kierkegaard is giving here is to see that we can think of time A as being like a line, and then we can take one point on that universal timeline as designating the stage that the infinite vanishing has reached. This gives us one instant that is different from the others, and so special or privileged. With this idea we arrive at the abstract concept of the "moment" (*CD* 86). The moment is the "limit" of time, the Latin *instans* or the Platonic *exaiphnēs* (*CD* 87–8). Call this kind of time, time as infinite vanishing that has proceeded to a definite point, "time B". Time B is thus a way of thinking about time A. Unlike time A, it has one moment that is special because it is the last moment so far attained. But this moment is conceived abstractly. It is still not the "present" Kierkegaard envisages, the *Øjeblikket* or *Augenblick*: what you see in the blink of an eye. When you blink your eyes as fast as you can, in between

---

6. This should not be confused with J. M. E. McTaggart's *A* and *B* time series, both of which contain relations of one sort or another (McTaggart 1908).

the blinks you take in a lot of content. So the "present", as Kierkegaard wants to use this term, is not abstract: it is "full" (*CD* 86).

In order to experience the present, we must take in a lot of content, and that "taking in" is an action that requires more than the passing moment to accomplish. We must somehow, therefore, stop the infinite vanishing, or in Kierkegaard's words we must "annul the succession": we must see a manifold of content that we in fact acquire sequentially as if it were given all at once (*CD* 86; in Hegel's term from "Sense-Certainty", we generate a universal). The content thus "sticks around" long enough to be noticed. In that respect, the present is like eternity, for in eternity also, everything sticks around. How, for Kierkegaard, do we come to "annul the succession"? We conceive time's "infinite vanishing", not on its own terms, but on the model of something else: of eternity, in which *all* succession is annulled. The present is thus when "time and eternity touch each other" (*CD* 87). Eternity thus structures, or prevails over, the common human understanding of time: "The moment [i.e. the *Øjeblikket*] is that ambiguity in which time and eternity touch each other, and with this the concept of temporality is posited, whereby time constantly intersects eternity and eternity constantly pervades time" (*CD* 89). Call this time C. Time C, for Kierkegaard, presupposes that we have some idea of what eternity is; we form an experiential hybrid between the motionless content of eternity and the final moment of time B.

Time C, then, comes from time A via a process that is itself temporal, one that requires our thinking and experiencing of time A in terms of time B. This is a complex argument, and it is not over, for there is something about time C that is not yet explained. So far, we have seen that time A, an "infinite vanishing", or homogenous succession of nows, becomes time B when we conceive of one part of that infinite vanishing abstractly and philosophically as the farthest point it has yet reached, thus privileging that part as the "moment". We then arrive at the content-laden experience of the "present" by annulling the succession of contents that is given in time B. But there is more to the present than this, for the present not only has content, but *we* are located amid that content. The "present moment" is *our* moment. The idea that a moment has distinctive content does not show how it is *our* distinctive content: the moment *we* are at. How do we get that?

As we have seen, the determinate content of the present is *our* doing. We can identify specific content within the moment only if we operate in terms of an analogy between the moment and eternity, for we need to "stop" the vanishing long enough to focus on something. The question is *why* we would do that: indeed, why we *must* do that. Kierkegaard's answer is going to be that we must do that because the present, with its content, is *our* present. It is because we are located at the present moment that it comes to have determinate content for us. But what locates us?

Yet again, Kierkegaard goes back to the Greeks. Plato, he says, was unable to get beyond the "moment" of what I call time B. He could not do that because he could not understand how it is that we are the "synthesis" of time and eternity.

He could not understand that because Plato, like the Greeks in general, had no concept of eternity (*CD* 88). This is a surprising claim, because Plato, from the *Phaedo* to the *Parmenides*, insists that the most basic reality is the "Forms": it is they that make our world what it is. And Platonic Forms, as Plato says over and over, are perfect beings that never change, never come into being and never pass away. This certainly *sounds* like eternity. What is it about eternity that Plato, and Greeks in general, could not understand?

They could not understand, says Kierkegaard, that eternity is our future. Certainly, we sometimes speak of eternity as if it were the future; in Christianity, it *is* our future, for we enter into it when we die. What Plato could not understand about eternity, then, is something that Christians do understand: that the eternal is our future. But this, too, seems unfair to Plato, who says, also over and over, that when we die, if we have lived a sufficiently philosophical life, we will join the Forms. Moreover, why should we think of eternity that way? The eternal is what intersects with the vanishing moment to give us the present. Why think of it in terms of the future? Why conflate the two? Part of the answer is that eternity, like the future, cannot be understood. Kierkegaard's criticism of Hegel showed that the temporal and the atemporal are utterly different from one another; Hegel's attempt to bring them together amounted to mere words. Since we are temporal beings, we cannot understand what is eternal, *at all*: "The eternal first signifies the future or because the future is the incognito in which the eternal, even though it is incommensurable with time, nevertheless preserves its association with time" (*CD* 89).

Plato could not understand that the eternal is our future because he could not grasp that the eternal, and the future, are unfathomable. He thought he knew what heaven is like, although he expressed it in myths (such as the myth of the "true earth"; *Phd.* 110b–114d). Aristotle was clearer about this: he said that the life of the Prime Mover, his version of God, is "a life such as the best we enjoy, and enjoy for but a short time – for it is ever in this state, which we cannot be" (*Metaph.* XII.7 1072b14–6). Plato and Aristotle conceived of eternity, in other words, as an infinite prolongation of the present, and not as an "incognito". And this inability to understand the unfathomable nature of eternity goes beyond Plato and Aristotle. In Chapter 1 I discussed Kant's efforts to establish the eternal – the pure idea of humanity under moral laws – as the goal, that is, the future, of the world. Hegel too, at least as Kierkegaard understands him, thought that he could lay out the (logical) structures of eternity and then "mediate" them with time. None of these philosophers, therefore, could get beyond the moment, that is, beyond the abstract conception of the final point so far of the infinite vanishing. On this basis, the whole of time is merely what has elapsed up to that moment: "time, if it is to be revealed by the determinations revealed in time itself, is time past" (*CD* 87).

The moment, as the final point (so far) on the universal timeline, is continuous with what went before it. But such continuity, however obvious to the Greeks and to later philosophers, is incompatible with Christianity. For Christians, the moment of Christ's death on the cross radically changed everything human: it was the moment of "atonement" and "redemption" in which mankind was "saved" (*CD* 90). Everything was immediately, and radically, transformed. Time thus becomes discontinuous: the moment after Christ's death is nothing at all like the moment before. We experience time in terms of discontinuity today because we are either Christians or live in the heritage of Christianity. But the death of God was a unique event. Why should the kind of discontinuity it evidences apply to *our* lives? If Christianity brings with it the idea that time can in principle be discontinuous, because it once was, is there something about Christianity that makes us conceive of our own time that way?

To put this differently, is there something that *makes us* move from time B to time C, that requires us to focus on the content around us because it is the content that is around us *now*? What makes us say that some particular moment is *our* moment? When must we take account of the specific circumstances that prevail *now*? When we must *do* something; or, more basically still, when we must *choose* to do something, that is, must commit ourselves to some course of action. Then, and only then, the fact that these particular states of affairs obtain right now becomes crucial. I can, in my imagination and with the help of history books, reconstruct in some detail the Age of Caesar. I can think myself into Caesar's position as he stood on the banks of the Rubicon, ready to step into it. I can imagine the breeze hitting my face as if it were his face, picture my reflection as he studies his in the water, pondering one last time whether to march on Rome or not. But this is all imaginative play, because I cannot act, or decide to act, in those circumstances. They were the circumstances for Caesar's choice, not mine; they do not prevail now. And I can only choose in the circumstances that prevail *now*.

In forming time C, or what could be called human temporality, we thus add two things to time B. First, we see the moment as having distinctive content, which means annulling the infinite vanishing and allowing specific content to come forwards. Second, we recognize that this content is *our* content: it is the circumstances prevailing over us right now. The reason they "prevail" is that they are the circumstances in which we must make a choice, and the formation of time C is necessary, in short, because we have to choose. The present is thus, for Kierkegaard, an *ethical* phenomenon. I "annul the succession" in order to take account of the manifold contents of the *Øjeblikket* because, and when, I must choose.

As an ethical intersection with eternity, the present has religious overtones for Kierkegaard. That is why he points to the Latin meaning of "presence", *praesentes dii*, meaning not merely the presence of the gods but their aid, in my actions (*CD* 86). But pagan thought was unable to get to the full nature of the present, because Christianity forces on each one of us a unique decision: the decision of whether to accept or reject the Christian message. That message for Kierkegaard includes three crucial things. One, which we have already discussed, is that your future is eternity. The second is that your eternal future has only two possibilities, which are equally unfathomable but as different from each other as it is possible for them to be: either eternal salvation or eternal damnation. And the third is that you have to decide, *now*, whether to accept that message, and live as a Christian, or not. The pagan religions – Kierkegaard does not discuss here any religions other than paganism and Christianity – do not force that "infinite" a choice on you. Hence, the present as the prevailing circumstances of action, has a deeper meaning for Christians – and, presumably, for those who consciously decide to reject Christianity – than for other people.

The present, because it is experienced on the basis of eternity as the future, is then extraneous to time as such, that is, to times A and B. To introduce it is to *rupture* the continuity of time. And this rupturing is central to our lives, because it is not restricted to Christ's death. It is also behind the idea of conversion, which is basically the idea that what I have been up to now, even on my most basic levels, is not what I have to be. I am free. I am in dread: "The possible corresponds exactly to the future. For freedom, the possible is the future, and the future is for time the possible. To both of these correspond dread in the individual life" (*CD* 91). We can only fully have a present, then, if we see it as the moment in which we must make an "infinite" decision – one that is far more than a mere life or death decision, for it regards eternal life or death. It is only through our capacity to decide, our freedom, that we fully have a present.

Dread follows on the discovery that one is free: that one has possibilities that are radically different from one's present and past; that one therefore has a future; and that one can sin, that is, become unfathomable – confronting, like Adam, a choice that one does not understand.

BEING A CHRISTIAN

In his *Point of View for My Work as an Author*, Kierkegaard says that the single theme of his whole work as an author is that of "becoming a Christian" (Kierkegaard 1962: 5–6). Kierkegaard will understand basic Christian doctrines in terms of the temporal schema that he has laid out here. For example:

- The deepest meaning of the Christian doctrine of original sin is that all humans are in the same situation Adam was in: we are all under commands that we do not fully understand because they relate to the future. What he did, we have all done (*CD* 90–91).
- The deepest meaning of the Christian doctrine of redemption is that we have the possibility of becoming good – that our future is radically open at every minute.

- The deepest meaning of the Christian doctrine of the Incarnation – itself the deepest doctrine of Christianity – is that the Eternal became human, that is, temporal. In the *Concluding Unscientific Postscript*, Kierkegaard calls this the "absurd":

> What now is the absurd? The absurd is – that the eternal truth has come into being in time, that god has come into being, has been born, has grown up, and so forth, precisely like any other human being, indistinguishable from other individuals.　　(Kierkegaard 1941a: 188)

So it seems that the most honest way to be human – to accept our freedom and so our full nature as in time, with a past, a present and a future – is to be Christian; only Christianity can make of you what Kierkegaard calls an "individual" (cf. Kierkegaard 1962: 107–38). Certainly Kierkegaard advocates this, but in a strange way, for his version of Christianity is a fearsome religion. It not only claims that you will exist eternally, but that your possibilities for eternity are as different as two possibilities can be: either eternal life or eternal damnation. It claims that only you can decide which happens. And it claims that you must make that decision *now*. As Kierkegaard puts it in a passage from his *Concluding Unscientific Postscript*, which he published under the pseudonym "Johannes Climacus" and which exemplifies these aspects of his understanding of Christianity,

> I, Johannes Climacus, born in this city and now thirty years old, a common ordinary human being like most people, assume that there awaits me a highest good, an eternal happiness, in the same sense that such a good awaits a servant-girl or a professor. I have heard that Christianity proposes itself as a condition for the acquirement of this good, and now I ask how I may establish a proper relationship to this doctrine. … It is Christianity itself which compels me to ask this question in this manner. It puts quite an extraordinary emphasis upon my own petty self, and upon every other self however petty, in that it proposes to endow each self with an eternal happiness, provided a proper relationship is established.　　(Kierkegaard 1941a: 19)

Christianity is thus the religion of dread *par excellence*; it is the most dread-ful thing in the world – ever. There are different ways to be a Christian that mitigate this dread, and which therefore are in "bad faith". Kierkegaard goes through them in detail.

First, you can call yourself a Christian while remaining a pagan. There is then no real sin, no real salvation, no real freedom, no real future – and no anxiety:

> The life of Christian paganism is neither guilty nor not guilty. It really knows no distinction between the present, the past, the future, and the

eternal. Its life and its history go on crabbedly like writing in ancient manuscripts without any punctuation marks, one word, one sentence after the other. It is … comical that the sum of rational creatures is transformed into a perpetual muttering without meaning. Whether philosophy can use this *plebs* as a category by making it a substratum for the greater, just as vegetative sludge gradually becomes solid earth, I do not know. Viewed from the standpoint of spirit such life is sin, and the least one can do is state this and demand spirit from it.   (*CD* 94)

In today's world this is "spiritlessness", and "Humanity qualified as spiritless has become a talking machine, and there is nothing to prevent him from repeating by rote a philosophical rigamarole, a confession of faith, or a political recitative" (*CD* 94).

There is no anxiety here; spiritlessness is "too happy, too content, and too spiritless for that" (*CD* 95). But anxiety is below the surface, disguised, because the task of keeping it away is directing the whole show (*CD* 96). In real paganism, which is far preferable to spiritlessness, anxiety is still there – because *fate* is there. Fate is a combination of necessity and random chance: necessary in that it is not under your control, and random because you cannot begin to understand it. When fate is central in human life, as it was in paganism, guilt and sin have no place: how can you sin or be guilty when everything about you is fated?

The clearest *Christian* version of this, and the second way to be an inauthentic Christian, is "genius". A "genius", in the strict sense, is someone who is led by something outside herself: her genius, or guardian spirit (*CD* 98). The genius (Hegel's term is, as we saw, "world-historical individual") is someone who would "rock the whole world", but is not exempt from fate (*CD* 99). Thus, the genius seeks to be his or her own unique self, but does not see this as a free choice, because the genius sees herself as being led by some other being. So you cannot decide to be a genius, and if you are one you see yourself as *compelled* to create, or win great battles, and so on. The genius thus denies her own freedom. Indeed, in order not to see that he or she is free, the genius avoids reflection altogether: "the genius does not turn inward into himself" (*CD* 99). But avoiding reflection does not spare the genius from dread: "The genius as such cannot apprehend himself religiously, and therefore he reaches neither sin nor providence, and for this reason the genius is found in the relation of anxiety to fate. There has never existed a genius without this anxiety, unless he was also religious" (*CD* 101).

The next step, and the third way to be an inauthentic Christian, is to be a *religious genius*, who does turn inwards. To turn inwards is to discover guilt: the religious genius is the creative person who actually feels bad when she hurts other people, or the general who regrets that thousands have to die in order that she can win her battles (*CD* 107): "To the degree that he discovers freedom, to that same degree the anxiety of sin is upon him … He fears only guilt, for guilt alone can strip him of his freedom" (*CD* 108). The religious genius is thus capable of repentance, and when this happens "Guilt … captures the genius who is religious, and this is the moment of culmination, the moment when he is greatest, … when by himself he sinks before himself in the depths of sin-consciousness" (*CD* 110).

Fourth, now that the awareness of sin is in the picture, the individual can become terrified of sin itself. This amounts to anxiety in the face of the concrete, "for no one ever sins on the average or in general" (*CD* 114; if one could do that, sin would not be unfathomable). Sin is a constant possibility, so this kind of person is in constant anxiety: the individual "shall be dragged through life to the place of execution" (*CD* 116). The way out of this torment, and the fifth way of being an inauthentic Christian, is to give up even trying to be good and embrace your own evil nature, in which case you come to fear the good, and are "demonic": "The individual is in the evil and is in anxiety about the good. The bondage of sin is an unfree relation to the evil, but the demonic is an unfree relation to the good" (*CD* 119).

To be "demonic" is the most important and most vicious way of being an inauthentic Christian. Since evil is a turning towards one's own individual, unfathomable nature, the salient characteristic of the demonic person is "shut-upness":

> The demonic does not close itself up *with* something, but it closes itself up within itself, and in this lies what is profound about existence, precisely that unfreedom makes itself a prisoner. Freedom is always *communicerende* [communicative] … unfreedom becomes more and more enclosed and does not want communication. (*CD* 124)

This refusal to communicate is what makes the demonic feel dread in the face of the good, for the refusal to communicate is what such dread is.

By "communicate", Kierkegaard does not mean to issue a set of true statements to another person. When I tell someone something that is true, I present her with something that she must accept, and this deprives her of her freedom. Kierkegaard wants another kind of language entirely, a language that neither lies nor speaks objective truth, but gets people to accept their freedom.[7] Such language can be ironical, as Socrates was; it can also include remaining silent, "closing your door" to others, not in order to be shut up with yourself but in order to get them out of themselves (*CD* 134). The demonic person, by contrast, rejects others; so rejects ongoing relationships with them; and so appears suddenly, like Mephistopheles, the devil in Goethe's *Faust* (*CD* 132). She has, then, a present, but it is a present that is full only of her own ego, and so the demonic

---

7. For more on this cf. Kierkegaard (1941a: 70–74, 169–224).

person is very boring. When she does communicate, nothing new comes forth (*CD* 133).

"Demonic" Christianity has two subtypes for Kierkegaard. One, the sixth form of inauthentic Christianity, is "freedom lost psychosomatically", that is, insanity of various sorts. The other, more important for Kierkegaard, is "freedom lost pneumatically", that is, spiritually. This seventh way of being an inauthentic Christian is very widespread, and he gives it a serious analysis. The loss of freedom he has in mind is, he tells us, the "loss of inwardness". What is inwardness? To understand this we must bear in mind that truth, for Kierkegaard, is individual, by which he means that "truth is for the particular individual only as he himself produces it in action" (*CD* 138). In other words, Kierkegaardian truth is, and must be, something you live by. Living by a truth, in turn, requires "certitude", that is, a willingness to entrust your life to that truth in the face of the fact that you do not know your future, and so do not know what living by this particular truth will actually bring you.

What Kierkegaard calls "the paradox of the age" (similar in form to Marx's paradox that the more the workers produce, the poorer they get) is that the more truth increases, the more certitude decreases; that is, there are more and more truths around that nobody wants to live by (*CD* 139): "With what industrious zeal, with what sacrifice of time, of diligence, of writing materials the speculators in our time have wanted to produce a complete proof of God's existence! Yet to the same degree that the excellence of the proof increases, certitude seems to decline" (*CD* 140).

What leads to this is reflection (*CD* 142): instead of *committing* ourselves to a belief as something to live by, we ask whether it is really true or not. We intellectualize things; we sacrifice the immediacy of commitment for the "mediations" of reason. Philosophy is very prone to this, of course; but so is biblical scholarship. When someone tries to prove that the Bible is either true or not true, she is missing the point of the Bible entirely: that it is to be lived by (*CD* 142). A successful proof *either way* would be a disaster, because it would deprive us of our freedom either to accept or reject Christianity. As Kierkegaard puts it in the *Concluding Unscientific Postscript*:

> Without risk there is no faith. Faith is precisely the contradiction between the infinite passion of the individual's inwardness and the objective uncertainty. … Without risk there is no faith, and the greater the risk the greater the faith; the more objective certainty, the less inwardness (for inwardness is precisely subjectivity), and the less objective certainty the more profound the possible inwardness.
>
> (Kierkegaard 1941a: 188)

We now know that inwardness is "subjectivity", but that does not tell us much about the nature of inwardness itself. You can give another synonym:

"earnestness" (*CD* 146). But that, too, is hard to define. Kierkegaard talks for a while about Rosenkranz, a psychologist (*CD* 147ff.), but gets his thread back: "Whenever inwardness is lacking, the spirit is finitized. Inwardness is therefore eternity, or the constituent of the eternal in man" (*CD* 151). This suggests that inwardness is conversion as an ongoing activity; for the "eternal in man" can be nothing other than the rupture introduced together with the present. To see this, we can note some things inwardness is not.

First, it is not the *denial* of the eternal in man, and so of the present. Only when the eternal is accepted can the future be radically other than what we want it to be – that is, radically awful – and then we are in dread about the good. Denying the eternal, and the present, are certainly possible, but a person who does this is, so to speak, "in denial":

> He may continue to deny the eternal as long as he wants, but in so doing he will not be able to kill the eternal off entirely. Even if to a certain degree and in a certain sense he is willing to admit the eternal, he fears it in another sense and to a higher degree. Nevertheless, no matter how much he denies it, he still cannot get rid of it entirely.   (*CD* 152)

Inwardness is also not conceiving of the eternal *abstractly*, as a sort of outside boundary to our daily lives, one that we never approach (*CD* 152). Nor is it giving eternity some sort of *aesthetic* presentation: "art is an anticipation of eternal life" (*CD* 153), and it is very nice, but you do not have to live by it. Nor, finally, is inwardness conceiving of yourself metaphysically, that is, as unchanging, as a pure "I = I" or as an immortal soul (*CD* 153). In sum, "Men are not willing to think eternity earnestly but are anxious about it, and anxiety can contrive a hundred evasions. And this is precisely the demonic" (*CD* 154).

So what is inwardness? Dread, we have seen, is the dread of possibility, of things being different. More precisely, it is the dread of freedom: dread of the idea that things will be different because of what *you* do. Accepting this truth – accepting that at every moment of our lives we are opened up to eternity and so are in dread – is inwardness.

An honest confrontation with dread teaches us, then. It teaches that all things can be different – that nothing, not even your own most cherished goals, has to be as it is: dread "consumes all finite aims and discovers all their deception" (*CD* 155). But this possibility becomes educative only in *faith*, which Kierkegaard, following Hegel, defines as "the inner certainty that anticipates infinity" (*CD* 157).

This, then, is inwardness: the inner certainty that the only thing that truly matters is your relation to eternity, that is, to God. Inwardness occurs, in other words, when the rupture brought about by the present brings you closer to God. The dread of things being somehow different for all eternity because of what *you* choose to do here and now is like a fire that burns away your interest in things of this world, in finite things. It leads you to faith in God: not in the sense that God will save you and what you love from destruction – that is paganism, an attempt to use God to achieve your own happiness – but in the sense that you can always turn to Him; "with the help of faith, anxiety trains the individual to repose in providence" (CD 161). The true communication of the individual is thus with God alone: it is communion. The other things, all of them –including the love of one's life, one's reputation in one's community, or the Church itself – do not matter. The aim is "to be alone with Him in a solitary place" (Kierkegaard 1962: 113).

CONCLUSION

Kierkegaard is the first exponent of continental philosophy to grasp the future as a problem, and, indeed, as an insoluble one. It is with Kierkegaard that we see, at last, why continental philosophy is so terrifying: because it makes us respond to, and that means recognize, something truly scary. Unlike Hegel, Kierkegaard does not dismiss the future, and unlike Marx he does not see the problem with it as merely one of how to make correct predictions about it. *Contra* Hegel, the future is all-important; and *contra* Marx, it is intrinsically unfathomable. The reason for both these things, in Kierkegaard's view, is that the future is eternity.

The basis for this claim, Kierkegaard insists, is Christianity. This lands him in religious trouble, in part because it leads him to justify Christianity on the grounds that it is absurd and dread-ful: indeed, that it is the most absurd and dread-producing of all things. This is hardly the way most Christians see the "good news", the gospel, of their religion.

As later continental philosophers will make evident, Kierkegaard's undertaking also runs into philosophical trouble. This is not because he makes the unphilosophical move of presupposing the truth of a particular religion, but because of the way in which he avoids doing this. This is by claiming that the objective truth of Christianity is irrelevant to Christianity itself. What true Christianity demands is just the greatest subjective certainty for a belief that is not merely objectively uncertain, but is the most absurd possible belief:

> Anything that is almost probable or probably, or extremely and emphatically probable, is something [one] can almost know, or as good as know, or extremely and emphatically almost know – but it is impossible to believe. For the absurd is the object of faith, and the only object that can be believed. (Kierkegaard 1941a: 189)

If the Christian story of the afterlife makes no sense, why should we believe it? Why should we believe anything? Kierkegaard's answer lies in the effects of that belief on us. Accepting the absurd story of Christianity makes us good people by giving us "inwardness". But why is inwardness good? Why should we adopt a morality that takes as its supreme goal being alone with God "in a solitary place"?

Kierkegaard's advocacy of solitude is not a mere pathology. It is the inevitable outcome of his insistence that faith itself must be an acceptance of absurdity. For what is absurd to the point of being paradoxical is something we cannot discuss with others, much less come to agreement with them about. This is perhaps clearest in his account, in *Fear and Trembling*, of Abraham (Kierkegaard 1941b: 27–37). Abraham has been told to leave his native city and go out into the desert with just Sarah, his wife; if he does this, his descendents will become a mighty people.

In an event that can only be miraculous because of Sarah's great age, she actually becomes pregnant and gives birth. God then tells Abraham to take this child, Isaac, to the top of Mount Moriah and kill him. This command, like the one that Adam received, makes no sense at all: how can Abraham become the father of a mighty nation if he kills his only child? And why should a lord who tells you to kill your child be obeyed at all? Abraham decides to obey; but he cannot explain this decision – it is too absurd. He and Isaac ride to Mount Moriah for four days, during which Abraham does not speak a single word.[8]

The future, of course, can be unfathomable without being absurd in this sense. Hegel, for example, admitted that nothing intelligible could be found in the future; but he hardly credited it with existential absurdity. What makes the future absurd, for Kierkegaard, is the action of God, who in Christianity makes our future eternity itself. Kierkegaard's invocation of absurdity thus comes at the precise moment when he moves into his version of Christianity: into his conflation of the future with eternity.

But there was another reason for conflating the future with eternity: to show how we arrive at the present, at the idea that what confronts us right now is the moral space in which we must act, rather than merely the outcome of the past that we must, *a là* Hegel, intellectually comprehend. But here Kierkegaard is simply wrong. The conflation of the future with eternity is not necessary for us to conceive of the present; denying that conflation does not land us back in time B, the kind of time that Kierkegaard attributes to Plato and Hegel. For even if we do not believe in eternity, the present remains for us the moment of choice and action; and as long as our future is open, our choices and actions can shape it. For the present is shaped, not merely by the past of which it is the outcome, but by the future, a future that, if it is open, is indeed unknowable. This is what makes the present moment more than merely the limit of the past: it is the prevailing circumstances with which we must deal.

---

8. *Fear and Trembling* was published under the revealing pseudonym "Johannes de Silentio".

We do not need Christianity to teach us this. Nietzsche, who was anything but a Christian, will teach it. The Greeks (*pace* Kierkegaard!) had a way of expressing it. They distinguished *to nun*, the now as the abstract limit of the past (and future, according to Aristotle's discussion in *Physics* IV) from *ta nun*, the currently prevailing circumstances. I have to take account of the latter when I have to choose. I must, for Kierkegaard, choose in light of a future that is, to be sure, radically more open than the future is for someone like Aristotle, and so unfathomable – but it need not be the Christian view of eternity.

Philosophically speaking, Kierkegaard's conflation of the future with eternity is not an acceptance of Christian doctrine in any traditional sense, but something even older and more traditional: the appeal to a timeless realm. Such appeal is hardly foreign to Kierkegaard. Consider this passage from the *Point of View for My Work as an Author* where he evokes the:

> eternity which arches over and high above the temporal tranquil as the starry vault at night, and God in heaven who in the bliss of that sublime tranquility holds in survey, without the least dizziness at such a height, these countless multitudes of men and knows each single individual by name. (1962: 111–12)[9]

Kierkegaard's difference with the philosophical tradition, however, is monumental – and revealing. It lies in his claim that the atemporal domain is not logically structured and so knowable, like Plato's Forms and (Kierkegaard thinks) Hegel's logic. It is the future, and so unfathomable. After Kant's failure to establish the noumenal realm as the final cause of nature, the atemporal can appear to us only as something that makes no sense.

If we avoid Kierkegaard's conflation of the future as unfathomable with the future as eternity, as later continental philosophers such as Nietzsche will do, his fundamental question remains: how do we take account of the future if it is intrinsically unfathomable? Philosophy cannot take such account, for him, because the future is not merely unfathomable but absurd: the future can only be encountered as eternity, which means in the form of the Christian story of the afterlife. Excising Kierkegaard's move from the unfathomabilty of the future to its eternality not only cuts the "Christianity" away from his thought, but also opens up the way to understand how to bring the future, in all its unknowability, into philosophy. This understanding, and the *philosophical* answer to Kierkegaard's question, will come only with Heidegger, seventy-two years after Kierkegaard's death.

---

9. Kierkegaard's objection to Hegelian logic, we saw, was that such logic was not atemporal enough: it contained movement. Also cf. Kierkegaard (1946).

CHAPTER 5

NIETZSCHE AND THE BOUNDLESS FUTURE

PRIMARY TEXT Friedrich Nietzsche, *On the Genealogy of Morality*
(*GM*; [1887] 1994)

In January 1889, in Turin, Italy, a drayman was whipping an old horse in the street: a common enough, although unpleasant, sight in those days. One of the passers-by, a thin man with pince-nez glasses and an enormous moustache, was terribly moved by the spectacle. He rushed forwards, threw his arms around the horse's neck to stave off the whip, and collapsed. Friedrich Nietzsche regained consciousness, but he was totally insane for the rest of his life.[1]

This was a transformation in Nietzsche's life as profound as any Christian conversion Kierkegaard ever envisaged, but in the opposite direction. Instead of an acceptance of radical freedom, it was a physiological collapse that virtually erased Nietzsche from the human race. Yet in a strange way it was the best thing that ever happened to him. During the previous ten years, in spite of worsening health, Nietzsche had written ten absolutely brilliant books. He is one of the true masters of German prose, indeed one of the very best writers ever to write in any language. But nobody read his books; in several cases he had to pay to get them published. Only after his collapse did the legend spread that his insanity was the result of seeing too clearly, deeply and honestly, and his reputation begin to grow.

Nietzsche, like Marx, was from a clerical family. His father, a Lutheran minister, died in 1849, when he was five; his younger brother, the next year. His mother took Friedrich and his sister Elizabeth, also younger, to live with relatives. In 1858, four years after Kierkegaard's death and twenty-six years after Hegel's, Friedrich's life began to improve, for he got a full scholarship to a very prestigious boarding school, Pforta. He then studied classical philology at Leipzig and in 1869, aged twenty-four, was appointed a full professor at the University of Basel in Switzerland. Leipzig thereupon awarded him a doctorate

---

1. For Nietzsche's life cf. Safranski (2003).

without his even having finished his dissertation, something virtually unheard of in Germany, then and now.

Nietzsche's training in classical philology was not entirely accidental. After the purge of the Young Hegelians (discussed in Chapter 3) German philosophers, under political assault, had retreated to philosophy's most recent bastion of tradition: Kant. But everyone knew that the best young philosophers had been purged for reasons of politics, and many suspected that those who remained were there for reasons of career. This, in fact, was often the case, and the result was as pure an outburst of charlatanry as philosophy has seen in the modern world:

> Men entered and left the [neo-Kantian] movement as if it were a church or political party; members of one school blocked the appointments and promotions of members of the others; eminent Kant scholars and philosophers who did not found their own schools or accommodate themselves to one of the established schools tended to be neglected as outsiders and condemned as amateurs. (White Beck 1967: V, 428)

Given all this, it is not surprising that creative young minds were drawn elsewhere: Nietzsche to philology and, somewhat later, Husserl and Frege to mathematics.

More positively, however, it is also true that a strong interest in classical thought is inherent in the very nature of continental philosophy. If everything is in time, then the foundations of our thought must be in time as well. They do not permanently underlie other things, as would an atemporal stratum, but are merely the historical circumstances from which other things begin. Since the Greeks are the farthest back that the Western philosophical record currently goes, everything begins with them. The closest thing continental philosophy has to a "foundation" is thus the historical record of Greek thought, and continental philosophy's concern with the Greeks did not begin or end with Nietzsche. The content of Hegel's philosophy, as Hegel scholar G. R. G. Mure pointed out, owes a great deal to Aristotle (Mure 1940: ix–xi). It is no accident that Marx's doctoral dissertation was on Epicurus, or that Kierkegaard's first book, *The Concept of Irony*, was on Socrates. After Nietzsche, the critical appropriation of Greek philosophy becomes an explicit and central concern of such major continental thinkers as Arendt, Deleuze, Derrida, Foucault, Gadamer and Heidegger, as well as the first generation Frankfurt theorists Adorno and Horkheimer.[2]

In any case, after a difficult start Nietzsche's life became very good indeed. Unfortunately the good part did not last. After ten years at Basel, Nietzsche had to resign for reasons of health. His colleagues, in further testimony to his schol-

---

2. The main exceptions to this will be Sartre and Beauvoir, who were deeply influenced by the ahistorical side of Husserlian phenomenology.

arly abilities, voted him a full pension. For the next ten years, Nietzsche used that pension to wander around Europe, writing the ten brilliant books that nobody read. He set pen to paper in many of Europe's most naturally beautiful places: the high mountains of the Swiss Engadine; the dark woods of the Bavarian Forest; the lovely villages of the South of France. This sounds like a wonderful life, but there were two serious downsides to it. First, Nietzsche was totally alone, living in boarding houses (his university pension was not *that* bountiful!). Second, his health continued to deteriorate: he became subject to terrible migraines, which kept him in bed for three or four days at a time. The least variation in his diet – any coffee, let alone alcohol, meat and other foodstuffs – could bring one of these on.

After Nietzsche's collapse in Turin, his mother and sister took him in. He lived for ten more years and died in Weimar, in August 1900. By that time, he and his works were quite well known; but, fatefully, they were now in the hands of his sister Elizabeth. She oversaw their republication in editions that now sold out, and also edited some of the notes he had left behind into what she and others called his "masterpiece", *Der Wille zur Macht* (*The Will to Power*). On the basis of this body of work, Nietzsche came to be understood as a German racist; when Hitler met Mussolini for the first time, he legendarily presented him with a Moroccan-leather-bound edition of the works of Nietzsche. Nietzsche's sister's house at Weimar, where he had lived the last years of his life, was turned into sort of a shrine; there is a famous picture of Hitler there, contemplating the bust of Nietzsche.

After the Second World War, then, and indeed well before it, Nietzsche's stock was low indeed. Who needs a Nazi racist philosophy? Fortunately for Nietzsche, a man named Walter Kaufmann had some suspicions about him. Kaufmann, himself a German Jew who had emigrated to the United States and become a professor of philosophy at Princeton University, undertook to compare the published versions of Nietzsche's works with Nietzsche's own original manuscripts, which were still available at the Weimar house. And he discovered that the racism was the product of Elizabeth's editing. Elizabeth was a racist and anti-Semite; she had edited her brother's works in such a way as to make him look like one as well. Kaufmann's book appeared in 1950; if it had not, few people today would be reading Nietzsche.[3]

NIETZSCHE, CHRISTIANITY AND THE GREAT NOON

Like Marx and Kierkegaard, Nietzsche exemplifies the very feature of temporalized philosophy that brought grief to the Young Hegelians: its inability to give full allegiance to any existing state of affairs. If all things are mortal, then

---

3. Kaufmann tells this story at Kaufmann (1956: 15–28).

everything around us will eventually pass away, and, perhaps, ought to do so. In this way, continental philosophy is always open to the possibility of a critical stance towards the givens of the day. Such a stance is by no means necessary, however; Hegel, perhaps in virtue of his refusal to think about the future at all, had avoided it. But subsequent continental philosophers carried it through: Marx in economics, and Kierkegaard with regard to established versions of Christianity. Nietzsche is probably most famous for his own scathing views on religion, especially Christianity. But we need to be careful about how we associate this critique with Nietzsche. Consider the following points:

The "purest flower" of the "Christian idea" is "ascetically contemplative monasticism". Christianity has had its greatest historical influence as a:

> religion whose earliest dogmas contain a condemnation of the flesh, and which not merely grants the spirit superiority over the flesh but also deliberately mortifies the flesh in order to glorify the spirit. I am speaking of the religion whose unnatural mission actually introduced sin and hypocrisy into the world.

Christianity's "unnaturalness" means that it is sort of a disease:

> [This] real idea of Christianity spread over the entire Roman Empire with incredible rapidity, like a contagious disease … We moderns still feel spasms and lassitude in all our limbs. … Sometime, when mankind regains its complete health, we will scarcely be able to comprehend the unnatural discord that Christianity has sown between the two.

As itself a disease, Christianity values most highly what is really most defective: its "mission" meant primarily "curbing the strong and strengthening the weak". Today, "the ultimate fate of Christianity depends on whether we still need it". It is not the will of God or the holiness of humanity that decides the value of Christianity, but merely our human needs.

Most people with some knowledge of Nietzsche will recognize the main outlines of his critique of Christianity in these passages, but they are not by Nietzsche. They are by Heinrich Heine, the great German poet – and a pupil of Hegel – writing between 1832 and 1835.[4] Is Nietzsche, who reckoned Heine among those few who had anticipated the future of Europe (Nietzsche 1989: 196), merely plagiarizing him?

No. Consider the last lines of Nietzsche's most famous work, *Thus Spoke Zarathustra*:

---

4. The quotes are from Heine's *Concerning the History of Religion and Philosophy in Germany* at (Heine 1973: 132, 280, 281). I am indebted to Terry Pinkard for pointing out the resemblances between Heine and Nietzsche.

"Well then! The lion came, my children are near, Zarathustra has ripened, my hour has come: this is *my* morning, *my* day is breaking: *rise now, thou great noon!*"

Thus spoke Zarathustra, and he left his cave, glowing and strong as a morning sun that comes out of dark mountains.

(Nietzsche 2006: 266)

Heine says the same things as Nietzsche; but Zarathustra's day is just breaking. Nietzsche, in other words, is talking about the future, while Heine, like a good Hegelian, thinks he is talking about the past. Christianity, for him, has *already* been overcome:

People have now recognized the nature of this religion, they no longer let themselves be fooled by promissory notes on heaven, they know that material things have their good side and are not totally evil, and they now vindicate the pleasures of the earth. (Heine 1973: 132)

In Germany deism ... was long ago overthrown in theory. Like many other things, it still maintains its position only among the mindless masses, a position without rational justification ... We have in fact over-thrown deism. We are free and do not want any thundering tyrant. Deism is a religion for servants. (*Ibid.*: 341)

Nietzsche too, of course, believes that Christianity has been overcome: God, after all, is dead. But there is for Nietzsche more overcoming to be done. The end of Zarathustra shows us someone walking confidently into the future – into a boundless future, the empty blue of the noon sky: "The great noon, where human beings stand at the midpoint of their course between animal and overman and celebrate their way to evening as their highest hope: for it is the way to a new morning" (Nietzsche 2006: 59).

The "great noon" that is coming upon us, for Nietzsche, is itself, like the night with which Hegel began the *Phenomenology*, a moment of transition, between the rise of the morning sun and its setting itself towards evening. The night to which it is the prelude is itself the prelude to a new morning, one that we cannot fathom, because we humans will no longer even be there to experience it. It is the time of the "overman": "That the human being is something that just be overcome, – that human being is a bridge and not an end, counting itself blessed for its noon and evening as the way to new dawns: [these are] the Zarathustra-words about the great noon" (*ibid.*: 158). As with continental philosophers in general, then, everything is temporal for Nietzsche. As he puts it in *Human, All Too Human*, "Everything, however, has come to be (*alles aber ist geworden*); there are no eternal facts, just as there are no absolute truths. *That is why historical philosophizing is necessary from now on*" (1986: 13, trans. mod., emphasis added).

Nietzsche differs from Heine – and from Hegel – in the way he sees himself responding to time. As with Kierkegaard, he takes the future to be both the most important aspect of time and intrinsically unfathomable. But this does not, for him, occasion Kierkegaardian *Angest* over one's eternal fate, for Nietzsche has abandoned eternity altogether – except as an object of passion. As the refrain from the "Yes and Amen Song" in *Thus Spoke Zarathustra* has it, "Never yet have I found the woman from whom I wanted children, unless it be this woman whom I love; for I love you, O eternity" (2006: 185).

Even eternity, for Nietzsche, counts only for its offspring.

ON THE GENEALOGY OF MORALITY: INTRODUCTION

On the Genealogy of Morality was published in 1887, two years before Nietzsche's final collapse. It is thus the product of a Nietzsche who has learned and developed over the course of his writings, but is not yet wrestling with his madness in the sometimes distracting ways of his final books. *On the Genealogy of Morality* is thus, perhaps, the most lucid presentation of Nietzsche's distinctive approach to time and his innovations in continental philosophy's effort to appropriate the future philosophically. Like all of Nietzsche's works it is aphoristic in nature, consisting of independent observations and trains of thought rather than a single overarching argument. In and around this, however, it is disciplined by an overarching methodological concept that Nietzsche calls "genealogy".

Like Marx's and Kierkegaard's, Nietzsche's account of the modern age begins by invoking a paradox: "we knowers" (in particular, philosophers and psychologists) are unknown to ourselves (*GM* 3). This paradox itself is testimony to Nietzsche's classical education and interests, for it was Socrates who adopted for philosophy the Delphic motto "Know thyself" (*gnōthe seauton*). Modern philosophers too, have sought to know themselves. To know what it means to think with a human mind is, for example, basic to Kant's philosophy, and Kant attempts, as we saw in Chapter 1, to use this knowledge to determine such things as what sort of government is best for humans, and where history should be viewed as heading. Self-knowledge is thus an important concern both for Kant and for the neo-Kantians dominant in Nietzsche's day. But somehow this knowledge is deficient for Nietzsche. And somehow philosophers actually like things that way; they seem to *value* their self-ignorance: "there is a good reason for this" (*GM* 3).

We can understand this "good reason" by asking: *what* is it that we do not know about ourselves? Nietzsche's analogy here is telling: we are like someone who, sunk in reverie, hears a clock striking and, startled, asks "What hour struck?" (*GM* 3). In fact, as Nietzsche specifies, the hour was noon. What we are ignorant of, then is the great noon: our position between past and future. The way to overcome our ignorance is to uncover what Nietzsche calls "the descent of our moral prejudices" (*GM* 4). But this is a difficult investigation because we "knowers" *like* our ignorance; perhaps because if we knew where our moral prejudices come from, we would have to admit that they are merely prejudices.

At this point, Nietzsche is in the Kantian "critical" camp in that he wants to trace things back to their origins, in the expectation that knowing their origins will reveal their nature (cf. *GM* 7). He seems also, however, to be following Hegel in that his project of "genealogy" is to trace not the one-step emergence of a representation from a faculty but a "descent", which as we shall see is a long and involved, and so temporal, process. But Nietzsche has never seriously read Hegel, who as I have noted was completely out of fashion in Germany in the second half of the nineteenth century. To see where Nietzsche is really coming from with this notion of "genealogy", we should look a bit more at the issues he thinks are involved in tracing the "descent" of moral prejudices.

At bottom, we are asking how our most basic moral ideas, the categories of good and evil, came to be. The obvious answer, and the one Nietzsche tells us he himself gave at the age of thirteen, is a theological one: from God. But making God the origin of the concept of evil means making him the origin of evil itself, presumably because one cannot do evil unless one knows one is doing it; if God had not given us the concept of evil, we could not knowingly sin. This was an issue for Kierkegaard, for whom, as we saw, God ended Adam's innocence, thereby making him free and so doing him a favour.

For the adolescent Nietzsche, the situation is much worse: God must be the "father of evil" (*GM* 5). Nietzsche is here alluding, of course, to a standard version of a standard argument against the existence of God: that the existence of evil is incompatible with that of an all-knowing, all-powerful and all-good creator. This is an argument Nietzsche accepts; elsewhere he sums it up as the view that "God's only excuse is that He does not exist" (Nietzsche 2005: 91).

But if our moral ideas do not come from God, they can only come from us: we must have invented them. In this connection, Nietzsche enunciates the most basic principle of his "genealogical" procedure: "Fortunately I learnt, in time, to separate theological from moral prejudice, and I no longer searched for the origin of evil beyond the world" (*GM* 5).

In general, Nietzschean genealogy allows only for natural, that is temporal, origins: things can only be explained by other things that preceded them in time.

Once we abandon the quest for supernatural origins another, even more important, question imposes itself. The purpose of tracing things back to their origins, for Kant, was to evaluate them: to see, for example, what kind of validity can be assigned to belief in God. This is where Kantian critique approaches our normal view of "criticism". But with no supernatural origins tolerated, the final standard by which we can evaluate beliefs is ourselves, which raises Nietzsche's ultimate question: have our moral ideas "obstructed or promoted human flourishing up to now"? Do they reveal and promote "our fullness, vitality and will of life, its courage, its confidence, its future" (*GM* 5)?

In short, Nietzsche understands the "descent" of moral ideas in much the same way Darwin understands the "descent of man": our morality has evolved, and it has evolved in order to aid and abet life.[5] But moral ideas, for Nietzsche, are not keyed to survival, as Darwinian evolution is. They are keyed to "human flourishing", a much more ancient idea first developed in Aristotle's account of *eudaimonia* in the *Nicomachean Ethics*.[6] Nietzsche will not be interested, then, in "survival of the fittest". He will be interested in "flourishing of the fittest".

We can now see more clearly where Nietzsche is coming from with his method of genealogy. First, he is coming from Kant: he means to evaluate our moral ideas by tracing them back to their origins. But for Kant, nothing important *originated* in history. All our important moral ideas, for Kant, are grounded in the structure of our minds. You "critique" belief in God, not by trying to decide whether God really exists, but by tracing that belief back to the structure of the human mind. This, then, is a one stage derivation: belief → structure of mind.

Because Nietzsche is on the other side of Darwin (and Hegel), appeals to anything atemporal are out of the question, and you must go to history to see where things come from. Because history consists of long and convoluted processes of change, things do not come to us from their origins in any kind of simple or straightforward way. Any idea or rule we have today has come down to us via a whole series of transformations. So the critique of moral ideas Nietzsche has in mind must show not only where moral ideas originally came from, but how they got down to us. It must show how they grow up, develop, change:

> We need to know about the conditions and circumstances under which the values grew up the developed and changed (morality as result, as symptom, as mask, as tartuffery, as sickness, as misunderstanding; also morality as cause, remedy, stimulant, inhibition, poison) since we have neither had the knowledge up to now nor even desired it. (*GM* 8)

This, Nietzsche says, is a radically new kind of question: "The vast, distant, and hidden land of morality – of morality as it really existed and was really lived – has to be journeyed through with quite new questions and, as it were, with new eyes: and surely this means virtually discovering this land for the first time?" (*GM* 8).

This new philosophical *topos* demands a new kind of investigation: the "genealogy of morality". But how new is it? Is Nietzsche really doing anything different from Hegel, once we have liberated Hegel from the atemporality foisted on him by traditional readings? Fully resolving this question will eventually require us

---

5. For Nietzsche on Darwin, see the "Introduction" (*GM* 9); in *The Gay Science* he traces Darwin's insight back to Hegel: "without Hegel, no Darwin" (¶357; reprinted *GM* 172).
6. For a discussion of *eudaimonia* see Cooper (1986).

to turn from Nietzsche's discussion of his method of genealogy to his practice of it. But *GM*, Essay II, §12, gives us a clue as to how Nietzsche differs, not only from Hegel as Nietzsche understood him, the "traditional Hegel", but from Hegel as I have presented him here, temporalized Hegel.

First, Nietzsche rejects all teleology: "The origin of the emergence of a thing and its ultimate usefulness, its practical application and incorporation into a system of ends, are *toto caelo* separate" (*GM* 55). Nothing, in other words, comes to be in order to serve a purpose; ends and purposes are foisted on things by us only after they come into existence. For Darwin, evolutionary change is the result of random mutations, which turn out – in a few exceptional cases – to be useful. For Nietzsche this holds, not only for natural beings, but for social institutions such as punishment. We may say that punishing wrongdoers is a deterrent to crime, but that is only a *post facto* interpretation; in reality as we shall see, punishment can be viewed as having come about for very different reasons. This kind of *post facto* assignment of purpose is one form of what Nietzsche calls "interpretation". Interpretation, for its part, is an exercise of power on the part of the interpreter: "Anything in existence, having somehow come about, is continually interpreted anew, requisitioned anew, transformed and redirected to a new purpose by a power superior to it" (*GM* 55).

In this respect, interpretation is one form of what Nietzsche calls "dominating":

> Everything that occurs in the organic world consists of overpowering, dominating, and in their turn, overpowering and dominating consist of re-interpretation, adjustment, in the process of which their former "meaning" and "purpose" must necessarily be obscured or completely obliterated. (*GM* 55)

In these passages, Nietzsche is indeed taking issue with the traditional Hegel. For that version of Hegel, history and nature are truly teleological: they come about in order to be manifestations of the Absolute. Since the nature of the Absolute is specified in Hegel's own philosophy, philosophical interpretation (or, as Hegel calls it, "philosophical comprehension") reveals the inner purpose or "truth" of the thing, in the sense of its final significance. Such interpretation, fixing the nature of things for all time, cannot be carried out by a mere human being, and so must be the work of some suprapersonal version of Reason itself: the Absolute. On this view, Hegel's philosophy claims to be the Absolute interpreting itself.

When we turn from the traditional Hegel to continental philosophy's temporalized Hegel, we find two things that must be distinguished from one another. On the one hand, the idea that in understanding something we assume a stance superior to it from which we use it for our own purposes is attributable to Hegel. In fact, it is precisely what I portrayed as Hegel's attitude as he looked upon Napoleon riding his fine white horse. While no one can know what was really in Hegel's mind at that moment, I hope that I showed how Hegel's philosophy leads to such an attitude. But we cannot go on and attribute to Hegel the view that philosophical thought has the capacity to fix, once and for all, what things are: to formulate their "truth". Neither he nor Nietzsche thinks thought can have that kind of power. Hegel's teleological reconstructions of history, as we saw, are foisted on the facts, just as Nietzsche claims they are; and Hegel knew this.

Hegel thus agrees with Nietzsche that teleological explanation does not tell you how things originate, and that in making teleological or other interpretations of things we set ourselves "above" those things. But Nietzsche is not merely rehashing Hegel. Their real differences come out clearly towards the end of the second quotation from Nietzsche above. Hegel would not accept the view that when an object is reinterpreted, its previous interpretations "must necessarily be obscured or completely obliterated". Older interpretations are, for Hegel, what a newer interpretation is built on; and if it is rational, it changes them only in minimal ways. For Nietzsche, however, new interpretations do not build on older ones:

> The whole history of a "thing" … can to this extent be a continuous chain of signs, continually revealing new interpretations and adaptations, the causes of which need not be connected even amongst themselves, but rather sometimes just follow and replace one another at random. (*GM* 55)

At any given stage in the development of a thing, the interpretation that formulates the "nature" of that thing may be replaced by another interpretation that is wholly new. This means that the future of a thing is open at all times: one can never know what interpretation will be placed over it next. The openness of the future, which Kierkegaard had shown to be constitutive for the human individual, is for Nietzsche constitutive of everything that develops, and so of history itself. The future is thus at work even in the past; events that occurred long ago had open futures at the time they occurred, and this means that history for Nietzsche has a "looseness" that it does not have for Hegel. The privilege that Kierkegaard had accorded to the moments of Christ's death and Christian decision are thus undone; every moment, whether human beings are even around or not, is "loose" for Nietzsche.

Finally – and here the contrast with Hegel becomes a decisive move beyond him –combining the view that the history of a thing is a series of interpretations with the view that these interpretations occur in random order means that no interpretation can be relegated to the past. A thing can be the object of many interpretations at once. As Nietzsche puts it: if the "meaning" of a thing is the use function assigned to it by a given interpretation (*GM* 55), then by the time a thing has accumulated much of a history it has "not just one meaning but a whole synthesis of meanings" (*GM* 57). A thing, then, is "ambiguous" in the sense that it can always be fitted into a number of teleological narratives. Because its future is open in this way – indeed, totally open, or infinite – no interpretation is ever final. The aim, then, is keep the future open and infinite (and the sky of the great noon blue) by multiplying interpretations, so that we are not bound to just one of them. As Nietzsche will put it in Essay III:

> Finally, as knowers let us not be ungrateful towards such resolute reversals of familiar perspectives and valuations. … To see differently, and to *want* to see differently, is no small discipline and preparation of the intellect for its future "objectivity" – the latter understood not as "contemplation without interest" (which, as such, is a non-concept and an absurdity), but as *having in our power* our "pros" and "cons": so as to be able to engage and disengage them so that we can use the *difference* in perspectives and affective interpretations for knowledge.   (*GM* 92)

Much of Nietzsche's writing consists in such "resolute reversals", even of things he has just said.

For Hegel, too, no interpretation (or philosophical "comprehension") is ever final; for him as for Nietzsche, teleological interpretations of the facts of the past are foreign to those facts. Things come about however they come about, and it is the business of the philosopher to trace the rational thread in history's chaotic tapestry. But Hegel, unconcerned with the future, does not seek to proliferate interpretations, or to keep the future open; he never mentions the possibility that there might be more than one teleological interpretation of history. That his philosophy is merely a perspective on the facts is one of his basic principles, once we understand him as a continental philosopher; that it is only one perspective among many is not.

"GOOD AND EVIL", "GOOD AND BAD"

Nietzsche now applies the views that all origins are historical, that the future is always radically open and that historical developments are therefore always contingent or "loose" to what really interests him: morality. This brings him before the conceptual contrast between "good and evil", which is the main binary of modern morality, and "good and bad", which is its ancient ancestor. The key to understanding what Nietzsche means by opposing these two conceptual pairs lies in what he means by the "pathos of distance". He gets at this by noting that current historians of morality trace our notion of goodness back to how we feel about someone who has done us a favour. "He is good" is the original moral judgement, and originally meant "he has done me a favour" (*GM* 12). Nietzsche, however, thinks that the original moral judgement was, rather, "I am good". And "good", like all predicates, draws a contrast. If I call one thing, or kind of thing, good, I am implying that another thing, or kind of thing, is bad: "I am good" thus goes together with "she is bad", where "she" is just anyone who is not like me (*GM* 12).

If this is so, Nietzsche has made an incredible discovery about our most basic moral category, that of "goodness": he has discovered that it was originally grounded in self-love, not in love of others. Somebody who was "good" in the original sense of the term loved herself, and so did not love those who were unlike her. Her basic moral feeling – as the Greeks would say, her *pathos* – thus included an aversion to those others, a desire to maintain distance from them. What kinds of reason can Nietzsche give for this overthrow of our commonly understood views?

He has four arguments. First, people who genuinely like themselves are strong – and rare. They are "noble, mighty, high-placed, and high-minded" (*GM* 12). They are the *doers* of society. And creating words is a kind of doing (*GM* 13). So it is the powerful who, originally, created our words: we can "conceive of the origin of language itself as a manifestation of power" (*GM* 13). This includes the words "good" and "evil", which would then reflect the self-love of the strong.

Second, the view that our idea of "good" originated in the feeling of gratitude towards another poses a puzzle, for it comes as a surprise to us today. Why? Nothing has changed: People still do favours for one another. Why do we forget that "good" arose in that context (*GM* 13–14)? This criticism, of course, also applies to Nietzsche himself. He will have to give his own explanation of how we "forgot" that "good" originally meant "like me".

The third argument consists of philological indicators: in all languages, "good" originally meant "high minded", and "bad" meant "common" (*GM* 14–15). "Bad" did not originally have any negative connotations, and the original moral judgement could be paraphrased as: "I'm good; you're bad; and that is fine". Thus, in Homer's dialect of early Greek, *hoi kakoi*, which in later Greek came to mean the "bad men", just meant "the common people", the ones whose only function in the *Iliad* and the *Odyssey* is to be witnesses to the bravery and skill of the heroes. Nietzsche locates similar developments in German, Latin and the Celtic languages. In spite of its widespread nature, this philology has gone unremarked, he says, because of the "democratic bias within the modern world" (*GM* 14).

Finally, we have a historical indicator: the great blond conquest of the ancient world (*GM* 15–16; this is now called the "Dorian invasion"). The result of this is that words for "bad" tend to be related to words for "dark skinned" (*GM* 15–16). Here we seem to have a tinge of the racist Nietzsche, but if we look closely we see that he is not saying that "blond is good". He is saying that because the conquering heroes *happened* to be blond, they took blond to be good; more generally, whatever was like them in any way was "good". So Nietzsche is not being racist here. He is doing something that many people, in his day and in ours, find even more threatening than racism: he is saying that what we do and do not value is a result of mere chance. It is determined by whoever *happened to win* the relevant battles. If Nietzsche had known, as scholars believe today, that the "Dorians" were not blond northerners but in fact another group of Mediterranean Greeks, his association of blondness with goodness would fail, but his underlying point would not be affected.

Here, then, is where Nietzsche goes decisively beyond Hegel. Both of them would admit that who wins a given battle on a given day is largely a matter of chance. But Hegel would say that the victory, *if it mattered at all*, can be sub-sequently grasped as an advance for humanity. If the Dorians conquered the ancient Mediterranean world, either something about their values and social organization can now be seen to have been superior to the peoples they con-quered, or their victory was merely another meaningless event in the "slaugh-ter bench of history" and can be safely forgotten by today's philosophers. For Nietzsche, chance historical outcomes can remain decisive for us today without representing progress in any way. History cannot be reconstructed as a story of the advance of Spirit to freedom and self-knowledge, but must be viewed as a series of accidents. Things could have been different, and our contemporary moral ideas, which are the outcome of history, may be no more than prejudices.

Another way to put this, as I have suggested, is that the future, for Nietzsche, is infinitely open and always has been. For Hegel, the outcome of an ancient battle would have been largely contingent, in the sense that it was not possible to predict in advance who would win it. But whoever won, the battle had only two basic possibilities: either it could be construed as making an advance for humanity, in which case it deserved to be philosophically remembered by later generations and eventually placed into Hegel's own narrative, or it could not. Nietzsche believes, by contrast, that at each stage of history humanity is striding into an unknowable future; the unfathomability, or openness, of the future is an operative force in history.

These four arguments show, in Nietzsche's view, that contempt for others was originally intrinsic to one's own moral worth. But actually the feeling involved here is not the kind of thing we usually associate with contempt; it is not an active hatred or even dislike. Rather, it is a simple recognition that you are infe-rior to me (and those like me). Because you are unlike me (and those like me), you must be far from me on the moral scale; and since I am good, you must be bad. I am not going to try to stamp you out: I may need you (if only as a witness to my merit). Nor do I hate you. I may even like you. Do not, however, try to get close to me. This attitude is what Nietzsche calls the "pathos of distance".

The birth of the priests

So now we have two groups: aristocrats, not by virtue of blood or descent but by virtue of merit, on the one hand; and common people on the other – really "common". And so things would have stayed, except there was another group (here comes Nietzsche's story of how we "forgot" how things originally were). The aristocratic group originally contained not only warriors but priests. Priests, however, were forbidden to fight; they could not act, and thus had no power (*GM* 18). This represents a "turning way" from action, and this unnatural inaction is, for Nietzsche, a disease:

> From the very beginning there has been something unhealthy about these priestly aristocracies and in the customs dominant there, which are turned away from action and which are partly brooding and partly emotionally explosive, resulting in the almost inevitable bowel complaints and neurasthenia which have plagued the clergy down through the ages.   (*GM* 17)

Since the priests are aristocrats, they think they are good. But they do not act, so they quite consistently decide that not acting is good. Those who do not act, in general, are those who are acted upon: the losers in life. The priests thus come to value these people. This inversion of the original state of morality expresses itself in words like these (*GM* 19):

> "Only those who suffer are good; only the poor, the powerless, the lowly are good; the suffering, the deprived, the sick, the ugly, are the only pious people, the only ones saved, salvation is for them alone, whereas you rich, the noble and powerful, you are eternally wicked, cruel, lustful, insatiate, godless, you will also be eternally wretched, cursed and damned!"

This "slave morality" is in opposition to the original morality of the strong: "The chivalric-aristocratic value-judgments are based on a powerful physicality, a blossoming, rich, even effervescent good health which includes the things needed to maintain it, war, adventure, hunting, dancing, jousting, and everything else that contains strong, free, happy action" (*GM* 18).

As history, this is rather impressionistic: why were there priests among the original warriors? Were they cowards? Why did they not only view themselves as good but also try to convince the common people that they were the good people? How did they succeed? Nietzsche makes no attempt to explain these developments; they are merely accidents, then, and could well not have happened at all. But it is one thing to claim that the facts of history show looseness in its development, and quite another to advance developments that you claim to be the facts, but for which you offer little or no evidence. Nietzsche's historical interpretation of the origin of our moral ideas is, clearly, only weakly supported by his four "arguments". Even if we agree with Nietzsche that knowledge is merely a set of interpretations that "overpower" and "dominate" one another, should not the persuasive power of an interpretation have something to do with its empirical support?

To ask this question is to miss Nietzsche's point. The basic issue for him is not whether his interpretation is true (we shall see his critique of truth near the end of this chapter), but, as we saw, whether it will obstruct or promote "human flourishing". It is from promoting human flourishing that true interpretive power derives, and Nietzsche clearly thinks his interpretation will do that.

Ressentiment *and the slave morality*

Behind Nietzschean ethics lies a moral psychology that Nietzsche has inherited from the German philosophical tradition. Like Kant, Fichte and Hegel, Nietzsche views the mind not as a thing but as sheer activity. This means you cannot be inert; you cannot just sit there. Which means, in turn, that if you cannot act, that is, cannot originate your own deeds, you must *react* to the deeds of others. The most healthy way of reacting to someone is to follow their orders, as the *kakoi* in Homer do. So there are leaders and followers, "good" people and "bad". But if you are "priestly", you cannot follow orders either, for you think of yourself as superior. Your active energy is there, but cannot be expressed in action; so it is forced back inwards. This in turn makes you angry and frightened, the emotion Nietzsche calls *ressentiment* (using the French word for "resentment"): "All instincts which are not discharged outwardly *turn inwards* – this is what I call the *internalization* of man: with it there now evolves in man what he calls his 'soul'" (*GM* 61).

Ressentiment is what you feel towards someone when you know they are superior to you, but cannot simply admit their superiority and follow their orders. A person of *ressentiment* is therefore a loser who is fixated on the winners, and looks *outside* herself for what is good: "'If only I were some other person!' is what this glance sighs; 'but there's no hope of that, I am who I am; how could I get away from myself? And oh – *I'm fed up with myself!*'"(*GM* 95).

The first judgement of this morality is: "I am bad". This negative judgement on oneself is, then, the core of the slave morality, as opposed to the original "master morality". Both moralities condemn what is different from them. In the noble or masterful person, condemnation merely takes the form of occasional mild contempt, when she or he actually has to deal with an inferior person. There is no *malice* in it. A noble person is having too much fun being themself to bother with malice. To the creature of *ressentiment*, by contrast, *hating someone else is the condition for loving themselves*. Hatred of others is central to their lives because it is the only thing that keeps them from hating themselves. "Whereas all noble morality grows out of a triumphant saying 'yes' to itself, slave morality says 'no' on principle to everything that is 'outside', 'other', 'non-self'; and *this* 'no' is its creative deed" (*GM* 21).

"Slaves" to *ressentiment* have to supplement their basic moral judgement – "I am bad" – with the judgement "and you are worse"; or "I am bad – but you are evil". "Bad" and "evil", then, are completely different moral concepts. "Evil" is the basic concept of slave morality, and is saturated with malice. For the master morality, on the other hand, the concept of "good" is basic. Its complement, "bad", "is only a pale contrast, created after the fact" (*GM* 22). The two moralities that are expressed through these disparate concepts are the exact reverse of one another.

Nietzsche is explicit that the slave morality came about as the result of a historical event or process, and he locates this in ancient Israel (*GM* 19). It was there that the priests sought and found allies among the common people: the many powerless ones whom the priests elevated to the status of "good" people. The essential characteristic of the Jews, he says is hatred – "the deepest and most sublime … the like of which has never been seen on earth" (*GM* 19). Nietzsche here sounds very anti-Semitic, just as he earlier sounded very racist. But careful reading shows where he is going. What does he identify as the "pinnacle of [Israel's] sublime vengeance" (*GM* 20)? It is the supreme example of somebody good, noble and powerful rejecting the pathos of distance and instead bringing salvation to the poor and downtrodden: Jesus Christ, God Himself, dying on the cross. Nietzsche actually has a great deal of respect for Judaism; even in these passages he says Jewish hatred "created ideals and changed values" (*GM* 19). But there is one thing for which he cannot forgive Judaism: that it gave birth to Christianity, a religion where even hatred cannot speak its name and must masquerade as love.

Nietzsche's moral psychology now contains four groups: the masters, who act and like themselves; the common people, who follow and are content to do so; the priests, who do not act but should and therefore turn their active force inwards; and, finally, those whom the priests create in their image, the slaves to *ressentiment*. The first two groups love themselves; the latter two do not, and must hate someone else in order to love themselves. Is there anyone else? Yes, says Nietzsche, somewhat cryptically (*GM* 27): there is also the vision of someone who makes all this worthwhile. It is only a vision, because in modern Europe true Nietzschean goodness is getting more and more impossible. Such a person is a "stroke of luck"; whether he will ever exist or not is part of the radical unfathomability of the future.

What makes this five part moral typology possible? That is the question of what makes the slave morality possible, because it is only when the slave morality is presented that the whole thing clicks into place. And what is that? In Nietzsche's view it is a defective *ontology*, a theory of what it means to exist, which says that most basically, things in general are not sheer activities but inert beings, "substrates", that somehow underlie the things they do. Originally suggested in Plato's *Phaedo*, this view was developed in Aristotle's *Categories*, from which it went into medieval philosophy and has come down to our day. It holds that every action has an actor that is more basic than, and often unchanged by, that action. This means that an actor might not have committed any given action: that people are free to act otherwise than they do; that the strong, there-fore, are "free" to be weak, so we should blame them for being strong (*GM* 28–9).

In reality, however, there are no such individuals; all that exists for Nietzsche, both inside the human mind and outside it, is forces:

> It is just as absurd to ask strength not to express itself as strength, not to be a desire to overthrow, crush, become master, to be a thirst for enemies, resistance and triumphs, as to ask weakness to express itself as strength. A quantum of force is just such a quantum of drive, will, action. In fact it is nothing but this driving, willing and acting, and only the seduction of language (and the fundamental errors of reason petri-fied within it), which construes and misconstrues all actions as condi-tioned upon an agency, a "subject", can make it appear otherwise.
>
> (*GM* 28)

Nietzsche's whole world, not just his moral psychology, is a world of forces, not of things (the overall set of such forces is sometimes called the "will to power"). Force, however, shows itself only in conflict with another force; power is evident only through the resistance it overcomes. Hence, all life for Nietzsche is conflict:

> What cannot be borne in the way of need, deprivation, bad weather, disease, toil, solitude? Basically we can cope with everything else, born as we are to an underground and battling existence. Again and again we keep coming up to the light, again and again we experience our golden hour of victory – and then there we stand, the way we were born, unbreakable, tense, ready for new, more difficult and distant things, like a bow which is merely stretched tauter by affliction. (*GM* 27)

The great noon is this hour of our temporary victory, but, because we are in time, it will not last. New nights will come, new challenges will arise, and some day we shall succumb to them. Only the "seduction of language", which splits things up into subjects and predicates, and so into substrates and actions, can make us think differently.

"GUILT", "BAD CONSCIENCE" AND RELATED MATTERS

For Nietzsche, as for Hegel and Marx, our modern world is what it is because of how it has come to be. For Nietzsche, as we saw, it has come to be through a series of accidents, which means that things could be fundamentally different from how they are. In *GM*, part II, Nietzsche applies his genealogical way of thinking to two further basic moral concepts: those of "guilt" and "conscience". These, too, were not always what they are now. They, too, have come to their present form via a historical process that was largely accidental.

Guilt is a basic moral concept because it defines what we are: it is what we feel when we fail to keep a promise, and humans are the animals that can make promises (*GM* 38). When we make a promise, we bind ourselves to be answerable in the future for shaping the future in a certain way. Nietzsche thus agrees with Kierkegaard about the importance of the future and of the fact that our actions can change it – although he does not take the further step of conflating the future with eternity. The relevant future for a promise is just the state of the world that I undertake to bring about: my posting your letter when I go to the post office, for example. It is by making promises that we select just one of the boundless number of possibilities that our future holds and commit ourselves to making it actual.

This means that when we make a promise, we convert the open, boundless future into a specific future, the one in which we shall keep our promise. This specific future does not belong to everybody; its is pre-eminently ours alone, and also includes everyone who will be affected by our keeping our promise. That we can "finitize" the future in this way will be important to Hannah Arendt and one of the main concerns of the third, French stage of continental philosophy. Nietzsche, however, takes it in a different direction: towards a reflection on the stability of the human will.

The future is so important to us that our basic attitude towards the past is "active forgetfulness", which clears our consciousness "to make room for something new" (*GM* 38). In order to make promises, however, we must be able to overcome our habitual "forgetfulness" of the past. We must retain the past, that is, remember it, so we shall not forget what we have promised. In order to keep a promise, and so to make one, you must therefore have an independent, durable will. If you have such a will, it is your immanent standard of value: it is what you most basically are. It is what you like when you like yourself. (Nietzsche is here, without saying so, filling in the "pathos of distance": I may like other people for being blond, or left-handed, or brown-eyed, if I have those characteristics, but, most basically, if I am "good" in the Nietzschean sense, I like them for having independent, durable wills.)

To be human is thus to be in a moral relation to time: you can relate to time in good ways or bad, that is, you can keep your promises and remember them – or not. When you make promises, you undertake to be responsible. And what keeps you responsible, what keeps you keeping your promises and keeps your will independent and durable, is your "conscience". Conscience is thus necessary to being a human at all. Where does it come from?

Conscience is what makes you feel *guilty* if you do not keep a promise that you have made, and the German word for guilt, *Schuld*, comes from *schulden*, to owe someone something, or to be a debtor. Thus, conscience cannot originate in some sort of internal experience like the still small voice that the Hebrew prophet Elijah hears when he is seeking God. It originates in an *interpersonal experience*. This follows from the view of the mind that we noticed before; the human mind is an active force, constantly related to things other than it which it is trying, in some sense or other, to conquer. Only *ressentiment*, as we saw, "internalizes" us, causes us to relate preferentially to ourselves rather than to other things, that is, to opposing forces.

The ancient German customs concerning creditors and debtors were rather stringent. If I owed you something and did not pay it, you were allowed to lop off one of my body parts. Nietzsche's question regarding these ancient customs is very acute. Why that? he asks. More specifically (and still more acutely): how does lopping off one of my body parts repay you for whatever damage I inflicted on you by not giving you what I owed you? What do you *get* out of it?

What you get out of it is pleasure. Lopping off other people's body parts is *fun*, "the pleasure of having the right to exercise power over the powerless without a thought" (*GM* 44). So when Nietzsche says that Kant's categorical imperative, the moral law, "reeks of cruelty" (*GM* 45), that is of itself no objection to it, in Nietzsche's view. What is objectionable is that the cruelty is towards *yourself*: you must surmount, deny, do violence to, your own inclinations in order to be a moral person, for Kant. Such "internal" cruelty towards yourself is unforgivable, for Nietzsche. But cruelty towards others? Bring it on!

> To see somebody suffer is nice, to make somebody suffer even nicer
> – that is a hard proposition, but an ancient, powerful, human-all-too-
> human proposition. ... No cruelty, no feast: that is what the oldest and
> longest period in human history teaches us – and punishment, too, has
> such very *festive* aspects. (*GM* 46)

So this is at least part of what it is like to be a "master", for Nietzsche: and a higher degree of the "pathos of distance", because I do not just despise other people from a distance, I enjoy hurting them. A master likes hurting other people and happily admits that fact; she is comfortable with it, and so with herself.

But it is not only the noble, or masters, who enjoy hurting other people. Even those who do not do things, who are not active – common people, slaves, priests – like it. Only they do not like to *do* it, because in general they are not active. Instead, they like to *watch*. Every violent film, television programme and video game attests to that today.

What conclusion does Nietzsche draw? That since everybody likes them, *pain and suffering are not evil*: "What actually arouses indignation over suffering is not the suffering itself, but the senselessness of suffering; but neither for the Christian, who saw in suffering a whole, hidden machinery of salvation, nor for naive man in ancient times, was there any such senseless suffering" (*GM* 48).

STATE, RELIGION AND THE GENEALOGY OF MORALITY

Nietzsche's view here can yield a theory of justice and a theory of community. We "owe" our community, which is the set of people to whom we make promises; and when we do not keep our promises to it we can be punished; that is "justice" (*GM* 49–50). Since the notion of justice is fundamental to conscience – we have a "bad conscience" when we feel we have committed an injustice – this account of community is essential to Nietzsche's genealogy of conscience. Two main forms of community are relevant to that genealogy: the state and religion.

Nietzsche's crucial question with respect to the state, as we might expect, is: how did it really start? And the answer is unsettling. First, the move was not "gradual and voluntary", but "a breach, a leap, a compulsion, a fate which nothing could ward off" (*GM* 62). It happened like this:

> The shaping of a population, which up to now had been unrestrained and shapeless, into a fixed form, as happened at the beginning in an act of violence, could only be concluded with violence – that consequently the oldest "state" emerged as a terrible tyranny, as a repressive and ruthless machinery. I used the word "state": it is obvious who is meant by this – some pack of blond beasts of prey, a conqueror and master race which, organized on a war footing, and with the power to organize, unscrupulously lays its dreadful paws on a populace which, though it might be vastly greater in number, is still shapeless and shifting. In this way the "state" began on earth; I think I have dispensed with the fantasy that has it begin with a "contract". (*GM* 62–3)

We know by now that Nietzsche is not praising the "pack of blond beasts" of the "master race". He is saying that if the state is basic to humanity, which it is, then it must have arisen out of conflict. This violent origin means that the state continues to be violent, and to do violence to everyone who inhabits it.

The state is unjust, for it begins, not with a promise – as in "contract" theories – but with a violent seizure of power. Unlike many German political thinkers, Hegel included, who see the state as the realization of freedom, Nietzsche sees it as freedom's enemy. In the state, the "instinct of freedom" is forced back on itself so that all you can control is yourself (*GM* 61). You then fall upon yourself with all the violence of "blond beasts" falling upon a docile population. You are continually attempting to control yourself, to make yourself better, to avoid sin: "Forced into the oppressive narrowness and conformity of custom, man impatiently ripped himself apart, persecuted himself, gnawed at himself, gave himself no peace and abused himself. ... This fool, this prisoner consumed with longing and despair, became the inventor of 'bad conscience'" (*GM* 61–2). Bad conscience is thus the form *ressentiment* takes in the modern state.

Religion, for its part, begins genealogically with ancestor worship, and with the feeling of being indebted to your ancestors (*GM* 65). Nietzsche has no problem with this. Everyone feels indebted to the people who begot and raised them. But as the generations go by, the original ancestors grow increasingly remote. Then we can no longer do things for them, so we do symbolic things: we *sacrifice* in their honour. We do this in the childish hope that somehow they will, like parents, give us what we need. But we often do not get what we need, and so we begin to fear: fear that we have not performed the sacrifice correctly. We come to *dread* the ancestors. And as more time goes on and our tribe expands, those ancestors grow more and more fearsome in our minds, until they become gods and finally coalesce into the figure of God the Father: father not just of me and my tribe, but of heaven and earth; the creator-god. Eventually God gets so powerful that our fear of him is literally unbearable; to gain some momentary comfort, we reverse the story. Now we say that God sacrifices for us. Hence the invention of Jesus Christ, the God who dies for us (*GM* 67–8). We have now contracted "the most terrible sickness ever to rage in man": Christianity (*GM* 69).

In Christianity, bad conscience is at its highest point, for the guilt we feel is guilt before God. At this point, since God is supposed to be other than this world, we are compelled to hate and struggle against all things of this world, against everything that we are. In the name of what? Of an imaginary entity, of a God whom we ourselves have invented; in the name, then, of something non-existent, of nothing. *Ressentiment* carried to its extreme in Christianity thus becomes love of nothing itself; in one of Nietzsche's many uses of the word, it becomes *nihilism* (*GM* 68; cf. *GM* 128).

Once he has torn down our ideals in this way, what does Nietzsche think he has left us with? With *a new ideal*:

> But some time, in a stronger age than this mouldy, self-doubting present day, he will have to come to us, the redeeming man of great love and contempt. ... This man of the future will redeem us ... from the great nausea, the will to nothingness, from nihilism; that stroke of midday and great decision which makes the will free again which gives earth its purpose, and man his hope again, this Antichrist and anti-nihilist, this conqueror of God and of nothingness – he must come one day.
>
> (*GM* 71)

This is far from the languid glimpse of a better future we had in Essay I, but it is also far from being a prediction. It is a *cri de coeur*.

ASCETIC IDEALS

Nietzsche has talked about masters and priests, and about common people and slaves. Now he is going to talk about philosophers, among other things. He begins (for my purposes; actually it is *GM*, part III, §6, the first five sections being remarks on Richard Wagner) by playing three philosophers – or, more precisely, two philosophers and a novelist – off against one another: Kant, Schopenhauer and Stendahl.

In *Critique of Judgment*, §2, Kant says that beauty is what pleases us "without interest" (*CJ* 204–5). When we find something beautiful, we are not impelled or required to take any action with respect to it, and so our pleasure is "disinterested". Stendhal, the novelist, on the other hand, said that beauty is a *promesse de bonheur*, a promise of happiness, so it tells us what we want to pursue, and therefore is an experience that carries a strong interest. Schopenhauer, a German philosopher who was a younger contemporary of Hegel, combines both: aesthetic experience, precisely by being without interest, does something very valuable for us – it quiets sexual desire. As with Stendahl, aesthetic experience does something for us, but that something is not telling us what we want to pursue, and thereby exciting our wills. Beauty *quiets* the will. This amounts, says Nietzsche, to the view that we seek beauty to escape being "tortured" by our desires (*GM* 80). And this, in a nutshell, is the ascetic ideal: the idea that somehow we can escape desires, not by acting on them, but by denying them with a "disinterested" experience.

This, Nietzsche thinks, is the origin of philosophy (along with many other things). Some people, to be sure, are by temperament genuine philosophers. For them, the ascetic ideal is freedom itself: "On seeing an ascetic ideal, the philosopher smiles because he sees an optimum condition of the highest and boldest intellectuality – he does not deny existence by doing so, but rather affirms *his* existence and *only* his existence" (*GM* 82). For people of this type, asceticism is a true "dominating instinct" (*GM* 85); it is an expression of what they are on a very basic level. Nietzsche has no problem with this. In fact, it bears some resemblance to our old friend the "pathos of distance". The philosopher "shuns light that is too bright, so he shuns his time and its day; he inhabits it like a shadow: the more the sun sinks the bigger he becomes" (*GM* 84). But this puts the philosopher very much at odds with a modern society based on *hybris*: on the habit of going after what you want regardless of whether you should want it or have it (*GM* 86–7). Opposed to this by virtue of their natural asceticism, philosophers must disguise themselves. In order to survive in a hostile climate, they have to make themselves and their ascetic ways feared, or at least respected. So they interpret the ascetic ideal, not as their own true natures, but as something imposed on them from outside, by the gods or by God. They became "ascetic priests". With this move, asceticism ceases to be something active – something the philosopher *is* – and becomes something reactive, something imposed on her.

Once it is no longer the proper pathos of the philosopher, asceticism becomes something that can be imposed on anyone: an ideal up to which we all should live. Asceticism is then formulated as the "ascetic ideal":

> The idea we are fighting over here is the valuation of our lives by the ascetic priest: he relates this (together with all that belongs to it, "nature", "the world", the whole sphere of what comes to be and passes away) to a quite different kind of existence which is opposed to it and excludes it unless it should turn against itself and deny itself. In this case, … life counts as a bridge to that other existence. The ascetic treats life as … like a mistake, which can only be set right by action – which has to be set right: he demands that we should accompany him, and when he can, he imposes his monstrous valuation of existence. (*GM* 90)

The ascetic ideal thus comes about through two moves. The first is to see asceticism as imposed on *me*; the second is to see it as imposed on *all of us*. What makes the second move possible is that in order to justify our personal asceticism we set up a domain that is opposed to "what comes to be and passes away": to the temporal order itself, then. Once we have a contrast to the entire temporal order, we are able to conceive of it as a whole and to issue blanket condemnations of it. The ascetic ideal is thus a way of evaluating life itself in general, a way that is at once *totally widespread*, since any race, place or class can adopt it, whatever their own individual nature, and *totally contradictory*, for it expresses *hatred of life* on the part of something that is a living thing *and nothing more*, which (Nietzsche being an atheist) has no immortal soul. It is "life against life" (*GM* 90–93). To hate life in this way is to hate everything you are, and to do so in the name of something that does not even exist: the atemporal realm that demands asceticism as the condition for adhering to it. It is to place yourself on the road to what Nietzsche calls "nihilism".

When this kind of nihilistic personality turns to investigate knowledge – to the ancient philosophical discipline of "epistemology" – its hatred of life leads it to see only error where the "instinct of life" sees truth: in the experience of our senses. Thus you get views such as that the physical world is only an "illusion", or the view – Nietzsche calls it a "dangerous old conceptual fairy tale" – that there is such a thing as a "pure will-less, painless, timeless subject of knowledge" (*GM* 92), that is, the idea that what we know is not always bound up with what we want or with the power we have to get what we want. As I noted earlier, instead of trying to get at the one truth – an enterprise that has brought untold harm to humanity – we should multiply perspectives, have those perspectives in our power and use them: "there is only a perspective seeing and a perspective knowing" (*GM* 92).

The ascetic ideal is not only contradictory but actually sick (*GM* 93), because it is what philosophy becomes when it cannot be honest and open about itself. It is thus an effort to preserve and heal a degenerating life. This degeneration is aided by two components of the ascetic ideal: nausea at humanity itself – disgust with ourselves and our lives; and pity for the very humanity that disgusts you, which means condoning its degeneracy because, in the final analyis, it is your degeneracy too (*GM* 94–7). When these come together you get sympathy for the nauseating, another example of nihilism (*GM* 94).

The true enemies of humanity, then, are the weak and the sick; the strong and healthy should stay away from them (*GM* 97), and so we are back yet again at the pathos of distance. Since we should avoid the sick, we should let the priests care for them – but we must be careful of such doctors ourselves, because they will wound us in order to cure us of that wound: "He brings ointments and balms with him, of course, but first he has to wound so that he can be the doctor; and whilst he soothes the pain caused by the wound, *he poisons the wound at the same time*" (*GM* 98).

Such doctors will nurture and channel your *ressentiment*, but will see to it that it never really goes away. (There follows an analysis of various ways of administering *ressentiment*, which I shall not go into.) At this point, things look pretty bleak. Humans, or at least Europeans, are dominated by the ascetic ideal: "I can hardly think of anything which has sapped the health and racial strength of precisely the Europeans as destructively as this ideal; without any exaggeration we are entitled to call it the real catastrophe in the history of the health of European man" (*GM* 113).

Trapped in nihilism and self-hatred, modern Europeans hate what they are not, namely strong and masterful people; and they cherish what makes them different from such people, namely their own weakness and degeneracy. They are trying, in fact, to get their lives over with so they can be saved and go to heaven. But heaven is a fiction, a story told by the priests to keep people in line, not so that the priests can hold on to power, for there are many other ways to do that, but because they hate themselves too. When the people are successfully kept in line by the ascetic priests, they become no more than a "herd" (*GM* 104–6): the unhappy citizens, as we saw earlier, of the modern state.

Means of priestly domination

To be sure, not all decency is destroyed. When you try to help others, even when that effort only comes out of your nihilistic depression (how wretched we are!), you increase, if only in the smallest way, your own will to power. When you join with others to form a community, even if it is only a "herd", you are trying to have influence: more will to power. And when your community grows and gets stronger, you are proud to be part of it. You inevitably start liking yourself, just a little. These are all forms of the will to power, and so good in themselves. But they can be used by the ascetic priests to hold the rest of us in subjection, for they can be manipulated to force the individual to value others above himself, thus denying the pathos of distance. They are thus the "innocent" means by which the ascetic priests enforce their domination (*GM* 107).

There are guilty means for this too: distortions of the will to power, brought about by the ascetic ideal. The feeling of "guilt" itself is an example. "Why am I miserable", you ask yourself. And the priest answers, "Because you have done something wrong. Your misery is your fault, because you have sinned. You can understand why you are miserable, then, if only you will hate yourself." So the idea of "sin" becomes all-important. Indeed, the biggest event in history was a sin (Adam and Eve in the Garden of Eden; *GM* 110). What is the real explanation for human misery? If we are in physical pain, there is no need to explain it: physical pain is just part of life and, as we saw above, is not evil. And if we are making *ourselves* miserable, the solution is to stop believing in the priests. Love yourself!

The will to truth

The ascetic ideal has ruined Europe: it has ruined its literature (by creating the New Testament; *GM* 113), its art and culture generally, its history. Finally, the ascetic ideal has ruined knowledge itself. Today's scientists do not believe in religious dogma, of course – they have escaped the priests. They seem to be the true opponents of the ascetic ideal, then: the "knowers" who mistrust the believers. Or are they?

> These "no-"sayers and outsiders of today, those who are absolute in one thing, their demand for intellectual rigour … they believe they are as liberated as possible from the ascetic ideal these "free, *very* free spirits": and yet I will tell them what they themselves cannot see – because they are standing too close to themselves – this ideal is quite simply *their* ideal as well, they represent it nowadays, and perhaps no one else, they themselves are its most intellectualized products. … These are very far from being free spirits: *because they still believe in truth* … Precisely in their faith in truth they are more rigid and more absolute than anyone else. (*GM* 118)

> The unconditioned will to truth is faith in the ascetic ideal itself. (*GM* 119)

Why? Because truth is not a physical or sensory thing. It is a "metaphysical value" (*GM* 119). Many truths, of course, are useful to us as living beings; modern medicine is full of such truths. But those truths are pursued on behalf of health. When truth is pursued "unconditionally", we are trying to get truths that hold independently of their specific circumstances, including the circumstances of why *we* think that truth is worth pursuing. Why do we want to know

121

something for sure, to decide some issue here and now? Why is this particular question or issue important? Who or what *made* it important?

The unconditioned will to truth tells us that these questions are not worth asking: truth is valuable in and for itself. Unconditional truth is pursued without reference to human flourishing, and so becomes an end in itself. It is merely another form of the ascetic ideal. If we seek to find genuine opposition to the ascetic ideal, art is a better place to look than science, because it is fully sensuous, and because it contains "quality lying"; when I write a novel or a poem, I am not pursuing truth (*GM* 121). A novel or a poem does not tell you something that really happened, but it opens up various perspectives on life for you to use as *you* decide. Art is thus much freer than science.

But what does Nietzsche mean here by truth? There are various traditional theories around, of course: three important ones today are the correspondence, coherence and pragmatic theories of truth. I shall not discuss them in detail, because Nietzsche's critique of truth can apply to any and all of them. This is because it is actually directed against a fourth thing that "truth" designates, a property of truth that is compatible with any of those three definitions: truth as the sole, sovereign goal of enquiry. What we will is a goal for us; so the "will to truth" is a will that takes truth as its goal. An "unconditional will to truth" is a will that takes truth as its goal no matter what. And truth in such a sense can never be attained, so it begins to sound a lot like heaven: a goal that we shall never reach. Because such truth is an unreachable goal, pursuing it requires us to deny life here and now, which is all we have. So the will to truth is a form of nihilism, of denial of everything.

What is the answer, then? The truths we actually attain are never unconditional: they are always conditioned by the fact that we have tried to attain them. We should therefore demote truth, in whatever sense, from a sovereign "unconditional goal" to a situated goal. What we are looking for in different enquiries varies with our purposes; it is not always truth. It can be many provisional but useful *perspectives*.

Will Europeans ever be able to think this way? Or are they simply too mired in Christianity and corruption? As with the other two essays, Nietzsche concludes this one on a somewhat positive note, more positive, anyway, than either the languid vision of Essay I or the *cri de coeur* of Essay II. For if all things are mortal, the ascetic ideal itself must be mortal: "All great things bring about their own demise through an act of self-sublimation: that is the law of life, the law of necessary 'self-overcoming' is the essence of life" (*GM* 126).

The will to truth destroys the ascetic ideal even as it serves it, and thus will eventually destroy itself. For the existence of the "other world" – of all the atemporal domains that have held humanity in thrall – is itself a lie, and the ascetic ideal teaches us that we must tell the truth at all costs. The will to truth, which grew out of Christian morality, has thus "destroyed" Christian dogma; all that remains, with the dogma gone, is to destroy the inhuman morality that it supported (*GM* 126–7).

Nietzsche thus agrees with Heine that "deism … was long ago overthrown in theory". He does not agree, however, that it has been overthrown in practice. On the contrary, Christian morality, with its appalling substitution of "good/evil" for "good/bad" is still supported by what is supposed to be its implacable enemy: the scientific love of truth, the last god.

CONCLUSION

Nietzsche's rejection of Christianity is as uncompromising as Kierkegaard's vindication of it. Both are future oriented, and this is what makes Nietzsche's attack on Christianity distinctive. After all, if we want to see Christianity identified as an intellectual disease and moral sickness, we need only read Heine. But for Heine, this unmasking of Christianity only means, *a là* Hegel, that Christianity is already a thing of the past. As to the future, Heine writes:

> I say it with conviction: our descendents will be finer and happier than we. For I believe in progress, I believe mankind is destined to happiness. … Even here on earth I would like to establish, through the blessings of free political and industrial institutions, that bliss which in the opinion of the pious, is to be granted only on the Day of Judgment.
> (Heine 1973: 281)

Heine's solemn faith in progress is entirely in the spirit of his teacher Hegel. To be sure, Heine goes right on to question his own faith, like a good Christian: "Perhaps mankind is destined for eternal misery, the peoples are perhaps doomed in perpetuity to be trodden underfoot by despots, exploited by their accomplices, and scorned by their lackeys" (*ibid.*). But Heine does not abandon his faith. In words I quoted at the beginning of this chapter, he continues: "the ultimate fate of Christianity thus depends on whether we still need it". We do not.

Nietzsche, by contrast, reserves the important work of overcoming the ascetic ideal, of which Christianity is the most powerful and creative component, for the future, and he is not sure whether it will ever happen or not. The closest he comes to predicting it, at the end of Essay III, is to point, as Marx and Kierkegaard did, to a contradiction in the present. Where, for Marx, the worker became poorer the more she produced, and, for Kierkegaard, the increase of scientific proof meant a decrease in inward certainty, so, for Nietzsche, the Christian imperative to tell the truth, once it is crystallized in ascetic science, destroys the lies of Christian doctrine. For all three, apparent contradiction serves the purpose Plato assigned to it as early as *Phaedo* 74b: it shows that something is unstable. But as Kierkegaard and Nietzsche realize, this cannot provide knowledge of how that instability is to be resolved.

With Nietzsche, then, continental philosophy breaks free from Marx's view that the future, while differing from the present, is enough like it to be predicted; and from Kierkegaard's view that among the many possibilities the future contains only two, unfathomable yet infinitely different from one another, which really matter: eternal bliss or eternal damnation. For Nietzsche, there is no certain revolution on the way, and there is no God to narrow the future's boundless possibilities into just two meaningful ones. The only way the future gets narrowed is when we make a promise. The Nietzschean future is thus wholly unpredictable, as empty as Hegel's "source of form". But it is something we cannot ignore, for we are heading straight into it.

If the future is radically open or, as I shall call it, "infinite"; if it is shaped by our interpretations, and our interpretations can follow one another at random; then anything can happen. This is not a possibility that we can respond to concretely, because it is so broad as to be abstract: there is nothing more to say about a radically open future than, precisely, "anything can happen". It is with the feeling of such boundless possibility, at once terrifying and invigorating, that Zarathustra strides forth from his cave.

The problem is that while Nietzsche has recognized that the boundless future is something we can specify, or "finitize", through our promises, he has not developed this insight. The infinite future with which he is left can be recognized in the abstract and metaphorically depicted, but it cannot be responded to *philosophically*: that is to say, in a way that is subject to rational norms and so can be rationally criticized. For if the future is infinite, anything can happen; and a future in which anything can happen gives us no guidelines about how to take it into account – it does not tell us, for example, *what* to promise. Nietzsche's future can be recognized in stories, poems and myths, and Zarathustra striding into the great noon is a wonderful image; but it springs from a philosophical *impasse*. Nietzsche has in fact moved far away from philosophy. Institutionally, his thought was formulated nowhere near philosophy departments, but by a solitary philologist wandering around Europe. Intellectually, Nietzsche abandons philosophical and even rational method in favour of such things as poetry, fables and aphorisms. Space is thus available, both institutionally and intellectually, to revivify traditional philosophy, which will be the task of Edmund Husserl.

What is needed to get continental philosophy out of its *impasse*, and to justify its own revival, is a way to make it methodologically complete. This requires getting beyond the abstract recognition that "anything can happen" to a way of thinking about the future that can show, in specific instances – the more specific the better – just where things are unstable and so are in confrontation with the openness of their *own* futures, not with the abstract "anything can happen" sort of future. This "concretizing" procedure, however, must not detract from the main characteristic of the future that Marx stumbled against, Kierkegaard uncovered and Nietzsche developed: that the future is intrinsically unfathomable. This is a tall order indeed. Filling it will fall to one of the pettiest figures in the entire history of philosophy, Martin Heidegger.

PART II

GERMANY AND AMERICA, 1900–1968

CHAPTER 6

THE RETURN OF TRADITIONAL PHILOSOPHY: EDMUND HUSSERL

PRIMARY TEXT Edmund Husserl, *Cartesian Meditations* (*CM*; [1931] 1960)

In the mid-1930s, a young woman from the privileged northern suburbs of Chicago came to Freiburg, Germany. Her purpose was to study with Germany's most famous living philosopher, Edmund Husserl. Husserl was then in his late seventies, and was known to her and the world as the founder of one of the twentieth century's most influential philosophical schools, "phenomenology". Since he had retired from his professorship at Freiburg, and as a world-famous philosopher had many demands on his time, she must have believed her main hurdle was getting his approval for her programme.

What she found was very different from what she expected. Because Husserl had been born a Jew, he was being persecuted by the Nazi regime, which had severed all his connections with the university. This governmental action had been implemented in a university order forbidding him (on 14 April 1933) even to set foot on the university campus. One week later, his younger associate Martin Heidegger was appointed Rector of the university (and, in one of the most notorious episodes in the intellectual history of the twentieth century, joined the Nazi party). One week after that, whether at Heidegger's instigation or not, Husserl was reinstated as a retired professor and was able again to receive his pension. The whole affair had lasted only two weeks, but things did not get easy for Husserl. Although he had protectors within the university, the Nazi government continued to make things difficult for him in every way they could; he was not allowed permission to travel to conferences, for example, and his pension, although restored for the moment, was not secure.

So the young Chicagoan's mission changed. Where she had originally planned to study with Husserl, now she would have to rescue him. In fact, she did both. In order not to injure his pride more than necessary, she signed up for private lessons in phenomenology, for which she paid at a generous rate. In this way, Husserl in his last years became a private tutor: not even a *Dozent*, the level on which Hegel began. It is hard to imagine that he did not see through her subterfuge, but he went along with it, presumably because he needed the money. In such fashion did Nazi Germany treat one of its greatest thinkers.[1]

Husserl's life had not prepared him for such a melancholy ending. He was born in 1859, not in Germany but in Moravia, which is today a part of the Czech Republic but in those days belonged to the Austro-Hungarian Empire. His father, a well-to-do clothing merchant, financed his studies, which were rather freewheeling. He began by studying mathematics at Leipzig, then transferred to the more exciting mathematical atmosphere of Berlin before moving on to Vienna, where he obtained his doctorate in 1883.

After a year in the army, mostly in Vienna, Husserl found his interests shifting from mathematics to philosophy. At the age of thirty-five he began studying philosophy in Vienna with Franz Brentano, a former Catholic priest turned Aristotle scholar. Then he went on to Halle, in Germany, to study with a student of Brentano's. There he was awarded his *habilitation* – a sort of second doctorate – in philosophy. Husserl began his professorial career in Göttingen, where in good order he made Associate (*Außerordentliche*) and *Ordinarius*, or full professor. In 1916 he was called to the University of Freiburg, where he spent the rest of his career.

Until close to the end, Husserl's was a typical professor's life: teaching and publishing, marrying and raising a family. Deeply patriotic, Husserl was sadly proud that his son Gerhart had been wounded in the First World War and his son Wolfgang killed. This did not matter at all, of course, so far as the Nazis were concerned, and when they came to power in 1933 his problems began. He was subjected to as much harassment as the Nazis could bring upon him until his death in 1938.[2]

NEO-KANTIANISM, KANT AND HUSSERL

By the end of the nineteenth century, philosophy in the German-speaking lands was beginning to work its way up and out of the morass into which it had fallen with the purge of the Young Hegelians. This revival took the form of the arrival of respectable versions of Kantianism, particularly in the south of Germany, where the "great south German Kant revival" took three forms: neo-Kantianism itself, which flourished in Freiburg under Heinrich Rickert and became established at the north German University of Marburg with Herman Cohen; logical positivism, which was centred in Vienna and moved to the United States when Hitler came to power; and Husserl's own brainchild, "phenomenology", which

---

1. This story was told to me by a friend of the young woman.
2. Details on Husserl's life can be found in Smith (2006).

he began developing in 1900 (one of Kant's early names for his own central project, which he would later call "critique", was "phenomenology").[3]

Husserl himself did not explicitly characterize his philosophy as a return to Kant, but issues and problems similar to those we have seen in the case of Kant crop up again for him, in particular the problem of how to explain the relationship of a realm of (putatively) atemporal truth to the changing world we actually live in. This residual Kantianism, as we shall see, means that, from the perspective of continental thought, German philosophy in the twentieth century in some ways re-enacts its path in the nineteenth. Just as Hegel's *Phenomenology of Spirit* "temporalized" Kant's atemporal account of the mind, so Heidegger will put the structures of Husserlian consciousness into time in his major work, *Being and Time*. The temporalized approach in philosophy thus arrives twice: once via Hegel's concern with the past, and again in Heidegger's concern with the future. Husserl and Kant play the role of atemporal foils for these two births. Sartre will pay a somewhat similar role in its third birth, in France.

Husserl's project was also inspired by his earlier work in mathematics. Mathematics is the most important challenge to temporalized philosophy, for the simple reason that numbers do not change. One, two and three are today just what they were when Pythagoras posited number as the inner core of reality; so are the relations among them. This *may* mean that numbers exist in some Platonically real way, as many mathematicians assume, in which case mathematics is an ally of traditional philosophy. Or it may testify merely to the faithfulness of human beings in manipulating socially agreed-on fictions, as Nietzsche and other continental philosophers would claim.[4] In any case, Husserl's philosophy, true to his own mathematical beginnings, was an attempt to revive traditional philosophy in Germany, not in the face of Hegel, Marx, Kierkegaard and Nietzsche, of all of whom Husserl is mostly unaware, but as against the low-grade forms of traditional philosophy that had taken over from Hegel after 1830.

Both Kant and Husserl, then, seek to restore traditional philosophy by placing it on an atemporal footing to be found in the structure of the human mind (or, as Husserl calls it, "transcendental consciousness"). Their common problem is thus that of how the (putative) atemporal side of the human mind relates to its (undoubted) changing, or "empirical" side. For Kant, this arises in two ways because, on his account, the mind has two sides: theoretical and practical.

Practically, as we saw in Chapter 1, Kant needed to explain how Reason, which was not in time, could have effects on the empirical world. This was to him a problem of ethics, since an action caused by Reason is a morally good one. Suppose, in some definite time and place, I perform a good act: I get up from

---

3. Kant, letter to Lambert, 2 September 1770 (Kant 1967: 59).
4. For a more recent statement of this view, cf. Hersch (1999).

my chair and go to cook dinner for my ailing grandmother. According to Kant, if my act is good, then Reason was its cause. But ten seconds before I get up from my chair, I am not performing any good act. I am just sitting there. What was my Reason doing then? Must there not have been some change in Reason itself in virtue of which it began to cause my good act? But if Reason changes, it must be in time. This, we saw, is one of the basic problems of the *Critique of Judgment*. We also saw that Kant does not resolve it satisfactorily.

The *theoretical* version of the problem is not really addressed by Kant. This would be the problem of how the (putatively) unchanging aspects of the human mind can be known, and known to be unchanging. Such knowledge certainly cannot be knowledge in Kant's standard sense, since (in the first words of the first *Critique*) "there can be no doubt that all our knowledge comes from the senses". It follows that either we know our minds through sensory experience, in which case our knowledge is merely empirical and cannot claim to be valid for all time, or we do not "know" our minds at all.[5]

The fundamental problem of how to relate the atemporal aspects of the human mind to its temporal side arises rather differently for Husserl, because he is uninterested in ethics. It lies for him on the side that Kant neglected: that of what Kant called theoretical philosophy. Husserl therefore devotes great efforts to solving the problem of how we can have knowledge of the atemporal structure of our minds, and, in this respect, Husserl can be said to be far more self-reflective than Kant. But in the minds of the philosophers we shall be looking at later, he is no more successful. Indeed, Heidegger's victory over him would be so complete that traditional philosophy mainly survives today, not as Husserl envisaged it, but on logical foundations established by Gottlob Frege.

Why do Kant and Husserl want atemporal realms in the first place? One reason, presumably, is just that philosophy has always appealed to such domains – and, in its mainstream anglophone version anyway, still does. (Today, after Frege, the "laws of logic" often stand in for Kantian mind, or Husserlian consciousness.) A better reason, for Kant, is that mind, which does not have an atemporal side, cannot be good; a morality that shifts with time is not, for him, a morality at all. Husserl's reason was rather different because, as I said, he is not very worried about ethics. What *does* worry him, from first to last, is science. In contrast to the doldrums that affected German philosophy, German empirical science was making great strides in the second half of the nineteenth century, on its way to such crowning achievements as the theory of relativity and quantum theory. In terms of prestige (and funding), empirical science had pretty much eclipsed philosophy, as it does to this day. Given the great and growing prestige of empirical investigation, Husserl sees only two solutions for a philosopher: either become a sort of scientist yourself, or make yourself

---

5. For a sophisticated discussion of this problem, see Waxman (1989: 271–93).

useful to science without actually assimilating what philosophers do to scientific investigation. Fearing that the first path will merely dissolve philosophy into the natural sciences, Husserl takes the second: philosophy is not supposed to become an empirical science itself, but it is to make itself useful to the scientific endeavour by *grounding* science. Just what that means will take a while to clarify, but an important part of it will be a very traditional appeal to atemporal truths.

THE CARTESIAN MEDITATIONS AND THE IDEAL OF RIGOROUS SCIENCE

Husserl's concern with science suggests that we should concentrate on his last book, *The Crisis of European Sciences and Transcendental Phenomenology* (1970a), or (as it is often called) the *Crisis*, which exhibits some striking parallels with the *Critique of Judgment*. Kant, as we saw, wrote the *Critique of Judgment* to salvage the critical standpoint in the face of people who thought that his philosophy was not historical enough. Similarly, Husserl, in the *Crisis*, confronts philosophers – primarily "existentialists" like Heidegger and Karl Jaspers – who think that phenomenology is not engaged enough with concrete questions. Both books are thus rescue efforts.

But Husserl's rescue effort, unlike Kant's, never really got going. Husserl wrote a great deal: his *Nachlaß* is some 45,000 pages, which amounts to five pages a day for over twenty-five years. Many of his manuscripts were edited and published by his students.[6] This is true of the *Crisis*, which was partly put together by Husserl and partly by other people, and is generally messy. Moreover, as its complete title indicates, the *Crisis* is not a revocation or modification of Husserl's earlier views on "transcendental phenomenology"; rather, it expands those views into a discussion of history. I shall therefore limit myself here to the *Cartesian Meditations*, which is a more focused account of Husserl's phenomenology.

The lectures that constitute the *Cartesian Meditations* were given in Paris in 1929, when Husserl was already seventy years old. He regarded them highly. Just the year before their publication, he wrote that the *Cartesian Meditations* "will be the major work of my life, a basic outline of the philosophy that has accrued to me … At least for me, [it will represent] a conclusion and ultimate clarity, which I can defend and with which I can die contented" (letter to Ingarden, 19 March 1930, quoted in Husserl 1970a: xxix). Even this text is messy, however. Because he wrote so much, Husserl tended to rewrite entire drafts of things. Although he did put the *Cartesian Meditations* together himself, he seems to

---

6. A particularly important example is the lectures *On the Phenomenology of the Consciousness of Internal Time* (Husserl 1991), which was put together by Martin Heidegger and Edith Weil.

have done so several times, for it exists in several different typescripts, often reworked, and it is hard to see which one is definitive.[7] The German publication was prepared from two different typescripts, but the English translator, Dorion Cairns, had a third typescript that had been given to him personally by Husserl; the English translation thus differs from the German edition at some points. It is also, alas, generally infelicitous; for the sake of intelligibility, I have altered it in my quotations.

Husserl begins the version published in English by proposing a "guiding ideal" (*Zweckidee*) of philosophy. True to his overriding concern with the relation between philosophy and science, he proposes that philosophy itself should be a science, or (in German) a *Wissenschaft*: an organized body of knowledge. Philosophy should, moreover, be a science of a special type: a rigorously "universal" science "out of absolute foundations"; that is, one that is composed of "absolute insights – insights beyond which we cannot go" (*CM* 43–4). The fallibility of empirical science is thus not what Husserl is after; he is seeking something more akin to the field in which he began his studies: mathematics.

If philosophy is to be absolutely grounded, these ultimate insights are not just arbitrarily chosen starting-points; they must themselves be absolutely indubitable, that is, insights that it is not even possible to doubt (*CM* 44). Thus established, these insights will also be stable, for in order to qualify as knowledge (*Erkenntnis*) they must be a "permanent acquisition" to which we can return at will (*CM* 51). With this, Husserl claims to have adopted Descartes' view that philosophy should provide a *fundamentum inconcussum*, an "unshakeable foundation" (or as Husserl puts it, a "radical grounding"; *CM* 45), not only for empirical science but for all intellectual activity. Because philosophy is the most general discipline, all other sciences and enquiries are founded on it in one way or another. Chemistry, physics and biology, for example, deal with different kinds of object. Philosophy, however, provides the theory of objectivity in general. Only when it is "radically grounded", and so rigorous, can they be.

There is a problem with this idea. On the one hand, philosophy needs, in Husserl's view, to exist as a rigorous science; for since it is the most basic of sciences, its disintegration and confusion have effects far beyond philosophy itself. In a call that will be echoed throughout the *Crisis*, Husserl concludes that "The entirety of human culture should have been led and thoroughly illuminated by scientific insights, and by this reformed into an autonomous culture" (*CM* 46). Such a philosophically guided culture would have been highly desirable in a Europe tending towards fascism (Mussolini had taken power in 1922; Hitler would do so in 1933).

On the other hand, none of the sciences we have today (i.e. in 1931) is actually founded in this way. Not even mathematics, in Husserl's view, is radically

---

7. See the discussion by David Carr in the "translator's introduction" (Husserl 1970a: xv–xliii).

grounded in indubitable basic truths. The "positive sciences", such as physics and biology, are pragmatically legitimized, of course, by their success in improving our lives. Things are worse within philosophy itself, which has been "broken up into a confused busyness" (*ratlose Betriebsamkeit*) (*CM* 46).[8] Philosophy not only does not know where it is going or why, but also does not improve our lives in the obvious ways science does (*CM* 46). What is the point of proposing as a guiding ideal for philosophy something that no science, nor philosophy itself, even approaches? Is there even any reason to think that it *can* exist? In the face of this problem, Husserl adopts his guiding ideal merely experimentally, "as a provisional presumption" (*CM* 49). Such empirical support as it has comes from what we can see is the "striving" of the sciences to gain such systematic certainty: "Nothing stands in the way of our living ourselves into scientific striving and activity, and thereby making *clear and distinct* what that activity is really after" (*CM* 50, emphasis added; cf. also 52–3).

That an idea is to be seen as that after which humans strive is nothing new. Reason, in Kant's *Critique of Judgment*, had just that status. But as we saw, Kant had argued for this status, in *Critique of Judgment*, §84, rather than just demanding that we "live ourselves in" to the striving after it. Husserl has begun his philosophical enterprise with a call to us to live a certain kind of life – the scientific life – in such a way as to develop, over time, an increasing familiarity with the basic nature of a certain phenomenon: science itself.

Husserl's ambitions are thus enormous: an absolutely certain systematic philosophy that will guide the entire culture, and this in the face of what was already, in 1931, a deeply and increasingly frightening landscape. How does Husserl think he can supply this? The answer occupies the whole of the *Cartesian Meditations*.

EVIDENCE

When we think about what it is to ground a piece of knowledge (*eine Erkenntnis*), says Husserl, we run up against the idea of "evidence" (*Evidenz*). The concept of evidence is then basic to the whole project of grounding cognition in general, and so that of rigorous science. It has little to do with "evidence" in the accepted English sense of the word. As the quotation above shows, Husserl adopts the ideals of "clarity and distinctness" for knowledge, taking the phrase from Descartes. Basically, for Descartes, an idea is "clear" when we can distinguish it from other ideas, and "distinct" when its content is clear.[9] "Evidence" is Husserl's word for this (see *CM* 116). In his first characterization of evidence, he calls it

---

8. That Husserl is basically correct in this harsh view of German philosophy at the time is documented in the quote from Lewis White Beck (1967: V, 428) near the beginning of Chapter 5.
9. See McCumber (1993: 100–102) for a discussion of this.

"A special judgmental opinion … in evidence the thing is present as itself, the state of affairs as itself" (*CM* 51). On the next page, we read: "Evidence is in the widest sense an experience of a being and of a being-thus, indeed a getting it-itself-spiritually-in-view" (*CM* 52). What does this seemingly impressionistic language mean? How does it help us found a science?

First, Husserl is up against the fact that no philosopher can define her most basic terms. Kant could not define "representation", and Hegel could not define "mediation" or "negation" (as Kierkegaard pointed out). Nietzsche could not define "power". For Husserl, the concept of evidence is basic enough to be undefinable. Nonetheless, it can be, if not defined, at least given a fuller and clearer characterization than Husserl has done here. He hints at the basic traits of such an account in the words following the first of the two quotations above: "and the judger thus as aware of himself" (*CM* 51). Evidence is a mode of *self*-awareness.

One common view – or perhaps dogma – of modern philosophy, common to figures as diverse as Descartes and Hume, is that the mind has certain knowledge of at least some of its own contents; Kant, as we saw in Chapter 1, founded his philosophy on the view that his own systematic approach guarantees such knowledge. Husserl, too, is a modern philosopher in this sense. So, as the Husserl scholar and phenomenologist Quentin Lauer has pointed out: "One need not be a phenomenologist to recognize (as did Hume, for instance) that an act of consciousness – be it perception, imagination, memory, or desire, is given in itself and as itself in such a manner that the subject of the act cannot doubt the being of the act" (1967: 151).

What is present to us "as itself", then, is acts of consciousness. Evidence, correspondingly, is an indubitable awareness of an inner content. It does not characterize my awareness of a blackboard, for example – of an external object – but my awareness that I am aware of a blackboard, that I am experiencing what *seems* to be a blackboard (even though it may in fact be a dream or illusion). Because evidences are indubitable, they are the appropriate grounding for rigorous science: "In that I, as a philosophical beginner, am striving towards the presumptive goal of true science, I can make or maintain as valid no judgment which I have not drawn from evidence, i.e. from experiences in which the relevant things and states of affairs are present *as themselves*" (*CM* 54).

Husserl introduces evidence in §4, and expands on it in §5, but only enough to distinguish different types of evidence. The first distinction I shall discuss, in §6, is between *complete* and *incomplete* evidence. Any evidence is burdened with vagueness that, being vague, is not itself evident. Suppose I am dreaming that I am seeing a stop sign. The dreamed stop sign itself is in no way outside my mind; but even within my mind, as an object of my awareness, it has a back side that I do not see, but which I "know" is there. Even in my dream, I "know" that if I go around the stop sign there will be a metallic surface, not painted red, which is its back side. This back side, Husserl says, is *vorgemeint*, expected. Also present in any experience are aspects that are *mitgemeint*, of which I am currently aware but peripherally, such as the post on which the stop sign rests, the street near which it stands, and its background generally. These, not being explicitly attended to by me, are left in a sort of unfinished state: they are, in Husserl's technical term, "unfulfilled" (Descartes would presumably call them clear but not distinct). To have a *complete* evidence of something would then be to experience it in all possible ways.

Crossing this classification of types of evidence is a different one: that of the apodictic versus non-apodictic.[10] As Husserl explains this distinction, every evidence is indubitable while it lasts:

> Every evidence is self-grasping of a being, or a being-thus, in the mode of "it itself" in complete certainty of this being, which therefore excludes all doubt. Not excluded, however, is the possibility that the evidence will later become doubtful, that being could present itself as [mere] appearance, for which sensible experience gives us examples. An apodictic evidence however has the special peculiarity (*ausgezeichntete Eigenheit*) that it is not merely as such the certainty of the being of the things or states of affairs evident in it but immediately reveals itself in a critical reflection as the utter unthinkability of the non-being of the same. (*CM* 56)

I can have this additional "critical reflection" even when my evidence is incomplete. If I have an evidence of a stop sign, an awareness that I perceive what seems to be a stop sign, that can change. Closer inspection (even in a dream) may reveal, for example, that what I thought was a stop sign was merely a cardboard replica of a stop sign. This does not, however, impeach the certainty of my earlier evidence, for it was certain that I *seemed* to be experiencing (or dreaming) a stop sign. But if my critical reflection reveals that some aspect of my experience *cannot* change, that it is "once for all or absolutely definitely ascertained" (*CM* 56), then I have "apodictic" evidence. An example would be if I seem to see two mountains side by side. I also see a valley between them, and it is *impossible* that I not see such a valley. Closer inspection will not make that valley disappear, unless it also makes the mountains disappear, or merge into one another.

The distinction between mere evidence and apodictic evidence is thus not a difference in the degree of our certainty; it is the difference between what in our experience changes and what will not. The kind of evidence that is going to be useful for grounding science is the apodictic kind, for Husserl has already said that knowledge is a "permanent acquisition". Husserl, then, is – like traditional philosophers before him but unlike Hegel, Marx, Kierkegaard and Nietzsche –

---

10. In earlier writings Husserl conflated this with the complete–incomplete distinction.

after truths that do not change, and so are not "in" time. Only such truths can be scientific, or philosophical: "Science … seeks truths which are valid once and for all and for everyone" (*CM* 52–3).

Finally, there is one last distinction among types of evidence, actually the first one that Husserl raised. This is the distinction between predicative and pre-predicative evidence (*CM* 52). Suppose I hate someone, and at a given moment am aware of this. In order to have a judgemental awareness of it – to be able explicitly to say "I hate Tom" – I have to give the name "hate" to what I am feeling. But of course things are complex; the term "hate" may not exactly apply to my feeling. That I know whether and to what extent it does is also a matter of evidence; pre-predicative evidence is what enables us to name things in our experience. Pre-predicative evidence is a rather mysterious thing here, and it will remain so because it is bound up with the nature of language, which, as we shall see, will remain a major problem for Husserl.

THE PHENOMENOLOGICAL REDUCTION

Our evidence for the existence of the world, says Husserl, is not apodictic (§17). What, here, is the "world"? Without presupposing too much, we can say that the world is where we live our everyday lives and act. The various distinct aspects of it are what empirical sciences study. And, Husserl says, it is *not* indubitable. Not only do individual sensory experiences often turn out to be false, but the whole of our sensory experience may be delusional: the world may be nothing more than a "coherent dream" (as Descartes had suggested): "The being of the world on the grounds of natural evidence of experience may no longer be for us a self-evident fact, but merely a phenomenon of what is valid for us" (*Geltungsphänomen*; *CM* 58). The key word here is "phenomenon". Whether external reality exists or not, it seems to, and so is an appearance, a phenomenon: and "as my phenomenon it is indeed not nothing" (*CM* 59).

Let us stop believing that the world exists, then, as a reality outside my mind. Of course, there is no reason to *deny* that either; we can just leave it open. When I do, my awareness of the world does not go away. Even if the world is only a coherent dream, it does exist, with *all* its content, in my mind – as an appearance. If I refrain from belief in the existence of the external world, then, I do not end up nowhere. I am redirected to my own experience of the world. To Husserl, this awareness is itself a "primordial life", the life of the ego.

Husserl calls this practice of refraining from taking the world as really existing "bracketing", or the "phenomenological reduction", or the *epoché*, the "holding back" of our natural tendency to view the world as really existing. When I perform this with regard to a particular experience of something, I place its content "within the brackets". Suppose I am looking at a tree. Normally, part of this looking is naively assuming, or, as Husserl would say, "naturally" assuming, that the tree is really there. If I stop making that "natural" assumption, my experience of the tree is not changed in any way: the tree loses nothing except its presumed existence outside the mind. The entire *content*, or, as Husserl calls it, the entire "sense" of the world, is thus within the brackets. Only its "existence" is outside them.

Within the brackets, the way something *seems* to me to be is just what it *is* – for me; I can wrongly perceive a real tree, but the tree "within the brackets" just *is* the tree as I perceive it. The tree itself, within the brackets, is thus present "as itself". It is there in evidence. When I apply the brackets, then, I restrict myself to merely what is evident. And here an absolutely grounded philosophy can get going: "The *epochē*, it can therefore be said, is the radical and universal method through which I grasp myself as a pure ego, together with my own pure consciousness in which and through which the entire objective world is for me, and is so as it is for me" (*CM* 60).

Why is the ego "pure" here? Husserl's answer would be that it is because nothing from outside can now affect it, since – as far as we are now concerned – nothing from outside can be known to exist. This includes not merely objects in space and time, but also culture, which comes to me from other people, who have also been bracketed out (*CM* 58–9). All content that comes from my experience of what is outside me – the entirety of what is called the "empirical" domain – has thus been, so to speak, disarmed; its validity is suspended by the brackets, so that I cannot use it in making inferences. Thus, my cultural tendency, as an American, to view freedom as freedom of choice is not, on this level, a valid way to describe freedom, but it captures what freedom *seems* to be to me. If I carry through this bracketing with respect to all conscious contents, then, I am freed from cultural presuppositions. What remains is the content of an ego simply as such, a pure ego, devoid of all interest (*CM* 74).[11]

Notice that Husserl has characterized bracketing as a *refraining*: we do not *go on* and do something. Taking the world really to exist is to do something *in addition*. In addition to what? To having the world as an appearance. The world within the brackets, although in a strict sense "unnatural" to us, is thus basic to having the world as really existing outside us. The pure ego is thus more basic than the real world: "The natural field of being is secondary in its validity as being, it continually presupposes the transcendental field" (*CM* 61). The pure ego is thus what Kant would have called a necessary condition for normal experience and normal life: it is "transcendental". In particular, since what is transcendental in this way is the mind itself, the pure ego constitutes what Husserl calls "transcendental subjectivity". Husserl thus calls himself, as did Kant, a "transcendental idealist".

---

11. There are obvious problems with this argument, which will be addressed in the Conclusion.

Now we have uncovered an absolutely certain domain: the existence of the pure ego is apodictic in nature, because its non-existence is unthinkable. Suppose it did not exist; then I am deceived if I think it does. But, as Descartes argued, if I am deceived I must exist. Therefore I cannot not exist: *cogito ergo sum*.

This appeal to Descartes' *cogito* will have important resonances in Sartre; but for Husserl, Descartes' formulation of his own insight is problematic. The problem, Husserl tells us in §10 (and has already told us in the Introduction and *CM* 61) is that Descartes saw "I think" as a premise for arguments, which would then form the science both he and Husserl are after. To do this, Descartes gave our primary experience of our own pure ego the form of a sentence: "I think, I am a thing which thinks."

For Husserl, transcendental subjectivity is not a set of certain premises for arguments, but a set of indubitable, basic or, as he calls them, "transcendental" experiences (*CM* 66). The pure ego is the primary and certain object of description, and the kind of science Husserl is after differs fundamentally from Cartesian science (and from Kantian critique) in that it is a set of descriptions, not of arguments.

As we shall shortly see in more detail, since thinking for Husserl is a form of experiencing, it always has its object, whatever it is that we experience in a given experience. It is unthinkable that there could be an experience without any object at all. The *object* experienced is thus integral to any *cogito*. What neither Descartes nor Hume saw, says Husserl, is that in the *cogito* the *cogitatum*, the object thought (or experienced), is given with the same immediacy and certainty as is the *cogito* itself. The basic structure of consciousness, behind which we cannot go, is thus not *cogito*, or even *ego cogito*; it is *ego cogito cogitatum* – I think a thought or (in slightly more Husserlian terms) I experience a something-experienced.

But if the *cogito* is apodictically certain, as Descartes showed, and if the *cogitatum* is integral to the *cogito*, as Husserl claims, how far does the apodictic certainty extend? Does it cover all *cogitata*, including the incompletely evident ones? What about the different modes of cogitation, such as perceiving, remembering, anticipating and so on? Is it possible that the absolute indubitability of transcendental self-experience is not limited to the mere abstract "I think a thought"? Might not:

> a universal apodictic experience-structure of the I (for example, the immanent temporal form of the stream of experience) extend itself through all particular givens of the real and possible self-experience – although they are not absolutely indubitable when taken individually.
>
> (*CM* 67)

Husserl does not answer this question here; it will be some time before he can do that. But the very fact that he asks it shows again that Husserl is seeking timeless truths within the "Heracleitean flux" (*CM* 86) of the pure ego. Instead of arguments that are always valid, he seeks descriptions that are always true. To show that such descriptions can be found, he must establish that the ego, as given in transcendental experience, exhibits enduring structures.

INTENTIONALITY AND NOEMA

There is also a problem about sensory experience. Perceiving is a mode of the *cogito*; it is somehow within the brackets. But unlike remembering, anticipating and so on, sensory perceiving has an object external to me. Now if no content is lost when we introduce the brackets, this externality also cannot be lost. So there must be some way in which we experience, within the phenomenological brackets, the externality of perceived objects. If the *epoché* preserves all content, in other words, then it must preserve that particular content of our experience that allows us to distinguish things in us from things outside us.

When I "perceive" a blackboard, the object of my experience is outside me. When I "remember" the blackboard, the immediate object of my memory is an image of the blackboard inside me. That is how we would "naturally" distinguish sensing something from remembering it. But phenomenologically, we are not allowed to appeal to the existence of things outside us. So how do we distinguish sensing from other ways of experiencing? There must be something about the experience itself that allows us to do so. To begin resolving this problem, Husserl must first explain in general what it is to be a *cogitatum*: an object of any kind of experience, be it memory, sense, anticipation or whatever. In this regard, he deploys his notion of "intentionality". This term has nothing to do with intending to do something or other, but comes originally from medieval philosophy.

We have already seen what Husserl is now calling "intentionality" when we noted that the *epoché* does not deliver us to a consciousness without content, that is, that the *cogitatum*, the object of awareness, is integral to all our experiences. Intentionality is one of the basic principles of Husserlian phenomenology, for he holds that there is in fact no such thing as consciousness without an object; as he says, "every conscious experience as such is in itself consciousness *of* this or that" (*CM* 71). The principle of intentionality thus states that all consciousness is consciousness *of*, or – in the terms we saw before – that every *cogito* has its *cogitatum* (*CM* 72).

What is it, then, to be the object of an intentional consciousness? Let us examine a case of sense perception. Suppose I am looking at a stop sign (Husserl's example is a die; *CM* 77–8). Moment by moment I receive different "presentations" of the stop sign: I walk towards it, then away; I walk to one side and then to another. In my visual field the stop sign is continually changing shape and colour. I know it is one single object in spite of these changes, not only because the different presentations resemble each other – they are all more or less red, for example – but because the changes in them are *continuous*. In other words, those changes proceed according to *rules*. So the individual *cogito* is not aware of its *cogitatum* in an abstractly empty way; any awareness has a constitutive structure. The structure is composed of some elements belonging to the *cogitatum*, which Husserl calls "noematic", and others belonging to the way I experience it, to the *cogito*. These he calls the "noetic" elements (*CM* 78).

The set of all the presentations I have of a thing, bound together by rules, constitutes what Husserl calls the "intentional object" (*CM* 79). The stop sign may or may not exist as what Husserl would call a "natural" object outside me. It certainly exists, however, as an intentional object within my pure ego. It exists there as just the rule-governed set of all experiences I have of it.

An intentional object is thus "immanent" to consciousness (*CM* 80); it is put together out of my own experiences, and is nothing over and above those experiences. The basic condition for my experiencing it is my ability to receive many different presentations of it, and to put them together according to rules: to perform the act philosophers call "synthesis" upon those experiences. The rules, of course, will vary with the type of object it is; if I walk around a horse, the syntheses will be different from those if I walk around a house. They will be still more different if I am hearing, say, a piece of music. There, too, I must put individual presentations – say, notes – together into a melody, and I have rules to follow in doing so. But they are not visual rules. And when I remember something, or fantasize it, the rules are different again.

In order for the different presentations to be put together by me, they cannot occur all at once; then they would already be together. They must come to me in succession. Since my perception of the object is continuous, the succession must also be continuous. On its most basic level, it is nothing other than continuously flowing time. My most basic and universal synthesis is the connection of what we may call the different moments of time to one another as they flow past; it is "immanent time" itself.

TIME AND PASSIVE SYNTHESIS

To be an intentional object, for Husserl, is, then, to be a set of appearances put together by the mind according to rules, much as it is for Kant. For Husserl, however, the most basic thing put together in this way is time itself, which is the object of the most basic synthesis: the "time synthesis". This synthesis, however, is of a special type, for its result stands before me as something I did *not* put together, as something that exists independently of me. Like other types of synthesis that result in objects that confront me as already made, the time synthesis is what Husserl calls "passive":

> In [active genesis] the ego functions as through specific ego-acts, as producing, constituting. … However, every level of activity presupposes as a lowest level a pregiving passivity, and following that up we come upon constitution through passive genesis. What encounters us in life finished, so to speak, as a mere thing existing (abstracted from all mental [*geistigen*] characters which make it knowable as e.g. a hammer, table, or aesthetic production) is given in the primordiality of the *it itself* in the synthesis of passive experience.   (*CM* 111–12)

Over and above the time synthesis, passive synthesis operates in accord with what Hume called the laws of association: resemblance, simultaneity and succession. When I see things resembling each other, coexisting or following one another with regularity, my mind automatically brings them together (*CM* 114).

Because the synthesis of time is passive, rather than something we do consciously, time can confront us as a "finished" object of awareness. It is then, in fact, my most basic awareness, the one that all others presuppose. This is my awareness of *time flowing past* in my pure ego: my "internal time consciousness" (*CM* 79). The time synthesis, being basic, is universal, in that it "governs" all other syntheses (*allwaltende*; *CM* 79). Because it covers all my experiences, it is responsible for the unity of my consciousness itself (*CM* 80).

The idea that objects are given to us as syntheses of presentations that come to us in time, for its part, is an extraordinarily important idea. It is not exactly new with Husserl. Kant had said as much, but – like Descartes – had not gone on and described that experience in more detail. He described, instead, the concepts of the understanding that governed that set of syntheses. In so doing, Husserl might say, Kant treated the temporal structure of our experience as merely a premise for further arguments, rather than as the realm of "transcendental experience" that it is.

The time synthesis plays an important role in Husserl's epistemology. Since he aims to found science itself on phenomenology, phenomenology must be able to provide a *complete* description of the conscious processes in the mind. Otherwise our mind may contain things that surprise us, which would mean trouble for any science founded on them.

All specific intentional objects, Husserl maintains, are formed by specific rules of synthesis, over and above the universal synthesis of the flow of time that they presuppose. They all run on its basis; and *since it is accessible to consciousness, they must be too*. All experiences of the ego, from the basic time synthesis upwards, will thus present themselves to reflection, that is, to phenomenological reflection, as temporally ordered: as beginning and ending, and as simultaneous and successive (*CM* 81). Hence, the mind is completely aware of itself, because all its operations and contents are entirely founded on this one basic operation. Consciousness, in other words, is completely knowable because it is a realm that is entirely closed to itself, as we already saw when Husserl said that putting the brackets in place removed all "interest" from the mind.

This view of consciousness as a closed realm is, like others of Husserl's views, not new with him. Berkeley's argument that there is no such thing as matter reposes importantly on the basic view that mind and matter are so different from each other that there is no way to fathom how matter could ever produce a mental experience (Berkeley 1982: 27, 29–32). If we suppose that the paint on the stop sign is a material object, it is impossible for us to explain how it is related to our subjective experience of the sign's red colour.

With his doctrine of passive genesis, or passive synthesis, Husserl has also found a way to deal with what Freud would call unconscious processes. They are not what Freud would call repressed, in the sense that they actually resist being brought to consciousness, but they are not obvious on the surface and need to be noticed. Phenomenology, as the practice of noticing them, can thus provide the kind of complete account of consciousness that Husserl needs. So Husserl's conception of passive synthesis is an attempt to preserve the complete knowability of mind in the face of the fact, known not only to Freud but also to Kant and other thinkers in his wake, that some mental processes are unconscious. For Husserl, these processes are activities of our mind, and so knowable with evidence; but, because they are passive, they seem to be things we do not undertake.

Husrerl has here bought the complete knowability of consciousness at the price of locating within the mind, instead of processes we cannot know, activities we cannot control. The way is thus open for the kind of postmodern doubts about human agency that we shall see in Foucault.

There is another implication of this for what would become postmodern theory. Time is, for Husserl, the product of a passive synthesis, and it provides in this way the unity of the ego. That means that the passive synthesizing of time is something always going on in our minds. Since it provides the unity of our ego, it is a condition for any awareness whatsoever. But to "synthesize" is to put things together. As Elizabeth Ströker (1993: 226–7) has pointed out, passive synthesis is therefore a putting-together of certain things. But what things? Upon what does it operate? What does it synthesize?

There is no way to say, because all determinate content varies. If I am aware of anything specific, then it is – precisely because it is *specific* – not something that I am always aware of. So there must be something that is there as the "material" of the passive time synthesis, towards which my mind is always directed, and which is even a condition for all the other things my mind does, but which cannot be known in any way.[12] Husserl thus salvages the complete knowabil-

---

12. As Ströker puts it, "Transcendental phenomenology must acknowledge something pregiven that was in principle withdrawn from achieving subjectivity" (1993: 227).

ity of mind by saying that the material of the time synthesis – the individual moments it brings together – contains nothing to be known. Even though we cannot say what it is, nothing about it escapes us. The material of the passive time synthesis thus becomes an empty activity of pure distinguishing that distinguishes nothing: an avatar of the famous Derridean "différance", which will come up in Chapter 13.

HORIZONS

We are still trying to see what kind of account Husserl can give, from within his brackets, of the peculiar nature of sensory experience. There must, we saw, be some feature of the experiences themselves that shows us that they are experiences of external objects. If Husserl cannot find some way to make this distinction, then it will be hard for him to show that one important characteristic of internal experience – that it is "evident", cannot be doubted while it lasts – does not extend to all our experience, and he will be in danger of claiming that we can have infallible experiences of sensory objects.

That Husserl should now be in danger of being driven to the absurd claim that our knowledge of sensory objects is infallible shows that – without acknowledging it – he has turned epistemology upside down. In standard modern theory of knowledge, the question is how we can come to know anything at all. Mind is viewed as an order of being unto itself, so different from the world that it requires utmost philosophical exertion to throw a bridge from one to the other. If you go back to Aristotle (and some of the medieval philosophers), however, you get the reverse problem: mind is on such a continuum with objects that it is hard to see how we can ever be mistaken. Husserl, too, has such a continuum, within the brackets: an intentional object is (so to speak) a shape of consciousness itself. He has thus returned to Aristotle. As with Aristotle in the *De anima*, Husserl's problem is not to show how we can attain knowledge, but how we can be mistaken. Although Aristotle was a primary concern of Husserl's teacher Brentano, Husserl never mentions Aristotle in this book, but, as Heidegger will show, Husserl is much closer to Aristotle than he seems to imagine.

Solving the problem of what in our experience tells us that its object is not merely intentional but outside us will require the whole conceptual apparatus Husserl has built up to this point: the accounts of evidence, intentionality, intentional objects (noemata), and the time synthesis. In §19, Husserl begins by claiming that "every actuality implies its possibilities". What he means by this is a bit complicated:

> My momentary awareness of any intentional object (noema), of any appearance of a thing, is part of an overall rule-governed system of such awarenesses. It is because of these rules that I can "synthesize" those

different appearances into appearances of a unified "intentional object." This means that my momentary awareness of some given noema is part of a larger sequence which includes previous nomata of that object that I have already had, as well as further noemata which may be yet to come. The noemata yet to come to me are, then, "potentialities" of the object.

The potentialities (or possibilities) in question – sides of the object that are not given to me in evidence but that are indicated by what *is* given to me – are of three kinds:

- aspects of the object we have not yet seen, or what Husserl previously called the *vorgemeinte* aspects of the evidence (properties the intentional object may come to have if, for example, we walk around it);[13]
- aspects we could see differently – *mitgemeinte* properties it has now that we are not attending to at the moment;
- aspects we could have seen – properties it had that were not presented to us – another form of *mitgemeinte* (CM 82).

The basic awareness brought by all three of these aspects of experience is an experience of possibility: a feeling that "I can do differently than I am doing". Our experience of an intentional object in general – sensed or not – is thus, for Husserl, a *gradual fulfilling* of it, as more and more of its aspects come to full evidence.

Any experience, therefore, leaves certain things open, or undetermined. If you see a door, for example, you know – without having to make an inference – that it has a back side. You do not know what the other side of the door looks like, but you have a vague idea. You are therefore "given" this back side, but in an undetermined way. Husserl's name for this lack of determination in an experience is "unfulfilment". An intuition can thus be more or less concretely filled out; when it is not filled out, it is unfulfilled. The set of unfulfilled aspects of a noema is the set of its horizons: "This leaving-open [of aspects], which is a moment contained in consciousness itself prior to their ... closer determination, which perhaps will never succeed, constitutes precisely what we call the *horizon*" (*CM* 83).

Because the horizons of an object are vague, not all of them will turn out to be aspects *of the object*. The other side of the door is part of its horizon, but so are the hall outside, the floor of that hall and so on. This is especially obvious in the case of the *mitgemeinte*, co-intended aspects. If I focus on the door, some parts of the door itself will be less focused on; but also present in an unfulfilled

---

13. Husserl sometimes calls this the "sense" of the object, although sometimes the unity of the object is its "sense" (cf. *CM* 83). In both meanings, "sense" remains opposed to existence.

way, and therefore "horizonally" present, will be its position in the wall, and so on.[14] All external, sensory objects have horizons of this sort: "to every external perception there belongs the reference from the *truly perceived* sides of the object of perception to those sides which are co-*intended* (*mitgemeinten*), not yet perceived but merely anticipated in an expectant way and at first in unintuitive emptiness" (*CM* 82). This is not only the case for external objects, however. The distinction between fulfilment and unfulfilment is basic to all consciousness as consciousness (*CM* 83), and so is a structure of intentionality itself. It applies to things we would ordinarily consider internal objects, such as remembering: the experience of remembering something, just like the thing remembered, has at any moment aspects that are not fully given to us and that we do not fully understand.

Because the distinction between fulfilled and unfulfilled intentions is a general structure of consciousnesss, so is the movement from unfulfilment to fulfilment. That movement is, we may say, the basic process that is added to the underlying time synthesis in our experiences of determinate content. So it applies to all experiences of objects, both internal and external. This means that we still do not have an answer to our question about how to distinguish sensory perception from various forms of introspection.

One thing we do have, as Husserl goes on to point out in §20, is an understanding of what phenomenology does. It does not analyse consciousness, as it were, from above, by furnishing accounts of its various structures and content. Rather, phenomenological investigation *enters into the temporal sequence of experience*, showing what is merely implicit in a given experience and so actualizing its potentialities, the various components of its horizon: "[Phenomenology] thus makes what is contained in the sense of the *cogitatum*, the merely unintuitive co-intended (such as the *back side*) clear by making present the potential experience which would make the invisible visible" (*CM* 85).

The way is now open to a view of phenomenology as a concrete discussion of the development of particular phenomena. This path will be taken by some phenomenologists, largely in the wake of Merleau-Ponty, but not by Husserl himself. For him, phenomenology, as "science", does not seek to follow out the unique structures of the way a particular experience gradually unfolds itself. Rather, it moves from the general to the specific. Starting from the most general

---

14. Note the difference between Husserl's account of noemata and Russell's account of sense-data (e.g. Russell 1959: 46–60). For Russell, as for Husserl, experienced objects are constructed out of basic sensory data. But for Russell, the construction comes about through inference. The sense-data that constitute the basic level of my empirical experience are in no sense vague; each is perfect and complete. The way it is ordered into my later and earlier experiences is not given in experience itself, but is something I *infer*. Russell thus accords a larger scope to inference than Husserl. Husserl would say that Russell, like Descartes, has missed an important aspect of our experience by turning too quickly to argument forms.

"typic" – the structure *ego–cogito–cogitatum* – it seeks the more specific rules that flesh that "typic" out in various ways (*CM* 87). That there are such more specific, but still general, rules is indicated by the fact that we class objects in various ways: spatial things, living things, substances, properties and so on (*CM* 86): "Every object … as such (including every immanent object) indicates a rule-structure of the transcendental ego. … Transcendental subjectivity is not a chaos of intentional experiences" (*CM* 90). Phenomenology thus ramifies into an organized set of "transcendental theories", each having to do with the rules by which we constitute and experience a particular type or region of objects (*CM* 88, 90).

TRUTH

Husserl is now able to discuss evidence again, and in more detail, now that the temporal structure of evidence bas been brought out. This structure consists in the fact that evidence normally occurs in a sequence that moves from less to more fulfilled. What evidence most instructively contrasts with, then, is not lack of experience but the relatively empty, unfulfilled "intendings", as I shall call them, which have not been given in full concreteness. We can see how this structure relates to Husserl's view of truth by noting that more fulfilled evidence is the *telos* of the merely intended:

> Evidence … indicates a possibility, and indicates it to be the goal of a striving and actualizing intention for any and everything which is intended or to be intended, and so it is an essential *basic character of intentional life as such* … Every consciousness as such itself either already exhibits the characteristic of evidence, that is it is self-giving with respect to its intentional object, or it is essentially directed upon being brought into self-givenesses, and therefore to synthesis of verification, which belong to the sphere of the "I can". (*CM* 93)

The emphasis in Husserl's account of truth is, then, on the *process* of confirmation (*Bewährung*). Confirmation happens when the gradual self-unfolding of an intentional object is "harmonious" (*CM* 97), or, as we may say, presents no surprises. On the other hand, it is also possible that in the gradual fulfilling of an intention, "instead of the [originally] intended itself a *different thing* (*ein anderes*) comes forth, at which the [original] positing of the intended fails and it takes on the character of nothingness" (*CM* 93). An object that is verified in this sense is not a "nothingness" but an actual object. As the title of §26 has it, actuality is the correlate of evident verification (*CM* 94).

Finally, in spite of the importance of its appearance within a sequence, any evidence is more than just its position in that sequence, because it can be *returned to*: once I have experienced something I can go back to it. Otherwise there would be no way for the "Heracleitean flux" of transcendental experience to yield enduring structures: no "standing and remaining being" (*CM* 96).

The evidences that go together to make up an intentional object are, of course, a finite set; they are experiences I actually happen to have had (even if they are "fantasy" images of the object; *CM* 94). A "true" intentional object, immanent to my mind, would be composed, then, of an infinite number of such evidences; this is what is meant, Husserl says, by (Kantian) talk of objects and truths *an sich*, or in themselves. This incompleteness of our experiences of intentional objects in general is, however, not a principled one, because it is grounded merely in what we might call human frailty: being merely me, I cannot ever have all the possible experiences of an object that would add up to the object's nature "in itself". There is, in other words, nothing *structural* about my consciousness that prohibits that.

Sometimes, however, the one-sidedness of the evidences we have regarding a particular object is structural or "essential", that is, not a matter of our own factual limitations, but something necessary and itself rule governed. We might call it a distinction in kind rather than quantity: it is not just that there are always more experiences out there to be had, but that this defines the kind of experience I am having from the very outset. Even if we had infinite time, in other words, we could not achieve complete evidence regarding the object. This is the case for all evidences that bring us before an objective world or its component objects. Such evidences:

> bring their object to self-givenness in an essential one-sidedness. This applies to nothing less than the sum of evidences, through which a real objective world [both] as a whole and according to some individual objects or other is immediately intuitively there for us. The kind of evidence proper to them is external perception, and it must be seen to be an essential necessity that for such objects no other mode of self givenness is thinkable.   (*CM* 96)

Within this structurally incomplete kind of transcendental experience, as our naive classifications of objects show, there are different regions, each of which can be characterized by a particular way in which the evidences proper to it are synthesized into objects.

Here, then, we have the distinction we have long been after between external perception and other kinds within the brackets. Although external perception, like other kinds, gradually unfolds itself in increasing evidence, that it can ever be complete is *in principle* excluded. Even the highest forms of confirmation will necessarily leave certain intendings unfulfilled, or reveal new unfulfilled ones (*CM* 96). The world is thus experienced as what Husserl calls "transcendent". It, and everything that exists in it, always to some degree escapes us, and is capable, then, of surprising us. The question now arises of how we know when the incompleteness of our experience of an object is due to human frailty and when it is due to the structure of the object itself. Presumably we have some sort of feel for this, although a fallible one (I may think a hallucination is external to me when it is not). One job of transcendental phenomenology is to explicate that feeling.

Husserl has now explained what aspect of our experience shows us that we are experiencing external objects. He has shown, in other words, how external objects can be excluded from the certainty of the *cogito*. Now he must show how far that certainty extends *within* transcendental subjectivity.

So far, we have found transcendental subjectivity – the set of our experiences viewed independently of the existence of the external world – to consist of the following:

- The pure certainty of the *ego–cogito–cogitatum*, that is, of the Cartesian "I think", understood as immediately and essentially including the various things I think (or experience), the totality of which is the ego. This structure can be formulated as "I experience intentional objects", where "I" is just a set of intentional objects and the experiences of them.
- The time synthesis: most generally, the unity of these objects is given through synthesis, that is, through what Husserl calls internal time.
- The temporal structure of gradual fulfilment: as we experience an object, our awarenesses of it grow more and more determinate and complete.

If we stopped here, there would be quite a lot of work for phenomenology to do. Entering into the temporal stream of experiences, it would at each stage direct attention to the aspects that as yet undeveloped, that is, still non-evident. It would bring these to complete evidence, or more complete evidence anyway, by attending to them, and in this way would enrich our experience of the world. This would be the kind of phenomenology we saw Husserl allude to in §20. Such phenomenology would, however, fall far short of Husserl's demand, at the beginning of the *Meditations*, for phenomenology to be a "science". For science, he believes, must yield "permanent acquisitions" to knowledge. This kind of phenomenology, by contrast, sounds more like a form of art criticism in which the critic takes someone whose perceptions of a novel or painting have revealed certain things, and then gets her to notice other things that she has not yet realized, or things that she could realize but does not, or things that she could have realized but has not. It would make phenomenology into an "appreciative" discipline.

In order to legitimize phenomenology as a foundational science, by contrast, Husserl is going to have to certify that there are further structures for it to deal with, structures that are indubitable, that is, to which the certainty of the *cogito* applies, and that are therefore structures of the pure ego. But the only structures of the pure ego that we have at this point are the three listed above: the threefold *ego–cogito–cogitatum*, the basic time synthesis, and the move from unfulfilment to fulfilment. How is he to flesh them out into a foundation for science?

THE EIDETIC REDUCTION

We have already seen Husserl claim that the ego can return to its evidences once it has achieved them, and he begins by restating this: "If I decide myself, for example, for the first time in an act of judgment in favor of something being thus-and-so, this fleeting act passes away – but I am now and remain, the ego-that-has-decided-thus-and-so" (*CM* 100). This is true even if I later revoke my judgement: I am still the ego that made that judgement. Through this I build a personal character, a "standing and remaining I" (*CM* 100), to go with the "standing and remaining being" we already have (*CM* 96).

In addition to the ego as the pure flux of the time synthesis – as being, over and above the changing contents of that flux, merely a pure empty "pole" of identity – we now have an ego that is a substrate of habit, that is, of abilities to replicate its past behaviour. This ego is capable of confronting enduring objects, and thus has an entire environment of things that matter to it (*CM* 102). "When I engage in phenomenological reduction, I recur to the transcendental ego and to this content which has been built up in it. I *find* in my ego the 'typics' that have been built up over time" (*CM* 103).

Some elements of these typics however, are independent of the particular set of events that have produced them in me. What makes this clear, in Husserl's view, is fantasy. Fantasy was introduced in §25 in connection with the concept of phenomenological verification. It comes from the concept of possibility that applied to horizons. When some aspect of a phenomenon has not been given, I am able to fantasize what it would be like (as when I imagine to myself the other side of a door). I can also, as Husserl pointed out there, fantasize what it would have been like to see the door in ways I did not in fact see it. Even after I have seen the other side of the door, that is, I can imagine it differently. Such fantasy, then, is always going on, as the *Mitmeinen* of unfulfilled aspects of an experience.

Generalizing this, we can say that, for any transcendental experience, I can imaginatively vary certain features of it but not others. If I vary my image of a table beyond certain points, for example, it is no longer an image of that table; but it is still a perception.

> We change the fact (*Faktum*) of this perception, while refraining from affirming its validity as existing, into a pure possibility, one among other completely arbitrary pure possibilities – but all of them possibilities of perception … The *Typus* "perception" attained in this way swings, so

to speak, in the air – in the air of absolutely pure beings thought-up (*reine Erdenklichkeiten*). Thus removed from all facticity, this *Typus* has become the eidos "perception".   (*CM* 104)

What happens, then, is this: the acts of consciousness that I perform leave a sort of trace, a *Typus*, in my pure ego.[15] By imaginatively varying the features of this *Typus*, I can expose what it is in it that does not change: the nature of the act of consciousness itself in which it comes to be. These natures or, as Husserl calls them *eidē*, are then permanent structures of my pure ego, or of transcendental experience. Since my variation is entirely random, or free, their *eidos* applies beyond them to all acts of that type: Husserl continues by saying that the *eidos*'s "ideal scope constitutes all ideally possible perceptions as purely thought-up". "The variations themselves are evident, since as conscious acts they are given as themselves. Therefore, their correlate – the eidos – is 'an intuitive and universal consciousness of universality'" (*CM* 105).

And finally, among the things that can be "varied out", so to speak, are all the peculiarities of my own ego, so that one of the *eidē* I come up with in this way is the *eidos* "pure ego" itself. Phenomenology thus has a method for studying the universal structures of the pure ego:

> If we therefore think of phenomenology purely according to the eidetic method as an intuitive, *a priori* science, then all of its researches into essences are nothing other than uncoverings of the universal eidos transcendental ego as such, which includes in itself all pure possible variations of my factical ego and this as itself a pure possibility.
>
> (*CM* 105–6)

This, then, is the second, or "eidetic" reduction. "Next to the phenomenological reduction, eidetic intuition is the basic form of all particular transcendental methods ... both together thoroughly determine the correct sense of a transcendental phenomenology" (*CM* 106). The universal form of all this, as we might expect, is time (§37). Time is, then, the most general *eidos*.

With this, Husserl has uncovered the full scope of transcendental subjectivity: it is a rule-governed set of acts of consciousness, whose rules are governed in turn by *eidē* or essences, which can themselves be made known. A number of questions impose themselves, however. Notice, first, that Husserl, in his examples, restricts eidetic variation to the noetic side of phenomenological investigation: that is, the *eidē* we can come up with in this way are the general

---

15. I leave Husserl's word *Typus* in German because that preserves the Aristotelian origins of the term: a *typos* for Aristotle was the trace of a perception remaining on in the mind, which then became a memory. The Greek *typos*, like our word "type", originally designated a physical imprint, as of a signet ring on wax.

types of intentional acts of consciousness. He does not seem to think that you could come up with the *eidos* of "chair", say, or table, in this fashion. It is easy to see why Husserl would *want* to restrict the scope of eidetic variation in this way. But what *grounds* can he give for that restriction? If he cannot justify the restriction, then it is possible for me, via eidetic variation, to come up with *eidē* of things like tables, moral acts and human beings. What controls will there be on this? The potential for abuse is enormous.

Other questions follow. Even in the noetic sphere, how do I know that the *eidos* I have uncovered is apodictic? How can the set of variations I actually perform tell me that the *eidos* applies to all possible variations? How do I know that my variations are "pure", that they are not guided by some hidden interest I have? In particular, how do I know that I have got rid of all characteristics of my individual ego in coming up with the *eidos* that I claim is that of the pure ego as such?

The eidetic reduction is highly controversial within phenomenology. Even people who accept the rest of Husserl have trouble with it. Others defend it, for example by saying that it is really the same thing as mathematical abstraction, or that the first (phenomenological) reduction is merely a form of it, so if you have accepted that, you may as well accept this. On that view, the pure ego is merely an eidetically varied natural ego.

INTERSUBJECTIVITY

Husserl does not claim, with this, to have fully carried out any sort of phenomenological investigation; the entirety of the *Cartesian Meditations* is only, as its subtitle says, an introduction to phenomenology. We might say, in fact, that his aim has not been to solve problems, but to open them up. Consciousness, which modern philosophers such as Hume and Descartes claimed to be a transparent realm of perfect self-knowledge, turns out to be a mysterious and complex realm, although still, if we are patient and careful, a fully transparent one.

There is one final major problem to be solved before Husserl's introduction to phenomenology is complete. This is the problem of transcendental philosophy or, for Husserl, *the* problem of transcendental philosophy. Phenomenology has now (if we agree with Husserl) uncovered the pure, apodictic and so unchanging structures of the pure ego; this makes it "transcendental". But in order to be transcendental *philosophy*, it must live up to transcendental philosophy's claim to "solve the problem of the objective world" (*CM* 121).

Idealism holds that the world can be explained in terms of the mind. Husserl has rethought the mind as the pure ego, that is, as a set of experiences. In order to deserve the title he gave himself – "transcendental idealist" (*CM* 61) – he needs to show how this conception of the pure ego can explain the existence of an objective world. Merely showing how we experience objects as external to ourselves, as he has done, will not suffice for this, because something truly "objective" is the same for everybody, and there is as yet no "everybody". There is just my own pure ego.

In §8, Husserl had shown that the ego is prior to the world, on the grounds that the bracketing was really a refraining from doing what we "naturally" do: attributing full existence to the world. But he did not show that there is such a thing as the objective world in the first place. He merely presupposed it, as the natural attitude does. Within the brackets, however, it cannot be presupposed. It must be explained. Husserl calls this kind of explanation "constitution". It is the basic concern of his more detailed phenomenological investigations: to take some feature of the "real" world and show how it is explained by traits of consciousness. The main example of constitution we have so far seen is the problem of showing how, within consciousness, some experiences show that they are experiences of an external world. We saw that Husserl, from within the brackets, was able to give an account of structural features immanent to sensory experience that indicated that it was experience of beings that are external to us.

What he did not show is that such beings are truly objective, that is, are the same for everyone. He has not, then, shown that there is such a thing as a "nature". And if there is no such thing as a nature that is the same for everyone, how can there be such a thing as science, which studies precisely that nature? How, if it cannot explain the possibility of the sciences, can phenomenology ground them? How, then, can it be the most basic science? To answer these questions, Husserl must show that the external world is objective, that is, does not vary from person to person. But in order to show that, he has to show that there are other people: he must constitute them, too, in terms of the pure ego (his pure ego). Thus, the first step in solving the problem of transcendental philosophy is to vindicate, phenomenologically, the existence of other minds: "The first alien thing-in-itself (the first not-I) is the other I. And that makes constitutively [i.e. phenomenologically] possible a new infinite domain of alien things, an objective nature and objective world as such, to which all the others and I belong" (*CM* 137). This is no small problem. We have uncovered transcendental subjectivity only after bracketing out all really existing beings. This, we saw, included other people. Has not transcendental phenomenology, relying only on my own access to my own pure ego, bought certainty at the price of being an intrinsically solipsistic undertaking? And if there is no phenomenological justification for talking about other people, how can there be one for talking about an "objective nature"?

> When I, the meditating ego, reduce myself to my absolute transcendental ego through the phenomenological *epochē*, have I not then become *solus ipse*, and do I not remain so as long as I engage in complete self-interpretation under the name of phenomenology? Is not phenomenol-

ogy, which wanted to solve the problem of objective being and thereby emerge as philosophy, to be branded solipsism? (*CM* 121)

Husserl's solution to this, which takes up most of the rest of the *Cartesian Meditations*, begins by defining nature in terms of intersubjectivity. It does not ask how nature can be known to exist *independently of* human minds, which would – if successful – end in a form of realism (*CM* 121–2), in which mind is no longer primary. Instead, he asks how nature can be known to be *the same for* all human minds (*CM* 123). The first step in this is to introduce yet another bracketing, one interior to transcendental subjectivity: "We look away from all constitutive achievements of intentionality which are directed upon the subjectivity of others, whether mediately or immediately" (*CM* 124).

With the entire interpersonal world bracketed in this way, we have what Husserl calls the "transcendental ownness sphere" (*transzendentale Eigenssphäre*), which consists in a solitary ego, with all its intentional experiences, confronting a world of non-human intentional objects. This world is not, to be sure, a nature that can (yet) be known to be the same for everyone, since there is no "everyone" but only my own meditating, or transcendental, ego. It is not the nature that science studies. It is a "level" of transcendental experience (*CM* 127–8).

There is one part of this non-human world, however, that I experience in a special way: as something in which I *schalte und walte*, that is, which immediately does my bidding, and through which I have experience of the rest of the own-sphere. This special object is my own body (*CM* 128). I can also, however, sense parts of this body as I can any other object: I can look at my hands for example, or touch my eye (*CM* 128).

> My body is thus given to me, on the one hand, as the privileged vehicle of my subjectivity. On the other hand, it is also given me as an object in the world, and these two ways of experiencing it must alternate: the "functioning organ must become an object, and the object must become a functioning organ". (*CM* 128)

Thus, although I am "outside" the world in the sense that my transcendental subjectivity constitutes it, I am also – paradoxically – part of it (*CM* 129).

When I see another body that resembles mine – another human body – I recognize it as another instance of the *Typus* "human body", that is, I see it as "body-which-is-controlled-by-an-ego" (*CM* 141). I then ascribe to it the various roles subjectivity plays in my own body, which means that I ascribe to it a *schaltend und waltend* subjectivity like my own. Because it is founded on resemblance, this is a case of passive synthesis: I do it automatically and without necessarily being aware that I am doing so. Since I constitute the other ego solely out of my experience of an other's body, I cannot know its contents:

"This other subjectivity which I have constituted remains, however, absolutely impenetrable to me: I cannot experience it directly at all. If I could, the other subjectivity would be merely a part of my own being, and the two egos would be the same" (*CM* 139).

In any experience of an external object, we have seen, there is necessarily, and will always be, a part of it that I do not experience. But in those cases, I can at least come to know it better: I can bring *some* of its properties to evidence. What distinguishes the case of an alien subjectivity is that I cannot even begin to penetrate it: the process of confirmation, of gradually increasing givenness, is here "a priori excluded" (*CM* 139). "My awareness of the other's subjectivity is entirely derived from my awareness of her body – from her behavior" (*Gebaren*; *CM* 144). I now experience the other's body as directed by a consciousness that remains, however, absolutely opaque to me. How can I attribute to her *specific* conscious contents: wishes, desires, thoughts?

Part of my experience of any object, we have seen, is that I know I could experience it differently. When I see a stop sign from one angle, part of its horizon is the stop sign viewed from other angles. If I see the world in general from here, I am also presented with the possibility of seeing it from over there. And this is what I do in the case of seeing the other's body: I imagine what the world would look like to me if I were where she is (*CM* 148). This also holds, Husserl says, for the higher psychic contents that I attribute to the other. These amount to the wishes, desires, thoughts and so forth that I would have if I were where she is (*CM* 149). I even attribute to her the logical categories in terms of which I experience objects in general (*CM* 155). And I attribute to her experiences of the same natural objects that I experience (*CM* 153). In this way, I constitute the other as existing in the same nature that I exist in, and that nature is itself constituted as a nature that is the same for everyone, that is, as objective nature.

This, finally, is how logical and mathematical categories are constituted as applying to all of nature, as eternally valid:

> In this way, incidentally, the transcendental problem of the specifically so called "ideal objects," in itself a most significant problem, is solved. Their supertemporality shows itself to be omnitemporality, as the correlate of their producibility at will and their reproducibility in any arbitrary point in time.　　　　　(*CM* 155–6, trans. mod.)

In particular, then, time itself is constituted as the universal structural form of nature itself (*CM* 156).

CONCLUSION

Now we can look back and see that Husserl has been building towards this all along. In his earliest discussions of *Evidenz*, for example, he had been careful to note that among the *mitgemeinte* aspects of an intention are the things that I could see but do not, and this element of fantasy has been present from the start. It is later used to develop the eidetic reduction, and now to show how I can know, although only indirectly, the contents of others' minds. Husserl's phenomenology is a marvellous intellectual construct; there is no disputing that. It is a single, beautifully constructed argument that is nonetheless checked at every step against the actual nature of our experience: one of the crowning achievements of early-twentieth-century philosophy.

However, there have been problems from the start. One is the matter of language, which first came up in the cryptic discussion of "pre-predicative evidence" in §4. Husserl claims that the phenomenological reduction eliminates cultural influences on the phenomenologist, because your culture is outside the brackets, and so in principle is excluded from what we find within them. What he does not take into account is that language itself is a vehicle of culture. When he describes what he finds in the pure ego, he uses the words of a particular language to do it; the word meanings of my particular language are not, then, "disarmed" by the brackets. "Real" phenomenology, it seems, would require a language all its own.

In general, every time Husserl claims to be uncovering structures that go beyond his own personal experience of the moment, he gets into trouble. The first of these was the *ego–cogito–cogitatum*. Why do concrete thoughts, intentional objects, always inhere in the structure of thought itself? Someone as bright as Descartes apparently did not think they did. Nor did Kant, if by "thought itself" we mean the pure unity of apperception he discusses in the first editions of the *Critique of Pure Reason* (*KRV* A 115–28): a unity that is without content.

Why is the first bracketing, the "phenomenological reduction", a refraining? Why is it that when we attribute existence to what we experience, we are doing something *more* than what we do in the brackets? We would not say that when we look at the world through a telescope we are refraining from looking at it with our eyes. We are adding something *to* our eyes. Why is not the phenomenological reduction, which Husserl admits is non-natural, something artificial: an artifice, an intellectual tool?

But if it is that, then the phenomenological attitude is founded on the natural attitude; it is a modification of it. Not only do Husserl's claims to be an "idealist" fall away, but if the phenomenological attitude is founded on the natural attitude, it will be affected by one important component of our natural lives: our cultures.

How do we know that the *eidē* uncovered by eidetic variation, in the "eidetic reduction", are not entirely due to our fantasy, mere figments of our imaginations? Husserl's answer is that we have repeated them in our previous lives; they are, we saw, "typics" built up over time (*CM* 100). But that only means that they are dependent on the experiences we have actually had, and so once again are culture bound.

Finally, Husserl's account of otherness is problematic, for it means that I can only understand others by attributing to them the thoughts and feelings I think I would have if I were in what I think is their position. It is an obvious fact that other people – especially people from other cultures – often think very differently than I do about even the most mundane things. So I cannot simply attribute my thoughts and feelings to them. But what thoughts and feelings can I attribute then? Ones I have never had?

These issues will bother Heidegger as he tries to appropriate the thought of Husserl. But the temporalized response to Husserl would be given most succinctly by Merleau-Ponty in the "Preface" to his *Phenomenology of Perception* ([1945] 1962). In it, Merleau-Ponty rejects Husserl's claim to have achieved atemporal truth. This is an issue on the most basic level of the mind, that of the time synthesis: "Since our reflections are carried out in the temporal flux on which we are trying to seize ... there is no thought which embraces all our thought" (Merleau-Ponty 1962: xiv).

In accordance with Husserl's doctrine of intentionality, for anything to be explicitly knowable, the knowing subject must be somehow detached from it. In order to have explicit knowledge of the time synthesis, then, we would have to be somehow outside it, and so outside time altogether. But that is not possible: we are always within the time synthesis, before some moments and after others. This means in turn that the time synthesis cannot be pure. If it were, then what it would synthesize would be completely homogenous, and we would not be able to distinguish any befores or afters; it would be what Kierkegaard called the "infinite vanishing", without any foothold for a present moment. This was why the "material" of the time synthesis, as we saw, was wholly abstract and unknowable. For Merleau-Ponty, by contrast, we are always within time, and so its moments are never completely homogenous; they exhibit concrete content. Since there are moments of time yet to come, there are parts of that concrete content that we do not know and cannot think.

If phenomenology is reflecting most basically on time so understood, then it is reflecting, not on a pure synthesis, but on something concrete and ongoing, and which, as the object of reflection, must be itself unreflective: "Radical reflection amounts to a consciousness of its own dependence on an unreflective life which is its initial situation, unchanging, given once for all" (*ibid.*).

The degree to which Merleau-Ponty posits unreflective or, better, prereflective life as unchanging and given all at once will be a problem for him (one that Heidegger will already block in his initial account, in *Being and Time* §7, of what a phenomenon is). The advantage for Merleau-Ponty in this postulation is that it enables him to maintain a concept of essence, or of what Husserl calls *eidos*. But such essences are for Merleau-Ponty not objects of philosophical contemplation in their own right, as they were for Husserl, but merely tools for unlockng the thickness of pre-reflective life:

> The need to proceed by way of essences does not mean that philosophy takes them as its object ... but that our existence is too tightly held in the world to be able to know itself as such at the moment of its involvement, and that it requires the field of ideality in order to become acquainted with and to prevail over its facticity.   (Merleau-Ponty 1962: xiv–xv)

"Ideality" is not simply there to be discovered, the way it is for Husserl and Kant, but is generated the way it is for Hegel in the *Phenomenology*'s opening section on "Sense-Certainty": as a way of coping with the fact that unconceptualized experience flees before we can address it. Such "ideality" for Merleau-Ponty, as for Hegel, is ultimately not concepts or categories, both of which are somehow supposed to be exempt from space and time, but words (*ibid.*: xv).

The phenomenological reduction, then, is never complete: "The most important lesson which the reduction teaches us is the impossibility of a complete reduction" (*ibid.*: xiv). Similarly, the fact that even the phenomenologist is caught up in the world on which she reflects means that the certainty Husserl attributed to phenomenological reflection falls away, and with it goes what Husserl called "apodicticity", or certainty for all time: "The self-evidence of perception is not adequate thought or apodictic self-evidence" (*ibid.*: xvi).

The phenomenologist, then, is in time, and time is always to some degree concrete. Honesty demands that these facts must be taken account of in her reflections. Since time did not begin with her, this is a demand that phenomenology become historical:

> The thinker never thinks from any starting point but the one constituted by what he is. Reflection even on a doctrine will be complete only if it succeeds in linking up with the doctrine's history and the extraneous explanations of it, and in putting back the causes and meaning of the doctrine in an existential structure.   (*Ibid.*: xix)

In thus temporalizing Husserl's phenomenology, Merleau-Ponty is not operating entirely on his own. His critique of Husserl is presented, from the opening words of the preface onward, as a clarification of what phenomenology really is. The reason for even suspecting that the true nature of phenomenology might diverge from Husserl's account of it is to be found in the work of Heidegger. From first to last in this text, Merleau-Ponty presents phenomenology as the joint creation of Husserl and Heidegger:

> One may try to do away with these contradictions by making a distinction between Husserl's and Heidegger's phenomenologies; yet the whole

of *Being and Time* springs from an indication given by Husserl and amounts to no more than an explicit account of the "natural concept of the world" or the "life-world" which Husserl, towards the end of his life, identified as the central theme of phenomenology, with the result that the contradiction reappears in Husserl's own philosophy ...   (*Ibid.*: vii)

Phenomenological reduction belongs to existential philosophy. Heidegger's "being-in-the-world" appears only against the background of the phenomenological reduction.   (*Ibid.*: xiv)

By his own account, then, what Merleau-Ponty is giving here is an explicit statement of Heidegger's rethinking of the nature of phenomenology, which he then attributes (rightly or wrongly) to Husserl himself. It is to Heidegger that we must turn to see the re-emergence in philosophy of all-devouring time, which Husserl thought he had escaped.

CHAPTER 7

THE FINITE FUTURE: MARTIN HEIDEGGER

PRIMARY TEXTS Martin Heidegger, *Being and Time* (*BT*; [1927] 1962);[1]
"The Origin of the Work of Art" (OWA; 1971a);
and "The Question Concerning Technology" (QT; 1977)

In September 1933, five months after Husserl was banned from the University of Freiburg, a casual visitor there might have found things quite normal. Preparations were underway for the start of Winter Semester. Classrooms and offices were getting their final cleaning and repairs; early-bird students were unpacking and greeting one another; and not a few professors were doing last minute revisions to their lecture notes.

Chemistry professor Hermann Staudinger, however, was having trouble concentrating. He was not alone. Beneath the veneer of normalcy they were trying desperately to maintain, many Germans were terribly worried about what the Nazi government, now firmly in the hands of Hitler, was going to do to their country. A smaller but still large number, including all but the most obtuse of Germany's Jews, was worried about what the government was going to do to them personally. Staudinger, although not Jewish, was in the latter group. He had been a draft dodger in the First World War, and had even published pacifist articles warning that technological advances had fundamentally changed the nature of war. This would hardly endear him to the war-loving Nazis, if it were to become known, and Staudinger was attempting to wait out the Nazi rule in Freiburg, as far as he could get from Berlin. In the interests of survival, he also was not drawing attention to himself by publishing or even doing research. He was deadwood by his own hand.

Staudinger's pacifistic activities were well known in Freiburg and attracted the interest of the university's recently appointed Rector, Martin Heidegger. Heidegger, for whatever reasons, saw fit to inform the government of Baden,

---

1. Page numbers refer to the German edition of *Being and Time* of 1927, which are given in the margins of Heidegger (1962).

the state in which Freiburg is located, of Staudinger's First World War activities. When the Gestapo made an enquiry, Rector Heidegger assisted them.

Having assured themselves that Heidegger's information was correct, the Gestapo summoned Staudinger and forced him to write a letter of resignation from the university, postdated six months. They told him they would decide what to do with the letter when that time had elapsed. With this hanging over his head, Staudinger suddenly became a most productive chemist indeed, turning his expertise in dyestuffs to a revamping of the German munitions industry. The result was that Staudinger not only did not leave the university, but was admiringly feted for his service to the Fatherland, at ceremonies that Heidegger, as Rector of the university, was required to attend.[2] The *Herr Rektor* presumably left early.

We may be pleased Heidegger's effort to do genuine evil, one of many, was foiled. What is interesting is that it was so ludicrous. The clownishness with which Heidegger pursued his various struggles simply points up how impossible it will always be to bring his thought and his life together into what we would consider a "rational" whole. He seemed, in fact, to have three different sides to his character, each as unlike the others as it is possible to be: he was at once a philosopher, a Nazi and a clown. Martin Heidegger as a person was little more than the unfathomable struggle among them.

That struggle began in the town of Messkirch, deep in the Black Forest of southwestern Germany, on 26 September 1889, five months after the birth of Hitler, and just four and a half months before Nietzsche's collapse in Turin. Like the surrounding community, Heidegger's family was devoutly Catholic; his father was the sexton in the local church. The pay was low and the living was difficult, but in high school Heidegger attracted the attention of a dynamic young priest in the area, Conrad Gröber.[3] This patronage got Heidegger a scholarship to the University of Freiburg in theology. He tried twice to become a priest, but each time was rejected because of a heart murmur. At some point, he apparently became unable to accept the Church's dogma. He never actually admitted to this: it would have cost him his scholarship, which in the Germany of that time would have sent him back to Messkirch. The main signal, to the local Catholics, was his marriage to Elfriede Petri, a Protestant, in a Lutheran ceremony. Church officials never confronted Heidegger openly about the propriety of taking money from a church you no longer believe in, but they seem to have turned against him. When he started applying for jobs, he conspicuously failed to get one, even when he was clearly the best qualified person. At one point, he and Elfriede were apparently living on handouts from her family.

---

2. The story is recounted at Ott (1988: 201–13), and at Safranski (1998: 273–5).
3. Gröber was later Archbishop of Freiburg, and in that capacity attended the banquet in honour of Staudinger that I mentioned above.

Heidegger's career was saved by the arrival in Freiburg of Husserl. Heidegger was never Husserl's student – he was too advanced for that – but he latched on to Husserl like a drowning man, which, professionally speaking, he was. At first Husserl thought Heidegger was just one of the band of Catholic students at Freiburg, but after a year he began to recognize how special Heidegger was, and got him a job at Marburg, a university town north of Frankfurt.

In order to keep that job, Heidegger had to publish a book. As the deadline for publication approached, he threw some manuscripts together and Husserl published the result as a special number of his journal the 1927 *Jahrbuch für Phänomenologie* (Yearbook for phenomenology). Heidegger then sent a copy off to the Ministry of Education. Several months later it arrived back in his office in Marburg in a plain brown wrapper, He tore off the wrapper and found the manuscript of *Being and Time* with one word rubber-stamped at the top of the title page: *ungenügend*, unsatisfactory. So he had to leave Marburg. By this time, however, *Being and Time* had been a wildfire success; legend has it that German Rotary clubs organized discussion groups on it. So Heidegger was able to get another job, as no less than Husserl's successor in Freiburg. His days of penury, at least of the financial kind, were over.

After the Allied victory in the Second World War, Heidegger was for several years forbidden to exercise any of the functions of a university professor, although he was always paid his salary. Once this situation ended, Heidegger resumed his professorial life, but was very alienated from the German academy. Most of his later work was given as talks to non-academic groups. He died in 1976.

BEING AND TIME

Like Hegel's *Phenomenology*, Heidegger's *Being and Time* is a book of great complexity and importance; and, like the *Phenomenology*, it was published under serious personal stress. In many ways, the German bureaucrats who rejected it were right. Although it is clearly a great book, *Being and Time* is also a rather bad book. Its thought is inchoate, its language intemperate, and it is haunted by unresolved issues such as the status and nature of "phenomenology" and of language itself. Heidegger himself, for his part, was not fond of it: after his return to Freiburg, when *Being and Time* was still at the height of its success, he went out into his backyard, made a fire and burned the second half of the book, which was never published. My discussion of it here, although less fiery, will be highly selective. I shall begin with the discussion of "phenomenology" in §7, where Heidegger outlines – although in a rough and tendentious way – some of the basic themes of his thought.

Phenomenology was, as we have seen, a highly developed method involving various kinds of "reduction" whose relationship to one another is controversial to this day. Heidegger took phenomenology over from Husserl, of course, but he took only the word, not the method:

> Here one does not have to measure up to the tasks of some discipline that has been presented beforehand; on the contrary, only in terms of the objective necessities of definite questions and the kind of treatment which the "things themselves" require, can one develop such a discipline. (*BT* 27)

If the discipline of phenomenology does not yet exist, then the word "phenomenology" has no meaning. Heidegger, in other words, has already repudiated his mentor Husserl, but has presented the repudiation as a general philosophical demand, namely that we should develop our methods out of the questions we are grappling with, rather than setting them up beforehand. Of course, the whole point of a "method" is to be set up beforehand, so Heidegger is rejecting not only Husserl's vision of the phenomenological method but also the centrality of method altogether. To be sure, he is doing it in Husserl's name: for he does it in the service of Husserl's slogan "to the things themselves" (*BT* 28). But for Husserl the "things themselves", whatever they were, revealed themselves only to the complex phenomenological method he himself had devised. In Heidegger's hands, by contrast, phenomenology is not so much a method as the repudiation of method itself.

The word "phenomenology" may not have a meaning, but it has a structure: it is composed of the two Greek words "*phenomenon*" and "*logos*". Heidegger now turns to these two words separately. In neither case does he respect their standard meanings, any more than he has respected the Husserlian meaning of "phenomenology".

The Greek *phainomenon*, for its part, has a good deal of structure: it is the present neuter middle participle of *phainein*, meaning to shine, show or bring to light. In the middle voice, this means to bring oneself to light, or to show oneself; and as a neuter participle, it refers to the action of doing this on the part of a thing. A "phenomenon" is thus something that brings itself to light as a thing, or, in Heidegger's gloss, "that which shows itself in itself". This means, although Heidegger does not put it that way, that a phenomenon is a temporal process. To be a phenomenon is not to be the object of a perceptual "snapshot" of some kind, but to develop in a certain way, so that the act of showing results in the thing shown. Heidegger has thus appropriated Husserl's view that the movement from less to more fulfilled is basic to our experience. Without such a movement, we cannot even be mistaken about things (*BT* 28). As he will attempt to show later on, this kind of self-clarification on the part of a thing, if we may call it that, is our experiential bedrock.

But phenomenality tends to be misunderstood, because it tends to be viewed in the context of what Heidegger (like philosophers generally) calls "appearance". On what we may call the "appearance-model", which has dominated philosophy more or less since Descartes and was most clearly articulated by Kant, the objects of our awareness are products of the interplay between our perceptual organs and the things that are really "out there". The things out there thus cause "appearances", which represent them but are, just by that, different from them.

Among the many incoherencies of this view are two already evident in Kant, and one pointed out by Heidegger. The more basic incoherence is that the things that are really out there, being different from the appearances we have of them, never themselves appear: they are what Kant called "things-in-themselves". The second, which follows on this, is that because things-in-themselves are very special kinds of thing, it makes no sense to say that they "cause" our appearances; causality as it is normally understood is a relation of different parts of our experience to one another, as when we burn our finger on a hot stove.

Heidegger adds to this that, on this view, "appearance" becomes ambiguous: an "appearance" is either an object of our experience, what is sometimes called a "perceptual content", or it is the overall process of manifesting oneself through such objects. Heidegger's point is not that this ambiguity of itself refutes the appearance-model. It is perfectly possible to distinguish the two senses in various ways or even, as English, does, to assign a different word to each ("appearance" and "appearing"). Rather, Heidegger's interest is diagnostic: a philosophical model that is intractably conveyed, over centuries, in muddy language – as this one has been – may well have something wrong with it (*BT* 30). In particular, calling both the process of manifestation and its result by the same name may lead us to concentrate on the result while overlooking the process altogether.

Given the problems with the appearance-model, it is perhaps surprising that philosophers have not tried harder to get beyond it, or at least express discontent with it, as Heidegger is certainly doing here. Their allegiance to it, which is still strong today, may lie in what Heidegger sees as one of its problems: that it tends to replace processes of manifestation with their results. This gives us a static picture of both the mind and appearances, or even of subject and object in general. Such a static picture of the mind is, to be sure, congenial to an atemporally oriented, traditional philosophical approach; it may be their devotion to that approach that leads philosophers to underplay the problems with the appearance-model. What they miss, in Heidegger's view, is the interplay of mind and appearance over the course of a thing's manifestation.

At the moment, however, Heidegger's replacement for the appearance-model is rather sketchy; the idea that phenomena consist in appearances following one another over time is merely an empty and preliminary, or, in Heidegger's parlance, "formal", conception of phenomenon (*BT* 31). What we need, but do not have, is a "phenomenological" conception of phenomenon.

Turning to the other half of the word "phenomenology", the Greek *logos*, Heidegger is even more peremptory. "Logos" is a protean word in Greek. Even in the hands of philosophers such as Plato and Aristotle, as Heidegger points out, its meanings are many and varied, embracing such disparate concepts as "reason", "judgement", "concept", "definition", "ground" and "relationship" (*BT* 32). These Heidegger dismisses in favour of seeing *logos* as equivalent to the verb *dēloun*, which means to make clear. *Logos* then becomes an action rather than an object, and Heidegger, following Aristotle, further associates this action with *apophainesthai*, to make something clear to somebody. *Logos* does this by emphasizing something about the thing talked about: it presents something *as* something.

In this way, *logos* participates in the process of manifestation that Heidegger has located within phenomenality. Speech, as a form of *logos*, is then a way of manifesting something, or of making it clear; but viewing speech in this way turns out to be a radical reconception of it. What Heidegger is saying is that if I say to you "Paris is beautiful", I am bringing you (and myself) into a particular relationship to Paris: I am showing you Paris *as* beautiful. What I am not doing is telling you what is somehow in my mind: I am not expressing to you my concepts or images of Paris and of beauty, and still less their interconnection. Rather, through my words I bring Paris *itself* to manifestation. Heidegger, in other words, does not view the mind as a sort of container for concepts (or images, or anything else). My words relate directly to things, even when those things are, physically speaking, thousands of miles away. Thus, the Greek definition of language as "*fōnē meta fantasias*", which is usually translated as "sound accompanied by an image" (where the image is the meaning), is translated by Heidegger as "an utterance in which something is sighted". The sound, in other words, is related directly to the thing, not to a concept or set of beliefs in my mind, or indeed to anything else "mental".

Heidegger is once again rejecting a view of Husserl's, for whom as we saw consciousness was a self-contained realm. Why does Heidegger do this? Partly because of one of his basic underlying motivations: he does not believe in the dichotomies of physical/mental, or of matter/mind, or of sensible/intellectual, and it is very difficult to talk about language in the traditional ways without appeal to such "binaries". Part of the motivation, however, is phenomenological: "To have a science 'of' phenomena means to grasp its objects in such a way that everything about them which is up for discussion must be treated by exhibiting it directly and demonstrating it directly" (*BT* 35). Phenomenological description must be direct, not mediated by concepts or images in the mind of the speaker or hearer of such description.

Language so understood cannot claim truth in the normal sense of correspondence or agreement with the facts. If I say "Paris is ugly", for example, I am traditionally understood as somehow "combining" a concept or image of Paris with the concept of ugliness in a way that Paris and ugliness – the city and the quality, not the concepts of them – are not in fact combined. But here, that is not possible: my words have made a direct exhibition of Paris as ugly, they have shown you Paris as ugly. How can they be "false"? In a Husserlian way: in that further experience of Paris does not bear out the statement that it is ugly. My statement is then disconfirmed, rather than confirmed, by future experience. To be "true" is then to be an early stage of experiencing something that is borne out in later experiences of that thing. As Heidegger will argue in §43, it is to stand in a particular type of temporal sequence.

Finally, we put these two Greek words to get our final word, "phenomenology". Since, on Heidegger's account, the words *phainomenon* and *logos* mean pretty much the same thing – a *phainomenon* shows itself, while a *logos* allows a phenomenon to be sighted – this is not difficult to do: phenomenology *apophainesthai ta phainomena*, shows the appearances.

Phenomenology and fundamental ontology

The idea that a phenomenon can be shown by words now leads to an enrichment of the notion of phenomenon itself. For if something that shows itself in itself can be made visible by logos, there must be some sense in which it does not simply show itself; otherwise we would not need *logos*, or, in particular, phenomenology, to lay it bare. This brings us to the "phenomenological" concept of the phenomenon:

> What is it that must be called a phenomenon in a distinctive sense? What is it that by its very essence is *necessarily* the theme whenever we exhibit something *explicitly*? Manifestly, it is something that proximally and for the most part does *not* show itself at all: it is something that lies hidden, in contrast to that which proximally and for the most part does show itself; but at the same time it is something that belongs to what thus shows itself, and it belongs to it so essentially as to constitute its meaning and its ground. (*BT* 35)

As with the traditional model of "appearance", that which lies open to us is not all there is; also "present" is something that does not show itself. But in contrast to the appearance-model, this non-apparent something is not a being that somehow lies behind appearances, causes them and never shows itself. It is, rather, a phenomenal component that can be *brought* to show itself.

The phenomenological concept of phenomenon is thus defined in opposition to, and so in conjunction with, the concept of concealment. What is concealment? Heidegger mentions three basic kinds. Something can be concealed in that it is as yet undiscovered, the way Einstein's $E = mc^2$ was as yet undiscovered in 1830. It can also be concealed in that it has been "covered over", that is, was once known but is known no longer; and this burial, finally, can be either accidental or necessary (*BT* 36). By the latter, Heidegger means that it is part of the nature of statements about things to be, in his sense, true or false: they can either contribute to the thing's self-manifestation, by helping us experience the thing more deeply; or they can stymie that self-manifestation, that is, "cover it over". Since nothing is forever, sentences inevitably lose their direct relation to what they are about and bury it over. Moreover the grammatical structure of a sentence ("S *is* P") tends to cover over processes; the way the appearance-model tends to cover up the process of manifestation is one example of this. Grounded in the assertional structure of language itself, such covering over is hardly adventitious or "accidental".

Phenomenology, for Heidegger, has two more salient features: it is "hermeneutical" and "fundamental-ontological". The need for it to be fundamental-ontological (and what that odd phrase means) can be seen from the account of *logos* just given, and becomes evident when we ask: how do we know that covering over is not happening with Heidegger's assertions in this very book? Must not the "things themselves" that the book is about be immediately available for everyone, so that Heidegger's assertions can be tested against what is evident to all of us?

Heidegger's book is about Being; that is why it is a work of ontology. Being is always the Being of some being or other (*BT* 37), so in the course of his investigation he needs to talk about some exemplary being. Only if that being is immediately available to his audience can what he says be checked against their own experience. Therefore, Heidegger begins *Being and Time* in such a way that the being *about* which he is talking is the same as the beings *to* whom he is talking. He talks about *our* kind of Being. In this, Heidegger presupposes that we can in fact do this checking – that is, that we not merely have Being in some way, since we are beings, but we possess it in such a way that we can become aware enough of it to check what he says about it against our own experience of it. He hypothesizes, in other words, that we have what he calls a "pre-ontological understanding of Being". This hypothesis is to be verified by the reader as the investigation goes on.

The account of human being, since it is that against which Heidegger's account of Being in general must be checked, is then "fundamental-ontological". Because it begins from a presupposition of this sort, Heidegger's undertaking is interpretive, or what he calls "hermeneutical" (*BT* 37–8). It is not merely a value-free description of ourselves, but a description carried out from a particular point of view that must be validated as it proceeds. To put this somewhat differently, among all our experiences and activities, there are some that manifest a feel for what Being is. Heidegger must show which these are, describe them accurately and show how they hang together in a (more or less) unified sense of Being. The set of those activities is thus the object of fundamental ontology. Heidegger's name for that set is Dasein, a word that has remained untranslatable and, thankfully, untranslated.

THE WORLDHOOD OF THE WORLD

Essential to the way in which things show themselves to us is "world"; indeed, Heidegger's standard way, in *Being and Time* of characterizing our nature is as "Being-in-the-world". Heidegger begins his discussion of the nature of "world" in §14, by asking how one could go about giving a phenomenological account of the nature of world. One way is simply to describe things in the world; if the world is merely the totality of things, this would eventually arrive at an overall account of world. A second approach is to determine, somehow, the basic nature of the being of things in the world – their "thingliness" – as traditional ontologists claim to have done. This traditionally means focusing on nature, since natural beings are considered to be more basic than artefacts or "useful things".

Both approaches have major presuppositions. The first approach presupposes that the world is merely the totality of the things that are in it, which would be a case of the classical fallacy of composition, and which Heidegger calls a merely "ontic" approach rather than a truly "ontological" one. The second approach presupposes that natural objects are somehow more fundamental than useful or valuable objects, which remains to be seen.

If both of these approaches have problems, is world an objective phenomenon at all? Perhaps it is in some sense merely subjective. Heidegger's answer, to be verified in his subsequent account of world, is that world is "a characteristic of Dasein itself", but one that we can get at only by investigating beings that we are not: beings in the world (*BT* 64). In accordance with the general nature of fundamental ontology, Heidegger will key this investigation to our everyday Being-in-the-world. This, however, is not cognitive in any traditional sense; it is not a kind of knowledge: "the nearest kind of association is not mere perceptual cognition, but rather a handling, using, and taking care of things which has its own kind of 'knowledge'" (*BT* 67).

Cognition, for Heidegger, is a "founded mode" of dealing with the world. We have already seen part of his criticism of it in his attack on the appearance-model in §7. That conception is founded on an ontology that posits two completely different kinds of being, subject and object, with cognition as the relation that connects them. As Heidegger argues in §13, this leads to two specific sets of issues. First, if subject and object are so different from one another, how can they be connected? We must ask: "How this knowing subject comes out of its inner 'sphere' into one that is 'other and external', of how knowing can have an object at all, and of how the object itself is to be thought so that eventually the subject knows it without having to venture a leap into another sphere" (*BT* 60).

In the most thorough working-out of the appearance-model, that of Kant, objects are constructed out of appearances when the Understanding applies the categories to them. This is not the least help in solving the current problem, however, for appearances are contents of our minds. The external object, the thing-in-itself, remains unknowable. Moreover, this philosophical problematic unfolds within the general presupposition that things of nature are more basic than other things, which means that "the question of the kind of Being of this knowing subject is entirely omitted" (a hyperbolic claim indeed; *BT* 64). Understanding the nature of our own minds thus requires understanding what Being in general is. It presupposes the fundamental-ontological investigation Heidegger is about to carry out.

Heidegger's response to the many and various problems of subject and object is not to answer them, but to evade them by claiming that our basic relationship to things is not "theoretical" (derived from the Greek word for vision), but one of handling and using things. On the most basic, everyday level, subject and object are not two radically different kinds of being, but merely user and used. Once we understand what this entails, Heidegger assures us, we will be able to see where the concepts of subject and object come from and thereby understand them, not as basic ontological categories, but as errors. As he put it in §14 (the last sentence is a handwritten marginal note in his own copy of the book): "As the categorial content of structures of being of a definite being encountered in the world, 'nature' can never render *worldliness* intelligible. Rather, the other way around!" (*BT* 65). Behind these appeals to the development of philosophy is another, more democratic impulse. It is, after all, a matter of empirical fact that theoretical contemplation of even the ordinary things around us has historically been the prerogative of a leisured class (cf. Arist. *Metaph.* I.1 981b). The other sort of encounter, with beings as ready-to-hand, has by contrast been engaged in as long as humans have worked. Heidegger's lower-class origins, presumably, made him sensitive to this.

Finally, handling things has not been attended to by theoreticians, not merely because of class prejudice and philosophical confusions, but also because it is "unthematic": the beings so encountered are not noticed explicitly in such encounter. When I use a hammer, I am unaware of it; if I focus on it, in fact, I will never hit the nail. The same is true of riding a bicycle, driving a car and so on.

The ontology Heidegger proposes in *Being and Time* is thus derived from our everyday experiences of things, experiences that manifest a general feel that we have for the kinds of thing we are dealing with. When this feel is for the most basic kinds of thing we deal with, it is our "pre-ontological" feel or "understanding" of Being itself. This understanding, as a feel for what things most basically are, is a "determination of the structure of their Being", rather than explicit knowledge of certain properties they have (*BT* 67).

At this level, our experiences of beings take only two fundamental forms. We can, of course, understand entities merely theoretically (as philosophers have traditionally done), contemplating or studying them as they "lie before us"; such entities are experienced as being "present-at-hand". More basically, as we have seen, we can encounter them in that we use them. In this case, which, according to Heidegger, corresponds to the ancient Greek sense of *pragmata*, they are "ready-to-hand" (*BT* 67ff.). The use to which a being ready-to-hand is put connects it with a number of other things in what Heidegger calls a "context of involvement". While I can, for example, place a pen before my eyes anywhere in the world and just look at it (as long as there is sufficient illumination and my eyes are good), if I am going to write with it I need to have paper, a writing surface, a certain amount of light and so forth. I also need something to say, someone to say it to and a language in which to say it. This yields a sort of "pragmatic spatiality" of its own: the pen is "nearest" the postcard, and also very near the postbox, which in fact is down on the street corner, while the glass of water on my desk is part of a different context of use and so is, pragmatically speaking, farther away, at least while I am absorbed in my writing.

This context or "totality" of involvement must be operative *before* the individual things is encountered, since the thing is encountered as functioning within that totality: if I were not going to write the postcard, and make use of the entire postal system in doing so, I would not be able to encounter the pen or the postbox as useful. In encountering them that way, I subordinate myself to the overall context: "When we take care of things, we are subordinate to the in-order-to constitutive for the actual useful thing" (*BT* 69).

If now we follow out the contexts of involvement within which we encounter beings as ready-to-hand, they get wider and wider. An encounter with something as mundane as a pen, to continue the previous example, ultimately refers us to matters like our command of language itself and our relations with those to whom (or for whom) we are writing. "World", for Heidegger, means the totality of these contexts of involvement.

In one of the most famous passages of *Being and Time*, Heidegger argues that world ordinarily becomes visible to us when equipment fails to function: fails to take us smoothly where we want to go. When that happens, the being is no longer equipmental. Instead of being unthematized, it becomes obtrusively present-at-hand:

> As a deficient mode of taking care of things, the helpless way in which we stand before it discovers the mere objective presence of what is at hand.   (*BT* 73, trans. mod.)

> Something is unusable. This means that the constitutive reference of the in-order-to to a what-for has been disturbed. References themselves are not [normally] observed, they are "out there" in our heedful adjustment to them … But in a disturbance of reference – in being unusable for … – the reference becomes explicit. The context of useful things appears not as a totality never seen before, but as a totality that has been continually seen beforehand in our circumspection. But with this totality world makes itself known.   (*BT* 74–5, trans. mod.)

169

This widening process of tracing out contexts of involvement is not endless, however: eventually it reaches a point that does not itself "fit into" any wider purpose or structure. This ultimate involvement is with Dasein, for the sake of which our various interactions with things and people are carried out (*BT* 84). In the same way that the pen refers to the postcard and postbox, they in turn refer to Aunt Bertha, to whom I am writing, and to my relationship with her. The meaningfulness of world always refers back to Dasein itself: either me myself, or others, or all of us indeterminately.

This account of the basic human activity as one of handling things within a context of involvement was widely perceived as philosophically revolutionary, as indeed it was; but it is not entirely without precedent in philosophy. One of its clearest antecedents is to be found in Aristotle's *Nicomachean Ethics*, which opens with the words: "Every art and every inquiry, just like every action and deliberation, is thought to go after some good" (*Eth. Nic.* I.1 1094a1–2, my trans.). Aristotle goes on to give examples of how goal-directed activities are embedded in larger pursuits – as bridle-making is embedded in riding and riding in warfare – all of them homing in on a single overarching goal, that of *eudaimonia* or human flourishing. Heidegger's often repeated formula for expressing the way contexts of involvement are embedded in larger contexts, *um-zu* or "in-order-to", is a German translation of Aristotle's *heneka hou*.

INAUTHENTICITY, AUTHENTICITY AND DEATH

Beings ready-to-hand are disclosed to me in terms of the uses to which they can be put. In such disclosure, they point to concrete characteristics of me, the individual Dasein who is to use them. My own personal work surface contains pens and paper and three by five cards, for example, rather than saws and hammers. The pipes I like to smoke while working are on the right, while the pens are on the left because I am left-handed, and so forth. The workspaces of other professors and students probably look rather different. A carpenter's or a surgeon's workspace is very different from all of them. These differences in our workspaces, however, do not usually go all the way to individuation; my workspace, while different from those of certain other people, is not as unique as I am. Put more generally, the Dasein referred to by the ready-to-hand around me is, very often, not the individual, unique person that I think myself to be, but a sort of average "mock up" of a human being.

Consider, for example, public transport. In my use of it, if I am to use it correctly, I have to be aware that it is intended to be used by people other than myself. Trains and buses do not necessarily run when I am there to catch them, and they rarely go exactly where I want to go. The existence of others is presented to me, in a non-thematic way, every time I hurry to catch a train, or pore over a bus map trying to figure out which bus to take; and this would be true even if, *per impossibile*, I always used public transport in the dead of night and never actually saw another passenger. The existence of other people is not something I need to step back and infer, as it is for Husserl, but inheres in my correct use of the technology in question, just as grasping a hammer by the handle is part of using it correctly. Public transport, along with other such ready-to-hand entities as clothing, books, typewriters and so on, thus refers, not uniquely to me, but to "the random, the average" (*BT* 71).

With this, we have Heidegger's account of what he calls "Being-with", the most basic mode of interpersonal relation for him. That his account of this develops it out of our encounter with tools, and the contexts of involvement through which tools address us, entails that our primary "relationship" is always to world; our relations to others, and to ourselves, are constituted in terms of our Being-in-the-world. If Dasein is not primordially alone in its world, then, it is not primordially face to face with other Dasein, either, *à la* Martin Buber (cf. Buber 1958). Dasein is, as it were, side by side with other Dasein, in that all are alike referred to by the concrete contexts of significance and purpose that make up their common world.

This means that the "others" who are given to Dasein in this way are not given as concretely distinct from Dasein itself. They are, as Heidegger puts it, others "from whom, for the most part, one does *not* distinguish oneself – among whom one is too" (*BT* 118). My Being-with others is thus a stratum of my own Being, which is average, random and indistinct from those others.

In §27 Heidegger claims there are only two attitudes an individual can take towards her own aspect of Being-with others. She can recognize it as what it in fact is, as merely one aspect of her Dasein, or she can treat herself as wholly identical with it. The latter is the usual case, says Heidegger (*BT* 131). Indeed, every time I function as indistinguishable from others, I function as identical with just one aspect of myself: the "dominance of the other" is taken on in Being-with itself (*BT* 126), in the sense that I act as others do and my actions are, to that extent, controlled by the "random, average" character of Being-with. In such cases, Heidegger refers to Being-with as the "they", or *das Man*, another Heideggerean term best left untranslated.

Das Man is thus intrinsic to Being-with others, and so to Being-in-the-world. It is a basic property, or "existential", of Dasein. As such, it cannot be overcome and left behind by authentic Dasein; authenticity itself is a "modification" of it and a sort of "breakthrough" from it (*BT* 129, 131; also cf. *BT* 179).

Das Man is thus a constant tendency of Dasein – and it is not restricted to "external" things such as public transport. It extends to our very activities of thinking and evaluating:

> We take pleasure and enjoy ourselves as *they* [*man*] take pleasure; we read, see, and judge about literature and art as *they* see and judge; like-wise we shrink back from the "great mass" as *they* shrink back; we find

"shocking" what *they* find shocking. The "they" which is nothing definite and which all are, though not as the sum, prescribes the kind of
Being of everydayness.   (*BT* 127)

The reason why Dasein ordinarily identifies itself with only that aspect of
itself which is "random and average", says Heidegger, is that Dasein is intrinsically "disquieted" by its "distance", or distinction, from other Dasein. The
reasons for this disquiet remain to be explored; but the mere fact that in this
disquiet Dasein measures itself against das Man (in Heidegger's term, "distanti-
ates" itself) means that Dasein takes das Man as a standard to which it tries to
conform, and so forsakes its own concrete individuality.

Thus, the bifurcation that the pimary dimension of Being-with undergoes
in its more concrete structures is not a dichotomy between alternatives of
equal weight. The world itself is always a shared world, and "refers" to me as
an average person; my inherent tendency is then to identify myself with that
average. Occasionally I rise above this, and take explicit account of the fact
that although world as such is always shared, certain of its aspects in certain
situations are not. Then I am being "authentic". But such occasions, although
important, are rare and painful.

Why the pain? Why is Dasein "intrinsically disquieted" by its differences
from others? One reason, which Heidegger points out in §27, is that by identifying myself with das Man I can "disburden" myself of responsibility for what
I do (*BT* 127). By adopting the moral and evaluative standards that das Man
prescribes, I absolve myself from having to judge, much less decide, anything
for myself. But there is another reason. My own love of the blues, the way that
music speaks to me in the depths of my Being, comes partly from my youth
in the Mississippi Valley and the train whistles I heard, as a small child, in the
Illinois night. As such, it will not outlive me; the Times Square subway station,
by contrast, will. To the extent that I can ignore the depths of my Being and
identify myself with mundane, but ongoing, structures such as the use of mass
technology or (on a more intellectual level) the values, prejudices and insights
that permeate my society as a whole, I can achieve a spurious sort of immortality (*BT* 249–67).

Heidegger's account of death in *Being and Time* is one of his most important,
and one of the most important steps in his restoration of temporalized philosophy. It is intimately connected to his views on authenticity. Its implications
are even broader than that, however, for it is here that Heidegger comes into
confrontation with Aristotle. We can begin to see this from a point Heidegger
makes in §49: that death is the "end" (*Ende*) of Dasein (*BT* 246–9), its result or
outcome: that towards which it is headed. On the one hand, this is obvious; but
Heidegger is also, I suggest, taking "end" in its specifically Aristotelian sense of
final cause or *telos*, which is not obvious at all, and in fact requires some serious
rethinking of what a "*telos*" is.

For Aristotle, the *telos* of a natural being is the form of that thing that has not completed the process of coming-to-be in that thing's matter. As long as this is the case, the being in question is not what it is eventually going to be if things go as they normally or naturally do. What it is eventually going to be is its "*telos*". When it becomes that, achieves its *telos*, the *telos* becomes its "form". Thus, the form of a human child, which, for Aristotle, is reason, does not yet have control of all the matter it will eventually control. Hence, the adult is the *telos* of the child. Heidegger has thus replaced human flourishing – which, as I noted above, for Aristotle was the overarching *telos* of human life – with death. But what can it mean to say that death is the *telos* of Dasein? What does Heidegger think death is?

Death as Dasein's unknown telos

At *BT* 250, in a singularly knotty paragraph, Heidegger gives a preliminary statement of some main points in his understanding of death. First, death is universal: it stands before, or impends for, all Dasein, which has to "take it over in every case" (*BT* 250). Second, as Dasein's *telos*, it is Dasein's most basic possibility, its "ownmost potentiality for being". Because of this, there is nothing in Dasein that escapes death: Dasein is "fully assigned" to it. Since nothing about Dasein can escape death, death undoes all Dasein's relations to other Dasein; we die entirely alone. Finally, Heidegger says a page later that we are reminded of all this in a particular feeling, which he discusses at greater length elsewhere: the feeling of "anxiety" or *Angst* (*BT* 251). This, of course, recalls Kierkegaard's concept of dread (*angest*). But for Kierkegaard death was not ultimate; it was our entry into our true future, eternity. For Heidegger, whose philosophy is not based in religion, death is final; even if we are immortal, we cannot know it. It is death itself, not the possibility of eternal damnation, that awakens dread in us.

Heidegger's more detailed discussion of death is keyed to his distinction between authentic and inauthentic. First, in §51, he discusses inauthentic views of death; then he shows, in §52, that a key component of this view implies that another, authentic view is possible; and then in §53 he tells us what that view is.

In §51 he claims that the "everyday" way we experience death is as present-at-hand, and so as decontextualized. While entities ready-to-hand are encountered through ongoing contexts, when something is present-at-hand those contexts have been buried over – and buried with them, in the case of death, our connection to death. This disconnected death is presented to us in two ways: as a discrete event in our lives that is still some way off, as a death that is essentially "not yet"; and as the death of somebody else, but nobody in particular, as the death of das Man:

> In such a way of talking, death is understood as an indefinite something which, above all, must duly arrive from somewhere or other, but is proximally not yet present-at-hand for oneself, and is therefore no threat. The expression "one dies" (*man stirbt*) spreads abroad the opinion that what gets reached, as it were, by death is the "they." In Dasein's public way of interpreting, it is said that "one dies," because everyone else and oneself can talk himself into saying that "in no case is it I myself," for this "one" is the "*nobody*." Dying is leveled off to an occurrence which reaches Dasein, to be sure, but belongs to nobody in particular.
>
> (*BT* 253)

This "tranquillization" of Dasein in the face of death does not so much conquer *Angst* as disallow it (*BT* 254). But it has a weak spot, for the "not yet" that it labours so hard to validate betrays two disquieting sides to our experience of death. These are explored in §52, and in turn point the way for the account of the authentic experience of death in §53. The first of these is that if death is not *yet* here, then it is coming, for certain (*BT* 255). This provokes Heidegger into a long discussion of the nature of certainty, which I shall pass over here. The second implication of the "not yet" is that if that is all we can say, then we are unable to specify just when death will come for us. It is possible at any moment, and therefore indefinite. Much as Derrida will later do with all manner of texts, Heidegger has here "deconstructed" the everyday attitude towards death: he has shown that the device that it uses to achieve itself, the "not yet" view of death, is, when pushed a little further, the very device that undoes it. When it is undone, another way of experiencing death becomes visible.

That other, "authentic" way of experiencing death is brought out in §53. The key clue here is that death is a "possibility". This, in turn, means that we relate to it as we do to possibilities. How is that? One way we relate to possibilities is in seeking to realize them. This is what we would be doing if death were our "end" in the full Aristotelian sense, but it will not work here because it would amount to seeking suicide, a quest that is neither authentic nor everyday but pathological. Another way is to realize the possibility in thought, that is, to try to imagine it in detail and otherwise "brood" (*grübeln*) over it. This too cannot work, because death:

> as possibility, gives Dasein nothing to be "actualized," nothing which Dasein, as actual, could itself *be*. It is the possibility of the impossibility of comporting oneself towards anything, of every way of existing. ... It knows no measure at all, no more or less, but signifies the measureless impossibility of existence. In accordance with its essence, this possibility offers no support for becoming intent on something, "picturing" to oneself the actuality which is possible, and so forgetting its possibility.
>
> (*BT* 262)

Part of being a possibility, then, is to be empty. Our ultimate possibility is wholly empty and in that sense could turn out to be anything; our death is utterly without measure. How do we experience this authentically?

We experience it as certain but indefinite, in other words as impending and as empty. Because of the latter characteristic, we do not experience death directly; we do not imagine it as an event. Rather, we see its effects in our lives as we live them. Heidegger's term for this is *Vorlaufen*, translated as "anticipation" but much more active than that; it literally means to "run ahead" to death. In this:

> one is liberated from one's own lostness in those possibilities which may accidentally thrust themselves upon one; and one is liberated in such a way that for the first time one can authentically understand and choose among the factical possibilities lying ahead of that possibility which is not to be outstripped. (*BT* 264)

It is the fact that we are going to die, at some unknown time, that requires us to make those authentic choices. If I were going to live forever, I would not have to choose a life partner. I could marry every other member of the human race and live a hundred years with each. Nor would I have to commit myself to a career, or to a community: I could be a farmer for sixty or seventy years, then open a legal practice in Sacramento or fish in Marseilles for a couple of centuries, and then enter a lamasery on the high slopes of Tibet. It is because we are mortal that the major decisions we make require us to let some possibilities go past *definitively*. The authentic experience of death, then, is commitment to the life we are leading now. And this commitment, finally, is "authenticity".

Our death thus structures our present to its very core. It means that each of us, always, is feeling along the edge of something radically unknown but impending, and the necessity of that groping is what it is for Dasein to have a future. We have a future, are *essentially* futural beings, because we are going to die. And we live coherent lives, rather than merely drifting, for the same reason. Death, as the "end of Dasein", thus performs the same function that a *telos* does for Aristotle: it organizes our lives around our basic commitments, or at least provides the impetus for us to do so.

We can also see that the radically unknown character of our death communicates itself back to everything else that we encounter as ready-to-hand. For to understand something as ready-to-hand is to understand its possibilities for us. And to understand those possibilities – in so far as they *can* be understood – is to understand them in terms of their possibilities in turn, and so on, until we get to the final possibility, which is totally unfathomable because it is our death. Nothing ready-to-hand can be fully understood, then.

In all phenomena, there is thus something that does not manifest itself, which integrates that phenomenon into our lives, guides our encounter with it and thus makes it cohere with itself. This something – Heidegger calls it Being – is non-manifest, but can, to some degree anyway, be made manifest by the attentive openness of the phenomenologist. It is the unknown and impending future of the thing.[4]

But Heidegger has not given a full account of how a thing can be made clear for us in terms of its future. For we have, in *Being and Time*, just two ways of encountering things: as present-at-hand, in which case they have no future and no past; and as ready-to-hand, in which case they are affected by their unknown futures but are themselves not thematized by us, and hence not known. Is there a way of encountering beings that allows them their temporal dimensions yet does not look away from them to their meanings?

"THE ORIGIN OF THE WORK OF ART"

This essay, from 1935, is perhaps Heidegger's most important single text, since it looks both backwards to *Being and Time* and forwards to his late writings. While its title suggests that its importance is limited to aesthetics, in fact it generalizes *Being and Time*'s account of death in significant ways.

Heidegger begins by pointing out that when we ask about the "origin" of the work of art, we run into a circle. Such a work can only originate, we think, in the activity of an artist. But what makes an artist an artist? The fact that she creates a work of art. Hence the circle: the work of art originates in the activity of the artist; but that activity can be artistic only if it creates a work of art. Common to both sides of this circle is, of course, art itself: artist and work are only artist and work if they somehow conform to what art itself is. But what is that? This is a question about whether, how and as what art in general exists. It is a question about what the philosophical tradition would call the "essence" of art, and Heidegger approaches it in a very traditional manner: he asks after the genus and species of art. Since works of art present themselves to us as a particular kind of thing, their generic nature is to be "thingly". Whatever it is that makes them works of art, their specific "workly" nature, then supervenes on this. What, then, is a "thing"?

Heidegger discusses three conceptions, taken from the history of philosophy, of what a thing is. Two of them appear to be of special importance to him: the views of the thing as a substance with attributes, and as matter and form. The substance–attribute ontology was first articulated by Aristotle at the beginning of his *Categories*. There, this view is derived from the subject–predicate structure of propositions, and so it is associable with "theoretical" approaches to things. The other view is, for Heidegger, derived from the nature of equipment: both form and matter, he writes, are ultimately determined by what a thing is to

---

4. I have discussed this part of Heidegger's thought extensively at McCumber (1999: 205–51).

be used for (OWA 28), and so the matter–form view sees things as equipment (OWA 26–30). The third, Kantian view of the thing as the unity of a manifold of sensible givens is treated at notably less length (OWA 25–6). One reason why the other two views are more important than this one, perhaps, is that they are respectively *Being and Time*'s categories of present-at-hand and ready-to-hand (cf. *BT* 66–72, 92–6). Heidegger is thus revisiting the ontology he had suggested in that book, and doing so in a self-critical way.

He argues, in fact, that both these views of what things are fail to capture a certain aspect of at least some things. From the point of view of the substance–attribute interpretation, this is the thing's *Eigenwüchsigkeit*, or "self-grownness", and its *In-sich-Ruhen*, or its "coming-to-rest in itself" (OWA 24–5).[5] From the matter–form point of view, it is the "self-sufficiency" of the class of things that are artworks (OWA 29).

These terms point, although not entirely clearly, to the idea that a "thing" has an internal, dynamic structure of its own. From the substance–attribute point of view, a "thing" is something that grows up by itself and comes to rest within itself. From the matter–form point of view, a "thing" is something that makes, and fulfils, demands upon itself: some parts or phases of it, we may say, place constraints that are met by other parts or phases. The qualities of self-grownness, coming-to-rest in self and self-sufficiency thus refer to the sort of internal dynamic that, we saw, was part of the concept of phenomenon advanced in *Being and Time*. Heidegger is, then, asserting that both the basic categories advanced in that work – that of the present-at-hand and of the ready-to-hand – fail to grasp fully the character of the thing as phenomenon.

The substance–attribute schema fails because it embodies an "assault" on the nature of the thing (OWA 24–5). It attempts to understand the nature of things in terms of a conceptual construct – the idea of substance itself – rather than in the phenomenological terms of our lived experience of them. According to the "metaphysics of substance", which we have also seen Nietzsche criticize, the determinate attributes of a thing inhere in an underlying "substrate". The substrate of a substance, since it underlies all its determinate properties, is itself indeterminate and so is not something we can ever experience; we must infer that it is there, which makes it a conceptual construct (OWA 25). The manifold phenomenal data we actually experience are viewed in terms of this construct, that is, as related to each other through the putative relation of each to the unknown "substrate" that is thought to support it: a model we saw Heidegger himself criticize in *Being and Time*, §7.

The understanding of things as "equipment", for its part, misses their internal dynamic because it too comprehends the thing in terms of something other

---

5. In the English translation, *eigenwüchsig* is rendered as "independent" and *In-sich-Ruhen* as "self-contained", thus missing Heidegger's careful contrast.

than it: here not a conceptual construct but the thing's very usefulness (OWA 28–9). In the terms of *Being and Time*, we encounter an entity ready-to-hand by looking beyond it to the context of its significance, and to the meaning it may have for an individual Dasein. Such an entity is defined in terms of its context, and, as we saw, encounters with entities ready-to-hand leave those entities unthematized. Encounters with entities as present-to-hand, since it leaves those contexts themselves unthematized, can hardly reveal their internal dynamics.

"The Origin of the Work of Art" thus begins with a critique of the ontology offered in *Being and Time*. Both the categories of ready-to-hand and present-at-hand, it argues, fail to capture what we might call the "phenomenality" of things: the way they present themselves to us in our daily experience of them. But is such a capture really necessary? Is there a phenomenality to things at all, or is Heidegger merely constructing an arbitrary concept and then criticizing other approaches (including his own previous one) for not capitalizing on it?

Heidegger's answer is that there is at least one class of entities that can and must be treated as "phenomenal" in the sense indicated: works of art. In discussing Van Gogh's painting of a pair of old shoes, Heidegger contrasts our experience of those shoes in the work of art with what he considers to be the peasant woman's experience of the originals.[6] She simply wears them, puts them on and takes them off, and in that context of daily use is not aware of them (OWA 34). It is we who see them, in the painting. They are equipment for her, but objects of explicit awareness for us.

This awareness is not a "theoretical" one, which would hypostasize the shoes as spatiotemporal objects with various properties: as substances. We are not, in the work of art, made aware of a series of propositions about the shoes that, simply because they are about the shoes, tell us little or nothing about their wearer. In a lyrical description of what the picture of the shoes reveals to us, Heidegger shows that the entire context of their use is evoked by the way the artist draws them: the rugged heaviness of their construction, the dark opening of their insides, the dampness of the leather as painted call up the climate, landscape and labour in which and for which they are worn (OWA 33–4). The whole work-world of their wearer shines forth in their presentation by the artist: "the more simply and authentically the shoes alone are [presented], the more directly and engagingly do all beings attain to a greater degree of being along with them" (OWA 56).

Van Gogh does not directly portray the relationship between the shoes and the world of their wearer. He does not, for example, paint the peasant woman actually wearing the shoes as she trudges through the fields. The shoes are not

---

6. Heidegger famously got this wrong, for the shoes Van Gogh painted were in fact his own. To correct Heidegger here, we can simply generalize his account a bit further: *someone* wore those shoes, trudged around muddy fields, walked slowly home in them, and so on; it was not a peasant woman, but a Dutch artist.

even portrayed as lying on the floor; they are in an "undefined space" (*BT* 33). The world of the wearer of the shoes, their context of significance, is evoked entirely through the portrayal of various facets *of the shoes themselves*.[7] This pair of shoes, worn through in just these ways, we may say, cannot be conceived apart from hard work in open fields. The shoes themselves, as presented in the work of art, do not merely "evoke" the work-world of their possessor; they define that world, and are defined by it. The interplay between the shoes and their context of significance is thus internal to the shoes themselves, and constitutes the "internal dynamic" of those shoes, that which makes them what they "truly" are as phenomena (OWA 35–6).

The work of art thus sets up its own context of significance: it "belongs, as work, uniquely in the realm which is opened up by itself" (OWA 41). Because this realm is opened up by the work, it is not a realm in which the beholder of the work normally lives: "in the vicinity of [Van Gogh's] work, we were suddenly somewhere else than we usually tend to be" (OWA 35). Where we usually are for Heidegger is in our own "everyday" world (*BT* 117–30), which is encountered in terms of entities ready-to-hand for us (or for those with whom we share that world) to use. Because we cannot use the shoes that Van Gogh paints, they do not constitute a part of our world. This is even more the case when the work of art presents a context of significance that itself is strange to us, as in the case of artworks that have survived from previous historical periods (OWA 40–41). The fact that works of art can remain meaningful even when the world that produced them has vanished only strengthens the contention that the context of significance the work "opens up" is independent of the overall context of significance that is the world of its beholders, or of its makers (*ibid.*). It is in opening up its own context of significance that the work of art is "self-sufficient" in a way that entities ready-to-hand within a pre-established world cannot be. Further, the process by which this realm is defined and explicated in the work of art is one of self-contained dynamic development, or *Eigenwuchs* and *In-sich-Ruhen*. Heidegger thus replaces the twofold ontology of *Being and Time* with a trichotomy of "mere" thing, equipment and work of art (OWA 29).

The context of significance opened up by a work of art is as unique as the work itself, and so is not part of the world of those who behold the work. They cannot use the work of art, and it does not "refer" to them as inner-worldly entities do. The work's context is thus a totality unto itself, and as such can be called a world of its own. It is, then, the function of the work of art as such, as Heidegger puts it, to "set up a world" (OWA 42; also cf. OWA 44). But what, here, does it mean to "set up" a world?

---

7. This, of course, is why Heidegger can wrongly claim that the shoes belong to a peasant woman.

We can approach this question by asking first what sort of situation precedes such setting-up, and here the answer is twofold. On the one hand, world arises only through and for human beings (OWA 44–5), and human beings, as we know from *Being and Time*, are always already in a world. So any world must arise from a previous world. The question of how this happens is one of the deepest in Heideggerean scholarship, and I shall hardly try to answer it here. This much, however, is clear: if world is the overarching totality of contexts of significance to which Dasein can be open, then a new world arises when people find themselves open to a new such overarching context.

Because the context in question is overarching, the new world cannot emerge from the old via any sort of dialectical negation or otherwise-conceived rational critique. If it did, the very concept of dialectical negation (or rational critique) would be one in terms of which both worlds could be understood: it, and not they, would be the "overarching" context of intelligibility. Thus, the emergence of a new world from an older one must be the emergence of something new and truly incommensurable with the old: "The truth that discloses itself in the work can never be proved or derived from what went before. What went before is refuted in its exclusive reality by the work" (OWA 75).

"What went before" is not simply abolished, then, by the work of art; it is merely "refuted in its exclusive reality", that is, the work makes available an alternative to it. It does this by presenting its new contexts to Dasein that already lives in a world, and as such already possesses certain ways of understanding and interpreting the significance of that world. Those previously acquired horizons must then persist as a sort of background, within and against which the new world emerges (OWA 66, 74, 77). Thus, worlds originate in works of art: art is historical, not merely in that it changes with history, but in that it grounds history (OWA 77) and so true human community (OWA 68).[8]

A work of art, in setting up a new world, brings us a specific future: not the infinite future of Kierkegaard's eternity, or the empty field of struggle that is the future for Nietzsche; and still less the unfolding of things already going on in the present that Marx tried to predict. But we do not yet have a complete account, even in outline, of the way this newness arises, for at least two reasons. For one thing, there are many "new worlds" spun from the heads of artists and thinkers.

---

8. This may sound, to contemporary ears, counter-intuitive in the extreme. Seeing in more detail how it is supposed to work will occupy us later; but we may note here that Heidegger understands "art" in an unusually broad sense. From what we have seen here, any creative act that opens up a new world is artistic for him. Such performances could include, for example, setting forth a radically new scientific theory, *à la* Einstein, or coming up with a radically new system of government, *à la* America's founding fathers. Heidegger's dismissive remarks about science as being "not an original happening of truth, but always the cultivation of a domain of truth already opened" (OWA 62) would then apply only to what Thomas Kuhn calls "normal science": science that is limited to puzzle-solving within an already accepted paradigm (Kuhn 1970: 33–4, 111, 119).

Only a few are accepted by society at large and become great art, and there must be something beyond imagination and whimsy to account for this (cf. OWA 49, 72). Second, phenomenologically speaking, there is more to art than ideas spinning from artists' heads: there is also the concrete, "thingly" character of the work of art, and this remains to be brought out (OWA 46).

EARTH

To every work of art there belongs a "material". In art at least, this material is not inert, for if it were there would be no way to distinguish the way a furniture factory turns out hundreds of virtually identical tables from the way an artist produces something unique from the materials at her disposal. A good sculptor pays attention, for example, to the grain of the wood she is carving, and seeks to bring it into her finished statue, in the spirit of Michelangelo's famous remark about the artist setting free forms that are already present in the individual piece of marble he confronts (cf. Heidegger's treatment of a similar statement by Albrecht Dürer at OWA 70). The material element of a work of art, then, is not inert but dynamic and configurating. Heidegger portrays the stone of a Greek temple not as a mere inert lump, but as interacting with the rock on which the temple stands, with the weather and sunlight, with the nearby sea and local life forms. These natural givens of the temple's site and material define it and are themselves evoked by it; they are thematized, or made explicit, in our encounter with it. They, like the world of the peasant woman, become what they "truly" are through their relation to the work of art that stands in their midst (OWA 42).

Heidegger calls this dimension of the work of art "earth" (cf. OWA 28, 42, 46, 48–9). Earth, we may say, functions here as a realm that I have elsewhere called a realm of "pre-significance" (McCumber 1989: 133). The prefix is important. On the one hand, the "pre-" indicates that the work of art comes from, belongs within and thematizes the natural significance of its site (OWA 46). On the other hand, as a realm of "pre-"significance, the earth is not significant itself: its significance remains latent, "undisclosable" (OWA 47). The work of art preserves this undisclosability: "The earth appears openly cleared as itself only when it is perceived and preserved as that which is essentially undisclosable" (OWA 46–7).

A given piece of wood, in other words, may have in it grains, colours and stress lines that enable it to be carved into a certain statue. The sculptor, if she is a good one, will allow herself to be guided by these, so that the statue comes about through a kind of collaboration between the sculptor and the wood. But the wood itself cannot bring forth the interrelations of veins and stress lines that make that statue uniquely expressible in it. And since the statue, even when carved, remains a thing of wood, that closed-offness never wholly disappears. The statue never loses its dependence on a domain that is inherently undisclosable. To put this more generally, world – the open space of meaningfulness

– is dependent on earth, the pre-significant realm, which, as "pre-"significant, always hides itself anew.

Heidegger goes on to call this mutual dependence of two active forces a "dispute" or "strife"[9] in which world seeks to open up earth and render it meaningful, while earth seeks to escape world and return to its primal concealment: "the repose of the work that rests in itself thus has its presencing in the intimacy of strife" (OWA 49–50, trans. mod.). It is its dispute with the domain of natural pre-significance, then, which gives the work of art a "resolute foundation" (*Entscheidendes*) and keeps it from being a mere play of whimsy (OWA 49).

This relates to truth in Heidegger's sense of "disclosure", of the removal of something from concealment, for in the strife of earth and world, specific meanings are brought forth and world itself is disclosed as meaningful. Hence:

> Earth juts through the world and world grounds itself on the earth only insofar as truth happens as the primal strife between clearing and concealing … Setting up a world and setting forth the earth, the work [of art] is the instigation of the strife in which the unconcealment of beings as a whole, or truth, is won. (OWA 55)

Art is thus connected to truth, but not to timeless truth that would exist "somewhere among the stars, only later to descend elsewhere among beings" (OWA 61). Rather, the work of art brings truth about in such a way that truth is dynamic. This dynamism, unsurprisingly, is an orientation to the future: because truth consists in the strife between world and earth, and earth is itself concealed, there always belongs to truth "the reservoir of the not-yet-uncovered, the un-uncovered, in the sense of concealment" (OWA 60). Earth, then, is not something that already exists somewhere "out there", sending new significance that is presented in the work of art. Rather, it is futural in character: the domain of the not-yet-disclosed.

Since the significance that comes to us in the work of art is radically new, it cannot be known in advance. The same is true, we saw, of our death: we know that it is coming but not when, and we have no idea what it will be like. As such, the future conveyed by the work of art shares the opacity of death in *Being and Time*. But the not-yet-disclosed of earth differs from that of death for Heidegger in two important ways. First, opacity is now generalized to all disclosure as such; the concealment with which truth begins is presented as our future itself, rather than as its final event. Second, this future, instead of being the single possibility of no more possibilities, is a whole set of concrete possibilities. It is thus a *specific* future. What was in the "reservoir of the not-yet" for Julius Caesar – including

---

9. *Streit*; the translation tones this down to "striving", which eliminates the Heideggerean undertone of linguistic contention.

such things as the Roman Empire, its fall and the triumph of Christianity over paganism – are not in our future today. The kind of future Heidegger is talking about is thus not infinite, like Kierkegaard's future-as-eternity or Nietzsche's limitless field of further struggle. It is a finite future – *our* future.

We, as humans and philosophers, are supposed to respond to this future with *restraint*. The future bestowed on us by the work of art is radically different from our present and "displaces" us from our current world:

> To submit to this displacement means: to transform our accustomed ties to world and to earth, and henceforth to restrain all usual doing and valuing, knowing and looking, in order to stay within the truth that is happening in the work. Only the restraint of this staying lets be what is created by the work that it is. This letting of the work be a work we call the preserving of the work.   (*OWA* 66, trans. mod.)

When we "submit" to the displacement Heidegger ascribes to the work of art, we begin dwelling in the world it opens up for us rather than the world we ordinarily live in. This makes us "preservers" of the work of art. We preserve a work of art when we confront it as a unique context of significance and allow it to reveal itself progressively as the unique phenomenon that it is, thus allowing it to project us into an entirely different world. This way of experiencing a work of art is a condition for its being a work of art at all (OWA 67).

To be a "preserver" of a work of art, then, is to allow our perceptions, and eventually perhaps our lives, to be guided by it. But as we have already seen, an artist is also guided by the earth of the work she is creating. Hence, the artist herself is merely one member of the community of preservers, and no more essential to it than the others (OWA 71, 78). While the work of art manifests its own createdness in that it preserves the mutual otherness of earth and world, thus showing that someone had to "create" the work of art, its ties to a *specific* creator and to the *specific* time and place of its creation, are undone (OWA 66).[10]

Heidegger's account of how to go about preserving a work of art is both minimal and negative: a mere matter of "restraint". What we are to refrain from in preserving a work of art is the kind of approach exemplified by the three accounts of "thingliness" discussed at the beginning of the essay: taking conceptual frameworks with which we are already familiar and carrying them over to a new experience, thus hiding from ourselves just how new that experience may be. Exactly how preservers join together to experience a work of art cannot be set forth in general, however, because every work of art is unique: "the proper

---

10. Like Hegel, Heidegger presents art as a social, communicative phenomenon by refusing to view it exclusively as the creation of an individual genius: both writers, in fact, refer to the creator as a mere "passageway" or "corridor" for the truth her work expresses (OWA 40; Hegel 1975a: 298).

way to preserve the work is cocreated and prescribed only and exclusively by the work" (*OWA* 68). Every work of art must be preserved in its own way.

LANGUAGE AS POETRY

As we have discussed it so far, "The Origin of the Work of Art" contains two major innovations on *Being and Time*. First, it enriches *Being and Time*'s twofold ontology into a threefold ontology of ready-to-hand, present-at-hand and works of art. Second, world is no longer ultimate, as it is in *Being and Time*, but is grounded and defined by something else: the realm of pre-significance, or the earth, which as futural is inherently "undisclosable" (OWA 42–3).[11] A third innovation is that language is now much more important than it was previously, for it plays an important role in the setting-up of worlds through art. On the one hand, as we saw, the earth offers only pre-significance, not significance, and this was in virtue of the fact that purely natural entities could not be "open" to one another. Language brings such openness about, not in virtue of being a set of propositions or an instrument of communication, but in its aesthetic function of opening up a world. The vehicle of such opening is the *name* (OWA 73).

This point depends on the fact that names always convey information about the object named. Any name in ordinary language tells us, at a minimum, that its bearer is important enough to have been responded to, at some time, by an act of naming. Most names, especially common names, tell us a good deal more than that. The name attached to a thing informs us, in more or less definite ways, what sort of thing the entity in question is. It conveys to the hearer of the name what sort of response she might make to such an entity under certain circumstances. In Heidegger's terms, names tell us *as what* the named entity is to be understood (OWA 73). That such is the case for common names, such as "horse" or "house", is indisputable; it has not always been held to be the case for names of individuals, or "proper names".[12] But there are, in fact, complex regulations for bestowing proper names on entities that deserve them, as is witnessed by the agonies that parents often go through trying to name their children. Certain names are more appropriate than others for certain types of entity: "Fido" is not, in English, an acceptable name for my son; but *Phaidōn*, in ancient Athens, was somebody's son. "Pikes's Peak" is not a good name for a

---

11. All "essential" social decisions are said to be grounded in this primordial dimension. Nothing a state or society does can ever be fully justified, then; all decisions, as grounded in something "concealed, confusing" (OWA 43f/55) are open to challenge.

12. Thus, for John Stuart Mill (to give an early example of this way of speaking), proper names are "denotative" but not "connotative": they "denote the individuals who are called by them, but they do not indicate or imply any attributes as belonging to such individuals" (Mill 1970: 20). A proper name, so viewed, designates an object, but conveys no information about it.

dog. And chickens, usually, do not have names at all; humans the world over, apparently, do not give names to what they are planning to eat.

The name of a thing thus brings it into, or in Heidegger's term "projects" it onto, a context of significance. In *Being and Time*, such projection was part of how entities showed themselves as ready-to-hand. Now they require to be named in order to do this. When such a "projective" naming occurs for the first time, it is "poetic" in nature; it places a being for the first time into a context of significance, which – since this is the first time – is new and unique, and so in Heidegger's sense artistic (OWA 73–4). Such language need not, to be sure, be what we would ordinarily *call* poetic. Although in "The Origin of the Work of Art" Heidegger discusses his realm of pre-significance primarily with reference to natural phenomena, he makes the same sort of point with regard to high-order philosophical conceptions as well: the principle of sufficient reason, for example, was "latent" within language for centuries before Leibniz gave it explicit formulation (Heidegger 1971b: 14), and this latency can be understood for Heidegger in the same way as the latency of the *Pietà* in Michelangelo's block of marble.

Heidegger is able to conceive of poetry in this way because he has shown that poetic language is, so to speak, earthly. As radically new, it is "detached" from the pre-existing world of the poet and her audience. This detachment means that by bringing earthly pre-significance into the openness of world, poetic language grounds and transforms world (OWA 74–6). If world is historical, then poetic naming, too, is historical in that, like all art, it grounds history (OWA 77).

In detaching poetic language from world, however, Heidegger has also detached it from other kinds of language as well, including not only conceptually abstract sorts of language but all ordinary language as well. Our everyday speech, after all, hardly consists in a series of breakthroughs to radically new contexts of significance, and Heidegger says (OWA 40) that he is considering only great works of art. Thus, the kind of language that is dealt with here has nothing to do with our ordinary efforts to find our way around in the world and to help others to do the same. As Werner Marx has put it for Heidegger's later works in general:

> The "everyday" modes of the Being of man, which played such an important role in *Being and Time*, are no longer studied. Nor is it asked how the creative modes of man might determine the everyday modes or whether and how these everyday modes are "derived" from the creative modes. The problems of the "self" in its capacity to stand in its own remain undiscussed. (Marx 1971: 214)

The next generation of continental philosophers – including German-educated philosophers of the stature of Arendt and the Frankfurt theorists Adorno and Horkheimer, as well as the French thinkers Sartre and Beauvoir –

will perceive the strange detachment of Heidegger's later thought from concrete realities as a trap they need to avoid. In this they will be joined by many other philosophers in Europe, America and elsewhere, and the result will be the most important explosion of social thought since Marx and Engels reshaped Hegel into materialism. Yet in escaping this trap, they will – from the point of view of temporalized philosophy – fall into another one. For their aversion to the later Heidegger will lead them to base their understanding of Heidegger on *Being and Time*, which will in turn lead them to understand the future on the model of death rather than that of earth. And this, finally, will lead them to miss two significant advances made in "The Origin of the Work of Art".

First, the essay sets limits to our knowledge in a particularly vigorous way. In saying that the knowable, meaningful aspects of works of art ("world") are dependent on unknowable, pre-significant aspects ("earth"), Heidegger is saying nothing new. Aristotelian form could not exist without matter, and Kantian appearances, according to Kant himself, needed Kantian things-in-themselves to be appearances *of*. In contrast to these familiar philosophical themes, Heideggerean earth is dynamic; its relation to world is not merely one of causality, but one of strife as it tries to maintain is undisclosedness in the face of world. And this means that the "reservoir of the not-yet", which conditions our experience of things, contains *specific* capacities for radical surprise. The future is not merely the general blankness of the unknown, as it was for Nietzsche, but a *particular* blankness that is already shaping our *particular* present. There are some things, then, that we can know our future will not contain. It will not contain the Greek understanding of Being, for example; that is proper to another time, to a bygone world. Nor will it include, if we are Germans, being ruled by Louis XIV; he belonged to France (or France to him). For Nietzsche and Kierkegaard, such things cannot be excluded from our future, for our future is entirely unknown, the dreadful unfathomability of Kierkegaard's eternity or the blue sky of Nietzsche's great noon.

Second, we begin to see from the later Heidegger how to allow for this in our thinking. Heidegger's characterization of this in "The Origin of the Work of Art" is negative: we are not to approach beings the way the three ontological views Heidegger criticizes do – with fixed conceptions (in this cases, fixed conceptions of what they have to be to be beings at all). Nor do we approach them with no conceptions at all, as if we did not already dwell in a world. Rather, we approach things by restraining our preconceptions: by refusing to accord them exclusive validity. We do not deny our usual ways of thinking and valuing, and so on, but we are ready to abandon them if our experience of the phenomena does not bear them out. This readiness-to-abandon is the meaning of the restraint Heidegger identifies as the basic nature of preserving, and so is not merely a subsidiary part of our approach. The central issue in any late Heideggerean interpretation of anything is whether or not our preconceptions should, in this particular case, be maintained or abandoned.

In Heidegger's later writings such as "The Question Concerning Technology", to which I shall now turn, to focus on whether a concept works or should be abandoned in a given case is to "question" that concept. On this later and more positive account, the way for thought to open up to the future is to formulate the right questions. The central insight of Heidegger's later years, from the perspective of later continental philosophy, is that the proper way to confront the future is not with Marxian predictions, or Kierkegaardian *angest*, or Nietzschean confidence, but by finding the right questions. This insight will be revised and exploited by "postmodern" thinkers in general.

QUESTIONING TECHNOLOGY

"The Question Concerning Technology" suggests this in its very title. It was published in 1953, when Heidegger was sixty-three years old. Like most of Heidegger's writings, it is very dense, and Heidegger's way of structuring his later writings is very untraditional. Heidegger says right at the beginning that the point of the essay is to ask questions, not to prove a thesis or even, ultimately, to suggest one. Moreover, the questions he will be asking are in a certain sequence, that is, constitute a "way": "We would be advised ... to pay heed to the way, and not to fix our attention on isolated sentence and topics" (QT 287).

Heidegger's concept of a "way" can be viewed as his late version of what *Being and Time* called a "phenomenon". Where a phenomenon was unified by Being, which gathered the stages of its gradual self-revelation together without being either one of those stages or any determinate property of the thing, so a Heideggerean way is unified not by the discipline of a theme or a thesis, but by something that, like the earth of "The Origin of the Work of Art", does not become clear: by something that is accessible only in and as questions. Thus, as you read through the essay, every so often you get a barrage of questions. Sometimes the questions take up an entire paragraph. These barrages of questions, eleven in all, are not, as they would be in other thinkers, orientating devices that stand outside the essay's basic argument. They constitute the main "joints" of the essay, and my account will focus on them.

Question 1: The fundamental question of technology: what is technology?

The fundamental question of the essay – What is technology? – is what, since Socrates, has been called a *ti esti* question: it asks what something is (QT 288). Heidegger answers it, although only provisionally, with statements of "what everybody knows". In this he is following another ancient guideline, which Aristotle called "dialectics". In Aristotelian dialectics, thinking begins not from what is true, as it does in conventional views of inference, but from what is *commonly accepted* (see Arist. *Top.* 100a20–24). What is commonly accepted about the nature of technology is in fact two things: that it is a means to an end, and a human activity. These two everyday truisms are closely related, because means and ends do not exist in nature, at least, not in nature as we view it today (Aristotle had a different view, which Heidegger will get to). They are imposed on it by our thinking, and so are products of human activity. When I see a river depositing mud in its delta, and say it is doing that "in order to" create farmland, I am viewing the river in anthropomorphic terms; in reality no such conscious process is at work in the river.

According to these everyday views, then, modern technology is a means, a set of tools. Our relevant human activity is to use it, and it is something we must use *in the right way*. If technology is causing trouble for us, then we must not be using it in the right way. It has somehow slipped from our control and turned against us. What we need to do, then, is to reassert our mastery over our tools, to start using them in such a way that they serve our purposes, rather then having unintended effects (in the sense that pollution, say, is an unintended effect of a factory): "The will to mastery becomes all the more urgent the more technology threatens to slip from our control" (QT 289). If we look at it this way, the problem is basically Nietzschean: we need to subdue technology by an act of will, assert our control over it. But Heidegger rejects this path. He asks us instead to question this everyday view: to make a supposition that technology is *not* a means, and is *not* a human activity. Then seeking to control it better may be precisely the *wrong* thing to do. Such an approach may miss the real problem because it misses the real nature of technology.

Note that Heidegger thinks it is perfectly correct (*richtig*) to say that technology is a set of instruments, means to ends, and also that it is a product of human activity. But these views, although correct, may not be true: they may not grasp the "essence" of technology. There are a couple of larger issues here. One, which will not be answered until late in the essay, is that of what an "essence" is. Another, more urgent, is: what does it mean not to be true but merely correct?

The term "human being" can be defined in many ways. We are the only apes with chins and earlobes, for example, so I could define "human being" as "ape with chin" or "ape with earlobes". We are the only animal that laughs; why can we not define human beings as "laughing animals"? Why does the philosophical tradition insist on calling us "rational animals"? Heidegger would answer that all the other definitions, while accurate to the facts and so "correct", do not tell us what we need to know. I am not greatly helped, in my dealings with Bill, if what I know about Bill is merely that he has earlobes and a chin. That Bill can laugh is more informative, but derivative: Bill can only laugh because he can perceive incongruities, and he can only perceive *incongruities* because he can perceive *congruities* – because he knows what normally happens in the world, and so because he is rational. So the ability to think is more basic than the ability to laugh. As a definition for human being, "rational animal" is thus more basic and more informative than its competitors, or, as Heidegger would put it, it opens up more possibilities for us. The definition of humans as rational animals gives us many clues as to how to deal with human beings: we can talk to them, lie to them, make promises to them and so on. It permits us to relate to them in a variety of ways: it gives us a "free relationship" to them. Hence, Heidegger says that "Only the true brings us into a free relationship with that which concerns us from [on the basis of] its essence" (QT 289).

The question of "free relationships" will come up again later. For the moment, what we have is a suspicion: maybe the essence of technology is not to be a means to an end, and instrument. This gives us a new question.

Question 2. What is the instrumental itself? Within what do means and ends belong?

In answering this question (QT 289), Heidegger first notes that to be a means is to be a sort of cause. But what is a cause? He goes back to Aristotle's standard account of the four causes: the matter out of which something is made; the shape or form that comes to be in the matter; the activity that puts the form in the matter; and the purpose for which this is done. We tend to look at these in terms of human activity: I shape the wood into a table so I can have a place to work. But we have many different ways of making things, and they do not have much in common.

Question 3. Why are there just four causes?

In fact, the Greek word for cause – *aitia* – did not, Heidegger notes (QT 290), originally have anything to do with making things. It meant "responsibility". The four causes are the kinds of thing that are most basically *responsible* for something else. Start with matter. Then, since a thing is not mere matter, you must add in the form: the specific way the matter looks to someone, or its "aspect". Third, you must add in the way the form and matter exist together in the thing; this togetherness, when it happens, is the final phase of the thing, the phase where it is "finally" what it should be. It is then the "final" cause (often misunderstood as a conscious purpose or goal, as when we say the river deposits soil "in order to" create farm land).

Finally, you need something that brings form and matter together in the final state of the thing: what Aristotle called the "moving cause". Here, and only here, you get to the idea of making things. Except it is not making as creating; it is a *bringing-together of pre-existing elements* (form and matter) into the final thing. The thing itself, indeed, was "there" all along, but it was latent, because dispersed. Think of all the food you are going to eat in your life: it is not all there today in some giant refrigerator, but is dispersed throughout the world. Producing something, then, is bringing its components together so that the thing itself is manifest. This sounds like Michelangelo and the statues again, and, according to Heidegger, it should. For as he points out, the Greek word for this activity of producing things is *poiēsis*: our word, poetry. Heidegger is thus generalizing his account of the work of art into a more general account of what we do when we make things.

According to the standard account, which even today is derived from Aristotle, when we make something we first think out what we want it to be, and then we try to rework some matter around until it resembles our picture. Heidegger is suggesting that making things is better seen as taking beings that already have a dynamic of their own (like earth in the work of art), and getting them to work together. Making things is not "producing" them out of our heads, but a gathering-together of elements that already exist somewhere. This is clearly a much more *respectful* way of looking at one's materials than viewing them as mere matter to be manipulated. It is also very close to peasant labour: when you cultivate a plant, you do not make it. You allow it to make *itself*, by giving it water and food and so on. You cultivate it. Heidegger generally has a cultivation model of production, which means that he does not think we are nearly as creative or powerful as we like to think we are.

This way of looking at human activity also makes it much more natural. For human activity so viewed merely piggybacks on processes of nature, which does this sort of thing all the time. Water and nutriment coming to plants is something that happens without farmers, without human intervention of any kind. Then we call it "nature" (*physis*).

Question 4. How does this happen?

Causality, understood as the Greeks understood it (and it is they who first started thinking about it in ways that would be preserved for future genera-tions; QT 293), is thus a complex process in which the most basic components of a thing – matter, form and finality – are brought together by a "moving cause", which *may* be a human being. Bringing together the components of a thing makes that thing manifest, whereas before it had been only a possibility latent in the components as dispersed. Because it makes things manifest, this process is a happening of "truth". The answer as to the "how" of causality, then, is that the *process happens as truth*.

Question 5. Wohin haben wir uns geirrt? Where have we strayed to?

This is a crucial question, for it reveals that the "path" of this essay has in fact been a "straying" or "wandering" (*irren*). Heidegger would insist – although perhaps not convincingly – that he did not set out to get us to this particular place. He merely asked questions that suggested themselves in turn, and gave answers one by one. But now we see that without intending to, we have come to the edge of a major insight: "Technology is therefore no mere means. Technology is a way of revealing" (QT 294). It is a way, not of looking at the world (which we could change at will), but of *having the world look to you*. It reveals things in certain ways, *as* certain things. Heidegger supports this view by pointing out that the Greek word at the root of our word "technology", *tekhnē*, refers in Aristotle to a kind of knowledge.

But this has all been developed out of considerations of Greek thought. Does it hold for modern technology, which is obviously very different from the "technology" of the ancient world (hand tools, oars, sails, carts, oxen)? Heidegger's answer is that if we simply pay attention, we can *see* that modern technology too is a way of revealing. But it is not a gathering-together of beings that have their own independent natures, as when Michelangelo brings a certain unique stone together with the equally unique story of David, both of these being ongoing things whose guidance the sculptor must respect. Rather, modern technology *ignores* the uniqueness and independence of the things it brings together in various ways: it "claims" (challenges or demands, *fordern*) the things, which it uses merely as instruments. It does not respect the things it deals with for their uniqueness and independence, but claims them as energy, which can be extracted from the thing and stored in various ways (QT 296). Since everything has a certain amount of energy in it, and modern technology cares only about that, from the point of view of modern technology all things are alike: they vary only in the amount of energy they contain. Hence, for Marx's capitalist, the workers were merely a source of "labour-power". That they had families, aspirations and cultural needs was of no importance in the capitalist system.

Consider, as an example of *ancient* technology, something dear to Heidegger: a peasant's field. The peasant turns the soil with the plough and opens it up so the seeds can receive the nutriments from the soil, air, water and sunlight. The peasant thus brings together soil, air, water, sunlight and the seed. So, of course, does modern planting equipment. But unlike the combine, the peasant does not change the field significantly. He does not need to level the field off so large machines can be used on it. Nor does he pour chemicals purchased from distant factories on to it so it can nourish plants that, of themselves, would never grow well there. The farmer cultivates the field, but he does not "claim" it. He lets it be the field that it was.

Claiming (*fordern*) is by contrast an "expediting" (*fördern*). It takes the field, or the wind, or the coal deposit, or whatever, and unlocks and exposes just one thing: the energy latent in them. In this way, it does reveal those things, or make them manifest. But it does not do this in such a way that they reveal their own unique natures. It reveals them for the sake of something else, for the energy they contain, in accordance with "maximum yield for minimum expense" (QT

297). This is done, finally, in order to have a stable supply of something or other: of electricity, or of foodstuffs, or whatever. The ultimate aim, then, is to "regulate and secure" nature.

Question 6. What kind of final state (unconcealment) does this tend to?

This leads ultimately to a situation in which everything is there for us just when we want it: "immediately on hand, [standing] there so that it may be on call for a further ordering" (QT 298). Heidegger calls this state *Bestand* ("standing reserve"). Modern technology thus tends to reduce everything to *Bestand*. Such things are no longer *Gegen-stände*, objects; they do not stand opposite to us, as the German suggests, for they come from our activity of reduction. They are "ours".

Question 7. Who does this?

We do it, but only on a superficial level (QT 299). The contractor who grades the hillside for a car park is claiming a chunk of nature as a *Bestand* for the cars (and the owners of the car park). But she is not wholly responsible for this: after all, she has to earn a living. No one individual creates this whole way of assaulting nature. Each of us does it because we must: because that is how things are done in our society. So each of us is "challenged" to operate in accordance with technology as challenging and expediting. Again, this can be compared with Marx: the bourgeoisie did not create capitalism; estranged labour is not the result of conscious activity of human beings. It has come about because of the way technology developed. Similarly for Heidegger.

Question 8. If man is challenged, ordered, to do this, then does not man himself belong even more originally than nature within Bestand?

We too, in our activities, are thus compelled to conform to the kind of revealing that is brought about by modern technology; the mere fact that companies have departments of "human resources" is an indication of this. A forester today who works for a large timber corporation may walk through the forest just like his grandfather did, but it is not the same, because he is an employee of a company that is going to chop down thousands of trees, changing – and perhaps destroying – the forest that his grandfather respected: "He is made subordinate to the orderability of cellulose"(QT 299). We could not change this even if we wanted to. Although we are the active force here, and for that reason not merely *Bestand* like other things, we are not in control. Nobody is.

Question 9. Where and how does this revealing happen if it is no mere handiwork of man?

Where it happens (QT 300) is everywhere, because revealing in general claims us *to our very core*; there is nothing in us that is not caught up in this way of being claimed by technology. How it happens is conveyed in Heidegger's overall name for this claiming and expediting, "which gathers man thither to order the self-revealing": *Ge-stell*. Here Heidegger takes over a word from ordinary German – where it means a frame for something, like a book rack – and uses it for his own conception, developed via his "wandering" or "straying" pathway of thought. *Gestell* is, then, Heidegger's name for the essence of modern technology. It denotes a frame that clamps down over everything, including us, and allows us to experience things – reveals them to us – only as potential energy or as commodities. The activity of *Gestell* is thus worlds away from the ancient conception of human action in the world as a bringing together of independent and unique components: as *poiēsis* or, I have suggested, cultivation.

Heidegger's thought has been following, or, more accurately, building, a "pathway". As we saw, that pathway led from question to question, without his worrying about exactly where he was trying to get to. But it has taken him someplace: to a new word – or, more precisely, to an old German word used in a new way – *Gestell*. *Gestell*, or "enframing", is the way modern technology reveals things to us: as a "standing reserve" (*Bestand*) of energy. Heidegger's path of thought, structured by questions, has led to the kind of thing he talked about in "The Origin of the Work of Art": to a new name, which locates what it names within a radically new context. Once we have acquired the word *Gestell*, Heidegger's pathway ends. After QT 301, the essay is no longer structured around questions in the way that it has been. The point of the questions has been to open up a set of phenomena and to experience them deeply enough to arrive at a name that conveys (to Germans, anyway) new contexts of significance.

Now Heidegger goes on to show how *Gestell*, his "new" word, can illuminate for us various other things that are going on, what sort of "danger" it presents to us, and what we can hope to do about it. The first topic in this regard is the nature of modern science.

Modern science is not, for Heidegger, at bottom a disinterested search for truth. This is because it has a presupposition that is too basic to be proved or disproved. This is the presupposition that nature is a "calculable coherence of forces" (QT 303). Because this presupposition of science cannot be proved or disproved, we cannot know whether it is true or false. If we adopt it, then, our adoption cannot be based on considerations of truth. Science is a search for truth – that is certainly a "correct" way to describe it – but only on the basis of this unprovable presupposition.

If scientists did not have this presupposition, they would never do experiments. It is therefore more basic to science than the experimental method itself:

"Because physics, indeed already as pure theory, sets nature up to exhibit itself as a coherence of forces calculable in advance, it orders its experiments precisely for the purpose of asking whether and how nature reports itself when set up this way" (*QT* 303).

If an experiment does not yield clear, quantified data, it is a "bad" experiment. Since our experiences of the world do not normally yield such data, physics gets further and further from experience. Where ancient physicists talked about balls and weights, things we can see around us, contemporary physics talks about quarks and mesons and string theory. Physics has pursued measurement so far beyond the bounds of experience that "its realm of representation remains inscrutable and incapable of being visualized" (*BT* 304).

What is Heidegger's problem with this? Does he think that nature is *not* a realm of calculable forces? No. He agrees with physics. What he is *questioning* (that word again!) is the idea that calculating the forces in operation around us tells us very much about *us*. The laws of physics could predict, for example, that the World Trade Center would come crashing down at some point; but knowing how that event occurred physically does not tell us what we really want to know about it. For the laws of physics, just because they are laws, tell us what *always* happens. They cannot capture the awful uniqueness of that event, or indeed the uniqueness of any event that affects us. That the World Trade Center succumbed to the first terrorist attack carried out by foreigners on American soil, thereby changing how each American felt about American soil, is not a matter for physics. Nor is it a fact of experimental psychology. It is a *historical* fact. Science can tell us how things happen regularly in the natural world. What it cannot tell us is how those happenings will affect us, as individuals, as communities, as nations.

What can? Nothing can. If the effects of 11 September 2001 followed from general laws, they would be predictable. But what 11 September showed is that our future is *radically open*. To be sure, *the* future – the set of all things that will happen in the universe – may be governed by laws of nature that we already know. But we cannot know *our* future: how those events will affect us. And this is not just true on the scale of world history and major events such as earthquakes or 11 September. Getting married, or getting a college degree, are also leaps into the unknown. Science, by contrast, deals with things in so far as they are calculable, which means in so far as they are examples of things that happen all the time: of laws of nature. It is thus predicated on a denial of the openness of the future. When we set science up as the model for all human knowledge, for Heidegger, we are pretending to ourselves that the future is predictable. This is an exercise in reassurance, but it is a delusional one.

This brings us again to what, from the perspective of continental philosophy, is the heart of Heidegger: his concern with our future. He thinks (rightly) that we are basically afraid of our future: of how wide it is, and of how it is going to end (with our death – the unpredictable inevitability). So we tend to deny that breadth of possibility by *narrowing down the future*. We tend to shrink the possibilities that we have. In all his writings, from *Being and Time* on, Heidegger seeks to develop ways in which the true width and breadth of our future can be opened up.

But he does not think that the future can be opened up to infinity, as Nietzsche and Kierkegaard thought; that, for him, would merely instate another kind of absolute. This is why he is so interested in questions, rather than answers. A question points us to a *specific* future: towards the quest for its answer. It is, for him, better to have a good question than its answer, because it is where we have questions that our future is open. As the final words of "The Question Concerning Technology" put it, "questioning is the piety of thinking".

Question 10. Does such revealing happen somewhere beyond all human doing?

Heidegger has now (QT 305) asked another question. But it does not move him forwards on his pathway the way the previous ones did, because it is not a new question. It is a return to question 6, which he is asking again. He is doing so in order to bring out another aspect of our relation to technology.

This relation, we saw, went to our very cores. Because of this, we are "claimed" by modern technology in a way even deeper than are the things of nature that modern technology destroys. Our relation to *Gestell* is, then, hardly a "free" one. But Heidegger, at the very beginning of the essay, said that his aim in writing it was to "prepare a free relation" to the essence of technology (QT 287). How is that even possible?

Everything for Heidegger, I said, is in time. This view has special implications for something that is basic. Let us say that a property is "basic" to us if we can have it without having anything else. Being a human is traditionally basic to me in this sense: no matter what colour eyes I have, or what religion, or what nationality: I can change all those things and still, more or less, be me. But if I am no longer human, it is hard to say that "I" exist at all. My humanity is therefore more basic to me than my eye colour, or religion, or nationality, in that it is only on the basis of it that I can have them. If I lose it, I lose everything. As long as I have the status of a human being – as long as I have the body and mind that make me a "rational animal" – I am me. If we put this notion of basicness into time, we get the idea that something is basic to us if we have it *before* we have anything else, not only logically but temporally. The state of having just that basic something is then the state in which we start out.

Being claimed by the *Gestell* is something basic to us, Heidegger has claimed, and so it is something that we have before we have other characteristics. As something that happens to us, it is something that "starts us off". Something that most basically starts us off is what Heidegger calls a "sending" (QT 305). A sending "sends" us on to a determinate pathway. It determines us, although not completely. It is our "fate".[13] When such a sending is really basic, like *Gestell*, it does not just determine us as individuals. It determines the "pathway" of our entire community. In this way, "it is from this destining that the essence of all history (*Geschichte*) is determined" (QT 306).

Our freedom comes in how we *respond* to this basic sending/destining action. For destining, like everything else, has its own unpredictable future. Just what possibilities a particular destining opens to us or closes off from us are therefore not knowable in advance. There is thus a *mystery* at the heart of all sending/destining, and this mystery allows us to be free: "All revealing belongs within a harboring and a concealing. But that which frees – the mystery – is concealed and always concealing. [Such] freedom consists neither in unfettered arbitrariness nor in the constraint of mere laws" (QT 306).

Since technology is a form of revealing, it is also a form of concealing: it puts us on to a pathway, but not one that we can fully understand in advance. Because of this, we know that there will always be some leeway for us. Although the basic parameters of our lives are given to us by our destining – in the case of modern humans, by *Gestell*, with all its unsavoury characteristics – we are not wholly determined by it:

> When we consider the essence of technology we experience enframing [*Gestell*] as a destining of revealing. In this way we are already sojourning within the open space of destining, a destining that in no way confines us to a stultified compulsion to push on blindly with technology or, what comes to the same, to rebel helplessly against it and curse it as the work of the devil. (QT 307)

The two come to the same because they are both ways of trying to attain mastery, in one case by using technology, in the other case by fighting it. A "free" relation does neither of these things. What does it do? It shows us how wide the possibilities are. And, says Heidegger, they are today very wide indeed:

(a) *either* we simply push forward with technology, as it demands that we do, in which case we become mere tools and cogs – mere *Bestand*;
(b) *or* we experience technology in its essence, that is, see it for what it really is, a way of revealing that leaves things loose for us (QT 307).

Placed between these extreme possibilities, we are in *danger*: "not just any danger, but *the* danger" (*BT* 308).

---

13. The German word for "fate", *Geschick*, is etymologically related to the word "to send", *schicken*.

Alternative (a) is possible because *Gestell* imposes itself on us as a way of seeing *everything*. It thus tends to grow and push out all other ways of experiencing things: to "drive out every other possibility of revealing" (QT 309), including, of course, the older sense of production as *poiēsis*. But it drives something else out as well: "Where enframing [*Gestell*] holds sway, regulating and securing of the standing reserve [*Bestand*] mark all revealing. They no longer even let their own fundamental characteristic appear, namely this revealing as such" (QT 309).

Since all revealing is partial and provisional, *Gestell's* tendency to instate itself as the one and only way to see things also tends to obscure its own nature as a revealing. When *Gestell* becomes the only way we can experience revealing, then, we cannot experience revealing *as revealing*: we cannot experience its partiality and provisionality. We cannot then experience our own basic nature, and are, so to speak, lost to our essence.

And now a way out begins to dawn.

Question 11. Might not an adequate look into what enframing is, as a destining of revealing, bring the upsurgence of the saving power into existence?

Here what is required is an understanding, not of "technology", which we are already beginning to get, but of "essence" (QT 310). An "essence" is traditionally understood in philosophy to be a specification of the basic nature of a thing: of "what" that thing is. So understood, technology's essence is to be *Gestell*, a particular way of revealing. Essences are also traditionally understood to be enduring, and this, again traditionally, means that they never change: philosophers as early as Socrates and Plato "think what endures as what remains permanently (*aei on*). And they find what endures permanently in what persists throughout all that happens in what remains" (QT 312).

This presupposes that there are two kinds of things: things that change, and things that do not. Everything we ever experience falls into the former class, but their essences, or as Heidegger calls them here Ideas, do not: you were once young and you will be old one day, but your basic humanity does not (supposedly) change in any respect. Yet, again traditionally, such an essence is not merely a passive something; it is what makes you what you are. After all, if you did not have your human essence, you would not be human; it is what makes you act and react in the ways that you do.

Heidegger has a more dynamic concept of essence to propose: a concept according to which that which most basically makes you what you are does not exhibit itself in a single set of specifiable characteristics. You have an "essence" in the sense that there is something that makes you you, but it has no single nature, it can change in fundamental ways, while you are still you. The manifold activities that make you you, then, are not exercised *by* anything determinate: they are simply there, pure activities. They unify you and make you what you are, but have no underlying nature of their own; they are a mystery. Heidegger's name for this activity of unifying that is not exercised by any "unifier" is "granting" (QT 313).

We can make this more comprehensible, and perhaps more plausible, by recalling what it was that unified our lives and shaped our identities in *Being and Time*. This was death, as the necessary but unknown limit to our lives. Granting, too, is an unknown but shaping force, but Heidegger does not identify it as death. Conceived more widely than the concept of death in Heidegger, it is closer to earth in "The Origin of the Work of Art", or to the finite Heideggerean future. Granting is thus the activity of the future, as the unknown that sets limits to what is and thereby unifies it. Because it is the future, it is open, although as a finite future it is not *boundlessly* open.

What Heidegger calls "challenging" is anything but a granting. Challenging provides no leeway, but has very specific criteria according to which it reveals beings: the calculations of maximal return, of security and order. So what is the relation between granting and the challenging that is the work of *Gestell*? The answer is that granting is more basic than challenging. For when destining first starts us off, its nature is unclear: that is when it is still "granting". As we move on, its nature becomes clearer, but that is secondary and, the future being what it is, temporary.

So technology is ambiguous. On the one hand, it is a challenging or claiming of beings, including most primordially man, a claiming that tends to instate itself as the only way we can experience anything. On the other hand and more deeply, it is the granting from which this challenging comes. To experience technology as both kinds of thing is to have a "free" relation to it. Since our ordinary relation to technology is to be challenged by it, this relation is only possible if the other side of technology – its revealing–concealing, "granting" side – is allowed into our experience.

Doing this, however, is the job of art. From this point of view, our problem today is that we have decided that art is something that is walled off from everyday life, something that we encounter only in museums or concert halls. We thus order it and store it up; there is an art market where people seek to get the highest return on their artistic investments. In short (as Heidegger argues in other writings) art, too, has fallen victim to *Gestell*. Only when we see art differently, not as a special kind of experience with no relation to the rest of things but as itself a way of revealing things in general, can we work towards a free relationship with technology. In particular, we must see *poetry* that way, for poetry, as the art of language, is the most basic art.

CONCLUSION

There is, obviously, much to criticize on Heidegger's "pathway" of thought. Given the undeniable influence of that pathway, such criticism is among the most important intellectual tasks of our time. Yet many of the criticisms made of Heidegger are vitiated by their own self-indulgence. One common form of this self-indulgence is a lazy refusal to take Heidegger seriously as a philosopher, that is, as someone who has reasons for what he says, reasons, moreover, that he honestly thinks are good ones.[14]

It we do not take Heidegger seriously as a philosopher, then it is hard to see why we should occupy ourselves with him at all. For in that case, his views amount to nothing more than the expression of a personal standpoint: the standpoint of a person, moreover, who was himself sufficiently odious to deserve dismissal rather than critique. Yet taking Heidegger seriously as a philosopher has serious drawbacks as well. For one thing, as we have seen, it requires a lot of heavy intellectual labour to see just what his philosophical warrants are and then to evaluate them. Furthermore, the latter enterprise carries the unpleasant risk that some of his more odious views may in fact be warranted, forcing us to accept them. From the perspective of continental philosophy, Heidegger's advance is clear, not so odious and twofold: first, he has uncovered what I call the "finite future"; and second, he has suggested that the appropriate way to take account of this kind of future is via the question.

Heidegger first presents the finite future in his account of death in *Being and Time*. While this insight clearly grew from Husserl's concern for accurate description of our experiences, Heidegger's account of death contained a major innovation on Husserl. We can sum this up by saying that Husserlian consciousness does not die, any more than it uses things. Thus, while both Husserl and Heidegger place time at the very basis of the self, the Husserlian time synthesis can in principle go on forever. Because as we saw it has no content whatsoever, it does not even matter if I die; the synthesis as carried out in other ego's would be exactly the same. For Heidegger, I experience time primarily as the time I myself have left, as *my* future. The finitude of this future is underwritten by my death, and it means that although I cannot know what my future holds, I do know that it will bring some things and not others, because there is simply not enough time for everything. The future is thus not a radically open horizon, like the eternity of Kierkegaard or the pure blue of Zarathustra's sky. It is specific and impending, although unknown. We saw how, on Heidegger's "pathway", this was developed: from death into earth, a component of great works of art, then of poetry, language itself, and finally of thinking.

---

14. For a paradigm of the genre see Wolin (1994).

Heidegger's pathway also brought into view increasingly rich, although never very rich, views of how we are to respond to this finite future. The main lesson of *Being and Time*'s account of authenticity was that we should not deny it; the first ingredient was a courageous honesty in confronting death. In the account of the "preserving" of the artwork in "The Origin of the Work of Art", there was added to this a general refraining from imposing one's own concepts and practices, themselves inherited from the past and so parts of one's "world", on the complex sequence of novel experiences afforded by the art work. When this combination of confronting and refraining is no longer instigated by great art, but becomes a practice of thinking in general, it requires us also to focus on certain as-yet-unknowns, while still refraining from forcing them into the open.

Heidegger's term for this focusing–refraining–confronting is "questioning", and with that we have the answer as to how, rationally, we are to take account of the unknown but impending future. Such reason is not the forward march of argument, but the quiet wandering of Heideggerean "error". Heideggerean wandering attends to what is questionable in a philosophical or other text: to the arguments that do not quite work, the odd choices of words that are unexplained or even unnoticed, the topics that should be discussed but are not. This attention to the undone and the unsaid, to the conceptual gaps in our knowledge that open up our future, stands as Heidegger's "deconstructive" counterpart to Hegel's dialectical reconstruction of the past.

One problem with the finite future, which will come to haunt not only Heidegger scholarship but subsequent continental philosophers, is that it narrows the scope of our action and so of our responsibility. On Kierkegaard's view of our future, for example, it contains just two basic possibilities, salvation and damnation. These are unfathomably infinite, and we are therefore infinitely responsible for what we make of our lives. For Heidegger, our future is unknown but specific; our possibilities are not infinite, but belong to what he calls the "reservoir of the not-yet" before which we are placed by finding the proper questions. This does not absolve mortals from all responsibility, as some suggest (most notably Habermas [1989]), because if the "not-yet-uncovered" contained only one outcome, we would not need questions to uncover it; we could predict it. But it does narrow the scope of human action, because it finitizes our future: there are certain things we cannot undertake.

With this, the basic temporal repertoire, so to speak, of continental philosophy is in place. Later continental philosophers – the Germans Arendt, Horkheimer and Adorno, and the French Beauvoir, Sartre, Derrida and Foucault – will be concerned to understand humanity as situating itself "between past and future" (to use one of Arendt's titles) – and will seek in their own thought to do that as well. In so doing, they will place themselves between history and the finite or infinite future. In their own very different ways, they will occupy, consciously and conscientiously, the space that all philosophers have always occupied: the temporal stretch between the Greeks and their own readers.

CHAPTER 8

ACTIVITY AND MORTALITY: HANNAH ARENDT

PRIMARY TEXT Hannah Arendt, *The Human Condition* (*HC*; 1958)

In the summer of 1941, a woman known today only as Mrs Giduz sat down to write a letter. Mrs Giduz, of Winchester, Massachusetts, was a proper person, and she ran a proper household. The Giduzes did not eat meat, and Mr Giduz was not allowed to smoke in the house, which meant that he was often in the garden. He was therefore envious of their boarder, a thirty-five-year-old refugee who had been placed with them on a language-learning venture. She, at least, was allowed to smoke in her room: which she did, like a factory.

The good order of the Giduz household, and Mrs Giduz's watchful enforcement of it, chafed the younger woman, who in addition to her smoking habits was no stranger to meat and whose romantic life, in her early years, would have thoroughly shocked her good landlady: it included a student–professor affair with none other than Martin Heidegger. More seriously troubling to the boarder was Mrs Giduz's uncompromising pacifism: she was opposed to American entry into the Second World War, which was understandably disturbing to a German Jew.

It was with astonishment that Hannah Arendt one day saw this rigid, strait-laced woman, ridden with so narrow a conception of bourgeois propriety, sit down and write a letter to her congressman, protesting in no uncertain terms the internment of Japanese Americans by the United States government, her own government. That a single individual, and a woman at that, might believe that her letter could have any influence at all on someone as powerful and prestigious as a US congressman not only shocked Arendt, but delighted her as much as the enforced proprieties of the Giduz household oppressed her. She wrote to her teacher and mentor, Karl Jaspers: "The basic contradiction of the country is the combination of political freedom and social bondage" (quoted in Young-Bruehl 1982: 164–6, esp. 166).[1] The relation of the social sphere to the political one would occupy Arendt for the rest of her days.

---

1. Young-Bruehl (1982) remains the standard Arendt biography.

Arendt was born in Königsberg, Kant's home town, in 1906, six years after Nietzsche's death in Weimar. She began her philosophical studies in Marburg, where she met Heidegger and watched him become famous. She continued her studies with him and with Husserl after Heidegger went to Freiburg, but soon terminated her romance with Heidegger and moved to Heidelberg to study with Jaspers. After Hitler took power she was interned briefly but fled to France in 1933, where, as a foreign Jew, she was interned again. In 1941 she and Heinrich Blücher, who had become her husband, fled again to the United States, where she spent the rest of her life. She died in 1975, a year before Heidegger.

THE QUEST FOR IMMORTALITY AND *VITA ACTIVA*

Like other continental philosophers, Arendt has a profound, even urgent, concern with the thought and society of ancient Greece. Such concern follows, I have suggested, from continental philosophy's temporalized approach: its view that everything is in time. If everything is in time, all origins are in time, and there is no such thing as a cause that begins a series of events but does not itself have a place within that series. The cause or origin of a historical process is, then, to be found in the earliest stages of that process. In view of this, it is only to be expected that when Arendt seeks, in *The Human Condition*, to explain what she means by *vita activa*, the "tradition loaded" phrase which for her characterizes the core of the human condition, she should begin by uncovering origins that are purely historical, specific and, indeed, Greek: "Our tradition of political thought … far from comprehending and conceptualizing all the political experiences of Western mankind, grew out of a specific historical constellation: the trial of Socrates and the conflict between the philosopher and the polis" (*HC* 12).

Arendt's project, in fact, has two main phases. First, she traces our concept of *vita activa*, or the active life, back to a single event in the history of ancient Greece, thereby showing that contemporary moral conceptions originate in contingent and long-ago events rather than in some unchanging cosmic or divine order. She then uses the humble, temporal beginning she has uncovered to criticize the entire subsequent tradition of philosophical and political thought, with which her own investigation is said to be "in manifest contradiction" (*HC* 16–17). In both these phases, Arendt's undertaking resembles that of Nietzchean genealogy. Indeed, by appealing to the trial of Socrates, Arendt is being more historically precise than Nietzsche, whose genealogical project relied, as we saw in Chapter 5, not merely on facts but on such thought constructs as the slave revolt and on such generalities as ancient Germanic customs regarding the payment of debts.

Arendt's basic criticism of the "tradition" is that philosophy has always subordinated *vita activa*, the active life, to *vita contemplativa*, the theoretical life. This is only to be expected, given that those who wrote about the two styles of life were philosophers themselves, and so personally committed to *vita con-templativa* (cf. *HC* 14–15). From that point of view, however, they were led to see *vita activa* as a life of busyness and disquiet, rather than as true freedom: "Traditionally and up to the beginning of the modern age, the term *vita activa* never lost its negative connotation of 'un-quiet,' *nec-otium, a-skholia*" (*HC* 15).

Again, as with Nietzsche, the philosophical perspective is *merely* one perspective; it can in no way claim a privileged position with respect to truth. And, as with Nietzsche, the problem with the philosophical perspective is that it is oriented to what is taken to be eternal. For Nietzsche, our experiences with what we think is eternal constitute what he calls the "ascetic ideal"; for Arendt, they constitute *vita contemplativa*, the contemplative or theoretical life. For Arendt as for Kierkegaard, however, eternal truth is a realm completely different from all human life and community, so true experience of it can come only, if at all, with death (*HC* 20). In her view, the precedence of *vita contemplativa* over *vita activa* is therefore at bottom a matter of preferring death to life. Although a mainstay of philosophy, this preference is not philosophically justified:

> My contention is simply that the enormous weight of contemplation in the traditional hierarchy has blurred the distinctions and articulations within the *vita activa* itself and that, appearances notwithstanding, this condition has not been changed essentially by the modern break with the tradition and the eventual reversal of its hierarchical order in Marx and Nietzsche. (*HC* 17)

If *vita activa* is proper to life, however, it is to life lived in view of death. For *vita activa*, in Greek views, comes only with mortality. This restricts it to humans, because in the Greek way of viewing things, only humans are truly mortal. The gods, of course, never die; but nor do animals. An animal for the Greeks, as Arendt presents them, is merely an example of its species: my cat's individuality, the features that set him off from other cats, are unimportant. He will die, but everything important about him will live on, because it belongs to his species, *Felix domestica*. And in Greek thought, which was long before Darwin, species are eternal: "Men are 'the mortals,' the only mortal things in existence, because unlike animals they do not exist only as members of a species whose immortal life is guaranteed through procreation" (*HC* 18–19).

Because we humans know that we are going to die, we care about ourselves in ways that other animals cannot. What we care about is our individuality. Humans are thus truly human in virtue of the most painful and unfortunate thing about them: their mortality. Their recourse, as humans, is to seek not eternity, which is death, but a this-worldly form of immortality. They want to create traces of their existence that will live on in this world after they are gone. Those traces are other people's memories of their great deeds: "By their capacity for the immortal deed, by their ability to leave non-perishable traces behind, men, their individual mortality notwithstanding, attain an immortality of their own and prove themselves to be of a 'divine' nature" (*HC* 19).

In asserting the superiority of the contemplative life over the active life, in Arendt's view, philosophers opted for a false victory over death, one predicated on the belief that heaven, where one goes after death, is better than earth. When Socrates, motivated by such a belief, embraced the death sentence imposed on him by the Athenian people, he began philosophy's traditional preference for *vita contemplativa* over *vita activa*. For Arendt, Socrates' embrace of death was misconceived, for we cannot know what awaits us after death. To avoid that misconception, and restore *vita activa* to its rightful place in human life, we must therefore go back beyond the "classical" Athens of Socrates to the "archaic" Greece of Homer (*HC* 41n., 82–3n., 194, 205). Since Arendt does not focus on this in detail, I shall fill in a few of the gaps.

The *Iliad* and the *Odyssey* are written about a world that is very, very tough, a world that (like that of the 1981 film *Mad Max 2: The Road Warrior*) has emerged from the collapse of an earlier, more advanced civilization (probably Minoan). In this world there is no stable social order and you have to fight, often physically, for everything. An important feature of this early (or "archaic") Greek worldview is the absence of belief in a decent afterlife. When you died, they believed, your life force was largely extinguished and all that was left of you was a "shade", a weakened ghost. Thus when Odysseus, in the *Odyssey*, actually visits Hades, he sees the shades of dear friends, but hardly any of them is strong enough even to speak coherently to him. Only the strongest of heroes, Achilles, is able to do so, and, in terrifying words, he tells Odysseus:

> No winning words about death to me, shining Odysseus!
> By god, I'd rather slave on earth for another man –
> Some dirt-poor tenant farmer who scrapes to keep alive –
> That rule down here over all the breathless dead.
> (Homer 1996: XI, 555–9)

We can imagine that if you accept this worldview, you must be absolutely terrified of dying, but what is the alternative? Not until Socrates would any Greek thinker say that the afterlife has the capacity to be better than the life we lead here on earth; his view, we now see, amounted to "a reversal of the Homeric world order" (*HC* 292). What, then, can a denizen of Homer's world hope for? Again, Achilles tells us:

> If I hold out here and I lay siege to Troy,
> My journey home is gone, but my glory never dies.
> If I voyage back to the fatherland I love,
> My pride, my glory dies
> True, but the life left to me will be long. (Homer 1990: IX, 499–504)

Only your undying glory, the memory of you that lives on among your fellow human beings, can provide a meaningful immortality, because only it can survive your actual death in any meaningful way; you yourself cannot. This means, in turn, that your acts of supreme valour must be witnessed by other people. A great act that is not seen by other people cannot be remembered by them, and so is no good at all. It was therefore a matter of more than life or death for the archaic Greeks to have a space where they could be seen to do great things. For the Homeric heroes, this was the battlefield; and for Arendt, the battlefield was the ancestor of the *polis*:

> What the Greeks themselves thought of [the *polis*] and its *raison d'être*, they have made unmistakably clear. The *polis* … gives a guaranty that those who forced every sea and land to become the scene of their daring will not remain without witness and will need neither Homer nor anyone else who knows how to turn words to praise them; without assistance from others, those who acted will be able to establish together the everlasting remembrance of their good and bad deeds, to inspire admiration in the present and in future ages. (*HC* 197)

Thus: "The *polis* was for the Greeks, as the *res publica* was for the Romans, first of all their guarantee against the futility of individual life, the space protected against this futility and reserved for the relative permanence, if not the immortality, of mortals" (*HC* 56).

If Arendt's emphasis on Greek philosophy strikes us as Nietzschean in intensity, her view that the primacy of theory over activity needs to be overcome reminds us of Heidegger's account of the humbler activities of everyday Dasein. But Arendt's central claim, that our most human activity is political activity, understood and justified as a quest for immortality, is missing from both. Nietzsche and Heidegger have little to say about politics, and what they do say is extremely unpleasant and often immoral. They are not, to be sure, mere Nazi racists; but they are at best, as we saw, elitists of an uncompromising bent.

OIKOS AND POLIS

The classical *polis* thus comes to serve the purpose of Homer's archaic battlefield, and Arendt develops her own more detailed views via a critical confrontation with classical Greek thought, particularly that of Aristotle. In *HC*, chapter 2, she begins this by distinguishing between the ancient *oikos*, or household, on the one hand, and the *polis* – as its name suggests, the "political domain" *par excellence* – on the other. These were kept strictly separate in Athenian life, and each had its own set of rules. The *oikos* was a private realm, and was the main unit of economic activity (*oikos* is the root of the modern word "economics").

In addition to living space, it included the family business or farm, and was directed towards providing the means of subsistence for the family (*HC* 28). It was ruled by a *pater* or father; paternal power, being derived from nature, was close to absolute. In the *polis*, which was the ancient home of the *bios politicos* or political life properly so called, power was restricted: political leaders had to take account of the diverse opinions and desires of those they led.

The ancient *oikos* and *polis* no longer exist, to be sure; but contemporary society contains descendents of them. As we shall see in more detail shortly, the most important change for Arendt is that, over time, the lines between *oikos* and *polis* have become blurred, which means that the modern political sphere is taking on some of the characteristics of the ancient *oikos*. The result is "society", in which the concerns of the *oikos* for the preservation of daily life have overstepped their ancient bounds and become of public concern. What is left of the ancient domain of the *oikos*, now that its basic concerns have moved into the political realm, is what she calls the sphere of "intimacy" (*HC* 38–9).

Because the *oikos* was geared to staying alive and perpetuating the species, it was a biological or natural type of community – indeed, animals have such communities (*HC* 24). As such, it was based on compulsion and ruled by necessity: people lived together in households "because they were driven by their wants and needs" (*HC* 30). This, in turn, legitimized violence: "Because all human being are subject to necessity, they are entitled to violence toward others; violence is the prepolitical act of liberating oneself from the necessity of life for the freedom of world" (i.e. of the polis, or "political" sphere; *HC* 31).

As Aristotle notes, *oikoi*, or households, historically preceded *poleis*, or political structures (*Pol.* 1252b–1253a). Arendt is saying that this order is not merely temporal but logical as well. A political order in the ancient Greek sense *presupposes* violence, because it is by violence that we first tear ourselves free from nature. In this view of the "prepolitical" state – of how things were before there were states at all – we thus find, as we do with Hobbes, violence (cf. Hobbes 1991: 86–90). Here, the violence is not a Hobbesian "war" of "each against all", but is channelled within the structures of the *oikos*. The power of the father over the *oikos* is no longer purely natural, then; but it is not yet rational or political.

The most basic of the *oikos*' channels for distributing violence was kinship (*HC* 24–5). Kinship, because it is based in nature, is a realm not only of violence but more generally of inequality. A child must do what the parent says or else be punished, and in so far as a woman's physical weakness in comparison with her husband sets the tone for their relationship – as it did in the Greek world Arendt is invoking – the wife must also follow her husband's orders. This, for the Greeks, is a "necessity" of nature; there is simply nothing to be done about it. In modern times, of course, we no longer see these inegalitarian and violent structures of family life as necessary. Thus, a father who beats his wife or children today is subject to legal sanction; but an ancient father had the power of life or death over his children, and Plato's *Euthyphro* begins by presupposing that a father is allowed to kill even his grown slaves.

In addition, although Arendt does not stress it here, the *oikos* was a domain of conformity. This followed on its hierarchical and violent nature: the members of an ancient household were compelled to act and think in certain ways, and because they shared a life together those ways were, on important matters, also shared. Ideally, then, a household had one interest and one opinion: that of the *pater*. This conformity also meant, as we shall see, that work within the *oikos* amounted merely to humdrum repetition of standardized tasks: cleaning the floors, cooking the food, beating the slaves. The *oikos*, then, was hardly a domain in which to win lasting glory – even for the *pater*.

Finally, the Athenian *oikos* was a realm not only of violence and necessity but, as Arendt points out later on, of privacy and seclusion. This too had its reason: the *oikos*, being the place where human beings lived according to nature, was the place where the great mysteries of *human* nature had to be confronted: the sacred events where life is not maintained, but is begun and ended, that is, birth and death (*HC* 62–3). These things, as natural life events and as mysteries, should not happen in public.

The *oikos*, then, was natural, need based, hierarchical, violent, conformist and mysterious to outsiders. The *polis*, by contrast, was the place where the *bios politicos*, the political life, was lived. It was, we have seen, the place where men (i.e. not women) tried to overcome their own mortality by gaining undying fame. What was its nature?

On Arendt's account, the Greek *polis* is the descendent of the Greek battlefield: it is the terrain on which individuals try to win glory for themselves. Even though it was no longer a literal battlefield, the political realm remained for the Athenians "agonal", a realm of contest and struggle (*HC* 41). As such, it had no hierarchy other than that of winner and loser (*HC* 33). Because it was a realm where you fought with others and others saw you win or lose, the *polis* did not die when you did and was a "common world" more permanent than an individual life (*HC* 28). Your role in it could thus provide you with a kind of substitute immortality, which meant that life in the *polis* was not something to which animals or gods could ever aspire; only humans, who know they are going to die, had access to it. And it was a realm you entered, not because you had to, but because you wanted to: because you wanted your fame to outlive you. The *polis* was thus the realm of "freedom", defined as the opportunity to engage in these struggles for immortality (*HC* 30–31).

Where the *oikos* enforces conformity, the *polis* requires a diversity of viewpoints. At least two are needed because, put most simply, you cannot be seen from where you are (*HC* 57). Since no one sees himself or herself, those who bear witness to my exploits must see them from perspectives other than my own, not just physically but intellectually. The people you fight are obviously different from you; that is why you are fighting them. But in order to fight someone, you have to share a lot with them, such as concern with what you are fighting about. Even more different from you should be the others in the political realm, the onlookers. For your victory will be all the more notable if you best somebody in a way that is recognized even by people who are very different from you and do not understand much about you. As opposed to the forced conformity of the *oikos*, then, "The reality of the public realm relies on the simultaneous presence of innumerable perspectives and aspects in which the common world presents itself and for which no common measurement or denominator can ever be devised" (*HC* 57).

This diversity of perspectives needs to be guaranteed. How can we be sure that enforced homogeneity will not take over? The answer, somewhat paradoxically, is the *oikos*, which is therefore necessary for the *polis* in several ways. First, your *oikos*, your private property, is located in a different place from the homes of other citizens. Because of its separate location – and because of the wall around it – it is a private place to hide and rest (*HC* 71). Second, and more importantly, it is the place where your natural needs are taken care of, so that you will have time and leisure to engage in the public sphere. Third, and most importantly, it is a realm that, because it is private, comes to differ from other *oikoi*, which you never really penetrate. Your family's values and needs and concerns are thus different from those of other families, and this guarantees a diversity of perspective on public matters: "Originally, property meant no more or less than to have one's location in a particular part of the world and therefore to belong to the body politic, that is to be the head of one of the families that together constitute the public realm" (*HC* 61). So, for all their differences, the *polis* is unthinkable without the *oikos*.

Finally, I said above that the polis was not a literal battlefield, but that was perhaps misleading. Already in Homer, struggles for glory took two forms that will not only survive him but will outlast classical Athens to remain crucial in Arendt's account of the "human condition" itself: those of speech and action. Achilles was therefore, for Homer, not merely the "doer of great deeds", but the "speaker of great words" (*HC* 25). By this is meant not that he is long-winded, but that he was someone who could not only best others on the battlefield but could sway their opinions in councils: he was better than others at making clear what the community needed to do. Speech itself was thus agonal, a form of action: "Finding the right words at the right moment, quite apart from the information or communication they may convey, is action. Only sheer violence is mute" (*HC* 26).

Within the *oikos*, speech was of a different order, for no struggle was allowed: the *pater* gave the orders, and everyone else followed them. Hence, within the *oikos* there was no contest and no glory; excellence and virtue are only to be found on the *polis*. Indeed, because language itself is a form of action, even the most theoretical of philosophers undeniably entered the sphere of *vita activa* – when they wrote or taught (*HC* 20). Viewed as action, speech also participated in the humanity specific to the *vita activa*: it was "the specifically human way of answering, talking back, and measuring up to whatever happened or was done" (*HC* 26).

SPEECH AND ACTION

Together with her distinction between work and labour, for which it furnishes the basis, Arendt's discussion of speech and action has been the most influential part of her thought. Speech and action are, for her, closely related and exhibit, in differing degrees, the two traits most distinctive of humanity itself: our capacity for self-revelation and our capacity to initiate new courses of events.

Everything, of course, differs from everything else. But humans are special because we can formulate our distinction *from* others and display it *to* those others. A cat acts, basically, like any other cat; but a human being, because of its mortality, wants to act as an individual – that is, differently from any other human being: "Speech and action reveal this unique distinctness. Through them, men distinguish themselves instead of being merely distinct. they are the modes in which human being appear to each other, not indeed as physical objects, but *qua* men" (*HC* 176).

Action is self-revealing, as Dante recognized (*HC* 175), at least to the extent that any actions reveals the intentions of the actor; that is why identifying yourself as the performer of a specific action means taking responsibility for it, rather than dismissing it as mere clumsiness or denying it as somehow compelled. But it is obvious, says Arendt, that self-revelation occurs more completely in speech than in action; it is easier to determine "who someone is" from her words than from her deeds, which are often ambiguous. Words thus complete the revelation of self brought about in acting:

> The action [one] begins is humanly disclosed by the word, and though [one's] deed can be perceived in its brute physical appearance, without verbal accompaniment, it becomes relevant only through the spoken word in which [one] identifies [oneself] as the actor, announcing what [one] does, has done, and intends to do.   (*HC* 179)

Just *who* is revealed in one's speech and actions is, however, generally unclear: not only are actions often ambiguous, in that any of a number of possible intentions may have produced them, but in both action and speech we are often unclear even to ourselves:

> It is more than likely that the "who," which appears so clearly and unmistakably to others, remains hidden from the person himself, like the *daimōn* in Greek religion which accompanies each man throughout

his life, looking over his shoulder from behind and thus visible only to
those he encounters.   (*HC* 179–80)

Speech and action must therefore be witnessed from elsewhere in order to
do what they are supposed to do, that is, reveal the nature of the actor to others
who can remember it or see that it is remembered:

> [I]n acting and speaking, men show who they are, actively reveal their
> unique personal identities and thus make their appearance in the
> human world, while their physical identities appear without any activity
> of their own in the unique shape of the body and sound of the voice.
>   (*HC* 179)

Human diversity is therefore the condition of both speech and action. Such
diversity requires both equality (sameness) and distinction (*HC* 175–6). If
we were not distinct from each other, we would not need speech or action to
reveal ourselves; we could do it telepathically. On the other hand, if we were
not somehow the same, we could never understand each other at all. It is only
within a space that is structured by an interplay of sameness and difference, that
is, a space of "diversity", that speech and action can occur (*HC* 176). The ancient
term for this space, of course, was "*polis*".

One reason we are unclear to ourselves is that, since we are unique, our
actions are as well. An action is therefore surprising, and "cannot be expected
[on the basis of] whatever may have happened before … The fact that man is
capable of action mans that the unexpected may be expected from him" (*HC*
178). To "act" originally meant, in the broadest sense, to initiate something; the
Greek word for this, *archein*, comes from the word *archē*, meaning beginning
(cf. "archaic"). An action, as a beginning, is something new and so unexpected.
So when we act in the strict sense, we do something no one else has ever done,
and we are unique in that (*HC* 178). It is thus the "initiatory" quality of action
that enables it to be the revelation of the uniqueness of the actor. This quality
is also shared, although less, with speech; speech and action are thus related by
the coexistence in them of self-revelation and initiative, and distinguished by
the differing weight they give to each (*HC* 178). These two dimensions coexist
in speech and action, we may say, because they are ways of taking up stances
towards the past and the future. What is revealed in both is the self of an actor
who has come to be within a "pre-existing web" of human relationships (*HC*
194), while the initiatory quality of action, and of speech in so far as it is action,
is its capacity to set something new in motion: to open up a new future.

Because action is always *unexpected* it is *unprecedented*, which in turn means
that it is *transgressive*, which means finally that it is *dangerous* (*HC* 190–91).
Action must thus have limits placed on it, in the form of reliable institutions that
will punish people who get too transgressive: laws (*HC* 195). By setting limits to

action, law helps keep open the physical and intellectual space in which it can take place. In the ancient world, this control on transgression was incorporated into the concept of action itself. An action, like anything temporal, has two phases: its beginning and its ending. In ancient languages, Arendt claims (*HC* 189), these were given two names. In Greek, *archein* designated the beginning of something while *prattein* designated its ending. In Latin, *agere* and *gerere* exhibited the same relation. In both cases, the former was the action of a single person, the latter of many: "Here it seems as though each action were divided into two parts, the beginning made by a single person and the achievement in which many join by 'bearing' and 'finishing' the enterprise, by seeing it through" (*HC* 189).

This originally cooperative conception of action, in which transgression was reined in *and completed* by the role of others in determining what has been done, came to an end when some people were permanently assigned to be "beginners" and others to be "finishers" of an action. At that point, the entire action was attributed to the person who began it, who was thereby designated as the "leader" (*archon*), while the others became mere "responders", or followers. We can recognize where this happened: in the *oikos*, where the *pater* (who could not transgress since his power was absolute) gave orders and everyone else obeyed. Nonetheless, the ancient conception of action as cooperative remains even today, in that a leader needs, and so depends on, followers (*HC* 190). So both sides are necessary even now; any action in the complete sense requires a diversity of people. Indeed, the ancient model of one person giving orders and the others following them – the model of the *oikos* – never worked, even in the *oikos*. Slavishly following an order is never just that; the response of the followers is always creative and so is a communal action of their own; it is the start of something different. All action – and we shall see this again – thus requires the cooperation of people, and that means the unification of the differing perspectives present among those people.

SOCIETY: THE LOSS OF THE POLITICAL

Certain concepts and distinctions that are still basic to our lives had, it seems, clearer outlines in the ancient world than they do today. The distinction between those who begin an action and those who complete it, and the relationship of action to speech, are among these. But things are also different now, most basically because "in the modern world, the social and political realms are much less distinct" (*HC* 33). The private structures and concerns of the ancient *oikos* have become public, and this has brought into being the realm of "society": "Society is the form in which the fact of mutual dependence for the sake of life and nothing else assumes public significance and where the activities of sheer survival are permitted to appear in public" (*HC* 46). In "society", then, a whole country (or, indeed, the whole world) is seen, so to speak, as one big family. In such a regime, the concern of politics is not immortal glory but the well-being of the citizens, that is, the preservation of their life and comfort. Giving individuals the opportunity to perform great deeds, or utter great words, has thus become irrelevant to public life. "Housekeeping" has become the function of community, and the political sphere has been replaced by "society".

This, Arendt claims, is historically new (*HC* 28). Even medieval times kept alive the notion that there was a distinct realm where one pursued excellence: the realm of the "sacred", religion (*HC* 34). But that is exactly where we see the line between *oikos* and *polis* beginning to blur, because when glory is reserved for religion – as saintliness – the things of this world are all the more given over to housekeeping functions. In keeping with the anti-political strain that Christianity retained from its days as a slave religion under the Romans, the medieval period thus encouraged the private virtue of "goodness" over the pursuit of public glory (*HC* 34). As public life descended into what had previously been private concerns, the whole feudal system, in Arendt's view, became one great system of housekeeping, with glory reserved for the Church.

The modern age has subsequently done away with the importance of religion altogether, eliminating the ecclesiastical vestiges of glory and leaving intact, on all levels, only the realm of "housekeeping". When this happened, no job was left for the *oikos* to do, for society had taken over its function. There was thus no need for a distinct realm devoted to maintaining life. But the need for *some* sort of domain outside the public domain was still there; it just shrank down into "intimacy". The family ceased to be the kind of real community that the *oikos*, for all its problems, presented, and became a union of hearts, which is not a very stable or enduring basis for human relations. Romantic love, which does not last long, became in theory the foundation of marriage, and thus crucially important (*HC* 39).

With the loss of the political come a couple of further losses. First, the organization of humanity into societies, rather than *poleis*, means that what had been defined as necessity has overcome freedom. Governments now have to supply their people with the means to a long and comfortable life, and this constrains their policies; indeed, public debate and action are only about that. Greatness is gone:

> It is decisive that society, on all its levels, excludes the possibility of action, which formerly was excluded from the household. Instead, society expects from each of its members a certain kind of behavior, imposing innumerable and various rules, all of which tend to "normalize' its members, to make them behave, to exclude spontaneous action or outstanding achievement. (*HC* 40)

Thus, the "social bondage" that Arendt found in America is symptomatic of modern societies in general. It is not that they are against greatness, but that, like the family, they enforce conformity: "Whether a nation consists of equals or non-equals is of no great importance in this respect, for society always demands that its members act as if they were members of one enormous family which has only one opinion and one interest" (*HC* 39). Moreover, the sphere of "society" is growing. In all "bodies politic", whatever the system, both the political and the private spheres have "proved incapable of defending themselves" against society's growing power (*HC* 47). We are moving towards a situation in which there will be only one huge family embracing all humanity (*HC* 46): not a "global village", to be sure, but something akin to a global *oikos*.

Private property, we saw, was founded on the separate and private character of the *oikos*. The rise of the social, being inimical to the *oikos*, is inimical to private property as well. It is directed instead to wealth, which is not one's unique situation in the world (as property was) but the unending accumulation of things:

> The enormous and still proceeding accumulation of wealth in modern society, which was started by expropriation – the expropriation of the peasant ... has never shown much consideration for private property, but has sacrificed it whenever it came into conflict with the accumulation of wealth. (*HC* 66–7)

Gradually, group after group within society came under the domination of society or got pushed out altogether until we get to the present stage:

> The rise of mass society ... only indicates that the various social groups have suffered the same absorption into one society that the family units had suffered earlier; with the emergence of mass society, the realm of the social has finally, after several centuries of development, reached the point where it embraces and controls all members of a given community equally and with equal strength. (*HC* 41)

An indication that this development has reached its end point, or is approaching it, is the existence and success of economics. Economic science finds conceptual purchase where people's behaviour is statistically predictable and so conforms to patterns. This means that economic analysis works only in large communities, where individual uniqueness is smothered under the weight of the "masses" and only a very few individuals have the opportunity to do great and unique things: "the larger the population in any given body politic, the more likely it will be the social rather than the political which constitutes the public realm" (*HC* 43). Statistics is thus anathema to Arendt:

The application of the law of large numbers and long periods to politics or history signifies nothing less than the willful obliteration of their very subject matter, and it is a hopeless enterprise to search for meaning in politics or significance in history when everything that is not every-day behavior or automatic trends has been ruled out as immaterial ... Statistical uniformity is by no means a harmless scientific ideal.

(*HC* 42–3)

LABOUR AND WORK

The idea that one social force has pushed aside all alternatives, enforced con-formity and accumulated wealth at the expense of private property should sound, in spite of obvious differences, a bit like Marx's view that the bourgeoi-sie has destroyed all competing classes except for the proletariat. I now want to examine Arendt's account of labour, in which she articulates her view of Marx as the supreme theorist of modern society, not, in her view, because he is a radical departure from previous thought, but because he encapsulates it: Marx is the most traditional, if the most acute, of modern thinkers. The distinction Arendt is now seeking to draw between labour and work cannot be found, however, in Marx or, indeed, anywhere in the tradition of political thought. It is one of her own, and most important, contributions. It will be taken up, as we shall see later, by Agamben.

In developing the *oikos–polis* distinction, we saw, Arendt relied on classical political theory; her account was largely taken from Aristotle. Her distinction between labour and work is another case of such critical reliance. For Aristotle, making (*poiēsis*) resulted in a product distinct from the activity by which it was made, and which therefore could last beyond that activity; action (*praxis*) does not, and is an end in itself (*Eth. Nic.* 1140b6–7). Arendt accepts this with regard to speech and action (*HC* 95), but thinks Aristotle's account of *poiēsis* needs to be complicated by distinguishing within it products that are unique and so enrich the human world, and objects that do not, such as made beds and cooked food. "Work" is thus like Aristotelian making in that it results in a permanent object, and like Arendtian action in that its products are unique. So, then, is the activity of making them. "Labour", Aristotle's *poiēsis*, is thus very different from "work".

Although political thinkers have ignored this distinction, at least some ordi-nary languages have preserved it (*HC* 80 n.3):

English:	labour	work
French:	travailler	ouvrer
German:	Arbeiten	Werken
Greek:	ponein	ergazesthai
Latin:	laborare	facere

This is rather contentious – these words do not in fact fall neatly into the two meanings Arendt claims for them – but the general outline of the distinction she wants to draw is clear enough. "Work" results in a finished and durable project (*HC* 91), which can then become part of the human world. "Labour" does not; it merely maintains life (*HC* 83) and, according to the ancients, was slavish and belonged in the *oikos*. The need for it was inherent in life itself, and so it was not specifically human (*HC* 84). But in fact ancient writers said this about work too (*HC* 85). They despised them both and did not really distinguish them; it was the medievals who began that distinction, by valuing work above labour (while, as we saw, reserving true excellence for the spiritual realm).

There are three efforts in modern thought to get at a distinction, if not between "labour" and "work" in Arendt's sense, at least between "praiseworthy" work and work that is just – laborious. The least important of these is the contrast, sometimes drawn by Marx, between intellectual and manual labour (*HC* 91–2); this idea is just an attempt by intellectuals to gain respect by claiming that they, too are "labourers". The distinction between "skilled" and "unskilled" labour is more serious but ultimately unsustainable, for all labour, even merely making beds, requires some degree of skill. Most important of all is Marx's distinction between "productive" and "unproductive" labour (*HC* 85ff.). Productive labour – or, as Marx calls it, "labour" – was what he praised in the proletarians; it was work that made a difference in the world, which enriched the "second" or human world in which we live (*HC* 86). Unproductive labour was of two kinds. First, it included the kind of thing done by servants (and pre-eminently women): laundry, making beds, cleaning houses, cleaning streets and so on. Second, the term also covered phoney labour: the rich man working hard at his stamp collection, or the manager who merely shuffles a few papers and calls some people on the phone.

What does productive labour produce? Marx assimilated labour to work by claiming that labour in fact had a product: labouring activity always produced something Marx called a "surplus". Once the worker had worked enough to maintain his or her own life, further work produced something that could maintain the life of others. Thus, we have not merely labour, but labour power: the ability of labour to produce more than is necessary for its own "reproduction" (*HC* 88). And thus, there is no need to distinguish labour from work; both produce something. It is just that what labour produces is not obvious.

Arendt thinks Marx is wrong about this. Her own distinction between labour and work begins from her view that labour "power" and the "surplus" are mere fictions that hide from Marx the true nature of labour: that it is *wholly* unproductive. Real labour, for her, does not produce anything but merely maintains life, and the things that it produces are reabsorbed into the life process by being consumed. Work, on the other hand, produces durable public objects that are not consumed but used (*HC* 94). What distinguishes work from labour is, thus, in the first instance, the permanence of the objects it produces. "Their proper use does not cause them to disappear and they give the human artifice the stability and solidity without which it could not be relied upon to house the unstable and mortal creature which is man" (*HC* 136). The permanence of the product carries over into the productive process, which (as Heidegger had also emphasized) must be guided by a conception in the mind of the maker: "the image or model whose shape guides the fabrication process not only precedes it, but does not disappear with the finished product, which it survives intact, present, as it were, to lend itself to an infinite continuation of fabrication" (*HC* 141).

Since work is the realization of an intention, it reveals the worker the way speech and action do; it belongs in what the ancients called the *polis*, rather than the *oikos*. Because its products are durable, they can become parts of what Arendt calls the "world": the common field of objects and concerns within which the antagonisms of the political life are enacted and decided (*HC* 94), and which is the contemporary version of the ancient *polis*. World as such has to be enduring because otherwise it could not give us what we have seen to be the only kind of immortality we can attain. It therefore requires enduring objects. Even speech and action belong to the public world only as works, for they must be witnessed by others in order to have any lasting existence at all (*HC* 95). In order to endure, however, they need to be reified: my words die away as I speak them, and my deeds are also fleeting. The only way I can gain immortality through my words and deeds is to write them down, or have someone else do it, in such a way that others will care to read them or read about them. At that point my speech, or my action, becomes a work.

The most basic difference between labour and work is, then, that the products of work belong in the public sphere, the *polis* or "common world", while the products of labour are in the *oikos*, or, now that society has moved so much of the *oikos* into the public sphere, are in society. Buildings, highways and works of art that endure for a long time, such as the *Mona Lisa*, are examples of worldly objects. Fruit, by contrast, is a product of labour and an object of consumption, not of work and use; so is the good order of a well made bed, which lasts only until bedtime. Labour is thus cyclical: something is produced and consumed (i.e. destroyed), then something else is then produced and consumed; as with animals, any individual uniqueness these objects may have is unimportant. A new work, by contrast, is a permanent acquisition for the community. What makes it permanent is that it is irreplaceable, and what makes it irreplaceable is that it is unique. This durability-as-uniqueness constitutes what Arendt calls the "worldly character" of the produced thing, whether it is "worldly" at all, or merely a matter of maintaining and enhancing life.

Work thus changes things in permanent ways, but this is a positive development only from the point of view of work itself. From the point of view of labour, a permanent work takes material out of the process of contributing to life and so is "useless" (*HC* 99–100). This is the point of view of political economists in general, who followed out the increasingly public nature of labour and saw human community as essentially a servant of the life process. In Arendt's view (as well, we saw, as his own), Marx did this more consistently than the earlier political economists; but he, too, fell into a contradiction. On the one hand, labour is, for him, as for the political economists, the "supreme world build-ing capacity of man" (*HC* 101); that is why he has to find a product for it to produce (the surplus). But labour, in fact, has nothing to do with our natures as beings who know we will die; it is fundamentally "unworldly". If human nature itself is to be liberated, then, it cannot be by means of labour. Marx, therefore, ultimately conceives of liberation as liberation from labour: "In all stages of his work [Marx] defines man as an *animal laborans* and then leads him into a society in which this greatest and most human power is no longer necessary" (*HC* 105).

In Marx's utopia, we will "fish in the morning and hunt in the afternoon"; labour will – somehow – no longer be necessary. Humbly put, Marx's claim that labour is the essence of humanity gets him into problems, because no one wants to be *just* a labourer. We can assume that Marx was too smart not to see this, and so the question rises of why he insists that labour is so basic. The answer, for Arendt, is that the concept of labour, unlike that of work, can make sense of something very important that Marx and other political economists saw going on around them. This was the gradual growth in wealth that has characterized Western modernity.

The replacement of property by wealth has thus masked the distinction between work and labour. Your property, in the ancient world, was your *oikos*: the specific place that made you different from other people and so qualified you for the diversity inherent in political life. Wealth, by contrast, is something that is inherently supposed to grow and accumulate: "What the modern age [has] so heatedly defended was never property as such but the unhampered pursuit of more property or appropriation; as against all organs that stood for the 'dead' permanence of a common world, it fought its battles in the name of life, the life of society" (*HC* 110).

Because of this association of wealth and life, it is not surprising that the body should be the source of property (e.g. for Locke).[2] To put this another way: accumulation has to start somewhere, and what it starts with has to be so much mine that nothing can ever take it away from me. My body is thus the "quintes-sence of property". The problem is that the body, as a mere living thing, is, like labour, completely "unworldly" (*HC* 115). In fact, labour is not, and cannot be, the source of property, for property originates in the world, of which, as we saw

---

2. "The *Labour* of his Body, and the *Work* of his Hands, we may say, are properly his. Whatsoever then he removes out of the State that Nature hath provided, and left it in, he hath mixed his *Labour* with, and joyned to it something that is his own, and thereby makes it his *Property*" (Locke 1960: 287–8).

in the case of the *oikos*, it is an essential structure. My property is my place in the world, which means that it is not something that should grow. Its function is rather to be unique, enduring and expressive of my individuality: my property is itself a work in the world.

My wealth, by contrast, figures as one stage in an unending process: that of accumulating wealth. In this it conforms not only to the nature of labour, but to that of life itself. Biologically speaking, I am not an independent entity; I am a process, a particular movement of matter from matter to matter. From dust I come, and to dust I shall eventually return. Life, in other words, is not individualistic. The Greek language expressed this in its distinction between *zōē*, which was the mere biological process of life, and *bios*, which was the unity of speech and action over the lifespan of an individual human being: a distinctively human *way* of life that could be morally evaluated and told as a story, and for which the person was responsible (*HC* 97, 184).

Since labour is understood in terms of what Agamben will call "bare life" – *zōē*, rather than *bios* – it too is not individualistic: it can be socialized, When it is, we have Marx's concept of "species being". "The form labor takes when it is socialized is, as political economists explored, the 'division of labor'. This is an important difference from work: work is specialized; labor is divided" (*HC* 123). What Arendt means by this is that work, like political life, requires diversity. It is what comes about when making something "requires different skills which then are pooled and organized together" (*HC* 123). The division of labour, as Marx conceives it, on the other hand, presupposes the qualitative equivalence of a whole mass of activities for which no skill is required: anyone could do any job equally well, because all the different jobs (as on an assembly line) are really the same job. Labourers on an assembly line, or elsewhere, are "the same and exchangeable" (*HC* 123). Unlike such labourers, workers in Arendt's sense are specialized. In making a movie or putting on a play, for example, all sorts of different kinds of people with different skills and perspectives, have to cooperate, and not just anyone can do their jobs.

Because the individual is of no importance in labour, labour can go on forever: like wealth and life itself, it can increase without limits. That is just what the economy is doing, and the work of the labourer then becomes twofold: to create and to destroy (consume). This is without natural limit, once society has unleashed it from the confines of the *oikos*, where the Greeks kept it; labour in the service of life can, as we have seen, take over everything. With the growth of "society", then, labour becomes increasingly important. It is freed, or emancipated, from its ancient subservience to world (*HC* 128). But the "emancipation of labour" may not be a gain for humanity. Although by blurring the lines of the *oikos* the growth of society has led to a decrease in violence (*HC* 129), or at least its randomization and internationalization, it has also meant that labour has taken over daily life. Nowadays you are either labouring, or resting so you can labour tomorrow, or consuming (destroying) so that others can labour tomorrow. Nothing else in life is "serious", and nothing at all can bring you glory. What is thus dismissed as "not serious", however, includes everything that makes life in a human community worth living: the chance to make a truly individual, and truly great, contribution to the enduring world we all share. "The danger [is] that the modern age's emancipation of labor will not only fail to usher in an age of freedom for all but will result, on the contrary, in forcing all mankind for the first time under the yoke of necessity" (*HC* 130).

This was on some level perceived by Marx, the most acute and clear-sighted social thinker of the modern age. But because he was not fully aware of the lessons of the Greeks – in particular of the real nature of politics and of why we need a *polis* – he failed to understand it and instead presented, as his utopia, the bizarre vision of a world in which labour was the essence of man but no one laboured any more, and in which the state "withered away" to be replaced by the administration of things, which is, for Arendt, precisely the triumph of society over everything else (*HC* 117).

POWER AND FORCE

Arendt has now opened up a series of distinctions within the modern world, all of which trace back to the ancient division between the *oikos* and the *polis*. On the one hand, deriving from the *oikos*, we have society, labour and wealth – all oriented to the biological processes of life or *zōē*. On the other, deriving from the *polis*, we have world, work and property, all centred on the individuality of speech and action as conveyed in one's *bios*, or way of life. A final distinction remains to be discussed: that between power and force.

Action, we saw, requires multiple perspectives. "Power" keeps the space for action open by allowing for the multiple perspectives that action requires to be unified by the common understanding of an action (*HC* 200). Only when we have a common understanding of what an action is, that is, of what it means in its context, can we fix on it; and, as Arendt puts it elsewhere, "Power corresponds to the human ability, not just to act but to act in concert. Power is never the property of an individual. It belongs to the group and lasts just so long as the group keeps together" (Arendt 1980: 349). What belongs to an individual in isolation is "strength", for example the natural strength of muscle power (*HC* 201): "While strength is the natural quality of an individual seen in isolation, power springs up between men when they act together and vanishes the moment they disperse" (*HC* 200).

Power, then, is the capacity of a group of people of differing views to express those views, talk them out, and come to a common plan or understanding of action. While it is tempting to think of power as the ability to command obedience, on Arendt's terms that is mistaken: power belongs to groups of people who unite their differing perspectives regarding a specific issue. Issuing commands is a matter of the strength of a single individual, or, sometimes, of the "force" of a group acting like one. As Arendt characterizes it here (*HC* 202), force is the use of violence against others. As merely violent, it is not a political or worldly phenomenon at all; it belongs in the sphere of life, for it threatens to take life away. The ultimate example of force is the tyrant, who is in a sense isolated from everyone else but who, precisely, seeks to use her strength against others (*HC* 202). Force may also, however, belong to a group, in which case it is the energy released by people who are all doing the same violent thing. When a group exercises force, then, its members have not come to their action via discussion and reasoned unification of perspectives, but are acting as a solitary individual would, often, although not always, because such a solitary individual has ordered them to do so. They are not truly acting politically at all. Because force, whether exercised by an individual or a group, is violent, it does not require true speech; it requires, not the unification of different perspectives, but only the giving of orders.

Power thus belongs in the *polis* or common world, with its diversity of viewpoints. Force requires the kind of conformity we find in the *oikos* or, in the modern world, in society. True government, for its part, rests on the kind of power that holds open the political sphere. The great political problem today is that what used to be the "political" sphere is increasingly "social", given over to helping people live happy lives, which (even in the "welfare state") can in principle be achieved by force. Arendt discusses various facets of this increasing sociality in the final chapter of *The Human Condition*. The discussion is essentially a detailed working out of the categories developed in the first four chapters, and I shall not go into similar detail here.

THE FUTURE AND NATALITY

Like all post-Hegelian thinkers, Arendt is deeply aware of the past, and takes it for granted that the categories by which we think and talk – the categories of the *vita activa* itself – originate nowhere but in history. But what about the future?

The Human Condition was published in 1958, just five years after "The Question Concerning Technology" but long after Arendt and Heidegger had gone their separate ways, intellectually and personally. Although some of its concern with technology as instrument and revelation sounds a bit like Heidegger's essay, the way that essay relentlessly sought to open up a future by finding the right questions seems foreign to Arendt's thinking. What, then, about the future? Is Arendt concerned with it at all? Or is she, like Hegel, exclusively interested with the past and the present, so far as the present is no more than the result of the past? Her answer to this relies on her point, noted previously, that as an expression of an individual human being, work and action are radically new:

> The life span of man running toward death would inevitably carry everything human to ruin and destruction if it were not for the faculty of interrupting it and beginning something new, a faculty which is inherent in action like an ever-present reminder that men, though they must die, are not born in order to die but in order to begin. (*HC* 246)

If I am to achieve undying fame by my actions, those actions must express my unique personality, and so must be unique themselves. This is why, as we saw, action is initiatory, and why transgression is basic to the political realm. But if human beings are capable of radically unique actions, they must themselves be radically unique. The birth of a human being is, then, the most radical of beginnings, because it is the beginning of someone who, through her unique creativity, can perform actions that no one else could perform: "The miracle that saves the world, the realm of human affairs, from its normal, 'natural' ruin is ultimately the fact of natality, in which the faculty of action is ontologically rooted" (*HC* 247).

Heidegger's emphasis on death goes together with his failure to perceive the "ontological" significance of birth. Marx perceived it, but not clearly enough. For "labour" – toil in the service of life – in fact has two meanings. One is Marx's: toil that merely maintains the life cycle. But when a woman gives birth, we also say that she "goes into labour" (*HC* 106). Labour in this sense is fertile, it increases the human world. It can have a certain joy about it, of a kind that is always missing even from work: joy in life itself (*HC* 107). Marx, as we saw, had procreation in mind when he tried to imagine a truly "communist" society. But labour as he defines it, that is, productive labour, "reproduces" the worker's life; procreating, for its part, merely reproduces the species.

The arrival of a new human being is for Arendt, by contrast, akin to what the creation of a new work of art is for Heidegger: the most originary possible upsurge of new meanings. Where Heidegger had restricted this to the rare and elitist realm of great art, Arendt locates it in each one of us. And here, Arendt – who never ceased to identify as Jewish, although in her own way – turns not merely to Jesus Christ, but to the Christian Gospels in general: "It is this faith in and hope for the world that found perhaps its most glorious and succinct expression in the few words with which the Gospels announced their 'glad tiding:' 'A child has been born unto us'" (*HC* 247).

But these words, the closing words of Arendt's exposition of *vita activa*, are not understood as Christians understand them: as referring to the God-man, a being unfathomably unique. Rather, she understands them as applying to any child, in the spirit of the Jewish mother who must ask herself, at the birth of her infant, whether or not that child is the Messiah: whether or not she or he is something unfathomably different from anyone yet born. Arendt's answer is a standing yes. She is never so Jewish as in this appeal to Christ and the Gospels.

CONCLUSION

Like continental philosophers in general, Arendt takes it as axiomatic that we are in time in every respect. That is why, in articulating "the human condition", she talks so much about the ancient Greeks. Since the basic premises of our life and thought can come only from history, the most important task of philosophy is – as with Hegel, Nietzsche, and Heidegger – to orient us to the past. This orientation, for Arendt, takes the form of recovering the true nature of *vita activa*, the active life in its distinction from theoretical and social life.

But we must also cope with the future. Arendt, we have now seen, understands the future in two ways. First, it is what I have just discussed: "natality", the unfathomable future of the newborn, together with the ongoing capacity to initiate radically new things that is most fully manifested by a newborn. This capacity, in so far as it belongs to us as individuals, is as radically mortal as everything about us. All claims to deliver us into a realm of eternal truth – whether this includes actually inhabiting such a realm, as religion promises, or merely knowing it, as traditional philosophy asserts – are illusory. And so our future is also, as in *Being and Time*, our death. The only realm in which we can live on after our deaths is the human realm, and the only honest quest for immortality is the effort to live on in the memory of other human beings.

This gives us the other sense of "future" for her: that which we try to control, at least to the extent that it will contain people who remember us. Arendt's own book is presumably written with this in mind:

> It is obvious that, no matter how concerned a thinker may be with eternity, the moment he sits down to write his thoughts he ceases to be concerned primarily with eternity and shifts his attention to leaving some trace of them. He has entered the *vita activa* and chosen its way of permanence and potential immortality. (*HC* 20)

Thus, the proper way for philosophy to take account of the future is not to open it up with questions, as for the later Heidegger, but to reinterpret the past in a way that will endure. This is not the "questioning" stance of the later Heidegger; it is not a refraining from action, but the most profound sort of action possible. Philosophy, like the rest of *vita activa*, is thus an effort to control the future. *Vita activa*, Nietzsche might say, consists of promises the actor makes to herself.

Arendt herself is far from saying this. But this *rapprochement* with Nietzsche can serve as a first indication that, with Arendt, continental philosophy has arrived at an extremely complex situation concerning how philosophers ought to take account of the future. When Nietzsche discussed the making of promises in *On the Genealogy of Morality*, Essay II, there was at least one implication of his views that he did not actually draw. This is that in making a promise, I *reduce* the boundlessness of the future (cf. *HC* 244). Instead of leaving the future wholly unfathomable, when I promise something I posit that just two of its infinite possibilities are particularly significant: either it will contain my keeping my promise, or it will contain my not doing so. My promise, as I will say, specifies and so "finitizes" the future. This was not the case for Nietzsche. While making promises was, for him, as we saw, an important activity – it defined what it is to be human – promising was important not because it finitized the future but because it indicated the possession of a "durable will" (cf. *HC* 245). Just what that will promised was not the issue.

For Arendt, by contrast, one "promise" is particularly important, and that is the promise of undying fame, the only kind of immortality possible for mortal beings such as ourselves. As far as it is philosophically significant, the future for Arendt, as for Kierkegaard, contains only two possibilities. But where for Kierkegaard these were the infinite unfathomabilities of eternal damnation or salvation, for Arendt they are the entirely temporal and comprehensible fates of being either remembered or forgotten.

In the wake of Heidegger, then, Arendt sees the future as finite. It is not boundless and so unfathomable. Rather, there are certain things that, as philosophically significant, the future does not contain, and these differ from person to person. We could extend this *rapprochement* with Heidegger by saying, although Arendt does not, that the issue of how precisely to attain undying fame – what works of art to create, what political policies to formulate and advocate – stands before each mortal individual as a question, one that opens up a specific, and so finite, future.

But Arendt is not merely following Heidegger here. For Heidegger himself, the future is finite from the start; it does not need to be "finitized" by making promises or in any other way. The philosophically relevant future, for him, is, we saw, that of a community: most basically, the community of preservers of a work of art. Those preservers, to be sure, were themselves finite in that they could not know what their future might bring; it was, within limits, unfathomable. But the action, and, as I noted, the moral responsibility, of any individual was bounded by the possibilities open to her community. Since communities differ, their futures differ. Thus, although our future is always less certain than we would like, no community's future is wholly open. Its limits are already there, in the "reservoir of the not-yet-uncovered". There was no discussion in Heidegger of how an individual might undertake, then, to "finitize" the future.

For Arendt, the future of a human being starts out as an infinite, and so blank, slate; this, we saw, was part of the meaning of natality for her. In order to be the future *of an individual*, the future needs to be reduced from this to something specific. It is Arendt's emphasis on the unique human individual, then, which leads her to emphasize what I am calling the "finitization" of the future. But an individual cannot, of herself, finitize the future; for this is achieved by the only promise that ultimately matters, that of undying fame. And that promise cannot be made by an individual to herself. It is the witnesses and potential witnesses

– those who will remember her – who must make it. This, Arendt says, is the real reason the Greeks invented the polis, which as an ongoing and organized political realm "was supposed to multiply the occasions to win 'immortal fame'" (*HC* 197). As opposed to being dependent on the chance presence of a poet, as Achilles was on Homer, "Men's life together in the form of the *polis* seemed to assure that the most futile of human activities, action and speech, and the least tangible and most ephemeral of man-made 'products,' the deeds and stories which are their outcome, would become imperishable" (*HC* 197–8).

Political life is thus, for Arendt, a compact to finitize the future. What holds us together in such life is ultimately "the force of mutual promise" (*HC* 244–5): the promise that if we contribute to the ongoing space of meaning Arendt calls "world", we will not be forgotten. Arendt thus sees the future, not as either finite (*à la* Heidegger) or boundless, (*à la* Kierkegaard and Nietzsche), but as an interplay of the two. This more complex view of the future will surface again in the French continental philosophers, particularly those most influenced by existentialist individualism: Sartre, Beauvoir and, to an extent, Derrida. Before looking at them, however, we must first examine a post-Heideggerean account of the finite future of a community: the account given by the Frankfurt theorists Adorno and Horkheimer.

CHAPTER 9

THE TWILIGHT OF ENLIGHTENMENT: THEODOR W. ADORNO AND MAX HORKHEIMER

PRIMARY TEXT Max Horkheimer & Theodor W. Adorno,
Dialectic of Enlightenment (*DE*; 1994)

On 22 July 1969 an old man walked out of a courtroom in Frankfurt, Germany. On the way he permitted himself a condescending smile in the direction of the defendant, a radical student leader named Hans-Jürgen Krahl. Krahl was on trial for trespassing; the old man, who had brought the charges against him, was his teacher, Theodor W. Adorno. The preceding February, Krahl had led a student occupation of Adorno's beloved Institute for Social Research; this was his trespass. His ensuing trial was the culmination of growing tension between, on the one hand, Adorno himself, his associate Max Horkheimer and the other "adult" spirits of the institute, and their own students on the other. The students claimed merely to be carrying into action the Marxist ideas and theories of the Frankfurt School. In their eyes, their elders – in particular, Horkheimer and Adorno – had ceased to be real Marxists long before. For true Marxism, the students argued, could not be merely a matter of theory. Was it not Marx himself who had written, in the "Theses on Feuerbach", that "the philosophers have only interpreted the world in various ways; the point is to change it?" (Marx 1994b: 101)·

Furthermore, Horkheimer and Adorno were too pro-American. To a degree this was understandable. The United States had not only given them personal refuge during the Nazi years but it had also ferociously fought the Nazis across western Europe, and so had been a general benefactor of humanity. It had also been with American support that the Frankfurt School had been able to re-establish itself in Germany after its wartime exile in New York and Los Angeles. But to the students, that was ancient history. By 1969, largely as a result of the Vietnam War, the United States had become a world villain to Europeans generally and to leftists in particular. The older members of the Frankfurt School refused to recognize this anti-Americanism as legitimate. Indeed, Horkheimer had gone so far in his pro-Americanism as to support the war. This was some-thing the students could hardly abide in any case; coming from someone who called himself a Marxist, it was intolerable. And so Adorno was walking out of the trial he had demanded, saying that he was going on holiday to Switzerland and would not be able to offer any further evidence against Krahl. Witnesses agreed that his head was high and his manner superior, but hostile stares and insults from the spectators in the courtroom let him know that he had lost: not so much the trial (Krahl was found guilty, given a three-month suspended sentence, and fined about $75), but something far more important – a whole generation of young people. In the words of a leaflet handed out during a dem-onstration at one of his lectures, "Adorno as an institution is dead". The following month, Adorno as a person was also dead, from a heart attack suffered while exerting himself in the Swiss mountains. The Frankfurt School passed into the neo-Kantian hands of Habermas, and (as I noted in the Introduction) temporal-ized thought died in Germany, the land of its birth.

The road to Adorno's final defeat was a circuitous one. He was born in 1903, to a middle-class family; his Jewish father was named Wiesengrund, but he took his Corsican mother's name early on.[1] His mother was an opera singer, and Theodor studied music as a child and then studied composition in Vienna for three years with Alban Berg. Then he went back to Germany and wrote a dissertation on Husserl. His associate, Horkheimer, was born near Stuttgart in 1895, so he was about six years younger than Heidegger. He was from a wealthy family, and completed his studies with a dissertation on Kant's *Critique of Judgment*.

In 1929, the *Institut für Sozialforschung* was founded in Frankfurt. It was privately funded by a young man whose father had made an incredible amount of money in the wheat trade in Argentina, and so was free from the kind of government interference that had shortened the careers of the Young Hegelians a century before. Horkheimer became director and hired the others, including Adorno. When the Nazis came to power, the members of the institute had to flee, being leftists and mainly Jewish. The institute itself was eventually recon-stituted in New York. Horkheimer and Adorno moved to Los Angeles and lived there for about four years, during which they wrote much of the *Dialectic of Enlightenment*. With the fall of the Nazis they moved back to Germany, where the institute became part of the University of Frankfurt.[2]

On 24 May 1968, the radical students occupied the university for the first time. They expected that Adorno would support them, but, as I have noted, he did not. Instead, he viewed their protests as merely another part of the total thought control exercised by the capitalist culture industry. This led to his final

---

1. Details of Adorno's life are from Jäger (2004).
2. For the history of the Frankfurt School see Wiggershaus (1994).

confrontation with the students, at Krahl's trial; but he had already been forced to resign from the university. Adorno as an institution was indeed dead.

MARX AND THE FRANKFURT SCHOOL

The Frankfurt School's mission, in so far as it had one, was to update Marxist philosophy in light of twentieth-century developments. True to Marx himself, the relevant developments were considered to be not merely in philosophy, but in the surrounding society as well. The most important of them, in the minds of the Frankfurt thinkers, was the rise of fascism. How could fascism, which was nationalist, racist and generally evil, have serious appeal to the working class? That it did have such appeal, in Depression-era Europe, was undeniable, but could not be explained in traditional Marxist terms. For Marx, as we saw, the working class was the "proletariat", the revolutionary embodiment of human liberation. Unlike other classes down through history, the proletariat was composed of people whose liberation would bring about the liberation of all.

Prior to the rise of the proletariat, one class could achieve dominance only by oppressing other classes, as did the bourgeoisie of whom we saw Marx speak so approvingly in *The Communist Manifesto*. But the bourgeoisie had achieved something no other class in history had ever attained: its dominance over society was virtually complete. Ending that dominance would thus, in Marx's view, end dominance altogether, which would end both class struggle and classes themselves. Even the bourgeoisie would be liberated by the victory of the proletariat: liberated from their need to control everything, a control that came at the price of obedience to market forces and so was oppressive. In Marxist terms, then, no progress was possible without the victory of the proletariat.

The proletariat was thus more than a mere object of hope for Marx; it was the necessary bearer of human progress. But it had for him one problem: its lack of revolutionary awareness. Proletarians were aware of their personal and local struggles, but had trouble seeing themselves as players with a common interest on the world stage. That is why communist practice was, for Marx, as we also saw, a kind of education, showing proletarians how their local struggles fit in with the larger global struggle for the workers. Without such awareness, the proletariat could never consciously undertake the revolutionary liberation of all people; it could never assume its historical destiny. The proletariat was essential to human progress for Marx, then, and communist teaching was indispensable to the proletariat. But such teaching could succeed only if proletarians were good people: if, beyond their selfish drive for their own liberation, they were willing to understand how their liberation required the liberation of all, and also willing to work for that enormous goal. Yet with the rise of fascism, the working class was turning anti-Semitic and nationalistic. Common cause among German, French, Italian and British workers was growing more difficult.

The essence of the revolution, and with it all hope for human progress, was threatened.

Fascism was thus, intellectually and historically as well as literally, a bullet aimed at the heart of Marxism. In *Dialectic of Enlightenment*, Horkheimer and Adorno respond to that intellectual bullet by biting it. Not only do they not see the proletariat as a progressive force in society, but they do not see *any* powerful group in society as progressive. This is not because they are burdened with "vulgar Marxist" dogma to the effect that the proletariat alone can be progressive, so that its distortion under fascism spells the end of all progressive forces. Their argument is broader and, on its broadest level, rests on the observation that all human groups are bound together by language. In the current situation, "There is no longer any available form of linguistic expression which has not tended toward accommodation to dominant currents of thought" (*DE* xii).

The fact that language itself had accommodated to fascism called for a rethinking, not just of Marx's appraisal of the proletariat, but of his entire hope that a just society would actually come about. That, in turn, required abandoning all of Marx's predictions about where the world was going. Marx was wrong, not merely in the predictions he made, but in the fact that he made predictions at all.

NEGATIVE DIALECTICS

The title "Dialectic of Enlightenment" shows, in its first word, that it is related to Marx (and, of course, Hegel). Its final word is also instructive, for when you talk about "Enlightenment" within the context of German philosophy, you are talking about Kant. Horkheimer and Adorno are not only trying to update Marx, then; they are trying to update Kant as well. And they are trying to do so by claiming that Enlightenment itself is dialectical. What they mean by "dialectics" is clarified, somewhat, in Adorno's *Negative Dialectics* (1966), written almost twenty years after *Dialectic of Enlightenment*, in which he defines dialectics as "the consistent sense of nonidentity" (Adorno 1973: 5). We can flesh this out a bit by noting that Hegel, the great rehabilitator of dialectics (after Kant had called it a *Logik des Scheins*, a logic of mere appearance; *KRV* B 86), would have agreed: dialectics is what he called "negativity", self-transformation, and is opposed to fixed identity. In the minds of Horkheimer and Adorno, however, Hegel did not develop this insight consistently. He practised "positive dialectics", in which everything somehow came to a final static identity in the "Absolute" (*DE* 24).[3] Their own kind of dialectics, being "negative", will have

---

3. As Chapter 2 showed, this is a misreading of Hegel, but a very common one.

no such stopping points: it will exhibit a "consistent" sense of non-identity by taking everything to exist only in order to be negated in turn.

Although advanced against Hegel, this also embodies a strong revision of Marx, for whom the achievement of communism represented a sort of social Absolute ("the riddle of history solved"; *EPM* 103), a final state of society in which all contradictions would be overcome and further negations, or transformations, of social structure would not be necessary. It is their view of dialectics as negative, then, that keeps Horkheimer and Adorno from making the kind of prediction Marx tried to make. What any prediction predicts inevitably gets taken to be a static outcome, even if it is not intended that way.

Adorno's synthesis of Marx and Kant comes out very clearly in *Negative Dialectics* when he identifies dialectics as the primordial form of thinking: "Thought as such, before all particular contents, is an act of negation, of resistance to that which is forced upon it; this is what thought has inherited from its archetype, the relation of labor and material" (Adorno 1973: 19).

That thought "resists" what is given to it is an unusual phrasing of good Kantian doctrine. What is ultimately given to us, in Kant's view, is sensory chaos: the completely disorganized "manifold". For Kant, as we saw in Chapter 1, the mind's "labour" is performed by the faculties: activities of the mind governed by principles that are *a priori* in the sense that they exist independently of the ways they are put to use on specific occasions. The faculty that brings the chaotic sensory manifold under the principles of space and time is intuition; the understanding supplies further ordering principles, in the form of its categories or "pure concepts". The actual bringing of an intuition under a concept – what Kant calls "subsumption" – is, then, performed by judgement, and judgement operates not only with "pure" or *a priori* concepts but with empirical ones. The results of this operation are objects. When I say "this is a horse", then, the "this", sensory data arranged in space and time, is furnished by intuition; the concept "horse" is furnished by the understanding; and bringing the two together so that the object is seen as an instance of a concept, that is, as an object at all, is performed by judgement.

But Kant, as we have seen, made no attempt to say where the structure and ordering capacities of our mind come from. At this point, Adorno assigns a Marxist origin: the struggle of mind to order the sensory chaos is a metaphor for the struggle of mind to form matter that Marx calls "labour". In *Dialectic of Enlightenment*, this labour is called "projection", and indeed "automatic" projection: "all perception is projection" (*DE* 187). It is grounded biologically, as a form of animal behaviour, and we need to project because the information our senses deliver us is only fragmentary: "Between the true object and the undisputed data of the senses, between within and without, there is a gulf which the subject must bridge at his own risk. In order to reflect the thing as it is, the subject must return from it more then he receives from it" (*DE* 188).

In order to obtain objects, then, we must work on the fragmentary data we receive from our senses. This in itself is nothing new. Husserl, Kant and Hegel, along with many others, had argued that objects must be constituted by the mind out of appearances, the presentations we receive from the outside world. Horkheimer and Adorno want to retain this idea in part, but without lapsing into "idealism", in the first instance of a Kantian sort. This seems hard to do, because idealism just is, traditionally, the view that objects are constituted by the mind; Horkheimer and Adorno's refutation of it, therefore, depends on just what they take it to be. To see this, it helps to note that Horkheimer's and Adorno's rejection of idealism comprises two stages. First, they claim that the mind constitutes not only objects out of its own projective activity, but itself as well. The subject, the knower or the self, "constitutes the 'I' retrospectively by learning to grant a synthetic unity not only to the external impressions, but to the internal impressions which gradually separate off from them" (*DE* 189).

This means that the "I" is not some sort of fixed unit, over and above its various constitutions of objects, and this is a first break with Kant, for whom the nature of mind is "fixed" in that mind operates according to pre-established, unchanging principles in constituting objects (*KRV* B xvi). Instead, Horkheimer and Adorno claim that the constitutions, or projections, come first. Only when the mind sees what it has done on specific occasions do general characteristics of its action become apparent; and the set of those characteristics is the only unity it has. Projection thus constitutes both mind and object. But this means that there is no reason to think that new experiences will not cause the mind to do things differently, as they do (for example) throughout Hegel's *Phenomenology*. On this more Hegelian view, mind and object co-constitute one another as they go along. All knowledge, including the mind's knowledge of itself, is empirical, and so changeable.

But although on this view objects need no longer conform to the mind's unalterable structure, there must still be a *rapprochement* of some sort between mind and object: the two, it seems, now co-create each other. We have, therefore, still not answered the question of how objects can be the result of the mind's labour, and yet still retain their independence from mind. Doing so leads Horkheimer and Adorno to a critique of the Kantian faculty that was supposed to bring concept and object together, judgement, and leads us to the heart of their thought.

For Kant, judgement brings pre-existing concepts together with given intuitions to form objects. In the view of Horkheimer and Adorno, judgement also has a problem: it is absolutist in nature. This is ultimately, for them, because truth is bivalent: it has no gradations. If a judgement is not wholly true, it is wholly false. What this means is that if my subsumption of an object under a concept is true, I have exactly captured at least one aspect of the object. If I correctly judge that the object before me is a horse, then it is a horse – and that is the end of it. Any judgement "must assert its content (however carefully formulated the latter may be) as something which is not merely isolated and relative. This is its essential nature as judgment. Truth, unlike probability, has no gradations" (*DE* 194). Such a thought, then, is not "negative"; it operates with a concept of fixed, or "positive" identity. Indeed, such identity is its goal. Judgement, then, has an intrinsic tendency to fix identities.

Kant got this all right. What he failed to appreciate is that the application of a concept to sensory data is always a leap beyond those data, which are fragmentary. In some ways, this is obvious. What I see before me as a horse may not in fact be a horse. In fact, what I see before me may not even really be an object in space and time. This may, of course, be the result of a wrong judgement, a misidentification on my part. It may also be that my concept of "horse" or "object" is itself somehow defective: if I have never made clear to myself the distinction between horses and mules, for example. Even if I have distinct concepts of "horse" and "mule", they may change in the future, for if our concepts are contingent products of our experiences, they can change over time.

For Horkheimer and Adorno, more than that is going on, however. What appears to be the fragmentary nature of sensory experience is not merely the result of defects in our sensory organs or our concepts or indeed of any other human frailty, but follows from something about things themselves: they are not self-coherent units, but are always other than themselves – changing and internally contradictory. The non-identity of a thing with itself, in fact, is the ground of concepts; it allows them to be formed. In a typically knotty passage, Horkheimer and Adorno assert:

> When the [individual] tree is approached no longer merely as [individual] tree, but as evidence for an Other, as the location of *mana*, language expresses the contradiction that something is itself and at one and the same time something other than itself, identical and not identical. Through the deity, language is transformed from tautology into language. The concept, which some would see as the sign-unit for whatever is comprised under it, has from the beginning been instead the product of dialectical thinking in *which everything is always that which it is, only because it becomes that which it is not.*
>
> (*DE* 15, emphasis added)

Mana, to some Pacific islanders, is a universal force that permeates all beings, animate or inanimate. When I see a tree as an instance of *mana*, or even just as an instance of treehood – that is, when I judge that the thing before me is a tree – I am moving on from the tree as it presents itself to my senses; in Hegelian parlance, I am "negating" the sensory tree. I do not do this at will, however; that would be to take the tree merely as an external starting-point for my own activity of negation, and giving precedence to my own subjective, negating activity, as Horkheimer and Adorno think Hegel did. Rather, I am impelled to do this by the fact that the tree is already negating itself; it is changing. Thus the thing before me can be called a tree only because it is already becoming what it is not: only because it is already becoming, and indeed has already become, something other than a mere instance of the concept "tree". But if it is changing, then whatever concept I apply to it – *mana* or tree or whatever – does not apply exactly.

We can now see how Horkheimer and Adorno have carried through their rejection of idealism. Mind does not wholly create objects, as Berkeley thought;[4] it does not constitute them according to pre-established principles, as Kant thought; and it does not constitute them by changing its principles, as Hegel presented it in the *Phenomenology*. This is because there is something in an object beyond concepts and principles, namely its disunity with itself. Our mind, in short, does constitute what we can perceive and say about things. But what we can perceive and say about things does not get all the way to their core.

When projection becomes judgement, it denies this, for it accepts truth as bivalent and uses concepts as ready made. Inherent in perception itself, that is, in the act of projection that any perception contains, is therefore the possibility that the thing may not be what I think it is. I may be wrong about everything; and for judgement, this possibility is devastating. My awareness of it becomes paranoid in nature: "paranoia is the dark side of cognition" (*DE* 195). This paranoia is, in a sense, fully justified. For it is not merely *possible* that things are not as I judge them to be; that is actually the case. The tree is a tree in that it impels me to apply that concept to it, and this very impulsion, grounded in its inner disunity, shows that it is unstable within itself. The aim of philosophy, then, is to combat this paranoia not by actually achieving the identity of thing and concept that judgement demands, but by showing that the demand is impossible to fulfil. It is as if someone attempted to treat paranoia, not by showing the sufferer that everyone is not in fact out to get her, but by showing her that they are – and should be, not because she is defective but because that is just how people are.

One thing this leads to is an extremely difficult writing style. Horkheimer, and particularly Adorno, do not hesitate to apply their view of the primacy of non-identity to their own words and sentences, leading to many gnomic and paradoxical formulations (such as "everything is always that which it is, only because it becomes that which it is not", quoted above). Many quotations from their work will thus require lengthy explanations, and any explanation at all is likely to be an oversimplification. Philosophy so construed is not something unique to philosophers; in spite of its difficulty, it is carried out in healthy human beings by what Horkheimer and Adorno call "reflection" (*DE* 195). Reflection, which we shall consider in more detail subsequently, is what projection becomes when it avoids the absolutism of judgement, although that claim,

---

4. See Berkeley (1982). This version of idealism is never entertained by Horkheimer and Adorno.

of course, is oversimplified. In any case, when my reflective capacity is impaired, I take objects simply to be what I say they are, which amounts to an inability to see that they will become other than they are: "The paranoiac reaction arises from inability to expect" (*DE* 199).

In its efforts to undermine the absolutism of judgement, philosophy is, as we shall see later in more detail, allied to art. A work of art resists the absorption of the material into the conceptual, or the particular into the general, because it has its own peculiar structure: "The work of art ... posits its own, self-enclosed area, which is withdrawn from the context of profane existence, and in which special laws apply" (*DE* 19).

This sounds like Heidegger's discussion of the "self-grownness" of the work of art, which we saw in Chapter 7; but it is also, and more illuminatingly, Kantian. In the *Critique of Pure Reason*, judgement is unproblematic: an empirical concept is applied to an intuition in virtue of some likeness (*Gleichartigkeit*) between them (*KRV* B 176). In the *Critique of Judgment*, however, Kant defines a beautiful object as one that pleases us "without a concept"; we can tell that an object is beautiful, but we cannot formulate explicitly what its beauty consists in (*CJ* 188–9). Such an object then gives rise, not to "determining" judgements, which could tell us that, but to "reflective" judgements, which produce a number of concepts, none of which captures the beauty itself of the thing (*CJ* 314). Reflective judgements thus constitute the beautiful object in so far as we can talk about it, but do not get to its core. What Horkheimer and Adorno are doing, from this perspective, is asserting that determining judgement is an illusion; all objects for them are like beautiful objects for Kant, because their inner dynamism – the fact that they are continually becoming what they are not – means that they cannot be captured even by the very concepts to which they give rise. It is thus not surprising that Horkheimer and Adorno should give to the "healthy" realization of this the Kantian name "reflection".

Paranoia is thus the impairment of reflection to the benefit of judgement, and its extreme form is anti-Semitism (*DE* 195). The anti-Semite simply projects an image of his own devising onto Jews, and takes them to be what he thinks they are. This is not only unhealthy as a matter of personal psychology, but is pathologically grounded in a totalitarian desire to dominate: "No matter what the Jews as such may [really] be like, their image, as that of the defeated people, has the features to which totalitarian domination must be completely hostile: happiness without power, wages without work, a home without frontiers, religion without myth" (*DE* 199).

Most frightening of all, to someone invested in stable identity, is that Judaism is founded on the hope that things will be different when the Messiah comes. The Jewish tradition, as we shall again see later, thus accords a basic place to expectation, as opposed to identity (*DE* 199). Because the Jews are resistant to the overall (Christian) order of Europe, do not play by its rules and are happy not to do so, they have become the privileged enemy of European paranoia; the unhealthy personal psychology of the anti-Semite becomes a political force of unbounded evil. But anti-Semitism is not merely a European sickness; it is more deeply rooted in the nature of cognition itself, in projection without reflection, or "blind subsumption" (*DE* 201).

THE CRITIQUE OF ENLIGHTENMENT

The Frankfurt School furnishes an important early impetus, if not the beginning, for the critique of Enlightenment, today associated with "postmodernism". We shall discuss postmodernism in more detail when we discuss Derrida and Foucault, two of the leading thinkers of "postmodernity". It remains today highly problematic: what is the problem with the Enlightenment? What can possibly be wrong with the idea that, as Kant defined Enlightenment, we should resolve problems by "the public use of reason" (Kant 1996a)? In fact, Horkheimer and Adorno basically believe that Enlightenment is a *good* thing: "We are wholly convinced – and therein lies our *petitio principi* – that social freedom is inseparable from enlightened thought" (*DE* xiii). They believe, however, that Enlightenment has gone astray because it has not been fully developed; or, as they would put it, dialectically developed. It has not been allowed to go beyond itself and become what it is not.

Enlightenment, like everything else, is dialectical in that it contains the seeds of its own surpassing. In order to develop dialectically, we may say, Enlightenment would for one thing have to continue its democratic insights into the economic sphere. Then economic decisions would be made by the people via the public use of reason, rather than by a few fat cats in corporate boardrooms. But for that to come about, the Enlightenment would have had to be self-critical: it would have had to see that its application of reason to politics, as in Kant, was only a halfway house. It would have had to incorporate *reflection*:

> [T]he notion of this very way of [Enlightened] thinking, no less than the … social institutions with which it is interwoven, already contains the seed of the reversal universally apparent today. If enlightened thought does not accommodate reflection on this recidivist element, then it seals its own fate. (*DE* xiii)

Enlightenment is thus doomed; for to develop, it must turn against itself by reflecting on its own "recidivist" element, that is, on what in it escapes its own view of itself. When Enlightenment bars such reflection, it denies its own dialectical mortality. When that happens with thought in general, as we saw, it turns to paranoia and fascism, both betrayals of Enlightenment. In order to become truly Enlightened and escape these evils, Enlightenment must accept reflection: it must turn against itself and become dialectical.

But dialectics must always be specific in its identification of the mortality of things; otherwise it becomes mere unverifiable speculation. What, then, is the *specific* problem with Enlightenment? To see this, Horkheimer and Adorno, like all good dialecticians, turn to history, comparing Enlightenment with what went before and with what comes after (what comes after being the most extreme component of fascism, anti-Semitism). The key to Enlightenment, we read right at the outset of *Dialectic of Enlightenment*, is the "disenchantment" of the world (*DE* 3). Disenchantment (*Entzauberung*) is a theme introduced into German thought by the sociologist Max Weber; it refers to the fact that, for premoderns, the world is a magical place, containing all kinds of strange spirits, genies, nymphs and so on (cf. Weber 1918). For us "moderns", by contrast, the world is merely matter in motion. Something has "disenchanted" it.

One excellent reason for disenchantment, of course, is that there are no such things as genies and nymphs. But that explanation cannot be the only one, because the fundamental categories in which we think are social categories. They are shared across a given society, and they are shared not because they are true – there are numerous cases of societies that not only believe in but are founded on myths – or simply because people happen to agree on them, but because they are useful to those in control of society: "This social character of categories of thought is not … an expression of social solidarity, but evidence of the inscrutable unity of society and domination" (*DE* 21).

To understand how disenchantment with nature became the norm in modern Enlightened societies, we must therefore see what made Enlightenment socially useful. And this was not its specific claims about such things as genies and nymphs, but a more general underlying claim about nature: that it contains nothing occult, nothing that cannot be understood. There are thus no natural obstacles to knowledge (*DE* 4). The social usefulness of this was captured by Francis Bacon in a passage to which Horkheimer and Adorno refer, but which they do not actually quote: "Human knowledge and human power meet in one; for where the cause is not known the effect cannot be produced" (Bacon 1939: 28). So, say Horkheimer and Adorno: "What men want to learn from nature is how to use it wholly to dominate it and other men. That is the only aim. Ruthlessly the Enlightenment has extinguished any trace of its own self-consciousness" (*DE* 4).

The real problem with genies and nymphs, then, is that they are inscrutable; a society in which they are widely believed to exist will be, as premodern Europe was, a society that fears to replace forests and waterfalls with car parks and dams. Concern with truth is a red herring here. It is posited by Enlightenment itself as the main issue in order to hide what Enlightenment really is, thereby extinguishing "any trace of its self-consciousness".

In its relentless pursuit of domination, "Enlightenment is totalitarian" (*DE* 6); it "behaves toward things as a dictator toward men" (*DE* 9). This is both a strong charge to make against Enlightened thought and the basic thesis of the book. One way Horkheimer and Adorno support it is to focus on something that is usually dismissed as an unfortunate weakness in Enlightenment thinking, a mere residual flaw that major thinkers like Kant and Voltaire never got around to eliminating: their anti-Semitism.

> The dialectical link between enlightenment and domination, and the dual relationship of progress to cruelty and liberation which the Jews sensed in the great philosophers of the Enlightenment and the democratic national movements are reflected in the very essence of those assimilated. The enlightened self-control with which the assimilated Jews managed to forget the painful memories of domination by others … led them straight from their own, long suffering community into the bourgeoisie … (*DE* 169)

The relationship between Enlightenment and anti-Semitism is not merely a contingent link.[5] It is a dialectical one, in which Enlightenment becomes what it is not supposed to be. This is most evident, not in those (many) Jews disfavoured by Enlightenment, but in those most "elevated" by it: those who were "allowed" to abandon everything Jewish and enter into the higher orders of Enlightened society. Enlightenment, treating everyone the same, thus made even Jews themselves anti-Semitic.

Enlightenment's oppression of Jews begins with its claim to understand them – a claim it also makes for everyone else: "[Enlightenment] allows no determination other than the classifications of the societal process to operate. No one is other than he has come to be: a useful, successful, or frustrated member of vocational and national groups" (*DE* 84).

Notice three things here:

(a) The knowledge claim the Enlightenment makes about Jews is the same it makes about everyone; the "good" races, the nationalities on which Enlightenment will look favourably, are also conceived as natural units.
(b) These natural units are biological – races. "Race" is thus the concept by means of which the Enlightenment is going to understand all that can be understood about human nature; Enlightenment is not only totalitarian, but deeply racist.
(c) The general way to understand someone is to see them as a member of a group that you understand. In the case of race, you can understand it because it is biological. In the case of, say, Catholicism, also a tradi-

---

5. As when Kant claimed, in a personal letter, that no Jewish painter could properly paint a nose ("Letter to Karl Leonhard Reinhold, May 11, 1789", in Kant 1967: 136).

tional foe of the Enlightenment, you understand it in other ways (e.g. as superstition).

The individual thus becomes a mere instance of a general concept. If the individual is a human and the generality is their "race", she may be frustrated by this: she may not like the group to which she have been assigned or the way that group has been defined. She may also, more in keeping with Horkheimer and Adorno's point here, not like the general idea of being reduced to her membership in that group. But as far as Enlightenment is concerned, she nonetheless signifies only in terms of her unalterable membership in a group whose nature has itself been determined. Such classing and cataloguing is part of what Horkheimer and Adorno call "administration" or "planning" (*DE* 131). It is the socially organizational counterpart of the absolutism of judgement, which says that its general concepts actually capture individuals: administration sees everything and everyone as instancing a concept, and then moves them around as it deems best. This kind of "administrative reason", as I shall call it for the moment, is, for Horkheimer and Adorno, very widespread in today's world. Kant "grounded [it] transcendentally"; the Marquis de Sade "realized [it] empirically" (*DE* 88). But it is also endemic in the people: "The regression of the masses today is their inability to hear the unheard-of with their own ears, to touch the unapprehended with their own hands – the new form of delusion which deposes every conquered mythic form" (*DE* 36).

The "masses" are thus prisoners of the classificatory schemes that have been inculcated into them. But this is not merely true today; its ancient origin is indicated by the fact that the inability of the people to truly use their own senses is first expressed in the "Sirens" episode of the *Odyssey*, where Odysseus has his men stop up their ears with wax so they cannot hear the fatal song. Its contemporary breadth is indicated by the fact that it is found where one might least expect it: in "socialism" (pre-eminently, in 1947, Soviet socialism): "By elevating necessity to the status of the basis for all time to come, and by idealistically degrading the spirit forever to the very apex, socialism held on all too surely to the legacy of bourgeois philosophy" (*DE* 41). And it is found in logic itself. As abstract thought, logic:

> treats its objects as did fate, the notion of which it rejects: it liquidates them. Under the leveling domination of abstraction (which makes everything in nature repeatable), the [people] themselves finally come to form that "herd" which Hegel has declared to be the result of the Enlightenment. (*DE* 13)

When we replace the words in a sentence with logical symbols, we lose their force in the particular circumstances of their utterance; if I say "I love you", formalization may turn this into something like $L(x, y)$, which suppresses all relation to myself, my love and whatever effects my declaration may have on our relationship (some of which I may not intend). Any utterance is issued in a unique set of circumstances, put forward with certain intentions in mind. Formalization turns it into something that could be said by any number of people on any number of occasions.

Logic, like Enlightenment thought in general, seems to be entirely modern, but for Horkheimer and Adorno it has its ancient affinities: with *moira*, fate or "fatal necessity". *Moira* treated all things alike, that is, made them go down or perish; and it was itself inscrutable.[6] Because logic "rules in every rationalistic system of Western philosophy" (*DE* 11), it presents its abstractions as the rational destiny, so to speak, of all things: the philosophical "fate" of any sentence is to be reduced to a string of symbols. Thought is thus confined to the most general and replicable of structures. The operation of logic is also inscrutable, in that by getting rid of their concrete content, it takes things out of the temporal order in which they belong and makes them incomprehensible. Why would anyone ever say "$L(x, y)$"?

What I am calling "administrative reason" is thus (like Heidegger's *Gestell*, with which it has obvious affinities) a global affair, infecting all aspects of contemporary life. It operates by reducing everything to merely an instance of a general concept, which can be fully understood. It does this in the service of domination. But in the name of what does it pursue domination? What is its real goal?

We all have goals. If you are sleepy, your goal is to get to bed. If you are hungry, it is to eat. But for Enlightenment, "we" humans are not merely natural beings. We have access, through our reason, to realms of truth that are *a priori* and so supernatural. And such truth must play a role in the formulation of our goal, especially in the formulation of our goal as humans, as members of a generality that itself, of course, is not empirically given. Our overall goal *qua* human being is, then, not natural:

> As soon as man discards his awareness that he himself is nature, all the aims for which he keeps himself alive – social progress, the intensification of his material and spiritual powers, even consciousness itself – are nullified, and *the enthronement of the means as an end* … is already visible in the prehistory of subjectivity.   (*DE* 54, emphasis added)

When we no longer see ourselves as beings of nature, nature becomes other than we and open to domination by us. But in elevating ourselves above nature in this way, we lose all concrete content to our lives. Then we can no longer say *why* we want to dominate nature – and domination becomes an end in itself.

---

6. For a general account of Greek views on *moira*, cf. Greene (1944).

Thus, Kant attempts to validate, as the goal of all human history, merely the empty rational idea of humanity under moral law: "the architectonic structure of the Kantian system … reveals an organization of life as a whole which is deprived of any substantial goal" (*DE* 88).

The goal of history, for Kant, is simply the opportunity for human beings to set their own purposes as individuals: a goal, to be sure, but a wholly abstract one. This contrasts, not only with more substantive goals such as we saw Marx try to formulate, but with the rejection of the idea that humanity has any goal whatever. Kant's contemporary Moses Mendelssohn expresses such a rejection:

> Progress is for the individual human being (*Mensch*). One person's path [leads] through flowers and meadows, another's across desolate plains or over steep mountains and past dangerous gorges. Yet they all proceed on their journey, making their way to the felicity or which they are destined. But it does not seem to me to have been the purpose of Providence that mankind as a whole advance steadily here below and perfect itself in the course of time.   (Mendelssohn 1969: 91)

For Mendelssohn, "felicity" is different for each human being; it is not even an abstract goal. For Enlightenment in its full Kantian form, Horkheimer and Adorno claim, there is by contrast a single goal, but the goal is what was formerly the means: administration, or domination, itself. Setting one's own purposes is then not merely a preliminary to pursuing and realizing them; it is the ultimate goal itself. This single vacuous goal means in practice that "Everything is looked at from only one aspect: that it can be used for something else, however vague the notion of this use may be. No object has an inherent value; it has value only to the extent that it can be exchanged" (*DE* 15).

When everything is looked at in terms of how it conduces to an entirely abstract, or "vague", goal, we cannot evaluate any individual thing because, since the goal is vague and abstract, we cannot know exactly how the thing conduces to it. We can therefore determine something's value only by comparing it, not with the goal, but with other means. Everything becomes, in Marx's term, a "commodity": it is valued only in so far as it can be used or exchanged for something else. In order to be exchangeable for something else, of course, a thing must be somehow commensurate with that other thing: there must be some more general category of which they are both instances. And so exchangeability complies with the basic thrust of Enlightenment, seeing things (and people) as merely instances of generalities.

Now that we have encountered the final strand in Horkheimer and Adorno's concept of Enlightenment reason, we can understand another name they give it: "instrumental reason". It is not merely reason that has no goal other than furthering the instrumental domination (or administration) of nature in the service of further instrumental domination of nature, but reason that does so by identifying things with concepts, that is, by operating in terms of unreflective judgement.

CULTURAL DIALECTICS

Since, as we saw, a work of art has its own "special rules", it insists on its own uniqueness and resists the paranoid classifications of judgement; in this, we also saw, it is paradigmatic of objects in general. It is unsurprising, then, that philosophy for Horkheimer and Adorno is importantly interested in artworks. This is especially true for Adorno himself, who, by family background and education, was deeply interested in music; but it also holds for Horkheimer, who wrote his dissertation on the *Critique of Judgment*. One important strand of the Frankfurt School is thus the birth of what today is called "cultural Marxism": the view that after Marxism's death as a programme for social change (at, we also saw, the hands of fascism), it lives on as a fruitful form of cultural diagnosis. Hence, when Horkheimer and Adorno apply their general views of the non-identity of concept and thing to the contemporary world, they do so indirectly, by way of a consideration of four specific cultural phenomena: the *Odyssey*, Sade's *Juliette*, the culture industry and anti-Semitism. The first three of these have to do with artworks and how they function in society.

As with all philosophies that assert, in the wake of Hegel, that philosophical knowledge comes only from historical retrospect, the claims Horkheimer and Adorno have made about the contemporary world stand or fall with the quality of their view of historical phenomena. These discussions are therefore very dense and very rich. They also have complex aims:

- To be comprehensive: Horkheimer and Adorno want to use their basic insights to illuminate as many features as possible of the phenomena they treat.
- To be rationally transparent: Horkheimer and Adorno want to make as much sense as possible of the phenomena.
- To be new: Horkheimer and Adorno want to show us new ways of understanding what they are talking about, in accordance with their general view that the old ways of understanding them have not exhausted them.

Because of this density and complexity, I shall not try to give anything like a full account of what Horkheimer and Adorno have to say in their discussions of these four phenomena. Since I have already discussed the main points of their treatment of anti-Semitism, I shall just touch on some points about the first three.

The Odyssey

Horkheimer and Adorno have told us, at the very beginning of the book, that the "program of the Enlightenment was the disenchantment of the world; the dissolution of myths, and the substitution of knowledge" (*DE* 3). Myth is thus important to Enlightenment, for it is myth that Enlightenment is to replace. Enlightenment seeks to replace myth for the same reason it does everything: to further administration for the sake of administration, or instrumental reason. It was in this name – that of the idea that "human knowledge and human power meet in one" – that Enlightenment set out to combat both the ancient spirits proclaimed by animism and their modern derivatives, the substantial forms and essences of medieval philosophy. The problem is that Enlightenment thought itself exhibits a dialectical discrepancy between its concept and its reality: while it claims to replace myth, it is in some respects mythic itself, that is, in true dialectical fashion, it turns into its opposite.

One important component of Enlightenment's attitude to myth (and to superstition in general) is that, as administrative, it *organizes* them. Thus, the mind for Kant synthesizes, that is, puts together, or "*organizes* the individual data of cognition into a system" (*DE* 81, emphasis added). But Homer was already doing that: the *Iliad* and *Odyssey* both take earlier legends, which had come down piecemeal, and organize them into disciplined tales of the wrath of Achilles and the homecoming of Odysseus (*DE* 43). This, moreover, is a *critical* organizing: there are some legends that simply do not fit, are not good enough for inclusion and so on. In its self-consciously critical functioning, Enlightenment reason thus becomes "dissolvent": it seeks to do away with things it reasons about. The general way it does this is to see them merely as useful for other things (thus, it sees religion not on its own terms, but merely as useful for capitalist domination). But the Homeric myths do this too. Homer dissolves nature by having Odysseus continually slip away from one part of it, one place, to another: "The epic adventures allow each location a proper name and permit space to be surveyed in a rational manner. Though [Odysseus] is powerless, no part of the sea remains unknown to him" (*DE* 46).

The story of Odysseus, as he frees himself from the mores and concerns of one concrete location after another, turns out to be the formation of something decidedly non-ancient. In leaving so many things and people behind as he voyages – a voyage that he finishes alone – Odysseus in fact constructs himself as a "modern" self, that is, one that is not particularized by where it grew up or bound by its culture, but is universal: "The self does not constitute the fixed antithesis to adventure. but in its rigidity molds itself only by way of that antithesis: being an entity only in the diversity of that which denies all unity" (*DE* 47).

Odysseus's self, then, is not something fixed from the outset. His voyage, seen in retrospect, shows a self moulding itself, across its adventures, into complete abstractness: "The self represents rational universality against the inevitability of fate" (*DE* 58). This active self-moulding takes the form of battle against the ancient mythic powers Odysseus finds in the various places where he lands: Cyclops, the Lotus Eaters, Circe, and so on. He vanquishes them with his wits, just as Enlightenment will later fight such superstitions with argument (*DE* 46). Odysseus' "enlightened" battle with mythic powers extends even to the divine realm; he deceives the Titan Poseidon, for example, by telling him that his name is Outis, "no one" (*DE* 64–7). Even the sacrifices that Odysseus and his men offer to the gods, which ought to venerate them, are often parts of larger plans to deceive them (*DE* 5), a clear indication that the ancient gods are not to be respected.

Finally, all this effort is in the service of no goal beyond itself. To be sure, Odysseus is trying to get home and see his wife and son, and Horkheimer and Adorno's argument becomes rather tortured here. But it is true that Odysseus continually gets embroiled in adventures that, if he were really trying to get home, he could have avoided (*DE* 54–5).

Juliette

The work of the Marquis de Sade is usually treated with abhorrence; Horkheimer and Adorno not only discuss it at length, but do so in terms of the stunning claim that Sade's sadism is merely a particular application of Kantian morality (*DE* 95). This is because of the way Sade introduces rational calculation into sex, both in the figure of the seducer and in the actual, highly choreographed scenes of pleasure that Sade depicts at enormous length: "Even injustice, hatred and destruction are regulated, automatic procedures, since the formalization of reason has caused all goals to lose, as delusion, any claim to necessity and objectivity" (*DE* 104).

For Kant, all natural drives have the same moral status: they are all morally neutral (*DE* 86). For Horkheimer and Adorno, Sade merely takes Kant at his word; in Sade's version of Kantian morality, reason applies equally to even the crudest acts. Since reason is stripped of all concrete goals, the sadism becomes an end in itself. This Enlightened degradation of love and of nature is, finally, seen clearly in its degradation of women, to which Horkheimer and Adorno devote some very important (and easily understood) pages (*DE* 109ff.).

The culture industry

The true aim of works of art, for Horkheimer and Adorno, is to "deny the commodity society by the very fact that they obey their own law" (*DE* 157). They are to resist instrumental reason by resisting the absorption of everything into general categories. A work of art does this by being complex and at the same time unique. This complexity means that it not only differs from other things, but that, as for Heidegger, it sets up its own unique way in which experiences lead to other experiences: its own logic (see *DE* 121). With this, Horkheimer and Adorno are reshaping Kantian aesthetics, according to which the non-identity of concept and thing is given in an experience for which no concept can be found: aesthetic experience. They are also reshaping the Heideggerean–Nietzschean view that art, because of its resistance to general categories, can present a social alternative: that in the face of political and economic domination that is only enhanced and ratified by science, we must turn to art for whatever freedom remains possible for us.

Such turning to art has become problematic today because art itself, for Horkheimer and Adorno, has been subordinated to instrumental reason. In the culture industry, this subordination is complete, as attested by the fact that culture "now impresses the same stamp on everything" (*DE* 120). This uniformity is not merely evident in the way Hollywood cranks out films and television programmes that are the same in everything but detail; it is also shown by the way Hollywood treats individuals. Those who act on the big screen – the film stars – are given enormous rewards, and become very rich and famous, but we can all see that they are basically just like us:

> The starlet is meant to symbolize the typist in such a way that the splendid evening dress seems meant for the actress as distinct from the real girl. The girls in the audience not only feel that they could be on the screen, but realize the great gulf separating them from it. Only one girl can draw the lucky ticket, only one man can win the prize. (*DE* 145)

We thus have a paradoxical relation in which the star is both just like us and infinitely more than we are allowed to be. So we, the audience, become the copies, the inferior or secondary members of a general class (*DE* 145). In this way, the audience itself is "administered": "Culture as a common denominator already contains in embryo that schematization and process of cataloging and classification which bring culture within the sphere of administration" (*DE* 131).

The nature of art is now broken in two. As true "art", we may say, it continues to respect dialectical individuality and offers a reservoir of resistance to administrative reason. But as "culture", it has been taken over by such reason to such an extent that Hollywood executives are only speaking rubbish when they say that they are only giving the public what they want. In fact, by elevating ordinary people into glamorous stars, they are *telling* the public what to want: "The attitude of the public, which ostensibly and actually favors the system of the culture industry, is a part of the system and not an excuse for it" (*DE* 122).

The public is no more allowed to follow its own desires than Jews were allowed by the Enlightenment to be Jewish. The public is thus reduced to mere instances of general categories, as Jews were reduced to mere members of the bourgeoisie. This reduction implies that the audience is passive, a passivity that is further enhanced in that the culture industry keeps the audience from reacting: "It turns all participants into listeners and authoritatively subjects them all to broadcast programs which are exactly the same. No machinery of rejoinder has been devised, and private broadcasters are denied any freedom" (*DE* 122).

Simply by broadcasting the same programmes nationwide, the culture industry homogenizes the public. The highest form of the culture industry, the talking motion picture, carries this the farthest, for it makes the audience into the most passive copies of the reality it portrays:

> The sound film, far surpassing the theater of illusion, leaves no room for imagination or reflection on the part of the audience, who is unable to respond within the structure of the film ... without losing the thread of the story; hence the film forces its victims [!] to equate it directly with reality.   (*DE* 126)

The culture industry thus converts its audience into a homogenous throng of passive desirers, thereby reducing it to that most traditional of Enlightened categories, matter (*DE* 147). And all this passivity and manipulation, so carefully induced, is in the service of what? True art teaches us things; learning its lessons requires effort. People who work hard with their bodies need, not further effort, but relaxation; art for them is not to instruct, but to amuse. And that is what the culture industry provides.

> What happens at work, in the factory, or in the office can only be escaped from by approximation to it in one's leisure time. All amusement suffers from this incurable malady. Pleasure hardens into boredom because, if it is to remain pleasure, it must not demand any effort and therefore moves rigorously in the worn grooves of association. No independent thinking must be expected from the audience; the product prescribes every reaction ... Any logical connection calling for mental effort is painstakingly excluded.   (*DE* 137)

The goal of the culture industry is, then, to provide amusement. But amusement is an abstract term; anything easy can be amusing. This means that art abandons any substantive goals: "The purposelessness of the great modern work of art depends on the anonymity of the market. Its demand pass through so many intermediaries that the artist is exempt from any definite requirements – though only to a certain degree" (*DE* 157). "Amusement" turns out to mean nothing more than administering the audience by reducing them to bored passivity, all in the service of rendering them disposable for further administration.

By the end of *Dialectic of Enlightenment*, Horkheimer and Adorno have linked phenomena as diverse as movies, the Homeric poems, capitalism, fascism, socialism and anti-Semitism into a single system grounded in the structure of knowledge itself. As such, it is a system with great stability:

> It is idle to hope that this self-contradictory, disintegrating [modern] "person" will not last for generations, that the system must collapse because of such a psychological split, or that the deceitful substitution of the stereotype for the individual will of itself become unbearable for mankind. ... Synthetically produced physiognomies show that the people of today have already forgotten that there was ever a notion of what human life was. (*DE* 156)

When oppression is that entrenched, is there anything to do but accept it? No wonder, we may suspect, that Adorno called in the police!

CONCLUSION

To say that there is a standing non-identity between individual and concept is not to deny the efficacy of concepts: "perception is only possible if the thing is perceived as something definite" (*DE* 194). Trees are trees, houses are houses, and Horkheimer and Adorno are German Jews, even though much of *Dialectic of Enlightenment* was written while they were in exile in Los Angeles and so were "Angelenos". The "concept" of a thing is not, therefore, a mere empty formula or arbitrary label. It informs us, so to speak, about what is going on at the heart of a thing. But it can do so only when we see that what is going on there is a struggle between the thing and its concept, a struggle that one of them must lose. Either the concept will be transformed by what the thing undergoes, or the individual will be administered into spiritual death.

This agonistic relation between a thing and its concept cannot be captured by any conceptual formula, which would merely be another concept; and so we could say that at the heart of a thing there is an unknown, a question. This puts us back in the realm of Heidegger, but with a crucial difference: thought for him, we saw, is a *series* of questions that, somehow, build a single "pathway" of thought. It is one thing, however, to see the core of a thing as posing *a* question, and another to see it as posing a *series* of questions. In the latter case, we are entitled to suspect that the next state of the thing will pose a further question that will somehow continue the series of questions already underway, and so on into the future. Moreover, since the questions arise at the core of a single individual, we often have some sense of what that further question will be: whatever awaits the German people in the future, it will not, for Heidegger, include their starting to speak French; then they would no longer be the "German" people, but something else entirely.

When we place at the core of a thing, not a series of questions, but merely a single question, a single non-identity of thing and concept, we lose that sense of identity preserving itself across discontinuities into the future. The resolution of the current question, whether it be in favour of the thing or the concept with which it struggles, will be the end of the thing, and we have no philosophical way to think about what will replace it. The future beyond the thing becomes wholly unknowable: the infinite blue of Zarathustra's sky.

At that point, dialectics turns negative. Horkheimer and Adorno, embracing this, refuse to make any image of the future, no matter how abstractly verbal. Not only can dialectics not predict, as Marx thought it could, but it also cannot prescribe or even suggest. But if it is to be critical at all, dialectics must at least be able to *diagnose*. What negative dialectics appears to uncover, for Horkheimer and Adorno, is everywhere a massive rejection, on the part of all aspects of society down to its very language, of dialectics itself, an insistence on the positive unity of thing and concept necessary, not for philosophical idealism, but for its social counterpart: administrative reason. Society that is predicated on such unbridled judgement can prolong itself only by refusing to see its recurrent failures as failures, instead positing them as successes. *Dialectic of Enlightenment* therefore seems to present a view of the future, not as some other state of affairs that will follow on the present, but as the present prolonged. Such views are presented in passages such as the last one quoted in the previous section, which asserts that it is idle to hope that present states of affairs will not last for generations.

The future most forcefully presented in *Dialectic of Enlightenment*, especially in its final two sections, seems uniformly bleak, a world in which masses of people, made passive by the media, numbly condone unspeakable crimes. Part of the reason for the global influence of Horkheimer and Adorno has been that this picture seems, to many, sadly like the current state of affairs. Not without reason: during the recent American presidency of George W. Bush, for example, absolutist judgement was explicitly advanced as the model for White House behaviour. In the words of a high administration official:

> The aide said that [journalists] like me were "in what we call the reality-based community," which he defined as people who "believe that solutions emerge from your judicious study of discernible reality." … "That's not the way the world really works anymore," he continued. "We're an empire now, and when we act, we create our own reality. And while you're studying that reality – judiciously, as you will – we'll act again, creating other new realities, which you can study too, and that's how things will sort out. We're history's actors … and you, all of you, will be left to just study what we do." (Suskind 2004)

This claim – that non-identity between vision and reality is impossible because the vision creates the reality – amounts to an embrace of projection on an imperial scale. In such a world, nothing could be truly understood, because everything would be reduced to administrative projections, and so would vanish beneath an unreflective repertoire of categories and concepts, as inscrutable and empty as the blue sky.

That this is not the only possibility envisaged by Horkheimer and Adorno is shown only elliptically, in part perhaps because what shows it is the most horrible of crimes, the extermination of the Jews. There are many strange things about that extermination, and Horkheimer and Adorno call attention to one of them: "Jews are being murdered at a time when the fascist leaders could just as easily replace the anti-Semitic plank in their platform by some other" (*DE* 207). According to the logic of administrative reason, whose omnipresence Horkheimer and Adorno have uncovered, anything that insists on its own uniqueness is to be eliminated. But there are many such things and people, for any minority group persists in its own identity. And there are many ways to eliminate them; the Enlightenment itself, as we saw, sought to eliminate Jews by offering them economic rewards for conforming to the dominant social order. So, why Jews, and why murder?

Horkheimer and Adorno identify Jews as the privileged enemy of fascism because of what they are taken to be, partly because of the projections made on them (disloyal wanderers, social parasites, etc.). But it is also because of something they really are: believers in a messianic hope, in the expectation that things can be different (*DE* 199). From the story of their liberation from Egypt to the words that conclude the Passover Seder ("next year in Jerusalem"), such hope has been central to Judaism. Paranoia is, we saw, the inability to expect; and in the minds of the paranoid, a group that refuses to relinquish expectation must be destroyed. But expectation is not restricted to Jews. We all live inescapably in expectation, because everything that confronts us poses a question. Jews are being killed because they represent and embrace this "human condition".

Because of the Nazi murderers themselves, then, the future of the Jews will not be a prolongation of their present, for they will collectively become either victims of genocide or survivors of it. This specific aspect of their future is not shared by humans in general; their future is being finitized, we may say, by the Nazis. The uniform future of administrative reason is thus denied, in the view of Horkheimer and Adorno, by the most unbridled form of such reason itself. In the face of the Jewish insistence on hope, administrative reason must refute itself by treating Jews differently from anyone else.

Messianic hope is a complex stance, and I shall not discuss it here. But what is it to *embrace* such hope, or expectation in general? It is to reverse paranoia, to admit that your current ways of understanding things, while necessary, do not tell you that they "truly" are for all time. This reversal, we saw, is reflection; and now we see that reflection includes identifying what it is that you are reading into things:

> In human society ... the [individual] requires an increasingly firm
> control over projection; he must learn at one and the same time to
> refine and inhibit it. ... A distinction is made between without and
> within, the possibility of distancing and identifying, self-awareness and
> the conscience. ... Reflection, the life of reason, takes place as *conscious*
> projection. *(DE* 188–9, emphasis added)

Making the distinction between within and without is the retrospective
constitution of the self with which this chapter began. In earlier times, people
learned to do this under the pressure of economic necessity. Now, we must
learn them under the wider and heavier pressure of Nazi genocide, which like
all administrative reason tells everyone: you are not allowed to be what you are.

"Constituting" mind and objects now means allowing both sides to come to
fullness separately, and yet enter into a kind of dialogue:

> Only in that mediation by which the meaningless sensation brings a
> thought to the full productivity of which it is capable, while on the
> other hand the thought abandons itself to the predominant impression,
> is that pathological loneliness which characterizes the whole of nature
> overcome. *(DE* 189)

Nature is "lonely", of course, in that it is unconscious: stones and trees can
hardly befriend one another. But it is also "lonely" when mind, which alone
could supply companionship, abandons nature in favour of projecting its own
categories onto it, thereby relating only to itself. Only a separation that allows
both subject and object to be what they really are – their own becoming-other
– can do justice to the fact that "The inner depth of the subject consists in
nothing other than the delicacy and wealth of the external world of perceptions"
(DE 189). Horkheimer and Adorno call the realization of this "reconciliation".
Reconciliation, the "considered opposition" of mind and object *(DE* 188–9),
is thus the true opening-up of the future. For in it the world confronts us, not
as the uniform gloom of administrative reason, but as an ongoing proliferation of concrete non-identities. As such, it is the ground of hope, and also "the
highest notion of Judaism" *(DE* 199). Reconciliation is not presented as a goal
in *Dialectic of Enlightenment*, much less as the goal of history itself; it cannot
be, if dialectics is to remain negative. Like Nietzsche's overman, reconciliation
is merely glimpsed from time to time, and often by allusion. Whether it will
ever come about on a social scale cannot be predicted: "The change depends on
whether the ruled see and control themselves in the face of absolute madness
and call a halt to it" *(DE* 199).

This is a large "whether". But reconciliation, the mediation of self and world
achieved through reflection and in the name of hope, is still something to which,
individually and in groups, we can aspire. An aspiration to hope is tenuous

indeed as a motive force in history, far more so than Marx's dream of an all-transforming proletariat. But it is something that critical theory itself, exposing absolutist judgements wherever they occur, can help bring about. Critical theory, as the disarming reflection on the "recidivist" components of Enlightenment (cf. again *DE* xii), on its inherent tendency to impose fixed identities on things, thus becomes Enlightenment's next dialectical stage. By means of it, "Enlightenment which is in possession of itself and coming to power can break the binds of Enlightenment" (*DE* 208).

PART III

FRANCE, 1945–2004

CHAPTER 10

THE FUTURE AND FREEDOM: JEAN-PAUL SARTRE

PRIMARY TEXT Jean-Paul Sartre, *Basic Writings* (*BW*; 2001)

In June 1940, a little less than a year before Arendt was to flee France and two months after the "phoney war" between France and Germany became all too real, a detachment of the German army surprised a small group of French soldiers who were more or less hiding in the small village of Padoux, in northern France. The French hardly constituted a cohesive fighting force; they had been wandering around in confusion and despair for several days. Most pathetic of all, perhaps, was their meteorologist. He was certainly an odd-looking soldier. Barely five feet tall, he had bulging eyes, the right of which was cocked up and to the right. He had with him a number of notebooks, which he had filled up with all sorts of ruminations. In one of them he had written: "Whatever men feel I can guess out, explain, put it down in black and white. But not *feel* it. I concoct illusions, I have the appearance of a feeling person and I am a desert" (quoted in Bertholet 2000: 208).[1]

This human desert enjoyed captivity as a German prisoner, for his little group of prisoners was the first non-hierarchical community he had ever been a member of. Family, school and church all had been authoritarian structures; only now, at the age of thirty-four, did he encounter fellowship. At the prison camp, he was able to wangle a room in the infirmary, where he continued to write. He organized discussion groups with other philosophically inclined prisoners. He even wrote and staged a play. In January 1941, he decided it was time to leave. He was physically unable to escape, but forged a medical certificate that did the job. He was sent first to the infamous staging area at Drancy, from which Jews would later be sent east, to their deaths; after six days of confinement there, Jean-Paul Sartre headed west, to Paris.

---

1. The overall story is in Bertholet (2000: 200–219).

He quickly became famous, not only for the quality and quantity of his literary output but for its diversity. Throughout his life he balanced philosophical treatises, often very technical, with an incredible number of plays, novels and short stories that explored the same issues in more concretely experimental ways. In 1964 he was awarded the Nobel Prize in literature – which he turned down: the only person ever to do so. After 1968, the tumultuous year that so affected France, Sartre devoted more and more time to matters of social philosophy, declaring himself a "Marxian": someone who does not agree with Marx or with the Communist Party but who recognizes that Marx is *the* thinker whom anyone, today, must take into account. But, as we shall see, his political interests were there from the start.

ETHICS AND PHENOMENOLOGY

The intensity of Sartre's ethical concern is unusual in twentieth-century continental philosophy. Heidegger, Arendt, Horkheimer and Adorno, Foucault and Derrida all begin, whether they say so or not, from a quasi-Hegelian standpoint in which the basic ethical unit is not the individual but the community. For them, as for Hegel, ethics is not a distinct part of philosophy; ethical matters are treated as they arise in social philosophy. Even Arendt's individualism, we saw, viewed human individuality as embedded within the matrices of *oikos* and *polis*.

Certainly, ethics does not fit easily with temporalized philosophy, because the kind of time into which that approach places the mind is not a simple, abstract passing away of things, or what Kierkegaard called the "infinite vanishing". Rather, it is time as history: as a set of concrete processes that are unfolding around and through us. Historical processes, in turn, are not located within or founded on individual minds. Rather, they pre-exist those minds, as the history of my country pre-exists me. Themselves the products of the efforts of many individuals, they provide the social and interpersonal contexts in which we must act, and in so doing they limit our action. On such a view, individuals rarely if ever begin things, and responsibility is always joint. The basic ethical unit – that which can be said to be good or bad – thus tends to be the community or even the entire society, developing over time.

Traditional philosophy in the modern era, by contrast, is built on a conception of the individual self as isolated from all other beings, and it tends to carry this over into its accounts of human goodness and badness. Indeed, for Descartes to think rightly *is* to be good:

> But the pure and genuine virtues, which proceed solely from knowledge of what is right, all have one and the same nature and are included under the single term "wisdom". For whoever possesses the firm and powerful resolve always to use his reasoning powers as correctly as he can, and to

> carry out whatever he knows to be best … will possess justice, courage, temperance, and all the other virtues. (Descartes 1985: 191)[2]

When Descartes put philosophy on the certain and secure foundation of the *cogito*, he also showed what he took to be the human path to goodness. But thought for Descartes is individual, and the goodness involved does not extend to communities or societies. Descartes makes this quite clear in the third maxim of his "provisional morality":

> to try always to master myself rather than fortune, and to change my desires rather than the order of the world. … Nothing lies entirely within our power except our thoughts, so that after doing our best in dealing with matters external to us, whatever we fail to achieve is absolutely impossible so far as we are concerned. (*Ibid.*: 123)

Husserl, as we have seen, accepted Descartes' view of the individual human mind as isolated. Although Husserlian consciousness and Cartesian mind were different kinds of thing, both were individuated and closed off; each constituted a realm unto itself. Unlike Descartes, Husserl avoided claiming that being a good thinker meant you were also a virtuous person. Indeed, he avoided ethics altogether, leaving it to later thinkers such as Levinas, Scheler and Sartre to develop his thought in that direction. Of these three, Sartre has been by far the most influential.

We can say that Sartre's ethics is the ethics that Descartes might have written had he been acquainted with Husserlian phenomenology. This is because the most basic claim of Sartre's ethics will be a version of the Cartesian thesis that to be a good person is to be a good *thinker*. In Sartre's case, being a good thinker works out to being a good *phenomenologist*, that is, to being someone who not only understands what a human being is, but who has the courage to accept this. The fundamental philosophical and human virtue, for Sartre, is, then, what I shall call "lucidity": the knowledge of what and who you really are. His ethics, and indeed his whole work as a philosopher, novelist and journalist, can be viewed as an attempt both to attain lucidity for himself and to instil it into his readers, particularly with regard to their nature as radically free beings. This does not mean that Sartre wholly rejects continental philosophy's concern with social philosophy. In addition to reading Husserl he has read Marx, and has been impressed enough to eventually, as I have noted, style himself a "Marxian". But because of his Husserlian–Cartesian heritage, he does not want simply to *begin* with social philosophy. He wants an ethics that is developed prior to, and so independently of, social philosophy: an ethics that is developed out of a

---

2. For Descartes' ethics as implicit in the later *Passions de l'âme*, see Cottingham (1986: 152–6).

phenomenological account of the individual human mind, or of what Sartre calls "consciousness". This, in turn, will provide the premises for social philosophy.

Part of what what gives impetus to Sartre's individualism is that, as we shall see, he agrees with Husserl that consciousness is a closed realm that must be explained entirely in its own terms. This in turn means that, when Sartre describes the basic structures of consciousness, history and society are not brought in as explanatory factors. This leads Sartre, in spite of his Marxist (and Heideggerean) concerns, to treat consciousness as something whose basic structures are unaffected by time. Although he does not seek to found the kind of "apodictic science" envisaged by Husserl, his thought is, like Husserl's, a kind of reawakened traditional philosophy, grounded in what are taken, if not explicitly asserted, to be atemporal truths. Like Husserl and Kant, although less overtly, Sartre thus serves as a "foil" for subsequent developments: later French thinkers, beginning with Simone de Beauvoir will undertake to place his discoveries about the mind back into a temporal context.

Although his ethics has become the most influential part of Sartre's thought, then, it is integrally related to the rest of his philosophy: he seeks to ground it in a theory of the human individual and to develop it into a social philosophy. My account of Sartre here will begin with the relatively non-technical account of his ethics in "Existentialism is a Humanism". Then I shall go on to treat the theory of consciousness on which those ethical views are based, before returning to a more deeply philosophical account of ethical matters to show how Sartre goes on to develop them into a social philosophy.

EXISTENTIALISM, HUMANISM AND ETHICS

Sartre's "Existentialism is a Humanism" is a defence of his philosophy that he gave as a lecture in October 1945, shortly after the war ended. It is in many ways a popular introduction to his moral and ethical thinking, but it is founded on one of the basic insights of the whole German philosophical tradition: the notion that the ego is not merely an inert thing, or substance, but a radical *activity*. To be sure, Sartre is not merely a French epigone of German thinkers; he holds Descartes in far too much esteem to be that. Another resource he is drawing on in formulating this view of the mind, although he does not explicitly discuss it much, is ancient thought. This is evident when, near the beginning of "Existentialism is a Humanism", he gives his famous statement of the basic principle of existentialism: that "existence precedes essence". This formulation not only makes use of the vocabulary of medieval Aristotelianism; it is immediately spelled out (*BW* 27–8) in opposition to Aristotle, whose name Sartre never mentions.

For Aristotle, the most basic component of a thing was its essence: the specific set of features that made it the kind of thing that it is. In his account of "equipment", Heidegger had suggested that Greek philosophers, including most especially Aristotle, arrived at this view by considering the way we make things. In order to make something, you must first have an idea of what *kind* of thing you are making. The painter does not have the exact image in her mind of the picture she is going to paint; she cannot, because too many things happen as she paints. But she has a general idea of what sort of picture it is going to be. So in general for all activities of making things. What the image and the finished thing have in common is, then, what Aristotle calls the "form". When you make a thing, you put its form into matter. In Heidegger's view, Aristotle had extended this to nature. The result was the general view that all things come to be as examples of pre-existing, specifiable *kinds* of thing: all things are essences given concrete existence. Because any thing has an essence, and because that essence is a specifiable set of properties, any thing must have certain properties, and cannot have others. Thus, in the philosophical tradition a human being is a "rational animal", with both a body and a mind, and this means that a human being has certain ways in which it should naturally act and live. Any divergence from these is literally "unnatural".

Later philosophers had ascribed this fundamental formative activity to God. God knows what a human being is, and he made you one. As a result, there are certain things you can do and certain things you cannot do: you can talk and laugh, and you cannot fly. If your essence was given to you by God, moreover, it is more than natural; you not only must but *should* live and act in such a way as to fulfil your God-given human nature. Not to do so is not merely unnatural; it is a *sin*. On such a view, our human essence must exist before we do; we cannot exist without it, and it is the source of our ethical standards. "Essence precedes existence" temporally, logically and ethically.

Still later philosophers – Sartre mentions Diderot and Voltaire, along with Kant – dispensed with God. But they still maintained that humans have a certain nature, a specifiable set of properties that we all share. And they all agree that we should act in accordance with that nature. Sartre's question is this: if God does not exist, why should our human nature have a normative claim on us? Where, in fact do we get our nature from? What is it? His answer is radical. Only God could give us a set of properties that we not only do share, on some levels, but must strive to share on *all* levels. Without him, no such thing as human nature can exist: "If God does not exist, there is at least one being whose existence comes before its essence, a being which exists before it can be defined" (*BW* 28). This means that there are no ethical requirements imposed on us by our nature (or our nature's divine creator). We are radically self-creative:

> Man first of all exists, encounters himself, and surges up in the world – and defines himself afterwards. To begin with he is nothing. He will not be anything until later, and then he will be what he makes of himself.

Thus, there is no human nature, because there is no God to have a conception of it. (*BW* 28)

This does not mean that we are entirely indefinite, nebulous creatures: Sartre
was a writer; Michael Jordan a basketball player; Bill Clinton a politician. But
it was not somehow decreed for Michael Jordan before birth that he would be
a great basketball player. He made *himself* into that: "Man is nothing else but
that which he makes of himself" (*BW* 29).

This is a very radical claim. What about circumstances? What about sheer
luck? If Bill Clinton had lived in France in the seventeenth century, he would
never have been President of the United States; he would not even have been
a politician, because he is a commoner. Michael Jordan could not have been a
basketball star then either, since basketball had not been invented. So why not
say that circumstances and sheer luck make you what you are? Sartre takes this
question very seriously, which does not mean that he can answer it. Here, he
makes three points:

(a) To say that circumstances make you what you are is a very lazy way of
looking at life: a denial of responsibility (*BW* 29). Sartre's own approach is
thus "alone compatible with the dignity of man, the only [theory] which
does not make man into an object" (*BW* 38–9).
(b) We are indeed, on some level, independent of our culture and circumstance. In words that could also have been written by Husserl, Sartre writes:
"I think therefore I am is the absolute truth of consciousness as it attains
to itself" (*BW* 38), that is, as it comes into being in a knowledgeable way.
If the *cogito* is "absolute truth", it at least must be independent of all culture
and circumstances
(c) Although he does not emphasize it here, Sartre does not ultimately hold
that circumstances do not matter at all. What he is saying, so to speak, is
that they provide the cards you are dealt, but what you do with them is
up to you: "We limit ourselves to a reliance upon that which is within our
wills, or within the sum of probabilities that render our action feasible"
(*BW* 35).

Point (a) is itself an ethical argument, claiming that the alternative to Sartre's
view is somehow morally inferior to it. Points (b) and (c) work out to the idea
that Sartre's view of radical self-creativity operates on a distinct, and basic, level
of what we are: of what he calls "human reality". He is not talking about how you
become something specific, like a basketball player or a writer. He is claiming
that in order to be *anything at all* you have to make yourself into that thing.
The question here is not "Why am I this rather than that?", but "Why am I
anything at all?": why do I live a life at all, rather than just be born, undergo
some things, and die? There is thus a basic level on which the human being is

radically self-creative, but when this raw creativity assumes specific form in a given individual, it comes up against circumstance and chance. Maybe Sartre, who was around five feet tall and had bad eyesight, could not have been a basketball player like Michael Jordan. But even to fail as a basketball player, he would have had to try, and nothing required him to try.

But now it seems that Sartre has just come up with a new definition of a human being: a human being is a being that has to make itself into something definite. Sartre agrees with this, in a way: "Although it is impossible to find in each and every human a universal essence that can be called human nature, there is nevertheless a human universality of *condition*" (*BW* 39). The common human *condition* is not a human *essence* because it is merely negative: a set of "limitations which define man's fundamental situation in the universe" (*BW* 39). The most basic of these limitations is that we have to work in order to be anything at all. Such a limitation, or condition, differs from an essence in that it has no normative status: it is simply a fact.

Instead of specifying a definite content for the human essence, Sartre has defined humanity by its lack of such content: by the fact that the human self is not something we are simply endowed with by virtue of being born, but must work to attain. This condition is, however, a universal and atemporal one, in that it applies to any human, no matter when or where they live. For Hegel, Marx and Heidegger, there is nothing to be said about a human being over and above the properties given her by her historical and cultural surroundings; history permeates us to our core. Although Kant and Husserl agree that a human being is affected by history on certain levels, they hold that she is also possessed of faculties (for Kant) or eidetic structures (for Husserl) that were the same for all humans at all times. Sartre's claim that humans can only be what they make themselves into is a much thinner view of the mind than Kant and Husserl had propounded, but it has the same atemporal status.

Sartre's view that radical self-creation is the human condition – that it is something all humans exhibit – thus places him closer to Kant and Husserl than to temporalized philosophy. It is also what allows him to develop his view into an ethics. "Ethics", as pursued within traditional philosophy, consists in general guidelines for how people should behave, and was traditionally founded on two things Sartre has rejected: the existence of God and of human nature. Because of this rejection, each human being for him is radically unique; everyone creates herself, but no one has ever before set out to create *my* self in *these* circumstances. Hence, as we have seen, there can be no general guidelines for such creation. How, then, can there be an ethics?

When I work towards some specific goal I have chosen, my commitment to that particular goal has to be seen in the context of my more basic project of self-creation: I am working towards being a certain sort of self. My commitment thus presupposes an "image of man such as [I] believe he ought to be" (*BW* 29). Although no one has ever been in my concrete situation before, there are other beings who, on their most basic levels, are as radically self-creative as I am: other human beings. And the image of human selfhood towards which I am working, being a product of the radical self-creativity I share with all other human beings, applies to them as well. When I choose something, therefore, I am implicitly saying that it is a goal towards which any human being should, in similar circumstances, work. So every decision that I make is a decision that I recommend to all other humans. I never choose, then, it is never just for myself. I choose as the representative of all humanity, and as such I am "responsible for all men" (*BW* 29).[3]

This is a high-pressure situation to be in, because since there is no God no moral guidelines are given to me for the decisions I have to make on behalf of everybody. Indeed, even if the Ten Commandments *were* given by God, it still would be up to me to figure out what they prescribe right here and right now. More realistically for Sartre, the same is true if I am under orders from another human being. There is always leeway in interpreting them; I must always "decipher the sign", figure out what my orders mean (*BW* 34–5).

The fact that we must choose without guidelines, yet choose for everybody, is what Sartre means when he says we are "free". Freedom is thus not fun at all; it is a truly fearsome condition. In viewing freedom itself as terrifying, Sartre thus agrees with Kierkegaard; but the reason for the terror is different. For Kierkegaard, working within what he understands to be a Christian context, what induces dread is the possibility of my own eternal damnation, even if I do not understand what that is. For Sartre, my anguish originates in the responsibility for all other human beings that I implicitly assume with my every choice. The fact that my choices are free, yet must claim to be valid for everyone, places me in "anguish" (*BW* 30). The human being is thus, in one of Sartre's most famous phrases, "condemned to be free" (*BW* 32).

This is the point of the moral dilemma Sartre discusses in *BW* 33ff.: that of the young man who must decide whether to join the Resistance or to stay with his mother, who needs him to care for her under the German occupation. What should he do? Sartre's response is twofold. First, nothing that anyone tells the young man can relieve him of the responsibility for his decision. Even if he goes to someone who gives him very definite advice, it is *he* who has gone to that person rather than to someone else. Why? Because to some degree he knows in advance what the other person is going to tell him. He can, for example go to a priest, but there were Nazi priests and Resistance priests, and he probably knew who was which. In fact (for Sartre tells us this is a real example, not something he has invented) the young man did not go to a priest at all. He went to Sartre.

---

3. We saw that, for Husserl, I know other people by projecting onto their bodies, which I perceive, the things I myself think and feel. Sartre here has given this an ethical twist: I project onto others my own ethical commitments, in the form of my image of what I think a human being should be, and I do this every time I act.

And the advice Sartre gave him was empty: "choose – that is to say, invent" (*BW* 34). This is, on one level, no help at all. But on the more basic level, Sartre hopes, he has clarified the young man's situation to him: that he is the one who is going to have to choose. And that is all Sartre can do for the young man. Anything more would be an attempt to take the responsibility of choosing away from him, and that cannot be done, not (merely) because that is immoral, but because it is impossible.

Empty advice is the only honest advice, then, which poses a further problem. Sartre seems to be saying that once you have admitted that you are free, and that your choice is not dictated by any set of moral standards that have been given to you from whatever source, then it does not matter what you actually choose. The young man can either stay with his mother or go and join the Resistance, and either is fine with Sartre – as long as he does it "authentically", that is, with lucidity, in the full awareness that it is his decision alone. But what if the young man made a third choice: to join the collaborators and even become a Nazi himself? It does not appear that Sartre could condemn this choice: "Whenever a man chooses his purpose and his commitment in all clearness and in all sincerity, whatever that purpose may be it is impossible to prefer another for him" (*BW* 42).

Sartre appeals here to the view that, in order to be a good person, you must make your choices in a certain way: with clear self-awareness combined with the honest courage that such awareness requires. You must, in other words, choose as a good phenomenologist, for phenomenology consists in coming to such lucidity about ourselves. To be a good person is thus also to be a good phenomenologist, a good thinker. The problem is that being a good phenomenologist and being a good person do not always seem to coincide. A phenomenologist, for Sartre, can attain honest clarity about anything whatever; but a good person cannot choose anything whatever. Suppose I choose, in full clarity and sincerity, to become a Nazi; indeed, I choose that for all human beings, which means, apparently, that I am recommending that all Jews commit suicide. To call such a view absurd does not do it justice; it is vile, and worse than vile. How can Sartre condemn it and its ilk? If he cannot, what good is his philosophy?

Sartre's answer shows the honesty that was so characteristic of him: no good at all. In order to salvage his entire philosophy, he has to show why it is impossible to choose, in all clarity and sincerity, to become a Nazi. He does so in a brilliant essay called "Anti-Semite and Jew" (Sartre 1948). No one can authentically choose to be a Nazi, or any kind of racist, because race is something you are born with. If I condemn any group of other people merely because of how they were born, I am also saying that I am immune to condemnation because I was born differently. And then I am denying that I am only what I make of myself. My birth, rather than anything of my doing, makes me morally immune to evil. Such a viewpoint *cannot* exhibit the lucidity and courageous honesty of a good phenomenologist, or of a good person. It is a lazy, cowardly lie, and as such the very opposite of what existentialism advocates.

This is a development of (a) above: the view that defining human nature is a lazy way of denying our own responsibility for our lives. Sartre articulates it in "Existentialism is a Humanism", although not as sharply, by saying that specifying what human nature is is always a way to exclude other people from that nature. It is not morally permissible, then, to define human nature; to do so leads not merely to irresponsibility but ultimately to fascism (*BW* 45), or even to Nazism. The true view of human nature is that it is constant "self-surpassing" (*BW* 45). We do not know in advance what humans are capable of, or what they can or should do. In doing what they do, they do not affirm some pre-existing human nature; what they affirm is that they are always seeking "beyond themselves" (*BW* 45).

Behind this is a view about time. Heidegger claimed in *Being and Time* that the future is radically open. Since we have no nature, we cannot know what we can become – until we have become it. Sartre agrees: "Man is, before all else, something which propels itself towards a future and is aware that it is doing so … Whatever man may now appear to be, there is a future to be fashioned, a virgin future that awaits him. … But in the present one is forsaken" (*BW* 29–32).

CONSCIOUSNESS

Sartre, like many philosophers, wants to give a comprehensive account of human life that will show us as much as can be shown about how to live as individuals and in societies. He also wants, very traditionally, to give an atemporal account of the basic nature of human life, and to ground that account in a broader account of the nature of things in general. After Descartes, however, the first thing the mind can know for certain is itself; and after Kant, metaphysical accounts of the basic nature of reality itself are decidedly out of favour. So Sartre, like Kant, has to develop his political and ethical thought out of an account of the human mind – which he calls, following Husserl, "consciousness". In taking the study of consciousness, or "phenomenology", as his starting-point, however, Sartre is following not merely Husserl but what, in *Being and Nothingness*, he designates as a general feature of "modern thought": "Modern thought has realized considerable progress by reducing the existent to the series of appearances which manifest it" (*BW* 70).

This evocation of Husserl's concept of an intentional object, however, goes beyond Husserl himself. Sartre does not merely "bracket" the existence of the world behind appearances, as Husserl did, but actually denies it. As Berkeley had argued in the eighteenth century (Berkeley 1982), if we can account for all our experience without appeal to things beyond them why make the appeal? "There is nothing behind the appearance, and since it indicates only itself (and the total series of appearances), it can not be *supported* by any being other than its own" (*BW* 73).

Sartre goes on to say that this post-Husserlian approach constitutes "progress" because it enables philosophy to escape a number of dualisms that have plagued it: interior–exterior (i.e. things in our minds versus things outside of them); appearance–reality; act–potency; appearance–essence. Avoidance of these constitutes progress, because philosophy that makes use of these dualisms must define them; explain how they come to be; and show how each side of a given dualism relates to the other. What, for example, is the precise meaning of the claim that some things are "interior" to our minds, and other things "exterior" to them? Why do things fall into these two categories? Is anything both internal and external to the mind? Is anything neither? And so on. For Sartre, such problems do not arise because on the phenomenological approach as he understands it – one that denies the existence of things other than appearances – we have not these dualisms but only the "monism of the phenomenon" (*BW* 70). On that approach, we have no exteriorities, potencies or essences, but only appearances, that is, phenomena.

There is one dualism, however, that remains even on Sartre's approach. As we saw in Husserl, the number of possible appearances of an object is infinite. New experiences of the thing are always possible, or as Sartre puts it there is always the possibility of "multiplying the points of view" (*BW* 71). This means that the object is not merely what our minds have experienced of it; there is always something more, even if that something more is not "exterior" to our minds. That something more is the infinity of points of view on the object. As with Husserl, this is what makes the object "objective": "Our theory of the phenomenon has replaced the reality of the thing by the objectivity of the phenomenon, and it has based this on an appeal to infinity" (*BW* 72).

What Sartre calls the "principle" of the series of appearances of a given thing (*BW* 71), and Husserl called its "rule", thus governs more – infinitely more – then the appearances we actually have of that thing. If the principle of the overall series is the "essence" of the thing (Husserl called it the "*eidos*"), then "The essence is radically severed from the individual appearance which manifests it, since on principle it is that which must be able to be manifested by an infinite series of individual manifestations" (*BW* 72).

Thus, the "principle" of a sequence of appearances is distinguished from the appearances themselves because of an absence: because it can govern appearances that we have not had, and never will, have. Our experience of any object, then, is defined by a *lack* (*BW* 86): by our awareness that our experiences of the thing amount merely to a finite subset of the infinite set of its possible appearances. To put this somewhat differently, we never possess an object securely; it always remains other than we are. Although he has reduced things to appearances, Sartre is thus not a "subjective idealist". He is not someone who believes that there is nothing to reality but what our minds create.

There is another component to consciousness for Sartre, however. An appearance must appear *to* something. What is this something? It cannot itself be an appearance, because that appearance would also have to appear to something. We would then have an infinite regress, which we could stop only arbitrarily, at which point the whole enterprise "falls away into nothingness" (*BW* 75). Consciousness itself, then, does not appear to us; it cannot be perceived. *All* its contents, as specific appearances, are other than it. Husserl had put this point by saying that consciousness is always consciousness of something that is other than consciousness itself: his principle of "intentionality". Sartre phrases it this way:

> All consciousness is positional in that it transcends itself in order to reach an object, and it exhausts itself in this same positing. All that there is of intention in my actual consciousness is directed towards the outside, towards the table; all my judgments or practical activities, all my present inclinations, transcend themselves, they aim at the table and are absorbed by it. (*BW* 76)

To say that all consciousness is "positional" or, as Sartre also says, "thetic" is to say that consciousness "posits" some definite appearance of which it is conscious. And that, we see, exhausts the nature of consciousness. Since all its content consists in appearances that are other than it, consciousness has no content of its own. It is a radical activity, and there is nothing specific to it over and above the things of which it is conscious, that is, the various appearances that it does not securely possess. Sartre is thus, typically for him, grounding the emptiness we saw in his "definition" of human nature in a feature of consciousness as such.

This account of consciousness is incomplete because, among other things, we must be conscious of ourselves: you cannot be conscious of *that table* without being somehow aware that you are conscious of it (*BW* 77). But this awareness of ourselves cannot be explicit or positional, because of the regress problem I mentioned above. Therefore there must be what Sartre calls a "non-positional" consciousness, a sort of "feel" that does not have a definite object: "every positional consciousness of an object is at the same time a non-positional consciousness of myself" (*BW* 78). With this we have our basic awareness of ourselves, or what Sartre calls the "pre-reflective cogito", borrowing Descartes' term for my fundamental knowledge that I think, but making that awareness even more basic by subtracting from it everything specific, even "thinking" itself (*BW* 78).

This non-positional, non-thetic, pre-reflective awareness of self is an ingredient in all consciousness. Where does it come from? Not from outside, from our experiences of objects, because then consciousness would be an effect of something that is not consciousness, and to that degree consciousness would not be fully conscious of itself – and so not fully consciousness. As Sartre puts this important point:

> It is impossible to assign to a consciousness a motivation other than itself. Otherwise it would be necessary to conceive that consciousness to the degree to which it is an effect, is not consciousness (of) itself. It would be necessary in some manner that it should be without being conscious (of) being. We should fall into that too common illusion which makes consciousness semi-conscious .... But *consciousness is consciousness through and through. It can be limited only by itself.*
>
> (*BW* 80, emphasis added)

This is a pretty amazing thing to say. When I am drowsy, or dizzy, or have had too much to drink, my consciousness certainly seems to be limited by physiological factors. Why would Sartre deny this?

First, Sartre is not alone here. As I have noted previously, modern philosophers in general – not only Descartes and Husserl but people such as Hume, Berkeley and Kant – have all held, in one way or another, that everything we can know is already "in" consciousness; whatever affects consciousness from outside cannot be known. This means that the effects of that unknown something would be also unknowable: they would be some sort of mysterious opacities showing up in my field of awareness.[4] But nothing in consciousness can remain unknown. So if consciousness is comprehensive (everything we can know is in it) and transparent (nothing in it cannot be known), consciousness cannot be affected by external things. When Sartre says (*BW* 81) that it is impossible for us to understand how physical states can change our mental states, he is echoing Berkeley's denial of the existence of physical things, and Kant's problematic claims about the thing-in-itself (which we saw in Chapter 1).

In order to provide us with comprehensive and certain knowledge, then, consciousness must be a realm entirely independent of physical things. It must be what Sartre calls an "absolute of existence and not [merely] of knowledge" (*BW* 81). Only so can consciousness be the "identity of appearance and existence", that is, a realm in which what appears to us is just what is, without reference to a set of appearances we have not had. And only so can consciousness be "the absolute" (*BW* 81), or, as Husserl had put it, can consciousness achieve evidence. The obvious problem with this is that Sartre has not ruled out the possibility that we can never achieve such certainty. It is one thing to say that *if* consciousness is to achieve certainty, it must be an entirely self-enclosed realm; it is another to say that this actually obtains. Sartre presumably thinks – as did Husserl and other modern philosophers – that the fact of such certainty is undeniable, and that he is merely explaining one implication of that undeniable fact.

---

4. As, we shall see, do Derridean *différance* and Foucauldian power, which bodes ill for Sartre's argument here.

In any case, the specific appearances of which we are conscious, plus our "pre-reflexive" awareness of ourselves, are all there is to consciousness. It is not as if we could become aware of our consciousness more definitely if we paid more attention; there is nothing to become aware *of*. Consciousness is, then, "total emptiness": the entire world is outside it (*BW* 81). It can be known completely, and is absolute, because there is nothing "in" it to be known.

This brings us back to the Germanic insight that the mind is a radical activity. We normally view perception as passive: as the reception into the mind of information from things outside the mind. But that cannot be the case for Sartre, because consciousness cannot be affected by what is outside it. Thus, there is no "passivity" in consciousness (*BW* 83). To be sure, my mind does not make the table I see. But it does not passively receive data from outside either; rather, in order to see the table I have to notice it, focus on it, turn to it. The table is not my doing – but my consciousness of it is: "Thus, to 'support passively' … is a conduct which I assume and which engages my liberty as much as to 'reject absolutely'" (*BW* 83).

That consciousness is a radical activity, not a thing, is one of two main upshots of this discussion. The other, as we have seen, is that this activity can have no cause beyond itself: "The existence of consciousness comes from consciousness itself" (*BW* 80). Here, Sartre again gives Husserl an ethical twist. What Husserl had called "passive synthesis" is identified by Sartre as a phenomenon of freedom.

SELF, NIHILATION, LACK

Consciousness, as an "absolute" domain unto itself, can be known only from within. No amassing of facts about consciousness can explain it to us at all, because in order to have a fact we must have an appearance, and appearances, being determinate objects of consciousness, are other than consciousness. This means that science (in the usual sense of the word) cannot reveal consciousness to us; only phenomenology can. And it means, further, that the only kind of consciousness we can know is our own kind: human consciousness. When we identify consciousness as human, it has further structures, albeit "empty" ones. These structures constitute what Sartre calls the "self".

We have seen that consciousness is: (a) radical activity; (b) a domain entirely unto itself, independent of all else; and (c) empty. Sartre's way of referring to all of these together is to say that consciousness is "for-itself". What makes these properties of *human* consciousness is that they exhibit a certain tendency, a direction. The first step in showing this is to contrast the nature of consciousness with the nature of an unconscious object.

The various things of which we are aware are, like the appearances from which they are compounded, very different from consciousness. They are not radical activities, but inert objects. They are not free, but behave as they do only when other things cause them to do so. They are not "empty" and do not have lacks the way consciousness does, then; they simply are what they are. Sartre calls this inert way of being the "in-itself".

Any object of consciousness, we have seen, is something that consciousness itself is not, because consciousness itself is entirely empty. To become aware of something is, then, an activity of seeing that thing as not-identical with yourself, of taking up a distance from it: "The for-itself is perpetually determining itself not to be the in-itself" (*BW* 157). Sartre calls this active distance-taking "nihilation", because it is carried out by the empty radical activity that consciousness is: by a "nothing" (*BW* 118). Nihilation is, then, the way the radical activity of consciousness comes about: it "*is not* – it is *made to be*" (*BW* 118, trans. mod.). As carried out by consciousness, nihilation comes – like consciousness itself – from nowhere. It is the "absolute event" (*BW* 119). Because nihilation has no nature of its own, it is defined entirely by what it nihilates. The objects of which I am aware – the "in-itself" in general – are, although different from consciousness, essential to it:

> The for-itself is perpetually determining itself not to be the in-itself. This means that it can establish itself only in terms of the in-itself and against the in-itself. ... The concrete, real in-itself is wholly present at the heart of consciousness as that which consciousness determines itself not to be.
> (*BW* 157)

Nihilation is thus perpetually unstable: what it is at any moment depends on what specifically is being nihilated. That is why, in concrete cases, nihilation is "made to be".

What, then, about my self-knowledge, the various appearances I have of myself? Are these not specific contents that can be assigned to my self? Sartre does not deny the obvious fact that we do appear to ourselves; we have already seen him claim that when I make any choice whatsoever it is in virtue of my image of the kind of person I want to be, that is, of my idealized self-image. But when I am aware of myself in such a specific way, I am also aware that what I am aware of is *not* myself: my self-image is not the basic level of my consciousness, which as we saw is empty. Nor, because it is determinate, can concrete self-awareness coincide with our primal, non-thetic self-feeling. I can never, as Sartre puts it, "coincide" with myself: "Of this table I can say only that it is purely and simply itself. But I can not limit myself to saying that my belief is [only] belief; my belief is the consciousness of belief" (*BW* 114).

In addition to my belief, I am also aware that it is I who am believing, and this "I" is not a specific awareness, but the pre-reflexive *cogito*. It is, then, a generalized feel, or non-thetic consciousness, of the radical, empty activity of consciousness itself. Because I am always aware of this, I am always out and beyond the sum total of my specific awarenesses, including those of myself. In other words: if you listed all the things of which I am aware at a given moment, you would have described my consciousness; there would be nothing left to add to your list. But you would not have described it *fully*, because you would not have described its basic activity of nihilation. That you cannot describe, because it is empty. You experience it only as a non-thetic "feel".

Thus, as a conscious being, I am always more than the set of all my definable properties. Where the table simply is what it is, I am what I am, and something more. Sartre expresses this in one of his most famous catchwords: "man is the being which is what he is not, and is not what he is". Of course, we are continually becoming other than ourselves, continually going beyond the present state of affairs, simply because we are in time. The moment you become aware of something, it has fallen into the past. It was one of the main defects of Descartes' account of the *cogito* as our basic self-awareness that he missed this fact:

> The Cartesian "I think" is conceived in the instantaneous perspective of temporality. ... If human reality were limited to the being of the "I think", it would have only the truth of an instant. ... But can we even conceive of the truth of an instant? Does not the cogito, in its own way, engage both past and future? ... Can we extend it without losing the benefits of reflective evidence? (*BW* 156–7)

When Descartes introduced the *cogito*, it seemed to be so basic to thought that it appeared to have a status like that of eternal truths (*BW* 154). For Sartre, however, this way of grasping the *cogito* operates only on a reflective level, because the *cogito* so conceived is explicit, a definite object of thought. It thus cannot be the pre-reflective awareness of ourselves that he himself posits as basic.

Sartre's desire to retain the "reflective evidence" of the *cogito* means that his "extension" of the *cogito* must remain entirely within the domain of consciousness itself; it cannot appeal to external factors. Nihilation cannot, then, be an effect of time; it must be entirely immanent to consciousness:

> To introduce into the unity of the pre-reflective cogito a qualified element external to this cogito [such as a lapse of time] would be to shatter its unity, to destroy its translucency; there would then in consciousness be something of which it would not be conscious and which would not exist in itself as consciousness. (*BW* 117)

For Husserl, the most basic level of consciousness was, we saw, the time synthesis; it was that which guaranteed the status of consciousness as an entirely self-enclosed, and therefore knowable, domain. For Sartre, making time basic in this way destroys the self-enclosed unity that consciousness exhibits and renders consciousness less than fully transparent to itself. Hence, Sartre's two arguments that consciousness is self-enclosed did not appeal to time, as Husserl's did. One, the argument that we cannot conceive of how something outside consciousness would affect consciousness, was, I suggested, Berkeleyan, rather than Husserlian. The other was more a requirement than an argument: the claim that the only thing we could know with certainty was consciousness itself, which presupposed that we could know something with certainty.

The pure, empty activity of nihilation is thus, somehow, prior to time, and so not in time. It is an atemporal structure, or more precisely an atemporal non-structure, on the basis of which Sartre tries to illuminate as much as he can about human life. Sartre is thus, in the end, a traditional philosopher. To be sure, the tradition is getting rather weak: instead of the robust atemporal subjects proffered by Husserl and Kant, we have the mere empty activity of nihilation.

I noted that, for Sartre, we perceive objects as objective in that we know that we have never experienced, and can never experience, all their appearances; and this knowledge is not inferential, but is given to us as the experience of a lack. Now he argues that we can only have it because of nihilation. We perceive the crescent moon as lacking fullness; we are aware that there are things about that moon that we have yet to experience. Taken on its own terms, the crescent moon conveys no such message; it is simply a crescent in the sky. It is only because we distinguish ourselves from it, are not wholly taken up with it, that we can see it as not yet what it will be: a full moon (*BW* 158). Only for us, then, are there lacks in the world; only for us can things be seen as not what they should or will be (*BW* 158). The fact that we can experience lacks means that human consciousness, or the for-itself, or human reality, also contains lack: "Human reality by which lack appears in the world must itself be a lack. For lack can only come into being through lack; the in-itself cannot be an occasion of lack in the in-itself" (*BW* 158).

Up to now, Sartre has talked about consciousness as empty. But it is possible to be empty without lacking anything; you can only lack something that you should have or want to have. To want something you do not have is to desire it, and so Sartre appeals to the phenomenon of desire as evidence that human consciousness, or the for-itself, is not only empty but actually contains lack: "Desire is a lack of being. It is haunted in its inmost being by the being of which it is desire. Thus it bears witness to the existence of lack in the being of human reality" (*BW* 159).

But that we *experience* lacks does not prove that we *are* a lack. The claim that human consciousness itself is a lack not only goes beyond what Sartre has established previously, but goes beyond his arguments altogether. The reason he gives for it – "lack can only come into being through lack" – does not establish that the (human) lack that brings lack (into the world) is entirely lack, and nothing more. The argument from desire, for its part, shows that desire is a lack, a point as old as Plato's *Symposium*, but this would prove that consciousness itself was a lack only if all consciousness were desirous, a possibility that Sartre does not mention. What is not getting discussed here, then, is the possibility that the empty activity of nihilation is not "lacking" anything. Indeed, if it really is a pure activity, to say nothing of the "absolute" foundation of consciousness itself and so of all human knowledge, nihilation *cannot* be a "lack".

Why, then, is Sartre so invested in characterizing nihilation as a lack? Nihilation, we may say, is Sartre's way of bringing content to the self without impeaching its status as an absolute, self-enclosed realm. The point is that while content is necessary to consciousness, this need not be content that consciousness has. It can be, rather, content that consciousness "lacks". Since ethics always deals with human nature in concrete situations, rather than with it as abstract, nihilation, the claim that consciousness *is* a lack – and so, paradoxically, "has" concrete content – is an important step in Sartre's transition from his theory of consciousness to his ethics.

We can see how this transition moves by noting that Sartre goes on to argue that lack can be experienced as *a* lack only if we have an idea of what it would be like for the lack to be filled: we can experience the crescent moon as not yet the full moon only if we know what the full moon is. So if we can experience ourselves as lacking, we must already have an idea of ourselves as not lacking.

But not to be lacking is to be what you are – it is to be in-itself. Thus, "Human reality is its own surpassing towards that which it lacks; it surpasses itself towards the particular being which it would be if it were what it is" (*BW* 161). So we are constantly aware, in a non-thematic way, of ourselves as lacking; we constantly experience ourselves as underway towards a state in which we will not lack, will not have to be beyond ourselves, will not have to change. We seek to coincide with ourselves the way the in-itself does:

> But this return to self would be without distance; it would … be iden-
> tity with itself. In short, this being would be exactly the self which we
> have shown can exist only as a perpetually evanescent relation, but it
> would be this self as substantial being. Thus human reality arises in the
> presence of its own totality or self as a lack of that totality.   (*BW* 162)

The empty transcending activity of consciousness, nihilation, becomes human when it seeks to transcend its own most basic self: to become, not for-itself, but in-itself. In this transcendence, we experience ourselves most basically as lacking content that we would like to have. But we can neither achieve such a state of "content-edness" nor even depict it, because attaining it would be the destruction of our human nature. This, then, is our ethical plight. But what is our solution? What can we work for?

TEMPORALITY

The main connecting link between Sartre's account of individual consciousness as nihilation, on the one hand, and the ethical views he had formulated in "Existentialism is a Humanism", on the other, develops out of his view of consciousness as lack. It is his view of temporality. Time, obviously enough, consists in the past, present and future; and Sartre treats it under these three main headings in turn. But he is not interested in time as it exists whether we are around or not, the way physicists are. As a phenomenologist, he wants to get at the ways we *experience* time, and how our experience of time provides certain structures to the ways we live. This he calls "temporality". Temporality, for Sartre, is thus a *human* phenomenon, and this is why it connects his account of cognitive mind to the lives we lead and thence to ethics. We saw earlier that nihilation could not be affected by time. Now we see that, for Sartre, our experience of time is grounded in nihilation, the same thing that gives us freedom. Hence, temporality is the connecting link between Sartre's account of consciousness and his ethics.

In his Nobel Prize address "May Man Prevail?", William Faulkner (who, unlike Sartre, did not turn down the prize) famously says, "The past is not dead. It's not even past" (Faulkner 1950). Sartre agrees: to say that something is in someone's past is not to say that it is over and done with, for if it were completely in the past it would leave no traces in the present and would be unrecoverable. When I talk about the death of the last triceratops, I am speaking of something unrecoverable in this sense. The general extinction of the species "triceratops" did leave traces on our world, which would obviously be very different if such dinosaurs were still around. But the species was effectively extinct, of course, as soon as there was no longer a male and female. The ensuing death of the very last triceratops, perhaps decades later, had, as such, no subsequent influence on earth's development. There is thus no link between us today and the death of the last triceratops.

When I say "Pierre was tired", by contrast, I am saying that there is a link between Pierre's fatigue in the past and the present situation. What is that link? Most basically, it is Pierre himself, for he is the single ongoing being who was tired and is tired no longer. It *is* a currently relevant fact about Pierre now that he *was*, at some previous time, tired (*BW* 165–6). Pierre is thus linked to his past, and I am linked to mine, no matter how much we both may try to deny it. This is true at every moment of my life, and most especially at its final moment, the moment of my death. At that moment, my past becomes my totality – it is all there is, and I am completely defined by it: "At my limit, at the infinitesimal instant of my death, I shall be no more then my past. It alone will define me" (*BW* 166). Thus, there is one moment when I do coincide with myself: when I die, I finally become an in-itself. "Death reunites us with ourselves" (*BW* 166), but only for a moment!

The past makes me into an in-itself because the in-itself is what does not move beyond itself, or "transcend" itself. The past, including my past, cannot change; it is "without possibility of any sort" (*BW* 167). And this is true not merely at the moment of our death, but at all moments of our life: "The past is the ever-growing totality of the in-itself which we are" (*BW* 167). It is the area of our being that is what it is (or was what it was) and so is that aspect of us that has no lacks. What can be defined about me is, then, my past; the present and the future are indefinable because of my basic activity of nihilation, the empty, and so indefinable, activity at the core of my being. As long as I am alive, I am engaged in nihilation – or nihilation engages itself as me – and so I am not wholly my past; I also have a present and a future.

But if the present and the future come about through nihilation, so does my past. For if my past is not simply various events that happened to me at previous times, but is what is currently relevant, then it is defined by way of my present. Past, present and future as aspects of temporality (rather than of time itself) thus come about through nihilation. Sartre is here even more traditional than Husserl: rather than making time basic to the self, as Husserl did, Sartre attempts to ground time in something yet more basic: nihilation.

To say that the past is grounded indirectly in nihilation is to say that it is defined through the present. What, then, is the "present" as we experience it? We can understand this by remembering that the term "present" is opposed to two sorts of thing. On the one hand, the "present" is opposed to the past and future; but it is also opposed to the "absent". When someone is taking a roll-call and I answer "present", I am locating myself in a particular place: not a physical place, but a social one (I can answer "present" during a conference call). I am present *to* something, and this is true for presence in general: to be present is to have a particular relation to other things.

Not every thing that exists at the current moment is "present", then; to be present means to be present *to* something. To what? Since Sartre is dealing with our experience of time, it means to be present to us: to the for-itself. Presence is thus the relation in which the for-itself defines itself against an in-itself. Since such definition is essential to the for-itself, as we have seen, this relation is what philosophers call "internal": it is a relation that defines the things it relates. "Presence to being implies that one is bound to that being by an internal bond … But this internal bond is a negative bond and denies, as related to the present being, that one is the being to which one is present" (*BW* 170).

Being present-to is thus a form of nihilation. Since nihilation is an establishment of non-identity, we are always escaping from that which is present to us, or, as Sartre prefers to put it, from that to which we are present.

> The present is precisely this negation of being, this escape from being inasmuch as being is there as that from which one escapes. The For-itself is present to being in the form of flight: the Present is a perpetual flight

> in the face of being. … It is a flight outside of co-present being and from
> the being which it was towards the being that it will be.   (*BW* 171)

This brings us to the future, which is "what I have to be insofar as I can not be it" (*BW* 171). I cannot be my future, simply because it is the future; but I *have* to be it in the sense that nihilation is always, in humans, a movement towards a future state. Just which future state varies, obviously. Like the past and the present, the future is grounded in nihilation. Sartre reminds us that "insofar as it makes itself present to being in order to flee it the For-itself is a lack" (*BW* 171). If we were not a lack, we would not flee the present and there would be no such thing as the future. Our movement towards the future is thus a movement towards something we lack, but which is still unknown. Sartre's characterization of nihilation as a lack was thus a step in deriving temporality from nihilation, for what we lack is what we shall (or should) be in the future. The future that he arrives at here is *my* future, as the set of things I currently lack: a version of what I have called the "finite future" first introduced into continental philosophy by Heidegger.

Our awareness of this future, Sartre says, is in the first instance a "non-thetic" awareness: that is, we are not, on this level, explicitly aware of the future to which we are underway. His example of this inexplicit awareness of the future is the way, when I am writing a sentence, I am only vaguely aware of the words in the sentence that I have not yet written (*BW* 173). I am aware that I *have* to write them, that I am on the way to writing them, and so that I presently lack them, but I do not know just which words they will be. And I am also aware that what I have yet to write is partly, but only partly, determined by what I have already written. I write, or in general I act, "in a world that has become and in a world that has become from the standpoint of what it is. This means that I give to the world its own possibilities in terms of the state which I apprehend in it" (*BW* 173).

Sartre's account of temporality thus leads to an account of action. Any action, exhibiting as it does human temporality, occurs in an already defined space. It has the kind of past Sartre has discussed above, one that persists in the present, and indeed in ways I must deal with. The future is distinguished from the imaginary, moreover, by the way in which it leads to action. I can imagine myself as President of the United States, and it is just barely logically possible that I will be President one day, but that possibility is not built out of my personal past. Nor is it something I can intelligibly work towards, given where I am today. If it were, it would be a future possibility rather than an imaginary one.

Sartre's discussion of temporality also enables him to give a more phenomenologically rigorous answer to the criticism, which we have already seen, that his concept of freedom is overly strong: I am, to be sure, free *now*, but I am not free to change my past, which persists into my present in all sorts of ways. Once again, Sartre is talking about temporality rather than time. He is not talking here about "the" future, the entire state of the world, say, three years from now. He is talking about the way *I* experience the future, and that is as *my* future: as what I can work towards on the basis of what I have become.

My future is not merely imaginary because it is limited by my past. But because I shall never attain it short of dying, the future is not something that wholly determines my actions here and now. It could only do that if there were no such thing as nihilation. Thus, "The future can only effect a pre-outline of the limits within which the For-itself will make itself be as a flight making itself present to being in the direction of another future" (*BW* 175).

While I can achieve specific goals, I can never achieve my future as such, for the future "does not allow itself to be rejoined; it slides into the Past as a bygone future" (*BW* 174). Three years from now, I will have achieved some of my current goals (I hope). But I will not thereby have attained my future. What I will have three years from now, if I am still alive, is a set of new goals constituting a new future (*BW* 174); the goals I have achieved or abandoned are my "bygone future".

The fact that I can never attain my future is the same thing, then, as the fact that I can never coincide with myself – can never attain a state of non-lacking:

> The For-itself can never be its future except problematically, for it is separated from it by a Nothingness which it is. In short the For-itself is free, and its freedom is to itself its own limit. ... Thus the Future qua Future does not have to be. It is not in itself, and neither is it in the mode of being of the For-itself since it is the meaning of the For-itself. The Future is not, it is possibilized. (*BW* 175)

FREEDOM

Sartre has now given an account of temporality in general, on the basis of his account of nihilation as lack. This has led him to an account of the temporality of action. How does all this relate to the central concept of his ethics, that of freedom? This is a complex question, but for the moment we can say that if I were not free, my future would be determined; it would necessarily come about. But because I am nihilation, am always distancing myself from whatever I am aware of, when I arrive at my future it will be, as we saw, a "bygone future": something that I am not. I will already be underway from it to another future. Hence, my future as such cannot be exhausted by any specific set of future states. It is always open.

To be sure, it is not entirely *indeterminate*. There is a "hierarchy of possibles", that is, of things that I have to do in order to go on and do other things: "But this hierarchy does not correspond to the order of universal Temporality. ... I am an infinity of possibilities, for the meaning of the For-itself is complex and cannot be contained" (*BW* 175). The "hierarchy of possibles" is merely *my* hierarchy, and indeed merely my hierarchy right now; there is no hierarchy that is inherent in the nature either of temporality or humanity, such that it would be imposed on me from without. Sartre's claim that there is no single end imposed on us all thus leads, via his account of temporality, to his conception of freedom. When Sartre gives his philosophically grounded account of freedom, it turns out to be a certain way of inhabiting time, one that, as with Heidegger, recognizes the openness of the future. Sartre approaches this in terms of the modern dispute between freedom and determinism. The defender of free will seeks to come up with an action – more properly, a moral decision – for which there is no cause. The determinist holds that all things, including our decisions, are caused. Both, however, locate freedom in the action. This, Sartre says, is where they are both wrong.

To be truly free. in the sense traditionalists advocate, an action would have to be unmotivated, for our motives constrain our actions (*BW* 182). But no act can be unmotivated, since it is part of the meaning of the term "act" that it be performed for a purpose. Something we do unintentionally is not an "act", but a random motion. Any act must therefore have a motive. But if an act is what it is through its motive, then to that extent it is caused by that motive. And if an act is caused, then it is not free.

Have the determinists won? Not in Sartre's view. Their argument fails because freedom really shows up when we try to answer the next question: how does a motive get to be a motive? Nothing is a motive just by itself. If I am stuck in a lift, my hunger pangs, no matter how intense, will not be the motives for any action I undertake, because there is simply no food around. In this situation, eating is merely something I can imagine; it cannot be a motive for any action. Thus, something can only become a motive when I make it a motive, and I do this by taking it as leading to something I am working towards: by committing myself to it through my basic activity of nihilation: "It is only because I escape the in-itself by nihilating myself towards my possibilities that this in-itself [my hunger pangs] can take on value as a motive" (*BW* 182).

Constituting certain things as motives is part of the way in which I nihilate on given occasions; that basic nihilation includes constituting the motive, committing myself to a certain possibility and actually moving towards that possibility. Constituting something as a motive for an action is therefore not a second action prior to and distinct from the action I am about to perform, but part of it: "It is in fact impossible to find an act without a motive, but ... this does not mean that we must conclude that the motive causes the act; the motive is an integral part of the act" (*BW* 182).

Action, end and motive thus form a whole in which each "claims the two others as its meaning" (*BW* 182). You cannot understand an act without understanding the state of affairs it was supposed to lead to (the end) and the way the actor related to that possibility (the motive). Nor can you understand the end *as* an end without understanding both the action that was supposed to lead to it and the motive that impelled that action. Nor can you understand the motive without understanding the end and the action. Each implies the others. In order for the determinist to be right, the entire complex of motive, act and end would have to be caused. But what sort of thing would cause all three? Nothing can, because we are back at the basic activity of nihilation, which cannot be further explained (*BW* 182). Thus, the organized totality of the action, end and motive is "the pure temporalizing nihilation of the in-itself, [which] is one with freedom" (*BW* 182).

What, then, is freedom? As a form of nihilation, it has no nature and so cannot be defined. You cannot look at various cases of freedom, abstract their common features and call that the essence of freedom (*BW* 183). If you could do that – if you could define freedom through what Husserl called eidetic reduction – it would not be free. So each of us must start with what really matters to us anyway: with our own freedom ("actually the question is of *my* freedom"; *BW* 185). But my freedom can only be understood in terms of temporality. It is the nihilation of the in-itself that I am – of my past (*BW* 184). To nihilate is to establish non-identity. So freedom is my capacity to establish non-identity with my past: to distance myself from it. And that is something that I cannot *not* do, even when I assign causes to my own actions:

> By the sole fact that I am conscious of the motives which inspire my action, these motives are already objects for my consciousness; they are outside it. I escape them by my very existence. I am condemned to exist forever beyond my essence, beyond the motives of my act. I am condemned to be free. (*BW* 184)

As we saw in "Existentialism is a Humanism", freedom is not to be found at the moment of choice. The young man who came to Sartre for advice had already "stacked the deck" just by coming to Sartre. And in fact, when it comes to a choice among defined alternatives, the decks are *always* stacked: decisions are always already made for us. By whom? By ourselves, in the course of defining those alternatives. Such definition includes not only the various ways we are going to achieve our goals but those very goals themselves.

Finally, determinism for Sartre is not merely an innocent philosophical doctrine. Since it holds that everything we do is susceptible of causal explanations, it aims "to establish within us an unbroken continuity of existence in itself" (*BW* 184). To advocate this is to deny humanity's "nihilating" nature, viewing it as an in-itself, or, rather, as a pseudo in-itself. This, however, is what racists, fascists and Nazis want to do; some form of determinism is always their philosophical rationale.

We saw that for Horkheimer and Adorno fascism was an outgrowth of something shared by all human beings: unconscious projection. Similarly, determinism, for Sartre, in all its complicity with those same social evils, is based on something all of us seek: on the denial of the for-itself. Human reality perpetu-ally tries to refuse to recognize its freedom (*BW* 184–5), and Sartre called our many attempts to deny our freedom "bad faith". Much of *Being and Nothing* is given over to analyses of such comportment. These analyses are often brilliant and illuminating; Sartre's gifts as a novelist shine in them.

SOCIAL PHILOSOPHY

Sartre's ethics is thus grounded in a phenomenological account of human reality that places at the core of our being the activity of nihilation. It is in virtue of this that we distance ourselves from everything determinate, including our own pasts, and it is in virtue of that, in turn, that we can freely adopt ends and constitute motives for our actions. But this all appears to end in a radical individualism that denies human community. For if to be aware of anything is to distance yourself from it, then in being aware of other people must we not distance ourselves from them? How, then, can there be any such thing as a human community? Is Sartre not caught in the desperation of one of his own most famous phrases: "hell is other people"?

In his "Search for a Method", the first part of his *Critique of Dialectical Reason* (1976), Sartre recognizes this challenge, and he considers it to be posed in its strongest form by Marx. Marx's attempt to predict the future, like all such attempts, had denied human freedom, for if the future is predictable with accuracy, what is predicted will come about of itself. Action on our part is therefore futile.[5] What Sartre calls "idealist Marxists" (*BW* 304), which is pretty much all Marxists at the time of his writing, have accepted this: we are not free, and the revolution will happen without us. But it is incompatible with Sartre's own version of existentialism, which posits a radical freedom at the core of every individual. Some middle ground clearly must be found between unpredictability of freedom and the lassitude of determinism. Engels had, in fact, attempted a formulation: "Men themselves make their history but in a given environment which conditions them" (*BW* 304). This poses three major questions for Sartre:

(a) Most specifically, as Sartre points out here, Engels's formulation is so vague that it merely evades the problem, which is that of when precisely are we conditioned and when are we not.

(b) More generally, the history we are making will lead to an ideal society: one in which humanity freely appropriates its own nature and in which we

---

5. This conundrum is not new with Marxism. In medieval times, predictive power was assigned to God, and this was called the problem of "divine foreknowledge". If God knows I am going to sin next Tuesday, what is the use of trying not to? For more on this see Zagzebski (2008).

finally become fully human. Only when it has arrived can we learn to live together freely and fully, and only on the basis of that ideal can we even imagine what we should do here and now. But for Sartre, there is no way of life, indeed no set of ways of life, that is going to satisfy human "nature", which is constant nihilation. If Sartre cannot talk about an ideal society, how can he talk about how we should live, or live together?

(c) Finally, as we have seen, consciousness is, for Sartre, a domain that is entirely unto itself, unaffected except by itself, and individual. This means that, on my most basic level, I am radically alone. How can the isolated ego live together in *any* way with others, let alone in an ideal way?

Sartre's answer to (b) and (c) is given at *BW* 326. Our material being, he says, is "a point of departure for a constant effort to establish lived bonds of solidarity". This effort itself is what he calls "revolution". In it, the radical activity of nihilation transcends the isolation of the individual ego, forcing it into relationships with others; this is his answer to (c). And this constant effort to establish relationships, rather than any final result, is itself the "ideal society" for Sartre; his answer to (b) is that nihilation itself is the social ideal. This all amounts to a major reformulation of Marx's concept of revolution. Revolution is now not merely a historical event that will lead to a better state, communism; it *is* that better state, and it is underway right now; it is a sustained ethical stance, somewhat akin to a lifestyle.

Sartre seems here to come perilously close to defining revolution as a form of what Horkheimer and Adorno call "instrumental" or "administrative" reason. That, we saw, was reason that had abandoned substantive goals and replaced them with what was formerly the means to those goals, so that we wound up with administration for the sake of administration. Here, we have revolution for the sake of revolution. This solves the problems that Marx encountered in trying to predict the nature of post-revolutionary society; but if it makes revolution merely a form of administration, it seems that the price was steep. What saves Sartre from this, in so far as he is saved, is that revolution is not administration. Administration, for Horkheimer and Adorno, proceeded on the assumption that things have identities that are fixed, immutable and known: that they are precisely what Sartre calls "in-itself". Revolution, by contrast, is grounded in nihilation and so begins from the opposite view: that human beings have no fixed identities, but are constantly recreating themselves. Revolutionary human beings, like all human beings, cannot be administered, either for Sartre or for the Frankfurt thinkers.

Sartre's first step in answering (a) is to embrace the contradiction between history as what we make and history as what makes us.

To be sure these (material) conditions exist, and it is they, they alone, which can furnish a direction and a material reality to the changes which are in preparation; but the movement of human *praxis*[6] goes beyond them while conserving them (*BW* 306). This contradiction is particularly acute in the current global situation, because so many people are being exploited: they are passive recipients of all kinds of bad things. And yet they have the capacity, Marx and Sartre both think, to transform this very situation: "man in a period of exploitation is at once both the product of his own product [i.e. of the economy] and a historical agent who can under no circumstances be taken as a product [of social forces]" (*BW* 305).

But we are not "products" of history in that it is a foreign force that makes and controls us from outside. History appears that way to me because I am not alone in my transforming it: "If History escapes me, it is not because I do not make it; it is because the other is making it as well" (*BW* 306). All humans together make history: the capitalist economy of which I am the "product" is itself the "product" of humanity's joint action. I am unaware of this because I am isolated from others and do not know of their struggles: "In this sense, History, which is the proper work of all activity and of all men, appears to men as a foreign force, exactly insofar as they do not recognize the meaning of their enterprise (even where locally successful) in the total, objective reality" (*BW* 306). Sartre has here brought together a whole series of concepts from previous continental thought. One is Husserl's conception of passive synthesis, according to which things that I do can appear to me as things already finished because my activity in constituting them remains ordinarily hidden from me.[7] Another is Marx's social concept of alienation, according to which the product of the worker's labour appears alien to him, a concept that Marx had in turn derived from Hegel. And a third is Marx's concept of communist revolutionary praxis, in which the communist teaches proletarians, who are engaged in local struggles, about one another and the overall meaning of their efforts.

The concrete understanding of history – of the forms it takes right now – is thus, for Sartre, a group effort, to which the entire human race must ultimately contribute. But bringing the entire human race together in any project is revolutionary praxis. The understanding of history is thus the goal of history: an understanding, and a goal, that can come about only through and as revolutionary praxis. This understanding is more specifically our goal as philosophers, and has not yet been achieved. We can understand the present day only in terms of its lack:

---

6. "Praxis" was Aristotle's term for the activity specific to a species (cf. McCumber 1988). Revolutionary activity qualifies as praxis for both Marx and Sartre because it expresses our nature as species being (for Marx) or as nihilation (for Sartre).

7. This conception was also implicit, although not openly stressed, in Kant's conception of critique, since if we were fully aware of the activities of our own minds, we would have no need of critique.

Thus the plurality *of the meanings* of History can be discovered and posited for itself only upon the ground of a future totalization – in terms of the future totalization and in contradiction with it. It is our theoretical and practical duty to bring this totalization closer every day. … Our historical task, at the heart of this polyvalent world, is to bring closer the moment when History will have only one meaning.

(*BW* 307)

Sartre has defended his concept of the isolated individual, but merely as a historical phenomenon to be overcome in revolutionary praxis, not as the "absolute truth" that the *cogito* and his own account of consciousness in terms of nihilation, the "absolute event", had made of it. Does this mean that existentialist philosophy, based as it is on that concept of the individual, is also to be overcome by revolutionary praxis? In order to show that this is not the case, Sartre must fill in Engels's formulation still more.

In praxis, we go beyond our particular situation because of need (*BW* 308). We transcend our situation in favour of another situation; we relate "positively" to that situation, and "negatively" to our current situation (*BW* 308). In other words, in so far as revolutionary praxis has a specific goal, it can only be one particular mode of human transcendence. As such, it is a historically specific way in which an individual defines himself or herself against the in-itself:

The structures of a society which is created by human work define for each man an objective situation as a starting point; the truth of a man is the nature of his work, and it is his wages. But this truth defines him just insofar as he constantly goes beyond it in his practical activity.

(*BW* 308)

Sartre has thus filled in Engels's formulation by seeing the "given environment" that "conditions" our "making of history" as the starting-point, not merely for that making but for revolutionary praxis conceived as nihilation itself, the basic human reality. He fills in Engels still more by identifying the current social environment as one that blocks this basic human transcendence or nihilation:

Every man is defined negatively by the sum total of possibles which are impossible for him; that is, by a future more or less blocked off. For the under-privileged classes, each cultural, technical, or material enrichment of society represents a diminution, an impoverishment; the future is almost entirely barred. (*BW* 310)

This brings Sartre to his first concrete example of revolutionary praxis in this section: a black airman in England who, although he was not a pilot, took a plane and flew it across the English Channel (*BW* 310). The airman wanted, by this, to show that he was unfairly blocked from being a pilot; more generally, he wanted to make the point that "a future possible for whites is possible for everyone" (*BW* 310).

Note three things here. First, this revolutionary activity is not the preplanned undertaking of a revolutionary group, but the unaided action of an individual, indeed, one who is uniquely isolated, flying alone over the ocean. Second, it is an action that *sends a message*, not a direct or violent attack on the status quo. Third, the message is addressed to both whites and blacks, that is, both to members of the actor's own group and to the British majority.

In addition, the content of the message is, as Sartre has just expressed it, equivalent to equal opportunity. This is in contrast to what is generally understood as the communist and socialist demand for equality of result. This demand is grounded in the view that if we all merely have equal opportunities to achieve prosperity, some of us are not going to make it, a situation that Marxism, and indeed socialism in general, takes to be unjust. Equality of opportunity, by contrast, is compatible with great disparities of living conditions, disparities that socialism and communism are supposed to eliminate.

Equality of opportunity is in fact associated not with European socialism, but with American capitalism. It is no weakness in Sartre that he should be advocating something like the civil rights struggle in 1960, when the *Critique of Dialectical Reason* was published. But it is hard to see how it is bringing him any closer to a critical reconciliation with Marxism. Indeed, Sartre seems to have jettisoned what was definitive of Marx's vision: the idea that the goal of history can be predicted in the form of the vision of a non-alienated society. What he has in fact defended is not traditional Marxism, but the view that revolutionary theory must take more account of the self-creative individual than its appeals to the "iron laws of history" have allowed it to do in the past. Sartre has argued that individual action, such as the airman's, must be allowed to count as revolutionary. But how can an action count as revolutionary if it is merely the action of an individual? If Sartre cannot explain this, he cannot explain how revolutionary praxis can overcome individual isolation, and this, as I pointed out before, is the central problem for a social philosophy that begins from an account of the isolated individual.

Sartre's answer, to begin with, is that the airman's action is aimed at transforming others, in particular, black people. The airman wants to show them not only that they can have the same possibilities as white people – that they already know – but that they can *demand* them. In that way, he seeks to transform his racial group from a passive group, sitting there and taking it in the face, into an active group that is transforming society: into a revolutionary group. How, in general, does this sort of transformation take place?

Sartre begins by constructing the minimal and most passive kind of human group: people waiting for the 7.49 bus in the Place St Germain in Paris (*BW*

312). This group is minimal in that these people do not know each other, or even look at each other. Each is going to a different place and coming from a different place, for they are in transition from their homes to their workplaces. Both home and workplace form much more cohesive groups than the group of bus-waiters these people are in at the moment. So the first thing about their isolation from one another as they wait for the bus is that it has been *produced* by a society in which people live at some distance from their work. Isolation is thus "the real social product of cities" (*BW* 313).

Modern urban isolation is something produced in modern cities, and so is not a basic feature of the human self. Indeed, the people waiting for the bus are not entirely without relation to each other. Although they do not actually look at one another, they can do so if they wish, and the fact that I am visible to others makes a great difference to my behaviour on any given occasion, as Sartre has established elsewhere (cf. "The Other", *BW* 221–43). And they all share the same need: the need to get to work. So they are united by that need and the means to fill it: by the bus itself; "the bus they wait for unites them" (*BW* 315). It is not, then, their need to get to work that makes them into this group. There are other ways they could get to work. What unites them, then, is the bus itself. And how does the bus treat them? What does it constitute them *as*?

It constitutes them as "interchangeable", fungible (*BW* 315). The bus will treat them all identically. One of them may be a doctor going off to perform a life or death operation; another may be heading off to pick pockets at the Eiffel Tower. The bus does not care. However much they may differ from each other in their concrete lives, on this very superficial level they are equivalent, and Sartre puts this in terms reminiscent of Heidegger's account of inauthenticity: "Everyone is the same as the Other, insofar as he is Other than himself" (*BW* 316). But this superficial equality leads to a problem: there are not usually enough seats on the bus. How to decide whom to admit? There is no way; as far as the bus is concerned, the pickpocket has a right to be there equal to the doctor's. It is not possible to tell who is "dispensable" (*BW* 316–17).

So there is installed at the bus stop a small device that gives you a number indicating the order of your arrival (*BW* 317). Now there is a way to tell who is going to be allowed on to the bus and who is not. And now the whole group is ordered. It is given a serial order, and is what Sartre calls a "series": the lowest form of group, in which each person is related to all the others only arbitrarily and superficially. This minimal group identity is imposed from outside, and indeed mechanically. But there is still praxis involved, because the bus and the ticket machine had to be made by people. Indeed, just taking a number is a very minimal praxis that constitutes the group:

> This [taking a number] does not mean that he helps to create an active group by freely determining, with other individuals, the ends, the means, the division of tasks; it means that he actualizes his being outside

> himself as a reality shared by several people, and which already exists
> and awaits him, by means of an inert practice, denoted by instrumental-
> ity, whose meaning is that it integrates him into an ordered multiplicity
> by assigning him a place in a prefabricated seriality.   (*BW* 321)

So we see what a more satisfactory group would be like: it would be one in which I, as a unique individual, can make my contribution to the project of the group as a whole, deciding on the goals, means and who is to do what: the things we do in nihilating deliberation, for Sartre. In such a group, "Everyone can regard himself both as subordinate to the whole and as essential, as the practical presence of the whole, in his own particular action" (*BW* 322). This sort of situation would be as if the airman, in Sartre's earlier example, could count on the fact that his action would actually "raise the consciousness", as Marxists put it, of his fellow black people: if he could know for certain that his solitary action, out of his own unique circumstances, would provide an essential benefit to the group.

Serial unity of this sort thus leaves a wide space for human individuality on a deeper level: one not produced in and by modern urban environments. To show this, Sartre takes up another minority, one very important in France and which, we saw, he has discussed elsewhere: Jews. His argument is that Jews ordinar-ily relate to one another in a "serial" way. They do not all go to synagogue or participate actively in Jewish life, but they all share the characteristic of being discriminated against by the majority. When something anti-Semitic happens, they are all in danger. And this means that each Jew is dependent on the behav-iour of every other Jew; if anyone does something wrong, everyone suffers at the hands of the majority (*BW* 323). When that happens, Jews – each in his or her unique life situation – become aware of themselves as a group. The people in the Place St Germain also become aware of themselves as a group when the bus comes and some of them start to get on. But getting on a bus is the action of an individual; it is only serially related to the actions of others getting on the bus. When anti-Semitism breaks out, Jews become a very different kind of group: a group that may need to take common action.

This, then, is Sartre's answer to the question of how the isolated individual ego becomes part of a social order: *social unification is always performed from outside*, through some exigency imposed by nature, technology, an enemy and so on. Isolation remains our common state; we unify in the face of an external threat.[8] So the serial group is minimal. Yet because it is capable of joint response to an outside exigency – be this something as terrible as anti-Semitic outbursts

---

8. Sartre has been rightly criticized for reducing Jewish life merely to banding together in the face of a hostile environment, rather than because of positive things. What this has to do with Sartre's own status as a member of one of France's historically most persecuted minori-ties – Protestants – is open to question.

or merely the arrival of a bus – it "furnishes the elementary conditions of the possibility that its members should constitute a [true] group" (*BW* 325).

The outside unifying factors that produce groups can be of many types, but for Marxists there is one overarching example of them: class exploitation (*BW* 326). A mere group of people becomes a class when its members see that they are being exploited by someone else: by the bourgeoisie. This someone else is, they think, what they themselves are not: active and unified; it is an active group. The exploited people, by contrast, are disunited and impotent: a merely passive serial group. But now they know what they should be (*BW* 327).

Thus, in the constitution of an active group we have, for Sartre, two active unities. One of these is already there, in the form of the others who are my enemy. The other consists of the other people my enemies are directed against, with whom I must unite. In the one group we have the givens of history that we do not create; in the other group we have our task as free agents. When we see this, we take over the inertia of our groups as something that can be changed, and as something for which we are therefore responsible: "I do not attribute inertia – which must constitute the real foundation of the group (as inertia which has been transcended and preserved) – to the active community; on the contrary, it is my praxis which, in its unificatory movement, takes responsibility for it" (*BW* 327).

Sartre's transition from the isolated, theoretical ego of Husserlian phenomenology to the communal identities that are advocated and criticized in a viable social philosophy thus passes through the ethical significance of nihilation. Nihilation is inherently individual and becomes communal only in the face of an external threat. What finally, makes a threat a threat? Need: "Without the original tension of need as a relation of interiority to nature, there would be no change; and conversely, there is no praxis at any level whose regressive or descending significance is not directly or indirectly related to this original tension" (*BW* 329). That is, we feel needs because we are natural beings: bodily beings. The laws of history, whatever they are, cannot lead to action unless their operation produces such need on the individual level:

> We have come to a vicious circle: the group constitutes itself on the basis of a need or common danger and defines itself by the common objective which determines its common *praxis*. Yet neither common need nor common *praxis*, nor common objectives, can define a community unless it makes itself into a community by feeling individual need as common need, and by projecting itself, in the internal unification of a common integration, towards objectives which it produces as common. (*BW* 329)

This is not possible unless there is already serial unity, a point that Marxists, and others, tend to ignore (*BW* 326).

CONCLUSION

Like Heidegger, Sartre undertakes to render phenomenology less of a purely theoretical affair than Husserl had considered it to be, and to bring it into contact with the lives we lead in our communities. The key requirement of those lives, for Sartre, is that they are to be lived lucidly. The foundation of his philosophy is thus an analysis of consciousness, an analysis that does not try to reduce consciousness to anything else but that seeks to explain it entirely in terms of itself. In order to do this, Sartre must locate within consciousness its single most basic phenomenon, so that he can use it to explain the others. For Husserl, there was no such single basic phenomenon of consciousness; consciousness was a whole host of *eidē* to be described rather than explained. Its most basic component, the internal time synthesis, was too abstract to be of much explanatory value.

For Sartre, the most basic component of consciousness is the activity of nihilation, in which we place a content "before" ourselves and thereby establish our non-identity with it. For Husserl, the otherness of conscious contents was a universal characteristic of all consciousness: "intentionality". For Sartre, nihilation is not a characteristic but an activity, and it is not only found in all consciousness but explains consciousness (in so far as it *can* be explained). Nihilation is thus *both* what we most basically are *and* what we most basically can know. His philosophy, like all philosophy in his view, is thus founded on "the absolute proximity of the investigator to the object investigated" (*BW* 66).

Sartre's attempt to explain the phenomenon of consciousness in terms of nihilation is technical to the point of being jargonistic. Behind the jargon is the point that nihilation gains practical significance when we carry it out on ourselves: when we take distance from our past as we are pushed towards our future. We are always doing this, so the moment our future becomes specific, as a concrete goal, it in a sense becomes part of our past: it is something we are already moving away from even before we have achieved it. Thus bound to nothing, we are radically free. We might say, then, that Sartre has given a traditional philosophical account of a very untraditional sort of mind. As what we both are and know, nihilation, like Descartes' *cogito*, has the status of an absolute, atemporal truth. But the mind that Sartre has described is a mind that, in the freedom of its nihilation, distances itself from all such truths.

To distance oneself from something is not to dispense with it entirely; I can only distance myself from things that are somehow present to me. This means that the future for Sartre is not the infinite expanse of Zarathustra's sky or the unfathomable infinitude of Kierkegaard's eternity. It is a field of "possibles" still conditioned by what has been nihilated, that is, by what has already been present. This field of possibilities is wider than I usually think it is, and indeed wider than I am comfortable with; but it is *my* future, not yours, and there are some things it does not contain. When I act freely, as I do in revolutionary praxis, I select one possibility from this wider field and work to make it actual: "It is by transcending the given toward the field of possibles and by realizing one possibility from among all the others that the individual objectifies himself and contributes to making history" (*BW* 309). But the field from which I have taken that one possibility is not an infinite expanse. Sartre thus follows Heidegger in conceiving the future as, so to speak, finite from the start. His interest in ethics pushes him to give the kind of account of moral responsibility that Heidegger did not bother with.

It will be the task of the next continental philosopher, Sartre's companion Simone de Beauvoir, to free his insights from the traditional grounding he himself gave them by making consciousness a less self-contained realm, showing it to be more open to outside influences including history and culture.

CHAPTER 11

THE FUTURE AND THE DISCLOSURE OF BEING: SIMONE DE BEAUVOIR

PRIMARY TEXT: Simone de Beauvoir, *The Ethics of Ambiguity* (*EA*; 1948)

On 26 August 1944, a triumphant Charles de Gaulle walked down the Champs-Élysées in a still-not-fully liberated Paris. In the cheering crowd was a tall, elegant woman accompanied by another woman. Suddenly shots rang out. They missed de Gaulle, but several other people fell to the ground. The two women, along with everyone else in the vicinity, ran from the snipers and eventually took refuge in a basement. In spite of the danger, Simone de Beauvoir spent the next couple of days moving around Paris, covering the liberation for a newspaper.

The sniping signalled the end of the German occupation of Paris. The war itself, and the Nazi government responsible for it, would last only another year. Beauvoir captured the joy of that time of transition:

> The age I lived in, which for ten years had revolved on a firm axis, now abruptly shifted out of orbit and dragged me with it. … The earth turned and revealed another of its faces to me. … No blade of grass in any meadow, however I looked at it, would ever again be what it had been. The ephemeral was my lot. … I seemed to have grown wings; henceforth I would soar above the confines of my personal life and float in the empyrean that was all mankind. My happiness would reflect the magnificent adventure of a world recreating itself afresh.
>
> (Beauvoir 1962: 473)

Beauvoir would spend the rest of her life reflecting on the "magnificent adventure" of a world that recreates itself moment by moment, if we will only let it.

Born in Paris three years after her companion Jean-Paul Sartre, Beauvoir outlived him by six years. *The Ethics of Ambiguity* was published in 1947, two years after Sartre's "Existentialism is a Humanism" and the same year as Horkheimer and Adorno's *Dialectic of Enlightenment*. Two years later, Beauvoir would publish one of the most influential books of the twentieth century, *The*

Second Sex, one of the first, and still one of the most brilliant, statements of the case for feminism ever produced.

Like Sartre, Beauvoir wrote novels and plays as well as philosophy. Her literary output was sufficiently brilliant that it is only in recent years that her philosophy has attracted serious attention. Much of her writing is very Sartrean, or he is very Beauvoirian. This is particularly true in the first section of *The Ethics of Ambiguity*, which is a basic statement and defence of existentialism. But even there, Beauvoir is an independent thinker. She puts things differently from Sartre, and disagrees with him on major issues, although the disagreements are very tactfully expressed. In particular, Beauvoir is less wedded to classical Husserlian approaches than was Sartre. She is less concerned with developing a theory of consciousness on its own terms than he was, and so she avoids much of his technical jargon, giving her substantive disagreements with Sartre a welcome stylistic pay-off.

FREEDOM AND THE DISCLOSURE OF BEING

Ambiguity takes many different forms in *The Ethics of Ambiguity*, but the most basic case of it lies in the fact that we are both natural and moral beings. We *live* this paradox: as natural we are passive, "crushed by the dark weight of other things". But morally we are free: pure internalities "against which no external power can take hold" (*EA* 7). Human freedom and natural determinism are both necessary yet mutually incompatible, and this paradoxical relation between them is the same one with which Kant's *Critique of Judgment* had begun. The point for Beauvoir is neither to resolve the paradox by rejecting one side, as determinists and free willists had done, nor to neutralize it by trying somehow to accept both sides, as Kant himself had undertaken. What we must do, in a more Kierkegaardian spirit, is accept the paradox itself and try not to deny its paradoxical nature.

To do this, Beauvoir turns not to the Christian Kierkegaard, but to the atheist Sartre. Her discussion of him at the beginning of *The Ethics of Ambiguity* proceeds, however, in terms he himself may have found somewhat foreign: "Man, Sartre tells us, is 'a being who makes himself a lack of being in order that there might be being'" (*EA* 11). This means, she says, that there is an "in order to" in the being of humanity: there is a point to our lives. That something is what she calls the "disclosure of being": "Thanks to man, being is disclosed and he desires this disclosure" (*EA* 12). Man accomplishes this disclosure in what Sartre called our fundamental activity of nihilation: "By uprooting himself from the world, man makes himself present to the world and makes the world present to him" (*EA* 12).

Suppose I am standing on a bluff looking at a river valley. That landscape, as seen from this point, would not be there if I were not there to perceive it. To "disclose being", then, means to reveal things as we experience them: a non-technical version of what phenomenologists, in Husserl's view, do scientifically. It makes no sense to say that we do not find joy in this.

This is already a major innovation on Sartre. In a couple of tactful paragraphs, Beauvoir suggests that this aspect of human existence – the idea that nihilation, our taking distance on whatever we are aware of, is not entirely without point but occurs in order that being may be disclosed – was not investigated by Sartre because on the level of his investigations, the idea of "usefulness" or "in order to" does not enter in (*EA* 11). This is why Sartre's great book, *Being and Nothing*, does not discuss ethics until its final pages. So Beauvoir claims to be merely drawing out ethical implications of Sartre's work. In fact, however, to say that nihilation has a point is to make it into something quite different from what Sartre took it to be, even if you are quoting Sartre in the process. For Sartre, nihilation was, as we saw, the constant core of human reality; it is simply what humans do and are, continually. If nihilation had a point, there would be a reason why it happens: it would not be a basic given, but would (in some sense or other) be grounded in something else. Moreover, if it were geared to the disclosure of being (whatever that is), it would be something that can be done well or badly: a "good" case of nihilation would be one that produced a "good" disclosure, or "more" of a disclosure, or something like that. As we shall see, this is exactly what Beauvoir says, but it is incompatible with what Sartre took nihilation to be: the absolute core of the human self.

In her defence of existentialism, Beauvoir encounters a problem that Sartre had also tackled at length: the criticism that since existentialism conceives of each individual as fundamentally isolated, it can deliver no theory about how we are to relate to each other – no ethics or politics: "It is said that this philosophy is subjective, even solipsistic. If he is once enclosed within himself, how can man get out?" (*EA* 16).

Traditional philosophers, she says, have had the same problem. Their solution is the one Sartre appealed to over and over: the "*cogito*", my awareness that I think. Although it is commonly formulated as "I think, therefore I am", in fact this awareness, if you look at it carefully, does not really refer to me as an individual. In so far as I am a thinking thing and nothing more, I have no properties that all human beings, who are also thinking things, do not also have. There is therefore nothing in the experience of the *cogito* that would not apply to anybody. Thus, for traditional philosophy, the idea that there is such a thing as universal humanity is given directly in my basic awareness of myself (*EA* 17–18). This does not hold for existentialism, of course, since (as Sartre has argued) there is no such thing as universal humanity; "human nature", over and above the empty activity of nihilation, is just a figment of our minds. What I do when I think, then, may not be what you do when you think. So for existentialists the *cogito* is no way out of solipsism, and the problem remains: "how could men, originally separated, get together?" (*EA* 18).

Once again, the important thing is not to deny this problem, by, for example, asserting that we have a common human nature that brings us together. But mere recognition of the problem is also not enough; it must be solved, in some way or other (cf. "before undertaking the quest for a solution"; *EA* 18). As Sartre did, so Beauvoir places this problem into connection with Marxism (*EA* 18–23), a discussion I shall pass over.

When Beauvoir returns to her paradox, she finds another problem with it: it seems that if existentialism is correct that we are free, then we can never attain our goals, because we will already be beyond them when they are attained. Therefore, to recognize that you are free is to recognize that you will never be satisfied. And if we can never be satisfied, what is the point in trying to achieve anything? "Must we grant this curious paradox: that from the moment a man recognizes himself as free, he is prohibited from wishing for anything?" (*EA* 23).

This way of putting the basic paradox of human freedom had its analogue in Sartre. On the level of individual consciousness, it was expressed in consciousness's paradoxical need to become in-itself, so that our basic desire is no longer to desire; Sartre had disposed of this lived paradox by denying that anything like that was possible. On the social level, it was treated as the problem of the status of revolution in Marx's philosophy, which Sartre solved by saying that that the path to the ideal life – the equivalent here would be the fight for satisfaction – was as close as we can get to the ideal life itself, so that the goal is not satisfaction but the search for satisfaction. On both levels, Sartre locates satisfaction only in the in-itself; lucidity then demands that we reject this in favour of the constant, but human, dissatisfaction. Beauvoir's answer is very different, because of her different view of nihilation. Freedom itself, she says, is ambiguous. On the one hand, we want to be something (as Sartre would say, to be an in-itself); and this goal, the goal of being a specific individual and nothing more, is always frustrated. But it is frustrated not because we are fated to continually transcend ourselves in dissatisfaction, but because we *will* ourselves to do so: we will ourselves to be the emptiness that discloses being (*EA* 23). And we do so because it is not merely satisfying, but joyful.

We can sum this up by saying that there is a positive side to Beauvoir's existentialism that is missing in Sartre. Nihilation is not, for her, merely an empty activity; that would make it "stupid" (here Beauvoir is, at least on the surface, talking about Epicurus, a Greek philosopher). Nihilation always wants to disclose being, to reveal things as they are in our encounter with them: "Human spontaneity always projects itself toward something" (*EA* 25). Instead of being solely a for-itself emptiness that distances itself from all things and can seek fulfilment only in trying to become in-itself, as we are for Sartre, for Beauvoir, we are beings that also enjoy our own emptiness, because our emptiness is what enables us to disclose being. This, although she does not stress it, is a second "ambiguity" affecting Beauvoir's ethics.

We saw that Sartre attempted to derive temporality from nihilation. The disclosure of being has a relationship to time that, although different from that of nihilation, is similarly close. As a projection "towards something", the disclosure of being is, or is the ground of, a temporal movement: it is the continual movement, not merely away from the past, as nihilation was, but towards a coming disclosure. Just what that disclosure is, is left open; that is why Beauvoir talks, not about the disclosure of this or that, but simply about the disclosure of "being". Freedom thus seeks disclosure of being, and as free beings we seek it too. It is Beauvoir's appeal to the disclosure of being that enables her to solve the current problem of why we seek specific goals even when we know they will not satisfy us. But what enables Beauvoir to say this, when Sartre could not? Why could Sartre not say it?

I suggest it is because something had changed in the world since Sartre published *Being and Nothing*, four years earlier. To be sure, the political situation was now radically different (the Allies had won the war and France was again free). But on the philosophical scene, which is intimately related to everything else for Beauvoir, something else had happened: Sartre had written *Being and Nothing*. Why would anyone care about that book? Why would anyone care, for example, that Sartre had laid bare the manifold structures of bad faith, of our recurrent denial that we are free? Sartre *must believe*, if he is asked, that humans have a desire to know the truth about their situation. But understanding the human condition is part of what Beauvoir calls the disclosure of being; so people must want to disclose being. Otherwise there is no point in doing philosophy. Attaining authentic clarity on our lives, or what I call lucidity, does not merely bring anguish, as it does for Sartre. It also brings joy.

Because *Being and Nothingness* takes nihilation, that is, our inescapable movement away from conscious contents, to be the single basic fact of human reality, it could not formulate the claim that nihilation, as the disclosure of being, is also positive. But if that claim were not true, no one would ever have written *Being and Nothing*, for its only purpose, as philosophy, is to disclose being. The disclosure of being is, then, the ambiguous movement both *away from* and *towards* conscious contents. Since such freedom is the constant transgression of boundaries, and so is the constant transformation of itself, to want it is not to will any *specific*, concrete goal; Beauvoir is in agreement with Sartre on that. But it does have a goal, and here she disagrees with him. We are always going beyond ourselves in order to disclose being, and to seek this is to seek existentialist freedom (*EA* 29). Freedom itself is thus a "universal, absolute end" (*EA* 58).

Beauvoir is not here returning to Hegel's view of human freedom as the goal of all history. Freedom, for her, has nothing to do with Hegelian reason, "reason in history", but (on this level) is simply our movement beyond what is given. Since this movement, as we have seen, is also a movement "towards something", it has a future on which it is directed, and is therefore temporal movement. Beauvoir thus remains within the framework of temporalized philosophy. But if she is not reinstating Hegel, in comparison with Sartre she is doing something almost as radical. The disclosure of being, we saw, is a movement towards the future, but not towards any specific future. As the disclosure merely of "being", it is a movement towards something entirely indefinite. The future towards which we move is thus one that can contain anything whatsoever. Beauvoir has thus, with her concept of the disclosure of being, reinstated the Nietzschean boundless future, as represented by the blue sky of the great noon into which Zarathustra walks. Beauvoir thus stands together with Arendt and against Heidegger and Sartre. Where the two men see the future as finite from the start, the women also see it as boundless.[1]

The status of freedom as absolute end means that we have moral standards (as we saw in Sartre's case as well, in the idea that a society does wrong to its members by closing off possibilities for them): "[Human existence] regards as privileged situations those which permit it to realize itself as indefinite movement; that is, it wishes to pass beyond everything which limits its power; and yet this power is always limited" (EA 32). Not only that, but in order to be truly indefinite, this indefinite movement – now grasped as "liberating" – must go beyond me: "It is only by prolonging itself through the freedom of others that it [freedom] manages to surpass death itself and to realize itself as an indefinite unity" (EA 32).

Once we see that freedom itself is our intrinsic goal, we see that we are intrinsically pulled to others; our basic nature, for Beauvoir, is social. Again, this is an implicit criticism of Sartre, who, as we saw, believed that social unification required a need or threat from outside. This in turn can be traced to Sartre's unambiguous view of nihilation as distancing; if the only way to become aware of other people is to distance yourself from them, it is hard to see how we can make common cause with them, or why we should. If a joyous attraction is basic to awareness, joyous attraction to other human beings is – as it is for Beauvoir – much easier to explain.

This argument – that our mortality requires us, in order to fulfil our nature, to relate to other people – came originally from Aristotle. He phrased it, however, in wholly different terms: those of biology. Why do people, or any living things, have children? It must be because they know, on some level, that they are going to die. Since individual immortality is impossible, he says (Gen. an. II.1 731b32–732a3), they try at least to gain immortality for their species, by begetting new members of it. Beauvoir has applied this argument to existentialist freedom. I seek the freedom of others because I value, not life, but freedom itself, which is ongoing nihilation. Since I myself am not ongoing, I must – and will – seek to

---

1. This may, of course, have something to do with the fact that, as women, Arendt and Beauvoir have futures that are not comfortably finite, à la Heidegger, but rigidly circumscribed.

make others free. Indeed, I cannot *not* do this, because that would amount to deciding against freedom – which is a contradiction: "Man cannot positively decide between the negation and the assumption of his freedom, for as soon as he decides, he assumes it. He cannot positively will not to be free, for such a willing would be self-destructive" (*EA* 33).

This has implications within the individual life too, of course. Freedom, for Beauvoir as for Sartre and Kierkegaard, is frightening. What do you do if you are too frightened of freedom to will it? You cannot will against it – willing yourself not to be free is a contradiction, and so "self-destructive" – so you must deny it. There are various ways to do this, and Beauvoir explores some of them in chapter 2. These modes of denial amount, then, to failure to fulfil the human condition; they are forms of dishonesty, or of what Sartre had called "bad faith".

CONSCIOUSNESS AND COMMUNITY

Freedom is basically a vitalizing force; it gives us "living warmth" (*EA* 41, in an important discussion of what it means to disclose being). But some people deny it, and this can be done in many ways. Some of those ways, moreover, are complex, coherent ensembles of various strategies. Each such ensemble has a certain set of rules, which hang together in such a way as to accomplish the denial. We can call them projects of denial, and in chapter 2 Beauvoir discusses no fewer than eight of them.

She begins with people who are not free, but who whose projects of denial are not their own doing. As in Aristotle, there are three such groups: women, slaves and children. The most important of these are children, because the state of being a slave or a woman is a state of being *infantilized*, of being treated like a child and, more importantly, of being made to believe that you are a sort of child (*EA* 37–8; Beauvoir's feminist concerns are showing here).

What is it then, to be a child? It is to be passive. A child finds herself in a world that she has not made, filled with Big People, who, she thinks, know what they are doing. She takes them for gods (*EA* 39) or, in the existentialist vocabulary, for humans who are in-themselves, who just are what they are and do not have to change. Since everything in her world is in-itself in this way, that is, in no need of change, the child has no idea that she herself can do anything differently from the way she does it. She is, as Kierkegaard would say, "innocent". Through her innocence, the child "escapes the anguish of freedom" (*EA* 36). But innocence, as Kierkegaard pointed out, cannot last: the child begins to wonder *why* she has to do things a certain way – such as brush her teeth. As she grows older, she comes to realize that Big People disagree with each other (*EA* 39). They make mistakes. They are often uncertain. On the one hand, such discoveries are liberating, because they teach the child that she is free not to do as she is told. But they are also, of course, scary:

> The adolescent finds himself cast into a world which is no longer ready-made, which has to be made; he is abandoned, unjustified, the prey of a freedom which is no longer chained up by anything.   (*EA* 39)[2]

> Our desire to be wholly in-ourselves is therefore a nostalgia for the carefree days of childhood.   (*EA* 40)

Here, the differences between Beauvoir and Sartre have widened still further. Recall Sartre's tortuous argument that the for-itself necessarily desires the in-itself. On Beauvoir's approach, that argument – and many others like it – is unnecessary. This is because Beauvoir does not have to explain consciousness strictly in terms of consciousness; she can explain it in terms of social situations. Consciousness is not, in other words, a self-enclosed realm that must be explained entirely in terms of itself: the game that Husserl and Sartre were both playing. Rather, we have the kinds of consciousness we do, in part at least, because of the kinds of communities we belong to and the personal histories we have.

This difference with Sartre is truly profound. We saw Beauvoir assert that Sartre had not discussed the point of nihilation – the disclosure of being – because it did not show up at the "level" on which he was working. It was on that level that the basic themes of Sartre's philosophy – nihilation, radical freedom and dread – appeared. Here, Beauvoir is challenging that very level itself, at least in the form that Sartre gave to it: that of a self-contained, independent stratum that can be explained only in terms of itself. She is thus challenging the heart of Sartre's philosophy, and doing so on behalf of history, community and common sense: doing so, also, without admitting it.

This implicit criticism of Sartre poses a very basic question: if the structures of mature consciousness are founded on childhood experiences; and if those experiences are of concrete individuals, whom the child sees as cases of the in-itself; and if the behaviour of those concrete individuals, and the ways the child relates to them, change over history – what happens to the absolute and ultimate core of the human self? Must not nihilation itself take on different forms over time? Would, for example, a small child whose relationships to adults had been predominantly abusive even desire to become "in-itself"? If Beauvoir were to answer no to this question, if she were to allow that nihilation itself changes over time, she would be doing for Sartre what Hegel did for Kant and Heidegger did for Husserl: purging his philosophy of its atemporal traditionalism. In fact, although her discussion of childhood indicates that this

---

2. It is testimony to the influence of Beauvoir's thought, and that of other feminists, that I can today use feminine pronouns when not directly quoting her.

pathway would be congenial to her, she does not explicitly take it. Her relation to temporalized philosophy thus remains, to a degree, ambiguous.

For Beauvoir, a child is not free, but also does not deny her freedom; she simply has not found it yet. People who have found their freedom, but have also found it too frightening to accept, actively deny it. Beauvoir's discussion of the ensembles of strategies for doing this constitutes the bulk of chapter 2. Like Hegel, she arranges these eight ensembles in an order such that each poses a problem or tension which can only be resolved by the next.

Projects of denial: Beauvoir's account of bad faith

The first, and worst, way to deny freedom is to be a "sub-human": to deny *all* disclosure of being, and so *all* joy and risk. This kind of person does not really invest herself in anything; she "is led to take refuge in the ready-made values of the serious world" (*EA* 44). But she does not commit to any of these values: "One day, a monarchist, the next day, an anarchist, he is more readily anti-semitic, anti-clerical, or anti-republican" (*EA* 44). The sub-human is thus uncommitted human energy, totally open to manipulation by others, because – like Heidegger's *das Man* – she has nothing she cares about, nothing she *dares* to care about. Which only means that the sub-human "makes his way across a world deprived of meaning toward a death which merely confirms his long negation of himself" (*EA* 44).

But that degree of meaninglessness is in itself scary. The next step in sub-humanity is to take just one ready-made value and commit yourself to it. This makes you a "serious person", a category Beauvoir takes from Sartre, for whom it denoted a form of bad faith. The serious person adheres consistently and of her own force to some social ideal or other, and so is not like the ever changing sub-human. But she does not really believe in that goal or cause, because she found it outside her, in the world as ready-made: "The thing that matters to the serious [person] is not so much the nature of the object which he prefers to himself, but rather the fact of being able to lose [himself] in it" (*EA* 47).

The serious person, like the sub-human, is dangerous, not because she is manipulable but because she is a fanatic: she is concerned with a single object or cause. She not only submits herself to this "object", or cause, but others as well: she becomes a tyrant (*EA* 49). Of course, not everything in her life is taken up by the cause; when that single value is not in play, the serious person "slips into the attitude of the sub-human" (*EA* 50), who has no values at all. Imagine a doctor who, when not talking about medicine, is just a stupid bore (*EA* 50).

The cause the serious person serves is not herself; it is an object. She is, therefore, inescapably detached from it. Her cause may be defeated, or it may be so transformed that it will no longer be *her* cause. So she worries about it, but her real worry is that it may escape her:

> Everything is a threat to him because since the thing which he has set up as an idol is an externality and is thus in relationship with the whole universe and consequently threatened by the whole universe; and since, despite all precautions, he will never be the master of this exterior world to which he has consented to submit, he will be continually upset by the uncontrollable course of events. (*EA* 51)

This can lead to rejecting the cause, and with it everything the serious person values about herself. Since identifying with the cause has not worked, she replaces it, not with another cause, but with nothing. This makes the serious person into a "nihilist". A nihilist rejects the ready-made values of the serious world, on the one hand, and thereby loses all meaning, becoming like the sub-human, but more deeply, because this absence of meaning comes to her only after a serious engagement with the world (*EA* 53). She does not simply mouth this or that blather that is out there, the way the sub-human does, but brilliantly hates all of it, like Baudelaire (*EA* 53). The nihilist is thus not merely dangerous, but actively destructive: "If [she] wills [herself] to be nothing, all mankind must be annihilated" (*EA* 55).

Like Nietzsche's ascetic idealist – and also like the existentialist – the nihilist thus distances herself from the current situation, but does not do so in favour of disclosure of being: "The nihilist attitude manifests a certain truth. ... The nihilist is right in thinking that the world *possesses* no justification and that he himself *is* nothing. But he forgets that it is up to him to justify the world and to make himself exist validly" (*EA* 57). This attitude, like that of the serious person, cannot be maintained across all of life. In other aspects of her life, then, the nihilist may retain some joy in living. In that case, she does not turn aside from what she does not believe in, but uses it destructively to show she does not value it; she becomes an "adventurer" (*EA* 58; cf. Don Juan, *EA* 60). The adventurer, too, is not without truth of a sort. She too is always beyond what is present to her: "If existentialism were solipsistic, as is generally claimed, it would have to regard the adventurer as its perfect hero" (*EA* 59). The adventurer is not a hero, however, in part because she is not always honest; sometimes she does care about something, such as her own personal advancement (*EA* 59). Sometimes her adventures even go along with serious devotion to a cause, as with Cortez (*EA* 59). And because she is adventuring, she meets other people; she is out there in the human world. But because she does not truly value anything, she treats everyone the same, and so, like Odysseus in the view of Horkheimer and Adorno, is "abstract" (*EA* 60).

The adventurer may perhaps become a moral person by realizing the require-ment of her own freedom, which she enjoys; then she undertakes to make others free, and is no longer an adventurer (*EA* 60–61). But the true adventurer "remains indifferent to the human meaning of [her] action" (*EA* 61). This is because in order to pursue her adventures in the human world, the adventurer must befriend the regime in power: "He will range himself on the side of the regimes which guarantee his privileges. He will make himself its accomplice, its servant, or even its valet. [His independence] thus turns into servitude" (*EA* 62).

Sometimes the adventurer even becomes the regime, takes power herself, in order to guarantee her own privileges: "But what he then knows is the supreme servitude of tyranny" (*EA* 62). Ultimately the adventurer, too, fails in her denial, because, she realizes, she will die and be forgotten. To be remembered, she needs other people (*EA* 63). So she tries treating *herself* as an adventure: she is no longer over and above the different objects she treats, but identifies himself with one of them. She becomes a "passionate person". The passionate person therefore has an absolute, like the serious person, but it is not something outside herself that she might lose. It is something with which she is wholly identified. Don Juan mistreated women and left them; but the passionate person loses herself entirely in a love affair because she identifies herself entirely with the love that she feels, as Kierkegaard identified himself with his love of God. Not only that, but because she is identified with this love affair, it must be unique to her. No one else can love this person in the unique way she does; because she is unique, her love must be unique. She alone sees the other person truly, she alone can truly love the other person ("no one loves you like I do!"; *EA* 64). Such a person defines herself as a lack, but not as the general lack involved in nihilation. She lacks only one particular object or person (*EA* 65). The passionate person therefore seeks to possess the object of her passion completely. But she cannot, because it remains "an external object which can continually escape him, he tragically feels his dependence" (*EA* 65). Thus single-minded, the passionate person withdraws "into an unusual region of the world, seeking not to communicate with other men. His freedom is realized only as separation" (*EA* 65).

This, too, leads to tyranny – to treating others as objects – and indeed to fanaticism (*EA* 66). Sometimes, however, the passionate person accepts that she can never completely possess her object. Then her love becomes "renunciation of all possession, of all confusion" (*EA* 67). Such a person comes to care genuinely about the other person, or whatever it is that her passion is for: "Passion is converted to genuine freedom only if one destines his existence to other existences through the being – whether thing or man – at which he aims, without hoping to entrap it in the destiny of the in-itself" (*EA* 66–7). It is already clear, then, that "No existence can be validly fulfilled if it is limited to itself. It appeals to the existence of others" (*EA* 67). But that is still frightening (*EA* 67). And so there are two further ways to go, ways that allow others their freedom but that do so incompletely because they appeal to something eternal which grounds the human world. They try to affirm that world only "in its eternal aspect and to achieve it as an absolute" (*EA* 68).

The first form of this is the "critic", who judges others in the name of "objective truth": a "superior, universal, and timeless value" (*EA* 68). Because she is in possession of this absolute value, the critic herself cannot be criticized. But she is still ambiguous, because she has *chosen* this value: chosen to make it central to her criticism. If she does not acknowledge this, she is not really committed to it and "is only the shameful servant of a cause to which he has not chosen to rally" (*EA* 69).

The "creative" person – artist or writer – does not merely accept a timeless value, but seeks to create something timeless, a work of art. But works of art tell us about ourselves; they are disclosures of being. A work of art, to be sure, is not an ordinary thing in the world; the artist is not "an engineer or a maniac" (*EA* 69). It discloses something other than itself. But the means by which it does this – the picture or novel itself – discloses existence in a supposedly timeless way: "Time is stripped, clear forms and finished meanings rise up. In this way existence is affirmed and establishes its own justification" (*EA* 69).

Because of this immortality, the work of art itself is absolute, and its creator can set herself up as absolute also. To avoid this, she must realize that "freedom itself is not to be engulfed in any goal; neither is it to dissipate itself vainly without aiming at a goal" (*EA* 70). Freedom is to pursue the goal of freedom itself, while realizing that no specific goal, and no specific work of art, can be ultimate.

Thus, freedom and the disclosure of being go together, and both require that we be bound up in a particular relation to other people: that of willing their freedom as well as our own. Without that, we are not free, but trapped in one of the morally deformed projects that Beauvoir has explored here.

We do not always recognize these interpersonal bonds for what they are. In particular, the young person – who has moved from the passivity of the child through the disillusion of the adolescent – does not appreciate them. Trying to exercise her new found freedom, she sees others as impeding this (willingly or not): "He sees in every other man, and particularly in those whose existence is asserted with most brilliance, a condemnation of himself" (*EA* 70).

But disclosure of being requires others; without them the world would be empty. So "If he is reasonable, the young man immediately understands that by taking the world away from me, others also give it to me … One can reveal the world only on a basis revealed by other men" (*EA* 71): on the basis, then, of history.

LIBERATION AND OPPRESSION

In the remainder of *The Ethics of Ambiguity*, Beauvoir is concerned to show that existentialism is a philosophy of liberation: that since my individual freedom requires the freedom of other people, each of us must strive to make everyone free. Her argument moves on two levels: one is a philosophical argument to that effect, while the other is a series of concrete examples that she thinks the general argument illuminates. I shall concentrate on the general argument.

At *EA* 129, Beauvoir distinguishes ambiguity from absurdity. Absurdity becomes problematic when it suggests that nothing means anything. If that is the case, there can be no ethics, because there is no point in doing anything: if any action had a "point" it would not be absurd. Ambiguity, which Beauvoir advocates, is, by contrast, the claim that while no basic meaning is ever fixed, existence has meanings, meanings that "must constantly be won", which we must produce through our free disclosing of being. Nothing has meaning in and of itself, then. Apart from us, the universe is indeed absurd. We give meaning to things by disclosing them as things that we value:

> All glorification of the earth is true as soon as it is realized. Let men attach value to words, forms, colors, mathematical theorems, physical laws, and athletic prowess; let them accord value to one another in love and friendship, and the objects, the events, and the men immediately *have* this value; they have it absolutely.　　　　(*EA* 129–30)

We disclose being, not merely by looking at it objectively, but in such phenomena as rejection, desire, hate and love (*EA* 78), for we reveal a thing in its meaning for us most basically by pursuing it or avoiding it. This has implications for liberation as a historical process, because it means that human freedom, the goal of liberation, is in a sense merely human loving and hating, rejecting and desiring: the disclosing of being. So we must not only will that humans be free, but must do so in a particular way: "to will man free is to will that there be being, it is to will the disclosure of being in the joy of existence; in order for the idea of liberation to have a concrete meaning, the joy of existence must be asserted in each one, at every instant" (*EA* 135).

Thus, we "must disclose the world with the purpose of further disclosure" (*EA* 74). But how can we liberate humanity while doing this – while asserting, in everyone and at every instant, the joy of existence? Why, in fact, does human freedom even require a process of liberation? If human freedom is disclosure of being, and we are always disclosing being, then freedom already exists, everywhere. And if disclosure itself is good, then all disclosure is good. It may seem that we are not forced to choose, that we can appreciate all disclosures equally. In that case, we do not need to do anything at all; in fact we should not; we should simply appreciate disclosure wherever we find it, that is, everywhere. Even Hitler and the Nazis were disclosers of being. We thus need not act; we should merely contemplate everything. Beauvoir identifies this attitude as "aesthetic", because it is detached and contemplative.

To paint a picture of something, to write a novel or poem about it, is to say that it is a suitable object for the hard work of artistic effort and so is to justify it (*EA* 77). Seen in this way, art can justify everything. But to take this power of art to mean that everything we can write a novel or poem about, or paint a picture of, is therefore justified is to go beyond the limits of art. For it rests on a deeper mistake: that of confusing the present and the past. The past (as Sartre had also pointed out) cannot be changed; it is the domain in which no further action is possible (*EA* 77). To take the view that we can simply contemplate everything people do because it is all equally disclosive of being is to say that nothing should be changed: that everything is, in effect, past. It is to deny what makes the present different from the past: that "it is the moment of choice and action" (*EA* 76), rather than of mere contemplation. It is because the present differs from the past in this way that we cannot value all cases of disclosing being equally. Some of them have to be fostered, others opposed: "man's project towards freedom is embodied in definite acts of behavior" (*EA* 78). For Kierkegaard, as we saw, it was our need to make a decision that broke the continuity between present and past; but that need itself was produced by Christianity's message that our eternal future was one of either salvation or damnation. Beauvoir, by contrast, assigns the leading role to time; it is because we constitute the present as discontinuous with the past that we need to take action, rather than the reverse.

Thus, human enterprises such as science, technics (technology), art and philosophy are all engaged in the project of human freedom; they are liberating activities. Science does not simply aim at truth, but "at the possibility of new discoveries" (*EA* 79). Indeed, all "the constructive activities of man take on a valid meaning only when they are assumed as a movement toward freedom" (*EA* 8). Outside that movement – outside liberation as the disclosure of being – the things we do have no meaning. Technological labour-saving devices, from washing machines to computers, are meaningless apart from what we *do* with the time we have gained. Art, too, as we saw reveals the transitory as an absolute, and thus presents new possibilities for us as well. And philosophy as a liberating activity? Beauvoir does not discuss that here.

To act is to change things, and so to oppose what we change. What we *must* oppose, then, is whatever stands in the way of human freedom, and that is oppression. Oppression, for Beauvoir, is, as far as the oppressor is concerned, basically a form of unawareness, a lack of what, discussing Sartre, I called "lucidity": "if the oppressor were clearly aware of the demands of [her] own freedom, [she herself] would have to denounce oppression" (*EA* 96). To be an oppressor is to deny the true meaning of your own freedom; it is to carry out one of the projects of denial Beauvoir has discussed previously. Her earlier account of those, then, was in the service of a more general account of oppression that she is only now giving. She is trying to show that one who oppresses others has already denied her own freedom, not merely that of the people she oppresses. Oppression is thus the denial of everyone's freedom, and once again my freedom is inseparable from the freedom of others.

When someone is oppressed, as Sartre had argued, their possibilities are diminished or blocked, and they are not able to disclose being freely. They are *forced* to love some things, and hate others, which means that their own individual capacity to decide freely on those things – to disclose being in their own way – is denied. They "consume their transcendence in vain", and their lives consist in "marking time hopelessly" (*EA* 83). They are adults who are treated like children.

Oppression is thus a basic denial of humanity. As such it likes to hide: to deny its own nature. It thus goes beyond mere lack of clarity to become a form of dishonesty. Oppression tends to hide, Beauvoir says, behind three different things that function as "excuses" for it:

- *Nature*: that some people are not allowed possibilities is necessary because nature decrees it, as in Aristotle's "slave by nature" (*Pol.* I.5–6), who simply was not equipped with those components of the human mind that would enable her to conduct her own life rationally (*EA* 83). The untenability of this, Beauvoir notes, has already been shown.
- *Tradition*: because we have always done things this way, we should keep doing them this way. This attitude "defends a past which has assumed the icy dignity of being against an uncertain future whose values have not yet been won" (*EA* 91).

The latter attitude presumes we know what the past was, and that the present, like the past, cannot be changed, or should not be. But more than that, it also supposes that the past understood itself. For the social practices of the past were believed, by the people who lived by them, to be the best possible way of doing things; otherwise they would not have accepted them. And if those people were mistaken about that, maybe those social practices were not the best. Living in slave societies, for example, Plato and Aristotle did not understand slavery: they took it for granted as the best way to organize economic labour. They did not understand what it really was. Thus,

> If the past [i.e. tradition] concerns us, it does not do so as a brute fact, but insofar as it has human signification; if this signification can be recognized only by a project which refuses the legacy of the past, then this legacy must be refused. (*EA* 93)

- *Utility*: when it is claimed that you have to be blocked in your aspirations because blocking you is useful (*EA* 95). Useful for whom, however? Usefulness is always *contextualized*: something can be useful to achieving this or that future state, or to this or that person, but there is no such things as pure or absolute usefulness. And the moment we admit that for something to be useful is for it to be useful *to somebody*, we are saying that it is useful for the disclosure of being, since that is what we most basically do. Since oppression denies the disclosure of being, it can never be truly useful (*EA* 95).

There is a fourth and final argument in favour of oppression: that freedom is *difficult*; that in fact the freedom of all cannot be achieved. The basic claim here is that in order to struggle against oppression, we must struggle against the oppressors, thereby denying them their freedom and treating them like things. We must, in other words, treat them the way they treat us. In order to fight the oppressor, then, we must treat her as a thing, deny her interiority; and this means making ourselves into external forces that force her to act in certain ways. And to do that we have to treat *ourselves* like things: as tools in the struggle. So in order to overcome oppression, we must not only treat the oppressor as she treats us, which is bad enough, but we must also treat ourselves that way. This argument is not a dissimulation of oppression, like the first three, but an attack on the notion of freedom itself. It claims that there are internal tensions within the concept of freedom that make it impossible to adopt freedom as the goal for all human beings.

THE ANTINOMY OF ACTION

Liberation, it now seems, can come about only through oppression. This is what Beauvoir calls the "antinomy of action". An "antinomy", according to Kant, is the claim that in order to accept one thing I must accept its opposite, and so must enter into a contradiction. Here, in order to realize my own freedom by fighting for the freedom of everyone from oppressors, I must cease to be free. To act against oppression, I must enter the world of external forces, must become a thing: "No action can be generated for man without its being immediately generated against men" (*EA* 99). In other words, in order for liberation to come about, some people have to be sacrificed: not merely the oppressors, but those struggling for liberation themselves. What could possibly entitle us to do this?

Beauvoir takes this final argument very seriously and treats it at length, in part because it incorporates elements of the first three. As always, the first thing about dealing with the antinomy at its core is not to deny that antinomy. Beauvoir examines four modes of such denial. The first two incorporate what we have seen is the first "excuse" for oppression: nature. In this case, it is a claim about the nature of human individuals in general.

The first way is simply to deny that individuals are important: as the old saying has it, you can't make an omelette without breaking eggs. The individual whom we mistreat is a zero, a nothing; the collective is everything (*EA* 100). But, Beauvoir points out, a collective is just a group of individuals, and $0 + 0 = 0$. If no individual is worth anything, then the whole human race is not worth anything, and there is no value in trying to liberate it.

The second way to deny the antinomy is a bit less extreme. It is to say that the individual does have worth, but their worth consists entirely in the way they move history forwards. We remember them for their sacrifice, but only for their sacrifice. The individual has value only in being surpassed towards the greater good (*EA* 103):

> The finite is nothing if it is not in transition to the infinite; the death of an individual is not failure if it is integrated into a project which surpasses the limit of life; the substance of his life being outside of the individual himself, in the class, in the socialist state; if the individual is taught to consent to his sacrifice, the latter is abolished as such, and the soldier who has renounced himself in favor of his cause will die joyfully; in fact, that is how the young Hitlerians died. (*EA* 103)

But this, once again, is just to say that the individual is nothing, because an "individual" is in fact more than the sum of her contributions to the cause or to history. On one level of her being she remains isolated from all such things, as Descartes showed (*EA* 105). So this too runs into the basic problem that "if the individual is nothing, society cannot be something" (*EA* 106). Only a philosophy that recognizes the infinite worth of each individual can truly appreciate the sacrifices that some of us must make (*EA* 107).

Finally, historical materialism – communism – denies the antinomy in two more ways. On the one hand, it claims that the sacrifice of individuals is *necessary*:

> [I]f only one way shows itself to be possible, if the unrolling of history is fatal, there is no longer any place for the anguish of choice, or for regret, or for outrage; revolt can no longer surge up in any heart. This is what makes historical materialism so reassuring a doctrine; the troublesome idea of a subjective caprice or an objective chance is thereby eliminated. The thought and the voice of the directors merely reflect the fatal exigencies of history. (*EA* 109)

Therefore, the orders of the "directors" cannot be critically reflected on; that is why "every authoritarian party regards thought as a danger" (*EA* 110–11).

Notice what Beauvoir has done here. To say that history is completely governed by iron laws is to conceive of history as a sort of natural realm, rather than as the field in which humans act freely. To tell someone to sacrifice herself because the laws of history require it is, then, to say that she must give up her transcendence, her capacity to disclose being, because of something natural. And that, we saw, was one of the principle lies of the oppressor. Beauvoir is implying that the Communist Party itself is an *oppressor*. This association of the party with oppression is even clearer in her final example of how to deny the antinomy of action. This is nothing other than utility, the third excuse for oppression discussed earlier (*EA* 111).

Finally, to say that someone's sacrifice is useful is not the same as saying that it is necessary because of the nature-like laws of history:

> It does not much matter that the action is not fatally commanded by anterior events as long as it is called for by the proposed end; the end sets up the means which are subordinated to it; and thanks to this subordination, one can perhaps not avoid sacrifice but one can legitimize it. (*EA* 111)

But there are no unconditional specific ends; the only unconditional end is freedom, and it is not specific. Another way to put this is to say, as Beauvoir already has, that nothing is absolutely useful, in and of itself; it must always be useful to someone or something, and is always conditional on a particular end in view. Only the "serious man" thinks there are specific unconditional ends (*EA* 111).

Thus "It is true that each is bound to all; but that is precisely the ambiguity of his condition: in his surpassing toward others, each exists absolutely as for himself; each is interested in the liberation of all, but as a separate existence engaged in his own projects" (*EA* 112). This appeal to utility is, then, a rationalization on the part of an oppressor, and once again the communists indulge in such oppression: when, for example, they decide that it is more useful to maintain the lives of party members, who are useful, than of non-party members (*EA* 114).

The upshot of all this is that we cannot deny the antinomy of action. In situations where some people are oppressed by others we must choose between the "negation" of one freedom and that of another. How can we do this? There is a clue when we remember that to be "useful" means not merely to someone or something, but, more generally, useful to a future state: usefulness has a reference to the future. And this is important, because it shows us the relation between the nothingness of an individual and their infinite value:

> Cut off from his transcendence, reduced to the facticity of his presence [what Sartre called his "in-itself"], an individual is nothing; it is by his project that he fulfills himself; thus, this justification is always to come. Only the future can take the present for its own and keep it alive by surpassing it. ... No action is possible without this sovereign affirmation of the future. (*EA* 115)

But what does it mean to "affirm the future"? Beauvoir argues that "future" has three meanings. In one, it is *my* future: the set of possibilities that I, on the basis of my past, can take as possible for *me*. This future "is the definite direction of a particular transcendence, and it is so closely bond up with the present that it composes with it a single temporal form" (*EA* 116). This is a future, then, that is connected to my present in that I can see how I can get there from here. It is thus even more specific than the Heideggerean finite future, which contains some things and not others but which is not necessarily something I know how to realize. I will call it my "practical future".

The second kind of future denies this continuity because it is not a human future at all. It is a future in which all problems are solved, and so there will be no necessity to move on from it; it is an immobile future (*EA* 116). This future does not "prolong the present", because it is unreachable from where any individual human is now. Indeed, it is so inhuman that it was originally conceived by Christians as the "messianic future", the Kingdom of Heaven. Moderns such as Kant and Marx have replaced this with the dream of progress, the hope that mankind would ultimately reach a state of such perfection that further change would be unnecessary (*EA* 116). But even when brought to earth in this way, the myth of progress still proclaims the possibility of the messianic future: a future in which all problems, or certainly all basic problems, are solved, humanity lives in harmony, there is no oppression, and there is therefore no need or possibility for further change. Such a messianic or "positive", that is desirable and unchanging, future is one that can totally deny the present:

> In the face of the positivity of the future, the present is only the negative which must be eliminated as such. ... The present is the transitory existence which is made in order to be abolished; ... it is only as an instrument, as means, it is only by its efficacity with regard to the coming of the future that the present is validly realized; reduced to itself it is nothing, one may dispose of it as he pleases. That is the ultimate meaning of the formula: the end justifies the means.   (*EA* 117)

From the point of view of the messianic future, the present can be sacrificed. This view of the future was what underlay the various claims we saw earlier about how the individual can be sacrificed to the collective, for the true collective does not yet exist.

Unfortunately, however, it never will, for no such messianic future is possible. Because we are free, we shall need to transcend future states in just the same way that we need to transcend this one (although maybe not just as much). Hence, the Marxist who came the closest to understanding things was Leon Trotsky, with his vision of "permanent revolution". Trotsky, of course, was killed by Stalin, in part because if the future is as revolutionary as the present, the current state of affairs is not exceptional, and exceptional behaviour, such as lying, stealing and killing people, as Stalin did, is not allowed. If revolution is humanity's permanent condition, as Beauvoir (and Sartre, as we saw) think it is, then we cannot take the view that morality is a luxury that we must dispense with right now, while after the revolution we can stop lying and killing. Humanity is always in revolution (or "at war"; *EA* 119), and moral norms are in force now as always. So the idea of a messianic future, in which humanity will be in a harmonious state that will never need to change, is just another lie.

But the messianic future and the practical future are not only the kinds of future. There is a third kind of future: the future we cannot understand. For we can know very little about the future, and even that is unsure:

> Our hold on the future is limited; the movement of expansion of existence requires that we strive at every moment to amplify [this hold]; but where it stops our future stops too; beyond there is nothing more because nothing more is disclosed. From that formless night we can draw no justification for our acts, it condemns them with the same indifference. ... In this perspective all moments are lost in the indistinctness of nothingness and being. Man ought not entrust the care of his salvation to this uncertain and foreign future: it is up to him to assure it with his own existence; this existence is conceivable, as we have said, only as an affirmation of the future but of a human future, of a finite one. (*EA* 120)

I can commit myself now to a goal that will come to be only after I am gone, such as the happy lives of my children. On that level, my future is concrete and practical; it is the set of goals and ends that I can commit myself to now. At some point, however, what will happen in the future is beyond my knowledge, and so is not something that what I do today can affect; I cannot take it as a goal, and so it cannot justify anything that I do today. My practical future thus fades into "formless night". This notion of the "formless future" is as unfathomable as the eternal future of Kierkegaard, or the boundless future of Nietzsche, but not because what it contains is infinite, or because it may contain anything whatever. It is because, as far as I can know, it contains nothing. It is therefore close to Heidegger's notion of death, and Beauvoir's invocation of it is as if she were pointing out the ultimate futility of Arendtian attempts to control the future by attaining undying fame.

THE CRITIQUE OF THE MESSIANIC FUTURE

Messianic futures were marketed heavily in the last century. Beauvoir's detailed criticism of them takes her into issues regarding the mutual relation of means and ends, the nature of revolutions and the justification of violence. It can seem dated, as can her careful development of an alternative conception of the future. But, in fact, the idea of a future so perfect that no further change is needed has been shaping Western civilization from the start; and it is still at work today. It was because the Homeric Greeks did not believe in a worthwhile afterlife that they fought for a finite future in which they would be remembered. With

Christianity, the idea of the messianic future – first formulated in Judaism – became explicitly basic to European civilization. For Christianity, the final future is not to be dismissed as formless and incomprehensible, but is to be affirmed as possible and important – indeed, all-important, for it is "eternal life" – even if, as with Kierkegaard, we have no idea what that means. Deprived of its religious grounding, this idea of the messianic future then became the idea that I can know and act for the future of all human beings, which explains the modern push towards a "universal science" (i.e. traditional philosophy, which Beauvoir did not discuss earlier).

> Instead of accepting his limits, [modern man] tries to do away with them. He aspires to act on everything and by knowing everything. Throughout the eighteenth and nineteenth centuries there developed the dream of a universal science which, manifesting the solidarity of the parts of the whole also admitted a universal power; it was a "dream dreamed by reason," as Valery puts it, but which was none the less hollow, like all dreams. (*EA* 121)

The claim that we can begin now to solve all humanity's future problems requires us to believe that we can understand everything now. Future generations will never be able to do to us what we regularly do to previous generations, namely, decide that they did not understand their own ways of life.

But this kind of universal, messianic future, we have seen, is impossible. What are we to do in its absence? The first thing to note is that the absence of goals in the ultimate, unforeseeable future does not mean that there are no goals at all. "It is in the interval that separates me today from an unforeseeable future that there are meanings and ends toward which to direct my acts" (*EA* 121). The unforeseeable future is absurd: there is no meaning in or to it. But my practical future, the specific goals and ends to which I can commit myself, does contain meanings, because in that domain I disclose them – allow them to come about – myself. When I look at those intermediate goals, rather than at the ultimate, messianic goal of an end to all oppression, I see that *I* define my goals, for the fact that my future fades into unforeseeability means that after a certain point there are no further goals to legitimize them. Since they cannot be legitimized by the future, or (as we have seen) by the past, they must be legitimized from the present, out of my current situation. And that means by me.

The problem with the messianic future is thus, most basically, that it is an end that supposedly imposes *itself* rather than being legitimized by *me*. Because it is, again supposedly, justified in itself, it is legitimate, as a goal, no matter how we get there: it seems to be ethically detached from the means by which we achieve it. So if we take freedom as our messianic end, it is permissible to use oppression to bring it about. Lying and stealing and killing are thus means to bring about the revolution, which in turn is a means to bring about the messianic end. But if our goals are things that *we* set up, and if part of setting up a goal as part of our concrete future is to see how you can get there from here, then the value of the goal is not independent of the way we get there, of the means we use to get to it. "The end justifies the means" is no longer valid; an end or goal that can only be attained by evil means is unacceptable as an end or goal. Thus "a democracy which defends itself only by acts of oppression equivalent to those of authoritarian regimes, is precisely denying all [democratic] values; whatever the virtues of a civilization may be, it immediately belies them if it buys them by means of injustice and tyranny" (*EA* 125).

Beauvoir's example of this is England's obsession with its own security during the Cold War, which led it to all sorts of vicious foreign-policy decisions.[3] But she does not condemn all actions of this type. In order to defeat an oppressor, we must, as we have seen, become oppressors ourselves. The point is to minimize this, and not to deny it.

The means can also become detached from the ends in the opposite way. If the future towards which we are working is remote enough, it becomes "messianic" and vague. Then the means, which are "nearer and clearer", themselves become the goal at which we aim, without having been carefully thought through, or "deliberately wanted". This is just a fall into what Horkheimer and Adorno called "administrative reason". Beauvoir's example of it is the "triumph of Russia", which was originally supposed to be merely a means for liberating all mankind (Stalin's policy of "socialism in one country") but which has now become "an absolute end for all Stalinists" (*EA* 125). What we are seeking, by contrast, is a situation in which means and ends confirm one another:

> This requires that each action be considered as a finished form whose different moments, instead of fleeing toward the future in order to find there their justification, reflect and confirm one another so well that there is no longer a sharp separation between present and future, means and ends. (*EA* 131)

Beauvoir discusses two ways in which the sharp distinction between means and ends is overcome. One way is to take our goal, which is in the future, and represent it here in the present. Such representation is not real; the end has not really been achieved, but for a few hours, we pretend to ourselves that all is well with humanity. This is the festival (*EA* 125). It is also one of the functions of art to fix this kind of moment in a more durable way (*EA* 127).

But the simplest way to affirm end and means jointly is simply to take your end as your means, and this is the nature of liberation, or, as Sartre called it,

---

3. A clearer example would be the United States, where fear of communism permeated society and produced long-lasting social transformations, including in philosophy itself (see McCumber 2001).

revolution. For liberation, truly understood, takes freedom for its means as well as for its goal; it does not make use of oppression today in order to achieve greater freedom in the future. Because freedom does not have a positive nature, it presents itself as a negative action – as "rejection" (*EA* 131): "In the moment of rejection, the antinomy of action is removed and means and end meet; freedom immediately sets itself up as its own goal and fulfills itself by so doing" (*EA* 132).

The pilot Sartre talked about, hijacking a plane to show black people that they did not have to submit to British racism, would be an example of this. In Beauvoir's words, such a person "lays claim to his existence as an absolute value; then he must absolutely reject what would deny this value" (*EA* 131). But the pilot is not abstractly affirming freedom. His action in fact has a very humble goal: to get to France. You see the enormous ambiguity of it: the pilot wants to fly across the English Channel – just a few miles – *and* to liberate his entire people. The very incommensurability between these two goals is crucial to his action; his means, the mere flying of a plane, has been brilliantly chosen. And this is also part of Beauvoir's lesson here. The earlier quotation reads, more completely, as follows: "In the moment of rejection, the antinomy of action is removed and means and end meet; freedom immediately sets itself up as its own goal and fulfills itself by so doing. But the antinomy reappears as soon as freedom gives itself ends which are far off in the future" (*EA* 132). There were many other things the airman could have done; he *could*, for example, have walked on to his base with a bomb under his clothes and killed everyone there. But that would have been to deny his own freedom in the most radical possible way, along with that of everyone he killed.

So even the act of rejection can be performed in different ways, if only because in rejection we are using our freedom to bring about freedom. Whether a given means is the right way to achieve a given end is then always an open question. There is, as Beauvoir says at the very end of this chapter, "a perpetual contestation of the means by the end and of the end by the means" (*EA* 155). All distinction between means and end is not abandoned. The "contestation" in question is the critical examination of each in light of the other: if I can only reach this end by that means, is it a good end? Given that particular end, is this means the best way to get to it? And it is always concrete: there are no general rules for it that can be of any help, because it is a matter of freedom bringing about freedom – a matter of liberation – and therefore has no positive nature. There are thus no recipes in ethics; it can only propose methods (*EA* 134), mainly the "method" of not denying the hard problems brought by the antinomy of action.

Sometimes, then, violence and oppression have to be used: "Thus, we challenge every condemnation as well as every *a priori* justification of the violence practiced with a view to a valid end. They must be legitimized concretely" (*EA* 148).

We now see that the title of this book has been mistranslated. In French, it is *Pour une morale de l'ambiguité*, "for a morality of ambiguity". In English it is *The*

Ethics of Ambiguity. But Beauvoir is not offering us *the* ethics, only *an* ethics, one that she advocates and tries to persuade us of, but which cannot itself be the final answer, for there are no final answers.

The important thing is then to keep in mind that the ends we choose are ends only because we choose them; there is no end in itself which is imposed on us, any more for Beauvoir than for Sartre. This is because to choose an end, to make it an end, is to make it part of my practical future, in two stages: first, I take it as something I *can* get to from here; second, I take it as something I *will try* to get to from here. But (Sartre to the contrary notwithstanding) I cannot choose for anybody else; there are no recipes. In particular, I cannot choose for those who will come after me. Intrinsic to my freedom is that others should be free, not that they should do what I think they should do. No specific end that I adopt can be the final end for everybody, regardless of what the myth of "progress" tells us. As Beauvoir puts it, our hold on the future is limited:

> Insofar as we do not have a hold on the time which will flow beyond its coming [beyond the arrival of the end for which we work], we must not expect anything of the time for which we have worked; other men will have to live its joys and sorrows. As for us, the goal must be considered as an end; we have to justify it on the basis of our freedom which has projected it, but the ensemble of the movement which ends in its fulfill-ment. (*EA* 128)

Our ends are *only* ours, then, they hold for our lives but no further. To renounce the messianic future is, in the final analysis, to accept your mortality: the idea that not only you, but everything you value and seek will one day no longer be valid, and so is mortal. And this bring us to what Beauvoir calls the most fundamental ambiguity of the human condition: "That every living moment is a sliding toward death. But if [you] are willing to look it in the face [you] also discover that every moment toward death is life" (*EA* 127). This is the same as the ambiguity with which she started out. On the one hand I am a free, interior being whose nature is to disclose being; on the other hand I am merely a natural object, prey to external forces that will one day destroy me and eventually will destroy everything I love and value. To live with this honestly is … to live.

CONCLUSION

The relationship between Beauvoir and Sartre is one of the most remarkable in philosophy's long history. It is testimony to the underlying strength of continental philosophy that its basic premises are so flexible as to allow room for two such creative minds, yet so compelling as to inspire collaborative lifetimes of thought. And this can be generalized: that the many creative minds of continental philosophy have been able to learn so much from one another is part of the strength of its basic premises, and part of why it has achieved such unparalleled influence today.

Beauvoir and Sartre, in spite of their disagreements, remained in constant dialogue until Sartre's death. There was a price for this, however: Beauvoir, the woman, had to be tactful in her disagreements with Sartre. Nonetheless, her thought, as I have discussed it here, contains a critique of Sartre that is broadly similar to the kind of critique that Hegel made of Kant and Heidegger made of Husserl. It is a critique that cuts away their traditionalist appeals to atemporal foundations, while retaining most of the rest of their thought. In the case of Kant, this meant ridding his thought of the transcendental status of the faculties, seeing the human mind as in all respects a product of history. For Husserl, it meant doing the same thing with the apodictic *eidē*, which phenomenology was to investigate, and turning them into what Heidegger called "phenomena" or, later, "ways". In the case of Sartre, all that was left of an atemporal mind was the empty activity of nihilation, and that too falls into the pitiless jaws of temporalized philosophy, when Beauvoir quietly notes that childhood experiences can affect its nature.

That nihilation can change its nature over time means that it was not all that empty to begin with, and Beauvoir captures this when she reconceptualizes nihilation as the "disclosure of being". For the nature of such disclosure, the how and why of it, depends at least partially on what is there to be disclosed. Such disclosure, to be sure, contains nihilation as one of its aspects: it is in part a movement away from disclosures already achieved. But it is also a movement towards something: towards content yet to be disclosed. It therefore has a purpose; and that, we saw, is what makes it "joyful". Because the content towards which the disclosure of being projects itself has not yet been disclosed, it lies in the future. We can thus view the disclosure of being as an interplay of the two kinds of authentic (i.e. non-messianic) future that Beauvoir discussed. The future as "formless night" in which "nothing more is disclosed" (*EA* 120) becomes, through us, something definite: a practical future towards which we can move.

The disclosure of being is thus Beauvoir's reshaping of what, in discussing Arendt, I called the "finitizing" of the future. By seeing the future in this complex way, Beauvoir is able to retain Sartre's most important innovation on Husserl: the view that ethics is not merely a further discipline of which the investigation of consciousness is independent, but intrinsic to it from the start. For the finitizing of the future, as the disclosure of being, requires the adoption of concrete purposes; and the conscious adoption of such a purpose has, from Aristotle on, been viewed as the core of ethical activity.

Sartre's effort to follow Husserl in giving an account of consciousness as an entirely self-enclosed realm led him into jargonistic excesses. It required an unambiguous starting-point, which he found in "nihilation", the distantiation of consciousness from its own contents. That Husserlian intentionality is really an achievement of this sort, rather than a merely given characteristic of consciousness, is an important insight, for it enabled Sartre to formulate a concept of freedom that is intrinsic to consciousness, and thus to give phenomenology the ethical bearing it lacks in Husserl.

But for Beauvoir it is only part of the whole, for in distancing ourselves from determinate contents we also vivify them. We bring them *as* conscious contents into what Husserl called "the primordial life of the ego", or, in Heidegger's term, we "disclose" Being. The fundamental movement of our consciousness is thus a movement *towards* as much as it is a movement *away from*. Sartre not only did not see this, but could not have, for it means that consciousness is positively affected by the external world on its deepest levels. This is a point he was not prepared to concede. For him, consciousness must be a realm unto itself, independent of all else, and nihilation is the way it expresses that independence. Once we no longer feel philosophically obliged to sustain that independence, the way is free to explain basic features of consciousness by such things as social relations and personal histories. When we see the positive, joyful side of human existence, we can also conceive of a positive relation to others that is intrinsic to our very nature as consciousness, something Sartre, for whom all social unity comes about in response to outside pressures, cannot do.

But to do all this, we must forsake Sartre's (and Husserl's) dream of an account of consciousness that relies only on consciousness. And it is not clear that Beauvoir's approach, by doing this, does not run into problems at least as serious as those Sartre comes up against. For the ambiguous unity of distancing and disclosure seems to impeach the unity of consciousness itself. If its positive side means that I am affected by other things on my own deepest level, what happens to the "proximity to self" that was so essential to philosophy for Sartre? If the disclosure of being occurs across a time interval, so must nihilation, for they are two sides of the same process. And in that case, the unity of the ego is fractured: it is always about-to-come-about, it is always already deferred. What happens, then, to phenomenology? What happens to philosophy?

CHAPTER 12

THE FUTURE AS RUPTURE: MICHEL FOUCAULT

PRIMARY TEXT Michel Foucault, *The Foucault Reader* (*FR*; 1984)

It was early 1956, and the good people of Uppsala, the famous old Swedish university town north of Stockholm, were on their toes. Day and night – and in the winter there was very little day – they had to watch out for a huge beige Jaguar, which was being driven around town by a crazed (and often drunk) instructor at the university. The instructor was a thirty-year-old Frenchman, and his temporary lectureship at the university was the lowest position it contained. His car, like his many convivial meals in the town's best restaurants, had been paid for by his well-to-do family back in France; his father was a doctor in Poitiers. Michel Foucault was not merely drinking and driving, however. He was working hard. In addition to his academic appointment, he was director of the local French cultural mission, the Maison de France. This meant organizing cultural events and sometimes giving impromptu talks at them. The harder he worked at this, the more popular the events became, and the more work there was to do. In addition, he was working on his thesis, which was on the history of science. He had discovered in the university library a fantastic resource: a collection of 21,000 documents, largely devoted to the history of medicine. As he worked through them on winter afternoons, the idea of a new way of doing history began to take shape in his mind.

Foucault's overstretched lifestyle suggests that a lid had come off in his personal life, that for the first time he was out from under something suffocating. That something was French decorum. Foucault's provincial family was solidly Catholic and thoroughly bourgeois, but Foucault himself was neither. He had realized early in life that he was gay. This caused serious (although not fatal) problems with his family, and led to his always defining himself as an outsider in French society. According to his later testimony, that had led to his escape to Sweden: "I have suffered, and I still suffer, from a lot of things in French social and cultural life. That is why I left France in 1956" (Eribon 1991: 74).[1]

---

1. The overall story of Foucault's time in Sweden is in Eribon (1991: 74–86).

Foucault liked Sweden enough to want to stay and defend his thesis there, rather than in France. But the Swedish professor he contacted, Stirn Lindroth, was a very traditional thinker and thoroughly discouraged him. The university also doubled his teaching hours, which would have made further work on his dissertation effectively impossible. And so in May 1958, Foucault packed up his Jaguar and headed for another job, in Warsaw. He spent the next ten years teaching in Poland, Germany and Tunisia. Only when he had become famous through his books did he return to France, where from 1969 on he taught at the prestigious Collège de France. There he was a "professor of the history systems of thought", a title he himself invented. Like many French intellectuals, he was always politically active in support of marginalized groups: in gay activist circles and in behalf of prisoners. He was one of the first people to die of AIDS, in 1984.

THE ORIGINS OF GENEALOGY

In addition to the generally Catholic intellectual tradition in France, Foucault can be said to have had two other traditions behind him. One was a tradition in the philosophy of science; the other, as we shall see later, was derived from Nietzsche.

The philosophy of science in which Foucault was educated was reacting to Einstein's theory of relativity.[2] In 1924, a French philosopher named Émile Meyerson, a friend of Albert Einstein, published a book that took a Hegelian approach to the origins of the theory of relativity. Taking a "Hegelian approach", for Meyerson, meant developing the theory of relativity out of the previous theory – Newtonian physics – in a step-by-step way, so that it exemplified the kind of continuous change that many Hegelians associate with rationality.[3] A younger Frenchman, Georges Canguilhem, was unconvinced. He agreed with Meyerson (and Hegel) that the theory of relativity could only be understood historically. But it seemed to Canguilhem that Einstein had radically revised, all at once, a number of basic concepts – space, time, causality, gravity – and that any philosophical reconstruction of the origins of the theory of relativity had to see it, not as a series of step-by-step revisions, but as a single massive break with previous physics.

The idea that history contains ruptures – that historical processes sometimes show sharp breaks with what went before – had been explored in Christian tradition, which locates such discontinuity in the transformative moment of Christ's death. Kierkegaard had insisted that a person's decision to accept the Christian message was no less of a rupture on the individual level. The idea of messianic

---

2. The story of this tradition in the philosophy of science is told in Gutting (2001).
3. For such an association see McCumber (1993: 149).

rupture had also carried over, as Beauvoir argued, into the political dream of a perfect future. Such dreams took special root in France, a country whose system of government was born in revolution and which has lived through periodic sharp crises ever since: the Paris Commune of 1870, the First World War, the Second World War, the Liberation and May 1968, just to name a few.

The existence of historical rupture cannot be denied; the facts are just too obvious, in France and elsewhere. On traditional views, however, such ruptures do not constitute the core of history; they are merely interruptions, usually unfortunate, in its ongoing progress. What came from Canguilhem's work in the history of physics was the insight that history is, so to speak, rupture-driven: that sharp breaks, rather than incremental progress, are what is basic to history. Foucault, who studied with Canguilhem, applied this idea of rupture to the social sciences. He thus formulated a project of tracing the history of the social sciences as a set of breaks or ruptures with what had gone before.

This project itself embodied a major rupture with previous philosophy. In his "Nietzsche, Genealogy, History", which I shall discuss in more detail in the next section, Foucault says that modern historicism in general "places within a process of development everything considered immortal in man" (FR 87). This breaks, not only with traditional ways of doing history of science (such as Myerson's), but with traditional philosophy in general. In Greek philosophy, our own human nature was generally considered to be immortal, as (for example) a Platonic Form residing in its own kind of heaven or an Aristotelian essence present in the matter of our bodies. In Christian thought, the individual human soul was considered to be immortal. The faculties of the mind, although not demonstrably immortal for Kant, were at least, somehow, not in time.

Hegel, as we saw in Chapter 2, opposed these views of atemporal truth; what is ontologically basic for him is not unchanging Forms or essences, let alone souls or faculties, but the dynamic process of history itself. Hegel therefore set himself against the idea that anything, in man or outside him, could be considered immortal, and so must be among those Foucault has in mind when he identifies modern thought as having put such ancient conceptions as the human form, essence or soul into a "process of development", into time. But, as we shall see in more detail later on, Foucault is not here making common cause with Hegel. He thinks that Hegel's conception of history, like those of modern thinkers in general, is at best a sort of halfway house. Although such thinkers make temporal developments basic to reality, they still see them as governed by supratemporal ideas or themes: characteristics that reside in a historical process from its beginning to its end and therefore give it a kind of unity. In Foucault's view, the focus on such themes abets the view that historical developments are continuous, in the face of the facts of discontinuity and rupture that history actually exhibits.

These modern unifying conceptions, unlike Platonic Forms or Aristotelian essences, have no other existence than the way they unify history; unlike their

Greek forebears, they are not realities subsisting on their own. Hence, for Hegel all of history is the development of one idea: that of freedom. And freedom has no existence outside the human history it unifies. The same is true of the concept of class struggle for Marx. Although freedom and class struggle take on different forms in different historical periods, however, at bottom something about them must remain unchanged. Otherwise, the unifying factor in the overall development would itself be disunified, and the development would fall apart into a mere series of episodes. Although Hegelian freedom and Marxist class struggle exist only in and through history, then, they are for Foucault ahistorical, and so atemporal, in that on their very basic levels they are unaffected by history.

For Foucault, the Hegelian move from factors that unify history from somewhere outside it to dynamic factors that unify it from within is not enough of a change because it still postulates unchanging reality. He wants to take the next step, which for him is a far larger one because it is a move beyond modernity itself: to one version of the fascinating hodgepodge of ruptures and captures that has conventionally been given the name "postmodernity". He wants, in short, to deny the guiding unities of history altogether. This has enormous consequences, both for theory and for practice. Practically, it tempts Foucault to question the efficacy of human action, because if there are no unified historical processes you cannot bring them along. The very concept of progress then becomes suspicious. Theoretically, it tempts him to deny, or at least to question, the possibility of truth. For truth too, in his view, is an atemporal ideal.

"NIETZSCHE, GENEALOGY, HISTORY": AGAINST METAPHYSICAL ORIGINS

This last claim brings us to Foucault's relation to Nietzsche, for, as we saw, Nietzsche had also claimed that truth was an atemporal ideal: the "last god". In "Nietzsche, Genealogy, History", a short but dense essay from 1971, Foucault uses Nietzsche to lay out the methodological basis for his own work. He has good reasons for turning to Nietzsche. One is that Nietzsche's concept of genealogy is itself the outcome of strenuous reflection on European history from the ancient Greeks on. By defining his own work in terms of Nietzsche, then, Foucault is able to confront the entire philosophical tradition, all the way back to the Greeks. He is thus picking up what we saw, in connection with Arendt and other figures, to be continental philosophy's concern with Greek philosophy. This concern had been masked in France by Sartre's grounding in Husserlian phenomenology, for if consciousness is an entirely self-enclosed realm, as it is for both Husserl and Sartre, then history – even the history of philosophy itself – will be irrelevant to it.

We saw that Arendt, like Nietzsche and Heidegger, was led to Greek thought by her interest in the origins of the ways we think today. This is the usual way thinkers are led to history; and it makes the study of history, traditionally, a study of origins. But Foucault is proposing, he says, a kind of history that "opposes itself to the search for 'origins'" (FR 77). How can this be? How can Nietzsche be interested in the Greeks, or indeed be a historian at all, if he is uninterested in origins? More fundamentally, what is an origin?

The notion of "origin" (*origine*, *Entstehung*), unlike that of "beginning" (*commencement*, *Anfang*), has become weighed down, over time, with some fancy philosophy. The Greek word *arkhē*, which Foucault (via Nietzsche) has in mind here, basically means: where you look for the beginning of something. In Greek it contrasts with *aitia*, which means the cause of something. Thus, the *arkhē* or "origin" of the Second World War in Europe was Germany's invasion of Poland. The "causes" of the Second World War, by contrast, go back for generations.

Origins are of two types. One, like the one I just gave, is an origin in time. The other kind of origin is somehow outside time, which means that it cannot be natural. It must, therefore, be some sort of supernatural power. When a human is said to receive her soul from God, or someone is said to perform an act of free will, we are invoking this kind of supernatural origin (*Wunderursprung*). In accordance with a philosophical usage going all the way back to Kant, I shall call origins that are considered to be outside time "metaphysical" origins. Metaphysical origins, as we shall see, can be of many very different types. Nietzsche, as we saw, rejects them all. So does Foucault.

We cannot reject metaphysical origins, however, unless we first uncover them. This is not easy, for because of their variety, metaphysical origins often do not look like metaphysical origins. As we saw Nietzsche argue, for example, scientists think they have rejected metaphysics; they define themselves as empiricist-minded seekers of the truth. But "truth" as they define it is not something in time; it is a relation or state of affairs that is defined to be time-independent. It is therefore metaphysical: indeed, the "last god". Much of Nietzsche's work consists in this sort of uncovering and diagnosing of metaphysical origins that do not seem to be metaphysical origins.

Like Nietzsche, Foucault rejects *all* metaphysical origins. He does not believe in any agency or power that is above nature. Why not? First and foremost, I suggest, because a supernatural agent, be it God, or Sartrean nihilation, or even just an idea such as "progress" or "modernity", is not in time. If God creates me as a human being, not only is he above time but the nature he gives me is as well. And if I do something out of love for a moral value, that value is (traditionally) postulated to be something that exists above time. The search for metaphysical origins thus "assumes the existence of immobile forms which preceded the external world of accident and succession" (FR 78).

The word "accident" here is important (as is the word "assumes"). That historical origins involve succession is obvious; they are events in time. But not all successions are accidental. Some things follow each other according to patterns or causal laws. Foucault seems to be saying that anything non-accidental is part of the problem. Why? Because if an event is not accidental, it comes about in accordance with a law of some sort. And a causal law that connects two events must hold not only for both of them, but for all events of a given type; otherwise it is not a "law". Such a law is then seen as something permanent, "immobile". However modern and scientific its validation may be, at bottom it is just another metaphysical origin.

We are now beginning to see something of the breadth and variety of what Foucault considers to be metaphysical origins. Any chain of events that is asserted to be non-accidental is being "metaphysically" understood. If it does not come from a supernatural act, it at least occurs according to a "metaphysical" law. Suppose I claim that the German invasion of Poland originated in certain specific events of the time, such as the German resentment of the Treaty of Versailles, or that it was encouraged by the antiquated Polish defences. Then I am in line with Foucault: I have not tried to explain the invasion in terms of any "supratemporal" law. But if I were to try to formulate a "law of history" according to which, say, any action produces an opposite reaction (if not an equal one), so that the Allied conquest of Germany was bound to lead to a German attempt to conquer the Allies in turn, then to Foucault I would be engaging in metaphysics, as much as if I said that God or the devil made the Germans invade.

So what happens to the permanent features of the world, a concept embracing everything from the causal laws of contemporary science to the guiding ideas of history to what both Plato and Aristotle (as well as Husserl) called *eidē*? We find "not a timeless or essential secret, but the secret [is] that [things] have no essence or that their essence was fabricated by a piecemeal fashioning from alien forms" (*FR* 78, trans. mod.).

In other words, there is not complete chaos; some things are "essential" in the sense of being basic to other things. But unlike Platonic Forms and Aristotelian essences, these "essences" have their own historical natures. They are not grounded in some eternal cosmic order, but are put together, when they exist at all, from things that do not in any sense belong together or have to go together: mutually "alien" forms (later on we shall see how this actually works for Foucault). It is not helpful, then, to understand Foucault as being opposed to origins altogether; he would hardly be a historian, of any stripe, if he were. Rather, he thinks we should try to find out where things come from, but rejects the traditional concept of *metaphysical* origin.

In addition to their atemporality, metaphysical origins have three other traits that Foucault rejects:

(a) *Unity*: For the Greeks, there could be nothing in the effect that was not in the cause; otherwise that thing would have come to be from nothing, which is unthinkable to them. Therefore, if there is unity in the effect – which there always is, just because it is "an" effect – there must be unity in the cause. On the contrary, says Foucault: "What is found at the historical beginnings of things is not the inviolable identity of their origin; it is the dissension of other things. It is disparity" (*FR* 79).

"Historical beginnings" are not only plural but they do not consist in plural factors cooperating to produce something new. Every origin is a *struggle*. Of what? Of precisely what Nietzsche had viewed as most basic: of forces seeking to overcome one another. When one force triumphs, you have a beginning or non-unified origin: non-unified because part of it is whatever it is that the victorious force was fighting against.

(b) *Perfection*: A metaphysical origin is supposed to be the place where a supernatural being intersects with the changing, accidental world we live in. Therefore, the point of origin is a moment of purity: "We tend to think that [the origin] is the place of ... greatest perfection, when they emerged dazzlingly at the hands of a creator or in the shadowless light of a first morning" (*FR* 79). On the contrary, says Foucault (again echoing Nietzsche), "Historical beginnings are lowly, not in the sense of modest or discreet, ... but derisive and ironic, capable of undoing every infatuation" (*FR* 79).

(c) *Truth*: Because the thing was most perfect at the moment of its origin, that moment was the place where the thing was the most rational, where it was most truly what it was, and where we could therefore gain the most perfect knowledge of it. It was where "the truth of things corresponded to a truthful discourse" (*FR* 79). While Foucault does not exactly deny the existence of truth here, he does say that truth should not have the supernatural dignity of a metaphysical origin: "The very question of truth, the right it appropriates to refute error and oppose itself to appearance, the manner in which it developed – does not this form a history?" (*FR* 79–80). Everything has a history, so if truth has a history, then truth is nothing special. And *that* is Foucault's point. Truth is not so special that we should pursue it at all costs; certainly, as Nietzsche also suggested, we should not make a god of it. Nor should we reject something merely because we call it "error".

That Foucault should call truth an "error that cannot be refuted because it was hardened into unalterable form in the long baking process of history" (*FR* 79) has led some to think that he rejects truth altogether, just as some people think he rejected origins altogether. But that is a way of avoiding his real challenges, for it reduces him to the philosophically familiar figure of the sceptic. Once again, a glance at Nietzsche will show us what Foucault is talking about.

In his essay "On Truth and Lies in a Nonmoral Sense" (Nietzsche 1979), Nietzsche points out that our sensory apparatus changes the sensory input it receives; colours as we see them are not really there in nature, for example. Nor are shapes. So in terms of capturing what exists independently of our minds, it is no more true to say "the sky is red" than to say it is blue. If no eye is around, the sky is without colour. Our sensory apparatus has, for Nietzsche, evolved not to give us an accurate representation of the world, but to give us the information we need to flourish and reproduce. Just what information that is, of course, varies with the circumstances. Hence, truth is perspectival; it is relative to need. The needs according to which we produce true statements, in turn, are not necessarily the needs of individuals; they may be the needs of an entire society or (as Horkheimer and Adorno also stressed) of a group within society. Thus, it is true to say the sky is blue, because that is how it looks to visually normal human beings who speak English. To be sure, it looks different to someone who is completely colour-blind. But even such a person, if she speaks English, can also call the sky blue, in which case she is not reporting her own experience but abiding by the rules of society. That is even more true if I am talking about values instead of colours: if, for example, I say that freedom is good or that homosexuality is bad. Social rules like these are not reflective of external reality, nor are they hard-wired into human biology. Just where Foucault thinks they come from will be seen shortly.

Foucault can be best understood, then, as agreeing with Nietzsche that truth exists but is perspectival (*FR* 90). In order to understand any statement whatever, it is necessary to understand not merely what it purports to tell us about the world, but whose needs it serves and how it serves them. All linguistic understanding is, in this sense, interpretation, and all truth therefore requires interpretation. Moreover, interpretation works best when it is truly creative, when it is a *changing* of the rules by which we speak, which leads us to see things in a new light (*FR* 86). If the rules are basic enough, you cannot argue for the change: as for Nietzsche, truly original interpretation is "violent" in nature (*FR* 86).

Foucault is here trying to change the rules by which we speak of history: to produce nothing less than a new interpretation of what history is. Moreover, since for temporalized thought history is the most basic reality philosophy can deal with, Foucault is talking about the most basic reality he can talk about as a philosopher; he is giving what traditional philosophers would call his theory of ultimate reality, his "metaphysics" (although he himself, as we have seen, uses that term rather differently).

HISTORY WITHOUT METAPHYSICS

Merely deciding to reject metaphysical origins in general is only the beginning of Foucault's project. In order to carry it through, we would have to identify all the different metaphysical origins we have attributed to history up to now. This means, first, that we must reconceive the *subject matter* of history. Historians tend to look at history as the great deeds of great men, but Foucault thinks that is just another form of metaphysical origin, because identifying what is a great deed or who is a great man includes positing "greatness" itself as a unifying idea, that is, as a metaphysical origin. If, by contrast, all origins are merely historical, then they are not only "lowly" and "derisive", but largely accidental. We should therefore pay attention to "the details and accidents that accompany every beginning" (FR 80).

In particular, historians should pay attention to the *body* (FR 80). Much of Foucault's work, in fact, concerns how people, at different times in history, perceive and live in their own bodies. This is yet another of his innovations, for we traditionally tend to overlook our physical embodiment. We tend, for example, to see the body as something that "obeys the exclusive laws of physiology" and so is strictly biological rather than historical. But this is not to see the body at all, because it understands the body as a case of unchanging natural laws and so – paradoxical as it sounds – as something supernatural. Foucault's deeper reason for paying attention to the body, however, is that the body is more exposed to accident than the mind. All kinds of thing can happen to you physically, from a tree falling on your head to cancer growing in your lung. But in the realm of the mind, you have nothing to fear but falsity, a reassuring claim that only exposes how fictitious that "realm" really is.

Like truth and everything else, the body has a history, and so it cannot be exempted from historical investigation: "The body is molded by a great many distinct regimes: it is broken down by the rhythms of work, rest, and holidays; it is poisoned by food or values, through eating habits or moral laws; it constructs resistances" (FR 87).

Foucault's rejection of metaphysical origins also has consequences for his views on how a historical process moves forwards from its beginnings and on where it goes after that. For him, as (again) for Nietzsche, any history continues to be accidental as it moves forwards from its accidental and conflicted historical beginning; otherwise it would have to have some metaphysical unifying theme. A history is not just accidental in its origins, then, but is a *series* of accidents, and so is discontinuous *at every point*, which means that no comprehensible reason can be given for how it moves along. Any historical process, like the event of its origin, is therefore the outcome of an intersection of forces – a "reversal" of their relationship:

> The traditional devices for constructing a comprehensive view of history and for retracing the past as a patient and continuous development must be systematically dismantled. History becomes "effective" to the degree that it introduces discontinuity into our very being – as it divides our emotions, multiplies our body and sets it against itself.   (FR 88)

Moreover, if historical processes do not have origins and do not move forwards from their beginnings in a smooth, comprehensible way, we cannot say that history is working towards a purpose. If we dispense with the concept of *arkhē* in dealing with history, then, we must also jettison that of *telos*. Foucault thus rejects, as we saw, the idea that history is moving towards an overall goal. This means that he rejects the notion of progress: "Humanity does not gradually progress from combat to combat until it arrives at universal reciprocity, where the rule of law finally replaces warfare; humanity installs each of its violences in a system of rules and thus proceeds from domination to domination" (*FR* 85).

In the eyes of many, this repudiation of the idea of progress gets Foucault into real conceptual trouble. For if history is nothing more than a succession of rules of domination that replace one another accidentally, why is he bothering to write at all? It is not clear that Foucault provides, or could provide, persuasive answers to this question. What he *has* done is distinguish his way of doing history, which sees it as a rupture-driven play of accidental forces, from the traditional metaphysical way, which sees it as moving continuously towards determinate goals from origins that are unified, perfect and true. But this raises another question for him. If his own way of doing history has such obvious advantages, why did anyone ever start doing history metaphysically? Where does metaphysical history itself come from? Not from the moderns: Foucault does not consider them to be all that different from the ancients. And among the ancients, the real villain is Socrates (*FR* 91).

At least Nietzsche, who was deeply concerned with the figure of Socrates, thought so. On Foucault's account, Nietzsche believed that because Socrates was willing to talk to anyone, and hence was a "man of the people", he made philosophy into something intended to please the common person. The impulse Socrates gave to the study of history was, then, a democratic one. The "Socratic" approach to history sees it as coming not from kings and heroes, but from the *plebs*, the people, and so as having a low origin. History thus began as demagoguery, literally "leading the people".

Foucault's own political instincts are much more democratic than Nietzsche's were. For him, there is therefore nothing bad about that "Socratic" moment, the moment of the man who would talk to anyone (*FR* 91). The problem for Foucault, in fact, is not that this low origin exists, but that it was seen as shameful, by those who like origins to be high flown. And so the historian has to cover up the origin of history – which is just the historian herself – by denying that very origin: in other words, by saying that history is not merely what historians do, but has a nature all its own. Then history *has* to be the way that it is, and everybody *has* to accept this. Like Nietzsche's ascetic ideal, history so construed "must hide its singular malice under the cloak of universals" (*FR* 91). It becomes something of universal import and validity, and another metaphysical origin.

Plato could have overcome this, in his critique of Socrates, and doubtless was tempted to do so (*FR* 93), but in the end he only "consecrated" Socratic demagoguery. His theory of Forms, which postulates a realm that is unchangeable and incorporeal, gave a rationale for Socratic hatred of the body and, with that, of reality itself. Hence, "It is necessary to master history so as to turn it to genealogical uses, that is, strictly anti-Platonic purposes" (*FR* 93). Thus, where Platonic history sees history as originating in a Golden Age when things were pure and true, genealogy must become "parodic", that is, it must show origins not merely as low but as laughably low: "Genealogy is history in the form of a concerted carnival" (*FR* 94). Foucault has just provided us with an example of such "parodic" genealogy, by tracing history, not back to an eternal essence or to some mighty intellect setting forth the future development of the field, but to Socratic demagoguery and Plato's failure to overcome it.

In Plato's own view, history operates with a basic concept of identity: things are identical with themselves because they approximate the Forms, which are truly self-identical. Genealogy, by contrast – like Adorno's and Horkheimer's negative dialectics – aims at "the systematic dissociation of identity" (*FR* 94). Our identities are fictional anyway – each of us is plural, a congeries of forces pulling in many directions: "The purpose of history, guided by genealogy, is not to discover the roots of our identity but to commit itself to its dissipation" (*FR* 95).

And finally, if truth is conformity to the rules of society, and if those rules are rules of domination of some by others, then "all knowledge rests upon injustice": truth is not morally superior to falsity, and possession of it gives no moral rights (*FR* 95). Plato's view that we should try to achieve knowledge, not in the sense of the knowledge of the many little things that make our lives better, such as how to build sewage systems, but knowledge of the overall structure of what is right and wrong in the universe, is thus not only delusional but vicious.

Nietzsche advanced his criticisms of Plato in the name of "the affirmative and creative powers of life", which he thought Plato despised (*FR* 97). Foucault too, finally and, as I suggested, somewhat inconsistently, appeals to a value, but it is not life. It is justice, which requires "The destruction of the man who maintains knowledge by the injustice proper to the will to knowledge" (*FR* 97). Here we see that history as genealogy is *critical*. For what most needs to be criticized is what we are most invested in, and nothing gets you more invested in something than thinking it comes from a higher or supernatural order of being. As soon as history stops being "pious" – as soon as it stops looking for metaphysical origins – it "has value as critique" (*FR* 81).

What, then, is "genealogy" for Foucault? It is very complex, and radically new. Here alone, I have identified at least ten specific traits of it. It is a way of doing history:

- that makes no appeal to anything outside time: no God or laws of nature shape history;
- that therefore rejects metaphysical "origins";
- that therefore sees things as beginning in accidents;
- that therefore sees history itself as accidental;
- that therefore takes "rupture" or discontinuity for its main category;

- that therefore sees the processes of history not as unified but as intersections of historical forces;[4]
- that therefore does not see history as going anywhere or aiming at anything or as "progressive";
- that therefore turns to what is accidental or temporal – is largely a history of the body;
- that ultimately aims, not at "truth" as normally understood, but at creative and useful reinterpretations;
- and in all these traits, is "un-Socratic".

DISCIPLINES

In 1975, Foucault published a book called *Surveiller et punir*. The English title, "Discipline and Punish", does not fully capture the sense of the French *surveiller*, which means to watch or oversee. The title in French thus connects two ideas that are normally considered to be very different, because merely looking at someone is a passive beholding of them, while to punish them is to act. The English "discipline" is both: to "discipline" someone is to subject them punitively to a set of rules, but an academic "discipline" such as philosophy or chemistry is a matter of knowledge.

Foucault had already published several works on the history of mental illness, dealing with how it came about that certain humans were classified as "crazy" or mentally ill, and were then locked up while other human beings tried to cure them. This, of course, was of personal importance to him given his sexual orientation. When he was a young man, it was quite common in some countries (such as the United States) for homosexuals to be incarcerated until they were "cured". In accordance with his concept of genealogy, Foucault does not believe that there is such *a* thing as mental illness, in the sense of a single property or set of properties shared by schizophrenics, bipolars, people with personality disorders and so on (to say nothing of homosexuals), which has always been the same and which justifies the rest of us in locking them up. That would be a metaphysical origin of the most vicious kind. His question, therefore, is: how did decisions about locking people up get to be made by people who considered themselves "scientists"? What did they think justified them, and how did they come to think that? How did they gain the power to enable them to make that sort of decision about other people?

Foucault is not, of course, denying that some people are mentally dysfunctional. But what makes someone dysfunctional, according to him, is largely

---

4. The set of all such intersections is what Foucault famously calls "power", which occupies a smaller role in his philosophy than is usually thought; Foucault's thought, as he repeatedly claims, focuses on "rupture" rather than "power".

unique to that person: a product of their biology and personal history. It is also, to a much larger extent than we like to think, a matter of what is accepted, and what is not, in the surrounding society. And what is acceptable in a society, and what is not, depends largely on who holds power.

Discipline and Punish is not merely a critique of the notion of mental illness. It is also a genealogy that treats the origin of the prison. But the *structure* of the prison, its "carceral" structure, is not limited to prisons; it is a general structure that, as Foucault puts it, could be "detached from any specific use" and applied in constructing schools, hospitals, asylums, factories and poorhouses.[5] Because of the generality of its form, moreover, this "schema is destined, without effacing itself or losing any of its properties, to diffuse itself in the social body" (Foucault 1979: 207). The form of the prison is thus the model for all sorts of institutions in modern society:

> And, distancing itself ever further from penality properly so called, the carceral circles enlarge themselves, and the form of the prison attenuates itself slowly before disappearing altogether. … And finally this great carceral network rejoins all the disciplinary mechanisms which function as disseminated through society.
>
> (*Ibid.*: 298; cf. generally 293–308)

In "Docile Bodies", then, Foucault claims that the same kind of disciplining found in prisons has also been applied in the modern army. The basic presupposition is that soldiers can be *made*: "out of a formless clay, an inapt body, the machine required can be constructed" (*FR* 179). The "classical age" (by which Foucault means the early modern era, rather than the ancients), thus "discovered the body as object and target of power" (*FR* 180). In itself, this is nothing new: in every society, "the body was in the grip of very strict powers" (*FR* 180). Ancient armies, after all, were full of well-trained soldiers. Indeed, the idea that the body is at bottom a kind of relatively "formless" clay is articulated by Aristotle (e.g. *Gen. an.* II.4).

What is new is the way in which this happens in the modern army. The control is much greater because it extends to the individual (*FR* 181). In ancient times, we may say, each soldier largely trained himself; for Aristotle, the form that controlled your body was *your* form, your own individual soul.[6] Today, by contrast, the aim is for the power of society to control the individual bodies of the soldiers. It is as if society wants to shove the soldier's individual soul out of the way and take direct, if invisible, control of her body, "exercising on it subtle coercion … obtaining holds upon it at the level of the mechanism

---

5. This is from a part of *Discipline and Punish* not included in the anthology to which my account here is keyed; see Foucault (1979: 205).

6. Cf. Heidegger's account of Aristotle's four causes in Chapter 7.

itself" (*FR* 181). This requires coercion that is not merely subtle but constant: it is not simply a question of trying to get the soldier to accomplish certain tasks on the battlefield, but to get her to hold herself and move in certain ways even when she is not soldiering. Nor is it a matter even of getting the soldier to look a certain way: it is a matter of getting her to *be* a certain way – "constraint bears on the forces rather than on the signs" (*FR* 181). The result is a kind of domination that is much more intense and generalized than domination had been previously, a domination that has some resemblance to slavery, although it achieves its goals without resorting to actual ownership of someone else. In contrast to slavery, this domination is methodical; there are certain rules that must be followed.

Where does a regime come from? As we might expect, genealogically speaking this new form of domination does not spring into being in a single act. Its "origin", to which Foucault sometimes gives the overall name of "power", is:

> a multiplicity of often minor processes, of different origin [themselves] and scattered location, which overlap, repeat, or imitate one another, support one another, distinguish themselves from one another according to their domain of application, converge, and gradually produce the blueprint of a general method. (*FR* 182)

So this particular form of domination was not always there: it is not written in the nature of things or of human society. Nor did it spring from the mind of a single military genius. It originated with people in different places, struggling with their own problems of how to train soldiers, hearing about something somewhere else and putting it together with their own ideas, and so forth. In all this, however, two basic things converged.

One was the discourse of physiology pioneered by Descartes, a kind of physiology that saw the human body as merely a complex machine. Foucault calls this the "anatomico-metaphysical register": metaphysical because the idea that we are physically nothing more than machines was not a scientific idea, which could be verified, but one that followed from a basic, non-verifiable view of what reality consists in and is therefore "metaphysical". The other side of the convergence was a "technico-political register": the need of rulers in the modern era to have armies consisting of large numbers of precisely trained soldiers. Soldiers could no longer just run out on to the battlefield and choose an opponent, the way they did for example in Homer's day. They had to operate complex machines, and an army came to be viewed as itself a huge machine. The soldier, correspondingly, came to be viewed as a sub-machine, a part of the whole: a cog.

The convergence of these two registers, or discourses, was accidental: it did not have to happen. Descartes came to apply mechanics to bodies because he was a mathematician, and wanted to view all bodies as mathematically describable;

hence, he denied the view that living bodies were different from other bodies. All bodies are just more or less complex machines.[7] Human bodies are different, to be sure, because, unlike rocks and animals, human bodies contain souls, although Descartes could never explain just how. But as bodies, they are merely mechanical phenomena, just like animal bodies or rocks. With this view, Descartes radically changed our view of what nature was. For Aristotle, nature was defined as the set of things that contained their source of movement within themselves (*Ph.* II.1 192b22–24). Nature was therefore governed by the essences of those individual things, not by laws. For Descartes, by contrast, nature is governed by laws that determine the movement of individual bodies with precision, so individuals have no leeway.

For modern military discipline, then, a human being is matter under control, as it was for Aristotle, but the control is not from within. It is not exercised by the individual whose body it is, but by society, through the training the solder undergoes. This training is supposed to be grounded scientifically; it is not merely the whim of society, but is (supposedly) based on a precise knowledge of how individual bodies behave. It is, then, something of which Aristotle could never have conceived: it is what Foucault calls a "discipline". "Scientific" disciplinarity is thus connected to precise observation; scientific principles are supposed to be developed by observing how nature is constituted. But observation in the modern era is not merely theoretical and passive, but also an essential mode of social control (hence the French word in the book's title, *surveiller*). So:

> In the course of the classical age, we see the construction of those "observatories" of human multiplicity for which the history of the sciences has so little good to say. Side by side with the major technology of the telescope, the lens, and the light beam, which were an integral part of the new physics and cosmology, there were the minor techniques of multiple and intersecting observation. (*FR* 189)

The military camp was one example of this (*FR* 189–90). Because it is aimed at reality, the observing gaze, like the domination it enforces, must be constant: "The perfect disciplinary apparatus would make it possible for a single gaze to see everything constantly" (*FR* 191). Thus, in modern disciplinary buildings, the lines of sight are all important. Those in charge must be able to see everything.

---

7. "I suppose the body to be nothing but a statue or machine made of earth, which God forms with the explicit intention of making it as much as possible like us" ("Treatise on Man", in Descartes 1985: I, 99).

DISCIPLINE AND NORMALIZATION

Disciplined surveillance, says Foucault, has become the norm for a wide variety of institutions. These institutions, as disciplinary, have their own regulations, more specific than the laws of society (*FR* 193). These local regulations tell you, as a member of that institution, what you are, what you must be and what you must become. Someone who transgresses them is punished (hence the other word in Foucault's title). But their effect goes far beyond that, for in the aggregate they present nothing less than a model for what human beings themselves should be:

> A meticulous observation of detail and at the same time, a political awareness of these small things, for the control and use of men emerge through the classical age, bearing with them a whole set of techniques, a whole corpus of methods and knowledge, descriptions, plans, and data. And from such trifles, no doubt, the man of modern humanism was born. (*FR* 185)

The disciplinary enforcement of an idea of what a human being should be, either in general or with regard to a specific institution, is what Foucault calls "normalization". On a social or national level, normalization is carried out primarily by the educational system, which in modern societies is obligatory for all. Its ultimate form is the examination. In an examination, each individual directly confronts the ruling power in the institution; the individuals do not engage each other: "It becomes less and less a question of jousts in which pupils pitched their forces against each other and increasingly a perpetual comparison of each and all that made it possible both to measure and judge" (*FR* 198). Like a medieval joust (or a hand-to-hand struggle in Homer's war), the examination tells you what you are in comparison with others: in this case, the other pupils. But since they are not directly there, you get this information from the ruler – the grader: "The examination enabled the teacher, while transmitting his knowledge, to transform his pupils into a whole field of knowledge" (*FR* 198).

Crucial to this modern form of observation is that the observer remain invisible, lest she be graded in turn, and this "distribution of invisibility" is what distinguishes modern power from ancient power. Traditionally, the powerful person was the one on whom the light shines. Now, the powerful remain in the shadows. They are not seen, and attention is focused on the lower levels: "It is the fact of being constantly seen, of being able always to be seen, that maintains the disciplined individual in his subjection" (*FR* 199). This kind of disciplinary observation, then, makes you into a particular kind of being: "the examination is at the center of the procedures that constitute the individual as the effect and object of power, as effect and object of knowledge" (*FR* 204). What it makes you into, of course, is what Foucault calls a "docile body": a body whose movements are controlled by those in power, not by your own individual soul.

The human being as a "docile body" is, then, a formless clay shaped and controlled by society itself, via specific sorts of rules. These rules claim scientific status but are really the results of complex historical convergences. These accidental convergences constitute what a human being most deeply is today. Again: "from such trifles, no doubt, the man of modern humanism was born" (*FR* 185).

CONCLUSION

For Sartre, as we saw, existentialism is a humanism, and human nature for him, as for traditional philosophers, is very special. Unlike most traditional philosophers, for whom our nature is to be at once animal and rational, Sartre refused any positive account of human nature, seeing it only as the empty activity of nihilation. But nihilation was uniquely valuable, for it was the phenomenological root of freedom itself, and in Sartre's philosophy of radical freedom, freedom is the most basic value. Everything else has value only because we freely value it. Nihilation was not only the source of all value in the world, but both what we most basically are and what we most basically can know. It thus constituted the "proximity to self" which, as we saw, was necessary to all philosophy for Sartre. Beauvoir, although she relaxed the phenomenological purism of Sartre's approach, can also be viewed as claiming that what we most basically are coincides with what we most basically can know, in consciousness's ambiguous mixture of nihilation and the disclosure of being. This proximity to self is now gone; what we most basically are, our own human nature, is not what we can most basically understand. Indeed, it is not something that we can fully understand at all, for even the most thorough and painstaking reconstruction of those accidental convergences can never be complete.

To be sure, the historical investigation of those accidental convergences is important, even all-important, for such self understanding as we can achieve. In this, Foucault agrees with such German philosophers as Nietzsche, Heidegger and Arendt. But historical processes are not, as they were for Hegel, things that we would want to carry forward or stymie, because in the end there are no historical processes. History is a scene not of developments, but of ruptures; and Foucault's concern is not to describe ruptures but to "multiply" them.[8]

The way to "multiply" ruptures for Foucault is, most basically, to recognize them. This means describing what went before and what comes after a given historical rupture, for a rupture, being empty, cannot be directly described.

---

8. See Foucault (1972: 16), where *multiplie* is translated as "seeking and discovering"; also cf. 7, 170.

What goes before and comes after a historical rupture are, as we saw, the various systems of rules for domination to which they give rise. These rule systems become accessible to historians when they are articulated in formalized disciplines and, less formally, in what Foucault calls "discourses". Those disciplines and discourses can then be preserved in texts. Foucault's philosophical enterprise, like Nietzsche's "genealogy", thus turns to historical texts in order to describe how various social practices – in Foucault's case, discourses – arise. This emphasis on description means that, unlike Nietzsche, whose efforts at history were often rather impressionistic, and who often resorted as well as to literary devices such as fables and poems, Foucault sticks to verifiable descriptions of specific texts; indeed, at one point he styles himself a "positivist" with respect to truth (Foucault 1972: 125–7).

This "positivistic" view of truth also characterizes Foucault's return to Heidegger. In this connection we may say that where Heidegger had earth, the unfathomable ground that brings forth world as its own contrast, Foucault has the ruptures out of which discursive systems take shape. Where the later Heidegger approaches earth with a series of questions, Foucault addresses rupture with detailed descriptions of social discourses: a welcome improvement on Heidegger's practice of paying scrupulous attention to the great words of a few poets and philosophers, while ignoring actual social trends and historical phenomena.

Foucault's kind of description, I have noted, provides no connection to the past. It also does not lead to a specific, finite future. Rather, what our future contains is absolutely unforeseeable, because history is a set of basic ruptures. Hence, Foucault is concerned with the radically open, Nietzschean future rather than the Heideggerean finite future. This applies even on the level of the individual: "Do not ask me who I am, and do not tell me to remain the same; leave it to our bureaucrats and our police to see that our papers are in order" (Foucault 1972: 17).

CHAPTER 13

THE FUTURE AND HOPE: JACQUES DERRIDA

PRIMARY TEXT Jacques Derrida, *The Politics of Friendship* (*PF*; 1997)

At the end of December 1981, as American philosophers were convened in Philadelphia for the yearly meeting of the American Philosophical Association, their French colleague Jacques Derrida was leaving a much smaller, but perhaps no less important, meeting in Prague. The conference was sponsored by Charter 77, a Czech dissident group, together with the Jan Hus Society, a French group formed to aid Czech intellectuals who had lost their jobs, and of which Derrida was vice president. Charter 77 was not an officially approved organization in the Czechoslovak Socialist Republic – to say the least – so the meeting had not received the required authorization from the Czechoslovakian government. At the airport, Derrida's luggage was searched, and drugs were found. The idea that anyone, let alone a prominent philosopher, would be smuggling drugs *out* of one of Eastern Europe's strictest police states was patently ridiculous; Derrida himself later said that he believed the drugs had been planted in his suitcase while he was visiting the grave of Franz Kafka. In any case, he was interrogated for eight hours, arrested and taken to prison. There, he was stripped, left naked for a time, and then placed in a cell. After twenty-four hours, intercession by the French government obtained his release, and he was placed on a train to West Germany. Unauthorized philosophizing was not to be tolerated in the Czechoslovak Socialist Republic.[1]

The state lawyer provided to Derrida for his "defence", who seemed to be quite aware that the whole thing was a charade, remarked at one point, "You must have the impression of living in a Kafka story". But Derrida, on the train back to Germany, was pondering something else: "How to describe all the archaic

---

1. This was not the first time the Czechoslovak Socialist Republic had sinned against philosophy. Four years previously, Czech philosopher Jan Patočka, one of the founders of Charter 77, had died at the age of sixty-nine after long interrogation from the Czech police (see http://en.wikipedia.org/wiki/Jan_Patočka; accessed March 2011).

movements that are unleashed below the surface. … All of this is part of such a common experience that I would not be telling it unless I could recapture some absolute singularity" (Derrida 1995: 129).[2] If Derrida can be said to have had a single philosophical mission, that would be it: to penetrate beneath the rigid, ritualized surface of life, where "a single voice on the line, a continuous speech … is what they want to impose" (*ibid*.: 130), and to uncover the manifold, ancient movements of absolute singularity that underlie that surface, oppose it and so make it possible.

The unique singularity known as Jacques Derrida was without question the most famous philosopher in the world during his life. Indeed, he was the philosophical equivalent of a rock star, as is indicated by the fact that two films were made about him. French by nationality, Derrida was born in Algeria to a Sephardic Jewish family that had migrated there from the Iberian peninsula. During Derrida's youth, Algeria was a French colony, and so when the Nazi collaborators of Vichy took over in France in 1940, they also came to power in Algeria. Shortly after that, at the age of twelve, Jackie (as he was known then) was sent home from school because he was Jewish. Then, when the Germans retreated and the Allies arrived, they left the Nazi racial laws in place for almost a year. As he later put it, Derrida, at the beginning of his teenage years, "was certain everything would end in fire and blood". As Algeria moved towards independence, the French colonialists packed up and headed for France. The Derrida family was not from France, but went there too, in 1949, primarily because they wanted a better education for him than he could get in Algeria. He studied at the Ecole normal supérieure and taught there and elsewhere in Paris until his death in 2004. Among his many visiting professorships was a yearly one at the University of California, Irvine.[3]

CHARLATAN OR PHILOSOPHER?

Although he was extremely famous and was feted far and wide, to many philosophers Derrida is a charlatan and a fool.[4] There are several reasons for this negative reception.

- As with other continental philosophers, Derrida's *style* is very difficult. I once heard him call his way of writing a "series of guerilla raids on the French language"; the basic idea is that he is not sure that the French language, whether in grammar or vocabulary, is adequate to say what needs

---

2. The story is told by Derrida himself (Derrida 1995: 128–9); also cf. Powell (2006: 151).
3. For information on Derrida's life cf. Powell (2006).
4. Derrida himself talks about this (Derrida 1995: 399–421).

to be said. The best way to read him, as with any highly original writer, is first just to relax and let it wash over you.

- His subject matter is virtually unknown in the anglophone world. Derrida was a historian of philosophy in the strict sense of the phrase. In Great Britain and the United States, "historians of philosophy" are almost always highly specialized: they usually deal in just one thinker or, at most, in the philosophy of one historical period. Like Arendt, Foucault and Heidegger, Derrida ranges up and down the history of philosophy, now talking about Plato and Aristotle, now about Kant and Heidegger, or again about various French thinkers. Although he wrote relatively little about medieval and Renaissance philosophy, he covered almost the entire sweep of ancient and modern thought.
- Derrida's way of dealing with philosophical texts is very original. Normally, a philosopher approaches the writings of some historical figure presupposing that that text is:
  (a) in form, a collection of arguments;
  (b) materially couched in unambiguous words from a particular language;
  (c) produced by a single philosopher;
  (d) written with the purpose of proving a single thesis.

These last four presuppositions are of very ancient date. In fact, they are, respectively, Aristotle's formal, material, moving and final causes (cf. Heidegger's discussion of these in Chapter 7), which have been the basis for literary and other forms of criticism for a long, long time. They lead us, then, to view texts as a particular kind of artefact, in which matter (a set of words) is formed (or arranged) by an author for a single purpose. That Derrida, who does not approach texts this way, would look so weird simply shows how very ingrained the Aristotelian way of looking at texts has become over the long history of the West. Derrida not only does not accept these Aristotelian causes as applied to literary or philosophical texts but he also does not even respect them. He tries to *undo* them. He:

(a) shows how arguments fail, sometimes because they are invalid but sometimes because, even if valid, they do not do the job they are supposed to do;
(b) takes words in meanings other than those the author intended, notices oddities in the way an author phrases things and draws all sorts of conclusions from that;
(c) focuses on intertextuality, on the ways in which a text contains thoughts and phrases from other texts of which the author may not even be aware but that guide her writing;
(d) will not assign any clear purpose to any text, and certainly not that of proving a thesis.

People who are wedded to traditional philosophy, and some who think they are not, often see this as mere anarchic fooling around, wholly unworthy of the high seriousness of arguing for theses. To Derrida, such traditionalists are seeking to perpetuate the exclusive validity or, as he will call it the "hegemony", of what is really just one set of rules for evaluating texts. Like the Czech border guards of whom he ran afoul in 1981, they want only "a single voice on the line".

DERRIDA AND THE HISTORY OF PHILOSOPHY

If Derrida wants to get below the surface of common life and open up the ancient forces at work beneath it to critical examination, the arcane discipline of history of philosophy seems an odd venue. Why, then, is Derrida a historian of philosophy? To see this we must consider what he calls the "hegemony of a philosophical canon" (*PF* 277).

The "canonical discourse" of Western philosophy, the set of major works by major writers that must be read by anyone who wishes to consider herself philosophically educated, is, of course, only one set of texts among many others. The works that Derrida actually discusses amount to only a small part of that. That they should be so indispensable not only testifies to their greatness but also constitutes what Derrida calls their *hegemony*. This high regard is at least responsible for their ability to silence other voices. As he puts it with regard to the topic of *The Politics of Friendship*:

> The history of friendship cannot be reduced to these [canonical] discourses. … But precisely to begin the analysis of the forces and procedures that have placed the majority of these major discourses in the major position they have acquired, all the while covering over, reducing or marginalizing the others, one must begin by paying attention to what they [these discourses] say and what they do. (*PF* 229)

Hegemony is thus a matter of "covering over, reducing or marginalizing" other discourses, containing other insights. It is a matter of *blocking things off*. Off from what? From us, as when the traditional, often useful, "Aristotelian" view of philosophical texts becomes the only way to view those texts, so that someone who approaches them differently is scorned and despised, and so not read.

The hegemony of certain discourses affects far more than the history of philosophy. Our lives are guided by certain basic concepts, which we employ to articulate ourselves and our aspirations, both to other people and to ourselves. Philosophy is one of the ways in which these guiding concepts get articulated; it is largely, although not only, philosophers who have created our concepts of freedom, causality, knowledge, truth, justice, friendship and so on. They have thus created the words we must use to understand ourselves and each other, and this gives them a great deal of power. Even non-canonical discourses have, over time, been affected by the restrictions and insights of the canonical tradition.

What is the remedy? It is not simply to sweep away the tradition; that makes no sense at all, for getting rid of that canonical tradition would simply mean that we had no words left in which to think and speak. Rather, we must accept the hegemony of the canonical tradition in general, while recognizing that even within that tradition there are other voices, other resources:

> Now if this tradition harbours within it dominant structures, discourses which silence others … a tradition is certainly not homogenous …. Our major concern will indeed be to recognize the major marks of a tension, perhaps ruptures and in any case scansions, within this history of friendship, the canonical figure of friendship. (*PF* 233–4)

The canonical discourses on friendship that Derrida discusses in the ten interrelated essays that constitute *The Politics of Friendship* are many: Plato, Aristotle, Cicero, Montaigne, Nietzsche, Schmitt, Bataille and others. In every case he is trying to get at the way friendship has been related to the political. Why so? Is he saying that politics is, or should be, founded on friendship? No. He thinks it already is. He is after all a Frenchman, and so a citizen of a country founded not only on *liberté* and *egalité*, but also on *fraternité*. This means that if friendship is hegemonically conceived by French society in a skewed way, the whole political structure will be skewed.

OLIGARCHIES: NAMING, ENUMERATING, COUNTING

Derrida begins with four words: *ō philoi oudeis philos*. These words, attributed to Aristotle by his ancient biographer Diogenes Laertius, occur surprisingly often in the canonical discourses on friendship that Derrida considers in this book. They are usually rendered as "O my friends, there is no friend". But that is paradoxical: if there is no friend, whom is Aristotle calling his "friends"? Aristotle, then, "must be saying" that there are no *true* friends. This means that there are different kinds of friendship, and only one of them is "true". This is what Cicero calls the "sovereign and master-friendship" (*PF* 2) and what Aristotle, in his own "canonical account" of friendship in *Nicomachean Ethics* (VIII and IX), calls "friendship of the good". For both ancient thinkers, this kind of friendship was the basic one; the other two main kinds, friendships of use and pleasure, can be understood only by comparing them to it.

The way we understand this odd sentence attributed to Aristotle (notice how careful Derrida always is to say that it is only attributed to Aristotle) shows several things, then, about our "canonical" understanding of friendship itself.

(a) It shows that in this canonical discourse the *who* of friendship has been subjected to the *what* (*PF* 6). You do not understand friendship by beginning with your friend and asking what about her makes her your friend. Rather, in this discourse friendship is a general structure, and you first get clear on that structure. Whomever that structure applies to is, then, a friend. A friend is not someone unique, then. It is a certain kind of person.

(b) It assures us that the basic structure of friendship not only exists but can be known, if only because friendship must be declared (*PF* 9). I cannot declare myself to be your friend unless I know just what friendship is. There is thus no mystery in the nature of friendship.

(c) This knowable terrain is itself structured, as we have seen, into true and not-so-true. True friendship for Aristotle is active – it is better to love than to be loved (*PF* 7–8) – and it takes time (*PF* 14). Because of this, you cannot have too many friends – for you have only a limited amount of time to live together with them.

But here we get a first problem. If friendship is or has a structure, it is something that endures over time. Indeed, as Cicero pointed out, true friendships may even outlast the friends themselves: when I die, my friend will live on, and since he is for both Cicero and Aristotle, in some sense "another me", an *alter ego* or *allos autos*, I too will live on in him: "Beyond death, the absolute future thus receives its ecstatic light, it appears only from within this narcissism and according to the logic of the same" (*PF* 4).

Moreover, my friend will remember me, and if it is great enough our friendship will even become *exemplary*, that is, it will be remembered by future generations (*PF* 4–5). Like the entire *vita activa* for Arendt, friendship on the canonical account is thus aimed at a certain kind of immortality, the kind that Homeric heroes seek: the immortality of fame that lives on after death. Friendship can give us such immortality because it is a reliable structure that can have exemplary instances (*PF* 22–3). As such, it is something that can narrow down the breadth of possible futures: whatever happens, you will be my friend, even after I am dead. When you are also dead and we have both been forgotten, at least friendship itself will live on.

But the very fact that I can have only a few friends belies this, for that comes about because I am *not* immortal. The reason I do not have time to form a great number of true friendships is because I am going to die. And when I do, to be honest about it, my friendship dies: "I do not survive the friend" (*PF* 13). When my friend dies part of me dies; I am no longer the person I was. Moreover, achieving true friendship is not easy. It takes time and effort to become a true friend. You must go through what Derrida calls the "ordeal of stabilization" (*PF* 16). And if this is difficult, it is not "natural" (*PF* 23); for if something is natural to us, we find it easy.

Aristotle's account of friendship, therefore, is not simply a "neutral" description of various features we find in our relationships with our friends. His understanding of friendship, and so the canonical philosophical understanding, and so *our* understanding, has been affected by some of the deepest of metaphysical issues: how things have structures; how an unchanging structure can relate to the changing things it structures; how activity (loving) is better than passivity (being loved); how what can be known is better than what cannot. Most basically, the canonical conception of friendship, Derrida points out, is a mixture of the timely and the untimely (*PF* 14). It is timely because friendship is the "act" of two people who will not live forever. Yet in its enduring structure and hoped-for exemplarity, it "dominates" time. It therefore makes us think of time in a particular way – as the prolongation of the present: "It opens the experience of time. It opens it, however, in determining it as the stable present of a quasi-eternity, or in any case from and in view of such a present of certainty" (*PF* 15).

We have now seen several ways in which the canonical concept of friendship seeks to stabilize time.

- My friend, my "other I", will survive me, so that after my death I will still go on.
- Maybe I will go on for quite a while, if others remember me too.
- Even if they do not, friendship itself will go on, because it is an enduring structure of human life.

The concept we have of friendship obviously shapes our lives in very important ways; and it has itself been crucially shaped by philosophers. Basic to this shaping has been a certain philosophical view of time, one that sees the future as the prolongation of the present, and so conceives it under the "logic of the same". The canonical account of friendship is thus a denial of the unpredictability of the future. Only so can it promise us any kind of immortality.

LOVING IN FRIENDSHIP: PERHAPS – THE NOUN AND THE ADVERB

Here, Derrida, like Foucault, moves to Nietzsche. He does this to expand his account of friendship into more general terms. Then he will turn to a thinker Foucault never discusses, the twentieth-century German social philosopher and lawyer Carl Schmitt, to examine the relation of friendship to politics. Since, as we saw, Derrida does not want to submit his discourse to the discipline of a *telos*, that is, a single goal towards which it all moves, his writings (like Heidegger's) tend to wander. My discussion of these essays (2–6) will be very selective.

It is important to note that when Derrida appeals to our desire for immortality to understand our concept of friendship, he is not just talking about personal psychology. Obviously nobody wants to die, and obviously we value things that keep us alive in whatever way we can stay alive: as mere memories in the minds of others, if need be. However, this project of immortality can go far beyond psychology. Political structures can be, and are, set up on its basis: to reassure the citizens that they are immortal. It can become a theme of art, as in the *Iliad* itself (cf. the discussion in Chapter 8). It can become basic to religions, as when Christianity proclaims the immortality of the individual soul.

As a historian of philosophy, Derrida is concerned with the ways in which this concern for immortality has infected the philosophical vocabulary. He gives a list of valued philosophical traits that have to do with immortality (*PF* 29), and it is quite a list: firm; constant; sure and certain; reliable; credible; faithful. These traits do not seem to have much to do with immortality. They are characteristics we want to see in such decidedly mortal beings as lawyers and bankers, to say nothing of such representatives of immortality as priests (and philosophers). Derrida's own term for them is *bebaios*, which comes from the Greek *bainō*, to step, and conveys the relief we feel when the stone on which we place our foot when crossing a river does not wobble. What does this have to do with immortality?

The answer can be found in Derrida's conception of hegemony. We like firmly fixed stepping stones because we want to be on our way without mishap; and our ultimate journey as immortals would be a never-ending one, persisting through all of time itself. Since things that we value here and now are often reduced versions of what we value most of all, which is a limitless and secure future, the underlying desire for immortality guides our preferences in the here and now: it has "hegemonic" status over them. In particular, because we value these traits they guide our quests, not only for friendship but for understanding. They tell us, for example, that when we are looking at a friendship we should not look at the passing or unique qualities of it, those that are due to the unique nature of the friends themselves and to what happens to them, but to the "firm and certain" underlying structure of what is going on. "Firm" and "certain", in turn, are adjectives that Descartes, the greatest French philosopher, famously used to describe the *fundamentum inconcussum*, the "unshakeable foundation" he sought for knowledge (cf. the discussion in Chapter 6).

Derrida then gives a further list: "What is not *bebaios* eludes it, and in so doing eludes another, even more impressive list of traits: consistency and constancy, presence, permanence or substance, essence or existence, as well as any concept of truth which may be associated with them" (*PF* 29). These more basic traits are more general than those of the first list, and serve to link them to what Derrida considers to be fundamental concepts of the "metaphysical" tradition: those that tell us what being itself is. They, too, are not descriptively neutral; they are not set up simply to capture faithfully the nature of the universe. They are designed, consciously or not, to guide us into uncovering, paying attention to and so valuing what is reliable here and now, the *bebaios*. They are thus further attempts to escape or dominate time itself.

If this is true of these terms, it is presumably true of many others derived from the philosophical tradition. I can add two more to the list. One is the term "act", which Derrida discussed in the first essay – friendship is an activity – since to act for Aristotle is to be fully yourself (see McCumber 1999: 41–2). The other is given on the last page of this essay: universality, which according to Nietzsche is "the cunning of all dogmatism" (*PF* 44). When I come up with a universal truth, I am escaping time itself because my truth holds for *all* time. Derrida and Nietzsche, whom he is discussing here, are not saying that such truths are impossible to obtain, as they are often held to do; they are asking us to examine just why it is that we want them so badly.

"Metaphysics", for Derrida, is the project of gaining hegemony within the tradition for concepts that valorize the *bebaios*, and thus to escape or dominate time. In his rejection of this, Derrida sides with Foucault's rejection of non-temporal origins (discussed in Chapter 12). Both philosophers think that everything is in time, and that the only honest thing to do is to recognize this. If metaphysics is the project of *not* recognizing this, of denying time, then a non-canonical account of friendship will have to be a non-metaphysical one. As we saw earlier, however, we cannot simply jettison the metaphysical tradition. Where would we be without such concepts as consistency and constancy, presence, permanence or substance, essence or existence and so on? We cannot, nor should we, stop valuing those things. But we can stop making the orientation to permanence, to the *bebaios*, our *exclusive* orientation: we can uncover, formulate and perhaps sometimes apply alternatives. But how do we do that? Where do we look for alternatives to the canonical tradition? Derrida's answer, we have seen, is that we should look for them in that tradition itself. The Western philosophical tradition is far too complex to be monolithic on any question, including this one. When philosophy speaks, more than one voice is "on the line". At this point, then, Derrida turns again to Nietzsche, hoping to find in him an account of a non-canonical form of friendship.

It turns out that Nietzsche, too, has "quoted" Aristotle's supposed saying, "O my friends, there is no friend", in his 1878 book *Human, All Too Human*. And he has turned it around:

> *Perhaps* to each of us there *will come* the more joyful hour when we exclaim:
> "Friends, there are no friends!" thus said the dying sage.
> "Foes, there are no foes," say I, the living fool.   (*PF* 28)

To the dying philosopher's vision of a world without friends, Nietzsche opposes the "living foolishness" of a world without enemies. But why is the idea of a world without enemies foolish? Schmitt, in Derrida's reading, will eventually tell us. But first there is another general consideration about time.

Nietzsche introduces these two sentences by telling us that saying this, and meaning it, may turn us into what only living fools can be: joyful. The first word of the quotation from Nietzsche is "perhaps", *vielleicht*. Each of us *may* become joyful by saying and believing this, or we may not; we *may* say it someday, or never. If the word "perhaps" were not there, Nietzsche would be simply making a prediction: claiming to know what is going to happen in the future, claiming thus to know the future, and in that claim foreclosing the future. But because he says "perhaps", his words hold the future open.

Canonical friendship, we saw, is oriented to the future, but to a predictable future, one that is a prolongation of at least certain structures of the present. So "To love friendship, it is not enough to know how to bear the other in mourning, one must love the future. And there is no more just category for the future than that of the 'perhaps'" (*PF* 29). Note that Nietzsche uses the word "perhaps" – or maybe it comes to him – just when he is formulating an opposition, in fact a reversal: the wisdom of the dying sage is converted into the foolishness of the living fool (*PF* 30). Accepting the possibility of this kind of reversal is what holding open the future means: allowing for the possibility of something radically new and different. Once we are ready to allow for that, we can (for example) ask questions, and eventually even (perhaps) answer them:

> No response, no responsibility will ever abolish the *perhaps*. The perhaps must open and precede, once and for all, the questioning which it suspends in advance – not to neutralize or inhibit, but to make possible all the determined and determining orders that depend on questioning (research, knowledge, science and philosophy, logic, law, politics and ethics, and in general language itself). (*PF* 38)

The innocent little word "perhaps", then, shows its true face when Nietzsche uses it here: it is a word that can *hold off* our certainties, *suspend* our questioning, *allow* questions to take form, and so make possible everything that depends on asking questions, which is quite a list of things. It does this particularly when we do not say "perhaps this" or "perhaps that", but when we have just said "perhaps" as if we could stop there. Because it gets in the way of answers, allowing us to slowly formulate and then experience questions as such, the "perhaps" has what Derrida calls a "teleiopoetic" function in language: it makes distance (*PF* 32).

What, then, is it to "think the future" (*PF* 36–7) in terms of the perhaps? It is to allow yourself not only to think of things that are only possible, but also to be guided in your thought by the pure holding-off of the "perhaps". It is to think the future as what it is, as unpredictable and so unknowable. It is also, for Nietzsche, to be a new kind of philosopher. Philosophers of this new kind are not bound to each other in any shared project, beyond that of thinking the future. And since the future is empty, it gives them nothing further to share with one another. They thus constitute a very odd sort of community:

> Friends of an entirely different kind, inaccessible friends, friends
> who are alone because they are incomparable and without common
> measure, reciprocity or equality. Therefore without a horizon of rec-
> ognition. Without familial bonds, without proximity, without *oikeiotēs*
> [hominess]. (*PF* 35)

These "friends" are not any determinable *kind* of person; the who of friendship is not here subordinated to the what. This kind of "friendship" is therefore not *knowable*. Nor does it have any *structure*, enduring or not, because
the structure of friendship is relational, and these people do not relate to one
another. And finally, since this whole kind of friendship is predicated on the
unpredictability of the future, there can be no concern for immortality in its
structure or definition.

Because the "who" of this sort of friendship is not subordinated to the "what",
anyone can turn out to be your friend: you do not even have to share a language
with her. The canonical discourse, by contrast, has always imposed prerequi-
sites on friendship, by excluding certain kinds of people from friendship. This,
Derrida notes, especially means women. Friendship as studied and praised by
millennia of thinkers is always male–male ("fraternity", after all, comes from
the Latin word for "brother"). Derrida recurs to this "chauvinistic" side of the
canonical conception of friendship repeatedly throughout the last twenty or so
pages of *The Politics of Friendship*. He considers a major advantage of the kind
of friendship that he has uncovered in Nietzsche to be that it is not restricted
to men.

We have thus uncovered a non-canonical account of friendship, right within
one of the most famous philosophers of the tradition: Nietzsche himself.
Friendship becomes non-canonical when it is directed upon the very thing that
philosophers (or "metaphysicians", anyway) try to obliterate: the thought of the
future as unknowable and unpredictable. In the "community" of non-canonical
friends, everyone is unique. Since to compare one thing to another requires
that they be similar in the respect in which you compare them, no such friend
cannot be compared with the others. In particular, no one is better or worse than
any other. Their overall relationship is thus a "community" without hierarchies.
But is it not also, then, a friendship that in fact is *without* community, and so
one that is not any sort of political fraternity? Its discourse, for example, is a
keeping-silent, for the philosophers have nothing to talk about to one another
(*PF* 54–5). How, then, can they engage in political debate or arrive at that most
precious of human terrain, common ground?

Nietzsche himself, of course, recommended separation, distance, rather than
community (*PF* 55); this was a main implication of his notion of the "pathos
of distance", discussed in Chapter 5. If I am a good person, thinks Nietzsche, I
should keep my distance from those who are not so good, rather than join into
a community with them. And I should certainly not try to help them!

We have swum in strange waters, and are heading into even stranger ones. The wrong thing to do, for Derrida, is to stop here because we do not like where we are going. That would guarantee that we would not learn any lessons from this. To see whether this strange view of friendship can be fleshed out any further, in the next two essays Derrida considers Schmitt. Schmitt is not someone for whom Derrida has any sympathy – he was in fact a Nazi – but he does pose the question of whether you can have politics without friendship. Schmitt's answer is basically no, because you cannot have politics without enemies and you cannot have enemies unless you have friends. Why are enemies necessary to politics? Plato's *Republic* shows us: the first step into a political order comes in Book II, when the ideal city gets enough goods that others are tempted to try to take them away, and it needs an army to defend itself. The crucial task of its defenders, according to Plato, is to be able to tell friend from foe: to know who is the enemy, and who the friend. Schmitt thus argues that all politics depends, for Plato, on the friend–enemy distinction.

In Schmitt's view, Plato was right; but the friend–enemy distinction is not one in which Derrida thinks we should place much trust. Plato himself, he notes, argues against it later in the book (*Resp.* 471b–c). There, having said that Greeks are all friends to one another and so do not have fierce wars, he then goes on and says that we (Greeks) should treat non-Greeks, or "barbarians", in the same way (*PF* 90), thus *prescribing* the erasure of the friend–enemy distinction ("Oh my enemies, there are no enemies!"). Moreover, this passage from the *Republic* shows that the distinction between friends and enemies was really, for Plato, a distinction in birth, in *physis* (*PF* 91). Distinctions in birth are hardly a basis for conducting political affairs today, unless, of course, one is, like Schmitt, a Nazi.

There is more. If politics is grounded on enemies, on what Schmitt recurrently calls the "real possibility" that someone will go to war with me, then the more intense the enmity the more intense the politics. And the most intense enemy I can have is *my own brother*. The famous image of Antigone's Theban brothers, Polyneices and Eteocles, fighting each other to the death is not specifically invoked by Derrida.[5] But it shows nicely that the friend–enemy distinction really has nothing to do with *physis* – with how you are born:

> There has never been anything natural in the brother figure on whose features has so often been drawn the face of the friend, or the enemy, the brother enemy. … The relation to the brother engages from the start with the order of the oath, of credit, of belief and of faith. The brother is never a fact. (*PF* 159)

---

5. Although at *PF* 262, in what seems to be a clear reference to *Antigone* (Soph. *Ant.* 904–12), Derrida talks about the brother as the figure of the irreplaceable in the family.

I have to recognize someone as a brother before he is one: "The brother is never a fact". Is the enemy?

RECOILS

In the canonical discourses on friendship that begin with and from Aristotle, true friendship and the political sphere have a fairly clear relationship to one another: "The work of the political, the properly political operation, consists in producing the most possible friendship" (Arist. *Eth. Eud.* VII.1 1234b22–3). True friendship encourages democracy, because friendship includes sharing things. In a democracy, people are equal and so share more things than they do if there is a political hierarchy (*PF* 197). Such friendship is also particularly human because it is founded on what Aristotle calls *proairesis*: the convergence of reason and desire that issues in action, as when reason tells me that my desire for a college degree requires me to sit down at my desk and study. Such convergence, for Aristotle, can be found in humans alone; animals do not have reason, and gods (for Aristotle) do not have desire. If friendship is associated with *prohairesis*, then, it is a properly human phenomenon.

But true friendship is also, as we saw, only one kind of friendship (*PF* 203). That there are different kinds of friendship, for Aristotle, means that it is possible for disagreements to arise about the nature of a specific case of friendship. I may think we are true soulmates, for example, while you consider us to be merely friends of convenience (*PF* 206). Such disagreements raise the question: what are the standards by which we should treat various kinds of friend? This issue is compounded because while friendship in general pulls towards equality, as we saw, there are, for Aristotle, certain kinds of it that do not: that of a god for a human, of the governor for the governed, the father to the son, the man to the wife (*PF* 206). Here, justice must be, not strict equality, but some form of pro-portionality. Which form? Proportionality according to merit, says Aristotle's biographer Diogenes (*PF* 207). And then he comes out with the original state-ment: "O my friends, there is no friend".

But here Derrida discovers an ambiguity. In Aristotle's original text, there are no diacritical marks. Depending on how we fill them in, the omega "Ω" can be either a vocative, as Derrida has translated it, or the dative relative pronoun, "to whom". In the latter case, the sentence is much less paradoxical: it says "to whom there are friends, there is no friend", that is, if you have more than one friend you do not have any (true) friend. Derrida calls this the "recoil" version of the statement. And unlike the canonical version, which originates with Diogenes, the recoil version really is found, differently stated, in Aristotle himself: in Book VII of the *Eudemian Ethics*.

There, Aristotle takes up the issue of how friendship can be reconciled with independence. His answer is that the most independent man (ultimately, for the *Nicomachean Ethics*, the philosopher) should have no friends: "Therefore the man who lives the best life must have fewest friends, and they must always be becoming fewer, and he must show no eagerness for men to become his friends, but despise not merely the useful but even men desirable for society" (Arist. *Eth. Eud.* 1244b10). The same argument is made at more length, again in different words, in the *Nicomachean Ethics* (IX.9–10). For Aristotle, then, "rarity is the virtue of friendship. He who has friends – too many friends – has no friend" (*PF* 212).

Both the canonical version and the recoil version are compatible with the Greek Aristotle actually wrote down, a Greek without diacritical marks. So which meaning is correct? We cannot decide. That would be to put just one "voice on the line". It is worth noting, however, that in certain respects the two do coincide. True, the canonical version is an address, while the recoil version is the reporting of a fact (*PF* 214). But we cannot put too much weight on this distinction; even in reporting facts I address someone – the person (or persons) to whom I make my report. Moreover, with regard to their content, both seem to be saying that there is never a sole friend: not that there are none, but there is never (just) one (*oudeis*; *PF* 215). For the Greek is not only undecidable as to whether the Ω is a form of address or a pronoun. It also turns out that the word translated as "no" in "there are no friends" literally means "not one". And while this normally would mean "not even one", it can also be taken more literally to mean "not just one". Taking it this way would give us, in the canonical version, "O friends, there is not just one friend", and in the recoil version, "To whom there are friends, there is not just one friend".

Read this way, both versions agree that *if you have one friend you must have more than one*. But this goes against the canonical view of friendship, in which your friend is someone to whom you can wholly give yourself, so that ideally there should be only one (*PF* 215–16). Moreover, if friends keep multiplying, I must give myself to different people – and since friends are "other selves", I am redefined by each new relationship. This means I must become different people as my friendships proliferate:

> *Canonical* or *recoil*, both versions speak to the infinite in the "none", the becoming "not one" of someone of either gender. This multiplicity makes the taking into account of the political inevitable. … It cuts across what is called the question of the subject, its identity or its presumed identity with self. (*PF* 216)

Both versions, in other words, invoke the necessary multiplication of friendships. And what do they say beyond this? Nothing, because in order to go beyond this we must choose which version we are going to pursue, and that choice cannot be made. We are left, in other words, with "perhaps" (*PF* 219).

So the *undecideable ambiguity* of the original sentence brings us back, although Derrida does not put it that way, to Nietzsche's non-canonical account of friendship. Friendship is merely a readiness to respond to whomever, on the part of whomever. Such friendship is not humanistic; not a matter of likeness or virtue (*proairesis*) between the friends; and not grounded in spending time together. Therefore, it is also not something we can work towards (*PF* 222). But this most minimal friendship, if not a goal, is a presupposition. For it is necessary for us to be able to address others in general, including those we do not know, and so to speak at all, and so to think at all:

> Friendship *par excellence* can only be human but above all, and by the same token, there is thought for man only to the extent that it is thought of *the other* – and thought of the other *qua thought of the mortal*. Following the same logic, there is thinking being – if at least thought must be thought of the other – only in friendship. Thought, in so far as it is to be for man, cannot take place without *philia*.   (*PF* 224)

In one of the later essays, "In Human Language, Fraternity ...", Derrida points out that this friendship is future-oriented: it is a call to a relationship that does not yet exist. As Derrida glosses it, "O my friends, be my friends, I love you, love me, I will love you ..." (*PF* 235). And in this regard it represents a risk on the part of the speaker, a risk that Derrida locates in the profoundly unsettling claim that it is better to love than to be loved, that is, you must first love in order to be a friend in order to be loved (*PF* 235).

Non-canonical friendship is a way of opening up a future, for at the moment that you make this call, you do not (yet) have a (single) friend: "O my friends, there is no friend". Thus, for Derrida, "Friendship is never a present given, it belongs to the experience of expectation, promise, or engagement. It is not satisfied with what is, it moves out to this place where a responsibility opens up a future" (*PF* 236). It is also, as expressed in this sentence, aimed at the past as well, for the minimal friendship must already exist in the form of the openness of other to the call (*PF* 236); otherwise they will never hear my call. It thus brings us before "a friendship, prior to friendships, an ineffaceable friendship, fundamental and groundless, one that breathes in a shared language (past or to come) and in the being-together that all allocution presupposes, up to and including the declaration of war" (*PF* 236).

Such future-opening friendship, then, is prior to politics in Schmitt's sense. It is also prior to determinate law, although not to law in general (*PF* 231), because it is a willingness to be responsible to one another, whatever that may turn out to entail. Derrida then asks a final question: "What politics could still be founded on this friendship which exceeds the measure of man, ... Would it still be a politics?" (*PF* 294). Derrida asks this, but does not answer.

345

CONCLUSION

So what has Derrida achieved by this? That is a complex question, and not one we are supposed to ask, because it presumes the value of the *telos*. Derrida's writing is not oriented to any specific goal or pay-off but (like Heidegger's) is a kind of wandering along. It should be justified at least in part by the light it has shed, along its route, on various ancient and not so ancient texts. In particular, it has thickened them up, shown that they are more complex and ambiguous than we are used to thinking. It is fascinating, for example, that so many writers on friendship should have returned, over and over again, to Aristotle's "O my friends …". It is even more interesting that that sentence should be so ambiguous.

But of course there is more. The particular texts Derrida discusses, in his view, have shaped our lives. When you go to nursery school or kindergarten, for example, you are often told not to bring anything to class unless you bring enough to share with everyone. You are not supposed to share whatever it is only with those in the class whom you enjoy being with and consider your friends, but with everyone, a group that, except for age, has been selected pretty much at random from your local community. So what would you say to the students whom you like but cannot share with? *O philoi, oudeis philos* (presupposing that you speak classical Greek): "O my friends, none of you is [can be] my friend".

One thing Derrida has *not* done is show how this new kind of friendship shapes our politics. Aristotle had said that friendship was the aim of democratic government, and at one point even says that friendship "holds the *polis* together" (*Eth. Nic.* VIII.1 1155a22–4). Nothing like that happens in this other version of friendship. Derrida has rather come up with a form of friendship that must be *removed* from politics, because it is removed from common action and debate. Indeed, the French title of the book is not – necessarily – about "politics" at all, for *Politiques de l'amitié* is more naturally read as "Policies of Friendship", that is, various ways of conducting it. The kind of non-canonical friendship Derrida has found in Nietzsche and Aristotle is non-political because, as we have seen, it precedes politics. As a friendship that respects the ineffable singularity of the individual, it is prior to the areas of common agreement on which political debate must be founded.

On a more general level, Derrida has undone a "hegemonic" discourse: he has stopped the canonical discourse from drowning out at least one other voice. This is a voice that talks about a kind of friendship that, unlike the canonical variety, does not presuppose that a friend is a particular kind of person, which does not subordinate the who of friendship to the what. Derrida has thus salvaged from oblivion a concept of friendship according to which a friend is defined by nothing other than a readiness to respond. This does not, however, somehow "refute" the canonical concept or make it obsolete. It is presented simply as an alternative to it, as a "perhaps".

Derrida's aim here is thus similar to Heidegger's project, in "The Question Concerning Technology", of providing an alternative to the *Gestell*. For Heidegger, this was in the service of the larger project of opening up the future. The importance of the future for Derrida is shown when he says, in a 2003 discussion of terrorism:

> [What is unacceptable about Bin Laden, etc.] is not only the cruelty, the disregard for human life, the disrespect for law, for women, the use of what is worst in technocapitalist modernity for the purposes of religious fanaticism. No, it is, above all, the fact that such actions and such discourse *open onto no future and, in my view, have no future.*
>
> (Borradori 2003: 113)

This is a very revealing thing to say. Of all the horrible things you can say about Bin Laden, the worst is that his way of doing things allows for no future.

Everything, of course, has a future, but as we saw with Heidegger, it is possible to deny this, as in fact we normally do. For the future is unknown, and therefore scary: as scary as the inevitable death that it contains. We may say that where Heidegger applies this to human beings – to Dasein – Derrida applies it to statements. Any utterance, like Dasein, then, has an unknown future: you cannot know when you say something how others are going to understand it. This breadth of future possibilities is, moreover, a characteristic of your utterance that needs to be taken account of now. How? One way is by bringing to mind how differently even a written text may be understood: how wide its future really is. This is what Derrida does with Aristotle and Nietzsche.

This is why the readings of Derrida by people such as Habermas and John Searle, which see him as a mere sophist who undermines moral norms and even the meaning of sentences, leaving us unable to understand one another, are so misguided.[6] As can only be expected of traditional philosophers, Habermas and Searle, like many others, read Derrida, so to speak, in the present tense. They take him to be asserting that utterances have no meaning here and now. What he is really saying, however, is that the meaning an utterance or moral norm has now does not determine what it will mean in the future, which, of course, is just a nanosecond away. To say that my words, when they arrive in your mind, will mean what I myself take them to mean is to attempt to control the future, just as the canonical concept of friendship attempts to do. And, as Beauvoir pointed out, all such attempts ultimately fail.

Derrida thus agrees with Heidegger that the future is unknowable and uncontrollable. But the future for Derrida is not merely finite, any more than

---

6. The Derrida–Searle controversy is treated in Derrida (1988); for Habermas's reading see Habermas (1987).

it was for Nietzsche or Foucault. True, when he talks about the "perhaps" he is, at least at first, talking about something specific: "perhaps this" or "perhaps that". But Derrida does not, as we saw, stop there. He goes on to postulate a pure "perhaps", one that simply says "perhaps" and stops there. Where, for Heidegger, the finite future was recognized in questioning, the infinite future to which Derrida appeals can give rise to nothing so specific as a question. This is why the perhaps, as he puts it, "suspends" questioning "in advance". And this is why the community of philosophers that Derrida finds in Nietzsche, committed to thinking the infinite future, is, as we saw, composed of "inaccessible friends, friends who are alone because they are incomparable and without common measure".

Still, the infinite future can, for Derrida, be finitized. Aristotle's address to his "friends" is coordinated to the possibility that the future will contain, among its boundless possibilities, friends. This address is not a Nietzschean or Arendtian promise, for it is not something that the person who utters it can undertake to bring about. It is not even an address in the full sense, because it is not aimed at anyone specific, but at people who may possibly exist in the future. It is more like a question, asking whether any such friend will ever exist. But unlike a Heideggerean question, this address has a very definite affect: the existence of such friends is something the utterer would like to see. We may say that, then, the address formulates a hope. Not the messianic hope to which Arendt alludes in the closing words of *The Human Condition*, but a humble, finite hope: "O my democratic friends …"?

PART IV

ONWARDS, 2011–

CHAPTER 14

BADIOU, RANCIÈRE AND
THE TIME OF EQUALITY

One could be forgiven for thinking that, by 2011, continental philosophy's distinctively temporalized approach, in which everything is mortal, was moribund itself. The anglophone lands remained generally in the grip of philosophical traditionalists, while continental philosophy's original habitat in Germany had dried up decades before. Already in his 2001 *Continental Philosophy: A Very Short Introduction*, Simon Critchley had characterized Germany as philosophically "becalmed", while in France, he found only Derrida himself "still very much going strong" (Critchley 2001: 124). and with Derrida's death in October 2004, the last of the great founding thinkers of French postmodernity went off into what Beauvoir had called "formless night". A certain amount of gloom seemed appropriate.

But gloom is nothing new in philosophy, and the temporalized approach originally pioneered by Heraclitus had known bad times before. The eighty years between Marx and Heidegger had been a dry period broken only by Nietzsche. The period between Heraclitus himself and Hegel had been far longer. Time and again powerful thinkers – thinkers of the stature of Kant, Husserl and Sartre – had summoned their intellects to restore traditional approaches. And yet continental philosophy had come roaring back. Could it not do so again?

FOUR CONTINENTAL PHILOSOPHERS

In this chapter and the next, I shall briefly discuss four contemporary philosophers who show that continental philosophy's temporalized approach is alive and vibrant today: Giorgio Agamben, Alain Badiou, Judith Butler and Jacques Rancière. They look somewhat different from their predecessors, if only because the very success of earlier continental philosophers has enabled, so to speak, two basic mutations in the current generation.

The first mutation is that contemporary continental philosophers are what I shall call secure in their canon. Philosophers from Hegel to Derrida were not; each suspected that his or her predecessors were seriously deficient on basic matters (and this includes, as we saw, even the tactful Beauvoir's attitude to her companion, Sartre). While earlier continental philosophers learned much from their predecessors, they thus felt obliged to lay sweeping foundations of their own: to establish major claims about history, power, Being, consciousness, *différance* and the like. When they discussed concrete matters, it was often as illustrations and outgrowths of those claims. Today's continental thinkers do not appear to feel such a need: they are free to take the groundwork as laid out by those who went before, and to focus their own thought more narrowly. Thus, Agamben is often viewed as a political theorist seeking to bring together Arendt and Foucault, as well as the German social philosopher Schmitt; Badiou moves from Cantorian set theory to articulate broadly Marxist views on art and politics, and entirely new ones on love; Butler engages the still young tradition of gender theory; and Rancière takes Foucault and the French Marxist Louis Althusser into issues of politics and aesthetics.

There are two important things this does not mean, and one that it does. First, it does not mean that today's continental thinkers are less important than their predecessors, or that their specialization condemns them to modest influence. Philosophy often becomes more useful when it becomes more focused; Hans-Georg Gadamer's application of Heidegger's grand insights about human life to the question of understanding texts, and Max Scheler's development of Husserlian phenomenology into the domain of ethics are recent cases of this. Moreover, today's continental philosophers, as we shall see, do not entirely abjure the larger concerns of their forebears; they just accord them less emphasis.

Second, that today's continental thinkers are secure in their canon also does not mean that they presuppose their predecessors in some thoughtless or dogmatic way. They can hardly do so, because the philosophical foundations bequeathed to them by those predecessors contradict one another at every turn. Today's continental philosopher is therefore obliged, at the very least, to make an intelligent selection among them, creating in the process her personal "canon". Moreover, the canonical works in question, being themselves instances of temporalized philosophy, are historical: to treat them as conveying changeless truths is to betray them. Today, years after they were written, they can have only such validity as is conferred on them by relentless and repeated scrutiny. This scrutiny is not, for the philosophers I shall discuss, a separate part of their thought. Although they do at times give explicitly focused accounts of their predecessors, almost every page of their thought exhibits engagement of some kind with those who have gone before.

What the security of today's continental philosophers in their canon does mean is that they can be understood only by understanding the rest of continental philosophy: the kind of overall understanding that this book has attempted to provide. This means understanding not merely the earlier continental philosophers on whom they explicitly base their work, but also those they did not choose for their own personal canons.

Part of the reason for this is the second major mutation in today's continental philosophers: that the development of their temporalized approach up to now has given them a full understanding of the temporality of thought. In the wake of Hegel, they understand that all philosophy grows from the laborious appropriation of previous thought; no one simply walks up to reality and starts writing down its basic features. In the wake of Kierkegaard and Nietzsche, they appreciate the absolute unboundedness of the future: the terrifying insight that nothing can be ruled out of it. In the wake of Heidegger, they also understand the finite aspect of that future; some possibilities are marked out for us as more immediate than others by our mortal appropriation of the past. And, in the wake of the postmodern thinkers, they realize that these two sorts of future, finite and infinite, are themselves in a variety of interplays: that the questions they ask and the promises they oblige will ultimately be validated by the further questions and promises they open up, and so on … forever.

Because of these two characteristics, the thought of today's continental philosophers has become what I call "situating".[1] This term is to be understood temporally: to "situate" something is to reveal its location between a partially comprehended past and a stubbornly questionable future. Situating, I suggest, has taken over from the traditional practice of critique, as pursued from Plato to Kant (and beyond). Instead of measuring things around us against some supposedly unchanging yardstick of value, situating philosophy seeks to establish the temporal limits of values and institutions, as Hegel himself envisaged in the *Philosophy of Right*:

> If it can be shown that the origin of an institution was entirely expedient and necessary under the specific circumstances of the time, the requirements of the historical standpoint are fulfilled. But … since the original circumstances are no longer present, the institution has thereby lost its meaning and its right [to exist]. (Hegel 1991: 30)

The four contemporary continental philosophers of whom I shall offer here brief, and perforce sketchy, accounts are chosen (from among thousands) for the ways in which their thought works to situate two kinds of thing: atemporality itself (in the case of Badiou) and that which, since Nietzsche, has given a name to what opposes the atemporal, life itself, in the specific forms of the constantly mutating domains of aesthetics and politics (Rancière), bare life (Agamben) and gender (Butler).

---

1. Cf. McCumber (2005) for a fuller account of this.

SITUATING SET THEORY: ALAIN BADIOU

Like Derrida, Albert Camus, Hélène Cixous and other prominent French philosophers, Alain Badiou was born in Africa, in Rabat, Morocco, in 1937. Like Derrida and Foucault, he was deeply marked by the sudden uproar, entirely unexpected, that overtook France in May 1968; but where they became postmodernists, Badiou undertakes to salvage some of the things postmodernism had placed into question. Among these are the enterprise of ontology and the concepts of truth and subjectivity.

Underlying this salvage operation for Badiou, as also for Rancière, is an attempt to salvage revolution itself: in the first instance from a Marxism that, by 1968, had hardened into dogma. Unable to find in the tumult and outrage of the general uprising the theoretically established characteristics of a genuine proletarian revolution, the French Communist Party acted (to use Daniel Singer's word) in various ways as a "brake" on the events, opposing the students and eventually supporting the government of Charles de Gaulle (Singer 2002: 10). This presented Badiou and Rancière with a problem that, in some ways, was almost the opposite of that confronted by Horkheimer and Adorno almost thirty years earlier. Where, for Horkheimer and Adorno, Marx's theory of the proletariat posited revolutionary potential where it no longer existed, for Badiou and Rancière it was unable to recognize revolutionary potential that was actually there.

In Badiou's most influential book, *Being and Event* (*BE*; 1988), we see what "salvage" means. Ontology had been originally placed into question by Heidegger, who, in a number of works – most explicitly in his "The Onto-theo-logical Constitution of Metaphysics" (Heidegger 2002) – had argued that the ontological attempt to give a single list of properties that distinguish what is from what is not inevitably justifies itself via an understanding of the most unified and self-contained being of all: God. Ontology is thus theologically founded: it is "onto-theo-logical".

Badiou agrees with Heidegger that resting an account of being on such a single being, and thereby privileging the category of unity itself, is untenable. This agreement with Heidegger is only partial, however, for Badiou thinks that ontology can be pursued without the kind of unity that Heidegger had attributed to it: "Ontology, if it exists, must necessarily be the science of the multiple as multiple" (*BE* 28). Heidegger was right, in other words, to question the feasibility of an account of being that proceeds from, and in terms of, a unified being; but he was wrong to think that this was the only kind of ontology possible at all. Not only is a truly "pluralist" ontology possible, but it has existed for over a hundred years, in the form of set theory. Mathematics, to be sure, has for Badiou always been a form of ontology; it is only with the establishment of set theory by the Russian/German mathematician Georg Cantor that mathematics could become a "pure doctrine of the multiple" (*BE* 43). Cantor's discoveries, like a work of art for Heidegger, thus opened a radically new world for Badiou. They represent a fundamental rupture with what had gone before, and Badiou does not attempt to find earlier versions of Cantor's insights in previous thinkers the way (for example) Hegel would.

When set theory becomes ontology in Badiou's sense, strange things happen to it. My aim is not to evaluate either the accuracy of Badiou's account of set theory or its validity as ontology, but simply to see what he does with it. The first of these is to move from Cantor to the formalization of set theory offered by Ernst Zermelo and Abraham Fraenkel in the early twentieth century. The reason for this move is that in the Zermelo–Fraenkel version, according to Badiou, there is no reference to "elements" of a set. An "element" in this sense is something that belongs to a set but to which no set belongs, that is, that has no subsets and thus is a sort of atomic ("uncuttable") unit; on the Zermelo–Fraenkel formalization such elements are treated as sets themselves. This is the final step in the direction of plurality. In the wake of it, "everything is a set" (*BE* 44): reality is, so to speak, sets all the way down.

Although this is the crucial insight that enables set theory to function as an ontology of the multiple, "functioning as ontology" does not, for Badiou, mean telling us what reality is really like:

> The thesis that I support does not in any way declare that being is math-
> ematical, which is to say composed of mathematical objectivities. It is
> not a thesis about the world but about discourse. It affirms that math-
> ematics, throughout the entirety of its historical becoming, pronounces
> what is expressible of being qua being. (*BE* 8)

In his later *Conditions* (2008), Badiou refers to his claim that set theory is ontology as "provocative and therapeutic", that is, as something other than lit-erally true (2008: 111). Set theory ontology, in the words of Oliver Feltham, is thus "performative" (*BE* xxiv):[2] it is not a discourse about realities that pre-exist it, but creates the realities it deals with. In this respect, it is like what Foucault calls a "discipline": just as madness was in a sense created by psychiatry, so being itself is created as pure multiplicity by set theory. Sets, then, do not exist in nature; they are created by us, when we group a multiplicity together and count them as one (*BE* 24).

The "count-as-one" is, then, a rethought version of the genesis of the uni-versal in the opening section on "Sense-Certainty" in Hegel's *Phenomenology of Spirit*, with the proviso that the components of the set do not follow one

---

2. Feltham's whole sentence is helpful here: "Set theory ontology is non-representational in that it does not posit being outside itself, but detains it within its inscriptions; in other words, it unfolds being performatively, in the elaboration of its formulas and their presuppositions" ("Translator's Preface", *BE* xxiv).

another in time, as they did for Hegel. In set theory, the orderings in a set are not necessarily temporal:[3] the members of a set can, in principle, coexist at the same time. That is what makes set theory, in its internal structure, atemporal.

Mathematics is often taken to be the paradigm of atemporal truth: who can imagine a time when $1 + 1$ did not equal 2? Since set theory underlies a great deal of mathematics (the concept of "number" itself can be given a set-theoretic definition), we might expect it to be the paradigm of the paradigm, the very acme, of such truth. But Badiou has now situated it in two ways. First, by tracing it, and therefore the sets it treats, back to Cantor, he has made it something historical. Set theory is what he will call a "condition" with which philosophy must deal, because it is the way of interpreting being that history, for the moment anyway, has imposed on us; but it is not a reflection of unchanging realities. Second, when we create a set by the "count-as-one", its existence is conditional on an operation of our minds: an operation that, of course, takes place in time. Badiou's assertions that set theory creates its objects, and his invocation of the "count-as-one", are thus the key steps in his "situating" of set theory.

Since unity is produced by the count-as-one, what precedes the count-as-one is not a count-as-many; it is not a multitude of units. Rather, it is more like a "count-as-none": the empty set, which has no subsets and is itself a subset of all other sets: "It is quite true that prior to the count there is nothing because everything [that exists] is counted. Yet this being-nothing – wherein resides the illegal inconsistency of being – is the base of there being the 'whole' of the composition of ones in which presentation takes place" (*BE* 54). It is possible, then, to have sets that do not have members: the first set constituted by a count-as-one has subsets only retrospectively, when we count them as ones. Such a set – one that has no components that have been counted-as-one – Badiou calls an "evental site" (*BE* 175). An example would be a Heideggerean work of art, which, as we saw, has a number of aspects that point us in various directions as we experience it. These aspects are not elemental, but complex; but they are not counted-as-one because their components have not been "counted" at all. Each aspect is wholly new.

When a component of such a site belongs to itself as well as to the site, that is, is taken on its own, Badiou calls it an "event". With this, Badiou is trying to capture the idea that an event cannot be reduced to the state of affairs that precedes it; it is, like the uprising of 1968 or the French Revolution itself, unique and genuinely new. When its components are counted-as-ones, if that happens, it becomes a complex event; Badiou's example is the French Revolution (*BE* 203). Such an event thus comes into being as an event via a twofold series of countings-as-one: the one that constitutes it as a set and the later ones that con-

---

3. Thus, in a "well-ordered" set, the ordering relation R is reflexive: for any x, xRx. In the kind of "universal" that comes out of "Sense-Certainty", the ordering relation is not reflexive: no component of the universal can precede or follow itself.

stitute its components as sets. These countings, again, are done by us; Badiou refers to the combination of them in a given case as an "interpretive decision". What counts as part of the French Revolution, and what does not, is thus up to the historians. The decision to recognize a multiple as an event is what Badiou calls an "intervention" (*BE* 202). The process of explicating and validating such an intervention is a complex one, embracing a great number of interpretive decisions. This process Badious calls a "fidelity": the "apparatus which separates out, within the set of presented multiples, those that depend on any event" (*BE* 233). That which performs this is the "subject" (*BE* 239).

Subjects thus come about as faithful attention to events. The "subject", as salvaged by Badiou, is thus very different from concepts of subjectivity found in such philosophers as Kant. It is not "substantial", that is, is not the kind of self-contained and enduring object that, for Kant, is studied by critique. It is not "transcendental", in that it does not bestow meaning on experiences from outside, as the Kantian mind did when it organized intuitions into objects. And, since it has neither of these statuses, it is not "necessary". It is, rather, "the local status of a procedure" (*BE* 392). As such, we may say, the subject always has a temporal location: *after* the event that it is trying to explicate, and *before* the "truth" that results from the explication (*BE* 331).

Things like interventions, interpretive decisions, fidelities and subjects are not accessible to set theory: they are operations and procedures performed in time, and so outside its scope. This means, in turn, that they are outside ontology, that is, outside being itself in so far as it is given in set theory. In this way, Badiou evades the bugaboo of what we may call "errant subjectivity": the fear that if we take a single intellectual step beyond those sanctioned by logical rules of inference we find ourselves in a realm of "psychologistic" caprice where subjective impulses are given free rein. This fear had haunted Frege, and was part of the motivation for Husserl's quest for a "universal" science "out of absolute foundations" (cf. Frege 1980; Husserl 1970b). In Badiou's view, some sort of subject is needed because set theory, like all mathematics, needs minds of some kind to deploy it. But according to him, the subject has no content over and above that deployment; the withholding of such content, in fact, is part of the meaning of "fidelity".

Badiou goes on to explore four basic types of fidelity. The local procedure of fidelity that traces out an event can affect the individuals as such, in which case it is what Badiou calls love; it can affect a collective through an individual, in which case it is either art or science; and it can affect a collective through itself, in which case it is what used to be called revolution (*BE* 339–40). These are the great transformations that stand outside ontology as set theory but reveal set theory's own temporality as an achievement of science. What makes them transformative is that they generate new truths. This makes them conditions for philosophy itself, which does not generate truths but "seizes" them, that is, recognizes that they are truths.

Exploring the way philosophy relates to its conditions thus means exploring science, art, revolution and love; and Badiou's explorations of these great themes have been some of the most influential components of his thought. He treats them in detail in *Conditions*. The guiding theme of these treatments is the necessity for philosophy to recognize these conditions of its existence *as* conditions, rather than falling into one of two traps with regard to them. The first trap is to detach philosophy entirely from one of the truth procedures, which is then viewed merely as another object or theme "out there" in the world about which one may (or may not) philosophize, rather than seen as something on which philosophy must partially base itself. Modern philosophy has fallen into this trap with regard to science, especially set theory. The second trap, as we shall see, is the reverse of this one: to attach philosophy to just one of the truth procedures at the expense of the other three. In such "suturing", as Badiou calls it, either the favoured truth procedure is accorded undue authority over philosophy, as poetry is in the later Heidegger, or philosophy attempts to exercise undue authority over the truth procedure, as happens when philosophers try to provide theoretical guidance to political practice.

We have already seen how Badiou deals with science, for mathematics is in his view the key science and set theory, as we have also seen, is the paradigm of mathematics. As the production of new truths, science continually moves beyond itself; at every such movement, philosophy must capture the innovations in concepts of its own, giving them a validation that lasts until science breaks with them. Since the capacity for breaking away from established concepts cannot itself be conceptualized, Badiou refers to it as science's "materiality". Since it escapes concepts in this way, science proceeds without regard to the conceptual fixities of a knowing subject.

In order to recognize science as the generation of new truths, that is, as a way of thinking rather than a body of results, and to see that way of thinking as its own condition, philosophy must "re-entwine" with science: mathematics, in particular, must enter "into the innermost structures of philosophy" (2008: 94). Philosophy, therefore, can no longer view mathematics as it usually does today: as the "grammar" of science or as a game whose significance lies in the rules that govern it (*ibid.*: 95). These are way of objectifying mathematics so that it becomes something philosophers think about as they think about anything else, rather than part and parcel of their own thought.

The unfortunate disjunction between philosophy and mathematics was brought about by Hegel, when, as we saw, he temporalized philosophy. This "temporalization of the concept" meant that the "ideal and atemporal character" of mathematics has no place in philosophy. Hegel disjoins philosophy from mathematics, in Badiou's view, when he supplants the mathematical concept of infinity with his own "true" conception, according to which infinitude is a "horizontal structure for the historicity of the finitude of existence" (*ibid.*: 97).

Hegelian infinity is a totality whose every component is historical, and therefore mortal.

This, Badiou claims, amounts to nothing less than an abrogation of philosophy's critical stance, in particular with regard to religion. The abrogation is complex, but in outline what has happened is that temporalized philosophy sees us as located, like everything else, within time. The temporal horizon of our knowledge lands us in things we cannot know: the thought of future generations (and perhaps that of long-past generations as well) remain opaque to us. This emptiness in our knowledge, says Badiou, haunts us as the place where God used to be: "God remains as that whose disappearance continues to govern us under the form of the abandonment, the dereliction, or the releasement of Being" (*ibid.*: 99).

History itself, then, has replaced God as the One that makes us what we are. Saving ourselves from this Heideggerean, and subsequently postmodern, version of piety requires embracing pure multiplicity, which amounts, as we saw, to incorporating set theory into philosophy, not as philosophy itself but as its ontology. Only when we thus "summon the solid secular eternity of the sciences" (*ibid.*: 99) can we fight God, so to speak, on his own ground: "There is only the infinite multiple which presents the infinite multiple, and the unique stopping point of this presentation [i.e. the empty set] presents nothing. Ultimately at issue is the void, and not the One. God is dead, at the heart of the presentation" (*ibid.*: 111).

Accepting mathematics as ontology does not mean, as we saw, accepting the current state of set theory as true, much less as eternally true. Mathematics is to be incorporated into philosophy not as a body of truths, but as a way of thinking; for as the production of new truths, even mathematics must change with time: "Mathematics is nothing other than *the human history of eternity*" (*ibid.*: 112, emphasis added).

Art has also long been excluded from philosophy. The key form of art in this regard is, for Badiou, poetry, and the recent philosopher who has done the most to restore their ancient connection is Heidegger. We have seen how, for Heidegger, a work of art is a disclosure of radical newness, and this, for Badiou, means that Heidegger recognizes art as the production of new truths. The vehicle of this production for Heidegger, we also saw, is the poetic name, in which a being is for the first time projected onto what thenceforth becomes its context of significance, and Badiou expresses this presentation of radical newness as a form of obligation: "the poem is therefore obliged to name the name, that is assert the name as an eventual naming" (*ibid.*: 51).

As the production of a new truth, a poem is not reducible to what went before, and as such is an event or an evental site. Poetry, and art in general, are therefore needed by philosophy. But philosophy cannot identify itself with art; indeed, it cannot privilege any of the four truth procedures, much less identify itself with any of them. This was Heidegger's mistake: attending to poetry at the particular expense of mathematics, he lost all sense of argument and so bestowed "sacral authority" on the poetic word (*ibid.*: 50). What philosophy properly does is make *localized* use of literary tropes and figures. When philosophy "seizes" on truths brought forwards in poetry, it should be in the service of its own argumentative structures:

> However, these occurrences of the literary [in philosophical texts] are, as such, under the jurisdiction of a principle of thought that they themselves do not constitute. … This deploying is carried out … under the general jurisdiction of a completely different style – as style of argumentation, of conceptual liaison, or of the Idea.   (*Ibid.*: 45)

Where philosophy "re-entwines" itself with mathematics, thinking along with set theory, as we saw Badiou do, it "places" literary *motifs* within itself (*ibid.*: 44). They occur at various points, but none of them governs, so to speak, the movement of the text.

If mathematics and art have been held too far from philosophy, politics has been too closely related to it, for when philosophers write about politics they tend to interfere with it: "The prevailing idea is rather that, in its determination of politics, philosophy determine the truth of what is at stake in politics" (*ibid.*: 153). The examples of this that most concern Badiou are versions of Marxism that presume to dictate what, in the here and now, needs to be struggled for and so to decide what the real struggles are, as when the French Communist Party attempted to "brake" the student revolt in 1968 because it was not a genuine case of class struggle. Such presumption follows from a misapprehension of the nature of both politics and philosophy; for it is politics, not philosophy, that is the generation of new truths. Philosophy's job is thus not to determine what is politically true or real, but to appreciate ("seize"; *ibid.*: 154) truths established politically in their character as truths.

As the generation of new truths, politics partakes of the radical newness of an event (*ibid.*: 155). Political activity is thus "rather a singular pathing in which the truth of a collective situation comes to light. But this pathing has no principle linking it to the races that have preceded it" (*ibid.*: 162). When philosophy arrogates to itself the role of a, or even *the*, political truth procedure, that is, tries to dictate to politics what it is or should be concerned with, the result is "disaster", the suturing of philosophy to politics (*ibid.*: 156). Examples of such disastrous suturing are the main categories by which philosophers have sought to identify political struggles as struggles for "community" (as in "communism"), "justice" and even "emancipation" itself (*ibid.*: 148–50).

This does not entirely abrogate philosophy's critical function *vis-à-vis* politics, however. Rather, it relegates it to what we might call a "post-political" stance, in which philosophy does not try to lead political struggle but reflects on political achievements: "The essence of a singular politics lies in the pathway of its procedure, and whether it does in fact comprise a truth-procedure is sayable only in the philosophical act, which for politics itself only ever constitutes a sort of inactive recognition" (*ibid.*: 154). Philosophy thus tells us something crucial: whether a given political struggle has, in fact, generated new truths. Much of what passes for politics in the contemporary world is not such generation, but merely the "regulated and natural development of liberal equilibria" (*ibid.*: 151; cf. 169), the administration and balancing of previously established power structures.

The one philosophical category that can be applied to politics without disaster is the only one that allows us to think of political struggle as the generation of new truths without imposing any vision of what those truths are supposed to be. This is the category of equality. Equality, as Badiou understands it, is the emptiest of political categories, for it claims only that no segment of society is to be accorded paradigmatic status for the whole (*ibid.*: 167). From the point of view of equality, then, politics is a matter of pure multiplicity, in which all political actions and actors are as equal to each other as the members of a set. Since all are equal, political truth may be generated anywhere. The political realm is not dictated to, but is held open for innovation: "Equality neither presumes closure, nor qualifies the terms it embraces, not prescribes a territory for its exercise" (*ibid.*: 173).

From the philosophical point of view, equality is thus the basic political value. When philosophy advocates any other, it closes off politics and takes away its ability to generate new truths. A philosophy that operates with the single critical category of equality thus maintains the proper relationship of philosophy to politics as its condition (*ibid.*: 159).

Finally, the truth procedure of love completes the other three. It plays this unusual role because, considered as a truth procedure (rather than merely an emotion or passion), love has a paradox at the core of its nature. In order to understand this paradox we must begin with Badiou's basic definition of love: that it is "an experience of the world, or of the situation, under the postevental condition that there are Two" (*ibid.*: 182).

Love is thus not the experience of a loved one. Still less is it a desire for the other, for desire (as we saw with Hegel) aims at some sort of unity with what is desired. Rather, in love I become aware, not of potential unity with another, but of what is almost the exact opposite of that: of the fact that the world is experienced both in the way that I experience it and in a second, radically different way. Badiou, following the French psychoanalyst Jacques Lacan,[4] calls these ways of experiencing the world "man" and "woman"; but in fact they have little to do with what Badiou at one point calls "empirical sex", although, as we shall see, they retain some overtones, and troubling ones, of very traditional views

---

4. For a brief account of Badiou's debt to Lacan as regards love, see Jöttkandt (2010).

of the sexes. I shall attempt to distance them somewhat from such traditional views without obscuring the overtones by adopting a locution Badiou often uses himself, calling them the "man-position" and the "woman-position". These positions are *radically* disjunct in that nothing at all in the experiences of the two is the same; there is no overlap between the world as experienced from the man-position and from the woman-position (*ibid.*: 183). There is also no third position, no sexually neutral standpoint from which the other two could be regarded and compared (*ibid.*: 183–4).

Like the other truth procedures, love is something that comes about: I am not always experiencing the world in terms of the Two, any more than I am always doing mathematics, writing poetry or struggling politically. When I become aware that the world is also being experienced in a way radically different from the way I experience it, we have love as "the advent of the Two" in an amorous "encounter" (*ibid.*: 184, 188). Although the amorous encounter has the uniqueness of an event, love does not end there; when the love is declared, it persists beyond the original advent of the Two as a series of enquiries into their radical disjunction itself. These enquiries, as joint efforts to understand what is radically different from both sides at once, constitute love as a truth procedure (*ibid.*: 188–9).

As the generation of radically new truths, the enquiries of love cannot be bound in advance to such things as the male or female "point of view"; truth procedures are not gendered, and nor, then, are the truths that they produce. If we take "humanity" to be the sustaining activity of the various truth procedures, we must then say that "there is only one humanity", the "content" of which would be merely the set of truths generated (*ibid.*: 184). And this, finally, yields the paradox Badiou locates in his concept of love: that it requires us to maintain both the radicality of the disjunction between the man- and woman-positions, the idea that there is no overlap between these two ways of experiencing the world, and the idea that truth is "generic", that is, that the procedures by which it is produced are the same for everyone.

Badiou's solution to this paradox gives love a special status among the truth procedures: it is love itself that unifies them, but it does so in different ways for the man-position and the woman-position. The woman-position unifies the four basic truth procedures around love itself, which thus grounds them and constitutes the essence (so to speak) of humanity. From the woman-position, the unity of the truth procedures is thus expressed as: "What will have been true is that we two were, and otherwise we were not" (*ibid.*: 194). For the woman-position, the experience of the world in terms of the Two is all there is to humanity. For the man-position, by contrast, the radical disjunction between the two ways of experiencing the world is radical but not basic: "What will have been true is that we were two and not at all one" (*ibid.*: 194).

From this position, the four truth procedures remain independent of one another; their unity is one on which they "metaphorize" one another (*ibid.*: 197), which in the original meaning of the Greek *metapherein* means that changes in one carry over to changes in the others, without any one of them underlying the others. For the woman-position, by contrast, love "knots" the other three truth procedures together:

> Woman is she (or he) for whom the particular subtraction of love devalorizes [humanity] in its other types, namely science, politics, and art, ... For the man position, things proceed differently: each type of procedure by itself gives birth to [humanity], without taking into account the existence of the others. (*Ibid.*: 196)

This bring us to an absence, and a question. We saw Badiou discuss the disastrous "suturing" of philosophy to politics, and we saw him criticize Heidegger's suturing of philosophy to poetry; and we saw him define "suturing" as, precisely, attaching philosophy to one of its conditions at the expense of the other three. Does it not follow that the woman-position "sutures" philosophy to love, for in that position the other three truth procedures are explicitly said to be "devalorized"?

Given the importance of suturing in other discussions it is notable that Badiou does not discuss the suturing of philosophy to love.[5] And so it appears that, for Badiou, either the woman-position's devalorization of three of the truth procedures is somehow not a suturing of philosophy to the fourth – in which case one is at a loss to see what it is – or that it is impossible to philosophize from the woman-position – which would be a fateful overtone of traditional sexism in his philosophy.

Badiou's criticisms of Hegel's temporalizing of philosophy, his claim that philosophy must appeal to "the solid secular eternity of the sciences", and such further claims as that "there is only one humanity", suggest that he is to be viewed as in league with Kant, Husserl and Sartre: that his thought is yet another attempt to restore traditional philosophy in the face of continental thought's ongoing rejection of it. On one level, this is indeed the case: Badiou clearly believes that if philosophy is to move forwards, it must reassert certain traditional values in the face, particularly, of postmodernism's relentless questioning of them. But Badiou's philosophical traditionalism has sharp limits, because the atemporal realm he advocates is empty. Philosophy for him contains not Kanian categories, Husserlian *eidē* or the complexities of Sartrean nihilation, but merely the demand to recognize truths produced elsewhere as truths.

That "elsewhere", of course, is the four truth procedures; and science art, politics and love are anything but atemporal. Not only do they produce radically

---

5. Badiou does suggest, in *Manifesto for Philosophy*, that this happens in the writings of Emmanuel Levinas (Badiou 1999: 67).

new truths that, as new, did not exist before they were produced, but also that very capacity for newness means that they may one day produce truths that cannot be classed as scientific, artistic, political or loving, in which case the truth procedures themselves will have morphed into something other than they are now. Philosophy's job is not, then, to provide some sort of atemporal truth freed from time and history, but to situate the truths of each procedure by showing how they fit together with those of the others, thereby *situating* them with respect to those others and so establishing their status as truth. In so doing, philosophy opens "a general space in which thought accedes to time, to *its* time, so long as the truth procedures of this time find shelter for their compossibility with it" (Badiou 1999: 38).

SITUATING ART AND POLITICS: JACQUES RANCIÈRE

Five years younger than Badiou, Jacques Rancière was, like him, a student of the French Marxist Althusser. Also like Badiou and many other French thinkers of his time, including both Derrida and Foucault, Rancière was deeply marked by the sudden uprising of May 1968. In Rancière's case this led him in the same direction as Foucault, with whose approach he acknowledges a "bit" of similarity (*PA* 50). Both thinkers look to the historical conditions that make various phenomena, and fields of phenomena, possible. Rancière calls such conditions "partitions of the sensible". What does this mean?

In *The Emancipated Spectator* (*ES*; 2009), Rancière explains this in terms of a letter from Gabriel Gauny, a French worker of the 1830s, describing a day in the countryside with two friends:

> What he recounted was nothing like the day or rest of a worker replenishing his physical and mental strength for the working week to come. It was an incursion into a quite different kind of leisure: the leisure of aesthetes who enjoy the landscape's forms and light and shade, of philosophers who settle into a country inn to develop metaphysical hypotheses there … By making themselves spectators and visitors, they disrupted the distribution of the sensible which should have it that those who work do not have time to let their steps and gazes roam at random …. What those days brought was … a reconfiguration in the here and now of the distribution of space and time, work and leisure.
>
> (*ES* 18–19)

The "sensible" here is just the overarching common world we live in and take for granted as a "system of self-evident facts of sense perception" (*PA* 12). In this respect, Rancière's conception of the sensible is akin to Heidegger's conception of "world" in *Being and Time*: both are names for the overall domain in which we commonly live and work. The structuring principles of the two, however, are very different. For Heidegger, as we saw, world is a totality of contexts of significance through which we move. For Rancière, this whole is "distributed": the world of Gabriel Gauny, like ours, is divided, for example, into city and country, as time is divided into work and leisure.

The sensible, Rancière says, is thus conditioned by space and time (the two great ordering principles of sensible intuition for Kant), as well as by the forms of activity we pursue within it (*PA* 12). These distributions are not neutral, for different people have more or less informally assigned spaces within the overall domain of the sensible: the worker belongs in the factory, which is usually in a city, and must take the train to the country in order to enjoy a few moments of leisure time there. We thus arrive at the common space, the sensible as such, from one or another particular position: "Having a particular 'occupation' thereby determines the ability or inability to take charge of what is common to the community; it defines what is visible or not in a common space, endowed with a common language, etc." (*PA* 12–13).

Since the primary way in which we know things is sensory (*ES* 56), distribution is most basically a process by which things become visible or invisible. What you can see depends on where you are situated, and different social groupings therefore have different points of view on the world. One key factor by which these social groupings are differentiated is the amount of say they have in how the common space of the sensible is itself distributed. Because of this inequality, the common space of the sensible can be contested, as different groups seek more say in its distribution. To be sure, Rancière does not reduce these groups to the kind of classes that Marx dealt with; one of the lessons of May 1968 was that class analysis, which posits as prior to the analysis a group of people who, whether they know it or not, have a common interest, could not account for the kind of sudden union of students and workers that captivated the world for those few weeks. In keeping with this, Rancière sees contesting parties not merely as economic classes but as more or less contingent groupings of people; this contestation is, then, the "distribution" of the sensible as a "polemical distribution of modes of being and 'occupations'" (*PA* 42), and is characteristic of politics in general: "Politics revolves around what is seen and what can be said about it, around who has the ability to see and the talent to speak, around the properties of spaces and the possibilities of time" (*PA* 13).

Politics, for Rancière, is thus a form of contestation – a democratic one:

> Politics is not tied to a determined historical project. … Politics exists when the figure of a specific subject is constituted, a supernumerary subject in relation to the calculated number of groups, places, and functions in a society. This is summed up on the concept of the *dēmos*.
>
> (*PA* 51)

This definition is highly condensed. Rancière formulates it by turning, like other continental philosophers, to the ancient Greeks: *dēmos* is the Greek word for the people, including not merely the leaders but everyone who belongs to the community. As such, the *dēmos* is outside (or "supernumerary" to) the established hierarchies and groupings that constitute the political order. The *dēmos* constitutes itself as a political factor, then, when that order is challenged: when groups resist the way the sensible is distributed in a given society. Arising in opposition to the established order, politics is always a contest for membership in the *dēmos*: for equality. Where, for Badiou, equality was the fundamental political value from a philosophical point of view, for Rancière it is basic to politics itself.

To sum this up, the manifold political facts and phenomena of a given time manifest a set of channels and procedures by which speech and visibility are distributed. Since they order and distribute the sensible world, these channels and procedures are "aesthetic" in Kant's broad sense:

> There is thus an "aesthetics" at the core of politics ... If the reader is fond of analogy, aesthetics can be understood in a Kantian sense – re-examined perhaps by Foucault – as the system of *a priori* forms determining what presents itself to sense experience. It ... simultaneously determines the place and stakes of politics as a form of experience.
>
> (*PA* 13)

This, to be kind, is a highly inflected reading of Kant. Kant had distinguished between "empirical" propositions whose truth or falsity is known via sensory experience and *a priori* truths, which are validated not by sensory experience, but by the mind alone. What characterizes the aesthetic domain, for him, is precisely the relative absence of such *a priori* forms: indeed, in aesthetic experience, all concepts are put out of play, and we have only the pure forms of intuition, space and time. Rancière's reference to Foucault clears things up a bit: the social and cognitive structures of the disciplines are, for Foucault, *a priori*, not in Kant's sense but relatively, in that they pre-exist the objects those disciplines study; indeed, they help constitute those objects. They are thus known, not independently of all experience, but only of the experience of the objects they are supposedly studying; they are part of the conceptual background with which we approach those objects. Aesthetics, for Rancière, is thus *a priori* only in a historical sense: it determines (to a degree) the specific forms art and politics take at a given time, but is itself the result of previous developments in both realms. As such, it is itself historical and so open to change by new developments in both politics and art.

In Kant's view, a thing of beauty escapes all conceptuality (cf. *CJ* 229–31); this is why Kant famously relegated the beauty of art to an inferior status when compared with the beauty of nature, for in setting out to create a work of art an artist always has a concept in mind, if only that of "work of art" (cf. *CJ* 299–301). For Rancière, this means that, with Kant, the relation between making a work of art and enjoying it is sundered, for the former uses concepts and the latter does not; as we shall see him say shortly, in a work of art "thought has become foreign to itself".[6] Because aesthetic experience presents to us, in an *a priori* way, the lack of further *a priori* structures, it frees us from the conceptualities and practices of our culture: from its "distribution of the sensible". It is on the "aesthetic" level of distribution that art and politics find common roots, and it is art that enables us to see things in new ways and thus to contest that distribution:

> These stories of boundaries to cross, and of a distribution of roles to be blurred, in fact coincide with the reality of contemporary art, in which all specific artistic skills tend to leave their particular domain and swap places and powers. Today, we have theatre without speech, and spoken dance; installations and performances by way of plastic works; video projections transformed into series of frescoes; photographs treated as *tableaux vivants* or history paintings; sculpture metamorphosed into multimedia shows; and other combinations. (*ES* 21)

Also called "aesthetic", in a second sense, are the many different practices by which things are actually made publicly visible, and which constitute what Rancière calls "art". One of Rancière's favourite examples of how a work of art can operate is Gustave Flaubert's *Madame Bovary*, in which, for the first time, "the adultery committed by a farmer's daughter is as interesting as the heroic actions of great men". Just by focusing on its unhappy provincial protagonist, *Madame Bovary* made a whole category of people publicly visible, and this went along with a democratic redirection of political energies and interests (*PA* 14, 55–6). As with Heidegger, then, a work of art is able radically to redirect our ways of experiencing, and on that basis to transform our behaviour and our communities: "On the one hand, the 'community of sense' woven together by artistic practice is a new set of vibrations of the human community in the present; on the other hand, it is a monument that stands as a mediation or a substitute for a people to come" (*ES* 59).

Heidegger might have written that sentence; but there are two major differences between his view and Rancière's. First, art and politics stood for Heidegger in a clear relation of priority: the work of art was a primary happening of truth and political practice was not. For Rancière, both domains arise in and through contestation. Art and politics are correlative, but are not coordinated in any tight way, if only because neither domain coheres tightly even with itself. Both are

---

6. For this view of Kant, see *ES* 64.

historically mutable, and neither can even be given an overall definition: "*art and politics* are contingent notions" (*PA* 51). In particular, as we shall see, they change over time. The importance of contestation, for Rancière, is his other salient difference from Heidegger; Heidegger's "community of preservers" of a work of art is, as we saw in Chapter 7, a group united by a common call, not one divided by issues of distribution.

What comes to the fore, then, when we consider art and politics together is, for Rancière, their contingency: that the political shape of an epoch is not a coherent system or a necessary development but depends, although only loosely and to an extent, on events in the world of art, and vice versa. Rancière's thought is thus a correlative situating of politics and art in terms of each other. We do this by seeing them in terms of aesthetics in Rancière's primary meaning: in terms of the realm in which the sensible is distributed and the domains of art and politics come together.

Rancière's name for the set of channels and procedures by which the sensible is distributed in a given society is "regime". A regime thus has the same kind of *a priori* status as a Foucauldian discipline, but is of considerably wider extent, since it applies to an entire political system. Like art and politics themselves, the nature of the regime changes over time. Indeed, Western history since the Greeks exhibits, for Rancière, three different regimes or distributions of the sensible, which came successively into being and are all still around today, meaning that they cannot be given any kind of Hegelian historical ordering (*PA* 51–2). The first of these, the "ethical" regime (*PA* 20–21), defines the arts in terms of who engages in them and of what they accomplish. Plato, who first articulated the basic outlines of this regime in *Republic*, Book III, characterizes art as the making of images, and many treatments of his views take that to be his "definition" of art. But the fact that art produces images does not suffice, for Plato, to distinguish it from other forms of human activity, since the whole sensible world is, for him, a mere image of the world of Forms; hence, Plato does not have a unified conception of art as such, but refers only to many different arts, ways of doing and making.

Still, some arts (such as the art of sandal-making) are, for Plato, "true" because they make images with precise ends in view; other arts (such as painting) are artistic "simulacra" because they are *merely* the production of images (*PA* 20–21). It is such "false" artists that Plato famously banned from his ideal city; but the ban, for Rancière, was not invoked merely because art is the making of images. Rather, the problem lies with who makes the images in question. The false arts make things publicly visible; but they themselves are made by mere artisans, many of whom are slaves, and they thus allow the common people to assume a role in visibility. Art "carries with it the syndrome of democracy" (*PA* 17). That is why it must be excluded from the rigid hierarchy of the Platonic *polis*, which confines slaves and artisans to the *oikos*. Plato's account of art is thus in the service of the elimination of contestation altogether, and misses the point of both art and politics; Plato's definition of justice as "everyone doing his own task" (*Resp.* 370c, 433d) is the epitome of this (cf. *ES* 20).

It is with Aristotle, who unlike Plato thought that sensible things were real and not merely mages of something else, that imitation becomes specific to art as we understand it. Sandal-makers, while still mere artisans, are, for Aristotle, making real things. Only artists make simulacra; and art's status as image becomes not merely unique to it, but its defining feature. With this, we enter the second of Rancière's three historical aesthetic regimes: that of "representation". Art is no longer defined in terms of who makes it and what it accomplishes, but in terms of what it is: an image. Art is now clearly conceptualized and separated from other concerns, so standards and norms for it can be elaborated. The result is a whole hierarchy of arts, classified by what a given art represents. Thus, tragedy is better than comedy, for Aristotle, because it shows people who are better than we, the audience, are; comedy presents people who are inferior to us (cf. Arist. *Poet.* 1448a).

Where the politics associated with Plato's view of art relied on the single distinction between artisans, on the one hand, and fully qualified citizens, on the other, Aristotle's redefinition of art brings with it a whole social hierarchy: "In the classical system of representation, the tragic stage would become the stage of visibility for an orderly world governed by a hierarchy of subject matter and the adaptation of situations and manners of speaking to this hierarchy" (*PA* 18). The "democratic syndrome" of drama, for Plato, has thus been overcome in the representational regime, and art has been salvaged for hierarchy.

The third, "aesthetic", regime appears much later and defines art objects not in terms of those who make them and what they accomplish, or in terms of other things that they represent, but solely in terms of themselves: an art object is "a form of thought which has become foreign to itself" (*PA* 23). That thought has become foreign to itself means, as with Kant, that works of art cannot be understood: they are co-productions of conscious and unconscious insight or works of intuitive genius (*PA* 22–3). Because they are estranged from thought, they are also estranged from the sensory order: that a work of art cannot be understood conceptually differentiates it from other sensory objects (*PA* 23). The aesthetic view of art thus maintains that a work of art is experienced as a unique kind of thing, but the specific way the definition characterizes that uniqueness – as a "foreignness to thought" – hardly works in practice, for everything is to some degree incomprehensible; as Kant himself points out, we can never fully understand the production of even a single blade of grass (*CJ* 400, 409). The realm of art is thus ready for great expansion: to declare something "art" is to say (against Plato) that it is something unique, but almost anything turns out (against Aristotle) to be capable of being viewed as unique in that way.

This expansion includes an expansion of the subject matter of art: the old hierarchies concerning what art should represent, and what it should not, are gone, and even the humblest of people can, as in *Madame Bovary*, find themselves in works of art (*PA* 32–3). Also gone is the old hierarchy of the arts themselves: not only comedy, but technical and mechanical pursuits such as photography and film can now be recognized as art on a footing with painting and poetry (*PA* 22).

All this enables art to become democratic. We saw how this happened in the case of Flaubert, but more is involved than merely devoting works of art to portrayals of ordinary people. The media of art also play roles in this; a novel does not require the complex financing and social organization of drama. Hence, the arrival of the aesthetic regime was a major change in both art and politics. Art can now be made by ordinary people; about ordinary people; and for ordinary people:

> With the triumph of the novel's page over the theatrical stage, the egal-itarian intertwining of images and signs on pictorial or typographic surfaces, the elevation of artisans' art to the status of great art, and the new claim to bring art into the décor of each and every life, an entire well-ordered distribution of sensory experience was overturned.
>
> (*PA* 17)

If politics is a realm of contestation, Rancière's own thought becomes political when he seeks to argue against other ways of categorizing art. He sees his three-fold classification in terms of contingent regimes as superior, in particular, to the conventional way of representing art in terms of "modernism". Modernism begins from a view of the aesthetic regime, but misunderstands and misuses it. It *misunderstands* it because it views it as the loss of representationality alone, as in abstract expressionism or in James Joyce's *Finnegans Wake*. Where the aesthetic regime is properly understood as art that has become recalcitrant to thought, for modernism the simple fact that art no longer depicts people and things suffices to define it. The "modernist" approach also *misuses* this view of art because it views it as the goal of the history of art in general, thus reduc-ing that history to a single linear progression, *à la* Hegel (*PA* 24). In so doing, it denies true novelty to art: all art is merely a development of what was there before it on the great path to modernism. And this is a denial of art's true tem-porality: "The idea of modernity would like there to be only one meaning and direction in history, whereas the temporality specific to the aesthetic regime of the arts is a co-presence of heterogenous temporalities" (*PA* 26).

Modernism in politics similarly denies novelty: it can see political revolu-tions only as realizations of ideas that already exist in theory (*PA* 27). (Thus, the French Communist Party viewed the uprising of May 1968 in the traditional terms of class struggle, and, unsurprisingly, repudiated it.) Revolutions under-stood as the applications of pre-existing theories are always seen as failures; and these failures give rise to philosophies that see modernity not as the final success of the human spirit, but as itself a failure: indeed, as a "forgetting" of what history really is (*PA* 27–8). This view in turn gives rise to "postmodernism", which takes forgetting to be so basic that it incessantly valorizes the forgotten, becoming "The grand threnody of the unrepresentable/intractable/irredeemable, denouncing the modern madness of the idea of a self-emancipation of mankind's humanity and its inevitable and interminable culmination in the death camps" (*PA* 29).

Instead of understanding the present age as the culmination of the past, and thus as something whose germ is present in all historical ages, and thus in turn as something that stands above history as its unifying principle, we should, for Rancière, situate art in its heterogenous temporality: in terms of the contingent coexistence of its various regimes with one another and with politics. In return, art will situate us, by making visible to us the current distributions of the sensible; and in that way it will guide our contestations of them. For art is not at all a matter of passive and private enjoyment, and "emancipation begins when we challenge the opposition between viewing and acting" (*ES* 13).

CONCLUSION

One common concern for both Badiou and Rancière is to find a way of freeing revolutionary political activity from a Marxism that, by 1968, had hardened into dogma; this concern both unites them with each other and distinguishes them from the younger continental philosophers I shall discuss in the next chapter, Agamben and Butler, who are less concerned with Marxism. In seeking to understand and justify revolutionary actions without appealing to Marxist, or indeed any other, theoretical presuppositions, both Badiou and Rancière turn to the notion of equality. This, we may say, is one thing that leads Badiou to "re-entwine" his thought with set theory: the presentation of "pure multiplicity" in which all members of a set are on an equal footing as members. It also leads Rancière to see revolution as a contest for equality with aesthetic dimensions. Rather than capturing set theory, politics and art in terms of a fixed set of theoretical commitments, both thinkers seek, in very different ways, to "situate" them: Badiou by showing philosophically how mathematics in general is, as one of four truth procedures, "the human history of eternity"; and Rancière by locating aesthetics with respect to the heterogeneous histories of its various regimes.

CHAPTER 15

LIFE AND GENDER IN AGAMBEN AND BUTLER

The final two philosophers we shall look at are, like Badiou and Rancière, not only flourishing today but hard at work. Unlike Badiou and Rancière, they are not in France: Giorgio Agamben is a professor at the University of Verona, in Italy, and Judith Butler is at Columbia University, in the United States. Such international presence is nothing new for continental philosophy, of course; Kierkegaard was a Dane, and Marx lived in variety of countries before settling in England. Something, however, has changed: continental philosophers born during and after the Second World War are no longer concentrated in France and Germany. Continental philosophy has become a decentralized network, pursued in a broad variety of locales around the world.

SITUATING LIFE: GIORGIO AGAMBEN

Born in 1942 and educated at the University of Rome, Agamben is the first continental philosopher in this book who has no clear memories of the Second World War. This does not mean that his philosophy ignores it, or that he somehow philosophizes as if the war had never happened. To understand the modern world, the one in which we live, requires, for Agamben, a confrontation with all the horrors of the mid-twentieth century and, most especially, with the Holocaust. Agamben's lack of concrete memories seems, however, to enable him to approach the horror of that time more conceptually, and hence more directly philosophically, than do his older colleagues.

In his 2008 *The Signature of All Things* (*SAT*), Agamben appropriates American philosopher of science Thomas Kuhn's conception of a "paradigm" (Kuhn 1970). The term is difficult to define, but for present purposes we can say that a "paradigm", for Kuhn, is the set of presuppositions and practices shared by the members of a scientific community. Like a Foucauldian "discipline", a scientific paradigm therefore has a constitutive role in determining what, in that community, is to count as true. The feature that Agamben finds most useful is that a paradigm, for Kuhn, is not a set of rules for conducting science, as is a discipline for Foucault, but is learned as something much more concrete: as an example of how to do science. Aristotle's account of motion in his *Physics* and elsewhere, as well as Newton's *Principia Mathematica*, thus count as "paradigms" in Kuhn's sense (*ibid.*: 12, 23). For Agamben, then, a paradigm is a "singular object, standing equally for all others of the same class, that defines the intelligibility of the group of which it is a part and which, at the same time, it constitutes" (*SAT* 17).

Thus defined, the notion of paradigm applies far more widely for Agamben than for Kuhn, who was concerned with scientific research; in particular, there are, as we shall see, paradigms in politics. In turning towards politics, Agamben rejoins Foucault (and other continental philosophers), and his appeal to Kuhn serves to highlight an important aspect of Foucault's "genealogical" approach. Because Foucault, as we saw, rejects metaphysical origins, he too must always discuss particulars: what accounts for any historical phenomenon can only be another historical phenomenon. Whatever in history is not merely accidental, and so unaccountable, must have a definite place in the sequence of things for which it accounts. When Foucault attempts to read off from his discussions of such objects the rules that they exemplify, we could say that he is attempting to determine their group "intelligibility": what relates them to other things of their "class". For both Foucault and Agamben, then, genealogy moves – as, indeed, with Nietzsche – "from singularity to singularity" (*SAT* 31).

Another similarity between Agamben and Foucault is more evident in Agamben's practice than in his reflection on it. This is that what Agamben is aiming at uncovering is the "kinship" among various historical phenomena. In order for Agamben's genealogical investigations to be worthwhile at all, such kinship cannot be obvious. Just as what is uncovered by phenomenology must, for Heidegger, be something that "proximally and for the most part does *not* show itself at all" (*BT* 35), so the kinships exposed by Agamben must "elude the historian's gaze", or at least be able to do so (*SAT* 31). If observable kinship is a form of similarity, then we can say that Agamben aims at bringing to clarity the underlying similarities among what appear to be diverse historical phenomena. What these phenomena need not do, in order to resemble one another, is *ground* one another. Agamben is not trying to explain how any set of historical phenomena arose from its paradigm; indeed, there is in his view no need for a paradigm and the class of things for which it serves as paradigm to be temporally related at all: "the *archē* [my investigations uncover] is not an origin presupposed in time" (*SAT* 32). As a singular thing, the paradigm is, of course, itself temporal, but whether it precedes or follows other things is not at issue. What matters is that it resemble other things enough that it and they can render each other mutually intelligible.

While Foucault also rejected the notion of metaphysical origins, he did not reject the importance of temporal sequence in this way. Thus, it is important for him that Christian writings on sexuality "borrowed" from earlier pagan philosophy, and his late investigations of sexuality seek to "proceed back from Christianity to antiquity" (Foucault 1985: 9–10, 15). Foucault's emphasis on the discontinuities in history means, to be sure, that what went before is less important for him than for someone like Hegel, but Foucault does not make an overall denial of its importance. Agamben too, in his actual work, does not deny the importance of historical sequences. He returns often not only to the Greeks, as is common for continental philosophers, but also to the systematic and abstract formulations of ancient worldviews achieved in Roman law. Thus, in *State of Exception* (*SE*; 2005), Agamben approvingly quotes the German historian Leopold Wenger concerning the ancient conception of *auctoritas*, which I shall discuss later: "*Auctoritas*, that is the fundamental concept of public law in our modern authoritarian states, can only be understood – not only literally but as regards its concept – starting from Roman law of the time of the principate" (quoted in *SE* 81).

As pursued in his *Homo Sacer* (*HS*; 1998) Agamben's effort to understand modernity thus requires a confrontation with ancient Greece. In his concern with Greek thought he builds explicitly on the work of Arendt and Foucault (*HS* 3–8); behind them are their mentors Heidegger and Nietzsche, and behind them all, as we shall see, is Hegel.

The modern political order, in so far as a distinctive one exists, tends to be viewed in terms of rulers wielding constitutionally limited power, on the one hand, and citizens bearing rights, on the other (*HS* 106). Agamben opts for an earlier conceptual binary, the Greek distinction between *bios* and *zoē*. One way to put this basic distinction is to say that any kind of life that someone would care to live is a *bios*; *zoē* refers merely to life as set of physiological processes, and hence is compatible with all kinds of misery. *Bios* thus has the fundamental character of what Arendt, whom Agamben is following here, would call the *polis* or world; *zoē* is the kind of life process she located in the *oikos*.

The distinction is an important one in the thought not only of Arendt, but of Plato and Aristotle. When Socrates tells Crito that "it is not life [*zoē*] which we value most highly, but living well [*to eu zēn*]" (*Cri.* 48b), "living well" means having something going on that is over and above your mere physiology: it means having a *bios*. In order to have that, you need to reflect on your life; Socrates urges in the *Apology* that "the unexamined life [*bios*] is not to be lived [*abiotos*]" (*Ap.* 38a). An examined *zoē* is not even an option, for we can hardly be aware of the many ongoing physiological processes taking place in our bodies at any moment. Indeed, as Nietzsche pointed out in *On the Genealogy of Morality*, we must remain ignorant of our physiology, for only so can we constitute ourselves as something over and above it; only when we do that can we "make room for something new, above all for the noble functions and functionaries" (*GM* 38).

"Noble" (*vornehm*) is perhaps the best word to translate what Aristotle, in a passage from his *Politics* that Agamben quotes in the "Introduction" to *Homo Sacer*, contrasts with *zoē*: *zēn kalōs*, or living nobly. In thus equating *bios* with living nobly, rather than merely with living well as Socrates had done, Aristotle is bringing in a technical term in his philosophy; *to kalon* the nominative form, designates for him the harmonious ordering of diverse components.[1] A "noble" life is one in which a variety of activities (most importantly for Aristotle, those concerning art and politics) are brought together harmoniously; such a life can be lived only by free citizens of a polis. Slaves and people who must devote all their energy simply to staying alive and reproducing themselves are excluded from it and relegated to mere *zoē*. Aristotle says as much in his *Politics* (I.2 1252b1–7), and it is why, in his *Poetics*, he restricts tragedy, the highest form of art, to the polis (1448a). *Zoē* is, then, the exclusive concern of family and village life; as Arendt pointed out, in the *polis* it is restricted to the *oikos* and does not appear outside its walls.

When Agamben proposes to understand the modern political order in terms of the ancient distinction between *bios* and *zoē*, he is making life into a central category of his thought; and as he does so, he situates it temporally. That *bios* changes with history is obvious; the harmonious integration of different activities will take different forms depending on the society one lives in, and ancient Greeks could not seek to integrate driving cars and playing video games into their lifestyles. But *zoē* too, as we shall see, has changed in modern times.

That Agamben undertakes this at all places him in the lineage not only of Arendt and Foucault, Heidegger and Nietzsche, but also of Hegel, the founder of temporalized philosophy. For the "bare life" that Agamben will take up is lived by the wretched creature we saw Hegel call the Bondsman; and it was life itself, the ever-changing nature of our mortal embodiment, that recurrently needed to be vindicated in the face of repeated claims to unchanging truth. For Agamben, the vindication comes about in an exceptional and unstable way. *Zoē*, which he calls "bare life", is present everywhere in society (as Hegel showed in the "Battle for Life and Death", you cannot do anything unless you are also alive). But where bare life was globally denied in Greek society outside the *oikos*, in modern societies, for Agamben, it is explicitly recognized by the political order, in the rare and unfortunate individuals who are allowed to appear in the political order as *nothing more than* bare life.

At this point (*HS* 25), Agamben invokes yet another continental precursor: Badiou. Since the many physiological processes that constitute bare life remain unknown to us, bare life is what Badiou calls an "evental site": it has nothing below it but the empty set. When such a site is allowed to "belong to itself", it

---

1. For a discussion of *kalos* and its appropriate translation in English see McCumber (1993: 112–18).

becomes an event; and this is what happens, for Agamben, when someone is publicly declared to be nothing more than bare life. This declaration, then, is what Agamben calls an "exception". Where an event for Badiou is generally anything to be traced with fidelity, the particular kind of event that Agamben calls an "exception" is, for him, something more: it is nothing less than the basis for the modern political order. "The entry of *zoē* into the space of the polis – the politicization of bare life as such – constitutes the decisive event of modernity and signals a radical transformation of the political/philosophical categories of classical thought" (*HS* 4).

Bare life structures the political order by being excluded from it, not, as the ancients did, by banishing it entirely, but by making it something visible only in a few exceptional places; bare life, the basis of everything human, is visible only when the person who has it has nothing else (*HS* 11). Thus, when we look at the Roman, the bandit, the outlaw, the werewolf, and – most importantly for Agamben – the Jew in the extermination camp (*HS* 104–11) as *homo sacer*, we see them as bare life – and we see ourselves as something else. All these specific manifestations of bare life within the political order are instances of the more general intrusion of bare life into politics, which reached its apogee in the Nazi death camps (*HS* 120).

Seeing others, and not ourselves, as bare life is not merely an unfortunate cognitive habit for Agamben; nor is it restricted to the Holocaust. It is crucial to modern concepts of sovereignty. Agamben explores this in most detail in *State of Exception*. A "state of exception" is a political situation, such as martial law (*SE* 4), in which the laws normally in force in a society are suspended in the face of some dire threat, as when Abraham Lincoln suspended *habeas corpus* during the American Civil War (*SE* 20–21). The laws are thus placed in a peculiar state: they are not abrogated entirely but remain, so to speak, "on the books"; in the state of exception, however, they are not applied. The result is "a zone of anomie [lawlessness] in which all legal determinations – and above all the very distinction between public and private – are deactivated" (*SE* 50).

Two features of this anomie are especially important for Agamben. First, the state of exception is, although lawless, itself legal: it is recognized as binding on and by the society for which it is invoked. Second, in being placed outside the law, the state of exception becomes apolitical. Not only is the "very distinction" between public and private, which we saw in Arendt to be fundamental to the political order, undone, but the subsequent distinction within the political realm between rulers and ruled is overthrown. Officials, deprived of their legal entitlements, are reduced to the status of ordinary citizens; while the citizens, called upon to defend the state, can act like magistrates, even killing people on their own initiative (*SE* 44–5, 48–9).

The state of exception is thus very odd indeed, and in much of the book Agamben discusses the efforts of both ancient and modern legal theorists to come to terms with it. The most important question is of how it can come about: in a society governed by the "rule of law", how can law suspend itself? "What must be inscribed within the law is something that is essentially exterior to it, that is, nothing less than the suspension of the juridical order itself" (*SE* 33).

The answer to this question is that the foundation of the law is not, in the case of the state of exception, considered to be anything that is itself legal, but something outside the law: the sovereign, the "anomic foundation of the juridical order" (*SE* 69). Agamben here adopts the definition of sovereignty proposed by Schmitt: the sovereign is the one who "decides the state of exception" (*SE* 1). Since the state of exception suspends the laws, they have validity only when the sovereign decides that there is no state of exception; and to make that sort of decision about the laws, the sovereign must be outside them, meaning that sovereign power is "entirely unbound by laws and yet is itself the source of legal legitimacy" (*SE* 70). When the laws are in force, moreover – when there is no state of exception – the sovereign exercises certain legally constituted powers. Sovereign power is thus, for Agamben, political power that is both constituted and constituting: the sovereign not only exercises the legally prescribed functions of an office, but creates and maintains those prescriptions in the first place (*HS* 41). The sovereign is thus legally *empowered* and also in possession of something higher and more elusive: the *authority* to constitute legal validity itself. Since authority does not come from the laws, but rather grounds them, it is vested in the sovereign as a living being (*SE* 69, 74–8).

We have, then, two distinct relations between law in general and that which is outside law, or life. On the one hand, the state of exception reveals that law is grounded in the living person of the sovereign, who can abrogate it. On the other hand, such power would not be possible unless it were possible to regard those on whom it is exercised as possible objects of any and all uses of power: as mere bare life. Thus "The sovereign and *homo sacer* present two asymmetrical figures that have the same structure and are correlative; the sovereign is the one with respect to whom all men are potentially *homines sacri*, and *homo sacer* is the one with respect to whom all men act as sovereigns" (*HS* 84).

The reduction of an individual to bare life is fully accomplished, then, only in "states of exception", when normal laws are suspended. But the exceptional can become the exemplary, and the oscillation between the two – between "I am not what that person is" and "I could become what that person is" – is crucial to political power in the modern world:

> Exception and example are correlative concepts that are ultimately indistinguishable and that come into play every time the very sense of the belonging and commonality of individuals is to be defined. In every logical system, just as in every social system, the relation between inside and outside, strangeness and intimacy, is this complicated.   (*HS* 22)

The state of exception is thus not "exceptional" in the sense of being rare; indeed it "tends increasingly to appear as the dominant paradigm of government in contemporary politics" (*SE* 2, 7). States of exception, Agamben notes, are found in post-Revolutionary France and under the rule of Napoleon; in the American Civil War; in most of the countries involved in the First World War, including the United Kingdom; in fascism and Nazism; and in the United States after 9/11 (*SE* 11–22). In all these, we see a "kinship" according to which a charismatic ruler, acting on his own authority, spends the legal order. None of these cases, to be sure, is the cause or origin of the others; but taken together, they show the exception becoming more and more exemplary of how the political order really functions.

Agamben has now rethought the distinction between rulers and rules in terms of the distinction between sovereign and *homo sacer*, and so of that between *bios* and *zoē*. The oscillation between exception and example allows him, finally, to clarify one of the most mysterious things about the ancient Roman conception of *homo sacer*: its very name. To be named *homo sacer* – or, today, to be excluded from society as Jews were in Nazi Germany – is something horrible; we are supposed to feel relief when we look at someone like that and think we are different. Yet the literal meaning of the Latin *homo sacer* is "sacred human being". Why would someone thus degraded be sacred? Because of what Agamben calls the "ambivalence of the sacred". To exclude something in a public way is to make of it something very important. When God forbids Adam and Eve to eat the fruit of the tree of knowledge of good and evil, they immediately become obsessed with it. To be eaters-of-the-fruit is something they do not at first wish for, and yet it is something they inevitably do become.

Just as the future of Adam and Eve in the Garden of Eden was, for Kierkegaard, completely incomprehensible to them, so for Agamben is the future of *homo sacer*: not because such a person does not understand her own transgression, for what she has actually done (or not done) is irrelevant to her status as *homo sacer*, which comes about (as we saw) through an event irreducible to its own conditions and so unfathomable. This event, depriving the *homo sacer* of the protection of the law, deprives her of family and property, and so of personal history, and so of a finite future. *Homo sacer* gets to ask no questions, and her future is as ambivalent as the sacred itself: anyone may kill her, at any time (*HS* 81–3).

With *homo sacer*, then, Agamben situates bare life itself, in two senses. First, he reveals its own temporality: cut off from the past, and with only death for a future. This, to be sure, is a characteristic of physiology in general – of *zoē* – but it constitutes the very identity of *homo sacer*. Agamben also shows how, in modernity, bare life has been given new meaning and importance: new life, as it were. Bare life is now the excluded and exemplary exception that enables the sovereign power of modern political institutions.

Although Nazi Germany's treatment of Jews was the most extreme example of this, in this respect the Holocaust was not unique; Agamben extends his analysis, we saw, to "every social system". On what appears to have been his last visit to the United States, in January 2004, a customs officer asked Agamben for his fingerprint. Agamben thus found himself in the position of being admitted to the United States, or excluded from it, on the basis of strictly physiological information, and to him this meant that he was being reduced, by the American government, to a version of *homo sacer*. He was obliged by his own teachings to reject this.

The laws of Athens taught Socrates the importance of living by your own teachings when they showed him the implications of escape from his death sentence:

> What arguments will you use, Socrates [after your escape]? The same which you used here, that goodness and integrity, institutions and laws, are the most precious possession of humanity? Do you not think that [if you do not live by your own teachings] Socrates and everything about him will appear in a disreputable light? (*Cri.* 53d)

Agamben, like Socrates, stood behind his teachings, and took the next plane back to Italy (Arenson 2004).

SITUATING GENDER: JUDITH BUTLER

The exceptionality of bare life, for Agamben, consists in its deprivation of all characteristics that would distinguish one bearer of it from another. This includes gender, which, according to Judith Butler, traditionally includes the "cultural meanings that the sexed body assumes" (*GT* 6). Butler, who was born in Cleveland, Ohio in 1956 and is today a professor at Columbia University, seeks in *Gender Trouble* (*GT*; 1990) to rethink this conception of gender, which she sees as limited by a "substantial model of identity" (*GT* 6). Gender should instead, she argues, be seen as a "constituted *social temporality*" (*GT* 141). What this means will take some time to explain; what is already clear is that Butler's underlying aim in this book is to reveal the temporality of gender, that is, (in my sense) to "situate" it.

In accomplishing this, Butler's first obligation (as with all continental philosophers) is to recognize the temporality of her own discourse, which means recognizing that it comes after other discourses on gender. She does this by engaging in a series of readings of a variety of previous gender theorists. These readings are at once detailed, subtle and provocative. Common to all of them is the view that previous discussions of gender have shared what we may call a particular discursive form, most clearly explored, I believe, by Ludwig Wittgenstein in his *On Certainty* (cf. Wittgenstein 1969: 22, 44). Wittgenstein proceeds there in terms of an analogy between scientific investigations and mechanical apparatuses. In both, there are a number of moving parts: components whose position is not fixed, as when you open and close a door. In the case of a scientific investigation (or, we may say, a discourse on gender), these are the propositions that can be challenged in the investigation itself, and whose truth value is therefore unfixed at the outset. But in order for the investigation to be coherent, there must also be some propositions that cannot be questioned within the investigation itself. These, Wittgenstein suggests, are like the hinges on a door: they form the axis on which the investigation turns.

The fact that any investigation presupposes the validity of certain propositions does not mean those propositions cannot be challenged; they just cannot be challenged within the investigation itself. Hence, for Plato, there was a separate form of enquiry that undertook to uncover and question the presuppositions of other investigations, a sort of "second-order" investigation, which he called "dialectic" (cf. Pl. *Resp.* 533c). Plato's own version of dialectic, of course, had a rather robust set of presuppositions of its own – the Platonic Forms, atemporal entities to which the terms we use must remain faithful – for whose existence Plato never explicitly argues. When Butler reads previous discussions of gender as self-contained discourses that, in one way or another, tacitly assume something basic as unchangeable, then, she undertakes a second task as well: that of not falling into the Platonic trap of positing something fixed and immutable as the presupposition of her own discourse.

Gender is often viewed in the way that the quotation above views it: as a set of cultural meanings assumed by something biological, that is, by a "sexed body". Sex is thus something fixed and unchanging, while gender varies with the surrounding culture. Like other phenomena, gender attracts discursive attention when it becomes questionable, and for Butler the realization that gender is questionable is expressed in Beauvoir's statement that "one is not born a woman but rather becomes one" (*GT* 8). If one *becomes* a woman, then being a "woman" is a matter not of biological givens, but of cultural meanings: "woman" is a category of gender and not of sex. Beauvoir does not, of course, call attention to this fact in order to underwrite the specific set of meanings that "woman" assumes in our time. Her purpose, as a feminist, is precisely to challenge them. Gender thus becomes an object of discourse when feminism throws it into question; it becomes an unfixed part of the investigation.

Yet it cannot be wholly unfixed: the very fact that "gender" is opposed to "sex" gives it some stability. Indeed, if feminism is going to criticize the specific ways in which gender is constituted in contemporary society, it ought to have a clear conception of gender itself at hand. Yet it does not: "Contemporary feminist debates over the meanings of gender lead time and again to a certain sense of trouble, as if the indeterminacy of gender might eventually culminate in the failure of feminism" (*GT* ix).

The need to question gender thus, paradoxically, leads to a need to determine it; and since gender is itself to be unfixed within the investigation, it must be determined or fixed in terms not of what it is, since that can vary, but of how it comes about. And for that we need something fixed and unchanging from which it can come about: some sort of determinate pregendered state from which the manifold meanings of gender can be produced by some agent or other. This, then, is "sex".

Such positing of an underlying identity occurs even in Beauvoir herself. We saw her criticize the self-contained view of consciousness that Sartre had inherited from Husserl, with the result that she maintains that even basic structures of consciousness may be affected by experience, and thus by factors outside consciousness itself (such as one's childhood upbringing). For Butler, however, Beauvoir retains the fundamental phenomenological dualism of mind and body (*GT* 12, 153 n.21). In this dualism, the mind is conceived as the *cogito*, which Husserl, in turn, inherited from Descartes. This makes of it a foundation so solid that the mind, for Beauvoir, "takes on or appropriates [a] gender and could, in principle, take on some other gender" (*GT* 8). Thus, it is not necessary in any great and cosmic sense that everyone exhibit the specific traits associated with a given gender; one *becomes* a woman, but need not. What *is* cosmically necessary, however, is that one be a "one": that there be some sort of identity, however abstract, that precedes what is often called "gendering". One can become woman, then, only if one is already something else; Beauvoir's discursive questioning of gender reposes on the presupposition of a fixed identity at a deeper level.

The situation is not helped by philosophy's traditional association of the mental, including the *cogito*, with maleness (*GT* 12). This suggests that "one" is not strictly neutral as to gender, but is already somehow imbued with the maleness traditionally associated with consciousness itself. Beauvoir, we might say, would have more trouble explaining how one "becomes" a man than how one becomes a woman, because on the most basic level everyone is already male.

We can already see that Butler's situating of her own discourse among those of her predecessors exhibits the characteristics of good philosophical reading in general: it is detailed, subtle and aggressive, in that it pushes beyond what the thinker actually says into the hidden dynamics at the foundations of her thought. In *Gender Trouble* Butler pursues such strategies into a wide range of discourses on gender, all of which attempt to show how gender – specifically, female gender – is produced in an individual from psychological or social factors. Thus, the other discourses on gender that Butler treats begin from similar recognitions that gender has a temporality – that our gender is not merely something presupposed in our lives but is something we become – and so requires explanation. They are thus what we might call discourses on "gendering". They view gender as something that comes about; and what they posit as unchangeable is ultimately what it comes about from: a pregendered, but "substantial", identity.

Sometimes that which becomes gendered is explicitly given a fixed identity, as with Beauvoir; other times this is avoided, but the productive factors themselves are given such identities, which implies that the "pregendered" being on which they act is also fixed. Thus, for Luce Irigaray, woman is "the sex which is not one", and so stands as something that, within a masculinist language, is unrepresentable (*GT* 9). But what makes woman that is a "masculinist signifying economy" with a global reach (*GT* 13). That the actions of this economy produce, worldwide, the same results not only shows that it itself exhibits a fixed set of characteristics, but also implies that what it is acting on is also, in certain ways, fixed. In particular, for Butler, Irigaray's version of feminism itself "uncritically mimics the strategy of the oppressor": feminism is the standpoint from which dominant significations can be designated as, one and all, masculinist, and so has a claim to universality, and so to being the kind of fixed standpoint from which such claims can be made (*GT* 13).

Exemplary of the invocation of such fixed standpoints with respect to gender, and also inspirational for many of them, is the work of Sigmund Freud. Freud's aim was, of course, to trace psychological phenomena such as neurosis back to humble origins in the experiences of early childhood. It is thus a form of what Nietzsche and Foucault called "genealogy", a fact that Butler recognizes in claiming to provide a "more radical" genealogy than Freud's (*GT* 65). Crucial to Freud's project is the idea that we become what we are by attributing to ourselves characteristics of a lost object of our desire: we cope with our loss by reassigning what we loved to ourselves, thus internalizing, if not the object we loved, at least certain traits of it (*GT* 57–8). In the case of gender, a boy comes to identify himself as masculine when he loses his desire for his father; masculinity comes about through the prohibition of homosexual desire (*GT* 59). Freud, to be sure, does not exactly foreground this in his account of gendering; much more prominent in his writings is the acquisition of mature sexual identity through the prohibition of the boy's desire for his mother, in the drama of the Oedipus Complex.

That the cultural prohibition of homosexual desire plays a role in the constitution of masculinity (and femininity) is something Butler will accept, but she challenges Freud's account of what this role is. If the actual prohibition that produces "mature" sexuality is double, then the individual must start out as by nature bisexual: desirous of both father and mother. The difference is that the prohibition of desire for the mother requires merely the renunciation of the object, while in the case of the father it requires also the renunciation of the desire itself (*GT* 59). The differing force of these two cultural prohibitions thus leads – usually – to individuals who are exclusively heterosexual.

Every human being thus starts out as bisexual, according to Freud, but desire itself, for him, is always heterosexual: the boy feels desire for his father in virtue of a "feminine disposition" within him, which coexists along with masculine dispositions: "bisexuality is the coincidence of two heterosexual desires within a single psyche" (*GT* 60–61). The fundamental heterosexuality of desire is, then, the fixed point around which Freud's genealogy of gender turns; it is that from which gender itself comes to be, when one kind of desire is renounced utterly. The problem with this is that Freud is forced to postulate two different types of masculine and feminine disposition (leading to four in all). The masculine disposition of the male bisexual, on the one hand, coexists with his feminine disposition, and is opposed to the exclusively masculine disposition of the "mature" heterosexual male on the other; the same is the case for the bisexual and "mature" female. What is the difference, here, between "bisexual" and "mature"? Does the masculine disposition somehow change once the feminine disposition is driven out? If so, why call them both by the same name? And if they cannot be distinguished, what reason is there to postulate a primary, pregendered disposition at all (*GT* 61)?

Indeed, it is possible to use Freud's own language to articulate a process of gendering that begins, not in precultural dispositions, but with the prohibitions themselves. When desire for the father is prohibited, the boy internalizes the lost object, not merely as an object of desire, but as an object of anger and blame: the father is perceived as withholding himself (*GT* 63). This withholding itself is then internalized along with other characteristics of the father, with the result that the boy formulates an "ego ideal" of masculinity as something to which he can never be adequate, and, precisely because he can never be adequate to it, he is condemned to try. For Butler, the whole process is, however, instigated not by a pre-existing desire for the father, but by the prohibition on any such desire itself (*GT* 64), as when, in Kierkegaard's version of the Garden of Eden, desire for the fruit is awakened by the prohibition on eating it. Butler's critique of Freud thus rejoins her reading of Foucault's late critique of the "repressive hypothesis". For Foucault, "Not only does the taboo forbid and dictate sexuality in certain forms, but it inadvertently produces a variety of substitute desires and identities that are in no sense constrained in advance, except insofar as they are 'substitutes' in some sense" (*GT* 76). "Substitute", here taken "in some sense", has no fixed meaning. We do not always know what a substitute is substituting *for*, and this means that anything whatever may turn out to be a substitute for something else. This, indeed, is a virtual axiom of temporalized philosophy, for which everything has a past and has therefore evolved from something else.

Although on specific occasions we may want to ask what preceded prohibitions such as the taboos on incest and homosexuality, there is no general need to do so. There is, therefore, no conceptual requirement, even for Freud, to view "Sexual dispositions as the prediscursive, temporally primary, and ontologically discrete drives which have a purpose and, hence, a meaning prior to their emergence in language and culture" (*GT* 65). Freud does this in order to view sexual desire from the start as heterosexual. Other discourses on gender, although often instituted by people opposed to these needs (personal or not) nonetheless follow Freud, although in various ways and at varying distances. A brief discussion of the basic points in some of Butler's readings will illustrate her overall approach.

Wittig gives an "inverted" reading of Freud in the sense that she views the process of gendering, which he regarded as the maturation of an individual from the original bisexuality to heterosexuality, as in need of reversal: "Polymorphous perversity, assumed to exist prior to the marking by sex, is [in Wittig] valorized as the *telos* of human sexuality" (*GT* 27). For Wittig, the original polymorphous perversity of a pregendered self is undone by the enforcement of the critical norms of compulsory heterosexuality; heterosexuality itself is thus posited as a "systemically integrated", and so unchanging, unit which can be challenged only by "the radical departure from heterosexual contexts – namely becoming lesbian or gay". But the idea that becoming lesbian or gay is a radical departure from heterosexuality *in toto* presupposes that heterosexuality is a fixed and unified standpoint, and inevitably attributes the same kind of unity to homosexuality (*GT* 27, 121–2). And this, for Butler, is not the case:

> My own conviction is that the radical disjunction posited by Wittig between heterosexuality and homosexuality is simply not true, that there are structures of psychic homosexuality within heterosexual relations, and structures of psychic heterosexuality within gay and lesbian sexuality and relationships. (*GT* 121)

A similar "binarism" is at work in the thought of Gayle Rubin, for whom undoing the cultural imposition of heterosexuality is not simply a matter of becoming gay or lesbian but of overthrowing gender altogether. This would make possible the return to a pregendered, and so ideal, form of sexuality, but in advocating this, Rubin is postulating a fixed distinction, not between heterosexual and homosexual, but between gender itself and sex (*GT* 74–5).

Similarly for other post-Freudian thinkers on gender. For Claude Lévi-Strauss, who bases his views on those of Freud but writes from the perspective of an anthropologist, the point of the incest taboo is to enforce exogamy by requiring that men exchange women, and so enforces a ban not only on incest, but at the same time on homosexuality as well (*GT* 41). This is an important clarification of Freud, in whom the double nature of the ban remains, as we saw, in the background, and it establishes the nexus between structuralist anthropology itself and psychoanalysis (*GT* 42). But it presupposes that what is primarily forbidden by the incest taboo – the primal state of endogamous heterosexual desire – is a "universal truth of culture" (*GT* 42), a fixed point around which Lévi-Strauss's investigations move. For Joan Riviere, writing in 1929, gender is induced from a "masculine identification" that underlies the assumption of womanliness as a "masquerade". Although Riviere avoids trying to show that there is a true womanhood beneath the mask – the mask is femininity itself – she still, in this, inevitably presupposes the identification of libido itself as "masculine" (*GT* 50–53). For Julia Kristeva, the original continuity between mother and child that is disrupted by the incest taboo then leads to gender (*GT* 82–3).

From this perspective, homosexuality – and specifically lesbianism – can be construed only as a "loss of self", or as psychosis (*GT* 86–7). In all these Freudian cases, in one way or another: "The taboo against incest and, implicitly, against homosexuality is a repressive injunction which presumes an original desire … which suffers a repression of an original homosexual libidinal directionality and produces the displaced phenomenon of heterosexual desire" (*GT* 65).

For Jacques Lacan, also influenced by Freud and Lévi-Strauss, the primary reality – not just of gender but of ontology itself – is the phallus (*GT* 43). But the phallus, as the desiring organ *par excellence* for Lacan, identifies with its object of desire. What is desired, that is, what does not *have* a phallus, must *be* the phallus: because men "have" phalluses, the woman must "be" one. For someone who has no phallus to be identified as a phallus means, in turn, to engage in a masquerade. Less important than what is masked is for Lacan (as for Riviere) the origin of the masquerade: the woman identifies as the phallus because (as for Freud) it is the lost object she would like to have but does not (*GT* 48). Having posited the desire for the phallus in both male and female as the fixed point in his own discourse, Lacan has a problem with female homosexuals. Their sexuality, he claims (on the basis of "observation") is not really a positive desire for women, but is a refusal of sexuality as such in the wake of a "disappointment" (*GT* 49). This view is necessary because for Lacan, as for Freud, desire is intrinsically heterosexual; it must be if the phallus is to play the role that it does in his thought.

Finally, even Foucault, with whom Butler has the most affinity, falls victim to his view of gender as a distortion of a more basic form of desire. While in his *History of Sexuality* Foucault criticizes the "repressive hypothesis" and advances something close to what will be Butler's own views (*GT* 91–3), in his discussion of the "hermaphrodite" Herculin Barbin (*GT* 96–106) he appeals to a conception of a pleasuring body that subsequently undergoes gendering (*GT* 97, 129–30).

In all these appeals to a pregendered or even presexual identity, Butler sees the same mistake: an appeal to what we saw Nietzsche, in Chapter 5, call the "metaphysics of substance". For Nietzsche, this was the claim that behind our actions there stand actors: enduring agents whose basic nature is unchanged by their actions (*GT* 20–21), and who therefore could have acted differently. Gendering is not, to be sure, an action; it is something we undergo. But the discourses that Butler treats all suggest that we could have existed, on some level, as the people we are if we had undergone it differently or not at all.

The upshot of Butler's critical readings of gender theorists is that we must conceive gendering without reference to any underlying substance that undergoes it, thus undercutting the notion of gender as something that "happens" to something else: "This production of sex *as* the prediscursive ought to be considered as the effect of the apparatus of cultural construction designated by *gender*" (*GT* 7).

Relying on the work of anthropologist Mary Douglas, Butler argues that the body itself – certainly its most erotic component, the skin – is produced socially, through various forms of cultural attention to bodily margins (tattooing, clothing, etc.). If the generative activities of culture can extend even to the skin, an aspect of corporeality that is implicated in all sexual relations, then we are at a loss as to what it might not extend to. In this way, Butler eliminates the "natural" substance on which previous accounts of gender relied. She has nowhere denied that there may be unchangeable biological facts about human beings; what she has argued is that no such facts can be known with sufficient exactitude to be able to anchor any of the discourses on gender currently available. Her strategy in "refuting" fixed points is thus akin to Hegel's in the *Phenomenology*: it is not that it is impossible to obtain unchanging truth, but that we today have no way to do so.

Butler's positive account of gender now faces two problems. First, can she articulate it without doing what the thinkers she criticizes have done, that is, introduce a fixed point of reference for the investigation? Or has she, like them, tacitly or overtly posited something unchanging, whether inside or outside the individual, as a fixed point for the process of gendering? Second, what happens to moral agency in her view? If every action is *affected* by culture, why are we not completely *determined* by our societies? If there is nothing pre-social underlying the procedures by which gender is imposed on us, how, in particular, can we hope to resist the imposition?

Once appeals to something fixed and underlying one's gender are abandoned, gender becomes a series of actions without an actor, or of performances without a performer. It consists merely in the repetition of gendered behaviour (*GT* 138). To have a gender is to behave in ways that others have behaved in the past; such behaviour is "not expressive [of an underlying identity] but performative" (*GT* 141). At its base we find, not the actions of any substantive self or body, but merely the fact of repetition itself.

This, to begin with, considerably broadens the nature of gender beyond "man" and "woman", "homosexual" and "heterosexual". Ancient Athenian males, for example, at various stages of their lives engaged in homosexual affairs (cf. Dover 1979). Someone growing up in that culture would adopt a repertoire of behaviours very different from those of someone growing up in contemporary Middle America, where one is either straight or gay; and so on across the whole panoply of human societies. Efforts to render all these diverse behaviours as more or less superficial accretions to an underlying binary – that of male versus female – can be abandoned. However, repetition itself seems now to be the "hinge" on which Butler's own discourse swings: our ability to repeat, or parody, the behaviour of others is the unquestionable anchor of Butler's account of gender as performance.

As a first step towards seeing that this is not the case, let us consider what most basically separates Butler from Hegel. For Hegel, too, we are nothing over and above our engagements with others. There is nothing to Hegelian spirit beyond the sum of its appearances; all is "phenomena", which was why Hegel wrote a "phenomenology" in the first place. When our engagements with others become linguistic, they perforce acquire a repetitive dimension, for the words I learn are those that others have used. But, for Hegel, the repetitions in verbal behaviour that constitute our identities have a *telos*, an overall goal, which Butler characterizes as the "adequation between the 'I' that confronts the world, including its language, as an object, and the 'I' that finds itself as an object in that world" (*GT* 144).

Repetition for Butler has no *telos*. That it is basic means that it simply is; it no more leads to a final state than does the daily rising of the sun. It thus escapes, for her, the teleological discipline imposed on it by Hegel. And without that discipline, it becomes creative; for, as continental philosophers from Kierkegaard to Deleuze and Derrida have shown, repetition is not exact replication (cf. Deleuze 1994; Derrida 1977; Kierkegaard 2009). To deny that would be to deny a basic characteristic of time: that no two moments in it can be exactly alike, because one has the other in its past. Hence, as Derrida puts it in his discussion of "citationality", the repetition of anything occurs in circumstances different from those in which what is being repeated itself occurred, and so *must* be, to some extent, different (Derrida 1977). Butler's use of the concept of repetition thus does not require the positing of anything fixed; there is no identity between the repetition of something and what it repeats. And this means that repetition is always creative or "parodic", not in the sense that later gender behaviour shows a conscious break with earlier behaviour, a notion that would reinstate the creative subject as a fixed point in Butler's own theory, but in the sense that it can never be anything else:

> The injunction to be a given gender produces necessary failures, a variety of incoherent configurations that in their multiplicity exceed and defy the injunction by which they are generated.   (*GT* 145)

> This perpetual displacement constitutes a fluidity of identities that suggests an openness to resignification and recontextualization. (*GT* 138)

We could not exactly repeat our forebears even if we wanted to. The experimentation to which this gives rise is moral agency enough for Butler, for it explains the ongoing mutations of what we currently call "gender" without reference to any mutating substance.

In connection with Hegel and Derrida above, I associated the repetitions involved in gender behaviour with those of language. While we all learn to speak from our early (and not-so-early) caregivers, we do not learn to say exactly what they say. The temporality of language itself has remained an important theme in Butler's later work, as she builds on the basic insights she originally developed with regard to gender. To be injured by a word, for example – as in the case of hate speech – that word must be used against us in a particular situation. It must, then, occur between a past and future that "cannot be narrated with any certainty", either by us or by those who insult us (Butler 1997: 3). And this is true of terms that sustain us as well: our bodies acquire cultural existence in that they are defined for us by what others call us: "Thus, to be addressed is not merely to be recognized for what one already is, but to have the very terms conferred by which the recognition of existence is possible. One comes to exist by virtue of this fundamental dependency on the address of the Other" (Butler 1997: 5). Tattooing and adornment, the cultural dimensions of skin, which we saw play an important role in Butler's account of gender, are particular forms of this broader, linguistic function: "The body implies mortality, vulnerability, agency: the skin and the flesh expose us to the gaze of others, but also to touch, and to violence … Constituted as a social phenomenon in the public sphere, my body is and is not mine" (Butler 2004: 26).

Our corporeality makes us vulnerable, for better or worse, to others: to their speech and their action. There is nothing in us that is not vulnerable in this way, and to understand our vulnerability is to understand how we are connected, again for better or worse, to others. To explore it is then, in Butler's view, to situate ourselves as the temporal beings that we are.

CONTINENTAL PHILOSOPHY TODAY: A FEW BRUTAL GENERALITIES

Even these brief summaries of just four contemporary continental philosophers show that they are very different from one another. In every case, however, they show a triple concern with temporality; and this concern can be generalized, I suggest, to most if not all "continental" thinkers, past and present. I shall present these generalizations in outline here:

I. Continental thinkers today seek to show the temporality of their *subject matters*.
   A. When Badiou discusses set theory it is crucial that it be seen, not as a truthful account of mathematical entities in the world, but as a discourse originating in what he calls the "Cantor-event" (Badiou 2001: 38): set theory opens up new domains in ontology but itself cannot be reduced to what went before.
   B. Rancière sees the contemporary interaction of art and politics as grounded not in the timeless natures of these two spheres, but in regimes that exhibit a variety of "heterogenous temporalities".
   C. Agamben views the contemporary political order as manifesting a kind of sovereign power that in turn derives from two Greek views

of life, as *zoē* and as *bios*. He locates *homo sacer* between the future of *zoē* – death – and its only relevant past, the public exclusion from all else.

D. Butler sees gender as "constituted social temporality", that is, not as a state or property that individuals have, but as a set of processes of creative repetition that constitute individuals.

II. All of them ask how the phenomena thus understood actively open up different kinds of time.

A. For Badiou, set theory as ontology brings us to faithful attentiveness, to tracing out events in ways that remain open to the unpredictabilities they have as events.

B. Rancière asks how a work of art inspires us to political contestation within a larger regime.

C. For Agamben, our future is given by *homo sacer* in the ambivalence of the sacred, in the space between seeing *homo sacer* as something we are not and as something we might become.

D. Butler asks us, when we accept that gender is creative repetition and see ourselves as gendered, to commit ourselves to such situated creativity: to "taking up the tools where they lie" (*GT* 145).

III. All of them seek to remain faithful to the temporality of their own discourses.

A. Badiou traces his own discourse on ontology back beyond Cantorian set theory to the hypotheses of Plato's Parmenides (*BE* 31–8).

B/C. Rancière and Agamben form their own basis categories by reawakening classical ones.

D. Butler devotes much of her book to careful readings of previous gender theorists, back to Freud.

In general (and this is the last of my generalizations), all the contemporary continental thinkers I have discussed here take up the thesis of radical newness articulated by Heidegger; and all, correspondingly, reject Hegel-style teleologies. In these ways, and many more, philosophers of today are carrying forwards the basic programme of temporalized philosophy in a critical way.

One reason continental philosophy is prospering today lies in the continuing soundness of its distinctive philosophical underpinnings. As I have presented such philosophy here, there are two of these:

(a) Everything is in time: everything has, in Hegel's words, a Before and an After different from its Now. Everything that exists has come into being, is changing and will eventually cease to exist.

(b) Philosophy must never allow itself to forget (a).

These, to be sure, must be understood correctly: not ontologically, as binding statements about the nature of all reality, or epistemologically, as statements about what we can know, but practically, as counsels of philosophical prudence. We can see their wisdom as such maxims if we begin with an objection to (a).[2] "Everything is in time" is, *ontologically* understood, itself a blanket statement if ever there was one. As such it is self-refuting, for it claims to hold for everything that ever has or will exist, and hence is itself the statement of an unchanging truth (or falsehood). *Epistemologically* understood, it is highly suspicious, for it shares the basic problem with all such statements: how could it (or its negation) ever be proved? How could we know that there are no eternal structures or truths?

If, however, we understand (a) as *practical*, a sort of philosophical advice, it becomes quite reasonable. Why not begin with philosophy as we do with everything else: with the knowledge that there are things that are in time, that come into being, pass away and change? I see them, hear them, smell, touch and taste them all around me. One of the recurrent lessons of modern science, indeed, is that things that do not seem to change – mountain ranges, the oceans, the stars themselves – have done so over time. Even the natural constants, such as Hubble's, increasingly seem to have evolved (cf. Smolin 1997). To pursue this to the very end, a cursory glance at Aristotle's *Analytics* will show that the very procedures of logic have changed over time, to the extent that his discussions of syllogistic inference are extremely hard to follow (see McCumber 1993: 186–93). In modern views of the standard syllogism:

(1) All humans are mortal.
(2) Socrates is a human.
(3) Therefore, Socrates is mortal.

Line (3) is the conclusion, as indicated by "therefore". In Aristotle's own deployment of syllogistic form, however, (3) is presupposed; the only way to find out that Socrates is mortal is to watch him die. The Aristotelian syllogism starts from that fact and explains it with the two other premises:

(1) Socrates is mortal (has died). This is because
(2) Socrates is a human, and
(3) all humans are mortal.

Where, now, are the timeless "laws of logic", the ones that govern both the ancient and the modern versions of the syllogism? In order to preserve them,

---

2. It is actually a family of objections, depending on what we think such terms as "knowledge" and "structure" comprise.

we must distinguish them from the different formulations they have been given in the history of logic from Aristotle on, which means that the laws themselves differ from the laws as we know them, for what we know is the formulations. This brings the paradoxical result that the laws of logic are unknown: "things-in-themselves" behind the "appearances" in which they are formulated.

The question then arises of whether we must also accept (b) above. Even if (a) is justified and we are to take it that everything is in time, may we not be allowed, in philosophy, to forget this on occasion? Quine thought so:

> Strictly speaking, as urged earlier, what admit of meaning and of truth and falsity are not the statements but the individual events of their utterance. However, it is a source of great simplification in logical theory to talk of statements in abstraction from the individual occasions of their utterance; and this abstraction, if made in full awareness and subject to a certain [technical] precaution, offers no difficulty.
>
> (Quine 1982: xvi)

> We may conveniently hold to the grammatical present as a form, but treat it as temporally neutral. … This artifice frees us to omit temporal information, or, when we please, handle it like spatial information.
>
> (Quine 1960: 170)

The pursuit of simplicity, the avoidance of difficulty and the love of convenience are classic signs not of prudence, but of exhaustion: in this case philosophical exhaustion. But why be exhausted? Why not admit into our thought the sophisticated tools for connecting with the past and opening up the future that have been developed by continental philosophy?

Certainly the temporalized approach to philosophy pursued by continental philosophy has been widely successful. Continental thinkers have transformed nearly all aspects of culture and society the world over. It is impossible to conceive modern religion without Kierkegaard, modern secularism without Nietzsche, modern art without Heidegger or modern society without Hegel and Marx. The critique of administrative reason by Horkheimer and Adorno, together with its allies in Heidegger and Arendt, has led to important innovations in the way social organizations are put together. Derrida has changed our view of literature and even architecture, where an entire approach has come to be called "deconstructive". Foucault has transformed our understanding of prisons, asylums, schools and other "normalizing" institutions. Beauvoir's feminism has reshaped our very families. Agamben, Badiou, Butler and Rancière are reshaping our understandings of mathematics, art, politics, gender and love.

Continental philosophy has also done a remarkable job of unlocking the history of philosophy. That philosophy even had a history, as opposed to a mere disconnected past, was still unknown to Kant, who looked upon his predecessors as instances of ahistorical types rather than as his own temporal basis. It was Hegel who realized that we have evolved out of our predecessors and that philosophy's ancient Delphic imperative – *gnōthe seauton*, know thyself – cannot be even partially achieved unless that evolution is understood. The first philosophers of the West, the Greeks, have thus received great attention from continental philosophers, who have illuminated the many ways in which we still depend on and struggle against them, and the medievals, and the moderns.

Continental philosophers have also come up with an astonishing variety of human and philosophical ways to respond to the future: with Kierkegaardian inwardness, Nietzschean and Arendtian promises, Heideggerean questions, Frankfurt School negative dialectics, Sartrean praxis, Beauvoirian disclosure of being, Foucauldian rupture and Derridean hope.

Moreover, continental thinkers have not done their great work because they were a random collection of geniuses; in fact, they were anything but that. The later ones have always carefully read and studied the earlier ones. Even more important, they have all remained true, if not to their predecessors – they were in fact rather ruthless in their mishandling of even their friends and teachers – then to the philosophical underpinnings of continental thought. It is those two underpinnings, in fact, that have made such thought so influential, for it means that they deal exclusively with what other philosophers, however insightful, treat mainly in passing: what Richard Rorty, speaking from the allied tradition of pragmatism, calls the "little mortal things" (Rorty 1989: 99).

"Little mortal things", of course, are what are important to us as we try to live our lives; continental philosophy's concern with them guarantees its relevance. Continental philosophers restrict themselves to such "little mortal things" more consistently, indeed, than does Rorty, who adopts the Wittgensteinian view I noted in discussing Butler. For him, our enquiries (or, as he prefers to call them, "conversations") remain structured by fixed sets of "final vocabularies" that express basic "agreements about what is possible and important" (*ibid*.: 9, 20, 48). As foundational to speech communities, these cannot be challenged, let alone changed, from within them (cf. McCumber 2000: 56–60).

Since for continental philosophers everything is in time, their own thought must be temporal as well; even their own "foundations" are not exempt from critical challenge. Philosophy's traditional escape route from miseries and dangers of human affairs – its ancient pretension to deal with a domain where nothing changes, and truth is eternal and necessary – is thus barred to them. As they have done since 1807, continental philosophers live and think today entirely in the shadowy rigours of Plato's cave.

FURTHER READING

1. THE COLLAPSE OF KANT

Allison, H. 2001. *Kant's Theory of Taste: A Reading of the Critique of Aesthetic Judgment.* Cambridge: Cambridge University Press.
Arendt, H. 1992. *Lectures on Kant's Political Philosophy*, R. Beiner (ed.). Chicago, IL: University of Chicago Press.
Caygill, H. 1995. *A Kant Dictionary.* Oxford: Blackwell.
Cohen, T. & P. Guyer (eds) 1982. *Essays in Kant's Aesthetics.* Chicago, IL: University of Chicago Press.
Deleuze, G. 1963. *La Philosophie critique de Kant.* Paris: Presses Universitaires de France.
Guyer, P. 1997. *Kant and the Claims of Taste.* Cambridge: Cambridge University Press.
Guyer, P. 1998. "Immanuel Kant". See Craig (1998), V, 177–200.
Guyer, P. 2006. *Kant.* London: Routledge.
Kemal, S. 1992. *Kant's Aesthetic Theory: An Introduction.* London: Macmillan.
Kuehn, M. 2001. *Kant: A Biography.* Cambridge: Cambridge University Press.
Lyotard, J.-F. 1994. *Lessons on the Analytic of the Sublime*, E. Rottenberg (trans.). Stanford, CA: Stanford University Press.
Pippin, R. 1996. "The Significance of Taste: Kant, Aesthetic and Reflective Judgment". *Journal of the History of Philosophy* **34**: 549–69.
Wood, A. 2005. *Kant.* Oxford: Blackwell.
Zammito, J. 1992. *The Genesis of Kant's Critique of Judgment.* Chicago, IL: University of Chicago Press.

2. HEGEL DISCOVERS THE PAST

Beiser, F. 2005. *Hegel.* London: Routledge.
Fackenheim, E. 1967. *The Religious Dimension in Hegel's Thought.* Boston, MA: Beacon Press.
Findlay, J. N. 1958. *Hegel: A Re-examination.* London: Allen & Unwin.
Horstmann, R.-P. 1998. "Georg Wilhelm Friedrich Hegel", J. Rushmer (trans.). See Craig (1998), IV, 259–80.
Inwood, M. (ed.) 1985. *Hegel.* Oxford: Oxford University Press.
Mure, G. R. G. 1950. *A Study of Hegel's Logic.* Oxford: Clarendon Press.
Pinkard, T. 1996. *Hegel's Phenomenology: The Sociality of Reason.* Cambridge: Cambridge University Press.
Pinkard, T. 2000. *Hegel: A Biography.* Cambridge: Cambridge University Press.
Pippin, R. 1989. *Hegel's Idealism.* Cambridge: Cambridge University Press.

Rockmore, T. 1997. *Cognition: An Introduction to Hegel's Phenomenology of Spirit*. Berkeley, CA: University of California Press.
Taylor, C. 1975. *Hegel*. Cambridge: Cambridge University Press.
Winfield, R. D. 1989. *Overcoming Foundations*. New York: Columbia University Press.
Wood, A. 1990. *Hegel's Ethical Thought*. Cambridge: Cambridge University Press.

3. MARX, CAPITALISM AND THE FUTURE

Balibar, E. 1996. *The Philosophy of Marx*, C. Turner (trans.). London: Verso.
Bottomore, T., L. Harris, V. G. Kiernan & R. Miliband (eds) 1991. *A Dictionary of Marxist Thought*, 2nd edn. Oxford: Blackwell.
Carver, T. 1987. *A Marx Dictionary*. Cambridge: Polity Press.
Carver, T. (ed.) 1991. *The Cambridge Companion to Marx*. Cambridge: Cambridge University Press.
Elster, J. 1999. *An Introduction to Marx*. Cambridge: Cambridge University Press.
Puchner, M. 2004. "1848, February: The Reinvention of a Genre". In *A New History of German Literature*, D. Wellbery & J. Ryan (eds), 577–81. Cambridge, MA: Harvard University Press.
Rockmore, T. 2002. *Marx after Marxism: The Philosophy of Karl Marx*. Oxford: Blackwell.
Singer, P. 2000. *Marx: A Very Short Introduction*. Oxford: Oxford University Press.
West, C. 1991. *The Ethical Dimensions of Marxist Thought*. New York: Monthly Review Press.
Wheen, F. 2001. *Karl Marx: A Life*. New York: Norton.
Wood, A. 2004. *Karl Marx*, 2nd edn. London : Routledge.
Zinn, H. 1999. *Marx in Soho: A Play on History*. Cambridge, MA: South End Press.

4. KIERKEGAARD'S DREADFUL FUTURE

Bloom, H. (ed.) 1989. *Søren Kierkegaard*. New York: Chelsea House Publishers.
Hannay, A. 1982. *Kierkegaard*. London: Routledge & Kegan Paul.
Hannay, A. 2003a. *Kierkegaard: A Biography*. Cambridge: Cambridge University Press.
Hannay, A. 2003b. *Kierkegaard and Philosophy: Selected Essays*. London: Routledge.
Mackey, L. 1986. *Points of View: Readings of Kierkegaard*. Tallahassee, FL: Florida State University Press.
Matustík, M. & M. Westphal (eds) 1995. *Kierkegaard in Post/Modernity*. Bloomington, IN: Indiana University Press.
Perkins, R. (ed.) 1985. *International Kierkegaard Commentary: The Concept of Anxiety*. Macon, GA: Mercer University Press.
Rée, J. & J. Chamberlain (eds) 1998. *Kierkegaard: A Critical Reader*. Oxford: Blackwell.
Weston, M. 1994. *Kierkegaard and Modern Continental Philosophy: An Introduction*. London: Routledge.

5. NIETZSCHE AND THE BOUNDLESS FUTURE

Allison, D. B. (ed.) 1985. *The New Nietzsche: Contemporary Styles of Interpretation*. Cambridge, MA: MIT Press.
Danto, A. C. 2005. *Nietzsche as Philosopher*, exp. edn. New York: Columbia University Press.
Hollingdale, R. J. 1999. *Nietzsche: The Man and His Philosophy*, rev. edn. Cambridge: Cambridge University Press.
Kaufmann, W. 1956. *Nietzsche: Philosopher, Psychologist, Antichrist*. Cleveland, OH: Meridian Books.
Nehamas, A. 1985. *Nietzsche: Life as Literature*. Cambridge, MA: Harvard University Press.
Safranski, R. 2003. *Nietzsche: A Philosophical Biography*, S. Frisch (trans.). London: Granta.
Schacht, R. (ed.) 1994. *Nietzsche, Genealogy, Morality: Essays on Nietzsche's Genealogy of Morals*. Berkeley, CA: University of California Press.
Sedgwick, P. (ed.) 1995. *Nietzsche: A Critical Reader*. Oxford: Blackwell.
Spinks, L. 2003. *Friedrich Nietzsche*. London: Routledge.

Vattimo, G. 2002. *Nietzsche: An Introduction,* N. Martin (trans.). Stanford, CA: Stanford University Press.

6. THE RETURN OF TRADITIONAL PHILOSOPHY: EDMUND HUSSERL

Carr, D. 1991. *Time, Narrative, and History.* Bloomington, IN: Indiana University Press.
Farber, M. 2006. *The Foundation of Phenomenology: Edmund Husserl and the Quest for a Rigorous Science of Philosophy.* London: Aldine Transaction.
Patočka, J. 1996. *An Introduction to Husserl's Phenomenology,* J. Dodd (ed.), E. Kohak (trans.). LaSalle, IL: Open Court.
Ricoeur, P. 2006. *Husserl: An Analysis of His Phenomenology.* Evanston, IL: Northwestern University Press.
Smith, D. W. 2006. *Husserl.* London: Routledge.
Steinbock, A. 1995. *Home and Beyond: Generative Phenomenology after Husserl.* Evanston, IL: Northwestern University Press.
Ströker, E. 1993. *Husserl's Transcendental Phenomenology,* L. Hardy (trans.). Stanford, CA: Stanford University Press.
Welton, D. 2002. *The Other Husserl: The Horizons of Transcendental Phenomenology.* Bloomington, IN: Indiana University Press.
Welton, D. (ed.) 2003. *The New Husserl: A Critical Reader.* Bloomington, IN: Indiana University Press.
Zahavi, D. 2003. *Husserl's Phenomenology.* Stanford, CA: Stanford University Press.

7. THE FINITE FUTURE: MARTIN HEIDEGGER

Dreyfus, H. L. 1985. "Holism and Hermeneutics". In *Hermeneutics and Praxis,* R. Hollinger (ed.), 227–47. Notre Dame, IN: University of Notre Dame Press.
Inwood, M. 1997. *Heidegger.* Oxford: Oxford University Press.
Inwood, M. 1999. *A Heidegger Dictionary.* Oxford: Blackwell.
King, M. 2001. *A Guide to Heidegger's Being and Time.* Albany, NY: SUNY Press.
Mulhall, S. 1996. *Heidegger and Being and Time.* London: Routledge.
Polt, R. 1999. *Heidegger: An Introduction.* Ithaca, NY: Cornell University Press.
Rée, J. 1998. *Heidegger.* London: Phoenix.
Safranski, R. 1998. *Martin Heidegger: Between Good and Evil,* E. Osers (trans.). Cambridge, MA: Harvard University Press.
Steiner, G. 1991. *Martin Heidegger.* Chicago, IL: University of Chicago Press.
Zimmerman, M. E. 1990. *Heidegger's Confrontation with Modernity: Technology, Politics, Art.* Bloomington, IN: Indiana University Press.

8. ACTIVITY AND MORTALITY: HANNAH ARENDT

d'Entrèves, M. P. 1994. *The Political Philosophy of Hannah Arendt.* London: Routledge.
Johnson, P. A. 2001. *On Arendt.* Belmont, CA: Wadsworth.
Kristeva, J. 2001. *Hannah Arendt: Life Is a Narrative,* F. Collins (trans.). Toronto: University of Toronto Press.
May, L. & J. Kohn (eds) 1997. *Hannah Arendt: Twenty Years Later.* Cambridge, MA: MIT Press.
McGowan, J. 1998. *Hannah Arendt: An Introduction.* Minneapolis, MN: University of Minnesota Press.
Parekh, B. 1998. "Hannah Arendt". See Craig (1998), I, 369–73.
Ricoeur, P. 1990. "Action, Story, and History: On Rereading *The Human Condition*". In *The Realm of Humanitas: Responses to the Writings of Hannah Arendt,* R. Garner (ed.), 149–64. New York: Peter Lang.
Young-Bruehl, E. 1982. *Hannah Arendt: For Love of the World.* New Haven, CT: Yale University Press.

9. THE TWILIGHT OF ENLIGHTENMENT: THEODOR W. ADORNO AND MAX HORKHEIMER

Bernstein, J. M. 1998. "Theodor Wiesengrund Adorno". See Craig (1998), I, 41–6.

Buck-Morss, S. 2002. *The Origins of Negative Dialectics: Theodor W. Adorno, Walter Benjamin, and the Frankfurt Institute*. New York: Free Press.

Gibson, N. & A. Rubin 2002. *Adorno: A Critical Reader*. Oxford: Blackwell.

Hansen, M. 1993. "Of Mice and Ducks: Benjamin and Adorno on Disney". *South Atlantic Quarterly* **92**: 27–61.

Hewitt, A. 2004. "1947: Snatching Defeat from the Jaws of Victory". In *A New History of German Literature*, D. Wellbery & J. Ryan (eds), 835–40. Cambridge, MA: Harvard University Press.

Hohendahl, P. 1997. *Prismatic Thought: Theodor W. Adorno*. Lincoln, NE: University of Nebraska Press.

Huhn, T. 2004. "Introduction". In *The Cambridge Companion to Adorno*, T. Huhn (ed.), 1–18. Cambridge: Cambridge University Press.

Jameson, F. 2007. *Late Modernism: Adorno, Or, the Persistence of the Dialectic*. London: Verso.

Jay, M. 1984. *Adorno*. Cambridge, MA: Harvard University Press.

Rose, G. 1979. *The Melancholy Science: An Introduction to the Thought of Theodor W. Adorno*. London: Macmillan.

10. THE FUTURE AND FREEDOM: JEAN-PAUL SARTRE

Anderson, T. 1993. *Sartre's Two Ethics: From Authenticity to Integral Humanism*. Chicago, IL: Open Court.

Beauvoir, S. 1984. *Adieux: A Farewell to Sartre*, P. O'Brian (trans.). New York: Pantheon.

Brosman, C. S. 1983. *Jean-Paul Sartre*. Boston, MA: Twayne Publishers.

Caws, P. 1979. *Sartre*. London: Routledge & Kegan Paul.

Flynn, T. R. 1997, 2005. *Sartre, Foucault, and Historical Reason*, 2 vols. Chicago, IL: University of Chicago Press.

Hayman, R. 1987. *Sartre: A Biography*. New York: Simon & Schuster.

Howells, C. (ed.) 1992. *The Cambridge Companion to Sartre*. Cambridge: Cambridge University Press.

Kamber, R. 2000. *On Sartre*. Belmont, CA: Wadsworth.

McBride, W. 1991. *Sartre's Political Theory*. Bloomington, IN: Indiana University Press.

Silverman, H. & F. Elliston (eds) 1980. *Jean-Paul Sartre: Contemporary Approaches to His Philosophy*. Pittsburgh, PA: Duquesne University Press.

Thompson, K. & M. Thompson 1984. *Sartre: Life and Works*. New York: Facts on File.

11. THE FUTURE AND THE DISCLOSURE OF BEING: SIMONE DE BEAUVOIR

Arp, K. 2001. *The Bonds of Freedom: Simone de Beauvoir's Existentialist Ethics*. Chicago, IL: Open Court.

Bair, D. 1990. *Simone de Beauvoir: A Biography*. New York: Simon & Schuster.

Card, C. (ed.) 2003. *The Cambridge Companion to the Philosophy of Simone de Beauvoir*. Cambridge: Cambridge University Press.

Grosholz, E. R. (ed.) 2004. *The Legacy of Simone de Beauvoir*. Oxford: Oxford University Press.

Holveck, E. 2002. *Simone de Beauvoir's Philosophy of Lived Experience: Literature and Metaphysics*. Lanham, MD: Rowman & Littlefield.

Moi, T. 1994. *Simone de Beauvoir: The Making of an Intellectual Woman*. Oxford: Blackwell.

Simons, M. 1999. *Beauvoir and The Second Sex: Feminism, Race, and the Origins of Existentialism*. Lanham, MD: Rowman & Littlefield.

Simons, M. (ed.) 2003. *The Philosophy of Simone de Beauvoir*. Bloomington, IN: Indiana University Press.

Sullivan, S. (ed.) 1999. "The Work of Simone de Beauvoir". *Journal of Speculative Philosophy* **13**(1), special issue.

Tidd, U. 2004. *Simone de Beauvoir*. London: Routledge.

12. THE FUTURE AS RUPTURE: MICHEL FOUCAULT

Armstrong, T. J. (ed.) 1992. *Michel Foucault Philosopher*. London: Routledge.
Bernauer, J. 1990. *Michel Foucault's Force of Flight: Toward an Ethics for Thought*. Atlantic Highlands, NJ: Humanities Press.
Bernauer, J. & D. Rasmussen (eds) 1988. *The Final Foucault*. Boston, MA: MIT Press.
Deleuze, G. 1986. *Foucault*. Paris: Editions de Minuit.
Gutting, G.1989. *Michel Foucault's Archeology of Scientific Knowledge*. Cambridge: Cambridge University Press.
Horrocks, C. 2005 *Introducing Foucault*, 3rd edn. London: Icon.
Hoy, D. C. 1986. *Foucault: A Critical Reader*. Oxford: Blackwell.
Lemert, C. & G. Gillian 1982. *Michel Foucault: Social Theory and Transgression*. New York: Columbia University Press.
Mills, S. 2003. *Michel Foucault*. London: Routledge.
Poster, M. 1989. "Foucault and the Tyranny of Greece". In his *Critical Theory and Poststructuralism*, 87–103. Ithaca, NY: Cornell University Press.
Rascevskis, K. 1983. *Michel Foucault and the Subversion of Intellect*. Ithaca, NY: Cornell University Press.
Visker, R. 1995. *Michel Foucault: Genealogy As Critique*, C. Turner (trans.). London: Verso.

13. THE FUTURE AND HOPE: JACQUES DERRIDA

Bennington, G. & J. Derrida 1999. *Jacques Derrida*. Chicago, IL: University of Chicago Press.
Caputo, J. D. 1996. *Deconstruction in a Nutshell: A Conversation with Jacques Derrida*. New York: Fordham University Press.
Deutscher, P. 2005. *How to Read Derrida*. London: Granta.
Niall, L. 2004. *A Derrida Dictionary*. Oxford: Blackwell.
Norris, C. 1988. *Derrida*. Cambridge, MA: Harvard University Press.
Powell, J. 2006. *Jacques Derrida: A Biography*. New York: Continuum.
Reynolds, J. & J. Roffe (eds) 2004. *Understanding Derrida*. New York: Continuum.
Royle, N. 2003. *Jacques Derrida*. London: Routledge.
Stocker, B. 2006. *Routledge Philosophy Guidebook to Derrida on Deconstruction*. London: Routledge.

BIBLIOGRAPHY

Adorno, T. W. 1973. *Negative Dialectics*, E. B. Alston (trans.). New York: Seabury Press.

Adorno, T. W. 2001. *Kant's Critique of Pure Reason*, R. Livingstone (trans.). Stanford, CA: Stanford University Press.

Agamben, G. 1998. *Homo Sacer*, D. Heller-Roazen (trans.). Stanford, CA: Stanford University Press.

Agamben, G. 2005. *State of Exception*, K. Attell (trans.). Chicago, IL: University of Chicago Press.

Agamben, G. 2009. *The Signature of All Things*, L. D'Isanto & K.Attell (trans.). New York: Zone Books.

Anscombe, G. E. M. & P. Geach 1961. *Three Philosophers*. Oxford: Blackwell.

Arendt, H. 1958. *The Human Condition*. Chicago, IL: University of Chicago Press.

Arendt, H. 1980. "On Violence". In *Self and World: Readings in Philosophy*, J. Ogilvy (ed.), 346–55. New York: Harcourt, Brace, Jovanovich.

Arenson, K. W. 2004. "In Protest, Professor Cancels Visit To the US". *New York Times* (17 January). www.nytimes.com/2004/01/17/nyregion/in-protest-professor-cancels-visit-to-the-us.html (accessed June 2011).

Bacon, F. 1939. *Novum organum*. In *The English Philosophers from Bacon to Mill*, E. A. Burtt (ed.), 24–123. New York: Modern Library.

Badiou, A. 1999. *Manifesto for Philosophy: Followed by Two Essays: "The (Re)Turn of Philosophy Itself" and "Definition of Philosophy"*, N. Madaras (trans.). Albany, NY: SUNY Press.

Badiou, A. 2001. *Logic of Worlds*, A. Toscano (trans.). London: Continuum.

Badiou, A. 2006. *Being and Event*, O. Feltham (trans.). London: Continuum.

Badiou, A. 2008. *Conditions*, S. Corcoran (trans.). London: Continuum.

Beauvoir, S. 1948. *The Ethics of Ambiguity*, B. Frechtman (trans.). New York: Kensington.

Beauvoir, S. 1962. *The Prime of Life*, P. Green (trans.). Cleveland, OH: World Publishing.

Berkeley, G. 1982. *Of the Principles of Human Knowledge*, K. P. Winkler (ed.). Indianapolis, IN: Hackett.

Berlin, I. 1996. *Karl Marx: His Life and Environment*, 4th edn. Oxford: Oxford University Press.

Bertholet, D. 2000. *Sartre*. Paris: Plon

Borradori, G. 2003. *Philosophy in a Time of Terror: Dialogues with Jürgen Habermas and Jacques Derrida*. Chicago, IL: University of Chicago Press.

Buber, M. 1958. *I and Thou*, 2nd edn, R. G. Smith (trans.). New York: Scribner's.

Butler, J. 1990. *Gender Trouble*. London: Routledge.

Butler, J. 1997. *Excitable Speech: A Politics of the Performative*. London: Routledge.

Butler, J. 2004. *Precarious Life*. London: Verso.

Cooper, J. 1986. *Reason and Human Good in Aristotle*. Indianapolis, IN: Hackett.

Cottingham, J. 1986. *Descartes*. Oxford: Blackwell.

Craig, E. (ed.) 1998. *The Routledge Encyclopedia of Philosophy*, 10 vols. London: Routledge.

Critchley, S. 2001. *Continental Philosophy: A Very Short Introduction*. Oxford: Oxford University Press.

Cutrofello, A. 2005. *Continental Philosophy: A Contemporary Introduction*. New York: Routledge.

Deleuze, G. 1994. *Difference and Repetition*, P. Patton (trans.). New York: Columbia University Press.

Derrida, J. 1977. "Signature Event Context". *Glyph* **1**: 172–97 .

Derrida, J. 1988. *Limited Inc.*, G. Graff (ed.). Evanston, IL: Northwestern University Press.

Derrida, J. 1995. *Points: Interviews 1974–1994*, E. Weber (ed.). Stanford, CA: Stanford University Press.

Derrida, J. 1997. *The Politics of Friendship*, G. Collins (trans.). London: Verso.

Descartes, R. 1985. *The Philosophical Writings of Descartes*, 2 vols, J. Cottingham, A. Kenney, D. Murdoch & R. Stoothoff (trans.). Cambridge: Cambridge University Press.

Dover, K. J. 1979. *Greek Homosexuality*. Cambridge, MA: Harvard University Press.

Eribon, D. 1991. *Michel Foucault*, B. Wing (trans.). Cambridge, MA: Harvard University Press.

Faulkner, W. 1950. "May Man Prevail" (Nobel Prize acceptance speech). http://nobelprize.org/nobel_prizes/literature/laureates/1949/faulkner-speech.html (accessed March 2011).

Feldman, K. & W. O'Neill 1998. *Continental Philosophy: An Anthology*. Oxford; Blackwell.

Findlay, J. N. 1958. *Hegel: A Re-examination*. London: Allen & Unwin.

Foucault, M. 1972. *The Archeology of Knowledge*, A. M. Sheridan Smith (trans.). New York: Pantheon.

Foucault, M. 1979. *Discipline and Punish*, A. Sheridan (trans.). New York: Vintage.

Foucault, M. 1984. *The Foucault Reader*. New York: Pantheon.

Foucault, M. 1985. *The History of Sexuality, II: The Use of Pleasure*, R. Hurley (trans.). New York: Random House.

Frege, G. 1980. *The Foundations of Arithmetic*. J. L. Austin (trans.). Evanston, IL: Northwestern University Press.

Garff, J. 2005. *Søren Kierkegaard: A Biography*. B. Kirmmse (trans.). Princeton, NJ: Princeton University Press.

Geuss, R. 1998. "Critical Theory". See Craig (1998): II, 722–8.

Glendinning, S. 2006. *The Idea of Continental Philosophy*. Edinburgh: Edinburgh University Press.

Golumbia, D. 1999. "Quine, Derrida, and the Question of Philosophy". *Philosophical Forum* **30**: 163–86.

Greene, W. C. 1944. *Fate, Good, and Evil in Greek Thought*. Cambridge, MA: Harvard University Press.

Gutting, G. 2001. *French Philosophy in the Twentieth Century*. Cambridge: Cambridge University Press.

Guyer, P. 2006. *Kant*. London: Routledge.

Habermas, J. 1979. "What is Universal Pragmatics?" In his *Communication and the Evolution of Society*, T. McCarthy (trans.), 1–68. Boston, MA: Beacon Press.

Habermas, J. 1984–87. *The Theory of Communicative Action*, 2 vols, T. McCarthy (trans.). Boston, MA: Beacon Press.

Habermas, J. 1987. *The Philosophical Discourse of Modernity*. F. Lawrence (trans.). Cambridge, MA: MIT Press.

Habermas, J. 1989. "Work and Weltanschauung: The Heidegger Controversy from a German Perspective". *Critical Inquiry* **15**: 431–56.

Hegel, G. W. F. 1952. *Phänomenologie des Geistes*, 6th edn, J. Hoffmeister (ed.). Hamburg: Meiner.

Hegel, G. W. F. 1953. *Reason in History*, R. Hartman (trans.). Englewood Cliffs, NJ: Prentice Hall.

Hegel, G. W. F. 1970–71. *Werke*, E. Moldenhauer & K. M. Michel (eds), 20 vols. Frankfurt: Suhrkamp.

Hegel, G. W. F. 1974. *Lectures on the History of Philosophy*, 2 vols, E. S. Haldane & F. H. Simson (trans.). New York: Humanities Press.

Hegel, G. W. F. 1975a. *Aesthetics*, 2 vols with consecutive pagination, T. M. Knox (trans.). Oxford: Oxford University Press.

Hegel, G. W. F. 1975b. *Hegel's Logic*, W. Wallace (trans.). Oxford: Clarendon Press.

Hegel, G. W. F. 1976. *The Science of Logic*, A. V. Miller (trans.). New York: Humanities Press.

Hegel, G. W. F. [1807] 1979. *Phenomenology of Spirit*, A. V. Miller (trans.). Oxford: Oxford University Press.

Hegel, G. W. F. 1983. *Philosophie des Rechts: Die Vorlesung von 1819/20 in einer Nachschrift*, D. Henrich (ed.). Frankfurt: Suhrkamp.

Hegel, G. W. F. 1991. *Elements of the Philosophy of Right*, H. B. Nisbet (trans.). Cambridge: Cambridge University Press.

Heidegger, M. 1927. *Sein und Zeit*. Special issue of *Jahrbuch für Philosophie und phänomenologische Forschung*, E. Husserl (ed.) **8**.

Heidegger, M. 1962. *Being and Time*, J. MacQuarrie & E. Robinson (trans.). New York: Harper & Row.

Heidegger, M. 1971a. "The Origin of the Work of Art". In his *Poetry, Language, Thought*, A. Hofstadter (trans.), 15–88. New York: Harper & Row.

Heidegger, M. 1971b. *Der Satz vom Grund*, 4th edn. Pfullingen: Neske.

Heidegger, M. 1977. "The Question Concerning Technology". In his *Basic Writings*, D. F. Krell (trans.), 284–317. San Francisco: Harper & Row.

Heidegger, M. 2002. "The Onto-theo-logical Constitution of Metaphysics". In his *Identity and Difference*, J. Stambaugh (trans.), 422–74. Chicago, IL: University of Chicago Press.

Heine, H. 1973 *Selected Works*, H. Mustard (ed. & trans.). New York: Random House.

Hersch, R. 1999. *What is Mathematics, Really?* Oxford: Oxford University Press.

Hobbes, T. 1991. *Leviathan*, R. Tuck (ed.). Cambridge: Cambridge University Press.

Homer 1990. *The Iliad*, R. Fagles (trans.). New York: Viking.

Homer 1996. *The Odyssey*, R. Fagles (trans.). New York: Viking.

Horkheimer, M. & T. W. Adorno 1994. *Dialectic of Enlightenment*, J. Cumming (trans.). New York: Continuum.

Hume, D. 1888. *A Treatise of Human Nature*, L. A. Selby-Bigge (ed.). Oxford: Clarendon.

Hume, D. 1894. *Enquiry Concerning Human Understanding*. In his *Enquiries*, L. A. Selby-Bigge (ed.), 5–165. Oxford: Clarendon Press.

Hume, D. 1985. *Essays Moral, Political and Literary*, E. F. Miller (ed.). Indianapolis, IN: Liberty Fund.

Husserl, E. 1970a. *The Crisis of European Sciences and Transcendental Phenomenology*, D. Carr (trans.). Evanston, IL: Northwestern University Press.

Husserl, E. 1970b. "Prolegomena to Pure Logic". In his *Logical Investigations*, 2 vols, J. N. Findlay (trans.), I, 53–247. London: Routledge and Kegan Paul.

Husserl, E. 1970c. *Cartesian Meditations*, D. Cairns (trans.). The Hague: Martinus Nijhoff.

Husserl, E. 1991. *On the Phenomenology of the Consciousness of Internal Time*, J. B. Brough (trans.). Dordrecht: Kluwer.

Jäger, L. 2004. *Adorno: A Political Biography*, S. Spencer (trans.). New Haven, CT: Yale University Press.

Jöttkandt, S. 2010. "Love". In *Alain Badiou: Key Concepts*, A. J. Bartlett & J. Clemens (eds), 73–81. Durham: Acumen.

Kant, I. 1967. *Philosophical Correspondence 1759–99*, A. Zweig (ed.). Chicago, IL: University of Chicago Press.

Kant, I. 1987. *Critique of Judgment*, W. S. Pluhar (trans.). Indianapolis, IN: Hackett.

Kant, I. 1996a. "An Answer to the Question: What is Enlightenment?" In his *Practical Philosophy*. M. J. Gregor (ed. & trans.), 11–22. Cambridge: Cambridge University Press.

Kant, I. 1996b. *Critique of Pure Reason*, W. S. Pluhar (trans.). Indianapolis, IN: Hackett.

Kaufmann, W. 1956. *Nietzsche: Philosopher, Psychologist, Antichrist*. Cleveland, OH: Meridian Books.

Kierkegaard, S. 1941a. *Concluding Unscientific Postscript*, D. Swenson & W. Lowrie (trans.). Princeton, NJ: Princeton University Press.

Kierkegaard, S. 1941b. *Fear and Trembling and The Sickness Unto Death*, W. Lowrie (trans.). Princeton, NJ: Princeton University Press.

Kierkegaard, S. 1946 "The Unchangeableness of God" (sermon of 1851). In *A Kierkegaard Anthology*, R. Bretall (ed.), 469–82. Princeton, NJ: Princeton University Press.

Kierkegaard, S. 1962. *Point of View for My Work as an Author*, W. Lowrie (trans.) New York: Harper Torchbooks.

Kierkegaard, S. 1980. *The Concept of Anxiety*, R. Thomte (ed.). Princeton, NJ: Princeton University Press.

Kierkegaard, S. 2009. *Repetition and Philosophical Crumbs*, M. G. Piety (trans.). Oxford: Oxford University Press.

Kirk, G. S. & J. E. Raven 1960. *The Presocratic Philosophers*. Cambridge: Cambridge University Press.

Kirmmse, B. (ed.) 1996. *Encounters With Kierkegaard*. Princeton, NJ: Princeton University Press.

Kolb, D. 1986. *The Critique of Pure Modernity*. Chicago, IL: University of Chicago Press.

Kuehn, M. 2001. *Kant; A Biography*. Cambridge: Cambridge University Press.

Kuhn, T. 1970. *The Structure of Scientific Revolutions*, 2nd edn. Chicago, IL: University of Chicago Press.

Lauer, Q. 1967. "On Evidence". In *Phenomenology: The Philosophy of Edmund Husserl and its Interpretation*, J. J. Kockelmans (ed.), 150–57. Garden City, NY: Doubleday Anchor.

Locke, J. 1960. "Second Treatise of Government". In his *Two Treatises of Government,* P. Laslett (ed.), 265–428. Cambridge: Cambridge University Press.

Marx, K. 1906. *Capital,* S. Morse & E. Aveling (trans.). New York: Modern Library.

Marx, K. 1988. *Economic and Philosophical Manuscripts of 1844 and the Communist Manifesto,* M. Milligan (trans.). Amherst, NY: Prometheus Books.

Marx, K. 1994a. *Selected Writings,* L. Simon (ed.). Indianapolis, IN: Hackett.

Marx, K. 1994b. "Theses on Feuerbach". In his *Selected Writings,* L. Simon (ed.). Indianapolis, IN: Hackett.

Marx, W. 1971. *Heidegger and the Tradition,* T. Kisiel & M. Greene (trans.). Evanston, IL: Northwestern University Press.

McCumber, J. 1988. "Aristotelian Catharsis and the Purgation of Woman," *Diacritics* **18**(4): 53–67.

McCumber, J. 1989. *Poetic Interaction: Language, Freedom, Reason.* Chicago, IL: University of Chicago Press.

McCumber, J. 1993. *The Company of Words: Hegel, Language, and Systematic Philosophy.* Evanston, IL: Northwestern University Press.

McCumber, J. 1999. *Metaphysics and Oppression.* Bloomington, IN: Indiana University Press.

McCumber, J. 2000. *Philosophy and Freedom.* Bloomington, IN: Indiana University Press.

McCumber, J. 2001. *Time in the Ditch: American Philosophy and the McCarthy Era.* Evanston, IL: Northwestern University Press.

McCumber, J. 2005. *Reshaping Reason: Toward a New Philosophy.* Bloomington, IN: Indiana University Press.

McTaggart, J. M. E. 1908. "The Unreality of Time". *Mind* **18**: 457–74.

Mendelssohn, M. 1969. *Jerusalem and Other Jewish Writings,* A. Jospe (ed.). New York: Schocken Books.

Merleau-Ponty, M. 1962. *Phenomenology of Perception,* C. Smith (trans.). London: Routledge & Kegan Paul.

Mill, J. S. 1970. *A System of Logic.* London: Longman.

Mure, G. R. G. 1940. *Hegel: An Introduction.* Oxford: Clarendon Press.

Nietzsche, F. 1979. "On Truth and Lies in a Nonmoral Sense". In his *Philosophy and Truth,* D. Breazeale (ed.), 79–97. Amherst, NY: Humanity Books.

Nietzsche, F. 1986. *Human, All Too Human: A Book for Free Spirits,* R. J. Hollingdale (trans.). Cambridge: Cambridge University Press.

Nietzsche, F. 1989. *Beyond Good and Evil,* W. Kaufmann (trans.). New York: Vintage.

Nietzsche, F. [1887] 1994. *On the Genealogy of Morality,* C. Diethe (trans.). Cambridge: Cambridge University Press.

Nietzsche, F. 2005. *The Anti-Christ, Ecce Homo, Twilight of the Idols, and Other Writings,* A. Ridley & J. Norman (eds.). Cambridge: Cambridge University Press.

Nietzsche, F. 2006. *Thus Spake Zarathustra,* R. Pippin (ed.). Cambridge: Cambridge University Press.

Nussbaum, C. 1996. "Kant's Changing Conception of the Causality of the Will". *International Philosophical Quarterly* **36**: 265–86.

Ott, H. 1988. *Martin Heidegger: Unterwegs zu seiner Biographie.* Frankfurt: Campus Verlag.

Pinkard, T. 2000. *Hegel: A Biography.* Cambridge: Cambridge University Press.

Powell, J. 2006. *Jacques Derrida: A Biography.* New York: Continuum.

Quine, W. V. 1960. *Word and Object.* Cambridge, MA: MIT Press.

Quine, W. V. 1982. *Methods of Logic,* 2nd edn. Cambridge, MA: Harvard University Press.

Quine, W. V. 1987. *Quiddities.* Cambridge, MA: Harvard University Press.

Rancière, J. 2004. *The Politics of Aesthetics: The Distribution of the Sensible,* G. Rockhill (trans.). London: Continuum.

Rancière, J. 2009. *The Emancipated Spectator,* G. Elliott (trans.). London: Verso.

Rorty, R. 1989. *Contingency, Irony, and Solidarity.* Cambridge: Cambridge University Press.

Rosen, M. 1996. *On Voluntary Servitude: False Consciousness and the Theory of Ideology.* Cambridge: Polity Press.

Russell, B. 1959. *The Problems of Philosophy.* New York: Galaxy.

Safranski, R. 1998. *Martin Heidegger: Between Good and Evil,* E. Osers (trans.). Cambridge, MA: Harvard University Press.

Safranski, R. 2003. *Nietzsche: A Philosophical Biography*, S. Frisch (trans.). London: Granta.

Sartre, J.-P. 1948. *Anti-Semite and Jew: An Exploration of the Etiology of Hate*, G. J. Becker (trans.). New York: Schocken Books.

Sartre, J.-P. 1976. *Critique of Dialectical Reason*, A. Sheridan-Smith (trans.). London: Verso. Originally published in French as *Critique de la raison dialectique* (Paris: Gallimard, 1960).

Sartre, J.-P. 2001. *Basic Writings*, S. Priest (ed.). London: Routledge.

Schelling, F. W. J. 1936. *Of Human Freedom*, J. Gutmann (trans.). Chicago, IL: Open Court.

Schiller, F. 1939. *Schillers Werke*, A. Kutscher (ed.). Berlin: Bong.

Schroeder, W. R. 2004. *Continental Philosophy: A Critical Approach*. Oxford: Blackwell.

Sedgwick, P. (ed.) 1995. *Nietzsche: A Critical Reader*. Oxford: Blackwell.

Singer, D. 2002. *Prelude to Revolution: France in May 1968*, 2nd edn. Cambridge, MA: South End Press.

Smith, D. W. 2006. *Husserl*. London: Routledge.

Smolin, L. 1997. *The Life of the Cosmos*. Oxford: Oxford University Press.

Solomon, R. C. 1988. *Continental Philosophy since 1750: The Rise and Fall of the Self*. Oxford: Oxford University Press.

Stepelevich, L. (ed.) 1983. *The Young Hegelians: An Anthology*. Cambridge: Cambridge University Press.

Ströker, E. 1993. *Husserl's Transcendental Phenomenology*, L. Hardy (trans.). Stanford, CA: Stanford University Press.

Suskind, R. 2004. "Faith, Certainty and the Presidency of George W. Bush". *New York Times Magazine* (17 October). www.nytimes.com/2004/10/17/magazine/17BUSH.html?_r=2&ex=1255665600&en=890a96189e162076&ei=5090&partner=rssuserland (accessed March 2011).

Taylor, C. 1975. *Hegel*. Cambridge: Cambridge University Press.

Waxman, W. 1989. *Kant's Model of the Mind*. Oxford: Oxford University Press.

Weber, M. 1918. "Science as a Vocation". Lecture presented at Munich University. www.ne.jp/asahi/moriyuki/abukuma/weber/lecture/science_frame.html (accessed June 2011).

West, D. 1996. *An Introduction to Continental Philosophy*. Oxford: Polity Press.

Wheen, F. 2001. *Karl Marx: A Life*. New York: Norton.

White Beck, L. 1967. "Neo-Kantianism". In *The Encyclopedia of Philosophy*, 8 vols, P. Edwards (ed.), vol. 5, 428. New York: Macmillan.

Wiggershaus, R. 1994. *The Frankfurt School: Its History, Theories, and Political Significance*, M. Robertson (trans.). Cambridge, MA: MIT Press.

Wittgenstein, L. 1958. *Philosophical Investigations*, 3rd edn, G. E. M. Anscombe (trans.). New York: Macmillan.

Wittgenstein, L. 1969. *On Certainty*, G. E. M. Anscombe & G. H. von Wright (eds). New York: J. & J. Harper.

Wolin, R. 1994. *The Politics of Being*. New York: Columbia University Press.

Young-Bruehl, E. 1982. *Hannah Arendt: For Love of the World*. New Haven, CT: Yale University Press.

Zagzebski, L. 2008. "Foreknowledge and Free Will". In *Stanford Encyclopedia of Philosophy* (Fall 2008 edition), E. N. Zalta (ed.). http://plato.stanford.edu/archives/fall2008/entries/free-will-foreknowledge/ (accessed March 2011).

INDEX

Abraham 95
Absolute, the 34
absolute theory 34
absurdity 89, 299
Achtung 25
action 209–11, 273, 275–6, 302–6
active forgetfulness 114
active groups 284
acts of consciousness 134
Adam and Eve 80–81
administration 237, 239, 278
administrative projections 247
administrative reason 237, 308
Adorno, Theodor 9, 17, 225–49
  brief biography 226–7
  Negative Dialectics 228–34
  synthesis of Marx and Kant 229
  see also Frankfurt School; Horkheimer, Max
adventurer 296–7
aesthetics 366
Agamben, Giorgio 352, 373–80, 389–90
alien subjectivity 154
alienation 279
ambiguity 288, 299
amusement 244
anatomico-metaphysical register 326
Anaxagoras 44–5
Angst 79, 173, 174
anguish 260
anomie 377
anti-Americanism, Frankfurt students 225–6
anti-Semitism 233–4, 236, 247, 283
antinomy of action 302–6
anxiety 80, 90–91
apodictic evidence 135

appearance model 19–20, 163, 167–8
appearances 19, 22
archein 210
Arendt, Hannah 9, 201–24
  brief biography 202
  future and natality 220–21
  labour and work 214–19
  oikos 205–6, 208, 213, 219
  polis 205–6, 207, 210, 219
  power and force 219–20
  society 211–14
  speech and action 209–11
  summary and conclusions 222–4
  temporality 202
  vita activa 202–5
argument from desire 269–70
Aristotle 5, 24–5, 143, 170, 172–3, 187, 189–90,
  214, 256–7, 327, 335–6, 342–3
armies 325–6
art
  allied to philosophy 233
  creation and enjoyment 366–7
  exclusion from philosophy 359
  experiencing 183
  job of 198
  as justification 299–300
  and politics 367–70
  as representation 369
  temporality of 370–71
  and truth 182
  see also culture industry; Heidegger
ascetic ideals 117–23, 203
atemporal domain 96
atemporal knowledge 17
atemporal objects 18–19

atemporality   30, 82–3, 130, 316, 318
atonement   87
auctoritas   375
authenticity   171–2, 174–5
authority   378
auxiliary conditions   25
awareness, through art   178–9

Bacon, Francis   235
bad conscience   116
bad faith   89–90, 295–8
Badiou, Alain   352, 354–64, 371, 389
badness   108
bare life   376–7, 379
basic and derivative, opposition of   38
basic properties   195
beauty   118, 366–7
Beauvoir, Simone de   9–10, 287–312, 381–2
    antinomy of action   302–6
    challenge to Sartre   294
    consciousness and community   293–8
    disclosure of being   288–93
    liberation and oppression   298–302
    summary and conclusions   310–12
bebaios   338
Being   166, 175–6
being-in-the-world   167
being-with   170–71
being-with others   171
beings, understanding   168–9
Berkeley, George   142, 232, 262, 265
Bestand   192
Bestimmungsgründe   25
Bewährung   146
bios   375
birth   221
birth of the priests   109–11
bisexuality   *see* sexuality
body   153–4, 217, 321, 325–7, 329, 387, 389
Bonaparte, Napoleon   31
bourgeoisie   60–61, 63–4, 227
bracketing   136–9, 151–3
Brentano, Franz   143
Butler, Judith   352, 380–89

Canguilhem, Georges   314–15
Cantor, Georg   354–5
Cartesian Meditations   131–3
catastrophe theory of history   54
categorical imperative   20, 115
causality   15, 23–5, 30, 190
causes, temporality   24
certainties   38–9

challenging   198
changing and unchanging   38
children   293–4
choice   260–61
Christianity
    as absurd and dread-ful   94–5
    Heine   123
    Kierkegaard   87–94
    Nietzsche   99–100, 117
    possibilities of eternity   89
    as religion of dread   89
Cicero   336
civilizations, Hegel's ranking   46–7
claiming   191–2
clarity and distinctness   133
class struggle   64, 66
classical thought   97–8
Climacus, Johannes   89
co-intended aspects   144–5
cogito   268, 289, 382
cognition   17–18, 167
commodification   239
communal activity   74–5
communication   91, 94
communion   94
communism   63, 73–4
    crude   73–4
The Communist Manifesto   60–64
community of sense   367
complete knowability, of consciousness   142–3
concealment   165–6
concept, of a thing   245
The Concept of Dread   79–81
conditions   356
confirmation   146
conflict   113
conscience   114–15
consciousness
    Beauvoir   311–12, 382
    Hegel   33–4
    Heidegger   164
    Husserl   138, 141–3, 255, 263–4, 268–9, 285
    non-positional   264
    and the object   40
    overcoming   40
    Sartre   256, 262–5, 268–9, 278, 285, 290,
        311–12
    ultimate truth as goal   36
constitution   52–3, 152
contemporary philosophy   351–3
contempt   109
contestation   309
context of involvement   169–70

continental philosophy
brief history   8–10
contemporary   389–93
continuity   7
ignorance of   1–3
importance   1
influence of   392–3
lack of explanation   2
philosophical bases   390–91, 393
as philosophical resonance of time   10–11
contradictions   33
conversion   88
correctness   188
creative people   298
*The Crisis of European Sciences and
     Transcendental Phenomenology*   131
Critchley, Simon   3–4, 351
critic   297–8
critical theory   249
Critique of Judgment   118, 131, 233
Critique of Pure Reason   233
cruelty   115
cultural dialectics   240–42
cultural Marxism   240
culture   29
culture industry   242–5; *see also* art
custom   16

damnation   88–9
das Man   171–4
Dasein   166, 169–76, 180
death   172–6, 182–3, 198–9
demonic, the   91–2
dēmos   366
Derrida, Jaques   10, 331–48
approach to work   332–4
brief biography   331–2
friendship   335–7
history of philosophy   334–5
loving in friendship   337–43
and Nietzsche   340
recoil   342–5
summary and conclusions   346–8
on terrorism   347
Descartes, René   6, 133, 138, 254–5, 268, 326–7
desire, argument from   269–70
determinism   23–4, 275–7
dialectics   58, 187, 228–34, 246
discipline, and normalization   328–9
disciplined surveillance   328
disciplines   330, 366
disclosure   182
of being   288–93, 298–9, 311

discourse of physiology   326–7
discourses   330
disenchantment   235
dispute   182
distantiation   172
distinction, and antagonism   34
distribution   365
of invisibility   328
diversity   3–4, 54, 210
division of labour   218
docile body   329
dominance of the other   171
dominating   105
Douglas, Mary   387
dread   88–9, 92–3, 173
dreams   80
dualisms   263
dynamism, of artists' materials   181–2

earth   181–4
education   63
efficient causality   24–5
ego   37, 137, 149
eidetic reduction   149–51, 155–6, 263–4
eidos   150–51, 263, 318
Eigenwüchsigkeit   177
elements, in set theory   355
empirical and noumenal realms   27, 29
end, action and motive   275–6
ends, choice of   310
enframing   193, 197
Engels, Friedrich   60, 277
Enlightenment   234–40
Entzauberung   235
epistemology   119, 143
epochē   136–9
equal opportunity   281
equality   361
equipment   176–8, 257
Erkenntnis   17
Erscheinungen   19
essences   5, 197–8, 318
estranged labour   66–72
eternal life   89
eternity   83–6, 89, 95–6
ethics   256–62
Hegelian   82
Kant   16, 20, 129–30
Sartre   254–6
in traditional philosophy   259
event   356–7
evidence   133–6, 146–7, 155, 265
evil   83

existentialism 256–62, 289
expectation 247
experience 16
exploitation 61
exteriority 263
external world, objectivity 152

faculties, reasons for 22–3
faith, and risk 92
family 63
fanaticism 297
fantasy 149–50, 155
fascism 227–8, 247, 276
fate 90
Faulkner, William 271
felicity 239
Feltham, Oliver 355
fidelity 357
figments of the brain 18
final causality 25, 27
Findlay, John 34–5
finite future 199–200
finitization 10, 223–4
for-itself 267, 272–3
force 219–20
forces 113
forgiveness 81
form 257
Forms 5, 16, 86, 322–3, 381
Foucault, Michel 10, 313–30, 366, 384, 386
 brief biography 313–14
 discipline and normalization 328–9
 Discipline and Punish 324–8
 disciplines 324–8
 "Docile Bodies" 324
 genealogy 374
 history without metaphysics 320–24
 on mental illness 324–5
 "Nietzsche, Genealogy, History" 315–20
 origins of genealogy 314–16
 summary and conclusions 329–30
four causes 189–90
Frankfurt School 225–49, 278
 in America 226
 critique of Enlightenment 234–40
 cultural dialectics 240–42
 culture industry 242–5
 development of Marxist thought 227–8
 dialectics 246
 foundation of 226
 Juliette 242
 Odyssey 241–2
 rejection of idealism 230–32

student protest 226
summary and conclusions 245–9
updating of Kant 229–32
 see also Adorno, Theodor; Horkheimer, Max
freedom 23–4, 27, 30
 Beauvoir 288–93, 298
 as communicative 91
 as constitution 52–3
 development of idea 47
 embodied in state 55
 Hegel 315–16
 Kierkegaard 88
 Marx 63, 69
 Sartre 260, 274–7
Frege, Gottlob 130
French Revolution 31
Freud, Sigmund 142, 383–5
 Freunde des Verewigten 58
friendship 335–7
 canonical and recoil 342–5
 and enmity 342
 loving in 337–43
 removal from politics 346
 types of 343
future
 Arendt 220–22
 Beauvoir 304–6, 311
 Derrida 345, 347–8
 finite 199–200
 finitization 223–4
 Foucault 330
 Frankfurt School 246–7
 Hegel 55, 65, 78–9
 Heidegger 175–6, 182–3, 194–5, 199–200, 223, 262, 347
 Kierkegaard 79–80, 94–6, 123–4, 200, 223
 Marx 65, 78, 123–4, 277
 messianic 305–10
 Nietzsche 109, 114, 123–4, 340
 as possible 88
 as radically open 194
 Sartre 273–4

Gadamer, Hans-Georg 352
Gattungswesen 69
Geist 33
gender 380–89, 390
gendering 382–5
genealogy 102–4, 202, 314–16, 323–4, 374, 383;
 see also Foucault; Nietzsche
genius 90
Germany 31
Gestell 193, 195–6, 198

globalization 61
goal-directed activities 170
goals 307–8
God 45–6, 103, 257
Godhead 34
good and evil; good and bad 107–13
goodness 107–9, 254–5, 261
granting 198
great noon 101–2
Greeks
    idea of death 204–5
    influence on continental philosophy 98
guilt 90–91, 113–15

happiness 28–9
Hegel, Georg 8, 31–56, 315–16, 353
    and Butler 387–8
    on dialectics 228
    distortion of philosophy by "Friends" 58–9
    early career 31–2
    ending Spirit's quest 39–40
    ethics 82
    final outcome 39–42
    history as rational 43–4
    Kierkegaard's criticism of 81–3
    on objects 231–2
    Phenomenology of Spirit 32–42
    Reason in History 42–51
    recapitulation of Phenomenology 41
    refusal to speculate on future 65
    self-referentiality 42
    summary and conclusions 55–6
    temporality 78, 129
    temporalization 358
    theory of historical state 51–5
    transformations in reason 44–6
hegemony 338–9
Heidegger, Martin 9–10, 159–200, 233, 257, 359
    authenticity 171–2, 174–5
    Being and Time 161–6
    brief biography 160–61
    criticism of 199–200
    on death 172, 182–3, 198–9
    development from Husserl 199
    earth 181–4
    and Foucault 330
    and Husserl 127
    language as poetry 184–7
    misunderstanding by later philosophers 186
    nature of thought 245
    and Nazi Germany 159–60
    "The Origin of the Work of Art" 176–81
    phenomenology 161–6

phenomenology and fundamental ontology
    165–6
    "The Question Concerning Technology"
    187–98
    shared role in phenomenology 157–8
    subject and object 167–8
    summary and conclusions 199–200
    on traditional philosophy 4
    worldhood of the world 167–70
    see also art; poetry
Heine, Heinrich 100–101, 123–4
Heraclitus 8
hermeneutical 166
hierarchy of possibles 274–5
Hirngespenster 18, 20
historical materialism 303
historical processes 321–3
historical ruptures 314–15
history
    continued importance 109
    as development of freedom 46–7
    goal of 239
    making 279
    use of individuals 48
    ways of doing 43
    without metaphysics 320–24
Hobbes, Thomas 206
Holocaust 247–8, 379
homo sacer 378–9, 390
homogenous vanishing 84
homosexuality see sexuality
Horkheimer, Max 9, 225–49; see also Adorno,
    Theodor; Frankfurt School
Human All Too Human 101–2
human condition 259
human cooperation 34
human flourishing 104, 111, 122, 170
human individual 47–8, 50
human nature
    Beauvoir 290, 292, 329
    Kant 29
    Marx 68–70
    Sartre 257, 262, 329
human temporality 87
humanism 74, 256–62
humanity 195
humans 28, 69–70, 188–9
Hume, David 6–7, 15–17
Husserl, Edmund 9, 127–58
    atemporality 130
    brief biography 128
    Cartesian Meditations and ideal of science
    131–3

Descartes 138
eidetic reduction 149–51, 155–6, 263–4
evidence 133–6, 146–7, 155
horizons 143–6
intentionality 139–40, 155–6
intersubjectivity 151–4
mathematics 129
nature 152–3
and Nazi Germany 127–8
phenomenological reduction 136–9
problematic elements of thought 155–6
residual Kantianism 128–9
in Sartre's thought 256
and science 130–33
summary and conclusions 155–8
time and passive synthesis 140–43
traditional philosophy 129
truth 146–9
hybris 118

I, relation to object 37
idealism 151–2, 230–32
ideality 157
Ideas 197–8
Ideas of Reason 18, 19–20, 24–5, 27
Iliad 204
immediate knowledge 35
immortality 292, 337–8
in-itself 267, 272
In-such-Ruhen 177
Incarnation 89
inclinations 25
incompleteness 148
inertia 284
infinite future 124
infinite vanishing 84–5, 156
infinity 358–9
initiation 210
innocence 80–81, 293
insanity 92
Institut für Sozialforschung see Frankfurt School
institutions, to control action 210–11
instrumental reason 239–40
intentional object 140, 144, 147
intentionality 264, 285
interiority 263
interpretation 105–7, 320
intersubjectivity 151–4
intimacy 206
Intuition 17–19
invisibility 328
inwardness 92–3
Irigaray, Luce 383

irrational state 51–2
isolation 281–2

Jews 247, 283
joyfulness 340
joyous attraction 292
Judaism 112, 233–4
judgement 230–33
Juliette 242
justice and community 116
justification 299–300

Kant, Immanuel 7, 8, 15–30, 49, 357
account of the mind 17–18
in Adorno's thought 229–30
aesthetics 366–7
after collapse 29–30
antinomy 302
appearance model 167–8
on art and beauty 233
atemporal knowledge 17
atemporality 130
basic Kant 17–21
causality of Reason 23–5
early reactions to 21–7
empirical and noumenal realms 27, 29
ethics 16, 20, 129–30
ethics: action, decision and will 26–7
failures of philosophy 21–2
final collapse 27–9
Frankfurt School 229–32
goal of history 239
in Husserl's thought 128–9
influence of Hume 15–17
model of knowledge 19–20
and Nietzsche 118
objects as syntheses of presentations 141
problems with 22–3
reasons for faculties 22–3
as systematic 21
traditional philosophy 129–30
two worlds 20
view of things 177
Kaufman, Walter 99
Kierkegaard, Søren 9, 77–96
Angst 79
Christianity 88–94
The Concept of Dread 79–81
criticism of Hegel 81–3
existentialism 79
isolation 77–8
reworking of Hegel 84
summary and conclusions 94–6

view of evil and sin 83
view of time 84–8
kinship 206, 374
knowledge 16–17
Krahl, Hans- Jurgen 225–7
Kristeva, Julia 385–6
Kuhn, Thomas 373–4

labour 67, 70–71, 214–19
Lacan, Jacques 386
lack 269–70, 273
language 155, 164, 166, 184–7, 388–9
Lauer, Quentin 134
law 210–11, 377–8
laws of association 141
Leibniz, Gottfried 6
Lévi-Strauss, Claude 385
liberation 217, 298–302, 308–9
living by truth 92
Locke, John 21
logic 82, 238
logical positivism 128
logos 163–4
love 25, 357, 361
lucidity 255, 300
luck 258

maleness 382–3
man-position 361–2
manifestation 162–4
manifold of sensible givens 177
Marx, Karl 8, 57–76
 Arendt's view of 214–17
 bourgeoisie 60–61
 brief biography 57–8
 The Communist Manifesto 60–64
 communists 63
 effects of proletarian revolution 63–4
 "Estranged Labour" 66–72
 historical perspective 64–5
 humanism 74
 influence 76
 labour as commodity 67
 political economy 66–7
 "Private Property and Communism" 72–5
 productive and unproductive labour 215
 proletariat 61–2
 purpose of humans 69–70
 response to critics 63–4
 reworking of Hegel 75
 Sartre's reformulation 277–8
 self-estrangement 72
 summary and conclusions 75–6

view of future 64–6, 76
 as Young Hegelian 59
Marx, Werner 185
material, as dynamic in art 181–2
materiality 358
mathematics 129, 354–64
matter-form 176–7
meaning 106–7
mediation 82, 83
Mendelssohn, Moses 239
mental illness 324–5
Merleau-Ponty, M. 156–7
messianic future 305–10
metaphysical origins 317–19, 320–21
metaphysics 18–19, 320–24, 339
metaphysics of substance 177, 386
Meyerson, Émile 314
military discipline 327
mind 17–18, 111, 266
Mitgemeinte 144–5
modern science 193–4
modern state 53–4, 55
modernism 370
modernity 53
moira 238
moment 84
moral goodness 28
moral law 25–6
moral prejudices 103
moral relation to time 114
morality 4–5, 20–21, 23, 26, 103–4
mortality 7–8, 17, 203–4
motivations 49
motive, action and end 275–6
moving cause 24, 189
Mure, G. R. G. 98
myth 241

names 184
natality 220–21
natural order 28
nature
 Aristotle 327
 Descartes 327
 Frankfurt School 238–9
 Hegel 46
 Husserl 152–3
 Kant 28–9
 liberation of mind from 21
 loneliness of 248
 and oppression 301
Nazism 247–8; *see also* Heidegger
needs 284

negation 83
negative dialectics 228–34, 246
negativity 82
neo-Kantianism 128
new worlds 179–81
Nietzsche, Friedrich 9, 97–124, 386
    ascetic ideals 117–23
    attitude to history 108–9
    birth of the priests 109–11
    brief biography 97–9
    and Christianity 99–100
    and Derrida 339–41
    editing and publication of works 99
    Foucault and 316–20
    On the Genealogy of Morality 102–7
    good and evil/bad 107–13
    guilt 113–15
    and Hegel 105–7
    on Judaism 112
    justice and community 116
    and Kant 118
    moral typology 112
    poor health 99
    priestly domination 120–21
    rejection of teleology 105
    religion 117
    ressentiment 111–13, 120
    seen as racist 99
    slave morality 111–13
    state 116
    summary and conclusions 123–4
    temporality 101–2
    "On Truth and Lies in a Nonmoral Sense"
        319–20
    will to truth 121–3
nihilation 10, 267–70, 272, 275–7, 280, 284–5,
    288–91, 311, 329
nihilism 117, 119, 296
noble life 375–6
noema 140, 143–4
non-moral beings 5
normalization, and discipline 328–9
norms 80
noumenon 19–20

object 36, 40
objective truth 65–6, 297–8
objectivity, of external world 152
objects 141, 154, 263, 269
Odyssey 204–5, 241–2
oikos 208, 211, 213, 219
ongoing past, as ultimate truth 37
ontology 112–13, 354

oppression, and liberation 298–302
original sin 88
origins 317
other-consciousness 33

paganism 88–90
paradigm 373–4
paranoia 232–3, 247
Parmenides 4
partitions of the sensible 364
passionate person 297
passions 49–51
passive synthesis 140–43, 153, 279
past 56, 272, 300
pathos of distance 109, 120, 341
peasant technology 191
perceiving 139
perfection 319
perhaps 340, 348
phainomenon 162
phenomenological reduction 136–9, 157
phenomenology 128–9
    as foundational science 148–9
    and fundamental ontology 165–6
    Sartre 254–6
    temporality of 157
    understanding of 145
    see also Heidegger; Husserl
phenomenon
    phenomenological concept 165
    as temporal process 162
philanthropic atheism 74
philosophical ethics 83
philosophical history 44, 55
philosophical tradition, alternatives to 339
philosophy 2–3, 16, 132
philosophy of science 314
physiology 326–7, 375
planning 237
Plato 4–5, 16, 85–6, 322–3, 342, 368–9, 381
poetry 184–7, 198, 359–60
poiēsis 214
polis 205–7, 210, 219
political economy 66–7
political power 378–9
political risk 2
politics 224, 342, 360–61, 365–70, 389–90
positionality 264
positive dialectics 228
positivism 330
possibility 144, 174–5
possible 88
postmodernism 142, 316, 371

power 113, 219–20, 326, 378–9
pragmata 168–9
pragmatic history 44
praxis 70
pre-predicative evidence 136, 155
pre-reflective cogito 264–5, 267
pre-significance 181–2
presence 272
present 272–3, 300
present-at-hand 169, 173, 178
present moment 84–5, 87–8, 91–2, 95–6
preserving art 183–4
priests 109–11, 120–21
primary truth 36
principles, making real 47
private property 66, 71
"Private Property and Communism" 72–5
pro-Americanism, Frankfurt School 225–6
proairesis 343
progress 263, 321–3
projections 229–32, 247
projects of denial 293, 295–8
proletarian revolution 63–4
proletariat 61–2, 227
promises 114, 222–3
proper names 184
property 63, 217–18
providence 45
public transport 170–71
pure ego 137–8, 150–52

quality lying 122
questioning 200
Quine, W.V. 5–6, 392

race 236–7, 261–2
radical activity, mind as 266
radical newness 390
Rancière, Jacques 352, 364–71, 389
rational state 51–2
ready-to-hand 168–9, 178
reason, as ideas of God 45
Reason 18–21, 23–5, 30, 129–30
Reason, Spirit and Absolute Spirit 33
recoil 342–5
reconciliation 81–2, 248–9
redemption 87–8
reflection 92, 141, 232–4
reflective history 43–4
reflective judgements 233
regimes 368
rejection 309
religion 53, 74, 117, 212

religious genius 90
renunciation 297
repetition 388
representation 369
repressive hypothesis 384
reservoir of the not-yet 186
respect, for moral law 25–6
ressentiment 111–13, 120
rethinking 3
revolution 278
revolutionary praxis 279–81, 285
Rickert, Heinrich 128
risk, and faith 92
Riviere, Joan 385
romantic love 212
Rorty, Richard 393
Rubin, Gayle 385
ruptures 314–15, 329–30

Sade, Marquis de 242
salvation 87, 88
Sartre, Jean Paul 9–10, 253–86
    "Anti-Semite and Jew" 261–2
    Beauvoir's discussion of 288–93
    brief biography 253–4
    development of Husserl 262–3
    ethics 256–62
    ethics and phenomenology 254–6
    existentialism 256–62
    "Existentialism is a Humanism" 256, 262
    extension of cogito 268
    freedom 274–7
    heritage 255
    humanism 256–62
    lack 269–70
    on oppression 300–301
    reformulation of Marx 277–8
    relations to Kant and Husserl 259
    "Search for a Method" 277
    self 266–70
    social philosophy 277–84
    summary and conclusions 285–6
    temporality 271–4
scepticism 42
schaltend und waltend subjectivity 153
Scheler, Max 352
Schelling, Wilhelm Joseph 34–5
Schiller. Friedrich 23
Schmitt, Carl 342, 378
Schopenhauer, Arthur 118
science 130–33, 193–4, 358
scientists 121
self-awareness 134, 264–5

self-consciousness 33
self-control 116
self-creation 257–60
self-estrangement 72
self-grownness 177
self-hatred 120
self-knowledge 102, 267
self-mediation 40–41
self-revelation 209
self-sufficiency, of works of art 179
self-understanding 49–51
sending 195–6
Sense-Certainty 35
Sensibility 17–18
sensible, the 365
sensory data, as fragmentary 230–31
sensory manifold 229
serial unity 283
serious person 295–6
set theory 354–64, 389–90; see also Badiou
setting up a world 179–81
sex, and gender 381–2
sexuality 383–7
Shaw, George Bernard 69–70
shut-upness 91
sin 83, 91
Singer, Daniel 354
situating philosophy 353
slaughter bench, of history 44, 48
slave morality 111–13
social bondage 213
social philosophy 277–84
social unification 282–3
society 206, 211–14
Socrates 48, 322
solitude 95
sovereignty 377–8, 390
space 18, 61
space and time 35–6
specialization 218
species beings 68–72
speech, and action 209–11
Spinoza, Baruch 6
Spirit 33, 45–6
spiritlessness 90
standing reserve 192
state 51–4, 55, 116
state capitalism 73–4
state of exception 377–9
staying power 50
Stendhal 118
strength 219–20
strife 182

Ströker, Elizabeth 142
sub-humanity 295–6
subject 36, 167–8, 357
subject–object split 34, 36–8, 40
subjectivity, alien 154
substance-attribute, view of things 176–7
substrate 177
suffering 115
surplus 215
surveillance 328
suturing 358, 363
syllogism 391
synthesis 85–6, 140

ta gignomena 5
taboos 384–6
technico-political register 326
technology
   ambiguity 198
   ancient 191
   Bestand 192
   causality 190
   four causes 189–90
   Gestell 193
   Heidegger 187–98
   means and ends 189
   possibilities of 196–7
   responsibility for 192
   revealing and concealing 196–7
   revealing as happening beyond human doing
      195
   revealing as happening everywhere 193–5
   unconcealment 192
   as way of revealing 190–92
   what is technology? 187–9
teleology, external and internal 27–8
telos 172–6
temporal succession 18
temporality
   Agamben 379
   of art 370–71
   Beauvoir 292
   Butler 388–9
   of causes 24
   contemporary philosophy 353, 389–90
   emphasis on 7
   of gender 380–89
   Hegel 78, 129
   human 87
   of language 388–9
   Rancière 370
   Sartre 271–4, 291
   success of 392

terms, problems of definition 134
terrorism 347
theoretical mind 17–18
theory of relativity 314
things 168, 176–81, 245–6, 263
things in themselves 19–20, 22, 163, 265
thinking 138–9
thought 245–6
Thus Spoke Zarathustra 100–101
time
    and basic-ness 195–6
    at basis of self 199
    bias in treatment of 5–6
    discontinuity 87
    as eidos 150
    vs. eternity 83, 85
    Husserl 199
    in Kant's philosophy 18
    Kierkegaard 84–8
    Marx 61
    moral relation to 114
    and passive synthesis 140–43
    rupturing continuity 88
    see also atemporality; future; Heidegger;
        Husserl; past; present; temporality
time synthesis 140–41, 149, 156, 199
tools, technology as 188
totalization 280
tradition, and oppression 301
traditional philosophy 3–8, 129–30, 202–3,
    259
transcendental consciousness 129
transcendental ownness sphere 153
transcendental philosophy 151–2
transcendental subjectivity 137, 138, 263–4
transition 83
transcendental subjectivity 148, 150
transzendentale Eigenssphäre 153
Trotsky, Leon 305
truth
    and art 182
    atemporal 136
    Foucault 319, 323
    Frankfurt School 230–31
    Heidegger 182
    Husserl 146–9
    Kierkegaard 92
    Nietzsche 121–3, 316
    objective 297–8

writing down 38, 42
truth procedures 358–64
typics 149
Typus 149–50
tyranny 297

ultimate truth 36–8
unconsciousness 33–4
Understanding 17, 19, 26
understanding 168
unfulfilment 144
unity 318–19, 356
universality and individuality 35–6, 38
unusability 169
utility, and oppression 301

Vernunftideen 18
violence 116, 206–7, 219–20
visibility 365
vita activa 202–5
vita contemplativa 202–4
Vorlaufen 175
vulnerability 389

wage labour 72
Way of Non-Being 4
Way of Seeming 4
Way of Truth 4
ways of understanding 187
wealth 213, 217–18
Weber, Max 235
Wenger, Leopold 375
will 29
will to truth 121–3
Wittgenstein, Ludwig 380–81
Wittig, Monique 385
woman-position 361–3
women 64, 66
work 214–19
works of art 178–9
workspaces 169
world 136, 147–8, 167–70, 172, 179–81, 365
world-historical individuals 54–5

Young Hegelians 59
young people 298

Zinck, Otto 77
zoē 375